THE RAIDER

THE RAIDER

THE UNTOLD STORY OF A RENEGADE MARINE AND
THE BIRTH OF U.S. SPECIAL FORCES
IN WORLD WAR II

STEPHEN R. PLATT

ALFRED A. KNOPF · NEW YORK · 2025

A BORZOI BOOK
FIRST HARDCOVER EDITION
PUBLISHED BY ALFRED A. KNOPF 2025

Published by Alfred A. Knopf, a division of Penguin Random House LLC, 1745 Broadway, New York, NY 10019.

Knopf, Borzoi Books, and the colophon are registered trademarks of Penguin Random House LLC.

Library of Congress Cataloging-in-Publication Data
Names: Platt, Stephen R., author.
Title: The raider : the untold story of a renegade marine and the birth of U.S special forces in World War II / Stephen R. Platt.
Description: First edition. | New York : Alfred A. Knopf, 2025. |
Includes bibliographical references and index.
Identifiers: LCCN 2024030355 (print) | LCCN 2024030356 (ebook) |
ISBN 9780525658016 (hardcover) | ISBN 9780525658023 (ebook)
Subjects: LCSH: Carlson, Evans Fordyce, 1896–1947. | United States. Marine Corps—Biography. | World War, 1939–1945—Commando operations—Pacific Area. | World War, 1939–1945—Campaigns—Pacific Area. | United States. Marine Corps. Marine Raider Battalion, 2nd—History. | Carlson, Evans Fordyce, 1896–1947—Travel—China. | Asia Pacific War, ca. 1931–1945. | Generals—United States—Biography. | Intelligence officers—China—Biography. | Special forces (Military science)—History—20th century.
Classification: LCC E746.C3 P53 2025 (print) | LCC E746.C3 (ebook) |
DDC 359.00973 [B]—dc23/eng/20241028
LC record available at https://lccn.loc.gov/2024030355
LC ebook record available at https://lccn.loc.gov/2024030356

penguinrandomhouse.com | aaknopf.com

Maps by Mapping Specialists

Printed in the United States of America

The authorized representative in the EU for product safety and compliance is Penguin Random House Ireland, Morrison Chambers, 32 Nassau Street, Dublin D02 YH68, Ireland, https://eu-contact.penguin.ie.

For Francie, Lucy, and Eliot

Night falls on China; the great arc of travelling shadow
Moves over land and ocean, altering life . . .

The dark will touch them soon: night's tiny noises
Will echo vivid in the owl's developed ear,

Vague in the anxious sentry's; and the moon look down
On battlefields and dead men lying, heaped like treasure.

—W. H. Auden, *Journey to a War*

CONTENTS

INTRODUCTION

MEET EVANS CARLSON—a tall, lanky, weatherbeaten New Englander with blue eyes and an aw-shucks grin who might be the most famous figure from World War II that you've never heard of. General Carlson (to use the rank they retired him with) was a legendary figure in the Marine Corps—when they still allowed him to command. He created one of America's first special operations forces, a battalion of Marine Raiders he trained to fight like Chinese guerrillas, and he led them to national fame during the early fighting in the Pacific. He was one of the most decorated Marines of his time, a war hero, a household name. They made a Hollywood movie about him in 1943. He introduced "gung ho" to the English language. According to a war correspondent in 1944, he was the most beloved officer in the Marine Corps to the enlisted men. But there are reasons you may not have heard of him.

When he died in 1947, the *Baltimore Sun* described Carlson as "the black sheep of the United States Marine Corps." His entire career was hounded with controversy, starting in the 1930s when, on a personal mission for President Roosevelt, he embedded as an observer with China's Communist army, traveled with them for months behind Japanese lines, and came out of the experience as an apostle of guerrilla warfare, convinced that the United States must work directly with—and learn from—the Chinese if it was to have any hope of stopping Japan. He was a maverick in the truest sense of the word, whose unorthodox ideas on leadership and military command alienated him from most of his fellow Marine officers, though none of them ever disputed his remarkable courage under fire. He may have been the black sheep, but his Raider battalion would write legends in the Pacific and some of the tactical features he pioneered would eventually become Marine Corps doctrine. In the small corner of the National Museum of the Marine Corps in Triangle, Virginia, that is devoted to Carlson and his Raiders, the sign under his portrait reads: "Colorful, visionary Evans Carlson emerged from the turbulent 1930s as one of the era's most controversial Marines." They could just as easily have left out the words "one of."

Carlson's life was riven by contradictions. He was a dyed-in-the-wool New Englander who found the key to his life's purpose in a foreign land. He was a ruthless battlefield commander who led his men in discussions of social progress and racial equality. He developed a profound sympathy for the people of China but could be a cold, even cruel husband and a distant father. He had lofty literary ambitions but never finished high school. He was deeply religious, the son of a Congregationalist minister, and also a devout admirer of the atheistic Chinese Communists. He was a man who took Emerson's writings on nonconformity to heart as a youth and lived his life by his own conscience, defiant of norms and the expectations of others, yet he found his lasting home in a military career that demanded conformity and obedience as its very lifeblood. He was a World War II hero who would be all but disowned by his service, pilloried as a suspected radical, and forgotten in the postwar era.

This is his story.

When we lift someone out from the fabric of their time to put them at the center of events, part of the background pulls away along with them. In Carlson's case, his life was woven into the grand drama of a world sliding inexorably into war—beginning in China, where his three tours as a Marine intelligence officer largely paralleled the long civil war between the Communists and the Nationalists that would end, two years after his death, with the Communist victory and the founding of the People's Republic of China. That civil war, which shaped China's twentieth-century destiny to an even greater extent than the war with Japan, began as Carlson first arrived in the country in 1927, rolled in waves through his returning tours, and reached its climax as he died in 1947. It was the central conflict of China's twentieth century, and it would shape the course of Carlson's own life as well.

And then, of course, there is World War II, which—as Carlson experienced it—began not with Hitler's invasion of Poland, or with Pearl Harbor, but with the Japanese invasion of China in 1937. For Western readers, China has long been, to use historian Rana Mitter's term, the "forgotten" theater of World War II, shadowed almost to the point of invisibility by the island-hopping campaigns of the United States in the Pacific. But Carlson's experience gives us a different perspective on these events because for him, the struggles in China and the Pacific were always two halves of a whole. His life formed a bridge between the United States and China in World War II, first as an observer in China, then as a combatant in the Pacific. By the end, he would be a voice in the wind: warning without being heard as the two countries' hopeful wartime alliance spiraled into disaster, giving way just a few years after the defeat of Japan to the slaughter of each other's soldiers on the battlefields of Korea. In the transpacific world we inhabit today—where the U.S.-China relationship is arguably the most important bilateral relationship on earth—we are still paying the price for what happened at the end of World War II. And Evans Carlson saw it coming.

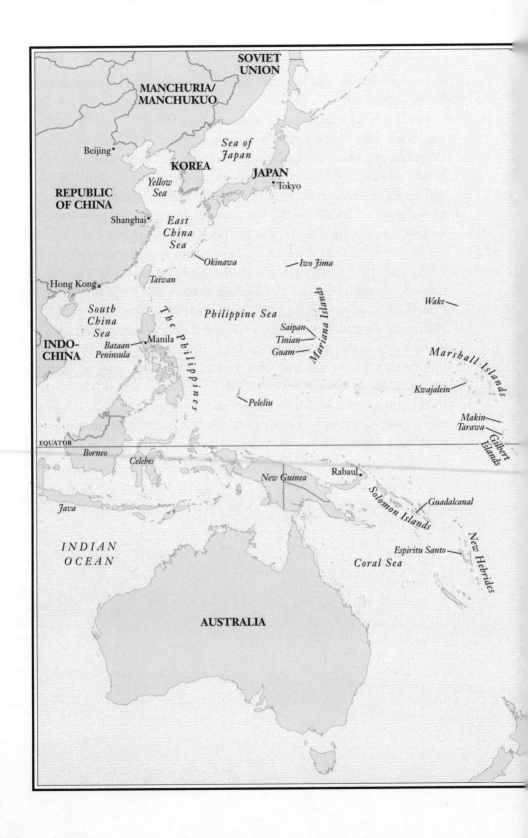

UNITED STATES

Camp Elliott
San Diego

Hawaiian Islands
Midway

Pearl Harbor

EQUATOR

The Pacific

| 0 | Miles | 1,000 |
| 0 | Kilometers | 1,000 |

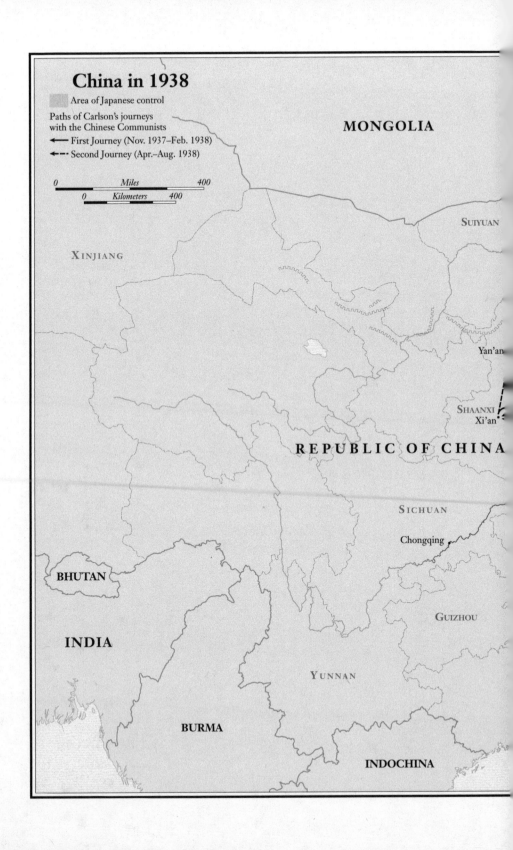

China in 1938

Area of Japanese control

Paths of Carlson's journeys
with the Chinese Communists

← First Journey (Nov. 1937–Feb. 1938)
←-- Second Journey (Apr.–Aug. 1938)

0　　　　Miles　　　400
0　　Kilometers　　400

MONGOLIA

SUIYUAN

XINJIANG

Yan'an

SHAANXI
Xi'an

REPUBLIC OF CHINA

SICHUAN

Chongqing

BHUTAN

GUIZHOU

INDIA

YUNNAN

BURMA

INDOCHINA

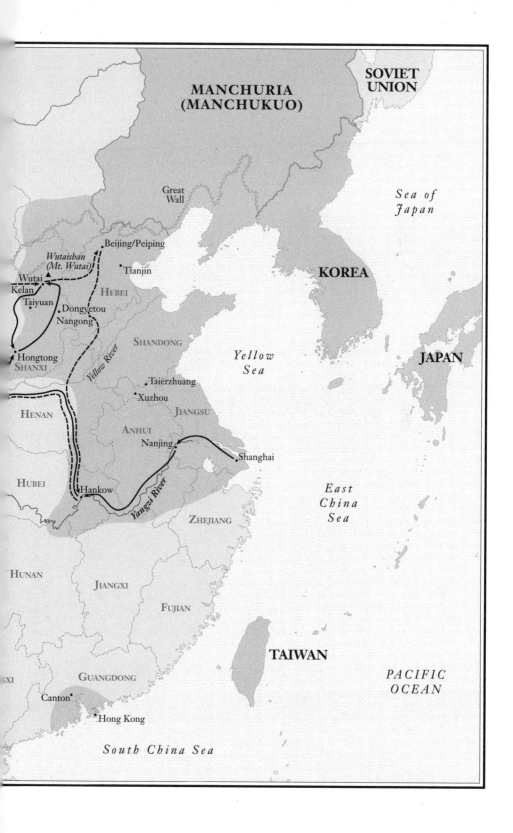

MANCHURIA
(MANCHUKUO)

SOVIET
UNION

Great
Wall

Sea of
Japan

Beijing/Peiping

Wutaishan
(Mt. Wutai)

Tianjin

KOREA

Wutai
Kelan
Taiyuan

HEBEI

Dongyetou
Nangong

SHANDONG

Yellow
Sea

JAPAN

Hongtong
SHANXI

Yellow River

Taierzhuang

Xuzhou

JIANGSU

HENAN

ANHUI

Nanjing

Shanghai

HUBEI

Hankow

Yangzi River

East
China
Sea

ZHEJIANG

HUNAN

JIANGXI

FUJIAN

TAIWAN

PACIFIC
OCEAN

XI

GUANGDONG

Canton

Hong Kong

South China Sea

THE RAIDER

THE GREAT ADVENTURE

Southern California, February 1942

O NE OF THE MEN in line was a dairy farmer from Minnesota who had signed up on December 12, five days after the attack. His brother was a Navy gunner at Pearl Harbor, and when he first went down to the recruitment office he still didn't know whether his brother was alive or dead. One was a high school student from Arizona who had dropped out in order to enlist. Others had been auto mechanics, policemen, and forest rangers. There was an insurance broker from Connecticut, a football star from Arkansas. There were railroad workers, bartenders, a mining prospector, and at least one labor activist. A few of them had previous experience as Marines, but most had just finished basic training when they heard about the new battalion putting out an outlandish call for volunteers. ("I want men who can walk fifty miles!" the recruiter shouted. "I want men who ain't afraid to die!") They all came together in this long, winding line outside a dusty administrative building by the parade ground at Camp Elliott, the Marine Corps base northeast of San Diego. One of them said it felt like they were cattle at a rodeo: the door to the building would open, one man would go through. The door would close. The line would advance a step. The other side of the door was a mystery.

They had all heard stories about the commanders. One was a name everyone knew: James Roosevelt, the president's son. He was executive officer, second in command. But it was unclear what he was doing here, in this particular unit. The one above him, the commanding officer, they didn't know much about, but the stories were wild. Most had only seen him from a distance. He was a tall, thin, gritty man with big ears and a shock of bristly gray hair. He was a major and his name was Evans Carlson, but among themselves they just called him the Old Man. Some said that he'd gone a thousand miles behind Japanese lines with the Communist army in China. Others said he'd fought the guerrillas in Nicaragua and learned their tactics. Word in the ranks was that he knew how to beat the Japanese. If you wanted to be one of the first ones into the war, they said, you had to get into this battalion. And so you came here and got in line with the others.

On the other side of the door was a spare room with two card tables where Carlson and Roosevelt were conducting interviews. The ones who got Carlson found a wiry-looking man on the other side of the table, his face leathery from exposure. He had sharp blue eyes that watched their reactions intently as he went through his list of questions. One of the men said it felt like having a preacher size you up. The questions were normal enough at the start. What do you do for a living? he asked in a slow, thoughtful voice. Can you swim? He wanted to know where they came from. Did you grow up on a farm? It was conversational. Some of the men lied, telling him what they thought he wanted to hear. The high school dropout pretended to be a ranch hand. The questions kept coming. Are you willing to suffer and go without food or sleep? Why are you volunteering for a service that might cost you your life?

As he went down the list, the questions got progressively stranger. Can you march thirty miles on a cupful of rice? What would you do if your buddy started panicking behind enemy lines? It wasn't at all clear what the answers to those should be. Do you think you could choke a man to death without puking? How often do you go to Sunday School? Those who passed the interview got his speech. He said the only things he could promise them were hardship and danger. When we go in, he told them, we won't be asking for mercy. And we won't be giving any in return, either.

Six hundred recruits made the initial cut from about six thousand candidates. They were loaded into jeeps and trucks and driven out through the scrub-covered hills to a remote valley studded with live oaks and date palms, the site of an abandoned chicken ranch called Jacques Farm that would be their base for training. There was only one farmhouse at the site and no barracks, so they pitched tents outside in a grassy field. The old farmhouse was the obvious place for the officers' residence, but when Carlson and Roosevelt arrived at the farm that night, they pitched tents outside just like the recruits. There was no officers' mess either; the next morning, one of the enlisted men found the president's son, Captain Roosevelt, standing next to him in the chow line. It was a bit strange, but it gave the young Marine a good feeling. "The morale of that outfit was something you wouldn't believe," he recalled later.

The men shared an enormous pride in being part of the select group training at Jacques Farm. "It is a crack outfit," one wrote home to his mother, "each man is hand picked. They have the most marvelous spirit I have ever seen." They were living in tents, sleeping on the ground, eating from mess kits, showering and shaving with cold water, washing their clothes in buckets. They trained seven days a week with no leave and they were climbing mountains in a foot deep of mud. "It's a rugged life," he said, "but we all love it."

A host of instructors came through Jacques Farm to work with them. Some taught them field tactics and riflery. Others were specialists in hand-to-hand fighting with knives and bayonets. One of them had just come back from training with the storied British Commandos, Winston Churchill's elite strike force in Europe. The higher-ups who knew about Carlson's experimental battalion liked to think of it as an American counterpart to the Commandos, but Carlson made it clear to his men that the fighters he was modeling them after weren't British. They were Chinese.

Given the urgency of the war, they condensed months of training into weeks. They scrambled through a bayonet course and learned how to scale cliffs. They learned the art of demolition, and how to land quietly on a beach at night in rubber rafts—the latter skill practiced away from camp, on the California coast. They got basic training in judo and other martial arts. They learned to fire Japanese rifles, in case those were the only weapons at hand. They practiced field stripping them and putting them back together blindfolded. In the field they wouldn't have the luxury of specific, narrow roles, so every man learned how to be a scout. Every man learned the basics of jungle hygiene and how to be a medic.

The standard firearms Carlson issued them were almost absurdly powerful. At the time, a regular eight-man infantry squad in the Marines carried six bolt-action Springfield rifles of World War I vintage and one Browning Automatic Rifle, a light, portable machine gun often referred to by its initials: BAR. By contrast, Carlson organized his Marines into ten-man squads, each broken down into a trio of three-man "fire teams" and a squad leader. Within each fire team, one man carried a BAR, the second a Thompson submachine gun, and the third carried the Army's new M1 Garand semiautomatic rifle—which would later be standard issue in the Marines, but they were the first to use it. The upshot of this density of firepower was that a single three-man fire team in Carlson's battalion effectively outgunned an entire squad of regular Marines.

At forty-six years old, Carlson was more than twice the age of the enlisted men, but he set the pace in their training. They would run a mile before breakfast and then hike up and down the surrounding hills all afternoon and into the night, stopping to cook their own meals of rice in their helmets on the way. The hikes got longer until they hit the promised fifty miles, returning to camp sometimes at three o'clock in the morning.

Carlson said he was going to teach them to march until blood came out of their shoes. "And at the end," he said, "I'm going to be there." To bring the point home, he stayed right by their side in their training—hiking with them, walking with them, running, eating, and talking with them. "You kind of felt good there, you know," recalled one of the Marines. "That man was wonderful." They grew to love him. "He would do anything we could do, plus some," said one. "He was a gutsy old man." "A corker," said another. "You couldn't find anyone better." They talked about him in hushed tones. "This Major Carlson," wrote one of the officers in a letter home, "is one of the finest men I have ever known."

Their physical training was unconventional enough, but it was in the group assemblies that Carlson revealed just how far he intended to depart from the familiar Marine Corps script. He called them "gung ho meetings," and since nobody had ever heard the phrase "gung ho" before, he explained it. He said it was a concept he had picked up in China. It meant working together. It was the secret to making them the most cohesive and effective fighting unit they could possibly be. They needed harmony in their ranks, he told them—full and complete trust in one another. The gung ho meetings would help build that trust. There would be no insignia on their uniforms in the field and no saluting. They were going to be equals, regardless of status. They were all in it together and the officers would lead by example, not by pulling rank. That was gung ho.

Carlson drilled it into his men that they had to understand *why* they were fighting. They had to believe in the righteousness of their cause at a deep, moral level. This wasn't just about Pearl Harbor, he told them. And it wasn't some revenge mission to "kill Japs." It was bigger than that. They were fighting on the side of democracy in a global war against fascism. He spoke at the meetings about the reasons why the United States was going into the Pacific. He talked about the ongoing war in China and everything he had seen and learned there. James Roosevelt chipped in as well, talking to the men about world politics, how the United States had gotten into the situation it was in. How the war against Japan related to the war in Europe. At one of the meetings, his mother, Eleanor Roosevelt, made a surprise appearance along with the secretary of the navy to congratulate and encourage the men—as if they needed another boost to their morale.

They spent a lot of time singing together at these meetings. They usually opened with the Marines' Hymn ("From the Halls of Monte-zuma") and finished with "The Star-Spangled Banner." They sang other songs Carlson taught them, and he encouraged them to start writing their own. "Singing helps a man to think," he explained. Sometimes he played a harmonica. He encouraged the enlisted men to speak up, setting aside time for them to ask questions about their training and talk about their lives back home. He pushed them to open up about the things they believed in, but he also tried to get them to talk about America's shortcomings and how it could be made a better society after the war, for all of its members. Because that, ultimately, was their stake, he told them. They weren't just fighting to win the war. They were fighting for a future that would be better than the past.

At the end of April, orders came from above that it was time for them to go. In a few days' time they were slated to depart in a transport for Pearl Harbor—to what remained of it, at least. From there, it would be onward into the vast, murderous Pacific that lay beyond. Admiral Chester Nimitz, the commander-in-chief of the United

States Pacific Fleet, described their battalion as "a striking force with strength out of proportion to its numbers." Later generations would call them special operations forces, though the term didn't exist yet. Their official designation was the 2nd Marine Raider Battalion, but they just called themselves the Raiders—Carlson's Raiders—and to a man, they were ready to follow him to the ends of the earth.

———

Carlson was pleased with the progress his men had made at Jacques Farm. To his mind, the young Marines of this battalion represented pretty much the best America had to offer. Given the chance, he thought they could utterly cut to pieces a Japanese force five times their size. They were as well prepared, in both body and spirit, as he could make them. The rest was in the hands of God. In his tent on April 29, 1942, he cranked a sheet of paper into his old Olivetti type-writer and began tapping out a letter to the president. He addressed it to Franklin Roosevelt directly, at the White House, which was a departure for him. For years, Carlson had been writing his letters to FDR in secret, addressed to the president's personal secretary instead of the man himself. That was the convention he and Roosevelt had agreed on back in the summer of 1937—back when Carlson was just a mid-career intelligence officer preparing for his third tour in China, before the events that had so completely upended the course of his life and now brought him to this place. The letters had been their private subterfuge for all that time—a secret line of communication from one Marine officer directly to the commander-in-chief, an end run around the entire military chain of command. But now circumstances had changed, and his letters didn't have to be secret anymore.

"Dear Mr. President," he began. "We are on the eve of the Great Adventure . . ."

PART I

LEAVING HOME

CHAPTER 1

THE TELEGRAM

AT FIVE O'CLOCK in the afternoon on January 8, 1927, a knock came at the door of Evans Carlson's apartment at the Rainier Hotel in Portland, Oregon. Carlson, a thirty-year-old Marine lieutenant from Vermont, was stationed in the downtown hotel with a platoon of Marines on temporary duty to protect the United States mail service at the neighboring train station. He and his wife, Etelle, were busy planning for a dinner party at the time and had not expected anyone so soon. Carlson opened the door to find a runner standing in the hallway with a telegram for him. He scanned the message: it contained orders for him to proceed immediately to San Diego, where he was to report for duty as training and operations officer for a new expeditionary force. This was it: his first overseas deployment as a Marine. He canceled the dinner party and stayed up late that night with Etelle packing up all of their belongings. Early the next morning, they boarded a train for San Diego.

Like Carlson, most of the 1,200 Marines in the expeditionary force were being reassigned from mail guard duty in the Western states—an uninspiring service where they rode the rails in their olive drab uniforms to protect the U.S. post from largely nonexistent train robbers. The rumors said they were headed for Nicaragua, so they were excited about the prospect of a fight, to say nothing of a change of scene. But once they were all assembled at San Diego—packed and ready to go, their wives and sweethearts all settled in nearby apartments—their orders to embark for Nicaragua never material-ized. A week passed, and the men were taken off standby. Finally, at the end of January, orders arrived sending them out from port without revealing a final destination. On February 3, they piled on board the rusty old tub of a transport USS *Chaumont* amid much waving and blown kisses from the pier, and departed for the unknown. Once they were far enough out to sea, Carlson learned that he was on his way to China.

He had been waiting for this day for the better part of five years. Not just for the prospect of his first combat deployment, but above all for China. Indeed, the hope of being sent there was one of the main reasons he had joined the Marine Corps in the first place. He was firm on that, though it is unclear why, or how, the idea seized him. The first he ever mentioned it to his parents was back in 1922 when he suddenly quit his civilian job without any explanation. "Hope to get out to China soon" was all he told them about his plans, in a cryptic letter that only made sense after he enlisted in the Marines a few days later. He didn't have any family connection to China, and had never expressed any kind of interest in it previously. If he had ever read a book about the country in his youth, he left no record of the fact. But even so, it wasn't such a far-fetched idea; a posting in China was the most prestigious overseas assignment in the Marine Corps, if not the entire U.S. military. And prestige aside, there was no place on earth more exotic to a young man from New England. For generations of restless wanderers like himself, the roads of the world eventually converged on the Middle Kingdom.

Carlson had traveled many of those roads. As a child, he ran away from home for the first time when he was barely twelve years old. It was distressing to his parents, especially his mother, but it wasn't entirely out of line with his family's history; his ancestors had not been the kind of people to sit still. Carlson's Norwegian grandfather had come to the U.S. as an orphan at the age of eighteen, promptly changed his name from Thorstein to Thomas, and then set out for California to dig for gold. After establishing a family in California, he left for the Klondike by way of the Chilkoot Pass with one son in tow and died there two years later. The son who accompanied him moved to Alaska and became a federal marshal. That son's brother—the one who hadn't come along—was Evans Carlson's father, Thomas Alpine Carlson, his middle name reflecting the fact that he was the first settler child born in California's Alpine County just south of Lake

Tahoe. Thomas took a different path than his brother and father—more a man of ideas than action, he moved back across the country to New York State to attend seminary and become a minister.

Evans himself was born in 1896 in the parsonage of a small Congregational church in the Catskill foothills of New York, the first child of his parents. He would never have a long-term home, either as a child or as an adult. A few months after his birth, his father made the first of what would be countless moves between New England churches—in this case taking over a small country parish in Weybridge, Vermont, where he also began attending classes at nearby Middlebury College. When on one morning the blond-headed, two-year-old Evans showed up in his father's English class at Middlebury, unaccompanied and tugging his little red wagon behind him, his family took it as an early sign of the boy's "adventurous" spirit. But these sorts of things always look obvious in hindsight.

The Carlson family was poor. His father's salary in Weybridge, where Evans's two younger brothers and a sister were born, was just $10 a week—roughly $16,000 a year in today's currency to support a family of six. Their meager lifestyle came as a shock to his mother, Joetta, who had been engaged for five years to Thomas before their marriage and should have seen what was coming. Joetta Evans was something of an American aristocrat, a thoroughly qualified member of the Daughters of the American Revolution whose ancestor Captain Jack Evans had served alongside George Washington in the French and Indian War. She claimed to trace her lineage back to the last royal family of Wales, and liked to reminisce to young Evans about the comfortable life she had enjoyed before her marriage to his father.

The Reverend Thomas A. Carlson was heavily preoccupied with his parish and his sermons and his studies—and, as Evans later came to see it, the hard work of keeping his downwardly married wife happy—so the boy was mainly left to fend for himself growing up. He was the very picture of a Vermont country child, clad in worn overalls and a straw hat, going barefoot in the summer. His father couldn't afford to buy him a bicycle so Evans "Yankee traded" for one but it had no chain so he would just push it to the top of a hill and sail back down again.

Evans admired his father insatiably, especially his high level of learning. One of the earliest memories he carried from his childhood was of exploring in his father's study in Weybridge or some other small-town New England parsonage, the tall bookshelves crammed to the ceiling with works in all of the languages his father could read—English, of course, but also Greek and Latin, German, French, and Hebrew. As a child, Evans picked up a desire to study and read, to better himself and somehow win his distant father's admiration. And although his father taught him a bit—the Greek alphabet, a little astronomy, some botany—for the most part in this, too, the boy was left to his own devices.

By the time he made up his mind to run away from home, his father's work had taken the family to a parish in Dracut, Massachusetts, where Evans was enrolled for a short time in a local school. An essay survives from his schoolwork that year, on the theme of "If I Had a Million Dollars"—which he most certainly didn't have. He said that if he had a million dollars, he would go to Harvard to study "liturature" and later, after traveling the world to further his studies, he would accept a position as "Professor of Liturature" at Yale. Such were the dreams of an eleven-year-old preacher's son in eastern Massachusetts.

He left home shortly after his birthday and started for the coast, determined to find work and make a new life for himself. In spite of his youth and lack of funds, he made it all the way up to Portland, Maine, nearly a hundred miles to the northeast of Dracut. There, he tried to get a job on a cattle boat but at twelve years old he looked so obviously young that nobody in the port city would hire him. What money he had ran out, and there was nowhere for him to stay, so in the end he had to return unhappily to his parents in Massachusetts. The family soon moved yet again, up to Peacham, Vermont, where Evans resumed attending school, but he continued to chafe at the confines of life with his family. Two years later, when he was fourteen, he ran away from home a second time, and this time he made it stick.

Carlson's desire to leave home seems to have been driven less by resentment of his parents per se than by a deep-seated urge to unburden himself and make his own way in the world. Ralph Waldo Emerson was at least partly to blame. The nineteenth-century New England philosopher was one of the boy's favorite writers, and Emerson's *Essays* was, for all intents and purposes, Carlson's Bible. He would carry a worn, pocket-sized copy of it with him for most of his adult life and could quote long passages verbatim. Emerson's essay on "Self-Reliance," in particular, spoke directly to Carlson as a boy, telling him that to be a true man he must be a nonconformist, breaking free from the expectations of others, including his family. "To believe your own thought," wrote Emerson, "to believe that what is true for you in your private heart is true for all men,—that is genius." At an early age, Carlson learned from Emerson that he must try to find his genius, his unique purpose in life. He had to learn how to listen to his own instincts rather than the instructions of others, to follow his inner spirit as a guide. "Nothing can bring you peace but yourself," Emerson told him. Running away from home was the boy's first step in what would be a lifelong search for that higher purpose in his life.

Evans wrote dutifully to his parents after setting out on his own, and though they knew where he was, they did not try to make him come home. "We were, of course, never happy to have him leave home so early," said his father many years later, "but his spirit was a restless one." His parents understood that once he'd had a taste of living on his own there would be no peace for anyone if they forced him to come back and live under their authority again.

At first, he found farm work in Vergennes, Vermont, just east of Lake Champlain, where he also attended the Vergennes high school and tried to get a bit more education. He was shy and awkward, and the local paper noted (somewhat cruelly) that when he was cast in an amateur play, he "almost failed to appear in the 'performance' and then in a manner in no way resembling either Barrymore." He was growing fast by that time, his child's body transforming into the lanky frame that would mark him as an adult. By age fifteen he could pass as a grown man and he got a job as assistant freight manager at a railroad junction in New Haven, Vermont. He knew a civil engineer who was a friend of the family, and the following year Evans followed him south to New Jersey to join a road-building crew, which put him the farthest from home he had ever been.

On October 14, 1912, the New York Giants defeated the Boston Red Sox by three runs in the sixth game of the hard-fought 1912 World

Series and New York City was electric with excitement. Evans, now sixteen and fully six feet tall, was working as a chain-man on a road surveying team in New Jersey, living in Newark with the civil engineer's family and going to night school to study mathematics and German. All anyone around him wanted to talk about was baseball, but Evans had his mind on other things. The day of the game, he had gone instead to see a naval review on the Hudson River, with President Howard Taft and the secretary of the navy in attendance. The energy of the tightly packed crowds along the riverbank, the grandeur of the immense ships sliding past, the sharp uniforms of the officers, all stirred something in him. The next day, he wrote to his father. "Say dad," he wrote, "if I ever got to where I wanted to join the navy enough to go and enlist would you give your consent?" He didn't know yet whether he actually would do it.

It took him less than a month to make up his mind, but it wasn't for the Navy. On November 5, Carlson was making his way into New York City to watch the presidential election returns on Park Row when he passed a storefront Army recruiter in Hoboken, New Jersey. On a whim, he decided to go inside. Woodrow Wilson would unseat Taft that day, and defeat Teddy Roosevelt's third-party Bull Moose candidacy in the bargain, but for Carlson it was the first day of a military career that would, against his own sometimes profound misgivings, span most of the rest of his life.

The recruiter asked him what branch of the Army he wanted to join, and since he liked horses, he said he wanted to be in the cavalry. The recruiter sized up his gangly physique and told him he was too tall. "Go to the field artillery," he suggested instead. He showed the boy a promotional picture featuring "dashing horses" (as Carlson remembered them) pulling an artillery caisson. Evans was sold. The only problem was his youth: the minimum age to join the Army was twenty-one, and he was only sixteen. But he was an exceptionally tall sixteen. So when the recruiter asked him his age he told him "twenty-two" to be on the safe side, and lied his way into the service.

After Evans vanished, the engineer he had been living with managed to track down his enlistment record at the Army recruitment office and cabled the Carlsons in Vermont to let them know what had happened. Evans's parents were shocked that their son had joined the Army—and what's more had lied to do so—but for two years already he had been out of their control. Moreover, he had already written to them about his interest in the Navy and they knew there was no way to keep him from it forever. So they told the engineer not to intervene—Evans would need to find his own way out. On the upside, his father thought that being forced to face the consequences of his actions might be the kind of education his wandering son needed most.

There was nothing glamorous about the Army Carlson joined. A brief initial stint in the Philippines appears to have left no lasting impression on him other than a tattoo on his left arm of the words "Manila 1913." It was followed by a longer period of service in Hawaii, but in spite of a great deal of time spent with artillery horses he didn't find it very inspiring. The other soldiers, as he later described them, were "scums—hard drinking and hard boiled." He tried to keep up with their drinking at first, but soon noticed that the soldiers that stayed sober got ahead, while the drunks remained at the bottom.

So he cut back on his efforts to fit in socially and began getting promotions. He became a clerk, then a corporal while he was seventeen, his age still unknown to his superiors. His conduct was impressive enough that he even went on to make sergeant—the first enlisted man from his battery to get such a promotion in ten years.

But when his commanding officer put him up to take the exam for second lieutenant, Carlson finally confided to him about his age, which by then was still just eighteen. That put an end to his upward trajectory—though at least the officer remained supportive, writing in a letter of reference that Carlson was "one of the best soldiers I have ever served with" and adding, apparently as an inside joke, that Carlson's abilities were "far ahead of his years."

There was a lot of dead time

Carlson as a boy in the Army.

in the Army and little to do for entertainment—"time hangs heavy on one's hands," he wrote to a friend back home—so he did a great deal of reading and started toying with the idea of becoming a writer. He knew he would never be a professor of "liturature," but he still hoped one day to be known as a man of words, a man with ideas— the kind of man his father would admire. At his barracks in Hawaii he read the novel *Martin Eden* by Jack London and felt an affinity for its title character, a self-taught writer from a poor and uneducated background. As Jack London told the story, Martin Eden did succeed in becoming a literary star in spite of his lack of formal education, though in doing so he turned darkly cynical about fame and the tastes of the publishing world. The book was hardly rosy in its conclusions (the protagonist eventually drowns himself) but its message of self-improvement still resonated with Carlson as a young Army sergeant who had never finished high school.

Carlson made it through his three years of Army service intact, and when he left in 1915 he tried his hand at civilian life. He dreamed of enrolling in college to become a writer, or at least studying to become a civil engineer, but he had neither the money nor the education for those paths, so he settled instead for a job as a surveyor for a road crew—the same job he had done before the Army, only this time in California instead of New Jersey. He found a room to rent in a town about seventy miles east of Los Angeles, where he met his landlord's daughter, a young woman named Dorothy Seccombe who studied piano in the city and occasionally visited home. Soon, they were married.

Carlson had only a year of domestic life with Dorothy before Pancho Villa's raid into New Mexico in 1916 led to his recall into active service by the National Guard. He hoped to be assigned to the expeditionary force that invaded Mexico to hunt for Villa and his army, but was disappointed when the Guard sent him to El Paso, Texas, instead as an instructor. A more hopeful opportunity for advancement came in 1917 with America's entry into World War I, by which time Carlson was twenty-one years old and could stop lying about his age. He hungered for service on the front lines in Europe—if he couldn't have education, he wanted action—but once again he found himself far from the center of events, stuck in the United States for most of the war helping train Army recruits in Arizona and Arkansas. On the plus side, unhampered now by his falsified age, he earned a quick series of wartime promotions, topping out at captain of artillery by February of 1918, when the Army finally sent his division to Europe. In the meantime, while they were in Arizona, Dorothy gave birth to their first (and only) child, a son they named Evans Junior.

The Great War did not, for Carlson, live up to its name. When he got to France, he was assigned to serve in his divisional headquarters rather than in any operational capacity, so instead of the action he had been hoping for, all he got was an administrative job in a mammoth bureaucracy. The closest he got to the fighting was in the fall of 1918 when his division was ordered to the front, but the war ended before they even got there. Armistice was declared, and three weeks later his division began shipping home. Not knowing what else to do with himself, Carlson stayed on and found a place on General John J. Pershing's staff in the army of occupation in Germany, investigating and verifying claims of bravery for medal nominations. It was a bitter pill, in that there were no opportunities left to demonstrate bravery himself.

War, as Carlson told a friend, was "an adventure or nothing"—and by 1919 it was nothing. As his hopes for further advancement in the Army evaporated, he felt his lack of education all the more keenly. In January, he wrote home to his sister, Karen, of the "ever increasing regret I have at not having the foundation of a college course to back up my own path in life." The context, painfully enough, was that his younger sister had just enrolled in college at Middlebury. Carlson tried to be gracious about Karen's good news, but it threw into relief the consequences of his own decision to run away from home at an early age. Yes, he had made his own way in life, but it had been mostly disappointing, and now—as his career in the Army stagnated—he wondered how things might have been if he had never left.

Carlson left the Army in October of 1919 to take another run at life as a civilian, and it started out promisingly enough: he found a job with the California Packing Corporation, the parent of Del Monte, as a canned fruit salesman in Montana. He loved the broad vistas and snowcapped mountains of Montana, the peaceful feeling of driving on long, rough country roads to visit provisioners in remote mining and timber outposts. Dorothy and one-year-old Evans Junior lived in Oakland, California, when he was on the road, but he enjoyed the solitude, initially at least, as well as the regular meeting of strangers that his job entailed. He was good at talking to people and felt like he might be going somewhere. But the money was so bad he could barely support his wife and son, let alone send presents home to his parents at Christmas.

Carlson's marriage to Dorothy ended in 1920. They had barely known each other before marrying, and barely lived together afterward, so it was perhaps inevitable. But one week he was writing to his parents to tell them "Our home is the happiest ever," and in the next letter he told them that he and Dorothy had separated. He was leaving her and the boy, and the marriage was over. The same minister who had married them supervised the divorce. Dorothy got almost everything; Carlson took only his personal effects and his typewriter. She got custody of Evans Junior and Carlson would spend no meaningful time with his son again until the boy was an adult.

Things only spiraled from there. Back in Montana, driving again along the slow, rutted roads between Great Falls and Bozeman, he found that selling contracts for canned fruit was no more fulfilling as a bachelor than it had been as a family man. And after the divorce he owed Dorothy $75 a month in alimony and child support, so his financial situation was even more precarious than before. The seasons passed with no improvement. His mood darkened; where once he had enjoyed conversations with the frontier dwellers he met as a salesman, he now found himself wishing for the company of educated, urbane men and women instead. He complained to his father that his work in Montana mainly brought him into contact with a rough sort of people who were his "mental inferiors." The work itself was "seemingly useless drudgery."

But Emerson still held him in thrall, and deep down he clung to the hope that he was meant to do something bigger with his life. "My one ambition," he told his parents in a letter from Missoula, "is to write, to interpret life as I see it, that others may see it in the same light and be inspired by the beauty of the art involved and wonder at the amazing manner in which all elements link themselves together." He said he was trying to understand "the phenomena of life"—the grand, overarching patterns of human existence. "I am constantly searching out new elements," he told them, "and connecting each up with the whole general scheme, which, when completed, will give me the power to perform my real purpose in life." That elusive, nearly divine purpose—he didn't know what it was, but he was certain it was out there, somewhere, waiting for him. Only he was pretty sure that he would never find it in the wilds of Montana.

In the winter of 1922, the packing company transferred Carlson to Oregon, where he drove his Ford up and down the coastal roads, plying his preserved pineapples and strawberries to storekeepers in the logging camps. It was a gorgeous piece of the earth, but among the towering cedar forests of the Pacific Northwest he felt even more alone and hopeless than he had in Montana. His job felt like a dead end. As much as he had come to dislike the Army by the end, he started wondering if maybe that had been the only chance he'd ever had to move upward in life. The idea kept nagging at him, until he finally broke down and wrote to the War Department to ask if he could reenlist. They replied that he could, but in light of the reduced size of the postwar Army he could not have his old rank back. He was proud of having been discharged as a captain, and had even been put up for major just before the Armistice. But if he rejoined now, the best he could hope for was second lieutenant—and that was if they gave him an officer's commission at all.

As desperate as he felt to find a way forward, Carlson still had enough dignity to resent the prospect of being demoted in the Army, especially as it meant that all his friends who had stayed in the service would outrank him. And so, in yet another of the acts of impulse that had characterized his life to this point, he decided in April of 1922 to throw his entire Army experience to the wind. Fourteen years after he first ran away from home to try to make his own way in the world, Evans Carlson washed the slate of his life clean and started over from the beginning again, hoping that this time things would turn out better. Without a word to Dorothy or his parents, he quit his job with the canning company. Then he drove his rambling Ford back down the coast to Oakland, where he walked into a different recruiting office and signed up as a private in the Marine Corps. When he reported for duty a week later, he told them that he wanted to go to China.

The Marine Corps that Carlson joined in 1922 was a small, increasingly elite force tasked primarily with security for American interests overseas. It counted only about eighteen thousand men in peacetime, restricted to one-fifth of the personnel in the Navy and no larger than a single division of the Army, but unlike the larger services, the Marines were frequently deployed. As the recruiting slogan went, they were "first to fight." Compared to the mundane existence of an enlisted man in the peacetime Army or Navy, most of whom were either based on U.S. soil or wedded to their ships, the Marines were, as one military historian has put it, "imperial America's fire brigade"—constantly shuttling around Latin America, the Caribbean, and as far as East Asia to intervene in local conflicts or provide protection to American civilians and businesses. It was a service in constant motion, a fitting home for a man who had always been in motion himself.

Beyond the prospect of going to China, there were other reasons the Marines were attractive to Carlson, the pettiest of which was that since his starting salary as a leatherneck would be only $30 a month, he wouldn't have to pay Dorothy the full $75 he owed her for alimony. On a more commendable level, though, it was a fresh start in a career he already knew something about and had an aptitude for. Nobody in the Marines knew him, so there was no shame in starting out as a buck private, other than his rather advanced age, which was an appropriate bookend to his time as a prevaricating sixteen-year-old in the Army. Since the Marine Corps was so much smaller than the Army or Navy, it offered Carlson a more promising chance to make a name for himself. It held out the lure of going back overseas and seeing more of the world and, unlike the other services, it promised him engagement with that world head-on rather than being holed up in some isolated base or confined to a ship.

"Well I'm back—in the service," he wrote to his father, who by this time had moved to a parish in West Rutland, Vermont. "And believe me, I'm so happy I am almost moved to tears." Carlson declared that he would rather be a private in the Marine Corps than a captain of industry in the outside world. "My heart is in the service and here

I must stay," he said. He assured his father that he would move up the ranks soon enough, and explained more about his desire to go to China. Specifically, it was the Legation Guard in Beijing he was hoping for, to join the permanent force of a few hundred Marines who guarded the U.S. diplomatic compound in China's capital. It was a legendarily comfortable assignment in a storybook locale about as far away from New England as you could get. With at least three servants to every officer, the Marines of the Legation Guard led easy, charmed lives that generally revolved around sports, marksmanship contests, and dress parades. All of the grunt work was done by Chinese servants so that even the enlisted men lived in far greater comfort than they would ever have enjoyed back home.

In spite of his request, however, the Marines did not need Carlson for China. Instead, they sent him to candidate's school in Washington, D.C. to become a commissioned officer. Once he was done with that, they posted him to their home base at Quantico, Virginia, as a horse agent for Smedley Butler, the commanding general of the barracks. Carlson was skilled with draft animals after all of his artillery experience in the Army, so he didn't mind getting his start in the Marines buying horses and mules for training maneuvers. China, though, would have to wait.

The Marine base at Quantico became a home to Carlson in a way the Army never had. He liked his fellow Marines, and they liked him in return. And he did start to move up the ranks, just as he had promised his father. He was a corporal by the end of May, only a month after his enlistment, and a year later he made second lieutenant. He felt a particular fondness for the enlisted men, with whom he got along easily because he had been one himself. He had clear memories of being a private in the Army and being so scared he couldn't bring himself to speak directly to his sergeant for the entire first year. ("He was like a god," Carlson recalled.) As an officer, he tried his best to guide and mentor the enlisted men, adopting what he considered a fatherly attitude toward them.

He was also quite a hit with the daughters of the senior officers. By his late twenties, Carlson had grown into a sharply handsome young man—six feet tall and straight as a ruler, trim and wiry with blondish brown hair, a square jaw, and a quick, disarming smile that made his blue eyes sparkle. His face, which in later life would be as craggy as the surface of the moon, was still smooth and boyish. The social life of a junior officer at Quantico was a busy and expensive affair, with a constant progression of dances, balls, dinner parties, and bridge games at the elegantly appointed homes of various colonels. His winter dress uniform and its accessories alone cost him more than $500, which essentially bankrupted him, and he needed a summer version as well. He had to borrow money from friends to cover the costs of the required wardrobe, and despaired of ever paying them back. But he was as excited at Quantico as he had ever been in his life—"I am right in my element," he told his parents. And his literary dreams continued to glimmer just below the surface. "I desire *very* much to write," he confided, hoping that once things settled down he might have "an abundance of time for literary work."

In the meantime, there were the women. "When my week's work is over," he wrote in a birthday letter to his mother, "it *is* nice to bask in the company of some good, wholesome girls." There was Jeannette, the daughter of a colonel, whom he declared in March 1923 to be the most extraordinary girl he had ever known. She had a mind that worked like "chain lightning" and a personality that was "sweet and charming beyond conception." Then, a few months later,

Carlson as a second lieutenant in the Marines.

there was Margaret, the daughter of another colonel. "I have a suspicion that I am falling in love," he told his parents in November— "really in love." So strong were his feelings for Margaret that he insisted he would die if he couldn't be with her. By December, he was certain she was the one. "She typifies everything that I hold worthwhile," he told his parents. The fact that she was already engaged to someone else, a Navy officer, didn't bother him. After "calm reflection and study" he concluded that she would just have to choose between them.

Whatever Margaret's choice might have been, Carlson forgot all about her (and Jeannette) a few weeks later, when he met a Girl Scout organizer named Etelle Sawyer while he was in Puerto Rico on a horse-buying expedition. Etelle, who had auburn hair and a radiant smile, was a fellow New Englander from Portland, Maine, who shared Carlson's yen for travel. When he met her, she was in San Juan running a training course to create a new Girl Scouts chapter for Puerto Rico, answering to Lou Henry Hoover, the Girl Scouts president and wife of Herbert Hoover (then secretary of commerce, not yet U.S. president). She was graceful, charming, and cultured, a college graduate and sorority girl, and with her Girl Scouts experience she was pretty much an ideal match for a military man. One friend described her as "the quintessence of the American character." Carlson fell hard for her (this was something of a theme for him). Soon they were spending entire days together and he couldn't bear to be away from her for more than a few hours at a time.

"Etelle loves me and is going to marry me," he announced triumphantly in a letter home from Puerto Rico in February of 1924. He was overwhelmed. Falling in love with Etelle was, he wrote in his typically melodramatic fashion, "a turning point in my life where tragedy was left behind and eternal love and happiness entered in." The "tragedy" to which he referred was, of course, Dorothy, whose claim to his finances continued to hound him and whose shadow had loomed over his previous attempts to find a new wife. "Eternal love and happiness" was his romantic side in overdrive. Etelle was already engaged when they met, to her brother's college roommate, but by the end of February Evans had convinced her to write home breaking off the engagement so she could marry him.

The glow followed him back to Quantico in March, where he kept trying to persuade his parents that Etelle wasn't just a passing infatuation like the others. "She was meant for me," he wrote to his father. "All obstacles in the path of our marriage should be swept aside." He knew what he sounded like. "You probably think me a nut for raving about Etelle the way I do," he joked to his parents. Apparently they did, though, for when Evans and Etelle were married a month later in her family's church in South Portland, Maine, neither of Carlson's parents attended the wedding. Afterward, he brought Etelle to their home in Vermont so they could meet her in person, but it didn't go well. His mother, Joetta, still had not forgiven him for abandoning Dorothy and Evans Junior, and she made it clear that she did not care for her son's new wife.

———

Carlson started to get some variety in his assignments after the wedding. He went to sea for a while on the USS *Nevada*, though he disliked being away from Etelle when the ship wasn't at port. In February of 1925 he started a nine-month flight course in Pensacola, Florida, and found that he loved to fly airplanes—especially over the blue-green waters of the Florida coast, Etelle happily encamped in a little house on the air base surrounded by flower gardens. The grassy expanse in front of their house was broad enough that sometimes he would land his plane there, right in front, and she would come running out of the house to greet him.

Carlson had been looking forward to flight school and told his parents that he had a hunch that he should be a pilot. "My hunches are always good ones," he explained. For the record, this was by no means true. Recently, for instance, he had told them of his hunch that the Marine Corps football team was going to beat Michigan, and they went on to get solidly trounced, 26–6. With regard to becoming a pilot, his hunch was spectacularly wrong. No matter how hard he practiced he just couldn't pass the stunt tests to get his wings. He was fine with basic flying and could do loops and tail spins well enough, but every time he tried the falling leaf maneuver, he failed. On one attempt he got so disoriented he nearly crashed his aircraft into the sea. The instructor cut him from the nine-month course after just four months, putting an end to his short-lived dream of aviation. And as if to compound his sense of failure, at the same time Carlson was being kicked out of flight school, his youngest brother, Tom, was graduating early from Middlebury College with Phi Beta Kappa honors after only three years of coursework.

By the time the Marines transferred the now grounded Carlson to Portland, Oregon, in the fall of 1926 to command the local detachment of the mail guard, he didn't have a great deal to look forward to. The disappointment of flight school stayed with him, and with the transfer to Oregon it seemed that his career in the Marines might turn out to be no more distinguished than his years in the Army had been. Protecting the U.S. mail was hardly the kind of command that invited distinction. Language of the recruitment posters notwithstanding, in the course of more than ten years in the Army and Marines Carlson's life had been mainly a quiet, routine existence of training, drills, and paperwork—of imagining, but never finding, the richer and more meaningful life that he still believed lay somewhere just out of his reach. For all of his hopes, his career in the military had turned out to be entirely devoid of the kind of adventure he had signed up for. That is, until the knock on the door, and the telegram, and the departure for China.

CHAPTER 2

SHANGHAI

CHINA IN 1927 was a shambles. The country's last imperial government, the Qing dynasty, had been overthrown in 1912, after more than two and a half centuries in power, to make way for a modern republic that never properly took root. The fifteen years between the fall of the Qing in 1912 and 1927, when Carlson arrived in the country, had been marked by disunion and internecine warfare. It was a period now remembered as China's "Warlord Era," when a broken republican government at Beijing held only nominal authority over an enormous, fragmented country of 400 million people in which the real power was in the hands of regional strongmen—the warlords—who had no particular allegiance to one another or to the republic of which they were supposedly a part. Warlords commanded their own armies and governed their own territories—some as large as a province, others as small as a railway line. They formed coalitions that went to war against one another. The country was internally divided, internationally weak, and existed in a constant state of crisis.

In 1927, however, a large and well-equipped military force calling itself the National Revolutionary Army was fighting its way up from the south on a campaign to reunify the Republic of China by conquering the warlord armies and forcing their leaders into a submissive alliance. The army's commander-in-chief—styled "The Generalissimo" by the foreign newspapers—was a slim, shaven-headed general named Chiang Kai-shek who gave fiery nationalistic speeches calling for the Chinese to unite and put an end to the presence of foreigners in the country. His army had a staunch foreign ally in the Soviet Union, which wanted a unified client state in China that could protect Russia's Asian frontier from Japan and the Western powers. To this end, the Soviets supplied Chiang Kai-shek's army with military advisors, armed it with Russian weapons and ammunition, and financed it to a large degree with Russian money. Chiang's forces had successfully taken control over the southern and central regions of the country in 1926, and by the early months of 1927 they were closing in on the international commercial center of Shanghai on the eastern coast. Shanghai, as it happened, was where most of the Americans in China lived, and it was for their sake—to protect them from Chiang Kai-shek and his National Revolutionary Army—that Carlson and his fellow Marines were on their way from San Diego.

For foreigners in China in the 1920s, the key term was "extraterritoriality"—which meant that in China, especially in the large sections of the major cities designated as foreign concessions, the Americans, British, and other citizens of foreign powers were entitled to live and go about their business free from the interference of the Chinese government and without even being subject to Chinese law. As a traveler's guide from the era explained, "If an American is arrested anywhere in China he must be handed over to the nearest American consul immediately. An American citizen is in no way subject to the jurisdiction of the Chinese courts." These extraterritorial rights had been coerced from China by force in a series of treaties with the weakened Qing government in the nineteenth century, and by the twentieth century they had come to full flower as the foreign districts became major centers of commerce, magnets for the accumulating wealth of the Republic. These concessions were still technically Chinese soil, but the foreigners who inhabited them—the International Settlement of Shanghai being the largest—lived in many ways just as they would at home. They laid out roads and public spaces and constructed buildings in their own countries' images. Whichever foreign power controlled a particular concession set up its own police and enforced its own laws.

The primary function of the United States military in China in the 1920s, as for those of Britain, France, and other outside powers, was to protect the extraterritorial rights of their own nationals. It was a highly distasteful arrangement to most Chinese—especially as the imperial government that had originally signed the unequal treaties (as they were known) had been dead and buried for more than a decade already. But the tenuous Republic that was born from the ashes of the Qing dynasty in 1912 had never been strong enough to assert China's sovereignty against the demands of the foreign powers. As much as republican leaders would have preferred to strip the foreigners of these coercive rights—and reclaim the concessions for China—they simply didn't have the power to do so. So the system had continued on into the 1920s, much to the frustration of Chinese nationalists, and much to the satisfaction of the foreigners who enjoyed their special privileges on Chinese soil.

But the National Revolutionary Army's campaign to reunify the country—the Northern Expedition, as it was called—promised something different. Propagandists who heralded the army's arrival and trailed in its wake bellowed anti-foreign slogans on street corners and rallied Chinese crowds into boisterous denunciations of Western imperialism. Publicly, Chiang Kai-shek vowed to take back the foreign concessions and repudiate the odious treaties from the nineteenth century that sapped China of her sovereignty. Privately, he went even further, writing in his diary that the British "regard Chinese lives as dirt" and declaring that the "parasites" in the foreign concessions should all be killed. "How can we emancipate mankind," he asked, "if we cannot annihilate the English?"

President Calvin Coolidge had not wanted to send any more American troops to China, despite the pleading of his commanders that Shanghai was in danger. Coolidge was uncomfortable with the whole notion of extraterritoriality—his State Department had in fact raised the prospect of abandoning it, but balked only because there was no stable government in Beijing with which to discuss a treaty revision. Furthermore, he was adamant that the United States should not become an aggressor nation in China; it must hold to the precedent of the past, in which America, at least as he understood it, had always been the "good" foreign power.

Americans like Coolidge at home (as distinct from many who lived and worked in China) had long imagined themselves a friendly, neutral party toward the Chinese, in contrast to the predatory European imperialists. When the British fought their Opium Wars in the nineteenth century, Americans remained neutral and publicly criticized the British. They took part only as observers—though as soon as the wars were over, they quietly and happily availed themselves of all of the new trading privileges the British had used their gunboats to win. Nevertheless, Americans back home missed few opportunities to try to undermine the British in China. In the very first diplomatic mission from the United States to the Qing Empire, in 1844 just after the first Opium War, the American envoy Caleb Cushing had offered to share weapons and other military aid with the Qing government that it could use to strengthen itself against the British and other Europeans.

The Qing dynasty did not express any interest in taking advantage of American military aid in the 1840s, but Americans continued to present themselves to China as a foreign power that preferred cooperation to conquest, a hedge against the rapacious Europeans. During the massive civil war in China known as the Taiping Rebellion in the 1850s and early 1860s, which overlapped with the U.S. Civil War, an American named Frederick Townsend Ward famously trained and led a small army of Qing troops against the Taiping rebels, who believed their leader was the son of God. Abraham Lincoln's minister to China, a former Massachusetts congressman named Anson Burlingame, forged a bond with the imperial Chinese leadership on the grounds that both China and the United States were trying to reunify their countries in the midst of civil war. China in that instance closed its ports to Confederate raiders like the CSS *Alabama*, with the prince regent of the Qing dynasty remarking to Burlingame how similar were the situations of his own dynasty and the Union, both of them faced with rebellions in their respective souths.

The Qing government liked Anson Burlingame so much that in 1867, after America's and China's respective civil wars were finished, they hired him to be part of China's first diplomatic mission to the United States. In Washington, he negotiated a treaty on behalf of the Qing emperor that allowed for free migration of Chinese to America, and Americans to China. Championed by American business interests, the Burlingame Treaty, as it was known, brought a flood of cheap labor to the American West—where the transcontinental railroad was built largely by Chinese workers—as well as to the South, where poorly paid Chinese took the place of emancipated slaves. In the other direction, the treaty unleashed a wave of American Protestant missionaries to China. They were protected by China's government thanks to the treaty, but deeply unwelcome to most of the Chinese themselves. America's business investments in China by the 1920s would still pale in comparison to Britain's (which were twenty times larger) but fully half of the Protestant missionaries in the country hailed from the United States. This, too, would feed into a general sense among Americans back home that their country had never been interested in profiting from China's weakness, but only wanted to help the Chinese people—or to be more specific, "save" them.

By the end of the nineteenth century, what had once seemed a hopeful new friendship in the wake of the Civil War and the Taiping Rebellion had turned far more cynical. A backlash against Chinese migrants in the United States led by Irish and other European immigrant groups who accused the Chinese of undermining them by working harder, for lower pay, led to riots and mob violence against Chinese workers in the American West. Anti-Chinese politicians succeeded in getting federal laws passed in the 1880s that restricted most Chinese from immigrating to America. By the time Carlson entered the Marines, in spite of the purported historical friendship between the United States and China, those restrictions were still in full effect and there were only about sixty thousand Chinese in the entire United States. There is no record of Carlson ever having met a Chinese person before he got to Shanghai.

The Americans who lived in China were considerably fewer in number than the Chinese who lived in America, but as a group they were far more powerful—especially the businessmen in Shanghai, whose lives of luxury stood in contrast to their more humble brethren who toiled as missionaries in the countryside. By the late 1920s there were more than four thousand Americans in Shanghai's International Settlement, living and going about their business with an air of superiority and entitlement. These American businessmen differed little from their European counterparts when it came to their racial views of the Chinese around them. Chinese were not allowed to become members of the American Club, for example—or even to be brought in as guests—no matter how Americanized they might be. Even as Chinese nationalists blamed foreigners and their imperialistic concessions for China's continued weakness, the Americans of Shanghai, like their European neighbors, tended to blame China for its own problems. Rather than seeing the International Settlement as some kind of affront to Chinese sovereignty, a wound in China's side left by the Opium Wars of the nineteenth century, many of them saw it instead as the model to which the rest of China should aspire. To their minds, the settlement was a beacon of civilized, modern life at the edge of a gargantuan and backward country. And they would be damned if they would let it be overrun by some horde of Chinese nationalists.

Carlson's battalion arrived at Shanghai on February 24, 1927, fired up and ready to get to work on its mission of—as he described it at the time—"taming the wily Chinee." Shanghai was an awe-inspiring city, a sprawling commercial and industrial center with a population in the millions. Within the International Settlement, it was a city of towering European-style banking buildings and wide boulevards, of gorgeously appointed restaurants and dance halls, of what seemed a thousand different nationalities coming together. It was a city of vast wealth, exemplified by the hideously luxurious foreign clubs with their long bars and elite memberships. It was also, once you stepped away from the main boulevards, a city of crushing poverty where millions of laboring-class Chinese lived in tiny homes crammed into a textile-weave of narrow, intersecting alleys. It was a city of ambitions and industry but also a city of vice and organized crime: gambling and prostitution and racketeering, from dice games and low-class brothels to its grand, high-society horse-racing track. Titillated Westerners liked to call it "The Whore of the East." A foreign missionary in the 1920s spoke for many of his brethren when he said that if God didn't destroy Shanghai then he would owe Sodom and Gomorrah an apology.

None of this was immediately apparent to Carlson, however, because when he arrived at Shanghai he wasn't allowed to get off his ship. Thanks to President Coolidge's reservations about American neutrality, the *Chaumont* tied up to a mooring five miles shy of the International Settlement, at the Standard Oil complex downriver;

and there the Marines sat, with orders to stay on board until and unless an actual threat to the American citizens in Shanghai should materialize. Carlson had finally made it to China, but there was nothing to see. Having just spent three weeks in the ship's cramped, foul-smelling quarters while crossing the Pacific, he and the other Marines were desperate for open space and fresh air, but they would get none of that. It was clear that they weren't about to start "taming" anyone.

Over the weeks that followed, Carlson's battalion got to go onshore only for brief bouts of drill exercise on the expansive Standard Oil grounds, and, on two occasions, to march on parade with other foreign troops through the International Settlement. Otherwise they were confined to their ship. With so little to do, the enlisted men spent most of their time lounging around on the deck of the transport, singing endless verses of an endless song they had made up, which went: "Oh, we all came to China on the *Chaumont* / Oh, we all came to China on the *Chaumont* . . ." Over and over. (Nobody had been able to come up with a good rhyme for "Chaumont.")

The British were delighted to have the Americans on hand to back them up against the Chinese, even confined as they were to their ship. The leading Shanghai British newspaper, *The North-China Herald*, reported that the American Marines made a "very fine impression, fellows whom any nation could be proud to claim as its own." It explained to its readers that the Marine Corps had a higher standard for enlistment than any other branch of the U.S. military. "Every man is picked for mental and physical capacity," it said. "Most of them are nearer six feet in height than the usual military unit, and they possess an *esprit de corps* which defies rivalry."

As operations and training officer, Carlson was responsible for his battalion's readiness to fight, and he welcomed the chance to march his men on parade because it gave them much-needed exercise. Second to that, he saw the parades as useful to "impress the Chinese with the strength and efficiency of the foreign forces." On the two occasions when they joined the other Western forces on parade, the Marines marched in formation through the streets of the settlement, the sun glinting off their nickel-plated bayonets. ("The flash of a bayonet has a decided moral effect on a mob," Carlson explained to his father.) A band marched in front, playing the Marines' Hymn, as the

U.S. Marines marching on parade in Shanghai, 1927.

lines of the combined foreign troops behind them stretched to a full mile. Large crowds of Chinese and expatriate spectators gathered to watch, and the Americans were the star attraction. One witness described the settlement's main boulevard, Nanjing Road, as being "choked with thousands eager for a sight of Uncle Sam's fighting men."

The question of whether the U.S. Marines would actually engage in combat with Chinese troops, or even civilian mobs, was highly controversial—mainly because doing so would mean abandoning America's pretense of friendliness toward China and, worse, actively supporting the British in China after nearly a century of trying to distance themselves. Back home, the *New York Evening Post*, for one, was fully in favor of joining forces with the British. While allowing that in the past the Chinese had always been "our historic friends," it argued that Chinese troops were now being armed, trained, and advised by the Soviets and should no longer be regarded as friendly. Even if an outright attack on Shanghai could be thwarted, it warned, Bolshevist-backed Chinese forces were sure to find ways to harm American interests, perhaps by sabotaging factories and setting fire to American homes. "It is a Bolshevik influence and a Bolshevik technique which are being applied in the threat at Shanghai," the paper insisted, and the thousands of American civilians at risk in the city needed the protection of their Marines. In the face of a common danger from the Chinese, the *Post* reminded its readers of a time back in 1859 when American sailors on an observation mission in the second Opium War came briefly to the aid of British marines under attack from Qing forces, under the justification—as declared by the American commodore at the time, and repeated now by the *Post*—that "blood is thicker than water." In other words, that white men must stand together against the Chinese.

This line of interpretation was heavily promoted by the British themselves. In a highly animated speech to three hundred New England businessmen in the metals industry, the British ambassador to the United States argued that through Moscow's influence, the "poor and ignorant Chinese coolies" were being stirred up to commit violence against foreigners. If the Russians succeeded in using Chiang Kai-shek to drive the British and other foreigners out of Shanghai, he declared, they would then dominate Asia themselves—and if *that* could happen, then "it will not be difficult to promote a Bolshevist revolution in Great Britain itself, which would be the precursor of similar revolutions in all European countries." He warned that unless Chiang Kai-shek and his National Revolutionary Army were stopped, the situation in China would give rise to a global communist revolution that could topple governments from the coast of Asia all the way to the ends of Europe.

From a more tempered perspective, *The New York Times* acknowledged that with Chiang Kai-shek's denunciations of imperialism and his vocal support for a new "world revolt" it was easy for outsiders to conclude that he and his army were anti-foreign Reds. However, the *Times* observed, the Chinese people had entirely legitimate grievances against the foreign powers—especially Great Britain, which, it pointed out, had been the "first of the Western nations to force her way into China for the sake of trade," and which "took a leading part in several expeditions against China." On the ground in Shanghai, the British with their "feeling of caste" had shown themselves to be every bit as racist in China as they were in India, and they had well earned the hatred many Chinese felt for them. Given this history, argued the *Times*, it was naïve to imagine that the Soviets were somehow turning the Chinese against foreigners. The Chinese had perfectly good reasons of their own to hate Westerners and want to drive them out of their country, no incitement from the Soviets needed. Even the most revolutionary of the Chinese, the paper believed, were serving their own country's interests rather than Russia's.

By the end of March, the National Revolutionary Army was outside Shanghai and the Chinese workers of the city rose up from within in massive labor strikes and armed pickets. Carlson's battalion finally got its orders to disembark from the *Chaumont* and take up a defensive position in a posh residential district at the northwest corner of the International Settlement. As they hoofed the three miles through the settlement from the dock where the *Chaumont* dropped them off, they could hear nearly continuous machine gun and rifle fire in the distance. Visually, the scene reminded Carlson of the Western Front in Europe, with looping entanglements of barbed wire and British soldiers patrolling the streets. Reaching their billets, the Marines set up their own patrols and sentry posts to protect the Americans in the vicinity from, in Carlson's words, the "depredations of Chinese mobs." However, President Coolidge was still adamant that the Marines should play a purely defensive role and avoid fighting with the Chinese, so the wider perimeter around the settlement was left to the British and others who had no such reservations. Yet the Americans were still ready to fight in the likelihood, as a writer in the *Marine Corps Gazette* put it, that "the front lines held by other international troops might be broken and thousands of fanatical Chinese would pour into the settlement."

Such incidents had already taken place farther inland. A few weeks earlier, at the city of Wuhu up the Yangzi River, activists from the National Revolutionary Army had whipped up a crowd of Chinese civilians and soldiers into such a fury that they went on to destroy the city's foreign clubhouse and customs office, forcing the foreign residents of the city to flee to Shanghai for protection. And more recently, on March 24, just two hundred miles upriver from Shanghai at Nanjing—the grand, walled city that Chiang Kai-shek had his eye on for the new capital of the Republic—rampaging soldiers from the National Revolutionary Army had looted and burned three of the city's foreign consulates and attacked foreigners in their homes, killing several of them. "You Americans have drunk our blood for years!" shouted a Chinese officer at the American consul, vowing that his men would kill every single foreigner in the city. In reprisal, a hastily assembled flotilla of British and American gunships sailed full speed up the Yangzi from Shanghai and shelled Nanjing from the river's edge until the Chinese authorities finally promised to restore order and protect the city's foreign residents from further harm.

Downriver in Shanghai, Carlson sensed that something big was about to happen. His own view aligned with those who believed that the Russian Bolsheviks were behind it all. Writing to his father, he predicted that Japan and Great Britain would soon declare war on the Soviet Union, and if that happened, then he expected the United States would join them and "grasp the opportunity to wipe the Bolshevists off the map, once for all." The Chinese forces that had overwhelmed Wuhu and Nanjing and now fought for control of Shanghai appeared to him little more than a proxy for the Soviets— surely Chiang Kai-shek's Nationalists with their hatred of foreigners and resentment of the old treaty concessions were being manipulated by puppet masters from behind the scenes. To his eye, it looked pretty clear that the global conflict between the Soviets and the Western capitalist nations was about to come to a head right there in front of him, at Shanghai. Carlson welcomed the confrontation. As for his own role and that of his fellow Marines in the matter, he told his father confidently, "Well, we're here for the job."

As it turned out, the Marines never did get to engage in fighting with the "fanatical Chinese." Chiang Kai-shek calculated that it wasn't worth provoking a war with the British over Shanghai when the rest of the country remained to be unified, so he left the foreign concessions alone and settled for taking control of the rest of the city from its warlord authorities. Carlson was disappointed. In the thick of the confusion, as Chiang's forces were fighting for control of the Chinese city, he had written home of his excitement. "It is a great show. I am enjoying it thoroughly," he told his parents. "I only hope we have a chance to wipe out a few of these [Chinese] before we get through." But in spite of flying bullets and mortar shells and a succession of false alarms and miscommunications in the tense days that followed, no direct fighting took place between the American and Chinese troops. The forces of the Northern Expedition captured Shanghai without invading the International Settlement, and by the beginning of May it was clear that any danger to foreigners had passed. They would not get to kill any Chinese. Rather than being recalled home, however, Carlson's battalion and the regiment of which it was a part—the 4th Marines, soon to be known by the enduring nickname of the "China Marines"—were instead settled into more permanent quarters in preparation for what would turn out to be more than a decade of garrison service in Shanghai, watching and waiting.

On April 18, Carlson wrote home that the situation in Shanghai was now "remarkably quiet." It wasn't really so quiet, though. There was a drama unfolding right around him of which he was unaware but that would shape the course of China's history for generations to come—and it would, in time, become central to his own life as well. Its basis was this: the Chinese forces that had marched on Shanghai did not represent some seamlessly unified movement. They were, instead, an uneasy alliance between two political parties who shared an interest in reunifying China but otherwise diverged in their visions of what should come next for the country. The larger of these two groups was the Nationalist Party, or the KMT as it was best known in English (short for "Kuomintang"), which traced its origins to the young radicals who overthrew the Qing dynasty in 1911. The KMT was originally the party of Sun Yat-sen, credited as the father of the 1911 Revolution, and it had its base of power in Canton, in the far south of the country. The armies of the Northern Expedition were largely the KMT's own Cantonese troops, as were the officers, most of whom had been trained at the party's elite (and indeed, Russian-financed) Whampoa Military Academy, near Canton.

The other party were the Chinese Communists. Founded in 1921, the Chinese Communist Party, or CCP, had a shorter history than the KMT and its numbers were much smaller. Only twelve delegates were present at its first meeting, and the party still counted barely a hundred members when it was invited the following year to form an alliance with Sun Yat-sen's KMT party to reunify China by force. The KMT possessed an entire government administration and an army, and so it did not need the fledgling organization of Communists in any essential way—they were mostly writers and teachers, more skilled at running discussion groups than fighting wars, and their numbers were scant in any case. But the KMT *did* need weapons, advisors, and other military aid from China's gigantic neighbor to the northwest, and the Soviets made their support conditional on the KMT's cooperation with the Chinese Communists.

That was in 1922, while Sun Yat-sen was still alive. Acting at the instigation of a Soviet agent, Sun formed a "United Front" between his Nationalist Party and the Chinese Communists, an alliance that was still in effect when Carlson's battalion was called to China. Members of the Communist Party were granted dual membership in the KMT and some held prominent political positions. As the Russians saw it, the Nationalists alone had the armies and the bureaucratic capacity to reunify China, but the CCP had the correct ideology of communism, so only by working together could the two parties fulfill Russia's hopes for a pro-Soviet revolutionary state in China.

Not everyone in the KMT leadership had been comfortable with the alliance, however, and after Sun Yat-sen died in the spring of 1925 the grounds of cooperation began to shift. For one thing, the Communist Party grew exponentially in size after a series of high-profile strikes and student marches that summer, sparked by the shooting of a striking Chinese worker by Japanese guards at a Shanghai factory on May 30, 1925. Initial protests were fanned into a wildfire when the British police opened fire on Chinese demonstrators. Communist-led anti-imperial protests exploded around the country, and with them rose the party's fortunes: by the end of the year the CCP would have more than ten thousand registered members, and by the following summer, thirty thousand. They were no longer the paltry, ineffective band Sun Yat-sen had originally allowed into the KMT. For another thing, after Sun Yat-sen's death the ambitious, thirty-seven-year-old military officer Chiang Kai-shek worked his way to the top of the KMT's ranks and—in spite of the resonance of his anti-imperial rhetoric with the goals of the Communists—he quickly grew to resent the Soviet Union's efforts to shape China's domestic politics and feared that the rising influence of the Chinese Communists posed a threat to his own personal power.

Even as the National Revolutionary Army succeeded in its conquest of the major cities of China's southern and central regions from 1926 into 1927, relations between the Nationalists and the Communists were breaking down. Still, Stalin pushed the Communists to maintain their alliance with Chiang on the grounds that they needed his military leadership if they were to have any hope of reunifying China. But once that was accomplished, he said, they could discard the Generalissimo "like a squeezed-out lemon."

By the time the army reached Nanjing in 1927, an energized Communist Party was organizing labor uprisings in cities throughout China, especially in Shanghai, where thousands of armed workers' pickets took to the streets. Given the close relationship between Soviet advisors and the Chinese Communists, senior KMT figures warned Chiang that their party was on the verge of being eclipsed and cast aside by a rival from within their own ranks. And so, in the relative quiet that followed the capture of Shanghai—just as Carlson's battalion was setting up its long-term barracks and he was feeling disappointment at the lack of "action" for him to be involved in—Chiang Kai-shek struck.

On April 12, 1927, Chiang declared the Shanghai workers' unions illegal. With ruthless efficiency, hit squads made up of KMT soldiers and allies from Shanghai's organized crime world massacred hundreds of Communists and labor organizers—in the streets of the city, in their homes, in offices, at hastily called meetings. Even as Carlson was taking stock of the peace and quiet after the transition of Shanghai into KMT control, Chiang's purge of the Communists was spreading through the city and out into the rest of the country in what would come to be known as the White Terror. By its end, thousands of workers and labor activists would be dead and the Communist Party would be effectively destroyed as a viable political force in China. Those Communists who could flee, fled—either into the deep countryside to escape the reach of Chiang's agents, or abroad to Moscow and elsewhere. Some went underground in Shanghai and other cities to continue organizing in secret, hoping to avoid discovery and someday resurface again.

By the end of 1927, this rupture between Chiang Kai-shek and the tattered remnants of the Chinese Communist Party was total. The United Front that Sun Yat-sen had brokered with Soviet encouragement was dead. Replacing it was the beginning of a civil war between the KMT and the surviving vestiges of the CCP that would embroil China for the better part of the next twenty-two years—and which, in certain crucial respects, has never ended.

By the fall of 1927, things were looking up for Carlson. On September 7 he was promoted to first lieutenant, a welcome increase in rank and pay, even coming as it did nearly ten years after his promotion to captain in the Army. He also started finding outlets for his writing, publishing short pieces for his fellow Marines in *Leatherneck* magazine and the *Marine Corps Gazette*, as well as the 4th Marines' regimental newsletter, *The Walla Walla*. Better still, Etelle finally arrived in China after nearly a year of separation. They set up a household in Shanghai together, which was worth it even though it cost a fortune. Rent in the International Settlement was comparable to a major city in the United States, and other expats told Carlson that in China it would be a loss of "face" if he or Etelle should do any manual labor for themselves. So like the other foreigners, they felt compelled to hire servants to take care of all their needs.

The two of them delighted in the insular social life of the settlement, hosting and attending dinner parties with other expatriates, dressing up for ladies' nights at the social clubs, watching the horse races. On the grounds of his being an officer, Carlson was admitted as a member to one of the most exclusive clubs in the settlement, the Shanghai Club. ("It is largely a British affair, and more conservative than the others," he explained to his parents. "I must be a conservative.") Carlson was busy with his work for the Marines, but he and Etelle still found time to read together and practice their Spanish and French, neither of them initially seeing any use in trying to learn Chinese. In time, Etelle found work as a teacher in an English school, which helped with expenses and paid the costs of furnishing their apartment. The two of them would go for long walks together through the International Settlement and sometimes into the city beyond, though Etelle preferred the company of foreigners

Etelle in a rickshaw.

and found it frightening when there were too many Chinese about. On one stroll they found themselves caught up in a sea of people in a factory district—"crowds of curious and often vicious-looking Chinese" as Etelle described them. She held tightly to Carlson's arm, begging him to get her out as soon as he could.

New as he was to China, Carlson's thinking about the country differed little from the example of the American businessmen in Shanghai. As with his visions of "taming the wily Chinee," he believed firmly that the Chinese people needed to be trained like children or pets to keep them subordinate to the white Anglo-Americans who ran the show in the concessions. Writing to his father early on, from the comfort of one of the Shanghai clubs that didn't allow Chinese guests, he said flat out that the only effective policy in China was to "teach these slant eyed people a lesson." Any Chinese who threatened foreign interests had to be "severely trounced," he said. Otherwise, "Just watch and see. They will lose all respect for foreigners."

The basic fact was that Carlson knew nothing about China or its people when he arrived in 1927, though there was nothing unusual about that. The same was true for most of his fellow Marines. But there was one thing that set Carlson apart, and that was his hunger for self-improvement. Still frustrated by his inability to go to college or study in any formal way, he was eager to take advantage of whatever practical education he could get his hands on, and as long as he was in Shanghai, he eventually decided that he might as well start learning what he could about China. The Marine Corps had no regular intelligence service in China at the time, and in that vacancy he sensed an opportunity to advance his career. He volunteered and, by the end of 1927, got himself appointed as the China Marines' first regimental intelligence officer.

Carlson set to work trying to learn what he could about the domestic situation in China. It was not easy. With no background training or mentorship, he was faced with trying to parse out who the major figures were in Chinese politics, how the new KMT government being founded in Nanjing was structured, and what the history was behind the seismic changes going on around him. He made friends with foreign journalists in Shanghai as well as with local Chinese government officials who helped orient him and keep him informed. He found it enjoyable and eye-opening work, and for the first time the friendly ease of conversation he had developed as a traveling salesman in Montana turned out to be professionally useful. He hired interpreters to translate some of the Chinese newspapers into English and started cultivating a network of secret contacts.

Carlson felt inspired by the sheer difficulty of his new assignment. Starting from nothing, he was trying to carve out a niche as an intelligence analyst, with a learning curve that was all but impossibly steep for a man with limited formal education and no prior knowledge of Chinese language or history. But it was the kind of intellectual challenge he had always wanted to believe he could succeed at, and according to his superiors, he seemed to have a knack for the job. By 1928, he was turning out weekly intelligence briefings on China that were shared with American diplomats, the Navy, and the Marine Corps all the way up to its headquarters in Washington. The more he devoted himself to the work of studying China, the more it began to consume him, obsess him, until it got to the point where little else seemed to matter. "I feel detached from the outside world," he told his mother once he was deep into it, "and my interest in any arena but China ebbs with each passing day."

Given that Carlson was based in Shanghai, and given that after 1927 Shanghai was firmly in the hands of Chiang Kai-shek and the KMT, his intelligence reports relied heavily, almost exclusively, on KMT-related sources. That, in turn, meant that as objective as he might have wanted to be, he essentially saw China through the Nationalist Party's eyes. He came to admire what Chiang was trying to achieve in his continued war to piece the Republic back together. "The Nationalists have accomplished a lot," he told his father in March of 1928. "I believe there is a better chance for a united China today than there has been since the inception of the republic." He particularly admired Chiang and the KMT for turning against the Communists in 1927, which he judged to be "their most important move."

Chiang Kai-shek had continued the Northern Expedition after purging the Communists in 1927, and in 1928 his Nationalist forces were still battling to recapture the old capital of Beijing and other major northern cities. On this count, Carlson's main intelligence reports were largely uninspiring accounts of the disposition of various warlord and government forces around the country (with the

KMT now claiming the mantle of "government"). Far more interesting, however, were a separate series of weekly reports that he began to generate specifically on communism in China. In those reports, he didn't just examine events and personalities within China itself; he also tried to link them into world affairs as part of a broader international phenomenon. So while the reports began with communist incidents in China, they then panned back to cover related news from the Soviet Union, Eastern Europe, the Middle East, and even Great Britain and the United States as their own homegrown communist parties threatened strikes and agitated for political influence.

These scattered spheres of communist activity around the world intersected most clearly through the orchestration of the Comintern— the Third Communist International—which was the Soviet Union's organ for promoting and coordinating worldwide revolution. The Comintern held varying degrees of sway over the native communist parties in other countries, and it had been a central source of struggle within the Soviet leadership itself: Leon Trotsky had viewed it as an internationalist organization for promoting revolutions around the world, while Joseph Stalin (the victor) saw it instead as a means of ensuring the security of the Soviet Union above all else—a policy he described as "socialism in one country." After 1927, with Trotsky expelled from the Central Committee and headed for a life in exile (and eventual assassination), Stalin decisively reoriented the Comintern to direct the other communist parties of the world to pursue activities specifically aligned with the needs of the Soviet Union—in other words, to subordinate their own national interests to those of Russia. As those interests related to China, Stalin had supported the alliance between the KMT and CCP as a means of ensuring Soviet influence in China and ultimately using the country as a defensive buffer against Japan. That meant that when Chiang Kai-shek had purged the Chinese Communists in 1927, he had likewise defied Stalin.

Carlson was well aware of the function of the Comintern, so the broad scope of his intelligence reports was intended to underscore the ways in which Chinese communism was not actually Chinese. So, for example, one figure who showed up regularly in Carlson's reports in 1928 was not Chinese but American: Earl Browder, a labor organizer from Kansas who would, by 1930, become general secretary of the Communist Party of the USA. Browder appeared in Carlson's reports as a Comintern agent who had been sent to China from the United States to help the scattered remnants of the post-purge Chinese Communist Party organize a series of anti-foreign uprisings in the major cities of China's east and south. Browder's activities, according to Carlson, included the recruitment of disaffected Nationalist soldiers as well as the "intensification of anti-KMT and anti-foreign propaganda"—in particular sending groups into the countryside to teach peasants that everything the foreigners possessed "was stolen from the Chinese people by the help of the 'Unequal Treaties.'"

The native Chinese communists, however, proved far more elusive than the foreign agents who moved among them. Most who appeared in Carlson's reports were accused rather than proven. They were magistrates, military officers, college students. Even a thinly based charge of communist sympathies was enough to merit execution as part of the ongoing White Terror. Carlson reported on raids in China's cities that claimed to uncover large stores of communist propaganda, or traces of Soviet advisors, or evidence of Russian weapons. He described mass executions—in one case, the shooting of three hundred accused communists at once with no trial. But he had no direct sources on these native communists—everything he knew was filtered through the KMT government and a local Chinese press that was aligned with it, so his intelligence reports rendered them just as the KMT did: as bandits, rampaging in the countryside, threatening China's social stability. They were a force of chaos and mayhem, but—as Carlson, following the KMT, was certain—it was just a matter of time until they were extinguished for good.

Whether or not the ones being executed were actually the ones causing trouble, there was no question that there *were* communists in the Chinese countryside, and their activities were real. On March 24, 1929, Carlson reported on an extensive uprising in southern Jiangxi province, in which four groups of "Reds" were ransacking the countryside, burning and looting towns and villages. "It is presumed," Carlson reported, "that the Red activities reported above are those of the 4th Red Army," a ragtag force of between four and six thousand soldiers that had been operating in central China ever since Chiang Kai-shek's purge in 1927. Those communist troops, as Carlson described them, were anti-foreign and reportedly offered rewards for information on the location of missionaries. They were "hardy ruffians and bandits," he wrote. Yet in a different report Carlson described that same army as "both well trained and well equipped," its officers mostly being former graduates of the KMT's prestigious Whampoa Military Academy. In either case—be they ruffians or well trained—as usual Carlson reported that a large group of handpicked KMT troops was on its way to fight them, "and it is expected that the Communists will be wiped out in the near future."

Through 1928 and into 1929, two figures kept reappearing in Carlson's reports—"notorious communist bandits," as he called them. Sometimes they appeared together, occasionally separate. They were reputed to be the leaders of the Red Army that was causing so much destruction in the countryside. In June of 1929 they made a typical appearance with their army, invading cities and extorting money, committing in his words "considerable murder, looting, and rapine." Attacked by government troops, the Reds "ravaged the countryside" before retreating to another province to "commit further depredations." Despite the constant efforts of government troops to root them out and destroy them, however, they just kept reappearing— here in one province, there in another. Were there four thousand in their army? Or just two thousand? Or were there ten thousand? His reports conflicted constantly. Carlson wasn't even sure of the two leaders' names. One appeared with decent regularity in his reports as Chu Teh. The other, though, was impossible to pin down exactly. Sometimes he appeared as Mao Che-tung. Or Mao Cheh-tung. Or Miao Tse-tung. Or Mao Chock-tung. Or, as their names would be written today: Zhu De and Mao Zedong.

———

The Marine Corps recalled Carlson to Quantico in the fall of 1929, and he shipped home along with Etelle and three tons of their furniture and other acquisitions from China. He looked forward to the home leave, but was already planning for his return to China to continue the intelligence work he had started. He asked the Marines for a short tour in Nicaragua to make some money, followed hopefully by a longer stint as a Chinese language student in Shanghai. They said that might be possible. The posting in Shanghai had been very good for Carlson professionally. By the time he left, there were seven

Marines under his command in the regimental intelligence office and *The Walla Walla* hailed them for their "systematic and laborious pursuit of the wily Chinese General, the insidious 'Red,' and the vociferous shouter of anti-foreign slogans." The Marines were sad to see Carlson go, it said, and they would especially miss "his famous grin, his eveready greeting, and his constant and neverfailing good humor."

With Etelle at his side, Carlson had made a place for himself in Shanghai that he regretted to leave. He was enormously popular in the foreign community. *The China Weekly Review*, a prominent English-language paper, reported just before his departure that Carlson probably had more journalist friends than any other military officer stationed in Shanghai. And it wasn't just the reporters who liked him: "Few officers have had such a wide acquaintanceship among the civilian community of Shanghai," said the paper, "and none will be missed more than Lieut. Carlson, and his charming wife."

It was nearly Christmas by the time they got back to Quantico. Carlson's parents had moved to a new parish by then, in Plymouth, Connecticut, which was convenient enough to the Marine base in Virginia that Carlson was able to drive up and spend Christmas with his family for the first time since he ran away from home nearly nineteen years earlier. His parents had aged greatly since then. His mother was now in a wheelchair. Nevertheless, he would remember that Christmas as a charmed one—snow in the trees, warm fires and wood smoke and the sound of Norwegian carols that his father had learned as a boy in California. Most importantly there was, finally, a welcome for Etelle in his family's home.

CHAPTER 3

BANDITS

FIVE MONTHS AFTER his Christmas in Plymouth, Carlson arrived at a run-down collection of mud houses in a mountain valley deep in one of the most isolated regions of Central America. The town was called Jalapa, and it lay just a few miles from the unmarked border between Nicaragua and Honduras. It had taken him more than a week to get there from the Nicaraguan capital in Managua—first a hundred miles by truck, then seventy miles on foot along jungle trails, and then a final leg on horseback into the mountains. He got there at the end of May 1930, already feeling homesick for Quantico.

For the duration of this tour, he would be an officer of the Guardia Nacional, a joint Nicaraguan-American military force established by the United States Marines, and remote Jalapa was to be his base of operations in the heart of what he described as "bandit country." It was a picturesque setting in the thickly jungled mountains, unlike any place he had ever been. The headquarters for his unit was a wooden stockade fort straight out of a Western movie, built from hewn tree trunks but with the modern additions of a looping tangle of barbed wire around the back and a Browning machine gun in front. It felt like a safe refuge in a dangerous region. "Only a fool would try to rush us here," he told his parents in a letter home.

Etelle wasn't with him, because there was no place for her in the mountains of Nicaragua, so this would be their second long period of separation. When he left for Central America, she went back to live with her parents in Maine. As much as he longed to get back to China, he had asked for this tour in Nicaragua for financial reasons; even separated from Etelle and sidelined from his project of learning about China, he expected the money would make it worthwhile. As an officer of the Guardia, he would be bumped up to a captain's rank and pay for the duration of the tour, and he was to be paid two salaries, one from the Nicaraguan government and the other from the Marines. Compared to opulent Shanghai, the cost of living in Nicaragua would be negligible—especially in Jalapa—so he expected to bank the surplus.

There had been one wrench in the works, however: the alimony he had been dodging since he joined the Marines finally caught up with him. Dorothy learned of his improved financial circumstances and demanded, through her congressman, the $75 a month he owed her from the divorce agreement. He countered that he would give her $35, and if she didn't think that was enough, he and Etelle would take custody of Evans Junior (now a boy of twelve) and raise him themselves. The Navy Department found in Dorothy's favor.

The United States Marines had occupied Nicaragua off and on since 1912, and when Carlson arrived in 1930 they were trying to effect a permanent withdrawal that had already been postponed several times. From a peak of over 5,000 Marines in 1928, their numbers had been reduced to about 1,500 by the time Carlson got there, and the rest were intending to get out as soon as they reasonably could. There was strong opposition to the occupation among the American public at large, but this reduction in the U.S. military presence represented less a change of heart on America's part than it did a grudging acknowledgment of the rise of nationalism in Latin America more broadly, compounded by economic reality: after the Wall Street crash in 1929 and the onset of the Great Depression, the costs of the occupation simply became insupportable. By 1930, the State Department was intending to leave the country in the hands of an elected government approved by the United States.

Catching what he thought was the tail end of this process, Carlson planned to spend a year with the Guardia before moving back to China. The Guardia itself was supposed to be handed over to Nicaraguan command shortly—the whole point of its creation had been to establish a combined army-police force that could maintain stability in the country after the Americans departed. But at the time Carlson arrived, the Guardia was still under American control. Nearly all of its commissioned officers were American, and they were appointed and removed without input from the Nicaraguan government. Furthermore, the ranks of the enlisted men were entirely Nicaraguan and there were strong tensions between them and the officers. Few of the American officers could speak Spanish with any fluency, so they had to rely on interpreters, or even gestures, to communicate with the men they commanded.

Carlson was put in charge of thirty-five men, all of them Nicaraguan except for one American lieutenant, and with that force he was expected to maintain security in a district roughly fifty square miles in size. Scale aside, his mission wasn't so far removed from that of the KMT's "bandit-suppression" forces in China. The Guardia's primary mission in 1930 was to put down an insurrection led by the revolutionary general Augusto César Sandino, whose forces were based in the mountains of New Segovia near Carlson's headquarters. Just as with the communists in China, the Sandinistas had been marked as "bandits" by the U.S.-backed government in Managua—even though, in this case, Sandino himself was from an elite family, while his followers were organized into an alternative government with departments of agriculture and education, appointed their own judges and police, and even minted their own coinage.

Sandino's followers were trying to build a national resistance movement against the U.S. occupation and the American-backed government in the capital. Sandino had been at war with the Guardia since 1927, and in that time he had established himself as an international figurehead of anti-imperial resistance—even in China, nationalist demonstrators carried Sandino's portrait through the streets of Beijing in 1928 when the city fell to Chiang Kai-shek's Northern Expedition forces. Sandino wasn't a communist per se, just a nationalist who wanted the U.S. out of Nicaragua—to the point of issuing an order, in 1931, to "kill all Americans and destroy their property." But as Carlson saw it, Sandino and his revolutionaries were just like the communists in China: criminals and hooligans with political pretensions who attacked towns, terrorizing the rural population and disturbing public order. This time, however, rather than watching from a distance he was going to be in the thick of it himself.

It was in Nicaragua that Carlson found himself in a shooting war for the first time. In all of his previous time in the military, never once had he been in any significant danger. His Army service in

World War I consisted mainly of training and bureaucratic work far from the front lines. His service in Shanghai had never gotten more treacherous than conducting motorized patrols in the International Settlement. Even in the campaign against Pancho Villa he had served only in a training capacity on the American side of the border with Mexico. But in Nicaragua he found himself on the ground for the first time, commanding soldiers of his own and leading them against a well-armed enemy in hostile territory. It was a new experience for him, and it turned out that he rather liked it.

The first time Carlson was nearly shot in Nicaragua, it was early on, when he was trying to track down the leader of a gang of thieves. Carlson had followed the man from a distance on foot, up a mountain and along a ridge to a pair of darkened houses. One had a door open at the side so Carlson went in, carrying a sawed-off shotgun. Inside, in the darkness, he could barely make out a form in the corner, sitting with its arms crossed, but he couldn't see its face. Carlson started to ask a question, when the shadowed figure opened fire at him from nearly point-blank range. Somehow, he missed. Carlson fell to the floor and fired his shotgun but the man escaped. Another time, he was in the capital, Managua, where a group of presidential guard soldiers had defied their officers. They were in the process of carrying away a machine gun from the palace when a Marine lieutenant by the name of Pigg tried to stop them. One of them shot Pigg twice in the head. Carlson arrived just as he was bleeding out. Without thinking, Carlson started barking orders and somehow managed to convince the guards to hand over their weapons so he could smell them and figure out who had killed Lieutenant Pigg. It wasn't until later that he realized how close he'd come to being shot himself.

Morale and discipline were terrible in the Guardia Nacional. When Carlson arrived, desertions were common and there had been multiple incidents of soldiers turning against their officers. On his way up to Jalapa, he stayed one night in a house whose walls were still riddled with bullet holes from a Guardia soldier who had machine-gunned his two American commanders there a month earlier. Carlson decided that he would try to get along better with his own men. As he saw it, the way to do that was to treat them with respect. Even if he might consider himself superior to the Nicaraguan enlisted men, he told his parents, "I try not to imply the fact by word or action." He would try to keep his personal attitudes to himself.

In that vein, from the outset he resolved to speak with his men only in Spanish, which he had been practicing in Shanghai. He also made an effort not to set himself above the Nicaraguans he commanded—if they had to walk, he would walk—so as to avoid giving them grounds for resentment. The fact that he was never shot by his own men suggests that he succeeded better than some of his colleagues in this regard. He also tried to do things a bit differently in terms of training. Not wanting to follow Guardia orthodoxy in fighting Sandino, he instead tried to find out what he could about how Sandino himself operated. It was his first encounter with guerrilla tactics. Sandino's forces were highly mobile, Carlson learned, and they tended to camp during the daytime and move at night to avoid discovery. Carlson concluded that the best way to fight Sandino would be to match the revolutionary using his own methods, so he trained his small force of Guardia soldiers to travel light and move quickly, and to be prepared to engage at any time of the day or night.

Carlson relished the challenges of his command. "I feel that I am accomplishing something," he told his brother, Tom, in a letter home. He said he found the constant presence of danger "stimulating." He especially loved leading his men on patrols—loaded down with ammunition and weapons, chopping their way through the jungle with machetes, destroying Sandinista campsites and safe houses. "What a sweet hike that was through the bandit country in the dark," he wrote home after one particularly long slog. He armed himself to the teeth—when he could go on horseback, he carried a .45 Colt in his waistband, a Springfield rifle hanging from his saddle, and a Thompson submachine gun on his left arm. He got himself into the best physical condition of his life from all the climbing and hiking in the hills. The local diet of beans, tortillas, rice, and eggs was basic but substantial, and it strengthened him. He gained fluency in Spanish. The mountain air was cool and sweet, the landscape rugged, the lower elevations densely covered in tropical foliage. It was absolutely exhilarating. "It is a great life," he told his parents.

There were downsides, though. He contracted malaria, which would dog him in recurring episodes for the rest of his life. Later in his tour, he would have to be evacuated home to the United States for medical treatment. And it was hard to be away from Etelle, though the many attractions of his rugged life in the mountains also made him, for the first time, wonder whether their marriage was really the right one for him. Perhaps he wasn't meant for domestic life.

The first watershed moment in Carlson's military career—and the first step on the path to his distinctive future as a Marine commander—came on the afternoon of July 9, 1930, when a report came in to his headquarters that a force of roughly a hundred Sandinistas had appeared a few miles across the valley in the town of Portillo, where they were said to be robbing houses and terrorizing the local population. Taking a detachment of sixteen of his men on horseback and leaving his lieutenant and the rest of the men to hold Jalapa, Carlson set off for Portillo to confront them. The numbers of his detachment were small to begin with, and four of the men deserted along the way, so by the time they reached Portillo it was just Carlson and twelve Nicaraguan soldiers on the hunt for a guerrilla force they expected would be at least seven or eight times their size.

Instead of turning back to try to retrieve greater manpower from Japala, however, Carlson seized the moment and led his small band straight into the mountain trails in pursuit. They tracked the guerrillas from a distance for several hours, through the setting of the sun and into the darkness. Around nine o'clock at night they made an initial contact and then fell back, continuing to pursue the guerrilla column through the night until it stopped for rest.

At two in the morning, Carlson launched a raid on the Sandinistas in their camp. Armed with Thompson submachine guns and full drums of ammunition, his men fired almost continuously into the camp over the course of a ten-minute battle. When one of the Guardia soldiers' guns jammed, he calmly took out his pocketknife, unjammed it, and resumed firing. Carlson's men were vastly outnumbered, but with surprise on their side they managed to rout the camp of guerrillas in the darkness, killing five of them and wounding at least eight others without taking any injuries themselves. They seized the camp with all of its supplies and a cache of weapons, including dynamite bombs, grenades, and rifles. They recaptured all of the stolen loot from Portillo. It was a clear victory, and to Carlson's knowledge it was the first time a unit of the Guardia Nacional had ever fought voluntarily at night.

His superiors in the capital took notice. Carlson's commander put him up for a medal on the basis of that raid, and back in Washington, the Navy Department approved the award in terms he couldn't even have dreamed of. Based on what they judged to be his "extraordinary heroism," they gave Carlson the Navy Cross, the second-highest combat decoration in the U.S. military after the Medal of Honor. In the award citation, the secretary of the navy commended Carlson for his great courage at Portillo, when he hunted down the column of guerrillas with just twelve native troops. He also complimented Carlson for having kept his Nicaraguan district "singularly free from banditry." Carlson was now officially marked as a bandit-hunter.

The Navy Cross may have been the first thing Carlson achieved after leaving home that genuinely made his parents proud. He stayed with them for a few weeks later that year in Plymouth while recovering from malaria, and after he returned to Nicaragua a local paper sent one of its reporters to interview them for a story. The reporter was especially excited about a cache of captured weapons Carlson had left with his parents as souvenirs. "Spoils of Battle with Nicaraguan Bandits Housed in Quiet Plymouth Parsonage," blared the resulting headline. The reporter mused that an unassuming minister's house on the Plymouth town green was "hardly the kind of place one would expect to find a collection of wicked looking knives and daggers," but he assured his readers that the Carlson home was a much safer place for those weapons than the "stronghold of Nicaraguan bandits" where they had come from.

The reporter wanted some sensation for his article, and Carlson's mother obliged. Joetta said that when Evans was a baby, she had put a little American flag into his hand "and he seemed to want to keep it there"—a patriot from birth, as it were. Now he was all grown up, and the reporter cited Carlson's great success in Nicaragua as proof that he had chosen "the life for which he is best fitted." The article lamented that the Carlsons had only been in Plymouth for a few years, and so the town only knew their son as a "strong-jawed, erect military officer who has made infrequent visits there." The attention was welcome, but a little embarrassing. "Gosh, that was a pretty strong article," Carlson told his parents when they sent it to him. "Better tone them down in the future."

———

In early December of 1930, after a little over six months at Jalapa, Carlson was recalled to Managua to serve as commander of the Guardia Nacional's headquarters in the capital. By that time, his experience had started to sour. He was feeling physically exhausted from repeated bouts of malaria and welcomed the return to the city. The excitement of leading armed patrols and fighting Sandinistas had worn off after a few months, and the constant stress of danger was getting to him. At Jalapa, his old restlessness had flared up again. Time was passing, but he didn't see what higher purpose he could possibly be serving by fighting in the jungle. His mood dimmed, and he gave up reading—he didn't touch a book for months.

When he came down out of the mountains, a new round of depression was kicking in, and by the time he reached the capital, he was deep into it. "The change in climate, relief from the long strain of duty in the bandit area, etc., operated to develop in me a decided state of mental depression, sense of futility, and general mental and spiritual exhaustion," he wrote to his family in a bleak letter a few weeks later. He was writing just after Christmas—he had let the holiday itself pass unmarked—and he apologized for his silence but said he hadn't been mentally capable of writing. Despairing of treatment, he resorted to alcohol and spent two weeks drinking heavily before his emotions began to level out again.

He had at least one thing he could look forward to, though: now that he was stationed in the capital, Etelle could come and join him. On March 13, she arrived after nearly a year of separation and they set up another new home together, in a house designed by a German architect. Their renewed companionship in Managua didn't have the same aura of effortless charm they had shared in China, though. Carlson's mood was still dark, and he felt something shifting inside him. Nevertheless, he resolved to work through it and wrote to his mother that the day Etelle arrived in Nicaragua was the happiest day of his life. In any case, he didn't expect they would be staying in the country very long, because the drawdown was continuing. Another group of Marines was set to return home on April 1, which would leave fewer than six hundred in the country.

March 31, 1931—two weeks after Etelle's arrival and the day before the Marines were scheduled to depart—was a busy day in Managua. It was the Tuesday before Easter and women crowded the central market with their children in tow because it was their last chance to lay in supplies for the holiday. The stores were all going to close at noon that day and remain closed for the rest of the holiday week. The president was out of town. Carlson was in his office in the twenty-acre walled compound that served as the headquarters of the Guardia Nacional and home to the 2nd Marine Brigade. It was a payday, so a line of enlisted men stretched out into the drill grounds below his window waiting for their salaries.

A small rumbling sensation came through a little after 10 a.m., but minor tremors were common in Managua so Carlson didn't think much of it until a few minutes later, when the floor suddenly whipsawed with a violent surge and threw him to the ground next to his desk. He tried to get up and was thrown to the floor again. By instinct—a sudden memory of a tornado when he was in El Paso—he crawled under the desk as the walls and ceiling fell to pieces. The front wall of his building gave way completely. Buildings all around were collapsing as a 6.1-magnitude earthquake savaged the city of Managua. The main quake took just six seconds, but with the after-shocks that followed, it was enough to flatten much of the capital.

After the initial quake subsided, Carlson got out from under his desk and climbed down through the rubble that had been the outer wall of the building, to the ground outside where he joined the Guardia soldiers and Marines in a frantic search for survivors in the remains of their compound. To the north, a dense, black cloud of smoke was beginning to rise over the city. Fires were catching, fanned by a strong, dry breeze. Uncontained, they would build into a confla-gration that burned through the capital for days. By the end, almost the entire city of Managua would be obliterated. Three-quarters of its sixty thousand residents lost their homes in the earthquake and about two thousand were killed—the greatest number in the central market, which had collapsed on the crowds of women doing their Easter shopping.

A Marine in the wreckage of the Managua earthquake.

The city was cut off completely. Most of the radio towers had collapsed and railroad tracks were buried in landslides. The main hospitals were destroyed. The prison was in ruins, the prisoners either being crushed to death in their cells or surviving to escape and run free. In the days that followed, Marines and Guardia forces scrambled to set up field hospitals to treat the thousands of injured civilians, and kitchens to feed the tens of thousands of homeless. The U.S. withdrawal was postponed indefinitely. As camp commander for the Guardia, Carlson took on a leading role in the relief mission. He was the primary liaison between the Guardia and the civilian population, orchestrating the mass burials of the dead and the chlorination of the water supply, as well as the feeding and medical care of survivors. As soon as an American ship became available, a few days after the quake, Etelle and the other Marine wives were shipped off to California for safety. She and Evans had been together less than three weeks.

———

Carlson's Nicaraguan tour wound up lasting years longer than he had originally expected, and China kept getting put off. After the earthquake, and a brief convalescent leave, the Marines appointed him chief of police in Managua. "I am not flattered," he told his parents, "for it is one of the most delicate positions in the Guardia." Since the job was based in the capital, he was under enormous pressure from politicians to do them favors. He didn't know how long he would last before falling afoul of one party or the other.

Carlson's duties for the Nicaraguan president, as chief of police, included rooting out ideological subversives, a task he carried out with zeal. He even went so far as to organize a secret police force to spy on suspected communist organizers. In one series of raids his men arrested twenty-one Nicaraguan communists and confiscated large amounts of what he reported to be "subversive literature." His spies had been gathering data on the suspects for weeks ahead of time. Carlson confided to his parents that he thought he probably should have just had his men shoot the communists dead instead of arresting them, because he didn't trust the Nicaraguan authorities to deal with subversives harshly enough.

Carlson's final months in Nicaragua ground him down, and his depression came back with renewed force. Trying to run a police force in a foreign city whose culture he barely understood felt, in his words, like hitting his head against a stone wall. At the end of each day he was a hollow shell. He told his family he felt like he had "lost all mental stimulus as well as imagination and vision." The physical exhaustion from malaria, his heavy responsibilities after the earthquake, the separation from Etelle, and ultimately a sense of existential angst about where his life was going left him despondent and barely functional.

It was a religious epiphany that finally broke the spell. "I accept God as the Creator and Supreme Being," he wrote suddenly to his family in August of 1932. Despite being the son of a minister (or perhaps because he was), Carlson had dodged the subject of religion for much of his life. He had gone to church now and then after leaving home, but was extremely judgmental of preachers and military chaplains; some, he liked, but many, including the Navy chaplain in Nicaragua, he did not. None of them could live up to his father. Furthermore, the nonconformist in him—thanks again to Emerson— was suspicious of organized religion. He did not want to be told what to think; he wanted to explore the world for himself and come to his own conclusions. His parents do not seem to have pressed him on the issue, but in Nicaragua, in one of the lowest depths of his depression, he found himself overcome with a sense of religious awakening unlike anything he had experienced before.

It was not, however, precisely the kind of religious awakening his father might have hoped for. Although Carlson now believed firmly in God, he could not bring himself to accept that Jesus Christ was divine. He said he believed that Christ was "the greatest moral teacher the world has ever known," but rejected the notion that he had come back from the dead. "I do not believe that he was any more the Son of God than any of the rest of us," Carlson told his family. It was an idiosyncratic creed that would stay with him—a strong and abiding faith in the Christian God, combined with an admiration for Jesus that was based not on his divinity but on his humanity. To Carlson's mind, this made Christ's moral example all the more relevant and accessible to mortals like himself. His revelation infused him with a newfound sense of certainty and clarity. "I feel at peace with the world for the first time in my life," he told his family.

As physically and emotionally grueling as it had become by the end, Carlson's service in Nicaragua greatly burnished his Marine credentials. Along with the Navy Cross, he came home with several other decorations, including two citations from the president of Nicaragua, later converted to medals, for his service in the aftermath of the Managua earthquake. In his work of burying the dead and keeping order in the capital, the president said Carlson had rendered his services "without regard for his personal interest and straining his capacities to the limit of human endurance." He also came home with a Purple Heart, which was awarded to him on the basis of a meritorious service citation from General Pershing at the end of World War I. When it was created in its modern form, in 1932, the Purple Heart was given not just for wounds in action but also, retroactively, for exceptional bureaucratic service like Carlson's. So his was for desk work, though most people would later assume that it was for being wounded in the Great War—an eventuality he would have vastly preferred. In any case, by the time he left Nicaragua, he was a rising star in the Marine Corps, on his way to building a chestful of ribbons.

In the fall of 1932, following what appeared to be a successful round of Nicaraguan elections, the U.S. State Department decided the time had finally come for the Marines to return home. The new

Nicaraguan president was inaugurated on January 1, 1933, and the Marines departed the next day. As chief of police, Carlson was tasked with security for the presidential inauguration as well as for the withdrawal of the American troops. When the last wave of Americans decamped from Managua, he rode on the last car of the last train out.

A sizable crowd of Nicaraguans had gathered to watch them leave. Gazing out from his train car, Carlson projected his own nostalgia onto them. "A curious silence lay like a cloak over the assembled multitude as the Marines entrained for Corinto and their homeward bound transports," he wrote in a saccharine piece for the *Marine Corps Gazette*. The Nicaraguans, he imagined, were inwardly mourning the loss of these brave young men from America who, "in their search for adventure, had found in this picturesque land an opportunity to aid a neighboring people to achieve a larger measure of peace and happiness."

It did not occur to Carlson during his service in Nicaragua that there might be anything wrong with the American military presence in the country. After all, to him it had been a straightforward humanitarian mission—training a national guard force that would make it possible for the Americans to end their occupation and leave the country in peace; helping to suppress the bandits, as he understood them to be, who were causing so much trouble in the northern part of the country; helping to restore public order and feed the hungry in the aftermath of a terrible natural disaster. He saw no reason to think other than proudly on what he had done there.

But by the time he left the country, there was an argument to a rather different end being circulated by one of his mentors in the Marine Corps: Major General Smedley Butler, one of the most decorated Marines of all time and the key military figure in America's imperial ambitions of the early twentieth century. Butler had long had a soft spot for Carlson, going back to his service as the general's horse agent when he was just starting out at Quantico. When Butler made an inspection tour at Portland while Carlson was commanding the mail guard there, a local reporter asked him why the Marines were so popular, and Butler replied, "It's because we've got a lot of officers like Carlson who take care of the men." In a 1926 letter he told Carlson that he was "a hell of a good officer." "You always do the right thing," he said, "and it is one of the misfortunes of this

wretched system of promotion we have that you are only a lieutenant. Only wish I could make you a major." According to a fellow
officer who knew both men at Quantico, Carlson was one of Butler's
"lifelong favorites."

By one reckoning, Smedley Butler had participated in at least
twenty-two different revolutions around the world by the late 1920s,
most of them in Central and South America. He had spearheaded the
original U.S. occupation of Nicaragua in 1912. But after his retirement in 1931, looking back on a military career that spanned four
decades, he began to brood on the moral logic of America's overseas
military interventions and his own role in leading them. After running for the Senate as a Republican in 1932 and being defeated at
the polls, he took a sharp anti-interventionist turn and began giving speeches—which he later published as a short book, *War Is a
Racket*—in which he argued that the United States had long been
sending its Marines overseas not to defend any essential national
interests but only for the sake of enriching a small number of well-
connected banking houses and giant business interests.

As he put it in an article for *Common Sense* magazine:

> I spent 33 years and 4 months in active service as a member of
> our country's most agile military force—the Marine Corps. I
> served in all commissioned ranks from a second lieutenant to
> Major-General. And during that period, I spent most of my
> time being a high-class muscle man for Big Business, for Wall
> Street and for the bankers. . . .
>
> I helped make Haiti and Cuba a decent place for the National
> City Bank boys to collect revenues in. . . . I helped purify Nica-
> ragua for the international banking house of Brown Brothers
> in 1909–1912. I brought light to the Dominican Republic for
> American sugar interests in 1916. I helped make Honduras
> "right" for American fruit companies in 1903. In China in 1927
> I helped to see to it that Standard Oil went its way unmolested.

Carlson did not share Smedley Butler's views (not yet, at least)
but he did have an inkling that everything wasn't quite as rosy as
some imagined. A few months before his departure from Nicaragua, he had reported in an intelligence memo that both of the major

political parties in Managua feared a revolution of some kind after the American withdrawal. His personal view was that the Guardia Nacional would not last long in its current form once the Marines were gone. And indeed it would not. In February of 1934, one year after the American withdrawal, Augusto César Sandino—who by that time had agreed to give up his revolution peacefully and support the elected government—came down out of the mountains to negotiate the terms of his disarmament with the new president in Managua. After one of their meetings, Sandino was leaving the presidential palace compound when a detachment of Guardia soldiers stopped his car and took him prisoner along with his brother and two of his generals. The soldiers took their captives to another part of the city, shot them, and secretly disposed of their remains.

The soldiers were acting under direction from Anastasio Somoza, the commanding general of the Guardia Nacional. After executing Sandino, Somoza turned the combined army-police force to his own ends, eventually deposing the elected president and employing the Guardia as the muscle to enforce his own family's dictatorship over Nicaragua for the next forty-plus years. Far from the idealistic force of democratic stability Carlson and the other American Marines had imagined they were leaving behind, the Nicaraguan national guard became instead a ruthless and partisan army of terror for Somoza and his family to wield against their domestic enemies, one of the most corrupt and feared military forces in Latin America. When Somoza first took command of the Guardia in 1933, he did so because the Americans chose him to lead it. Carlson had worked with him to make the transition.

CHAPTER 4

THE OLD CAPITAL

CARLSON FINALLY MADE IT back to China in March of 1933. Reunited with Etelle, he looked forward to resuming the intelligence work in Shanghai he had left off at the end of 1929. "I plan now to make myself an authority on Far Eastern affairs," he told his parents when he arrived. "That seems to be the theater towards which the eyes of the world are turned now." Much had happened in the three and a half years he had been gone. Since the nineteenth century, China had been the grounds of intersection for many of the world powers: Russia, Britain, America, France, Germany, Japan, and others all sounding one another out in its neutral, semicolonial territory, each with its own claims and ambitions for the country's future. But by 1933 it had become clear that, of all of them, the country whose ambitions in China were far and away the greatest—and the most ominous—was Japan.

The initial target of Japan's imperial ambitions on the Chinese mainland was Manchuria, the vast northeastern region of the country that lay due west of the Japanese home islands, just beyond Korea. It was the original home of the Manchus who ruled the Qing Empire, and for most of the long span of their reign, the 600,000-square-mile territory (more than double the size of Texas) was closed to Chinese migration and was kept essentially as an enormous hunting preserve for the Qing emperors and their Manchu courtiers. By the time the dynasty fell in 1912, more than 250 years of restricted migration had left Manchuria with a relatively sparse population and enormous reserves of mostly untapped natural resources.

Japan's modern rise began in the nineteenth century as a response to Western imperialism and the realization that Britain, France, and the other European nations were carving the world up into their own zones of control. To survive in such a world, some Japanese believed, their country had to learn to compete head-to-head with the imperial powers—that is, to become one of them. As one Japanese official put it in the 1880s, Japan could either take its seat at the table in the grand feast of imperialism, or it could be served up as the main course. One of the first steps in Japan's expansion was a war with China in 1894–1895 in which, after soundly defeating China's poorly coordinated navy, Japan took control of Taiwan as its first major colony. Taiwan had been a territory of the Qing Empire since the seventeenth century and before that a Dutch possession, but under Japan's control, the children of Taiwan attended Japanese schools, learned to speak Japanese, and were brought up to think of themselves as subjects of the Japanese emperor. It was a showpiece for Japan to demonstrate to the world its capacity for colonial government.

The expansion continued by increments. In 1910, Japan formalized control over Korea, for which it had been competing against China and Russia since the late nineteenth century, and the next frontier to the west of the Korean Peninsula—beckoning with its vast resources and low population—was Manchuria. Through aggressive treaties and backdoor dealing in the 1910s and '20s, the Japanese gained special privileges there—territorial concessions, the stationing of economic and military advisors, preferential loan treatment, and rights of development in the territory along the routes of a railroad system, the South Manchurian Railway, control of which Japan had won from tsarist Russia in 1905.

The South Manchurian Railway would be Japan's central artery of expansion into Manchuria, a linear colony of sorts. To guard the railroad zone, Japan fielded a military force, the Kwantung Army, whose superficial charge was to protect the railroad from bandits but whose actual function was to establish a permanent Japanese military presence in Manchuria. By 1930, there would be over 200,000 Japanese workers in Manchuria under the watchful protection of the Kwantung Army, most of them white-collar employees of the many mining, industrial, and agricultural subsidiaries of the South Manchurian Railway, which in aggregate became the most profitable corporation in Asia.

What might otherwise have been a gradual buildup of Japanese power in Manchuria through the settlement of Japanese subjects and economic development in the railway zone gave way in the early 1930s to a military invasion. The tipping point was the Great Depression, which devastated Japan's export economy and bolstered factions within the country that wanted more aggressive expansion and—for the sake of protecting Japanese trade—to carve out a larger piece of the world that would be Japan's alone. They wanted a sphere where Japan would be unanswerable to the Western powers and their liberal post–world war order which, as many Japanese saw it, gave the greatest benefits to the Westerners themselves. An already divisive political caste in Tokyo frayed to tatters. Japanese politicians who sought to uphold international norms were sidelined by protests or in some cases assassinated, bringing far-right figures to power in their places. In Manchuria, certain aggressive commanders of the Kwantung Army acted with increasing independence from their superiors and from the civilian government in Tokyo, cheered on by a public hungry for economic relief and proof of their national strength.

On the night of September 18, 1931, just outside the Manchurian city of Mukden, soldiers of the Kwantung Army, operating without the knowledge of the home government (let alone its permission) set off a bomb near the track of the South Manchurian Railway and blamed it on Chinese saboteurs. Claiming self-defense and a right to provide security for their people and their investments in Manchuria, the Kwantung Army used the faked explosion as the excuse to launch a full-scale military offensive against the Chinese forces in Mukden. They soon overwhelmed the city, took control, and began to advance on the other cities of the region.

Even as Japanese reinforcements poured into Manchuria from Korea, China's leader Chiang Kai-shek was trying to concentrate his own military power on destroying the Chinese Communists, who persisted inland. Judging that he had no hope of stopping the Japanese by force, he decided not even to try, and sent no assistance to the Chinese warlord troops who tried in vain to hold Manchuria. The Japanese Kwantung Army, facing no meaningful resistance, went ahead with its plans of conquest and occupied the full span of the region by the spring of 1932. On March 1 of that year, less than six months from the date of the faked explosion at Mukden, a committee of local officials controlled by the Kwantung Army declared Manchuria to be independent of China.

As a concession to Western nations who were wary of Japan's growing power, the Japanese did not set up Manchuria as a colony as they had done in Taiwan and Korea. Instead, they created the cosmetic fiction that it would be an independent country. In a mockery of Woodrow Wilson's principles of self-determination, which had under-ridden the post–World War I order and the founding of the League of Nations, the new, ostensibly independent nation of "Manchukuo" (meaning "nation of the Manchus") was established in March of 1932, purportedly by the Manchus themselves who lived there. To rule the puppet state, the Japanese found the ideal puppet ruler in the person of Aisin Gioro Puyi, the last emperor of the Qing dynasty, who had been just a little boy when his dynasty fell in 1912. He was now twenty-six years old and the Japanese dragged him out of obscurity and installed him on the throne at Changchun, the new capital of Manchukuo. As "chief executive," Puyi began to go through the motions of ruling the nation of his allegedly self-determining fellow Manchus while answering always to his Japanese handlers behind the scenes.

In his own capital at Nanjing, Chiang Kai-shek justified his failure to stand up to the Japanese with the slogan "First unity, then resistance"—meaning that until the Communists were defeated and China was fully unified, there was no point in trying to resist an outside invader like Japan. Instead, he appealed for help internationally, asking the League of Nations to intervene in Manchuria on China's behalf. Although Chiang had made his name denouncing Western imperialism, he embraced the League as a means of strengthening his weak hand against the Japanese, and indicated that China was ready and willing to play a role in the international institutions founded by those same imperial powers.

For its part, the League, founded in the wake of World War I with the goal of ensuring world peace, revealed the true depths of its ineffectiveness with its feeble response to Japan's aggression in China. After a certain amount of hand-wringing, a commission was sent to the region in 1932 with representatives from Great Britain, the U.S.,

France, Germany, and Italy. The commission studied the situation in Manchuria and issued an ambivalent report declaring that yes, the Chinese had been wronged by Japan and the independence of Manchukuo should not be recognized, but it also allowed that the Japanese had legitimate economic rights in China and Manchuria which they were entitled to protect. China would get a vote of confidence, but no aid.

Such a timid protest on the part of the League of Nations served only to cement the resolve of right-wing figures in Japan that their country should pursue its own interests freely, unrestricted by the petty reservations of the declining Western powers. Accordingly, when in February of 1933 the League voted 42 to 1 (the lone dissent being Japan's) to approve a toothless resolution disapproving of Japan's control of Manchuria, Japan withdrew from the League entirely. Meanwhile, aggressions on the Chinese mainland were continuing. In a bloody month-long episode in the winter of 1932, on the excuse of avenging an attack on a group of Japanese monks, the Japanese navy bombed Shanghai from just offshore, killing an estimated ten thousand civilians and flattening large sections of the city outside the International Settlement.

The truce that restored peace to Shanghai in 1932 established a zone in the city within which Chinese troops were forbidden to operate. It was a deeply humiliating concession, especially layering as it did over the enduring International Settlement, where the Chinese government likewise had no power. In a similar vein, in May of 1933, Chiang Kai-shek's forces in the north signed a military truce that tacitly acknowledged Japan's control of Manchuria and other parts of North China. As with Shanghai, Chiang's officers agreed to the creation of a vast demilitarized zone, this one between Manchuria and Beijing, where the Chinese were forbidden to station troops that might "threaten" the areas under Japanese military control. Such concessions were shattering to Chinese morale and national dignity—and provoked a great deal of popular anger against Chiang—but if nothing else they at least secured a temporary peace. Not that Japan would stay satisfied forever with Manchuria, valuable as the territory might be in the near term.

Carlson was excited to be back in China. "I feel more in the center of world affairs than I do in New York," he told his parents in a letter from Shanghai. And while the people of China themselves may have had no particular reason to mark his return, the foreign community was glad to have him and Etelle back. The British-owned *Shanghai Times* said that Carlson's "many friends" would be delighted to hear that he was returning, given that on his last tour he had been "one of the most popular officers of the 4th Marines, both with leathernecks and civilians." It wasn't the same place they had left, though, and he could feel the changes all around him. By this time, Shanghai's population had swelled to bursting with refugees from the Japanese in the north—counting its new population, the city was now the fifth largest in the world. He and Etelle saw the rubble from the Japanese naval shelling the previous year, "blocks and blocks of nothing but ruins," as Etelle described the scene—and that was after a year of reconstruction.

Carlson warmed up his old contacts in Shanghai and picked up where he had left off with his intelligence work. In spite of all of his expectations to the contrary, the Chinese Communists had not only continued to hold out against Chiang Kai-shek's now six-year-long effort to exterminate them, but if anything they seemed even stronger and better organized than when he had left. By 1933 the motley, poorly equipped Red Army Carlson had reported on during his first tour had grown to more than 100,000 soldiers. Under the leadership of Mao Zedong and Zhu De, this faction of Communists had established a stronghold in the mountains of Jiangxi province, in central China, where it governed an area of more than ten thousand square miles and a population of three million people as a "soviet"—an independent, rural communist state.

Even as Chiang all but ignored the Japanese invasion of Manchuria, he was banking everything on his crusade to crush the Communists in their Jiangxi base. His truces with the Japanese, and the de facto acknowledgment of Japan's control over Manchuria, served, for him, the primary purpose of allowing him to avoid sending his forces into North China and commit them instead to his internal campaigns. To improve his armies, he had recruited a succession of German military advisors, most notably General Hans von Seeckt, who modernized Germany's military after World War I and laid the foundations for what would be Hitler's Wehrmacht. When Carlson arrived in 1933, Seeckt was helping Chiang to reorganize the KMT's military along similar lines.

The centerpiece of Chiang's anti-Communist strategy was a series of five major encirclement campaigns in the early 1930s to flush out the Communists from their heavily guarded base in Jiangxi. In the final campaigns, starting in the fall of 1933 and lasting into 1934, thousands of multistory blockhouse fortifications were constructed along radiating lines, enveloping the Jiangxi Soviet from a distance. Over a thousand miles of military roads were built to connect the forts. The hope was that in whatever direction the Communist scouts might try to probe, they would find nothing but hardened and entrenched Nationalist forces waiting to destroy them.

In contrast to his avoidance of conflict with the Japanese in Manchuria, Chiang committed fully 800,000 troops to his final campaign against the Communists in Jiangxi. But in spite of his numerical and financial advantages, he failed to contain them. In October of 1934, facing strangulation by the KMT encirclement, roughly eighty thousand of the Communists successfully broke through Chiang's lines and escaped on foot for what would come to be known as the Long March—a four-thousand-mile exodus through China's west, over snowbound mountains and across raging, un-spanned rivers, pursued incessantly by Chiang's forces. Of the eighty thousand Communist soldiers and administrators who abandoned the Jiangxi Soviet in October 1934, only about seven thousand would make it to the end of the Long March—some deserted along the way, while untold numbers were killed by disease, cold, exhaustion, and Nationalist weapons. But among those who survived to help build a new base of defense the following year at the city of Yan'an, in northwest China's Shaanxi province, out of the reach of Chiang's forces, were the men who would be the core of the future Communist leadership. Mao Zedong and Zhu De were still among them, and by the time they reached Shaanxi, Mao had risen to become one of the party's overall political leaders, while Zhu De was the commander-in-chief of its armed forces.

In August of 1933 Carlson secured a transfer to the Legation Guard in Beijing, his original hope from when he first enlisted in the Marines in 1922. The Marines of the Legation Guard were ostensibly the defenders of the American diplomatic compound (though from what, at this point, was unclear), and their presence in Beijing dated from the Boxer Rebellion of 1900, an anti-foreign uprising in the late Qing in which peasant sectarians known as the "Boxers" killed hundreds of American and European missionaries. At the peak of the crisis, the Boxers had laid siege to the legation quarter where the foreign diplomats and their families lived. A joint, eight-nation army invaded Beijing to break the siege of the legations and crush the Boxers, after which the United States and other party nations, including Japan, gained the right by treaty to station permanent military forces in the capital. The American force, the Legation Guard, had since 1905 been the responsibility of the Marines, and when Carlson joined them in 1933 there were five hundred men in their ranks. Carlson's position was as post adjutant and "school and morale officer," which gave him day-to-day responsibility for the education and welfare of the enlisted men in the Guard.

Central as China may have been to world affairs, there was something otherworldly about Beijing in 1933. For one thing, it was no longer the capital. In 1927 Chiang Kai-shek had moved China's capital to Nanjing, near Shanghai, midway down China's east coast—and Beijing, which had been China's center of government since the Ming dynasty in the 1400s, was now just a northern city with fading memories of grandeur. For another thing, it wasn't actually called Beijing anymore. "Beijing" (or "Peking" as it used to be written) means "northern capital" in Chinese, and after it was deprived of that status, Chiang's government renamed it "Beiping" (written at the time as "Peiping"), meaning "northern peace." Nevertheless the American Legation, which would become a full-fledged embassy in 1935, remained in Beijing/Peking (as many who lived there preferred to keep calling it), so the five hundred Marines of the Legation Guard remained there as well. The ambassador would visit Nanjing now and then for business, but he maintained his primary residence in the old legation building.

Carlson was accustomed to the sprawling, cosmopolitan city of

Shanghai with its modern buildings and jazz clubs and bustling international culture. Beijing, by contrast, was low-lying, dusty, and quiet. It was less visibly affected by the Western imperial presence than Shanghai and had far more of its traditional, tile-roofed architecture intact, including the mammoth red-walled Forbidden City complex where the emperors used to live (and which now boasted a giant portrait of Chiang Kai-shek on its front gate). The city felt more historical to Carlson, more essentially Chinese than Shanghai had been. "Dynasties and revolutions, civil wars and famines come and go," he wrote in a letter home, "but Peking moves serenely on down through the ages apparently oblivious of the passing of time or the progress of civilization." It was the exotic China that Westerners dreamed of— "the China you read about," as Carlson liked to put it—and it didn't let him down.

It was a comfortable life in the Legation Guard. His temporary bump up to captain's pay had expired when he left Nicaragua, but the perks of expatriate life in Beijing made up for the lower salary of a first lieutenant. The Carlsons' new house was larger than the apartment they had rented in Shanghai, as rents were less expensive up north, and servants in Beijing cost half of what they did in Shanghai. They also had an inside connection with the American ambassador, Nelson Johnson, whose wife had been in a chapter of the same college sorority as Etelle, so they got to stay in the ambassador's quarters and use his car when he was away in Nanjing on business. On a

Evans and Etelle in Beijing.

typical day, Carlson worked in his office until the early afternoon, then came home for lunch with Etelle and an hour of Chinese language study. The later afternoon was given over entirely to polo— riding, playing practice matches, tending to the animals. He was back on the horses he loved, and the mounted detachment of the Legation Guard gave him three ponies of his own.

Beijing also reawakened Carlson's latent literary ambitions, for he had more time on his hands for reading and writing. The pace of life was much slower than in Shanghai, and his responsibilities less grueling than in Nicaragua. "I have many personal ideas that I want to develop, and which require time for reflection and study," he wrote to his parents from the city. There was a vibrant intellectual community in Beijing—English-speaking Chinese scholars with degrees from American and European universities, foreign professors of various kinds teaching and conducting research, journalists covering China for European and American newspapers, diplomats, Protestant missionaries with their own particular linguistic and historical interests. He became secretary of the American Association of Peiping and presided over dinner parties of more than a hundred guests for occasions like George Washington's birthday. He joined a discussion group on "world panaceas" at a Protestant church, for which he made a presentation on Naziism. It was the community of high-minded people he had longed for when he was selling canned fruit in Montana, though it turned out he had to come all the way to China to find it. "Not much money," he reported to his parents, "but lots of intellectual inspiration."

Among Carlson's new friends in Beijing, one stood out in particular: a young reporter from Missouri named Edgar Snow, a slim man nine years younger with wavy hair and thick eyebrows, who had written a few books already and was at that time piecing together a living as a freelancer. Snow was Carlson's first real writer friend, and he had just gotten married to another American journalist, Helen Foster, who wrote under the pen name "Nym Wales" but was known to her friends as Peg. Carlson and Edgar Snow had first met each other back in 1929 in Shanghai, when Snow was fresh out of journalism school and Carlson was near the end of his first tour. They were close enough then that Carlson had tipped Snow off that the Shanghai Municipal Police were keeping a file on him, for suspicions that he had been a labor activist in the United States and was consorting with radicals in Shanghai (charges that Snow hotly denied). In Beijing in 1933, Evans and Etelle met Edgar Snow's new wife, Peg, and they hit it off immediately. The two couples soon became the center of each other's social lives.

On weekends the four of them would travel together to the Western Hills outside of Beijing, where a friend rented an old Buddhist temple

Edgar Snow and Evans Carlson.

as a mountain retreat. Carlson had developed a love of trail hiking in Nicaragua, and he set the pace with his long legs while the others did their best to keep up. Together, they tramped through the hills and valleys, visiting temples and crumbling sections of the Great Wall. At home in Beijing, they lounged in their courtyards talking about the Big Questions of the world—of the future of fascism and democracy, of the New Deal, of socialism and the prospects for world peace, of what might come from Japan's continued aggression in China.

Edgar and Peg Snow adored Etelle, whom Edgar, apparently forgetting that she was from Maine, described to his mother as "a lovely Southern girl whose specialty is tea with raisin crumpets." But they could also sense the frictions in the Carlsons' marriage. It had been a difficult few years. First, there was the weight of separation while Carlson was in Nicaragua, a time when he discovered his love for climbing mountains and forging through jungles on mounted patrol, a rough existence that didn't square well with married life. Then, so soon after being reunited, he and Etelle were separated again by the earthquake. It is possible that having a child might have drawn them closer together—not that it had worked with Dorothy—but Etelle suffered at least two miscarriages, one at very late term in China that left her shattered.

Evans knew how badly she was hurt inside—he revealed as much in letters to his parents—but his inclination was to soldier on. Peg Snow recalled one of their long hikes in the Western Hills on a hot day in 1933 when Etelle just couldn't keep up. It wasn't long after her first miscarriage and she was pregnant again and feeling sick. As Peg told it, Etelle was clearly exhausted but Carlson would not slow down to let her rest. Peg asked her why she didn't just hire a few porters and ride in a sedan chair instead of walking. Etelle said she couldn't because Carlson wouldn't approve. "Evans wouldn't like it," she told Peg. "You have to be a good sport no matter what. I never let him know how I feel." She had her second miscarriage a few months later.

The aspiring writer in Carlson envied the fact that Edgar and Peg Snow were bonded by their shared love of paper and pen. Peg told him that even before she met Edgar in person she had already fallen for him because she admired his writing. It was a kind of relationship Carlson had sometimes fancied for himself. When he first met Etelle in Puerto Rico, in 1924, he wrote home about how the two of them were reading and editing each other's compositions—an article in his case, a report to the Girl Scouts in hers. Their editorial changes improved each other's writing, he said, and showed "We are in accord in every respect." This, to him, was the height of romance—an intellectual courtship based on writing and reading together. By 1933, however, he no longer felt like Etelle was measuring up. Not only had they stopped writing together; he hardly ever even let her borrow his typewriter anymore. Etelle considered herself a traditional kind of wife and tried to keep her husband happy by not complaining or criticizing. Carlson, though, was finding himself less and less content to be paired with a Girl Scout of impeccable social manners; he wanted a partner with big ideas and strong opinions who would challenge him and argue with him. In short, he wanted a marriage like the Snows had. "Keep criticizing and pushing Ed," he once told Peg. "It is the making of him."

When they reconnected in 1933, Edgar Snow had just gotten a $750 advance to work on a new book. It was a considerable sum,

Carlson and friends in the hills outside Beijing.

enough to cover a year's worth of living expenses in China. And the whole concept of an advance was new to Carlson—the idea that a publisher would pay you up front, and you could then write freely without having to worry about money. It sounded like a dream to him. There were limitations, though; to get the advance, Snow had to write on the topic his publisher wanted. And in this case, the publisher wanted something that was basically impossible: a book about the Chinese Communists. Snow had enough integrity that he didn't want to write a book based on hearsay and rumor, but none of the foreign reporters knew anything concrete about the Communist leaders beyond the reports from the KMT about how violent and destructive they were and how much they hated foreigners. There was no way to get to their base in Jiangxi province, which at that point still lay behind the heavily militarized, radiating lines of the KMT's final encirclement campaign. Snow had accepted the assignment in "a moment of optimism," as he put it, but soon realized that he would probably have to give up on the book and return the advance.

Carlson's attitude toward the Chinese people was different this time around. There was no more talk of "slant-eyed people" or the "wily Chinee." His outlook had changed as a result of his tour in Nicaragua, where he came away believing that any success he'd had as a commander of troops for the Guardia, or as chief of police in Managua, had been because he had tried to respect the Nicaraguans by speaking Spanish as much as possible and, above all, because he had tried to look beyond their many cultural differences to see them as equally human. This was hardly a common view for an American Marine in Nicaragua at the time, and it only crystallized fully for him toward the end of his tour, as part of his religious awakening. In the same letter from Managua where Carlson told his parents about his newfound belief in God, he also told them about his changing views on racial difference. "The human heart is the same the world over," he told them. "It responds to kindness, sympathy, toleration, consideration. The sense of right and wrong is deeply imbedded in the minds of all civilized people."

Such a view had its own kind of naïveté, assuming as it did that everyone was the same inside, and it also begged the question of who was "civilized," but it was well intentioned nonetheless and it caused him to think differently about how Americans should treat the people of other countries. In the wider world, he told his parents, there was "a growing sense of equality among all people, especially those who have forcibly been kept submerged by the so-called upper classes." And though he phrased this in the abstract, as a "growing sense" out there in the world, it was something he was starting to believe himself: that people should be thought of as equals.

As it applied to Carlson's second tour in China in 1933, this shift in his thinking made him wish for a deeper understanding of Chinese culture. He was serious about trying to become a Far Eastern expert, and knew that being able to read and speak Chinese would be a cornerstone of that career. He also now accepted that there was much more to culture than just words. And so, as he started basic Chinese lessons in Beijing, he also began to scour the libraries of the foreign legations and missionary colleges to find books he could read in English about the country's longer history.

This process of educating himself about China wasn't just for his own benefit. As "school and morale officer" for the Legation Guard, he felt responsible for setting an example that the other Marines could follow, and he thought they, too, could stand to learn a bit more about the country where they were based. In 1934 he received permission from the commander of the Guard to start a Chinese language course for the Marines in Beijing. He also took over editing their in-house newspaper, *The Legation Guard News*, where he used his editorial page to encourage the men to use their free time wisely by enrolling in the Chinese class. He pitched it as a way for the Marines to improve themselves and engage more deeply with the world around them. "Life can be made a glorious experience by those who have the will and courage to live vigorously," he told them. "Think it over, and then organize your free hours with that in mind."

Carlson happily refashioned himself as the Legation Guard's in-house amateur China expert. When the excavation for a new recreation hall in the Legation compound turned up some old coins and shards of ancient pottery, he started a museum. With permission from the ambassador, he invited a prominent Chinese scholar and some foreign historians to study the objects, then welcomed the general public to come view the collection. Ambassador Johnson took to calling him "the curator." Carlson also convened a Chinese history contest for the Marines, for which they had to prepare answers to seventy-five questions ranging from ancient historical traditions to the politics of modern China. The questions came up nearly to the present, asking about the terms of the treaty that ended the first Opium War, the failure of the Taiping Rebellion in the mid-nineteenth century, and the roots of the 1911 Revolution. The winner got $60 worth of books about China.

Learning Chinese, studying philosophical trends of earlier dynasties, and analyzing the rebellions and wars of the nineteenth century were hardly the kinds of activity the Marines in Beijing had occupied themselves with in the past, but in the eyes of the colonel in charge of the Legation Guard it was a welcome change. He supported Carlson's work and agreed that Americans needed to understand the Chinese better if the two peoples were to get along. As evidence of at least modest success in his efforts, Carlson could point to the fact that after the enlisted men started learning Chinese, the number of disciplinary cases involving them getting into fights with the Beijing locals diminished significantly.

The foreign press took notice. *The China Weekly Review* announced that there was a "new life" in Beijing, "injected into it by the (of all things) American Legation Guard." To the astonishment of the more conservative foreigners in the old capital, the United States Marine Band was playing free concerts in a local park and making visits to Chinese universities "to the delight of the students." Carlson's commander told the paper that he viewed the Chinese not as potential enemies (as his predecessors had done) but as "honored colleagues." Echoing Carlson, he said the way to avoid conflict between peoples was through understanding and learning about one another. He wanted the Marines to get to know the Chinese "as friendly neighbors." To that end, he invited a school of Chinese military cadets to inspect the American Legation compound for the first time ever, which prompted fits of apoplexy from the neighboring Europeans. ("We're supposed to be here to keep the Chinese out," one of them sputtered, "not let them in.")

The *Review* noted with approval that thanks to Carlson's Chinese

U.S. Marines teaching Chinese cadets how to play baseball.

school, "now many a marine is busily poring over Chinese phonetics and radicals." The Americans were teaching Chinese cadets how to box and play baseball, while the Chinese were teaching them martial arts and swordplay in return. It was an unprecedented moment of friendliness between the militaries of China and the United States in Beijing, and the paper (edited by an American) heartily approved. The fewer walls there were between the Chinese and foreigners, it said, the better.

Carlson also began socializing with Chinese officials during this second tour. It began slowly. "Evans and I had our first Chinese dinner the other night at a Chinese restaurant here," reported Etelle from Shanghai in April 1933. Of course, being Shanghai, most of the guests at the dinner were British, but at least two of them were Chinese, so that was progress. She and Evans fumbled with chopsticks to try to fit in.

In Beijing, he became more serious about paying his respects to Chinese military officers. In May of 1934, he was tasked with showing around a visiting American general named Bradman, and convinced him to call on several of the civil and military officials in the city. It was an unusual show of respect from foreigners who typically looked down on their Chinese counterparts, and the Chinese generals seemed delighted, welcoming Bradman and Carlson with banquets and military salutes. They met with the mayor of Beijing as well as the general in charge of troops in the region. They were hosted for an especially lavish banquet at the old imperial Summer Palace by the KMT minister of war. Etelle was seated directly next to the minister, and as he didn't speak English, she got to use some of the Chinese she had been practicing. Carlson wrote home that it was the best food he had ever tasted. In return, Carlson engineered reciprocal visits for the Chinese generals with full honors at the American Legation. "The Chinese were overcome," he told his parents afterward, "for no foreign guards had ever received them before as equals. In fact, no foreign military men had ever called on them officially before."

When Carlson's tour in Beijing concluded in the summer of 1935, he left China without knowing what his next assignment would be, just that he had been approved to spend part of the following year studying foreign affairs at George Washington University, an opportunity that absolutely thrilled him. He was also promoted to captain, marking his third time at the rank after the Army and the Guardia Nacional. Carlson left Beijing as the model of a cultured Marine officer—tall and courtly, poised and confident, he charmed nearly everyone he met. There would, in his life, usually be a few people around who secretly loathed him, resenting his easy manner or the way things always seemed to shape themselves around him, but for now the critics were quiet and his admirers were effusive. He was the "quintessential American Christian officer and gentleman," wrote Helen Foster Snow, "more West Point than any West Pointer." And Etelle played the role of an officer's wife to the hilt. "They were the model couple in the Marine Corps," wrote Peg, "and aware of it."

An unexpectedly large crowd turned out to see them off at the Beijing train station. Ambassador Johnson and his wife were there, along with the commanders of the various foreign guards, the secretaries of legations, many of the enlisted men, and a number of old friends. The new editor of *The Legation Guard News* said they were going to run Carlson's picture on the cover of the next issue. Carlson was unnerved by all the attention, but found it encouraging as well. At the very least, he told his parents, "it indicates that people realize that my efforts during the past two years were well intentioned." By contrast, he found the Japanese on his ship home—which stopped at Shimonoseki, where the treaty ceding Taiwan to Japan had been signed in 1895—to be hostile. "They were nasty," he told his father. The customs agents in particular wanted to know exactly where he had been in China, and seemed highly suspicious of a notation in Carlson's passport indicating that he had been into Japanese-controlled Manchuria.

CHAPTER 5

WARM SPRINGS

CARLSON WAS SUPPOSED to report to Quantico when he got back to the United States, but there was a bit of leeway in the timing, so after he and Etelle made the Pacific crossing to California they decided that, instead of continuing by ship through the Panama Canal, they would drive across the country and see the full span of the place for themselves. In August of 1935 they bought a second-hand Plymouth sedan in San Francisco and spent the next month on the road, stopping at the major sights along the way. They visited the nearly finished Boulder Dam (now the Hoover Dam), which Carlson declared to be "the most magnificent man made monument to modern science and industrialism I have ever seen." They went to Zion National Park, where they marveled wordlessly at "the majesty of God's handiwork." They picnicked on the Continental Divide and reveled in the Americana of small towns with their children's parades and marching bands. They hunted for relics of the old Oregon Trail and the Pony Express and admired the colors of the desert. Carlson was still fascinated with higher education, so they made a point of visiting college and university campuses along the way. At night, they stayed in auto camps, sometimes in a tourist cabin if it wasn't too expensive. The car only had to be repaired once, and on the long, empty stretches out west they managed to average nearly fifty miles an hour. With the wind in their hair and the whole breadth of the United States to explore, it was a glorious trip that gave the two of them some much-needed time for just themselves. To judge from his letters home, that drive across the country was the happiest he and

Etelle had been in a long time. It was also the happiest they would ever be again.

When Carlson got back to Quantico, the Marines gave him a new assignment that had nothing to do with China, though it would turn out to have everything to do with China as well. In either case, it was a total departure from the trajectory of his previous work: they assigned him to perform guard duty for the president. Franklin D. Roosevelt kept a residence in Warm Springs, Georgia, where there were therapeutic mineral baths thought to be beneficial to polio victims like himself who suffered from paralysis. Roosevelt's Warm Springs residence, where he went to bathe and swim in the buoyant pools, was known as the "Little White House," and in November of 1935 he was planning to spend Thanksgiving there with his family. Carlson was posted as second in command of a detachment of sixty-five Marines that would provide security for the president at the site as an adjunct to the Secret Service.

Carlson had been an admirer of Roosevelt ever since his first run for president in 1932, when Carlson was in Nicaragua and feeling roundly disappointed in Herbert Hoover for his weakness on foreign policy. "Looks like Roosevelt is going to ride into the White House," he told his parents in a letter back then. "I hope so. We are all for him down here." In 1934, when he was living in Beijing, he credited Roosevelt's statesmanship with helping to prevent the outbreak of a full-blown war between China and Japan. He saw Roosevelt as a strong and moral leader who understood Asia and genuinely cared about the little guy. It was a special honor, then, to get to meet the man himself, even if at somewhat of a distance.

Roosevelt's Warm Springs residence was a sprawling, leafy compound in the hills about seventy miles south of Atlanta with green lawns and land that rolled away into the trees at its edges. The main section contained a guesthouse and servants' quarters, as well as the Little White House itself—a trim, camplike white cottage of Georgia pine with a columned portico that echoed the original in Washington. The Marines got their own section of the estate to pitch their tents on, which they dubbed "Camp Roosevelt." About a mile away in an open-air complex of their own were the mineral baths: broad and rectangular pools, white-painted, fed with pleasantly warm water piped from a neighboring spring.

It wasn't exactly taxing work. Mostly, Carlson stood by the pools while FDR floated. The air was cool, the water warm, and there weren't any particular threats to the president's safety. In truth, it wasn't actually very interesting in the day-to-day, except that now and then Roosevelt would break through the wall of formality between himself and his guards and come visit with the Marines on more intimate terms. There were surprise visits—sometimes, FDR would come careening unannounced into their camp in his modified Plymouth, much to the delight of the enlisted men as they scrambled to attention in whatever state of dress they happened to be in (which on at least one occasion meant underpants). For the officers, there were occasional invitations to the main house for polite conversation over tea by the stone fireplace.

The easygoing charm that had won Carlson so many friends in Beijing and Shanghai had its effect on the president's family as well. The president himself was busy and usually distant, but during Carlson's time at Warm Springs he got along especially well with Roosevelt's oldest son, James, a tall, prematurely balding man who was eleven years younger than Carlson and lived very much in his father's shadow. By the time the president moved on from his Thanksgiving holiday and Carlson returned to D.C. to start his coursework at George Washington University, he and James could count each other as friends.

The time at Warm Springs only deepened Carlson's admiration for the president. Roosevelt had spent a substantial portion of his family fortune to purchase the land at Warm Springs and establish a foundation for polio victims, of whom there were several in residence at any time. On one chilly Sunday evening, Carlson was along as Roosevelt went to church in the foundation's main building. It was a small congregation, made up mostly of other polio patients and a couple of Secret Service members, but the Episcopalian bishop of Atlanta gave the sermon. Carlson had prepared the president's wheelchair for him, but Roosevelt insisted on walking into the service instead—slowly but deliberately, hiding the incredible effort it cost him to move erect on a contraption of heavy leg braces. But he did it, with a cane in one hand and a man holding his other arm, and Carlson realized he was doing it for the sake of the other polio patients in the room, to show them the power of human will to overcome adversity. "He's a great man—and don't you forget it," he told his parents afterward.

While the duty at Warm Springs gave Carlson good stories to tell, it was only occasional work, mainly during holidays, so his coursework first at George Washington University and then at the Marine Corps Schools in Quantico occupied most of his time and attention in the following year. After spending so much of his life envying those who had been able to go to college, GWU was Carlson's first chance at formal, post-secondary education at a civilian institution, and he did better than he had expected. When he got a B in his seminar on International Law and Relations, it sent him over the moon. "Not bad for a non-college graduate!" he wrote to his parents.

His coursework on American foreign policy was especially eye-opening, and it inspired him to write a thesis on the American Marines as an instrument of diplomacy in the Far East, which he later published in the *Marine Corps Gazette*. What he learned about the subject matter did not match with his initial expectations, however. In particular, it was from his advisor, a Professor Charles Hill, who chaired the political science department, that Carlson first learned about "dollar diplomacy" and the ways in which America's foreign policy in the early twentieth century mainly sought to create conditions abroad that would benefit American business interests, just as Smedley Butler had argued. It was a disorienting perspective that deflated some of Carlson's pride in the work he had done in Nicaragua. "I was shocked by what I learned of our intervention in foreign nations," he later told an interviewer when reflecting on his studies at George Washington University. "I suppose I had taken too much for granted about our American idealism."

Carlson put in three stints at Warm Springs, the last of which, for three weeks in November of 1936, conflicted with his classes in Quantico, which he found frustrating. For all of the honor of serving at close quarters for the president, Carlson was keen on finishing his coursework and getting back to China as soon as he could. The work at Warm Springs thus became something of a distraction, if a pleasant one. But the president seemed to like him, which was flattering—he had even singled Carlson out beyond the confines of

Warm Springs, inviting him and Etelle to come have lunch at the White House, much to the envy of the rest of Quantico. And Carlson's admiration for Roosevelt continued to grow. After Roosevelt's landslide reelection in 1936, Carlson predicted that he would "prove, by virtue of his second administration, to be one of the greatest of all our Presidents." So while he might grouse about missing his classes for Warm Springs, his duty was to Roosevelt. "I would go to hell for him," he told his parents.

In February of 1937, Carlson learned that the Marine Corps was going to send him back to China that summer, and this time, he would get to be a full-time language student with no other responsibilities. He was ecstatic. He wrote a letter to Nelson Johnson, who was still ambassador, to share the news that they would be seeing each other again. "It is almost too good to be true," he told Johnson. "Needless to say, I shall make the most of my opportunities." Learning to read characters would be his primary goal, but he added that it was "hardly less important to become acquainted with the people, and understand their design for living." He yearned to travel again, to get to know the people in China better, not just study them in books. After his foreign affairs coursework he felt certain that it was only a matter of time before China regained its proper place in the sun, and he wanted to be there when that happened.

But as he looked ahead to his third tour in China, with travel, exploration, and study on his mind, Carlson made one significant change from before; this time, he decided he would go alone. He did not want domestic life in Beijing again. He did not want to have to worry about Etelle's happiness or safety when he was away from home. So he told her that she would have to stay in the U.S. and fend for herself while he was gone. She was devastated—as was his mother, who worried that his second marriage was heading down the same path as his first. But he was adamant. "Tell mother to keep her shirt on and not to worry about this separation of mine," he told his father. "It doesn't bother me."

Friends in the military pressured him to abandon the idea of separation—it didn't look good socially in the Marine Corps. Etelle was very well liked, and the breakup of their marriage could damage his career prospects. But Carlson dug in his heels. "My separation from Etelle has caused quite a commotion, and strong pressure is being brought to bear on me to return to her," he told his father. "That only strengthens my determination." For her part, Etelle, true to form, tried to be conciliatory and accommodating, to keep her hopes up in case things might work out in the end. She enrolled in a graduate program at the University of California at Berkeley to study East Asian history. She would also take up residence at Berkeley's International House—if she had to stay in the U.S., she would let the world come to her. They negotiated an alimony that he would pay her while they were separated. Not long afterward, however, he asked if he could reduce it so he could afford to bring his sister, Karen, to China with him, presumably to maintain his household in the absence of a wife. For once, finally, Etelle stood up to him and said no.

In March of 1937, Carlson made his final trip down to Warm Springs, this time in an advisory capacity to check on the status of "Camp Roosevelt" under its new commander. He did not want to take yet another break from his schoolwork, but the White House had requested him by name. He wasn't really sure why, as the duty at Warm Springs wasn't especially complicated, and he worried that his presence might provoke resentment from the officer who had replaced him. In any case, he made the trip as requested, and on his last afternoon there, the president invited him for tea. Carlson was delighted by the invitation but thought it a bit strange when he learned that none of the other Marine officers had been invited. It turned out to be an intimate group of the president's inner circle. Among the guests were William Bullitt, the American ambassador to France (and previously to the Soviet Union), and Roosevelt's private secretary, Marguerite "Missy" LeHand, to whom Bullitt had briefly been engaged. The president's son James and his wife were there as well. After the tea service was done, Betsey Roosevelt, James's wife, took Carlson aside and asked if he would stay for dinner, which he did, pinching himself when he learned he would be seated between Bullitt and LeHand, right across the table from Roosevelt himself.

It was a lively dinner of stories and reminiscences. The dining room was cozy, with dark-stained pine walls hung with nautical art. Roosevelt and Bullitt did most of the talking early on, but with Carlson there, the conversation turned naturally to China—they quizzed him on his Chinese, on the proper pronunciation of "Peiping" and the names of other Chinese cities. Carlson warmed up, and ventured a joke about how hard it was to be a Roosevelt voter when he came from Vermont and had a wife from Maine (those being the only two states FDR lost in the 1936 election). Roosevelt laughed, and talked about his long family history with China. His Delano ancestors had sailed regularly to Canton as merchants in the old China trade of the early nineteenth century, back before the first Opium War (and though it didn't come up in the dinner conversation, FDR's original family fortune had depended to no small degree on the sale of that drug in China). Roosevelt told the story of his grandfather Delano taking his nine children to China during the Civil War, and how one dark night off the Cape of Good Hope their ship crossed paths with the Confederate raider *Alabama*. They blacked out their ship's windows and remained silent, narrowly escaping detection by the Confederates. If they hadn't, said Roosevelt, he probably wouldn't be there to tell the story.

That evening was one of the most memorable of Carlson's life—the runaway son of a poor preacher from Vermont, sitting at a table in Georgia laughing and swapping stories of China with the president of the United States. It was magical, surreal. Somewhere in the course of the evening's conversation, Carlson happened to mention that he would be going back to China soon, in just a few months. Roosevelt took note. It's possible he already knew. At the end of the evening, just as the guests were leaving, Roosevelt called Carlson aside and told him he'd like to see him privately sometime before he left the country. Carlson wondered whether he really meant it, or if he was just being polite.

He wasn't just being polite. An invitation to the White House arrived in due course, and Carlson met privately with the president on July 15, the day before he was scheduled to depart for the West Coast en route to China. It was no time too soon for him to be getting back, for the news from Asia had turned ominous. It appeared something big was coming. Clashes had been reported between Chinese and Japanese troops in North China, in the vicinity of Beijing. Trains carrying Chinese reinforcements from Nanjing were said to be converging on the old capital, prompting accusations by Japan that they were in violation of the demilitarized zone. On the morning that Carlson met with Roosevelt, *The Washington Post* reported that three million Japanese army and navy reservists had been notified to ready themselves in case of war. "Future developments are unpredictable," said the general in charge of Japan's reserves, "but we must be prepared for the worst in order to preserve the empire."

There is no transcript of Carlson and Roosevelt's conversation that day, but in the course of their meeting they came to an arrangement. Roosevelt wanted to know what was really happening in China—the unvarnished truth—and he had decided that Carlson was the man he trusted to get it for him. To avoid any interference from others in the military or the State Department, he asked Carlson to communicate with him directly and secretly, sending his reports in the form of personal letters addressed to Missy LeHand. Nobody outside the three of them—Roosevelt, Carlson, and LeHand—was to know of this arrangement; Carlson would tell no one of its existence. More specifically, Roosevelt made clear that he wanted the full picture of China, with an eye toward its potential to resist the further aggressions of Japan. If it came to war, could the impoverished, agrarian Chinese somehow muster the strength to stand up to one of the largest and most technologically advanced military forces in the world? There was nothing distant or abstract about his curiosity, for behind Roosevelt's interest in China's fate lay the deeper question of America's place in the Pacific world.

Going all the way back to Carlson's original, impetuous decision to enlist as a private in the Marine Corps in 1922, and continuing through his tentative early efforts at intelligence work in Shanghai and his more recent efforts to learn the Chinese language, he had been steering his future toward China by some unplanned combination of impulse and gut instinct without ever having a clear sense of where it might lead. But now he had a mission. When Roosevelt extended his invitation on that summer morning at the White House, the scattered pieces of Carlson's life fit together at last into a coherent whole. He would no longer be a mere language student. Now, he would be the clandestine eyes and ears of the president—a president he revered—and he knew that what he discovered in China could have profound consequences for the future of his own country. That old, enduring mystery from his Emerson-infused childhood—to find his intended path in life, to unlock the secret of his true purpose—

was, it seemed, finally starting to reveal its contours. And so, when Carlson boarded the SS *President McKinley* at Seattle two weeks later, alone, for his return passage across the Pacific to Shanghai, he did so with a rising sense of certainty that somewhere, under the darkening clouds of war that loomed over Asia, lay his destiny.

PART II
CHINA WAR

CHAPTER 6

INTO THE CATACLYSM

THE BOMBERS DRONED high above Shanghai in two squadrons, points of configured darkness against an otherwise perfect sky. As they neared their target, they shifted formation—falling into a single-file line and following the leader as he dove down over one of the densely crowded civilian districts of the city, pulling the others along behind him like pearls on a string. One by one, they unloaded their bombs over the Chinese Civic Center building, which stood out from the skyline with a distinctive dome. Watching through his binoculars from the upper deck of the *President McKinley*, Carlson could just make out the red suns on the undersides of their wings. He heard a series of delayed thumps and saw smoke rising from the dome as the civic center burned. The *McKinley* was on its final approach to Shanghai now, running a gauntlet between the vessels of a Japanese naval fleet that flanked both sides of the river. Carlson had counted eighteen Japanese warships at anchor—three cruisers and fifteen destroyers, their guns aimed low toward the city. Others were coming up the river behind them on the same course. It was the morning of August 18, 1937, and the war had already begun.

The tumblers had all clicked into place while Carlson was preparing to return. It began with a bizarre sequence of events in December of 1936, when Chiang Kai-shek's campaign against the Communists in Shaanxi province ground unexpectedly to a halt. The commander of Chiang's anti-Communist forces, a former Manchurian warlord named Zhang Xueliang, known as the "Young Marshal," was based with his army at the city of Xi'an, an ancient capital and the gateway to China's northwest. He had orders from Chiang to mount a final assault on the communist base at Yan'an, which lay 150 miles to the north. That assault—which Chiang Kai-shek declared would be "the last five minutes" of the civil war—was to be the decisive blow against the Red Army, destroying it once and for all. But after receiving his orders, Zhang Xueliang's army did not move. Instead, Zhang pleaded with Chiang that his troops were restive, and potentially mutinous, because they wanted to fight the Japanese instead.

Outraged, the Generalissimo flew out to Xi'an himself, arriving on December 4 with a large crowd of advisors and bodyguards. He set up a headquarters in a hot springs resort outside of the city and proceeded to grill each of Zhang Xueliang's senior officers in turn, learning from them that there was indeed broad sentiment in favor of redirecting China's military toward fighting the Japanese in Manchuria instead of the Communists at Yan'an. The Generalissimo, however, would tolerate no dissent. When the Young Marshal reported that ten thousand students from Xi'an were marching toward Chiang's headquarters to protest the Japanese occupation of Manchuria, Chiang shouted: "Let them come and I can use a machine gun to kill them!"

Thinking he had cowed Zhang, the Generalissimo planned to fly back to Nanjing on December 12. But early on the morning of his departure, a detachment of Zhang's bodyguard forces stormed into Chiang's headquarters, shooting dozens of his guards. Chiang escaped through a back window of his bedroom, climbing over a wall and running up a snowy path into the mountains, wearing only his nightclothes and a thin robe in the winter cold. He had no shoes. He slipped and fell along the way, hurting his back. He lost his dentures. The Young Marshal's soldiers found him the next morning, hiding in a cave, shivering and nearly frozen. "I am the Generalissimo," he told them. "Kill me, but do not subject me to indignities." They took him prisoner. And then the Young Marshal notified the Communists by radio.

As it turned out, he had made an alliance with the other side. The Communists had long been issuing public calls for Chiang Kai-shek to stop the civil war and turn his armies against the Japanese. As far back as 1932, when Chiang sat back and let Manchuria go, the Communists declared war on Japan from their base in Jiangxi. Of course, it was an easy thing for them to do at the time, Jiangxi being separated from the Japanese in Manchuria by more than a thousand miles. But at Shaanxi, in their northern base after the Long March, they had renewed their call for national unity, for all of the Chinese to fight together against Japan, and that message had succeeded in winning over Zhang Xueliang. His original base of power had been in Manchuria, and his father—the Manchurian warlord before him—had been killed by the Japanese, so his desire to avenge his father and see Japan punished for its invasion of his homeland ultimately trumped the loyalty he had pledged to Chiang Kai-shek.

The kidnapping of the Generalissimo took the Communists at Yan'an by surprise, but it presented them with an unprecedented opportunity to take revenge against their number one enemy. According to one of his comrades, Mao Zedong laughed "like mad" when he got the news. They now had Chiang at their mercy—him, the murderer of untold thousands of their kind. And yet they did not, as one might expect, have him killed. Mao wanted him executed, preferably after a public trial. Others in the Communist leadership did as well, but Stalin intervened by radio, promising Soviet military aid on the condition that the Communists use the kidnapping to force Chiang to agree to a new United Front. Stalin wanted what he had always wanted—a unified China that could protect Russia's eastern flank from the Japanese. And that need for protection had only increased in urgency in the weeks leading up to Chiang's kidnapping, for Japan and Nazi Germany had just sealed an alliance against communism— the Anti-Comintern Pact—which was directed squarely at Stalin and threatened the Soviet Union with the possibility of simultaneous wars on both its Asian and European frontiers.

Stalin feared that if the Communists should encourage the Young Marshal to execute Chiang Kai-shek, it would only lead to a disintegration of the KMT with its many inner factions. A right-wing group within the KMT could take power and make an alliance with Japan, which would free the Japanese to send their Manchurian forces into Siberia. And Stalin's fears were well founded, for at that very moment Chiang's chief rival in the KMT—a man named Wang Jingwei—was in Germany, meeting with Hitler to discuss the possibility of China signing on to the Anti-Comintern Pact.

Chiang Kai-shek was widely seen as the only man in China with the prestige and influence to hold the KMT together and keep a lid on its factionalism. Stalin needed him, and so he was willing to let past insults slide. The Chinese Communists at Yan'an ultimately did as well, buckling to Stalin's demands and swallowing their desire for revenge. On Christmas Day of 1936, the Young Marshal let Chiang go free, with a verbal agreement that the KMT and the Communists would form an alliance in a new United Front. It was nothing less than what the public had wanted all along; when Chiang arrived safely back in Nanjing, thousands of people turned out in the streets to celebrate his return. The war against Japan, they believed, could now begin.

Although the anti-Japanese United Front signaled that the CCP and the KMT would work together again, the old resentments and mistrust did not simply vanish. Chiang hoped to use the alliance to make the CCP leaders renounce communism and subsume their army under his control. The Communists, for their part, publicly celebrated the alliance even as certain of their leaders—Mao in particular—intended to use the détente as a means to strengthen their own hands for an inevitable resumption of civil hostilities in the future. Nevertheless, the alliance formally satisfied the condition of unity in Chiang's slogan of "First unity, then resistance," which had been his justification for avoiding confrontation with the Japanese since the invasion of Manchuria in 1931. Now that the civil war was on hold and the Communists were ostensibly no longer a threat, he had run out of excuses. And from the massive public outpouring of support that had followed the announcement of the United Front, it was clear that the people of China were no longer willing to acquiesce quietly to Japan's aggressions. Once all of this was established, it was just a matter of time before a minor incident—in this case, a small skirmish between Chinese and Japanese troops near the Marco Polo Bridge outside Beijing on July 7, 1937—would explode into a full-blown war.

The *President McKinley* dropped anchor at a safe distance from the city to release its passengers onto a tender, and almost nobody besides Carlson got off. Shanghai was a city people were fleeing from, not trying to visit. The British and Americans had already evacuated thousands of their citizens from the International Settlement and, after

Carlson disembarked, the *President McKinley* did its part by loading up with American evacuees, mostly women and children, before casting off to return downriver and convey them to safety in the U.S.-controlled Philippines. It was impossible, at any rate, for the ship to proceed any farther into China, for Chinese forces had sunk several steamships on top of one another in the Yangzi River as a barricade to prevent Japanese naval vessels from approaching Nanjing.

The area around the customs jetty was eerily quiet as Carlson disembarked from his tender and stepped into the International Settlement. The familiar masses of people who normally crowded the waterfront streets were gone. The bustling traffic of bicycles and cars and trucks and rickshaws that created so much noise at all hours was gone as well. The tall, elegant office towers and hotels of the settlement's main street were boarded up and sandbagged. The hotel where he had planned to stay had a blackened, gaping hole in its roof from a bomb that had blown out the top three floors. "This is not the Shanghai I have known," he wrote to his parents.

Shanghai was now the eastern front in the war, bearing the full brunt of the Japanese invasion, and this time Chiang Kai-shek was determined to make a stand. He had drawn his line here, just two hundred miles from the capital at Nanjing, deploying most of his best, German-trained troops to fortify the city and its environs outside of the International Settlement. His hope had been to draw Japanese forces away from Manchuria by forcing a second front at Shanghai, and he would ultimately commit some 300,000 troops as a desperate firewall against Japan's invasion of the east coast. But the dense concentration of Chiang's forces at Shanghai—against the counsel of his German advisors—rendered them all the more vulnerable to Japan's artillery, especially the naval artillery on the warships anchored in the river. Meanwhile, the Japanese had already succeeded in landing ground troops and were flooding the wider region with their own forces.

It was clear to Carlson that he would not be returning to Beijing for language study. Not only did the assignment seem pointless in the face of the war, but Beijing had already fallen to the Japanese. He needed a new assignment. The admiral of the U.S. Asiatic Fleet, Harry Yarnell, was stationed in the river at Shanghai on his flagship the USS *Augusta*, and after Carlson arranged a room at the American

Club and dropped off his luggage, he hired a boat to row him out to the *Augusta* to get new orders. Admiral Yarnell gave him a temporary appointment with the U.S. naval attaché's office—an ad hoc position that made Carlson one of several naval intelligence officers detailed to the U.S. embassy (which by this time had formally moved from Beijing to Nanjing). Officially, he was still a "Language Student Officer," though he described his position to his parents as being "assistant to the Assistant Naval Attaché." Whether there had been any kind of coordination behind the scenes, the vague new assignment meshed perfectly with Roosevelt's desire for him to report on the status of the Chinese military, for the affiliation with the naval attaché's office gave Carlson a great amount of leeway to travel where he wanted—pending permission from the Chinese authorities. If they gave him that permission, he would be free to observe the war up close.

In the meantime, no travel was needed because the war was all around him. Formally, the fighting at Shanghai was restricted to the Chinese areas of the city outside of the International Settlement because Chiang Kai-shek did not want to provoke the British or Americans by sending his troops through their concession (though the Japanese, with fewer compunctions, and with their own extraterritorial rights, encamped in its northern section and used the settlement as a shield for their naval artillery on the river). It was impossible to keep the war out entirely, though, and stray bombs still found targets in the supposedly safe parts of the international zone, some dropped accidentally by Chinese aircraft and others by Japanese ones.

Carlson's first glimpse of an aerial bombing had been from a distance, but for many in Shanghai, including the foreigners inside their enclave, the bombings were an immediate, devastating experience. A *New York Times* reporter captured the visceral feeling of terror when a bomb landed a short distance from his car on a crowded shopping street in Shanghai. "There was a tremendous, sickening lurch of the ground," he wrote, "accompanied by a shattering explosion so close that my eardrums and my windpipe seemed to be affected. It must have been as much as two minutes that I sat in the car, stunned and unable to move, conscious only of the fact that debris and rubble from the buildings kept showering down." It felt as if time had

Aftermath of an aerial bombing, Shanghai, 1937.

stopped. "For as much as four minutes," he went on, "if the bomb is a big one, nothing moves except swirling smoke and thick dust, and there is no sound except the continued tinkle of falling broken glass and the rumble of crumbling masonry. After about four minutes the wounded begin to moan and shriek and try to drag themselves away; then come the sounds of the sirens and the ambulances, and then the tempo of shocked life picks up with terrifying reality."

Being so close to the war—and yet mostly safe inside the International Settlement—was both exhilarating and unsettling. Foreigners enjoyed watching Japanese bombing raids from the rooftops of their apartment buildings or through the high glass windows of their luxurious hotel dining rooms. "Nowhere else is a great metropolis likely again to have a ringside seat at a killing contest involving nearly a million men," wrote Edgar Snow. He compared it to the Battle of Gettysburg being fought in Harlem while the rest of Manhattan looked on. But for any observer who actually confronted the suffering and destruction of life happening on the other side of the glass, it was hard to insulate oneself completely.

Carlson ventured out from the safety of the concession to get as close to the Chinese lines as possible, and on several occasions he got to within a few dozen yards of the fighting. "Never to my dying day do I expect to witness a spectacle as tremendous or as moving,"

U.S. Marines watching the fighting in Shanghai from a rooftop.

Carlson wrote to Roosevelt after one of these occasions. "Seventy-five yards from us two armies were fighting to the death, employing most of the implements of war known to modern science." In a letter home, he told his parents it was "the greatest show on earth, from the spectators' standpoint," but added that he was depressed by the death all around him. "I think I can be content to retire and lead a peaceful life when this is over," he told them.

Carlson had started writing letters to President Roosevelt even before he arrived in China, and from Shanghai he fed him his observations—at least, as much as he could understand of the war in its early days. "Pictures are always distorted when viewed at close range," he wrote a few days after his arrival, acknowledging the impossibility of grasping the broader patterns of history while standing as an observer on the ground in a single moment. But he went out on a limb anyhow and predicted it would be a turning point in the history of the region, and not just for China and Japan. "It is, I believe, a turning point in our own relations with the Far East," he continued. "It appears that Japan intends not only to extend her influence over the northern half of China, but to eliminate foreign commercial competition as well." As he saw it, Japan's ultimate goal was to dominate the economy of China at the expense of the United States and the other Western nations who traded there. But the Japanese had already been ascendant in China, he said, and they could probably have achieved dominance over its economy without need of further war. So why were they fighting? What was their ultimate purpose? He did not know.

Edgar Snow had left his home in Beijing when the Japanese invaded, and he and Carlson reconnected in Shanghai. Snow had witnessed the pitiful defense of Beijing by northern Chinese warlord troops, and was disgusted by Chiang Kai-shek's refusal to send sufficient reinforcements from Nanjing, preferring instead to reserve his best forces to defend the territory close to his capital in eastern China. By the time Snow and Carlson met up, Snow had gotten an assignment to report on the war for the *New York Herald Tribune*, so the two men were both observers of a kind. Together, they charged around the outskirts of the International Settlement to watch the battles between Chinese and Japanese troops as they shifted through different districts of the Chinese city, snapping photos from a safe distance.

It was a rolling front, not always predictable. Snow, for his part, was impressed with the stoic heroism of the Chinese soldiers in their trenches as they suffered constant, vicious bombardments from the Japanese air and naval forces. Their "sense of fatalism" and "absence of nerves," he wrote, were "assets in Chinese troops which it is doubtful if any Western race possesses." Be that as it may, he could also have applied those epithets to his companion, for Carlson had learned in Nicaragua to be a fatalist himself. One corollary of his religious awakening had been that he now carried a certain equanimity about the possibility of death. If God meant for him to die, Carlson believed, it would happen no matter what he did to avoid it. By the same token, if he was not meant to die then there was no reason to be afraid. As he later put it, "When my time comes there is nothing I can do about it. No point in dodging, for there is as much chance of dodging into [a bullet] as away from it." It was a useful trait for wartime, though he realized that he was hardly the only person who felt this way, especially in a time and place like Shanghai in 1937.

In spite of the sense of invulnerability many foreigners felt inside the settlement, their actual safety was never guaranteed. One afternoon in November, Carlson and Snow made their way to the French Concession in the far southwest corner of the foreign district, to a power plant that abutted the wall of brick and barbed wire that separated the concession from the Chinese city. They were looking for a vantage point from which to observe a battle along the sluggish creek on the opposite side of the perimeter wall. The power plant's water tower was the highest point around, reaching about a hundred feet in the air, and it had a platform near the top that looked like a good place to watch the battle. They started climbing up the open staircase anchored to its side but only made it partway before a torrent of bullets started peppering the cement wall of the tower and they dropped to the ground under a shower of concrete fragments. A Japanese machine gun across the creek had targeted the water tower and kept a steady aim there, hammering away as Carlson and Snow ducked into the main power plant building for cover, windows shattering and debris from the ceiling falling around them.

When the machine gun paused, they crept back out and were met by hundreds of retreating Chinese soldiers in broken disarray, climbing over the wall into the French Concession, picking their way through the barbed wire on its top in hopes of finding safety inside. The ones who made it over the wall threw their rifles to the ground in jumbled piles to show the French police that they were only seeking sanctuary. Edgar Snow stared at them—up close, they looked to him younger than Boy Scouts. Then he looked around and noticed Carlson was gone.

Carlson had spotted a puddle of blood on the ground just below the water tower. Looking up, he saw a pair of feet dangling off the edge of the roof. Without a word to Snow, and in spite of the machine gun, he dashed up the exposed staircase to see if he could help. He found seven men on the platform at the top, all foreigners. They were lying facedown, huddled together in terror, pressing themselves into the thin surface. One was already dead, shot through the head and groin. Three others had also been hit by the machine gun and were bleeding profusely. They had all gone up earlier to watch the battle, thinking they were safe in neutral French territory, and were trapped when the Japanese gunner started firing at them. A Japanese military spokesman would later insist it had been an accident, but given the concentration of the fire Carlson refused to believe they weren't the intended target. The ones who survived only did so because the platform was higher than the gunner's nest and he couldn't quite hit them as they lay flat. Edgar Snow's account in the *New York Herald Tribune* cited Carlson's "prompt action in going to the rescue" for saving the wounded men's lives, but Carlson wanted none of the credit. "If I had not done so, someone else would have," he wrote to FDR. The man who was killed was a British war correspondent. Armistice Day had been a little over a week earlier, and he still had a red poppy in his buttonhole to commemorate the dead from World War I.

The fight for Shanghai was the first major battle in the Sino-Japanese War, and it was an unmitigated bloodbath. Chiang Kai-shek's decision to send the majority of his elite forces into Shanghai in hopes of decisively repelling the Japanese was a disaster, and though they managed to hold off the invading forces for three months—a resistance that Chiang calculated was necessary to impress the Western powers with China's resolve, to make it more likely that they would come to China's aid—in the end his best divisions were nearly obliterated: Chiang's forces suffered a breathtaking 187,000 casualties at Shanghai, nearly two-thirds of their total strength. The Japanese, for their part, had expected a quick walkover victory of the kind they had experienced in Manchuria and were shocked by the resistance. Neither side expected the long, grinding battle in the streets and in the air that destroyed much of the Chinese city, turned its residents into corpses and refugees, and cost a crippling military toll. The sheer density of bombing and artillery fire in such a tightly packed urban setting was itself unprecedented—military observers at the time estimated that the district of Shanghai just north of the International Settlement had received "the heaviest concentration of fire ever laid on one piece of earth." The Japanese, in contrast to the Chinese, lost fewer than ten thousand killed, and a little over thirty thousand men wounded, but even those numbers were far higher than they had expected, with the result that even in victory, the soldiers of the Japanese army came out of Shanghai with a bloody, ravenous lust for revenge.

For years, there had been reports of atrocities committed by Japanese troops in Manchuria, but in Shanghai the Americans saw up close for the first time the sheer, wanton sadism of the Japanese army toward ordinary Chinese civilians. "One phase of this war which I had not expected," Admiral Yarnell reported to the chief of naval operations, "is their ruthless cruelty toward the Chinese. Killing of non-combatants is an ordinary occurrence." As an example, he forwarded the report of a Marine officer who had witnessed a Chinese laborer being attacked by a Japanese soldier at Shanghai. The Chinese man, an employee of the Shanghai Power Company, was working on a dock when, without any provocation, a Japanese soldier slammed the butt end of his rifle into the man's face. When he fell to the ground, the soldier stabbed him through the arm with his bayonet and then kicked him until he fell into the river. Another group of Japanese soldiers happened to be passing up the river on a launch at the time, and when they spotted the bleeding man thrashing in the water, instead of helping him they raised their rifles and started taking potshots at him for fun. A boat from the power company rowed out to rescue the man, and a Navy corpsman tended to his wounds until an ambulance arrived to take him to the hospital.

What Carlson saw of the Battle of Shanghai convinced him that the Chinese could never stand up to the Japanese in traditional, positional warfare. Chiang Kai-shek had sent the best forces he had, but even then their weapons and other equipment were in many cases inferior to the Japanese, who had not only bested Chiang's 300,000 troops with only 90,000 of their own but had inflicted devastating casualties in the process. Japanese artillery was far superior to China's and the air war was hopeless—China had too few aircraft, and too few pilots to fly them, so they could only mount small nighttime raids against the Japanese positions, while the Japanese flew sorties at will against the Chinese ground forces and the city around them. The Chinese side at Shanghai was, he concluded, doomed from the start.

However, he was still impressed by the bravery he saw in the Chinese troops—their willingness to hold their positions even against incessant aerial bombardment, their determination, which he called their "will to endure hardship," in trying to hold the line at Shanghai. They may have been savagely beaten, but they were no cowards. They just needed better weapons, better training, and better leadership. They had potential. "The Japanese have found that China is not the 'push over' that they expected," he wrote in a letter home from Shanghai. "Despite a marked inferiority in aircraft and artillery, China has given a good account of herself. I would not be surprised to see her fight this war to a draw."

Edgar Snow was a welcome companion to Carlson during the Battle of Shanghai, but one fact loomed above everything else when they reunited in 1937, which was that during Carlson's absence from China, Snow had gone to see the Communists. Long after he finished spending down the $750 advance (which he never did get around to giving back to his publisher), a lull in fighting between Zhang Xueliang's forces and the Red Army in the summer of 1936 had opened the possibility for Snow to slip over to the other side and perhaps get to write his book after all. He had gone in early July, and managed to spend four months with the Red Army at Bao'an, their headquarters before they moved to Yan'an, during which time he interviewed most of the Chinese Communist leadership with the help of interpreters. By October of 1936 he was back in Beijing with Peg (who soon left for her own trip) and by the time he and Carlson reconnected in the fall of 1937, Edgar had finished the breathlessly written manuscript of what would become the single most famous book on China of the twentieth century: *Red Star Over China*, Snow's account of the Chinese Communists on the eve of World War II.

Carlson read a draft of Snow's manuscript when they were together in Shanghai, and he practically felt the earth shift beneath him. According to Snow, the Communists in North China weren't anything like the media reports (or Carlson's own intelligence reports) had made them out to be for all those years. He said they were in fact friendly, not hostile. They were well organized, not dissolute bandits. They didn't hate foreigners. They seemed open to an alliance with the United States. Most importantly, as far as Snow could tell, they weren't in the pocket of the Soviets; to him, they appeared to be working entirely in China's interests, not Stalin's. As the *New York Times* review of Snow's book would put it the following year, "the significance of Red China is not that it is red but that it is Chinese." Meaning that if Edgar Snow was correct, then the forces at Yan'an represented a homegrown movement in China, not some local arm of an international conspiracy under the Comintern. "The

'Red bandits,'" said the *Times*, "bear a close resemblance to people whom we used to call patriots."

Edgar Snow wasn't a disinterested writer. He had a career to pursue, and he wanted a book that would be suitably dramatic and pathbreaking; in a letter to Ambassador Johnson he described *Red Star* as "a world scoop on a nine-year-old story." From the outset he envisioned his book as a travelogue, toying in his diary with calling it "I Went to Red China." In its pages, he would play the role of the intrepid young American reporter, penetrating into the secret recesses of the Chinese Communist headquarters and throwing open its gates for all the world to see. For that plan to work—for the book to be as good as he hoped it would be—the Communists had to oblige. They had to open up to him fully. And they did (at least, he thought they did), especially Mao Zedong, who told his life story to Snow over the course of several nights in a candlelit cave, an account of the making of a Chinese revolutionary that would form the backbone of the book and captivate liberal imaginations around the world in the years that followed.

Along with Mao, Snow interviewed most of the Communists' major political and military leaders—though not the one about whom Carlson had the greatest curiosity: Zhu De, the commander of the Red Army. Zhu De was away while Snow was in Bao'an and they never met, so all Snow could do in his book was relate stories about him as told by others, and speculate. As Snow thus described him, Zhu De was a disarmingly pleasant person—"a quiet, modest, soft-spoken, old-shoe sort of man" with "kind eyes." Physically, he was short and stocky, but with "arms and legs of iron." Yet somehow, this unassuming, stocky man with his kind eyes had successfully defied Chiang Kai-shek's much larger and better-equipped forces for nearly a decade. He was unquestionably a tactical mastermind—even the official U.S. intelligence reports, post-Carlson, had acknowledged him to be "an extremely competent, determined and resourceful leader" and "a very clever and able tactician." Edgar Snow nevertheless imagined him as a ruthless killer. "It would be naïve to suppose that Zhu De has not found it a 'revolutionary necessity' to send men to the firing squad," wrote Snow, but he left it up to the reader to decide whether the blood on Zhu De's hands was that of a surgeon or an executioner.

Snow and Carlson came at the question of Chinese communism from completely different perspectives. Snow was a journalist, a left-leaning one who was highly critical of Chiang Kai-shek's authoritarian government—which, as Snow described it, was closer to the fascists of Germany or Japan than anything resembling a democracy. Snow had published a number of derogatory articles about Chiang and the KMT, and he was a friend of Sun Yat-sen's widow, the older sister of Chiang Kai-shek's wife, who was, unlike her younger sister, a prominent supporter of the Communists. For all that Edgar Snow's journey to Bao'an felt to him like a daring adventure in which he met with incredible, timely luck, it was at least partially engineered for him by the Communists themselves, who welcomed Snow because they knew of his leftist politics and the likelihood that he would be both sympathetic to their cause and capable of publicizing it to the wider world. Whether or not they determined the outcome by setting the conditions of the meeting, he did ultimately give them that publicity.

Carlson, on the other hand, was a Marine whose personality was built on a conservative foundation. There was nothing radical about him, other than his dawning belief in the equality of mankind, which he kept mainly to himself. To judge Carlson from the outside, he was what he was: a fairly traditional military officer who had written derogatory reports on communists and guerrilla "bandits," and who had actively hunted them down in Nicaragua, both in the field with the Guardia and as chief of police in Managua rooting out communist subversives. Carlson was interested in China, but mainly in Chiang Kai-shek's version of it. Unlike Snow, who was so critical of the KMT, Carlson typically spoke of Chiang Kai-shek and his wife in deeply admiring terms. ("The Generalissimo displays marvelous fortitude and unswerving determination to continue to resist," he wrote in one of his letters to Roosevelt. "Madame Chiang is a human dynamo. . . . They are true leaders, and a source of inspiration to the whole nation.") So he was hardly a potential "recruit" for the Chinese Communists like Snow had been. But he had an open mind—he had shown that in the past—and it was no small matter that he was friends with Edgar Snow, who saw him as a kind of thinking-man's Marine officer.

The other major difference between Carlson and Snow was that Carlson's interest in the Communists was almost entirely military in nature. He wanted to know far more than Snow could possibly tell him about how exactly Zhu De and Mao Zedong's forces had managed to hold out for so long against the KMT—and, further to that, what resources they might be able to bring to bear against the Japanese. He was not especially interested in their politics; he wanted to know how they fought. Above all, though, he loved the idea of an adventure. So he got Edgar Snow to write him a letter of introduction to Mao, and started making preparations to find his own way up north to the Communist base in Shaanxi province.

Carlson gathered his supplies in Shanghai in mid-November. He wanted to travel light, but it would be cold up north so he bought some sturdy boots, a fur hat, and a sheepskin-lined coat. Also a sleeping bag and a haversack that he could sling over his shoulder. He got a simple kettle for boiling water, a pair of chopsticks, a bowl, a cup, and a small basin for washing and shaving. He packed a few articles of clothing, his shaving kit, and some first-aid supplies. He also threw in his harmonica and a bit of reading material, including his worn copy of Emerson's *Essays* and an issue of *Reader's Digest*.

He sent a quick radio telegram to Etelle that she shouldn't expect to hear from him for a while. It felt like a long time since their first, tentative experience of a Chinese restaurant together in 1933; now she was far away in Berkeley and he was preparing to leave the boundaries of the Shanghai international enclave for parts unknown. Even in Beijing they had lived in the legation compound, which in material terms might as well have been American soil. But now, for the first time, he was going to travel afield in China—during wartime, no less—and as he had first learned to do in Nicaragua, he intended to try to live like the people he encountered. For the duration of the trip, he planned to eat what the Chinese people around him were eating, he would sleep where they slept. He would try to experience life as they experienced it. He had his long legs to carry him, and his pack contained everything he needed. There was something tremendously liberating about it all.

When Snow had gone to find the Communists at Bao'an in 1936, he took advantage of the cease-fire between Zhang and the Red Army to cross the lines without permission from any outside authority. But by the time Carlson began seeking his way north, the advent of the anti-Japanese United Front and the alliance it created between the KMT and CCP had made an aboveboard trip possible—and since he worked for the U.S. government it was necessary that it be so. Admiral Yarnell and the naval attaché readily agreed to support Carlson's planned observation work. And though Carlson wouldn't know until he got to the north whether the Communists would let him in, his letter from Edgar Snow seemed about the best introduction he could hope for. For now, the tricky part was how to get permission from Chiang Kai-shek.

Carlson caught a steamer up the Yangzi River toward Nanjing, its lower deck crammed with refugees with their belongings wrapped up in makeshift bundles of blankets and quilts. The grand city of Shanghai was in ruins as it faded behind them. Charred skeletons of factories smoldered. Dozens of fires still burned in the distance. The route to Nanjing would skirt the flank of the Japanese army, which had moved on from Shanghai and was advancing toward the capital along the Yangzi, so Carlson had to take a succession of conveyances to get around them—first the steamship, then a canal boat towed by a barge, then a fifteen-mile stretch of walking, another river boat, and finally a military train packed to the ceiling with retreating Chinese soldiers. In all, it took four days to cover the two hundred miles to the capital.

Early on in the journey, on the airy upper deck of the steamship where the foreigners rode in comfort, Carlson met an American airplane salesman who said he could "fix things" with Chiang's top foreign advisor, William Donald. Donald, an Australian, had been in China since the 1910s and was by 1937 the most trusted foreigner in the KMT government, practically a member of Chiang's family and especially close with Chiang's wife, who called him "Gran." Donald—whose admirers later dubbed him "Donald of China" in a feeble attempt to equate him with Lawrence of Arabia—had earlier been an advisor to Sun Yat-sen during the 1911 Revolution, and even claimed to have written the speech in which Sun proclaimed the founding of the Republic. Remarkably, in spite of his long service in China (or perhaps "typical of" would be better), Donald couldn't speak a word of Chinese. He also proudly refused to eat Chinese food. "Never touch the stuff!" he told a pair of visiting British writers in 1936. "It ruins my stomach."

Nanjing was in chaos as Carlson arrived. The proud capital of the Republic was being disassembled into its component pieces as the population tried to evacuate. Boats packed with refugees and their possessions left slowly up the Yangzi toward the central city of Hankow, nearly four hundred miles farther up the river to the west, which would be the next redoubt if Nanjing should fall. The trains in the station had been commandeered to carry heavy equipment to safety—airplane engines and the like—while the roads were jammed with trucks carrying other war materials down to the docks to be shipped upriver. The stores were closed, the banks closing. Buildings had been painted a blackish gray to make them less visible at night. Air raid sirens howled as the Japanese freely bombed the city. The foreign diplomats had already uprooted and moved west to Hankow and Carlson found only four men left in the American embassy. Most of the Chinese government had already decamped for Hankow as well.

Yet Donald was still there with his master the Generalissimo, and the airplane salesman succeeded in arranging an audience for Carlson that very afternoon. Amidst the bedlam outside, with Japanese bombers roaring overhead and civilians scrambling for their shelters, Carlson asked Donald if he could secure Chiang's permission to travel north from Xi'an to the Communist base area. The meeting was apparently polite enough, but as soon as he left, Donald—who didn't know Carlson from Adam—called up his friend James McHugh, an assistant naval attaché and one of the four men who remained in the American embassy, demanding to know who the hell was "this man Carlson, who claims to be a Marine," who had just come asking for the Generalissimo's permission to go through the lines at Xi'an. He said Chiang Kai-shek wouldn't hear of such a thing.

McHugh said he would look into it, then scoured around Nanjing until he found Carlson and the airplane salesman at their hotel, where he told Carlson ("rather curtly," in McHugh's words) that he should have contacted McHugh first, rather than rushing in willy-nilly to see the Big Man. McHugh went on to lecture Carlson that he didn't realize how delicate the situation with the Communists still was, and the chances of him actually getting through to see them was "dimmer than he thought."

Carlson and McHugh went back years together, though they were hardly good friends. McHugh, a Naval Academy graduate, was the younger of the two but considered himself the more experienced China hand. As an unobtrusive individual who always followed the rules, he harbored an instinctive resentment of Carlson, the charming extrovert who seemed always to be departing from the script. Privately, he considered Carlson a "collector of medals" who couldn't be relied upon to stick around and do his quiet duty (like McHugh himself). He was also bothered that Carlson kept his own counsel, and called him a "queer duck" behind his back. McHugh's mood at the time may have been especially ungenerous as he was dealing with a chronic gastrointestinal problem that caused him to fart constantly. On this occasion, McHugh took some pleasure in dressing Carlson down for not keeping him informed, but once he felt he'd chastened Carlson suitably, he acknowledged the value of the trip—and recognized that there was no one better for it. In McHugh's eyes, for all of Carlson's faults he was still a "first-class soldier" and a man who could "take it." He was well suited to the dangers of crossing over into a war zone no Western military observer had yet seen.

Carlson really might have done well to approach McHugh first, because as it happened William Donald was McHugh's most valuable intelligence asset. In exchange for a monthly retainer, Donald had been feeding information to McHugh secretly since the late 1920s. Indeed, "Donald of China" was the main reason for any professional success McHugh ever had, basically setting him up as a direct conduit of information from Chiang Kai-shek's household to the American government. In this instance, McHugh worked the chain of connection in reverse, explaining to Donald that if Chiang was to have any hope of getting American aid for the war against Japan, then the United States needed clear, firsthand information on what was happening throughout China, not just in Nanjing.

It took a few days, but by the morning of November 27 Carlson was in possession of an elaborate pass, more than a foot long on each side and endorsed by the Generalissimo himself, permitting him to travel freely into the area controlled by the Communist army. As McHugh later wrote in a rather sad, self-serving memoir of his career for which he never found a publisher, Carlson was so grateful to him for the pass that "he almost burst into tears." Carlson, in his own notes, said nothing of the kind.

Now that he had his pass, Carlson booked passage on a British steamer upriver to Hankow, hoping to continue from there by train to Xi'an and points north. The steamer wasn't going to depart until late that night, so he had a free afternoon in Nanjing, which he spent visiting with the KMT general who commanded the city's defenses. The general had vowed publicly to defend the capital "to the last man," and Carlson was impressed with his determination but stunned by the literalness of the pledge. The Chinese forces defending Nanjing had their backs to the Yangzi River, which was a mile wide at that point, meaning that it would be impossible for them to retreat in the face of a Japanese advance. Be that as it may, the general told Carlson that he planned to make the Japanese pay dearly for the city. Carlson's steamer sailed from Nanjing at three o'clock the following morning. Two weeks later, on December 13, 1937, the last of the KMT's defenses collapsed and the Japanese army swept into the city, unleashing one of the most grisly atrocities of World War II, the horrific Rape of Nanjing, in which rampaging Japanese soldiers massacred hundreds of thousands of unarmed civilians in the broken Chinese capital, speared babies, set fire to the elderly, and raped upwards of twenty thousand women.

CHAPTER 7

THE REDS

THE CITY OF XI'AN was far enough inland that it had not been directly touched by the war with Japan, but when Carlson arrived on December 3 he could feel the echoes of the fighting all around him. The city's hospitals were overflowing with casualties from the front. Wounded soldiers hobbled along the streets with newly amputated limbs. Xi'an was the capital of Shaanxi province and the central city of the northwest, a walled settlement in a broad, flat plain bounded to the south by high mountains. In earlier times it had been China's imperial capital, and the Qin emperor, who unified China in the third century BC, lay buried nearby in his vast mausoleum protected by subterranean armies of terracotta soldiers—still waiting, in 1937, to be discovered.

Carlson arrived late at night and took a room in a guesthouse. In the morning, he went down to the local office of the Eighth Route Army, as the Red Army had been renamed after its incorporation into China's national military. He gave them his letter of introduction from Edgar Snow, showed them his pass, and put in a formal request to be allowed to visit Yan'an. The office was simple and plain with just a few pieces of furniture. The walls were dominated by portraits of Mao Zedong and Zhu De, along with Chiang Kai-shek, who had his place on the wall now that the Communists were allied with him in the United Front. There was also a portrait of Sun Yat-sen, the leader of the 1911 Revolution; and last, a lone foreigner, Karl Marx. The soldiers on duty struck Carlson as a "smart looking crowd," and their light blue cotton uniforms embodied the United Front: their caps bore the radiant white sun insignia of the KMT, while they wore the red star of the Communists on their left breast. The officer in charge promised to radio Carlson's request to Mao at Yan'an, but advised that it might take a while to get a reply.

While he waited, Carlson settled into his quarters and started getting a feel for the city. There were thousands of students in Xi'an from universities in Beijing that had been uprooted and evacuated en masse to escape the Japanese occupation. The students spent their mornings marching around the city streets in formation with their classmates, singing patriotic songs and keeping themselves prepared to move their schools farther into the interior if needed. There was a strong Russian presence as well, marking the Chinese terminus of a supply route extending from Moscow through Xinjiang province in the far northwest. (Part of Chiang Kai-shek's rationale for making his stand at Shanghai at the outset of the war, rather than in the north, had been to keep the fighting as far away from this supply line as possible.) Carlson saw convoys of Russian trucks carrying Russian supplies, driven by Russian drivers. They moved mainly at night, he learned, and the Chinese government tried to keep them as invisible to the general population as possible. There were also Russian pilots, mechanics, and aircraft, all on loan from Stalin. Almost all of these materials and personnel were destined for use farther south. Throughout the war with Japan, the Soviets would send the bulk of their military aid to Chiang and his KMT forces, prompting the Communists to complain that the bourgeoisie got all of the guns and aircraft while all they got were crates of Marxist literature.

The initial response from Yan'an came on December 5, and it was positive. Mao Zedong approved Carlson's visit and said there was an escort on its way to bring him north to join the Communist army. Not to Yan'an, though, for the army was on the move in southern Shanxi province (which bordered Shaanxi to the east, the closeness of their spellings in English being a perennial source of confusion for foreigners). Carlson would be able to join the army's leaders at their field headquarters. Five days later, he got the call that the escort had arrived at the Eighth Route Army office and was ready for him. He packed up his haversack, slung it over his shoulder with his sleeping bag, and hurried over to the office. His guide turned out to be a young officer named Yin, accompanied by four sentries with Thompson submachine guns who would be their bodyguards for the journey. "None speaks English," Carlson wrote in his diary, "and I do not speak much Chinese, so we get along famously."

They spent that day on a backbreaking ride in a third-class train carriage eighty miles east to Tongguan, in neighboring Shanxi province. From the train station, he followed his escorts through the dark streets to a mud-walled compound that contained another Eighth Route Army office. They gave him a place on the floor to sleep, and he rolled out his sleeping bag and made the best of it. Over the following days he and his escorts continued their trip: first across the mile-wide Yellow River on a sailing junk, then north on a rough road by a small private bus. Houses were designated for them to sleep in at night, and the roads were tough going. When the roads gave out, his escorts bundled him onto a horse for the remainder of the journey.

Carlson was quite taken with the behavior of the Communists he traveled with, as well as those who greeted him at the Eighth Route Army offices during his planned stops along the way. They struck him as being poor and unadorned, but generous. They went out of their way to feed him well and tried to make him comfortable, which embarrassed him as he didn't want to be the recipient of any greater comforts than they were used to themselves. They didn't seem to realize how willing he was to put up with hardship, which he found touching. "All of these people are astonishingly honest and straightforward," he wrote in his diary. "I like them."

As for what Carlson might otherwise have expected from the members of a communist party, the issue of *Reader's Digest* he brought along on his trip contained a fine illustration. In an article titled "A Professor Quits the Communist Party," the professor in question told the story of his two and a half years as a member of the Communist Party of the USA, which had recruited him through a group at his university. He described the absurd affectations of membership—everyone taking a new name when they joined, always with the prefix "comrade." He described his fellow members as humorless and self-aggrandizing. "Every meeting had a conspiratorial undertone," he wrote. "Fascists were lurking in every corner of the city." Anyone who got excited and spoke too loudly at a meeting "was immediately hushed." His wife joined the party as well, and she made the mistake of cracking a little joke about Stalin's mustache at one of the meetings, which made the room go silent. "This is war, class war," the organizer told her sternly, "and if we don't defend the Soviet Union we are traitors to the working-class movement."

The point where the professor decided to quit was when one of his comrades was excommunicated for having the temerity to say that he intended to vote for Roosevelt in the 1936 election instead of Earl Browder, the Communist candidate. Leaving was a sad affair, he said, but he couldn't take it anymore: the endless rules, the pointless secrecy, the sanctimony, the paranoia, the overbearing solemnity of everything, the demands that all of his actions and even his thoughts follow the party line. By contrast, the members of the Chinese Communist Party Carlson met on his way north from Xi'an seemed to him to be cut from an entirely different cloth. With their friendliness and easygoing generosity, they gave him the same initial impression that Edgar Snow had gotten, namely that the communist movement in China appeared to have taken a form that bore little resemblance to its joyless and pedantic manifestations elsewhere.

———

By December 15, Carlson and his escorts were within a day's ride of the Eighth Route Army's field headquarters. Carlson got up before dawn to join a company of soldiers in their training run up a terraced mountain behind the town where he had spent the night. The run turned into a race, the young Communist soldiers scrambling with him up the side of the hill with gusto. Once they reached the top, panting and breathless, they gathered in a circle and the men asked if Carlson would sing them an American song. He said he couldn't sing very well, but he had his harmonica with him, so he played the Marines' Hymn, "From the Halls of Montezuma." They seemed to like the tune, and hummed it as their marching song on the way back down to the town.

By ten that morning he was off on horseback for the final leg with his bodyguards. They rode for five hours and arrived in the late afternoon at the Eighth Route Army's military headquarters, a low, rough house of brick and tile in a small village of Hongtong county a few miles from the county seat. Carlson dismounted, tied up his horse, and waited. After a little while, as he recorded in his diary, "a stocky short man of about 55 strode out from an inner compound and approached me with extended hand, his face wreathed in a genial smile of welcome." Carlson had seen his face before, most recently adorning the walls of the Eighth Route Army offices on his way up from Xi'an. "I recognized the features of Zhu De," he wrote, "the famous commander of the Eighth Route Army."

In a young Communist army, Zhu De was the old man. He had turned fifty-one in 1937, seven years older than Mao (and a decade older than Carlson), and he had not only lived through the 1911 Revolution against the Qing dynasty, he had fought in it. Like Carlson, he had been born poor—though "poor" was a relative term, insofar as the gradations of poverty in China ran so much deeper than they did in New England. His family were tenant farmers in Sichuan province, working a field of a little over three acres for which they paid a rent they could scarcely bear. According to the story his family told him, when he was born his mother was in the middle of cooking rice for the family dinner. She lay down and birthed him in the kitchen, then got up and finished cooking the rice. His parents had thirteen children in total, five of whom they drowned as infants because they could not afford to feed them. The eight who remained were still more of a burden than they could support, so when Zhu was six years old they gave him away to a wealthier uncle who had the means to provide the boy a Confucian education, in hopes that he could one day pass the civil service examinations and become a Qing imperial official.

Zhu De's early life did not by any stretch point him toward the military. His family wanted no such thing—with the classical education his uncle had given him, he was supposed to become a scholar, an official. But in the ferment of Han Chinese nationalism that would soon explode into the 1911 Revolution against the Qing dynasty, many young students who had never planned on taking up arms found themselves drawn into martial life. Zhu De

Zhu De.

was one of them, and in his case he would spend the rest of his life there. Traditionally, the military was a disgraceful path for an educated man in China to follow, but things were changing. Reforms undertaken by the Qing dynasty in the early twentieth century aimed to build a more modern military (the "New Army," as it was known), which would feature higher pay, newer weapons, and most importantly, an educated officer class trained in military academies on the model of West Point or Sandhurst. It was becoming more respectable, even if his family didn't believe that yet. And so in 1909, he traveled south with a friend to Yunnan province on China's far southwestern border, in hopes of enrolling in the prestigious Yunnan Military Academy to become an officer in the New Army. He would never return to his home village again.

The academy rejected him when he first applied—they had a strong preference for natives of Yunnan province and he was from Sichuan. So he enlisted instead as a common soldier to gain some basic military experience and then reapplied under a false identity, pretending to be from Yunnan. His childhood name had been Zhu Daizhen, but now he gave himself a different one, Zhu De. The new identity got him into the academy (and gave him another point in common with Carlson, who had lied his way into the Army). For the next two years Zhu De studied at the Yunnan Military Academy, where he also joined a local cell of the secret organization under Sun Yat-sen that was planning a nationalist revolution against the Manchu government. When the revolution broke out in 1911, Zhu De played his part as a company commander in a Yunnanese army led by his mentor at the military academy. After the overthrow of the Qing dynasty and the founding of the Republic of China in 1912, he stayed on at the academy as an instructor, having established a reputation as a capable officer. In his teaching, he specialized in field tactics and marksmanship, but the peace that followed the revolution was short-lived, and as the Republic broke down into warlordism, he left his teaching post to take up a rising series of commands in various forces engaged in the warlord fighting in Yunnan and Sichuan.

Zhu's first taste of guerrilla warfare came in 1913 when he was assigned to garrison duty for two years in the mountainous border region between China's Yunnan province and French Indochina (today's Vietnam). Battling hill tribes and bandit groups that were highly adaptive and moved effortlessly through the difficult terrain, he had an eye-opening experience similar to Carlson's in Nicaragua. Like Carlson, he concluded that the best way to fight the bandits in the hills was to use their own tactics against them. Zhu came away from that assignment appreciating for the first time an irregular, fluid style of warfare that would eventually become his stock-in-trade. By the 1920s, with a decade of practice under his belt, he was known widely in Chinese military circles for what he called his "mobile partisan tactics"—a hybrid of his experience on the Indochina border and his European-style training at the Yunnan Military Academy, which he combined into a style of fighting largely distinctive to himself.

One of Zhu De's trademarks was that he stayed exceptionally close to his men on campaign, which he could do because he was every bit as strong physically as they were. He also prepared exhaustively for every engagement, studying the topography, planning every minor detail in advance. He relied on extensive reconnaissance to get a clear picture of the enemy position from every possible angle and tried to earn the sympathy of the noncombatants who lived in the areas where his troops operated. It was essential, he explained to an interviewer in 1937, to maintain "good relations with the people." Good weapons also helped, he said, as did politics—for as he believed, if the men understood the political situation then they would be fighting for a principle and they would have stronger morale as a result. Beyond that, all one really needed was experience. "The more you fight," he said, "the better you are able to grasp the situation."

The Communists never recruited Zhu De, instead it was he who went looking for them. He was an avid reader thanks to his childhood education and academy training, and his first interest in communism was sparked by a book he read about the Russian Revolution of 1917. Having worked hard for Sun Yat-sen's revolution against the Qing dynasty, he was profoundly disillusioned by the eruption of warlordism in the late 1910s and felt that China needed more substantial changes than the Republic had provided. The model of the Bolsheviks seemed to provide an answer. He went on to read everything he could find in Chinese about the Russian Revolution, as well as the Great War in Europe.

In 1922, he left Yunnan and traveled all the way across the country to Shanghai and then Beijing to try to make contact with the newly founded Chinese Communist Party but could find none of its members. In Shanghai, he met with Sun Yat-sen, who suggested he go to America to study instead. This was an alluring prospect; Zhu De had studied George Washington's writings at the military academy and admired the American Revolution—which he understood mainly in Chinese terms, as a revolution of "volunteer farmers." (Someday, he predicted, the farmers of China would fight for their freedom and independence in the same way.) But at that point, if he was to go anywhere outside of China, he wanted most of all to go to Germany—both so he could study military science from the masters and to see the destruction from the Great War for himself. So instead of America, he traveled to Europe, by way of India, eastern Africa, and Egypt.

It was in Germany that Zhu De finally found the Chinese Communists. Zhou Enlai, who would be China's chief diplomat in the future, was there along with a number of other early members of the party, taking part in work-study programs. Zhu joined their ranks even as he studied German and continued his military training in Berlin and Göttingen. All told, he would spend three years in Germany, learning military science while engaging in covert political work among the Chinese students. Twice, he was arrested by German authorities, and though they did not detain him for long, they deported him in 1925. He moved on to the Soviet Union for a year, and then returned to China. As a dual member of the Communist Party and the KMT during the first United Front, he was placed in charge of a military training school and the police force in the city of Nanchang, in Jiangxi province. After Chiang Kai-shek's purge of the Communists in 1927, which Zhu De survived, he helped organize an uprising of former KMT troops in Nanchang and openly began fighting for a communist revolution. In the spring of 1928, at the foot of the Jinggang mountain range on the border of Hunan and Jiangxi provinces, he met Mao Zedong for the first time—a dreamy-eyed former student with moppish hair and a thick Hunan accent. In the years to come, the two would become so inseparable that many just referred to them as "Zhu-Mao," as if they were one person.

Both Zhu De and Mao Zedong agreed that the survival of the Chinese Communist Party depended above all on its army—as Mao put it famously at the time, "Political power comes from the barrel of a gun." In the nine bitter years from 1928 to 1937, the two men founded, trained, and successfully commanded the military body that became known as China's Red Army, from the uprisings in central China that Carlson had struggled to report on from Shanghai in 1928, to the years of the Jiangxi Soviet in the early 1930s, and through the grueling, four-thousand-mile Long March that brought the skeletal remains of their army to northern Shaanxi province in 1935. With the establishment of the anti-Japanese United Front in 1937, the Communist troops were officially redesignated as China's Eighth Route Army and Zhu De was appointed its commander-in-chief by the central government. Throughout the growth of this military force—the progenitors of today's People's Liberation Army—Mao and Zhu had continued to work closely together, dividing responsibility according to their own natural inclinations: Mao, with more of a philosophical bent, was the army's leader in political and higher-level strategic thought, while Zhu, the fighter, was its top field commander and tactical guru. Together, they made for a formidable combination.

Carlson found Zhu De to be self-effacing and gentle, hardly the sharp-edged figure one would expect of a military commander. Helen Foster Snow met him when she made her own trip to Yan'an just after her husband, and she described him as having "that rare kind of personality which is immediately and universally appealing to nearly everyone." She asked Zhu's wife what his most distinctive traits were, and the first thing his wife replied was that he was kind by nature. The second was that he always took full responsibility for even the smallest matters, and he loved to be part of the daily life of his men. He enjoyed talking with the common soldiers, playing basketball with them, passing the time. With his sweet manner and gentle eyes ("liquid brown," as Helen Foster Snow described them), and with his broad smile and catlike grace of movement, he was as far from a strutting, epauletted "generalissimo" like Chiang Kai-shek as one could imagine. He earned the respect of his men not by instilling fear in them, but by caring for them and sharing their hardships, and in return they positively worshipped him. He was the most unorthodox and compelling military commander Carlson had ever met.

Carlson felt an almost immediate affinity for Zhu De, as if they had been waiting years to meet each other. And in a sense, they had—or at least, Carlson had. During his year at George Washington University and the Marine Corps Schools, Carlson had spent a lot of time thinking about the nature of military leadership, especially how an ideal leader should relate to the men he commanded. He published his views on the matter in an article for the *United States Naval Institute Proceedings*, where he argued that a great leader must be humble and tolerant, and he must cultivate loyalty by making it "part of his lifeblood" and practicing the same loyalty toward the men below him that he did toward his superiors. But above all, Carlson wrote,

> the true leader practices the precepts which he advocates. He is devoted to the interests of his men, and when campaigning with them in the field he subjects himself to the same hardships which they are required to endure. And out of the crucible he finds that there has been forged a spiritual bond between him and his men which will enable them, collectively, to accomplish seeming miracles.

That article was written at Quantico and published before Carlson had ever met Zhu De. But it described the Communist general's style of leadership—his humility, his devotion to his own men, the spiritual bond they shared—as perfectly as if Carlson had written it afterward and based it on him. Which is to say, Zhu De appeared to be the true leader, or worker of miracles, Carlson had been looking for.

They spent several hours talking together that day, first in Chinese, with Carlson's limited vocabulary, and then for a longer time in English, with the help of a young writer from Shanghai named Zhou Libo, who was tasked with being Carlson's interpreter during his stay with the Eighth Route Army. Carlson explained his mission as a military observer from the U.S. naval attaché's office, while Zhu De, in turn, told him about the goals of the Eighth Route Army—specifically, "to rid China of an enemy that sought to make of her a vassal state." In the course of the conversation he explained to Carlson that the Chinese Communist Party did not intend to try to make China into a communist state in the near term. Rather, he said, they understood that China had to become a multiparty democracy first, as a necessary first stage. He said they were open to working toward this goal with any foreign country that would treat China as an equal. Carlson left the meeting in something of a daze. Reflecting on the encounter that night, he wrote in his diary, "I felt that I had found a friend and a true leader."

They would spend a great deal of time discussing military matters over the days to come, but in the bigger picture it was Zhu De's mention of democracy that captivated Carlson the most, for he had always understood communism in terms of subversion and dictatorship. But here, it seemed, was something more constructive. To Carlson's ear, Zhu's words seemed to imply that the soldiers in the Eighth Route Army were actually patriotic nationalists first, and communists only second. Above all else, they were simply fighting for China's freedom, and they were willing not only to share power with the KMT to achieve that end, but also to continue that sharing of power after the war was over.

It is worth stepping back for a moment to see how much of this was true. What Zhu De told Carlson did indeed represent the official line of the Chinese Communist Party at the time. However, the party's espousal of democracy was also a snapshot in time, a product of the specific moment when Carlson happened to be visiting. The goal of multiparty democracy had been enshrined in the formal agreement between the KMT and the CCP to establish an anti-Japanese United Front, wherein the Communists agreed to abandon their pursuit of land reform, the expropriation of property from landlords, and other fundamental communist goals they had pursued with vigor during the era of the Jiangxi Soviet in the early 1930s, in favor of subordinating their military to the command of the central government and working together with the KMT toward a democratic state.

When Carlson encountered them in 1937, the Chinese Communists had renounced their antagonism to the KMT and publicly reoriented themselves toward a unified, national war against Japan, even to the point of publicly expressing support for their erstwhile enemy Chiang Kai-shek as the leader of the country. Under such circumstances, democracy was an attractive goal—in the absence of a winner-take-all civil war, it was their party's most promising route toward gaining power on the national scale. In a speech in September of 1937, a week after the agreement on the United Front was made public, Mao explained: "Communism will be put into practice at a future stage in the development of the revolution. At the present stage the Communists harbor no illusions about being able to apply it now, but will carry out the national or democratic revolution as required by history." In an interview published in the Communist *Liberation Daily* newspaper a few weeks before Carlson's arrival, Mao stated that his party advocated a "united democratic government" which should "grant the people all necessary political freedoms, especially the freedom to organize, train, and arm themselves for self defense." He predicted that China would "definitely get to a system of universal suffrage."

On the surface then, what Zhu De told Carlson about the desire of the Communists for democracy was true. Behind the scenes, however, the situation was far more complex than Carlson could know. The leadership of the Chinese Communist Party—and thus its plans for the future, and its relations with the Soviet Union—were very much in flux at that time. Carlson had arrived at Zhu's headquarters just two days after the conclusion of an important Politburo conference at Yan'an that entailed a reshuffling of the party's top leadership to give greater influence to a faction of Chinese Communists who had just returned from Moscow. Mao, who had never been outside of China, let alone to the Soviet Union, managed to hold on to his place at number two in the party's political hierarchy but the three slots below him were filled with the new arrivals from Moscow.

The leader of the Moscow faction was a man named Wang Ming who had spent several years working closely with the Comintern and was understood to be Stalin's choice for party leadership in China. He attacked Mao at the conference, accusing him of being insufficiently supportive of the United Front (for being, in his words, too far "left"). The line from Moscow, through the Comintern, was that the Chinese Communists had to embrace the United Front and cooperate fully with Chiang Kai-shek in the war against Japan. Mao himself had never been inclined to subordinate his own party's interests to those of another, be it in China or in Russia, but he was pragmatic enough to yield to Stalin's will at the time of Chiang Kai-shek's kidnapping at Xi'an, and he continued to do so in December of 1937.

So although the Chinese Communist Party indeed supported a multiparty democratic state at the time of Carlson's arrival, the primary reason it did so was not because of Mao, but because of Stalin.

Carlson felt like a new man. "Up early today," he wrote on December 16. "The air here is bracing. It is grand to be eating a diet of substantial foods, and living a rugged life with no frills." This was precisely what he had come for. He spent much of that day with Zhu De and other leaders of the Eighth Route Army, including Lin Biao and Peng Dehuai, the latter of whom would, for a later generation of Americans, be known best as China's top field commander in the Korean War; Carlson found him "gruff in manner."

They grilled Carlson for news of the international situation and for his assessment of the comparative strengths and weaknesses of China and Japan. They were interested in all aspects—political, economic, military, diplomatic. In contrast to the overwhelming politeness and formality he had grown accustomed to from his social calls on KMT figures in Beijing and Shanghai, he felt that with these men he could be honest and direct. "I gave it to them straight from the shoulder," as he put it. They especially wanted him to tell them his impressions of the strong and weak points of China as a nation, and he was surprised by how open they seemed to criticism. "I have never seen Chinese so interested in correcting their faults and so keen on gaining knowledge," he wrote in his diary. "Above all, I have never seen Chinese who were so self-effacing." After he was done, they gave him his turn to ask questions, and he quizzed them about their army and their plans for the war with Japan. They spent five hours talking that day, and then Carlson joined Zhu De for dinner.

Carlson's admiration for Zhu De was cemented over the following days through long discussions about how he ran his army and trained his troops. Never had Carlson encountered a military commander who was at once so hardened and effective, and yet so disarmingly personable. On the evening of his third day at the headquarters, Carlson attended a stage play put on by Ding Ling, one of China's leading writers, who had come from Shanghai to join the Communists as a cultural worker after the KMT murdered her husband. Her troupe called itself the War Area Players, and it turned out when he got

Zhu De and Carlson.

there that the evening's event had been staged in his honor. Zhu De introduced him to the crowded audience of soldiers and townspeople as an observer from the U.S. naval attaché's office, telling them how much he appreciated Carlson's "fair criticisms" of the Chinese war effort. It was necessary, he said, to know your faults before they could be corrected. Carlson's language skills weren't strong enough to comprehend everything in the performance that followed, but he enjoyed the singing and the comedy acts, and especially Ding Ling's opening speech, which he said "sparkled with patriotism."

What left the most lasting impression on Carlson, however, was not the dramatic performance itself but rather a feeling of connection that came over him in the course of the evening. After making the rounds, Zhu De had come over to Carlson, beaming his wide, unassuming smile, and took Carlson's hands happily in his own with a squeeze. He sat down next to Carlson on his bench and there they stayed, side by side, the general continuing to hold Carlson's hand for several minutes as innocently as if they were lovers or childhood friends. Such a gesture was not so unusual between close friends in an informal Chinese context, but for Carlson it was an intimacy he had never experienced with another man. It stirred him deeply.

.   .   .

"What a magnificent fighting machine this is," Carlson wrote in his diary. He was spending several hours a day in close conversation with Zhu De, usually followed by dinner together and sometimes activities in the evening. When the general was needed elsewhere, Carlson talked with his chief of staff. They talked about the history of the Chinese Red Army, its policies and practices, the state of the war with Japan. Zhu De and his officers were remarkably unguarded—it seemed like no topic was off-limits. They sketched out battle plans for Carlson, re-creating past skirmishes with the KMT and the Japanese. They gave illustrations of the tactics they had used, gambits and deceptions unlike anything he had ever seen. He found himself astonished by their "ingenuity and imagination."

One of the central principles he learned from Zhu De was that in this army, the line between politics and the military was an exceptionally blurry one; the training of their soldiers was at least as much psychological and moral as it was physical. The men all took part in "political training," which, as he understood it, served mainly to develop in them the desire to serve willingly and selflessly. Communist soldiers were trained on the principle that "individuals should follow an upright course of action because it is right, and because it is the right thing to do." In addition, there was a unique closeness between the officers and the common soldiers. The leaders took the men into their confidence. They explained to them why they were engaging in a fight, "so that they go into battle with their eyes open." The result, he later reported, was a "strong bond of understanding between leaders and fighters." It was those two facets of their training, he concluded—their indoctrination to serve selflessly on the one hand, and the deep bond between the officers and men on the other—that had made possible the Red Army's endurance against Chiang Kai-shek's much stronger and better-equipped KMT forces in the past, and might predict their similar endurance against the Japanese in the months and years to come.

Carlson was similarly fascinated by what Zhu De told him about the army's use of the civilian population. They organized local peasants in the areas under their control into armed militias they called "partisans," with the goal of mobilizing all of the Chinese people to take part in the resistance against the Japanese and thereby amplify the strength and capability of the regular army. Thanks to the partisans, he was told, the main body of the army did not have to guard its own lines of communication—that was done by armed, trained peasants, who likewise engaged in sabotage work against the Japanese when they came through, by tearing up railroad lines or poisoning water supplies. Trained partisans also helped the army with reconnaissance and intelligence work, which gave them an edge over the invaders. This made it far easier for the army to move secretly, to avoid direct engagements against superior forces, and to strike without warning. Their tactics, as Carlson learned, relied heavily on surprise and subterfuge. This was the same Red Army whose imminent destruction he had predicted many times over as a Marine intelligence officer. But now, as he learned the full details of how they had managed to survive, his views on them changed. Their story, he now wrote in his diary, was "thrilling . . . the story of a brilliant military effort."

In the fall of 1937, the Eighth Route Army was still a relatively small force, consisting of 45,000 troops in three divisions. All three divisions had moved into Shanxi in September, at a time when about 100,000 government and provincial troops were attempting to hold back the Japanese advance from Beijing. By early November the government lines had broken, and on November 6 the Japanese army captured the Shanxi provincial capital, Taiyuan, which precipitated a chaotic retreat to the south by the KMT forces and a near-abandonment of the region by the central government. In the vacuum of power that ensued, with local government functions breaking down, the Communists stepped in to fill the gap, taking the lead in Shanxi for the first time. Since then, the fighting in Shanxi had shifted away from the positional warfare of the KMT toward the smaller-scale guerrilla tactics of the former Red Army. Given the enormous numerical and material advantages of the Japanese, the Communists limited themselves to minor engagements, though back in September they had achieved one significant victory in a battle at Pingxing Pass near the Great Wall, where Lin Biao's forces destroyed a Japanese convoy with a thousand-man escort. Insofar as that battle had been the first Chinese victory in the war, their morale was high.

The Japanese had advanced into Shanxi so swiftly that they were unable to garrison the countryside behind them, so a brigade of two thousand men from the Eighth Route Army's 115th Division, under command of an officer named Nie Rongzhen, had managed to establish a military base at Wutaishan, a sacred Buddhist mountain area northeast of Taiyuan and well behind the Japanese lines. There, Nie's men were attempting to assert control over a territory of forty thousand square miles—the size of Ohio—and hold it against Japanese attacks from multiple sides. Their goal was to organize the local Chinese peasants for resistance and establish a semi-independent elected government over as much of the region's population of ten million as possible. As soon as Carlson understood the situation there, he knew he wanted to go. He asked Zhu De for permission to go north, up to Wutaishan, to see Nie Rongzhen's forces in action. Zhu De looked a bit startled when he asked, but then regained his composure and told Carlson that of course that could be arranged. A patrol was heading north to bring supplies to the Wutaishan base in a few days, he said, and Carlson could accompany them.

Carlson was fully absorbed in everything he was learning in Shanxi, but on December 23, shortly before his scheduled departure for the north, the events of the wider world intruded. Carlson took a long walk that day to visit a family of British missionaries who lived in the county, and they asked him to stay for dinner. There were some recent newspapers in their house, and Carlson was able to read in detail for the first time about an incident that had taken place earlier that month near Nanjing. Japanese aircraft had bombed a U.S. Navy gunboat, the *Panay*, as it lay at anchor in the Yangzi River. It was a serious attack: four American sailors were killed, nearly fifty were injured, and the *Panay* had been sunk.

When Carlson got back to the Eighth Route Army headquarters that evening, he and Zhu De and a few of the other commanders sat around a charcoal fire, warming themselves and talking through the significance of the attack on the *Panay*. A report had just come over the radio that the United States was preparing a naval fleet at San Diego for service in East Asia, and it seemed possible that America was about to go to war against Japan in reprisal.

"So we sat around the charcoal fire at HQ," Carlson wrote in his diary, "and prognosticated about what would happen if America, France, Russia, and Britain should line up against Japan, Germany, and Italy." They were years ahead of the course of events, but on that cold December night in 1937 everyone around the fire seemed to agree that if America and China should ever become allies against Japan, it would bode well for their relationship. Carlson said that China might seem strange at first to American troops, but he knew they could adapt just as he had done. Zhu De, for his part, said that if the United States and China were to fight together against Japan, then after the war was finished surely a "clear bond of friendship" would unite the two countries going into the future.

CHAPTER 8

AGNES

Z HU DE WAS NOT the only person Carlson met at the Eighth Route Army headquarters who made a lasting impression on him. The other was a fellow American who happened to be there at the same time, a writer named Agnes Smedley who would play a significant role in Carlson's life. Agnes was a friend of sorts of Edgar Snow, and though she and Carlson had never crossed paths before, he knew her by reputation (every foreigner in China did). In the fall of 1937 she was in her mid-forties, a short, tough, quasi-bisexual, radical left-leaning journalist with a sharp flop of graying hair over her high forehead. She was a staunch feminist and failed spy who could ride horseback and shoot a gun. At the time he met her, her preferred attire was an old Chinese Red Army uniform, in green cotton with a bright red star on the cap.

Agnes had been born poor in Missouri, and raised poor in Colorado, and she would fictionalize her early life many times over, most famously in a 1929 memoir, *Daughter of Earth*, that was translated into multiple languages and made her a minor celebrity—Carlson had read it, which is how he knew of her. But the basic reality of her childhood was simply that it was unhappy. She made herself out to be the impoverished daughter of a Colorado coal miner, though the truth was that she was only mostly impoverished, and her father was not a miner but one of the aboveground workers, wielding a gun, who terrorized those same miners. This, however, did not stop her from later identifying herself with the miners or any other number of marginalized peoples whose causes she took up in her life. Her father was a part-Cherokee alcoholic who, with rare exceptions, failed to provide for the family. He was abusive, at least until 1907, when a fifteen-year-old Agnes stood up to him when he threatened to hit her mother. The father quieted somewhat after that, but he regularly abandoned his family. Her sickly mother, who died early, was reduced to taking in laundry and hosting boarders to feed her children. For a time, Agnes's family was supported by an aunt who worked part-time as a prostitute.

Agnes liked trying on different names, fashioning new personas to protect the vulnerabilities of her real one. She had never felt comfortable in her own skin—partly from a vein of depression that ran through her family, and partly from growing up self-consciously "ugly and poor," in her words. As a teenager she gave herself the alias "Marie Rogers," which she would continue to use off and on throughout her life. Her preferred style of dress tended toward the masculine, and for a period in her late teens she called herself "Georgie" and worked as a traveling magazine salesperson. Later, as a student at a teachers college in Tempe, Arizona, she embraced her Cherokee ancestry and renamed herself "Ayahoo" (the name, fittingly enough for its artificiality, wasn't even Cherokee, it was Navajo). As Ayahoo Smedley, she fashioned herself a female cowboy, with a revolver in a holster by her bed and a dagger she used to open her mail.

By her young adulthood Smedley had formed fierce ideas about the status of women. As she wrote in *Daughter of Earth*, "I began to see that a girl could be beautiful, or she could command respect by intellectual ability, a show of power, a victory." She had no interest in being the beautiful one. She never wanted to marry, after seeing what it had done to her mother, though in her life she would do so twice. And so bitter were Agnes's memories of her childhood that one of the firmest pledges she made to herself was never to have children of her own. A failed first marriage to a Socialist Party dilettante in California led to two unwanted pregnancies, the first of which drove her to attempt suicide. Both ended with illegal abortions that were devastating in their own right. She did not learn about birth control until her mid-twenties, when she was living in New York's Greenwich Village and working with Margaret Sanger, the founder of the American Birth Control League (later to become Planned Parenthood). The two maintained a lifelong friendship.

Smedley arrived in China for the first time in December of 1928, crossing the border from Russia into Manchuria as a thirty-six-year-old reporter for the leftist German newspaper *Frankfurter Zeitung.* By then she had cemented her radical bona fides by involving herself deeply in the Indian nationalist movement, and her second husband—whom she had just abandoned in Germany—was the Indian revolutionary Virendranath Chattopadhyaya. After a few months in Manchuria and Nanjing, she settled down in Shanghai in the summer of 1929, just after Carlson left for Nicaragua. She would stay in Shanghai for the next seven years as a reporter and, for at least part of the time, as a makeshift spy for the Comintern, which had recruited her in Berlin.

In the international city of Shanghai, Smedley felt as free as she had ever been in her life. Unattached, sexually liberated, and armed with birth control, she made hay while the sun shone. "Out here I've had chances to sleep with all colours and shapes," she wrote to a friend in 1930. "One French gun-runner, short and round and bumpy; one fifty year old monarchist German who believes in the dominating role of the penis in influencing women; one high Chinese official whose actions I'm ashamed to describe, one round left-wing Kuomintang man who was soft and slobbery." She shared an apartment with an American woman, to whom she declared her intention to "take sex like a man" and then proceeded, in that friend's words, to bring home "anything in pants that she found around town."

Smedley wove herself into a lively web of Chinese and foreign radicals in Shanghai, a group that included underground Chinese communists and left-wing writers, Soviet spies, and the odd Western housewife looking for a bit of adventure. Many of these contacts were linked through reading groups at the leftist Zeitgeist Bookstore in Shanghai, a Soviet front organization. She worked briefly with Earl Browder while he was still in China, though she wasn't much impressed with him (she called him "an idiot"). But in her service to the Comintern she did what she could to help the underground communists in Shanghai, offering her apartment for meetings and mail drops, relaying information by radio between the remnants of the Chinese party and Moscow—where, according to an associate of her handler, she had "a very high standing."

Smedley and Carlson never overlapped in their Shanghai years, so unlike Browder she never made it into his intelligence reports, but the foreign authorities in the International Settlement certainly kept a wary eye on her. To the British secret police, who tracked her assiduously because of her involvement with Indian nationalists, she was "a well known radical writer," while the French police in Shanghai had her down in their files as a "notorious American anarchist." In the pro-KMT Chinese press she appeared as "an American who represents Soviet Russia," and "an American journalist in Shanghai who is known to be in sympathy with the communists . . . [who] has now become very active in communist affairs."

The center of Agnes's universe in Shanghai, and her true love in spite of all of the men she had associated with, was a German reporter named Richard Sorge. Sorge—or "Sorgie," as she liked to call him—was polished, daring, and devilishly handsome with thick, dark hair and blue eyes. He had a motorcycle, which he liked to drive at break-neck speeds through the streets of Shanghai, Agnes on the back with the wind whipping through her hair, feeling—in her words—"grand and glorious." They first met in early 1930, and spent the spring and summer of that year as lovers in Shanghai and then Canton in the south. In May of 1930 she wrote to a friend, "I'm married, child, so to speak—just sort of married, you know; but he's a he-man also and it's 50-50 all along the line, with he helping me and I him . . . I do not know how long it will last; that does not depend on us. I fear not long. But these days will be the best in my life."

Their romance was not just an innocent one, though, for the "help" they gave each other was of a highly specific kind: although Sorge pretended to be a journalist, he was in reality an agent of Russia's military intelligence service, the GRU. In the world war to come, he was destined to play such a major role in the theater of espionage that Ian Fleming, the author of the James Bond novels, would call him "the most formidable spy in history." Sorge had sought Agnes out when he first arrived in China, offering her a letter of introduction from a "mutual acquaintance in Berlin" and asking her to help him build an intelligence-gathering network.

Agnes would never amount to much as a spy—she was too head-strong and impetuous for the profession, her moods too mercurial. She was undisciplined and resistant to following orders. But she loved the theatricality of tradecraft—the false names, the codes, the entering of her apartment by climbing first to the roof—and she did show a remarkable talent for putting other spies into contact with one another. As Sorge's lover and associate, she acted as his match-maker in Shanghai, connecting him to the people who would become his most successful assets in the years to come.

One of these matches was a German woman named Ursula Ku-czynski, whom Agnes recruited personally. Ursula idolized Smed-ley as a writer, and was at first overwhelmed by Agnes's willingness to be her friend ("I could not understand why a person of Agnes's stature should want to spend her time with me," she wrote). Once Agnes was certain Ursula could be trusted and had the right politi-cal mindset, she secured permission from Moscow to recruit her as a spy and turned her over to Sorge. Ursula would eventually become Sorge's lover herself, supplanting Agnes at the center of his atten-tions, much to Agnes's jealous fury. But in a practical sense, his time was better spent with Ursula, for she would prove far more capable than Smedley at spycraft. Under Sorge's tutelage, Ursula Kuczynski entered the service of the Soviet Union and became "Agent Sonja," one of their most successful operatives in World War II and, after the war, in Great Britain, where she ran networks of secret agents across Europe and relayed nuclear secrets to Moscow, all the while passing unnoticed as a quiet and mannerly mother of three.

Agnes had been involved lightly with the Chinese Communist underground since her arrival in Shanghai in 1929, but by the mid-1930s, after Sorge left China and her own attempts to build an intel-ligence network for the Comintern failed, the Chinese became her primary cause—and, indeed, her highest object of loyalty. She grew disillusioned with Soviet policy toward China, especially how the Russians were trying to direct the Chinese Communists to act in Russia's interests rather than their own. She opposed the calls for a second United Front, and resisted Comintern demands that she stop criticizing Chiang Kai-shek. Meanwhile, under unrelenting pressure from Chiang's secret police, the Communist underground and its network of foreign sympathizers in Shanghai was ground down to almost nothing, to the point that the CCP decided in 1935 to dissolve its remaining party organs outside of the Red Army's immediate zone of protection—namely, the Jiangxi Soviet, and later Yan'an. Smedley's fraying relationship with the Comintern was severed completely in 1936 as Stalin's paranoia consumed the Soviet Union from within and Smedley's backers in Moscow disappeared one by one. By the time Carlson met her, she was on her own.

Agnes had gone to Yan'an in February of 1937 to join the Communist leaders with the same goal Edgar Snow had, of writing a book about them. But by the time she got there, Snow had already come and gone and he had interviewed Mao before her, so she was furious about being scooped and did not know what to do next. There was another American at Yan'an at the time, an oddball doctor named George Hatem who had come out with Edgar Snow and stayed on afterward to do medical work. Hatem knew Agnes well from Shanghai—they ran in the same radical circles—and he suggested she interview Zhu De instead, since Edgar Snow hadn't gotten to meet him. "The fighters love him," he told Agnes. "He is their father and mother."

Hatem took her to meet Zhu, whom she—being Agnes—immediately embraced and kissed on both cheeks. Hatem, not to be outdone, followed suit and "kissed him resoundingly, then stood back to observe his handiwork." Zhu De, it would seem, had a good deal of patience. Agnes then gave a long introduction of herself, mentioning in passing that Chiang Kai-shek had put a bounty of $25,000 on Zhu De's head, at which point she started walking in circles around him, appraisingly, while Hatem "ran his hand over General Zhu's shaved head," murmuring, "Hum-m-m-m-m!" When their joke was done, Agnes gave Zhu De a sheaf of Shanghai press clippings from over the years announcing his death, which he seemed to enjoy.

Agnes Smedley in Chinese army uniform.

Agnes was larger than life, but the stories told about her back in

America were even larger. After she made a series of pro-communist radio broadcasts during the Xi'an Incident in 1936, where she was the only American at the scene of Chiang's kidnapping, *The New York Times*, citing "reliable sources," cast her as a leader of the campaign to create a communist state in North China and credited her with a "spectacular role" in convincing Zhang Xueliang's soldiers to defect to the Communist side. *Life* magazine called her "Mao's American ally" and said she specialized in women's rights. In March of 1937, when she was in Yan'an, the journalist Upton Sinclair—who had known her since 1916 when she was, in his words, "a young schoolteacher, very pretty"—wrote a profile of her for *Liberty* magazine under the title "America's Amazing Woman Rebel in China," where he described her as a "little-known Iowa schoolteacher who has leaped into sudden fame as a fighting leader." He made Agnes out to be not just a visitor to the Eighth Route Army, but in fact one of the principal leaders of the whole Chinese communist movement, and said she had convinced the Chinese to "prefer her teaching to anything of their own." He predicted that if her cause should fail she would be beheaded and forgotten—but if her side should win, she would be remembered forever in China just as the Americans remembered Lafayette or the French remembered Joan of Arc.

For her own part, Agnes—who was nothing even remotely resembling a leader of the Chinese communist movement—appreciated the attention but took occasional, pro forma pains to refute the public stories about her. After Upton Sinclair's account caused a stir in the Chinese foreign community, she took to *The China Weekly Review* to deny any affiliation with the Chinese Communists. "These statements are utterly false," she wrote to the paper's editor. "I am a free writer, writing freely without direction from any individual or organization . . . neither now, nor in the past, have I had any organic connections with any Communist Party anywhere." She did not, of course, mention her past involvement with the Comintern. Nor did she mention that the only reason she was not a member of the Chinese Communist Party was because when she applied to become one, they had turned her down.

Evans Carlson and Agnes Smedley met for the first time when he was on his way to a basketball game with Zhu De. The general made the introduction. That evening the three of them went to Carlson's room to talk and when Zhu De had to leave, Agnes stayed on for several hours. "She is grand," Carlson wrote in his diary that night. "Straightforward and no frills. She has ideas and a mind of her own . . . she has an attractive personality and a quality of voice and facial animation which bespeaks deep emotional feeling." There could hardly have been two people more different than the two of them—the tall, straitlaced, mostly conservative, and devoutly religious Marine captain on the one hand, and the short, gender-bending, libertine, radical feminist self-styled revolutionary on the other—which may be why such sparks flew when they met in Shanxi. Carlson had never encountered a woman like her before.

Agnes herself was guarded about their first meeting. When she later wrote of it publicly, she made out that he was the suitor and she was the skeptic, unimpressed by his overtures. As she wrote in an account of her travels with the Eighth Route Army:

> When I heard that Carlson had arrived, I decided to give him a wide berth. My experience with American officials in China had not been enviable. Most of them thought of the Chinese as "Chinamen" who took in washing for a living; I didn't like their religion, so to speak. . . .
>
> One day I was sitting on a mud bank watching two Army units in a basket-ball game when Zhu De came up behind me and asked me to meet one of my countrymen.
>
> "I've long wanted to meet you, Miss Smedley," Captain Carlson said.
>
> "Well, now you've met me," I remarked, and turned back to the ball game.

She was pretty well convinced that he couldn't be trusted. In a letter some years later, she insisted that when they first met she believed he was a military spy sent by the American embassy and the Marine Corps. "While the 8th Route Army had nothing to hide," she wrote, "still I realized that the American capitalist class which rules our Government had always been and would always remain a mortal enemy of any Chinese democratic movement. . . . Thus, when an American officer turned up in the 8th Route Army headquarters, I regarded him not only as a spy against that army, but a traitor to the principles on which the American Republic had been founded."

For all of her suspicions, however, their growing attraction was undeniable. The morning after their first long evening of conversation, Smedley sent him coffee, which began a regular routine for the two of them. For the next two weeks they were hardly ever apart. She found him innocently charming. "Carlson was a very long, lanky man," Smedley wrote—"so bony, in fact, that he looked loose. But when you went walking with him you found that he was as firm as the farmers of his native New England. There was an air of utter simplicity about him which I first thought must be a cunning disguise." Each day they had their coffee together and then went for long walks through the surrounding countryside. In the evenings, they lingered until late in his quarters, talking about the world and China and their lives and the Eighth Route Army. "Agnes Smedley and I breakfast regularly now," he wrote in his diary on December 19. "It is good to have companionship and she is a grand companion." He was still struggling to capture in words what made her so fascinating. She was "frank and forthright," he wrote; "she speaks and writes with great earnestness of feeling and evidences of an appreciation of nature and of a deep sympathy for suffering humanity."

Even as Smedley was drawn in by the charms of Carlson's personality (and, friends later insisted, his Nordic good looks), she gave him up as a loss politically. In her eyes, he was too American, too naïvely confident in the principles on which he had been raised to ever truly understand the Chinese revolutionaries (or herself, for that matter). Despite his background of poverty, and having made his own way in the military, she thought he had "accepted without question the whole outlook of capitalism." She scoffed that the complex politics of the Eighth Route Army appeared to him simply as idealism. "He, like so many Americans, seeks the 'good man,' the good individual," she wrote. "He can justify America's occupation of Nicaragua—he was an officer in that army of occupation—by telling me incidents in which he performed individual good acts and rooted out corruption. He knows nothing of the basic principles which motivate the Communists throughout the world, and which motivate the Eighth Route Army."

Given how wrong he was for her, Agnes tried not to reveal how taken she was with Carlson. When she later talked about their time with Zhu De's army, she always underscored her suspicion that he was an agent of the imperialists. But the reality of their interactions was much softer: breakfast, long walks, heartfelt conversation. It was a romance set against the backdrop of a guerrilla war in North China—a platonic romance, we shall assume, for there is no firm evidence to the contrary, though the rumors about them would swirl nonetheless. As late as 1979, Helen Foster Snow, who outlived them all, wrote to Carlson's son to convey her horror that a studio in Hollywood was preparing to make a TV movie called "Evans Carlson and Agnes Smedley," about their romance in 1937, based on supposedly "confidential and private information." (To her relief, they never carried through with the project.)

Above all, the two Americans bonded over their shared admiration for Zhu De. Agnes had been interviewing the general in preparation for writing a biography of him. Carlson was trying to learn everything he could about the Eighth Route Army and was mesmerized by the leadership principles he saw at work. He told Agnes that Zhu De was only the second actual, practicing Christian he had ever known in his life, after his own father the minister. When she laughed at the thought of Zhu De being a Christian, he said that it wasn't the "hymn-singing, grace-saying Christians" he was talking about. What he meant was that Zhu De was only the second man he had ever known who truly put Jesus Christ's teachings to work in his life, even if he didn't know the first thing about Jesus himself. Zhu De worked for the poor and oppressed, said Carlson. He practiced brotherly love without "grabbing as much as possible for himself." It was an opinion he would hold on to. China's "so-called communists," as Carlson began to think of them, were in reality Christian democrats without knowing it.

Agnes wanted to go to Wutaishan with Carlson to gather more material for her book, but when she brought it up with Zhu De and some of the other leaders, during a dinner with Carlson a week before Christmas, they were clearly uncomfortable. They told her it was too dangerous. Agnes replied that she wouldn't be the only one in danger—everyone who was going along with him would be in danger. She added that she was bigger and stronger than Zhou Libo, the young writer who was going along as Carlson's interpreter. Zhu De demurred. He didn't want her to risk a trip to the front, but he also did not want to anger her because she was a useful ally and a friend. He told her that anyone who went along with Carlson would have to be able to shoot a gun. Agnes immediately replied, "I'll shoot, I was raised in the West." But you're a woman, said Zhu. And that was exactly the wrong thing to say. Agnes flew into a rage, shouting at him over the table: "I'm not a woman because I choose to be!" After a tense few moments, she added: "God made me this way"—and that broke the ice. The atheists around the table all shared a good laugh.

More gently, Zhu De told her they would rather she stay alive and do her writing than die crossing the Japanese lines, but in the end he relented and said she could go, adding that he would send along a large bodyguard force to protect her. Having won her point, she confessed to Carlson that she knew she shouldn't go when the leaders had such reservations. Carlson consoled her that it wasn't just that he was a man; he had the better part of twenty years of military experience and she had none. They finished their dinner and went outside to play basketball. When Carlson left on the day after Christmas, Agnes stayed behind.

Carlson didn't know it, but there were more pertinent reasons the Communist leaders didn't want Agnes accompanying him to the front. Top among them was that she was a known troublemaker; the main reason she was at Zhu De's field headquarters in Shanxi province rather than at the Communist capital in Yan'an was because she was no longer welcome in Yan'an. Back in the spring of 1937, Smedley's enthusiasm for the Chinese Communists had flowered to the point that she formally applied to become a member of the Chinese Communist Party. It wasn't an impossible request, though neither was it a common one for a foreigner—only one American, her doctor friend George Hatem, had been accepted into the party. Nevertheless, her hopes were sufficiently high that when her application was turned down, she threw a fit—bursting into sobs and becoming almost hysterical. She never forgot the rejection, and took it out on other foreigners who visited at Yan'an, toward whom she was territorial and jealous—often refusing to speak to them and spreading rumors about them behind their backs. She overlapped in Yan'an with Helen Foster Snow, who would go to her grave insisting that Agnes was a lunatic. "The rule was 'stay away from Agnes Smedley,'" wrote Snow in 1979, "because she could not be trusted five minutes and also she was a psychiatric case and could not work with anyone else at any time."

The breaking point with the Communist leaders had come in the summer of 1937, just before the start of the war with Japan. After the thinning of their ranks in the Long March, the population of Communists at Yan'an was almost entirely male: there was only one woman for every thirty men. Most of the women who were there were the wives of the senior leaders, and they set a highly moralistic tone. But Agnes, who had always loved a party, decided to try to whip up some social life among the revolutionaries nonetheless. She set up a phonograph player and started teaching the men how to dance to American tunes like "She'll Be Coming 'Round the Mountain" and "On Top of Old Smokey." Her partner in crime was a young Chinese actress from Shanghai named Lily Wu, who acted as her interpreter at the dusty base and lived in the cave next to hers. In a city with so few women, the objectively striking Lily was a magnet for the men, who began flocking to the nightly dance lessons.

Smedley's dancing parties raised alarm among the wives of the senior cadres, who saw them (in Agnes's words) as "a kind of public sexual intercourse." She relished the scandal. "I have a reputation for corrupting the Army," she wrote to Edgar Snow in April. "It does not worry me at all . . . I haven't 'corrupted' Mao yet, but I shall do so soon." Mao did eventually join the lessons, and not only started learning how to foxtrot but also became increasingly fond of Lily Wu's company. He wrote her poems, and visited Agnes's cave frequently with a guard, where they drank tea and talked with Lily Wu acting as interpreter. Mao asked Agnes pointed questions about her love life, and whether she had ever experienced romantic love of the kind the English poets Byron and Shelley wrote about. Agnes understood that these questions were really directed at Lily.

Mao's wife at the time, a woman named He Zizhen, became suspicious of all the time Mao was spending in Agnes's cave with Lily, and late one fateful evening in July, she caught him sneaking into Lily's own cave alone. She barged through the entrance to confront them, screaming at Mao for consorting with a "bourgeois dance hall strumpet." Agnes, in her own cave next door, heard the commotion and quickly put on a coat and ran over to find He Zizhen hammering away at Mao with a long-handled flashlight. When she was done thrashing her husband, she turned on Lily Wu and scratched her face with her free hand. Lily ran to hide behind Agnes, who became the new object of He Zizhen's anger. "Imperialist bitch!" she shouted at Agnes. "Get back to your own whorehouse cave!" She went for Agnes with the flashlight, and Agnes hauled back and punched her as hard as she could. One solid blow, and it laid Mao's wife out flat on the floor. It didn't take long after that for the leaders to inform Agnes that it was time for her to leave Yan'an.

Roosevelt's secretary Missy LeHand had been writing to Carlson to give him encouragement on the president's behalf. "I cannot tell you how interested we all have been in your letters," she told him in October; "The President asks me to tell you to please keep it up." In November she sent a concerned note that they had not heard from him in some time "and we are all interested to know how things are going with you." On December 23, 1937, she sent him Christmas greetings on behalf of FDR. "We are all thinking about you," she told him, "wishing you luck and envying you a little the excitement you are having." His heart surely would have lifted when he read the line that followed—"My chief loves your letters"—but that one would never reach him, as she had addressed it to him in Nanjing, and by the time the letter arrived in San Francisco to be forwarded to China, Nanjing had fallen to the Japanese.

Even as she was writing that note in Washington, Carlson was busy drafting the next installment of his own side of the correspondence on a borrowed typewriter. He had not written to LeHand since leaving Nanjing because there was no longer a secure postal system, but he was heading north soon, to Wutaishan in the occupied zone—where it would be even more difficult, likely impossible, to get a letter out—and he felt the information he had already gathered was significant and urgent enough to risk paying a British missionary to carry a letter for him to a safe destination. In the letter, he said he had just learned of the bombing of the *Panay* but was still in the dark as to what America's response would be. As he well knew, the sinking of the *Maine* in 1898 had helped to precipitate the Spanish-American War, and the German attack on the *Lusitania* had brought America into World War I. So it seemed possible that the bombing of the *Panay* could herald the start of a war between Japan and the United States—and if that were the case, then he felt the intelligence he had to share was all the more urgent.

Specifically, he wanted Roosevelt to know what he had learned about Zhu De's army because he thought China would be a natural ally for the United States in the case of a war with Japan. He explained that the Communists had developed "a style of military tactics quite different from that employed by any other military force in China, and, indeed, new to foreign armies as well." Their army was agile and fluid—he described it as being like an eel squirming in and out between the Japanese enemy's units, or a swarm of hornets attacking an elephant. "They strike and disappear, cut lines of communication, attack repeatedly during the night so that the opponents cannot sleep," he wrote. He said they were finding ways to fight the Japanese that no other Chinese army could yet approximate.

Carlson explained to FDR that the Chinese Communists were not just formidable fighters but also remarkably easy to get along with, "quite unorthodox in their mental processes, in their conduct and in their action." They were "habitually direct in speech and action." They were welcoming and cordial, with none of the stiff formality that made regular Chinese officials difficult to deal with. He reserved his greatest praise for Zhu De, whom he described as "a kindly man, simple, direct and honest. He is a practical man. He is humble and self-effacing. And yet he is forthright in military matters." He told the story of Zhu De holding his hand at Ding Ling's performance. It was a "gesture of affection and confidence which was spontaneous and genuine," he wrote, "and it touched me deeply. But that is the kind of man he is."

Although Carlson supported all parties in China, it was clear from the letter where he believed China's best hope for the war against Japan lay. Zhu De, he told Roosevelt, had commanded the Red Army through its survival of Chiang Kai-shek's five encirclement campaigns; he had led them on the Long March; and as far as Carlson could tell, he had won multiple victories against the Japanese in the north, a feat yet to be achieved by Chiang Kai-shek's KMT forces with their stumbling retreat from the most important cities in eastern China.

Carlson advised Roosevelt that if the United States and China should become allies against Japan, American troops would need to be educated in advance to erase their prejudices about the Chinese people. (This, from the man who had come to China ten years earlier wanting to teach the "slant eyed people" a lesson.) "The knowledge which our American people possess of China and the Chinese is very meager," Carlson wrote, "based largely on the Chinese laundrymen they meet in their home towns, or on what the foreign missionaries tell them." To combat this, he thought American troops should be instilled with the willingness to understand the Chinese and cooperate with them as equals. Echoing his conversation with Zhu De about the hopeful possibilities for an alliance against Japan, he told Roosevelt that if it came to war, a feeling of "close comradeship" could be encouraged between the American and Chinese troops, which not only would enable them to undertake combined operations, but would also (and this he underlined) "result in a closer bond of friendship <u>after the war.</u>"

Carlson's enthusiasm positively flowed off the edges of the page, but he was sufficiently self-aware to know that he might sound compromised. To be so candid about his admiration for Zhu De and the Eighth Route Army was to risk being dismissed as a partisan himself or a zealot. But he had the solidity of his past career to fall back on. He had never expressed sentiments like these in any of his reports or letters before. And so, really, all he could do was to try to reassure Roosevelt that he hadn't somehow lost his head. "I am impartial in my attitude towards political parties, especially abroad," he wrote. "I seek only honesty, intelligence and selflessness in public officials. I recognize them no matter where I find them."

Carlson said the Chinese he had met in the former Red Army

were, as a rule, intelligent, honest, and direct. They were open-minded and took criticism well. You could talk and act with them just like you would with an American. And then, the kicker: that the Chinese Communists were not hell-bent on communism in the near term, but aimed instead to help build a free and democratic China, with an "honest government . . . in which the people had a voice." They wanted to improve the living conditions of the poor and underprivileged (which, he added for Roosevelt's sake, "has a familiar sound"—implying that the Chinese Communists might as well be New Dealers). The ideals of this particular Chinese army, he maintained, were ideals that any American should celebrate and encourage.

Carlson said he knew it wasn't enough simply to relay what he had learned at Zhu De's headquarters. He had to see the army's operations in the field for himself, to confirm the reality of what he had been told. He wanted to see the partisans at work, to judge with his own eye the army's success in organizing Chinese civilians. And that, he explained, was why he had decided to continue north into the areas where the Eighth Route Army operated behind Japanese lines. "I must *see* how these ideas and theories work out in practice," he said. His plan was to depart the following morning, on December 25, with a detachment of Zhu De's troops. And yes, he assured Roosevelt, he was aware of the irony that he would be leaving for the northern front with an army of Communists on Christmas Day.

The intensity of those weeks at the Eighth Route Army headquarters was not easy for Carlson emotionally. Even as his mind processed his unexpected epiphanies about Zhu De's army, he was entering into an intense and equally unexpected entanglement with Agnes Smedley. He felt as if he had learned the greatest secret in the world and Agnes was the only other American he could share it with. On Christmas Eve, after Carlson was done with his paperwork, she came over for coffee and peanuts and they talked as usual about their hopes for the future of humanity, though the conversation took a sentimental turn. Carlson pulled out his harmonica and they spent part of the evening singing together by candlelight. Agnes, fitting with her social-revolutionary persona, sang Black spirituals, while Carlson played

Christmas carols from his childhood. They sang "The Battle Hymn of the Republic" together and tried "Silent Night" but couldn't remember all the words. He played the Marines' Hymn, and then "My Country 'Tis of Thee" while Agnes stood and pounded out the lyrics in the strongest voice she could muster.

Carlson's confusion of emotions came to a head later that night after Agnes had gone and he could let his Christmas Eve with her sink in. He reflected on the personal struggles that had brought him to this strange place in his life. "This is Christmas Eve. Think of that!" he wrote in his diary. Just a year ago, he and Etelle had been happily ensconced in their home on the Marine base at Quantico. "And now look at the darned thing!" he wrote. "What a hell of a mess I have made out of my emotional life. And all because I seek perfection—a mere illusion." He had left his wife behind, had almost no contact with her, wouldn't even be able to send a letter until he was back in a part of China under KMT control. In the meantime, he had found another woman who argued with him and inspired him and stirred his conscience in ways Etelle never had. He wrote fondly of Agnes that night, "She has had a hard life—has had tough breaks and she is a thoroughgoing crusader." But he had seen the softness and vulnerability that lay behind her brash armor. "She has a tender heart," he concluded. He felt divided, wondering at the forces that had fractured his private world.

For all the affection he felt for Agnes Smedley, Carlson was wary enough of her that he didn't trust her with his letter to Roosevelt. That was his best kept secret. But since she was planning to travel down to Hankow after he left—not of her own accord, but because Zhu De had asked her to move on and she was no longer allowed back in Yan'an—he gave her a separate letter to deliver to Nelson Johnson, the American ambassador he and Etelle had been close with when they lived in Beijing. "This is probably the most interesting experience of my life," he told Johnson. "What I have seen since my arrival in the zone of the Eighth Route Army is a revelation." He related some of the same news as in his letter to Roosevelt, but his purpose in this case was more pointed: to leave a record in case he should fail to return. "I am going to the front at my own request and somewhat against the advice of Commander Zhu De," he wrote. "If

I am killed, no blame is to be placed on him or on the Chinese government." He promised not to take any unnecessary risks, but said it was impossible to observe military operations while sitting safely in a headquarters far from the occupied areas. As if to amplify the dramatic effect of the letter, when Agnes arrived at the temporary quarters of the United States embassy in Hankow a couple of weeks later to deliver it, she marched into Johnson's office dressed in her full Chinese Red Army uniform, red-starred cap and all. She claimed it was the only suit of clothing she possessed anymore.

CHAPTER 9

INTO THE NORTH

U P EARLY ON THE MORNING of his departure, Carlson rolled his sleeping bag into a tight bundle and packed his belongings into his haversack. Agnes Smedley came over for a final breakfast. They went out to the south wall of the town to meet up with a patrol that was heading north to bring supplies to Nie Rongzhen's 115th Division in the Wutaishan region, behind the Japanese line of control. The distance there was about 230 miles overland to the northeast, but the direct path ran through the provincial capital, Taiyuan, which was occupied by the Japanese, so their planned route was circuitous and ranged much farther, giving Taiyuan a wide berth. Zhou Libo came along, partly to continue as Carlson's interpreter and partly because he was an aspiring writer and wanted to document the war zone for readers in China.

Carlson and Zhou Libo did not carry weapons, but an escort of twenty-eight soldiers in two squads accompanied them for protection. Between the soldiers of the patrol, the two squads of bodyguards, and a handful of travelers that included Carlson and Zhou, there were forty-five men on horseback or on foot in the group and fourteen draft animals laden with boxes of bandages, medicine, and other supplies. Zhu De came out to see them off. Agnes and Carlson said their goodbyes. As they were getting ready to depart, two Japanese planes swept down out of the north, flying low in the distance, but they did not seem aware of the army headquarters. They dropped a couple of desultory bombs on the city of Hongtong, the county seat a few miles to the east, then turned back north and disappeared. Once they were gone, a small advance guard of the patrol set out first on the road, followed by the rest of the column in a long, single-file line.

Leaving the familiar valley and heading north, Carlson's patrol rode into a dusty and inhospitable loess landscape. Desolate, tree-less mountains rippled all around them, fringed with ice from frozen streams that looked to Zhou Libo like silver chains hanging from the hillsides. When the cold got to be too much for them, they got off their horses and walked to generate warmth. Ancient, gnarled trees, brown and leafless, stood sentry at the sides of the deeply rutted road.

In the villages they passed along the way, the peasants seemed glad to see them. Some offered the soldiers walnuts, a delicacy they used to ship to the northeastern city of Tianjin for export until it fell under the yoke of the Japanese. Now there was no market for them. The rural economy had been broken by the war, and many busi-nesses were closed in the towns they passed through. The land was mostly dry and bare, and the locals said it had been a long time since it had snowed or rained. The memories of a drought-induced famine that had killed millions in North China less than a decade earlier were still vivid—the eating of bark, the withered corpses—and now, to the north of them, there were the dead from the war. There wasn't much left beyond mere survival and, for some, to find ways to con-tribute to the war effort, even if that just meant offering food to the Communist soldiers passing through.

They were still far enough south of the Japanese occupation forces that they felt safe. Aircraft sightings were rare and the local county governments were still in the hands of officials loyal to Nanjing. There were other Chinese forces in the region besides the Commu-nists, mainly provincial troops under control of the Shanxi warlord, who was loyal to the KMT. Carlson wasn't terribly impressed with them (nor with their leader, whom he met later). Occasionally they encountered deserters from those forces, who struck him as "shifty-eyed fellows." Some had become bandits. A few days out from Hong-tong, Carlson saw a larger body of provincial troops drilling in a field and as far as he could make out, all they were doing was marching around, learning how to goose-step like Germans. What a waste of time, he thought, at a time when men needed to learn how to fight.

Carlson may have been the first American military observer in Shanxi, but he was hardly the first of his countrymen to visit the province—Protestant missionaries had been operating there since the late nineteenth century. When Carlson came through in 1938, he encountered an American named Ernest Wampler, of the Church of the Brethren, who had been based there for several years and whose residence predated the Communists' arrival. Wampler maintained a small chapel for his converts and a handicrafts school to give the local villagers vocational training. He had been there for the start of the war with Japan the previous summer, and his congregation had set up an aid station on the road serving millet porridge to the refugees fleeing from the north.

In spite of the deep mutual mistrust between Protestant missionaries and the Communists, Wampler's impressions of the Eighth Route Army largely supported what Carlson was seeing. He recorded that the Eighth Route Army soldiers who had recently moved into the area appeared "very well behaved." Even as they had to crowd into nearby villages, where sometimes the number of billeted soldiers was greater than the populations of villagers themselves, he saw that instead of taking over farmers' homes, they preferred to pack themselves into Buddhist temples and other largely empty buildings so as not to interfere with the lives of the locals. The locals, in return, did everything they could to help—they shared their household effects and brought the soldiers food (which, Wampler noted, the Eighth Route Army soldiers always paid for). Local women made the soldiers shoes and other garments. As he saw it, the local population seemed well protected, and in no way endangered, by the Communist army's presence.

A few days before Carlson's arrival, a young Eighth Route Army officer had come to visit Wampler, explaining that a "rather important American official" was coming but his unit knew nothing about American customs so he hoped the missionary might be able to help them. The officer was worried that his unit's housing would be too cold for the American guest. Wampler offered to let Carlson stay in his own cozy home, but when Carlson arrived, with what Wampler judged "a rather large staff of interpreters and aides" (meaning Zhou Libo, his orderly, and the bodyguards) there were too many of them to fit.

Carlson said that rather than dividing up, he preferred to stay with Zhou Libo and the others in their quarters. He did, however, join the missionary's family for a Western New Year's dinner. Wampler, like so many others, found Carlson "a very pleasant man to meet." Carlson in return took a shine to Wampler and his wife, whom he found "honest, earnest, straight forward people," which to Carlson's mind was about the highest praise you could give someone. "They practice what they preach—in a quiet way," he wrote in his diary. He thought it was a shame that more American missionaries weren't like them.

Zhou Libo, however, was more suspicious of Wampler. As a communist, he resented the presence of Christian missionaries in China. He noted that Wampler had been teaching the local peasants to raise an imported breed of sheep, and suspected that a number of the farmers had been "baptized in capitalist religion" at the same time they were being baptized in capitalist agriculture. Nevertheless, after talking with the American missionary for a while he decided Wampler was a sincere man, and he appreciated that the missionary seemed eager to find common ground. Wampler told Zhou, "Jesus was a social activist. Therefore, he is also a socialist, and so he is a comrade of yours." In other words, morally speaking the Christians and Communists in China were on the same side—which was something Carlson, from a different perspective, was already in the process of concluding for himself (though in his case, unlike Wampler, it was because he doubted that Jesus was actually divine, and likewise doubted that the Chinese Communists were actually communist).

Carlson and Zhou Libo spent the first days of January in the county seat where Wampler was based, waiting for their patrol to continue north. The county administration put on a grand show for Carlson, of a kind that would be repeated many times on his journey north. On the cold, windy morning of January 2 the county magistrate assembled about eight thousand supporters outside the walls of the city. The partisans and self-defense forces formed up in lines and Carlson was invited to inspect them as they stood at attention. They carried a hodgepodge of different weapons, everything from rusty old swords and ancient, muzzle-loaded muskets to modern, light machine guns. Many simply carried spears. The leaders had set up a reviewing platform, adorned with a captured Japanese flag, where they asked Carlson to stand as the crowd marched in formation in front of him, singing military songs and chanting nationalistic slogans: Down with Japanese imperialism. Unite to defeat the Japanese fascists. China fights for the peace of the world.

All of the fuss left him feeling suspicious. A large banquet followed the review, where his hosts ate almost nothing even though there was enough food to feed half the column. The same would be repeated, against his protests, by local non-Communist officials at further stops along the route. He wrote in his diary that there was too much "keqi" for his tastes—*keqi* being one of those Chinese words that foreigners preferred to use in the original because it seemed to them to defy easy translation. It meant politeness, but a particular kind of formal, ceremonial politeness that Carlson, for one, found forced and insincere. He saw it as only so much "bowing and scraping" and "ceremonious exchange of platitudes." He wanted to be an invisible observer, not the center of attention, though that would not turn out to be an easy thing to accomplish.

Their column continued its progress the next morning, its length expanding with the addition of 250 soldiers from the Eighth Route Army's 129th Division who were returning to their headquarters farther north in the province. There was also a propaganda group that seemed to consist entirely of young boys of about twelve years old. One of the boys—"little devils," the Chinese soldiers called them—explained that he was in the army because his father, who wanted to send one of his sons to fight, had drawn his name from a bowl. Another, who was fourteen, said that he had joined the Red Army when he was eight. Zhou Libo asked him if he missed home and he said no, he didn't. Zhou asked why he joined the army. He said he joined to save China, and to save himself.

Carlson hardly rode his horse at all, preferring the exercise of walking each day's leg of the journey. Two more days brought them to the headquarters of the Eighth Route Army's 129th Division. By this time, Carlson was starting to notice patterns. The Communist headquarters were always in small villages, not in the cities nearby that would have been more convenient and comfortable, yet where there was also a greater risk of Japanese air raids. And the farther north they went, the more Japanese overcoats he noticed being worn by Chinese troops. Most of their supplies came from the enemy, which had been true of the Red Army all the way back to its ori-

Chinese partisans, with a "little devil" in the front row. Photo by
Carlson.

gins a decade earlier, when half of the soldiers had no firearms at
all but were trained with sticks in hopes that they could eventually
retrieve rifles from dead KMT troops. Even in 1938, different units
of the Eighth Route Army carried better or worse weapons depend-
ing on whether they had been fighting KMT or provincial warlord
troops before the establishment of the United Front. The commanders Carlson encountered were fond of showing him their collections of Japanese war booty—veritable museums of captured rifles
and grenades, uniforms, condensed food rations, flags, diaries, and
photographs. Occasionally there were pieces of Japanese airplanes.
He made notes on their dimensions and the materials used in their
construction.

As he had done in Zhu De's headquarters, Carlson spent hours
talking to the leaders of the 129th Division to learn how they had
been fighting, of the tactics and outcome of their engagements with
the Japanese. And as with the leaders at the army's headquarters,
these commanders also wanted to know about the international situation, especially what he knew about Japan's plans and the possibility
of American support for China. He fell back on his coursework at
George Washington University to go through what he understood of
Japan's long-term relations with China. He told them that Japan had

been intent on invading China since 1590, when the shogun Toyotomi Hideyoshi envisioned invading Manchuria and then moving the Japanese emperor to Beijing and proceeding to conquer the rest of China, along with much of Southeast Asia and India.

Carlson wanted to encourage the men he was speaking with, so he told them that in recent generations Japan had met with no major defeats or serious obstacles to its expansion in northeast Asia—until now, in China. The Japanese simply hadn't expected to meet with such fierce resistance at Shanghai, he said. They thought Chiang Kai-shek would capitulate quickly, but now the war was becoming a crisis for Japan. Between Manchuria, North China, and the region around Shanghai and Nanjing in eastern China, there were more than a million Japanese soldiers committed to the Chinese mainland, with another million likely being mobilized. They would exhaust themselves. Japan, he told the officers around the table, was in the process of learning that it was not, in fact, the top-tier world power it imagined itself to be. If you can just continue to hold out, he told them, the world's sympathy for China will grow, and with it will come their willingness to send aid.

Carlson began to warm up to the partisans and self-defense forces—the "masses," as it were—always on display, standing in amateur formation at the villages and towns his column passed. The more he saw of them, the more he became convinced that they were genuinely patriotic Chinese peasants rather than just well-orchestrated scarecrows arranged for his benefit by local officials eager to impress the American. And it likewise became clear just how important it was that he *was* American—the first representative of the U.S. government (or any other Western government, for that matter) to come view the war up close, to talk to people face-to-face, which meant he was the first person who stood a chance of conveying to the outside world that Chinese people far beyond the ranks of the KMT armies were trying to do their part to hold out against Japan. Their hopes for the message he might bring home were reflected in the unbounded enthusiasm people showed when he came through. At one town along the way, he noted in his diary, "people came pouring off the terraced village above to the trail below. They carried banners and flags, formed [a] line quickly—children, young and old men—and saluted. They were welcoming an American comrade and very genuine about it." At other towns, people regularly turned out and cheered as the column passed. Sometimes it seemed the entire town was out by the road with banners. He never got over his aversion to banquets and "keqi" government officials, but he found himself increasingly moved by the sentiments of the ordinary people he talked with.

It was also clear that many of the local officials had hopes for American intervention that were patently unrealistic. Some seemed to imagine that Carlson's arrival marked the beginning of a formal American military presence in North China. Banners pasted to the walls of homes in one village his column passed—which Carlson couldn't read, and it is unclear whether anyone translated them for him—proclaimed "Welcome, American patriots, to join China's war of resistance." A companion banner read, "Welcome, American military forces, to fight in the war in China." Such assumptions of American involvement disturbed Zhou Libo, not just because they were so mistaken as to the reasons for Carlson's mission but because they implied weakness on the part of China. Carlson was just there to observe and ask questions, not to be some kind of a savior. Zhou hoped that the guerrilla warfare Zhu De had pioneered would allow his fellow Chinese to hold out against the Japanese on their own, without need of American aid. As he saw it, it was only when you did not need to rely on foreigners for help that they might actually help you.

When local officials questioned Carlson directly about American intervention, he tried to deflect them with vague assurances that the American people were sympathetic to China, and that the two countries had always enjoyed friendly relations in the past. If the officials continued to press him, demanding to know why America hadn't yet joined the war, he tried to turn it around. If Mexico were an imperialist power and it were trying to invade the United States, he asked them, would China feel compelled to intervene? That seemed to work up to a point, but he knew they weren't always satisfied. "They would usually still murmur that America was the defender of democracy and liberty," he told Roosevelt. "The Chinese seem to be pretty well sold on that idea."

Zhou Libo made for a fine companion. In his diary, Carlson described him as "very sympathetic, understanding, and self-effacing," and said he didn't know what he would do without him. Zhou liked Carlson as well, though he held himself at a bit of a remove. One night early on in their journey, Carlson pulled out his harmonica to entertain the men in his quarters with some music. By the glowing light of a candle, he played "The Star-Spangled Banner" and "La Marseillaise." The songs sounded majestic to Zhou Libo, but they also made him reflect on the differences between himself and Carlson. He decided that the reason Carlson could have such a carefree and playful manner was because he came from a country that wasn't under invasion. "First you need to have a free and independent country," wrote Zhou in his diary, "and only then can your personal life be happy and joyous."

Zhou liked to keep track of what Carlson read at night after he finished writing in his journal. Carlson hadn't brought much—just Emerson, his *Reader's Digest*, and some pamphlets on geography and economics. Carlson read to him sometimes from Emerson's essays. "Emerson was a great man," he told Zhou. On Abraham Lincoln's birthday in February, they spent part of the evening talking about the former president. Zhou said he admired Lincoln very much, and recited a quotation he had memorized in English: "I am not bound to win, but I am bound to be true. I am not bound to succeed, but I am bound to live up to what light I have." The quote was apocryphal (there is no evidence Lincoln actually said it) but for a young man who had set his life's course on the salvation of his country, they were powerful words nonetheless.

In the course of their journey together, Zhou the young communist developed a certain respect for Carlson, and through him, for America. He wrote that even though Carlson was an "old soldier" who was sixteen years older than himself, Carlson's character and principles were so youthful that Zhou felt like they were of a similar age. He said that even as he helped Carlson as his interpreter, Carlson helped him as well. "He shared some of his war experience with me," wrote Zhou, "but most importantly, he showed me that there is a different kind of American—not sly and greasy like the ones you see in the movies, though still of course without the clear ideology of a socialist. They lack understanding of many problems, but for those things that they do understand, and do believe, they hold on to them loyally forever. This kind of person naturally gives great weight to his personal friendships, though America's national interests still come first."

Carlson's faith, Zhou went on, was the "simple and pure faith of a military man." His life wasn't ruled by "some empty and illusory God" but rather by his country's concrete interests and his own personal achievements. "America's realism and the progressive spirit of Russia are two of the great treasures of mankind," the young Chinese communist concluded, "and Carlson is the model of an American realist." Zhou Libo published his diary that year in Chinese, though when it was republished years later, when positive words about America were no longer so welcome in China, most of these statements about Carlson would be expurgated.

As the weeks passed, Carlson began to understand more fully how the self-defense forces were used. There were two levels of volunteers below the level of the army. Below the partisans—mostly young peasants who fought as adjuncts to the Eighth Route Army—were

Self-defense forces armed with spears. Photo by Carlson.

the local militias, or "self-defense forces," that were typically made up of people who did not qualify to become partisans, either because of age or ability, so they were basically local militias of young boys and old men. These forces were organized by the magistrate, the ranking civil official in any given county, and their primary purpose was to provide local security, especially to ferret out Japanese spies. The Japanese paid generously to Chinese peasants to bring them information—"Han traitors," the other Chinese called them. The ones Carlson encountered, or at least was aware he had encountered, were already dead, their severed heads impaled on spears as a warning to others who might betray their fellow Chinese.

The self-defense forces, armed as they were mainly with swords, spears, and ancient muskets, would be useless against the Japanese army, but that was not their job. Their job was policing the ordinary, nonaffiliated peasants in their areas, who were even less well armed than they were. They organized patrols and set up local sentries to check travelers for passes along the roads and mountain trails, and in cooperation with neighboring counties they served as a node for transmitting information on Japanese troop movements to the nearest Chinese military headquarters. They also helped with the removal of wounded soldiers, whom they carried on stretchers to the county line and then handed over to the self-defense forces of the neighboring county—and so on, until the wounded reached a hospital of some kind. When the Japanese army approached, they helped orchestrate the evacuation, moving people as well as food supplies and other useful materials to safety in hopes that they would not be captured. And finally, they served a propaganda purpose as well. They kept the local population on alert and built support for the war by holding regular meetings where they sang patriotic, anti-Japanese songs to keep everyone's spirits up.

The farther north they went, the more strongly Carlson and Zhou Libo could feel the presence of the Japanese who had come through before them. In one village, a group of old men were burying three of their neighbors. One had been shot for refusing to kneel before a Japanese soldier. Another was shot for failing to follow instructions shouted at him in a language he could not understand. For the third, they said, there was no reason at all. The houses in this impoverished region were built of mud and soil, and the wood of their window frames and doors was a precious commodity—even firewood was scarce, and children had to walk miles to collect it for their families. The Japanese apparently knew the local value of wood, for as Carlson passed through villages they had recently occupied he could see where all of the window frames and doors had been ripped out and burned out of spite. ("What vandals!" he wrote in his diary.) The harvests of grain the people stored carefully on their roofs to survive the winter were also burned. In some cases, where starting a fire apparently hadn't been convenient, Japanese soldiers had defecated and urinated on the peasants' food stores before moving on.

The images of death and cruelty were overwhelming. In a town early on, it was the remains of a series of Japanese aerial bombings, which had destroyed several hundred homes in a town that had no military presence. The local girls' primary school lay in ruins and they could see scraps of family letters and student papers lying among the rubble. In another village farther north, several witnesses told them how the Japanese had imprisoned two hundred people in a building, then ordered one of the villagers to set it on fire. When he refused, they disemboweled him with a bayonet. They repeated this process until someone finally obeyed. The villagers said there were pigs and sheep inside the building as well, and as it burned, the screaming of the children blended with the howls of the dying livestock. The Japanese soldiers just watched, laughing all the while.

Each story blended into the last, forming a litany of rape, murder, and sadistic violence against unarmed civilians. Japanese soldiers had killed more than three hundred people on the first day of their occupation of one village Carlson passed: on average, one for every family in the village. They raped the young women and then shipped them off in trucks to become "comfort women"—sex slaves—for the Japanese army. Some of the women never made it to the trucks, having been raped to death on the ground.

Even the lesser crimes were heartbreaking; at one small town, a middle-aged farmer came out to the road and pleaded with Carlson and Zhou Libo to come and bear witness to the place where all of his grain had been burned by the Japanese. They said they couldn't go. Zhou wrote in his diary that it was too easy to envision the scene they would find—the pile of black ashes where the man's precious crops had been stored, the old farmer, weeping into his large, rough hands. They had seen enough suffering already. Most of the town's residents had fled for safety, and the old farmer was one of the first to come back. The empty town felt like a vast burial ground, and they were relieved when it was time for the column to move onward.

The formal Japanese line of control was the Zhengtai Railway, which cut across the upper half of Shanxi province, part of the east–west line that connected to Beijing. As the Japanese depended on it for moving supplies and personnel, it was well protected with garrisons in the major towns along its length that sent out patrols to guard its more remote sections. Carlson's column had been growing as it gathered more travelers from each base they visited—it now numbered about six hundred men (and one woman) as well as a veritable herd of pack animals. To get to the rear base areas, the entire slow-moving column had to cross the railroad together. Even with the information they had from the local self-defense forces, finding a safe place and time to get across with such a large body of people and animals was not easy.

They made their first attempt in mid-January, but had to abort when they learned that the Japanese had recently occupied the county just north of where they planned to cross. So they continued east for sixty miles, parallel to the railroad, aiming to cross at a small town named Dongyetou. After beefing up their escort forces with two more companies of armed soldiers, they stopped to spend the night at a village two miles to its south. While they were unpacking their bags, however, a peasant from the self-defense forces rushed in with the news that an active Japanese column of seven hundred soldiers was just a few miles away, approaching Dongyetou, likely on a foraging mission. The ranking officer in Carlson's escort forces, a twenty-one-year-old regimental commander named Chen, took the escort soldiers with him to investigate, and asked Carlson to wait behind with the noncombatants—the orderlies, the kitchen section, the radiomen. Carlson said he would prefer to come along, but Chen said nothing interesting was going to happen.

Carlson could hear the firing of artillery a few miles away as the Japanese shelled Dongyetou, and it was maddening not to be able to go along and watch close-up as he had done in Shanghai. At the same time, however, he realized now that his presence would be a serious distraction for the commander—if an American observer should be killed on Chen's watch (or perhaps even worse, captured), the whole Eighth Route Army might suffer; certainly the KMT officials in Hankow would play it to their own advantage and tell the Americans that the Communists were to blame for his death. Carlson had written his letter to Ambassador Johnson absolving the Communists of responsibility, and he had left a similar one with Zhu De as well, but it was a more sensitive situation than a letter could compensate for. In any case, Carlson, in spite of his frustration, did not want to argue with a fellow officer in front of his men—especially one as young as Chen—so he reluctantly agreed to wait out the engagement with the orderlies and radiomen. They were directed to retreat to a village up in the mountains a little ways to their south. Fifteen minutes into their hike, just as they were starting up the trail toward their refuge, Carlson turned around to look at the view back down the slope and watched as an advance force of Japanese cavalry swept into the village he had just left.

That evening, Chen came back to their camp and rolled out a map to show Carlson the situation. There were two Japanese columns in the area, he said, and it looked like they were trying to converge on Dongyetou. The crossing would now be impossible, but he had sent out scouts in search of weak points in the Japanese lines of communication and he was going to keep moving with the escort forces and see if they could find an opening to cause some damage to one of the columns. Carlson asked again if he could come along and Chen demurred. Changing the topic, he asked Carlson what he would do with his forces under this scenario. Carlson said he would attack each of the Japanese detachments separately, before they could join forces. He said Chen should choose the sites of engagement carefully. Chen agreed. Carlson asked one more time if he could come along. Chen urged him again to stay in the rear.

He wound up being stuck at camp for four days with his diary and his Emerson essays, practicing Chinese with Zhou Libo while Chen's detachment played cat-and-mouse with the Japanese forces in the vicinity. It began to snow and soon the hills were covered in white and the trails were obscured. One of the other men who had been

told to stay behind was a wounded officer who was on his way back
to the rear areas. He consoled Carlson by reminding him that their
mission was to cross the railroad safely, not to fight. "He is right, of
course," wrote Carlson in his diary.

On their third attempt, a week later, they finally made it across.

The dogs started barking even before they came down into the valley,
approaching the small town. It was a cold, clear January night, the
wind searing along the unforested loess hills and slipping through
the valleys. They had been marching since early that morning, crossing a succession of mountains in single file on narrow trails through
the jagged landscape, not daring to stop for more than a quick meal
of rice. The railroad tracks ran through here, just beyond the town.
After the failure of their earlier attempts, this time seemed more
promising. Everything was quiet except for the dogs. There was
no shouting, no sound of gunfire, no visible evidence of a Japanese
patrol. The moon was not yet up and they carried no lights, so their
blue uniforms looked black in the inky darkness. The column moved
quickly, silently, the men walking softly on the same worn, felt-soled
shoes they had used to cover the hundreds of miles on their way here.
They did not talk. They were under orders not to cough.

Carlson did not feel afraid. Rather, he had never felt more alive in
his entire life. He breathed deeply in the cold night air, opened his
mind to the sounds of the dark town as it came into view. His previous
escort, the regimental commander Chen, had stayed behind with his
own forces while a different battalion, led by an officer named Kong,
was shepherding them across. Warmed by his heavy, fur-lined coat,
Carlson looked to the young battalion commander to find out what
would happen next. The Japanese held this town, but there were not
enough of them to keep constant patrols in such a vast, inhospitable
part of the country. In the stillness that emanated from the town, he
could sense that this might be the opening they had been probing for.

Kong indicated silently that it was time. He took Carlson by his
hand, gripping it tightly, and together they ran, swiftly and breath-
lessly, down into the darkened town. Against the symphony of the
dogs he could see glimpses of motion—a company of soldiers sent
ahead to protect their flank, holding a position at the edge of town

as Carlson and the battalion commander ran past. If there were civilians left in the town they did not show themselves—but there was no way to know if one of them had gone off to alert the Japanese, so still, they ran. Then they were through the town, and pushing onward—through the valley, across a small river, up an embankment, and toward the raised railroad crossing. Hand in hand, they ran until it felt safe. Then Kong let go of Carlson, gave a quick salute, and turned back for the rest of his men.

They couldn't stop there for long, so close to the railroad, so once the entire column of six hundred had made the crossing they continued into the mountains again, back onto the loose, rocky paths, with the North Star blazing in the sky ahead of them. They climbed again, then descended into a valley, and climbed one last mountain, their eighth peak of the day, and at the top they finally rested. Carlson's watch said 2 a.m. The men—boys, really, they seemed to him— were exhausted, but no one had been left behind. They sprawled on the ground in weary disarray and went to sleep. They had covered nearly fifty miles on foot since setting out for the railroad crossing the morning before. They had barely eaten, and barely rested, but there were no complaints. They had slipped past the enemy's line of control without firing a single shot.

Carlson was still awake. A half-moon was beginning to rise on the eastern horizon, revealing the pale, deep yellow outline of distant hills. A billion stars burned above in their sharp intensity as a cold wind sheared across the mountaintop, making him shiver in his coat. Exhausted and enthralled, he looked around him at the boys in their blue jackets sleeping on the ground in the bitter cold, these young would-be defenders of their country, and thought to himself that here, around him, was the foundation for what could be one of the greatest military forces in the world.

CHAPTER 10

THE OTHER SIDE

O NCE THEY WERE across the railroad tracks, the other side of the line of control was in some ways eerily similar—similar landscape, similar people, no obvious markers to show that they were now in occupied territory. But the presence of the Japanese was now all around them. What had been a one-dimensional approach as they traveled north from Hongtong county now became a moving chess game with Japanese forces potentially coming from any direction. Carlson's patrol moved furtively, relying on local peasants to give them information on where the Japanese patrols had been spotted, so they could keep their distance—all the while keeping an eye out for spies in the pay of the Japanese who might betray their own location.

As they made their way farther north into the mountains to visit the base at Wutaishan, the reality—which was the most eye-opening aspect of the entire journey for Carlson—was that the Japanese were spread so thinly in northern Shanxi that the Chinese guerrillas were able to move through them and behind them with practiced ease. Carlson found himself on the opposite side of his experience in Nicaragua—now he was one of the free-flowing guerrillas, like one of Sandino's men, moving through the spaces left in the defenses of the better-equipped but all-too-scant foreign occupation forces.

As long as Japanese patrols were in constant danger of ambush by the Chinese guerrillas, they tended to hold together in larger columns for safety, congregating mainly in the cities and other strategic points. Enormous swaths of the countryside remained effectively in the hands of the Chinese, in spite of the invasion. Furthermore, the movements of the larger Japanese columns were so laborious, and the stream of useful intelligence from sympathetic peasants so comprehensive, that it was relatively easy for small, quick-moving patrols like the ones Carlson traveled with to simply weave around the Japanese forces, engaging only under circumstances that suited their own advantages. The Communists took him on a circuitous route, crossing and recrossing, backtracking and flanking, to reach their destination while keeping a safe distance from the enemy. So remarkable was their success in doing this that in spite of Japan's public claims (and the rest of the world's understanding) that Japan was now in full control over the areas of northern China where he traveled, in the course of his journey behind the lines Carlson would see hardly any living Japanese soldiers at all.

Carlson found that the Communists in North China were just as adept at staving off the attacks of the Japanese as they had been with Chiang Kai-shek's forces in the ten years of civil war. At any rate, the Japanese army's efforts to root them out paled in comparison to the KMT's mammoth encirclement campaigns. The main base and center of the border government, as it was called, was fixed in a highly advantageous valley surrounded on all sides by mountains that the Japanese were unable to penetrate safely. As he interviewed Chinese commanders in the rear areas, Carlson took careful note of what they had learned about the weaknesses of the Japanese military— their dogmatism, the inability of foot soldiers to exercise autonomy, their overreliance on their mechanical and material advantages—all of which, said the Chinese commanders, made them especially vulnerable to guerrilla attack. The officers in Zhu De's army knew that nothing could be gained from confronting the Japanese head-on, but significant results could still be achieved by harassing and confusing them, raiding their supply convoys, throwing surprise attacks at their weakest points, and drawing them into difficult terrain that played to the guerrillas' strengths. "Those are good mountains," said one of the members of Carlson's patrol, gesturing at the hills around them as they traveled through a narrow, steep valley one afternoon on their journey. Zhou Libo asked if he meant because they were beautiful. He said no, it was because they would be good for an ambush.

Carlson was moved by the kinds of deprivation the guerrilla fighters put up with as they operated in cold, dangerous conditions with few comforts. They were desperately short on medical supplies and had few doctors. They had hardly any equipment, other than what they could steal from the Japanese. With little or no rear support of their own, each man in a given unit carried several days' rations of dried grain in a long sock slung over his shoulder, which was nearly all he would eat on the march. On one afternoon in January, as Carlson's group passed a battalion on the move, the commander had a company of his men draw up to greet Carlson. "I was very much affected," wrote Carlson in his diary later. "The idea of these men pausing in their life and death fight with the Japs to do honor to me as a representative of America. They are great fighting men, these boys—only two out of a hundred have overcoats. Their food is poor—but they plug along. And their work is effective."

By the end of January, Carlson had seen enough that he was anxious to get down to Hankow so he could write up his reports. He and Zhou Libo left Wutaishan at the start of the Lunar New Year. They attached themselves to a different patrol continuing westward across the top of the province, then south toward Hongtong again. But the Japanese had taken advantage of the start of the new year to launch a major offensive in Shanxi, and once Carlson was safely back across the railroad line, he and Zhou Libo quickened their pace to stay ahead of a Japanese advance that was coming up from behind them. On February 6 he saw Eighth Route Army soldiers blowing up railroad bridges on a line that paralleled the north–south road. He started hearing the drone of Japanese aircraft a few days later as they began bombing the towns in the area in preparation for the army's approach. One afternoon, a Japanese plane flew right overhead as he watched, fascinated, from his billet. It released its bomb, which glinted briefly in the sunlight as it separated from the plane to begin its long, accelerating arc downward. It landed a few hundred feet from him with a deafening, earth-heaving blast.

Carlson was stunned but unharmed. He was still taking stock of the damage from the bomb when a truck arrived to carry him and Zhou Libo south for the desperate final leg of their journey. The Eighth Route Army was giving them a truck and driver to speed them along their way, which was just as well because the partisans were already at work tearing up the roads and building tank traps to block the Japanese mechanized units that were heading their way.

Just thirty minutes after the bombing, they were packed up in the truck and the driver was off, speeding madly south along a twisting highway through the mountains, passing work gangs engaged in planting explosives to blow up the road behind them. As far as Carlson could tell, they were the last vehicle to make it through the mountains while the route was still passable.

They tried to make a stop to rest and eat at a town along the way, but when they arrived a sentry told them that a Japanese column was now only three miles to the east of them. The driver insisted they leave immediately—even if they could stay ahead of the Japanese, they still needed to get through before the roads were cut off. The truck blasted onward through the night, the driver refusing to make any more stops until two in the morning, after they had put eighty miles of distance behind them.

After a few, furtive hours of sleep, they were transferred into another truck, part of a convoy continuing south. They made slow progress as the road was crowded with provincial troops marching north to confront the Japanese. The provincial soldiers looked terrified: listless, dragging their feet along sluggishly as their officers rode beside them on horses, shouting orders. Carlson's truck periodically had to veer off the side of the road as Japanese aircraft roared down from the north looking for the Chinese troops. Spotting a column on the road, the Japanese planes would bomb them, then bank and turn around, flying low on the return with their machine guns blazing as the soldiers flattened themselves on the ground.

Carlson made it through and arrived back at Zhu De's headquarters on the afternoon of February 19, nearly two months after he had left. He was just in time, it turned out, for the entire headquarters operation was packing up to move north the next day. In light of the Japanese offensive, Zhu was moving closer to the front so he could take up a more active command. But he spared three hours that evening to debrief Carlson about his trip and talk about future plans. Zhu said the situation was serious; the Japanese had sent five divisions into Shanxi, about 100,000 troops in total, likely with the goal of pushing through to Shaanxi province to the west, toward Xi'an, which would put them within range of the Communist capital at Yan'an. The central government had put Zhu De in charge of the overall Shanxi theater, expanding the forces under his command by the addition of seven divisions of provincial troops ("the poorest of the lot," thought Carlson). It was a thankless assignment. Carlson guessed that the KMT had given the communist general this assignment mainly so that if he failed to hold back the Japanese they could blame him for it.

Carlson got up early the next morning to say goodbye to Zhu De, but the general was up earlier and came to Carlson's quarters first, announcing himself with a "Good morning!" in English. They talked again for a while, and Zhu De advised Carlson to go to Hankow as soon as possible because Shanxi was becoming too dangerous. Carlson did not record most of what they discussed, either then or the previous evening, but the encounter reaffirmed his feeling of affinity for the Chinese general. "I have met few men in this world who have inspired me with the confidence, or for whom I have felt the deep affection, that I do for Zhu De," Carlson wrote in his diary. "He is a really great man. Great because he is humble and self-effacing, because he is direct and frank in words and action, because he *loves* people and wants to see them happy."

Carlson walked with Zhu De to the outskirts of the town where the pack train was preparing to leave. The entire headquarters of the Communist army—their records and maps, their books and paperwork, the documents they had captured from the enemy, their plans for future operations—all of it had been packed into crates that were being loaded onto fifty draft mules, while a similar number of men acting as porters carried long poles over their shoulders with metal boxes hanging from the ends. The soldiers were singing, and their packs were festooned with branches and leaves to act as camouflage against Japanese aircraft. Zhu De came over to Carlson one last time and embraced him, then went back to rejoin his men. The column set out in single file, a long, slow, winding progression to the northeast. Carlson stayed watching them for a full hour, until the last of them finally vanished into the distant mountains.

———

For the ten months beginning with the fall of Nanjing in December 1937 and lasting until October of 1938 when it, too, would be overrun by the Japanese, Hankow was the capital of China in retreat. It was a period, wrote Agnes Smedley, when the months were as crowded as decades. The central Chinese city on the Yangzi River was really three cities in one—Hankow, the site of the old foreign concessions, Wuchang, where the government and central military command resided, and Hanyang, an industrial center (today, the three are known collectively as Wuhan). It was a place of desperation and intrigue, darkening under the shadow of the Japanese army's encroachment from Nanjing. "All kinds of people live in this town," wrote the British novelist Christopher Isherwood after he visited in 1938—"Chiang Kai-shek, Agnes Smedley, Zhou Enlai; generals, ambassadors, journalists, foreign naval officers, soldiers of fortune, airmen, missionaries, spies. Hidden here are all the clues which would enable an expert, if he could only find them, to predict the events of the next fifty years."

Agnes had come down to Hankow in early January 1938, after Carlson left for the north, but she found the city a difficult place to live. Branded as a Red, she was unwelcome at the Lutheran guesthouse where most of the foreign correspondents were staying. She eventually found a home with the Episcopalian bishop of Hankow, an American named Logan Roots who had a liberal outlook that had earned him the nickname "The Pink Bishop" from the others in the foreign community. (Agnes herself preferred to call him "Comrade Bishop.") With an upstairs room of Roots's spacious mission house as a base, she threw herself into an effort to raise funds to send supplies to the Eighth Route Army. She gave several speeches a day around the city about the terrific deprivation of the Communist soldiers on campaign. The Chinese women's community rallied to her cause, wives of the elite working side by side with war orphans to sew gloves and darn socks for the soldiers up in Shanxi. Some of the women wrote little personal notes which they rolled up and tucked into the gloves they sewed. "My parents were massacred by the Japanese," read one. "More power to you, valiant avenger."

Carlson arrived in the city on February 28 with a story to tell. He had gained five pounds of muscle from all the walking and felt as strong as an Olympic athlete. He had covered over a thousand miles with the Communist guerrillas, most of that distance on foot. Among the wealthy, fashionable urban crowd in Hankow he made for an almost comical apparition with his battered traveling outfit of old, rust-colored riding breeches, and a rough tweed jacket he wore over a thick, hand-knitted sweater. He carried his pipe with him, which, according to one of his friends, "he either puffed or handled as a Chinese storyteller handles his fan to express an idea, a thought, a situation."

Carlson had been there and back; he had gone behind the Japanese lines in North China and said it wasn't like anyone had imagined. The Eighth Route Army was trying to build a new kind of Chinese resistance there, he told anyone who would listen, a rural society with organized peasants and democratically elected local leaders. The Communists were teaching poor, illiterate farmers the arts of sabotage and guerrilla warfare and trying to instill them with a sense of patriotism to China, giving them both the means and the desire to fight back against the Japanese. The Chinese in northern Shanxi had not given up, he said. Far from it. He had seen greater hope up there than he had seen anywhere else in China—certainly more than he now saw in Hankow.

Carlson was the first outsider to witness firsthand the process by which the formerly threadbare Red Army, now the Eighth Route Army, was expanding its scope in the rear areas. From the 45,000 soldiers under Zhu De's command at the beginning of the United Front in 1937, by the end of 1938 there would be almost 160,000 of them, and by 1939 there would be 270,000. By 1945, the army that the Communists were recruiting and training from China's peasantry would count more than a million soldiers in its ranks. Carlson had observed the beginnings of this project, and he was rightfully astounded by what he had seen.

In Hankow, Carlson reconnected with Agnes as well as the remnants of the U.S. embassy staff. He moved into an apartment with James McHugh (who made nice, in spite of his personal feelings about Carlson). And he set to work writing up his experiences in an official report for the naval attaché's office, along with a less formal and more emotional version for Roosevelt's eyes only. "The Chinese Communist group (so called) is not communistic in the sense that we are accustomed to use the term," he told Roosevelt in his first letter from Hankow. He said that as far as he could tell, they did not seem to be engaged in the communization of land or redistribution of property. "I would call them a group of Liberal Democrats," he offered, "perhaps Social-Democrats (but not of the Nazi breed)." He said they seemed fully devoted to the United Front and supported Chiang Kai-shek as the leader of the country. He told FDR that the Chinese Communists had developed and perfected tactics for resistance against the Japanese army which, if the KMT would adopt them as well, could allow the Chinese as a whole to "smother" the Japanese invasion by cutting off their lines of communication and preventing ammunition and food supplies from reaching the front lines. He predicted that a prolonged guerrilla war on a massive scale could exhaust the Japanese Empire's will to fight long before it depleted China's enormous resources.

Hankow was crowded with Chinese and foreign reporters who had congregated there after being driven out of Shanghai and Nanjing by the advancing Japanese, and they practically broke down Carlson's door to get interviews with him. He obliged, and their stories went out into China and across the globe. Carlson chose to emphasize the positive—rather than dwelling on stories of Japanese atrocities in these interviews, he highlighted Chinese resilience and high morale instead. Edgar Snow quoted him in *The Saturday Evening Post* saying the Eighth Route Army was the "most mobile" military force he had ever seen and its soldiers moved "freely back and forth across the Japanese-held railways." A Chinese journalist from the *Xinwen Bao* relayed Carlson's news to his readers that the guerrillas of the Eighth Route Army were attacking the Japanese rear. He explained that the Communists had been unwilling to let Carlson risk the danger of traveling into the Japanese areas until he wrote a letter absolving them of blame if anything should happen to him. Even the Communist press in the United States took notice of the wire reports—the *Daily Worker* ran a photograph of Carlson and Zhu De on its front page in April, though its interest was in the Chinese general rather than Carlson himself ("Chu Teh and U.S. Marine," read the caption). Zhu De "has sworn to fight the Japanese invaders to the last ditch," it reported, adding: "The son of a Chinese farmer, he was schooled in the Chinese classics and likes to play baseball."

A few days after Carlson's arrival in Hankow, *The New York Times* identified him as a United States Marine Corps intelligence officer who had just returned from Shanxi, "where during the past three months he had marched the length and breadth of that province with units of the formerly Communist Eighth Route Army." He was, said the *Times*, "the first foreign military officer to accompany the Eighth Route Army, or indeed any Chinese military force, in an actual campaign." It recounted his adventures with the Communists—crossing the Japanese lines almost at will, "tramping in bitterly cold weather, often in forced marches," eating "the simple army rations of millet and turnips." And he had brought back good news for the United States: "Everywhere," it stated, "Captain Carlson was warmly welcomed, often being greeted with demonstrations in which slogans were shouted and posters displayed stressing Chinese American amity." That was perhaps the most unexpected news: that the Communists in China wanted an alliance with the United States.

In addition, Carlson brought back testimony to just how permeable the areas of Japanese control in Shanxi province actually were—so permeable, in fact, that "control" seemed to overstate the situation. In areas of the map that had been blacked out as Japanese territory, the Communists were building an army of partisans, training peasants in resistance and sabotage work, and even, in the case of Wutaishan, establishing their own new governments, quasi-democratic ones, administering territory as if it were independent. For all the unstoppable power of the Japanese army when it faced Chinese ground troops head-on in positional warfare, Carlson brought back the first concrete evidence that the area the Japanese were trying to conquer was so vast and topographically complex that all they could properly do was hold on to the cities and major railroad junctions. The rest still belonged to the Chinese. Behind the Japanese lines in North China, said Carlson, life for the Chinese peasants had regained far more normalcy than the outside world might expect.

Carlson felt energized. He had celebrated his birthday just before arriving at Hankow, and it was a moment to step back and take stock. "I am 42 years old today," he wrote in his diary, "think of that! And I am only just beginning to live." He felt like he was finally entering a stage in life where his actions might bring benefit to other people—something his father the Congregationalist minister had taught him was the highest calling in life. "It has taken me 42 years to discern the true facts of life," he wrote. "I am at peace with myself now." In Hankow, he did everything he could to get his message out to the world—through his formal report, his letters to Roosevelt, and his many media interviews—but once that was done, he wanted to go back in, to return to the north and travel farther afield than he had gone on the first journey, to try and see whether the Japanese occupation was as porous everywhere as it had been in northern Shanxi.

In the meantime, there was heavy fighting underway in east-central China between Chinese government troops and the Japanese, and Roosevelt wanted the full picture, so in late March Carlson took a side trip to see how China's more traditional forces were faring. The active front was at Taierzhuang, a small walled town in Shandong province near the city of Xuzhou, which occupied a major railroad junction about 350 miles northeast of Hankow. Two Japanese armies were attempting to converge on Xuzhou—one moving south from Beijing and the other coming north from Nanjing—with the goal of closing the pincer and capturing the railroad junction, which would give them full control over eastern China's north–south rail lines and complete their conquest of the east coast. It would also give them access to the perpendicular east–west line, so once Xuzhou was in hand, the two Japanese armies could join forces in a campaign along the westward rail line that would ultimately allow them an open approach to Hankow from the north. Chiang Kai-shek considered the preservation of the Xuzhou railway junction to be absolutely critical to the defense of Hankow, and it was at the small town of Taierzhuang, a few dozen miles northeast of Xuzhou, that the Chinese forces were trying to turn the Japanese back.

Carlson traveled up to Xuzhou by train with a sizable group of observers, including several Chinese and foreign print journalists as well as an American film crew from a group called History Today. The leader of the History Today group was a Dutchman named Joris Ivens, who had recently come to China on the heels of making a successful documentary about the Spanish Civil War with Ernest Hemingway called *Spanish Earth*. His group in China included the renowned *Life* magazine photographer Robert Capa, and they intended to capitalize on the success of *Spanish Earth*—which had given Americans their first close-up view of the fighting between the republicans and the fascists in Spain—by giving a similar treatment (sans Hemingway) to the war in China.

When Carlson met them, the History Today crew were intensely frustrated. Chiang Kai-shek had refused them permission to travel up to Shanxi to film the Eighth Route Army because he didn't want any publicity for the Communists, and for the past six weeks they had been restricted to Hankow under the close supervision of KMT censors. The trip to Taierzhuang was the first time they had been allowed into the countryside at all, and Joris Ivens wrote to a friend that Chiang's government was giving them "one hundred times more difficulties" than they had encountered in Spain.

Ivens was a unique figure at the cusp of World War II, the first filmmaker to introduce American viewers to the idea of a "people's war," where the combatants included not just trained soldiers but also ordinary citizen volunteers. His documentary on Spain had dwelled closely on individual fighters, humanizing them and showing how soldiers and farmers could be two sides of the same coin, could even be the same person. The war in China had some similar qualities— especially the parts of it Carlson had seen—so Ivens looked forward to filming the story of an innocent, peace-loving, agricultural popu- lation locked in mortal combat with a mechanized, fascist invader. The film crew arrived with a strongly sympathetic eye for the Chi- nese, and it was no coincidence that much of their financial backing had come from the Chinese American business community in New York City.

It was fortunate for Chiang that he had allowed all these foreign observers to come to the front at Taierzhuang, for at that walled town they were on hand for the first significant victory of Chinese govern- ment troops in the entire war—or, as Ambassador Johnson put it in a telegram to the U.S. secretary of state, "the first defeat that Japanese troops have suffered in the field in modern times." It was a battle that would provide fuel for propaganda for years to come, but as Carlson judged (and as the filmmakers would as well, showing his influence) the Chinese victory at Taierzhuang stemmed mainly from the ways in which the Chinese forces there had borrowed tactics from the Eighth Route Army. Carlson was impressed by the willingness of the Chinese at Taierzhuang to fight up close and to attack at night, when the advantages of the Japanese army's airpower and artillery were less decisive. As a simple matter of willpower, the battle at Taierzhuang showed that in hand-to-hand combat the Japanese soldiers were no match for the Chinese who fought on their own soil.

The battle for Taierzhuang was hard-fought in close quarters, house by house. And it was savage: fought first with artillery and machine guns, then with swords and grenades, and finally with fists and with teeth. Estimates ranged up to twenty thousand men killed on either side, and the aftermath of the battle made for stunning documentary footage. Smoking ruins of houses, mangled corpses of soldiers and civilians, dead livestock. The Japanese had been forced to withdraw from the town when they ran out of ammunition, and as Carlson and the others began exploring the next day, the first of the townspeople were beginning to trickle back in, rooting around for their meager possessions among the piles of broken stone and brick. One man they encountered said he was hoping to find his hammer in the rubble where his house had been. His wife was searching for the grinding-stones they used to sharpen their knives. The muddy ground was almost impossible to traverse, broken by shell-craters and trenches and shallow graves, barricaded by charred roof-beams, the surface a carpet of twisted metal from artillery and bomb shrapnel. Carlson hadn't seen such devastation since France at the end of the Great War.

The chief of staff of one of the Chinese generals walked Carlson through the battle. The Japanese had been typically overconfident, he said, and they had sent in too few divisions to hold the town. They also relied too much on their artillery to clear a path for their infantry, so the Chinese troops this time had dug deep shelters to withstand the shelling and remained in position to meet the Japanese head-on with machine gun fire when they tried to advance. "The Japanese infantry fights by the drill book," he explained. "When the drill-book instructions don't work, they are lost." This matched with what Carlson had been learning in the north—that the Japanese, by virtue of their sharply hierarchical military structure, were especially vulnerable to surprise attacks and unexpected situations. Their infantry soldiers simply were not trained, or allowed, to think and act on their own.

Not that the individual Japanese soldier was anything to be trifled with. The Communists had practically moved mountains to keep

Carlson at a safe distance from the Japanese forces in the north, but after the battle at Taierzhuang, while he was exploring the remnants of the destruction, he had his first close encounter with a Japanese combatant. It was a noncommissioned officer, a sergeant, who had been wounded in the battle and had used his helmet to dig a hole in the ground to hide in, covering himself with a blanket for camouflage. Carlson passed by the spot in the early evening the day after the battle ended, in the company of the History Today cameramen and a patrol of Chinese soldiers. As they passed, the Japanese sergeant reached up from under his blanket and started firing at them with a sidearm. They scrambled for a ditch on the other side of the road and a strange, long firefight ensued.

The Chinese soldiers shot repeatedly at the Japanese man with their rifles, but he was protected by his hole and they couldn't hit him. Whenever there was a lull in the firing, he would reach up and fire his little gun again. He refused to surrender. Eventually, one of the Chinese soldiers lobbed a hand grenade at him, but it fell wide of the hole and the blast had no effect. Someone threw a second grenade, which also missed. This went on for several minutes. Finally, one of the grenades exploded close enough to expose his hiding place and a Chinese soldier ran across the road to shoot him at close range while he was stunned. But the Chinese soldier's rifle jammed and it wouldn't fire. And he had no bayonet, so he just started slamming the bare muzzle of his rifle into the Japanese man's face, over and over, until it was an unrecognizable, bloody mass. The other Chinese soldiers then crossed the road quickly to strip off the man's clothes and empty his pockets. Carlson was absolutely stunned—both by the Japanese sergeant's refusal to surrender, and by the brutality of the Chinese soldiers when he wouldn't.

The victory at Taierzhuang gave new energy to the Chinese who had retreated to Hankow, but its impact on the war itself was fleeting. Chiang was unable to muster a forceful counterattack while the Japanese were back on their heels. His top German advisor, a General Alexander von Falkenhausen (who had taken over from Seeckt), was beside himself. "I tell the Generalissimo to advance, to attack, to exploit his success," he vented to Carlson in Hankow. "But nothing is done." Eventually, the window of opportunity closed. The Japanese sent in sufficient reinforcements to recapture first Taierzhuang, then

Xuzhou, and by May they would resume their advance toward Hankow. And Taierzhuang, as it turned out, was the last battle for which China would have help from the Germans. Hitler had recently recognized the independence of Manchukuo, an affront to China that revealed his preference for the Japanese. By June, two months after the battle, Hitler would order all of Chiang Kai-shek's German advisors to return home.

The German military mission—which was twenty strong at this point—had been in China helping Chiang modernize his KMT armies for more than ten years, predating the rise of the Nazis, and its members had no desire to abandon China. Chiang, furthermore, protested to the German government that he couldn't allow his advisors to go because they knew his most sensitive military secrets (and it was a simple inference that, in Berlin, those secrets would surely find their way into Japanese hands). All the same, on June 22, 1938, the German ambassador in Hankow gave Chiang's advisors twenty-four hours to sever their connections to the Chinese government or be charged with high treason. They acquiesced, and left for good on July 5, departing from Hankow in a train emblazoned with a gigantic swastika on its roof to protect it from Japanese bombers. Chiang had only the Soviets left to help him. In the final count, Taierzhuang would prove to be nothing more than a brief moment of hope in a vast ocean of despair, and by its end China would be more isolated than ever.

Back in Hankow, Carlson faced constant reminders of how far out of step he was from the other Americans in his views of the Eighth Route Army. Other intelligence officers and some of the U.S. diplomats mocked him behind his back for his admiration of Zhu De and the Communist fighters. One admiral joked that if the Chinese Communists were anything like Carlson said they were, they should have sprouted wings. James McHugh openly challenged Carlson to debates in front of the ambassador, where McHugh argued Chiang Kai-shek's side against Carlson defending the Communists. The KMT officials Carlson met with showed no interest in the information he had brought back from Shanxi—the lone exception being Chiang himself. After Carlson told him about the close relations between the army and the peasants in North China, Chiang turned to his underlings in the room and told them, "Spend less time riding in cars and more time getting close to the people."

Carlson was appalled by the decadence of the upper-class Chinese in Hankow—how the children of the wealthy elites danced and dined their way through the evenings as if the war had nothing to do with them, as if soldiers weren't dying by the tens of thousands a few hundred miles away. It stoked the contrarian in him, made him more provocative than diplomacy might otherwise warrant. On one evening, Ambassador Johnson brought him along to a dinner with a group of KMT officials and other members of the powerful class, where Carlson stood up and made a bold toast in Chinese to the *laobaixing*—the "common people"—which brought the room's conversation to a standstill. There was silence, a wooden response from his hosts. Nobody drank. He wasn't alone in sensing the disjuncture; on their way home after the dinner, Johnson confided to him: "These people are prepared to resist, but only to the last drop of coolie blood."

Carlson felt much more at home with Agnes Smedley, with whom he resumed his long conversations about Zhu De and the Eighth Route Army. He visited with her at the Episcopalian mission, which the other foreigners had taken to calling "The Moscow-Heaven Axis" now that Agnes was living there. He dined with Agnes and Bishop Roots and leftist Chinese writers and Communists like Zhou Enlai who were based at Hankow as part of the United Front. At one of these dinners, Carlson and Zhou Enlai established that they had both been in Shanghai in 1927, the year Carlson first came to China with his battalion of Marines and their nickel-plated bayonets, though of course the two of them hadn't met then. "We didn't have much to do with the American Marines," Zhou told

Zhou Enlai, Agnes Smedley, and Evans Carlson in Hankow.

him. "We used to see them marching down the streets trying to frighten us."

He also socialized with the remaining staff of the U.S. embassy as well as the foreign journalists in town, but he was restless. He didn't want to sit idly in Hankow with the war at a distance. He wanted to be back in a place where he was learning something new. Carlson's superior officer in China was the naval attaché, a Navy commander named Harvey Overesch who was a former college football star with a massively square jaw. Other than a few outings together to the Chinese lines during the Battle of Shanghai, they had rarely seen each other. Overesch was based in Japanese-controlled Beijing, while McHugh (the assistant attaché) covered Chiang Kai-shek from Hankow, and Carlson (the assistant-to-the-assistant) roamed all over the place. But Carlson crossed paths with Overesch briefly in Hankow in April, after the battle at Taierzhuang, and they discussed his future plans. Overesch assured Carlson that as long as his health would stand it, he was free to continue his observation trips.

There was, however, one thing that Overesch wanted to address. He wasn't happy about all the attention Carlson's travels had gotten in the press. He reminded Carlson that it wasn't his job to talk to American reporters—that was the job of the naval attaché and the diplomats in the State Department. In the same vein, he told Carlson to stop speaking to Chinese audiences as well because it undermined the authority of the ambassador and could confuse the United States government's message in China. On the whole, their conversation was friendly but Overesch still made his point. He ended by telling Carlson to use more discretion in the future and stop speaking to anyone outside official channels. Carlson's hackles went up. As he understood it, Overesch was telling him that he was just a Marine and so he had better keep his mouth shut. Carlson assured Overesch that he could do that, and left soon after for another tour with the Communists up north.

He had no intention whatsoever of honoring the agreement.

CHAPTER 11

CROSSROADS

A S CARLSON TRAVELED north from Hankow on his way back up to Xi'an in late April, the railway stations were crowded with military trains headed toward the Xuzhou front, their cars full of young soldiers singing patriotic songs. From the other direction, trains packed equally full of the wounded and maimed returned from the carnage. "It gets under my skin to see these youngsters—so full of enthusiasm, going off to the slaughter," he wrote in his diary. "I have seen so much death."

He had already gained a broader view of the war in China than most people, certainly more than any other foreigner, but his second journey into North China would be nearly twice as long as the first, covering roughly two thousand miles over the course of three months. He succeeded in traversing the full span from Suiyuan province (now part of Inner Mongolia), through Shanxi and Hebei, and finally to Shandong on the east coast by the Yellow Sea. He traveled by any means he could find: on foot, on horseback, on rickety trucks and buses. And in the receding areas where the Chinese still controlled the rail lines, he could travel by train. In the course of the trip he would cross deserts and climb mountains, picking his way through the rear areas along the lines of guerrilla communication.

Officially, Carlson's mission was to observe the military situation in North China. He was supposed to learn about the Japanese army's tactics and gauge the extent of Chinese efforts to organize resistance. Those would be the subjects of his formal report for the naval attaché's office when the trip was over. But when he left Hankow he also had a more personal goal in mind that had more to do with his growing feelings of sympathy for the Chinese than his responsibilities to the Marine Corps. He wanted to know how far Japan's occupation of North China really went, because if—as the evidence from his previous trip had suggested—it was true that most of the countryside was still in Chinese hands, then that was something he thought the outside world should know. It would be compelling evidence that the Chinese could hold out against Japan indefinitely—and if that were known widely, it could attract greater moral support for China and perhaps foreign aid as well. So while his mission of observation was on behalf of the United States, he privately hoped it would help serve China's interests as well.

Carlson visited Yan'an for the first time on this trip. The capital of the Chinese Communists was something of an otherworldly Shangri-La to the eyes of foreigners. As one visitor described it in 1939: "In Yan'an, in the wild and mountainous northwest, the skies are blue and the air is sweet to breathe. It is a lovely place, a remote valley set among high hills honeycombed with caves. An ancient pagoda and the crumbling walls of the original city bombed into nothingness by the Japanese in 1938, are the only reminders of the past." Most of the leaders lived in caves carved into the hillsides outside the city proper. The more people who arrived to join the communist movement, the more caves they dug out, and there were miles of them by the time Carlson arrived.

A good number of foreign journalists and Western radicals had come through before him, the latter group mostly hoping to become advisors or assistants of some kind. There was something magical there, most of the visitors agreed; Chinese Communists who had spent time at Yan'an measured other areas by their resonance with the perfection of the capital. It was a city of caves and dust, but infused with an intoxicating sense of optimism, a feeling of being part of a better future in the making. It was also, by virtue of its being the center of the Chinese Communists' political world, a place of much greater suspicion than the army bases where Carlson had traveled previously. He was watched there, he could feel it. He was quizzed about the photographs he took. A Comintern agent accused him outright of being a spy. A sense of nervousness pervaded Yan'an that hadn't been present in Zhu De's world.

As a military officer, Carlson was the only foreign visitor of his kind—neither a journalist nor a radical—and when he first got to Yan'an, he made it clear that he was a Marine doing intelligence work. "I do not want to pry," he told his handlers. "Anything you want me to see, please show me and I will be content." According to an acquaintance with connections in the Communist leadership, the directness and humility of Carlson's approach was far more welcome to them than the many self-aggrandizing Western leftists who made pilgrimages to Yan'an expecting to be embraced as comrades and who freely pointed out everything they thought the Communists were doing wrong. Carlson, by contrast, made no pretense that he was ideologically one of them, or that he had any advice or guidance to give. He was just an observer, he said, reporting to the U.S. government. He was there to learn, and he was modest enough to recognize that he was the one asking for favors, not the one granting them.

The top of Yan'an's political apparatus was the general secretary of the Communist Party, a near-recluse named Zhang Wentian, but the center of its intellectual orbit was Mao Zedong, and Carlson met him at the end of his first day in the capital. Mao made for a stark contrast to Zhu De. Where Zhu De had been grounded and lighthearted, Mao was ethereal and distracted. Where Zhu De had been ascetic and disciplined, Mao affected the radical intellectual's disdain for social norms; he preferred to sleep in the day while the others held their meetings and study groups, and he stayed up most of the night writing and talking and slurping tea. He paid little attention to grooming or hygiene. He spoke softly but had a crude mouth and swore like a peasant. He picked fleas out of his belly button while talking to interviewers. Every social signal he emitted indicated that he considered himself someone who lived on a different plane than the ordinary people around him, unhampered by the same norms.

It was not immediately apparent to Carlson when he first met Mao in 1938 that this was a man who would one day make all of China bend to his will. But it was clear that he had a magnetism that set him apart from the other leaders. Like the others, Mao lived in a cave carved into a hillside. It was smooth-walled and warm, with a door set into a brick wall at the entrance to keep out the elements. The ceiling was high enough to stand, the furniture simple. They spent four hours that evening talking in Mao's cave as the walls danced with the light of flickering candles. He appeared younger

Mao and Carlson.

than Carlson expected, dreamy and artistic. Through an interpreter, they talked about the war in China and the international situation. Mao repeated to Carlson what Zhu De had told him, that the Communists intended to continue the United Front after the war was over, in order to establish a "real democracy" in China.

They also talked about Europe, and Carlson was fascinated by how the forty-four-year-old Communist interpreted the situation there. Mao said that in the immediate term Great Britain would only go to war against Germany if Hitler invaded France. If Hitler attacked eastward instead, invading Czechoslovakia, he said Britain "would not become involved" (which indeed turned out to be the case at Munich a few months later, when British prime minister Neville Chamberlain chose appeasement over confrontation with Hitler). This mattered for China, said Mao, because if Russia had to face the threat of Hitler's Germany alone, without the support of Britain and France, then Stalin would likely pull back from helping China because he would not want to risk a war with the Japanese as well. As for the United States, Mao made the expected pitch for American support—which was the most concrete benefit this meeting with Carlson could bring him. He said that he believed the United States had been of great assistance to China in the past, and expressed his hope for an alliance where China, Russia, and the United States could join forces to surround Japan from all sides.

Carlson learned from others at Yan'an that Mao's ideas were subject to constant scrutiny by the other Communist leaders. His stature was rising, but he was not yet the unrivaled leader of the party he would eventually become. Carlson speculated in his formal report that their scrutiny of Mao's ideas and plans was because "they realize he is a genius, and is subject to the propensity of all geniuses to occasionally conceive impractical ideas." Nevertheless, even as the general tenor of Yan'an was to diminish Mao by depicting him as just one comrade among many, Carlson sensed his singular importance and credited him with a startling talent for evaluating political factors, both in China and abroad. To Roosevelt, Carlson called him a "dreamer" who possessed "an uncanny faculty of piercing through to the heart of a problem."

Carlson would never feel the same kind of affinity for Mao Zedong that he felt for Zhu De. With Mao there was none of the joy, none of the affection there was with the general, none of the feeling he had with Zhu De that they were like long-lost companions with a shared mindset. He would never pretend to understand Mao the way he felt he understood Zhu as a military commander. They would never hold hands. But Mao was still more forthcoming than Chiang Kai-shek had been, and when Carlson left their meeting—stepping out from the warm cave into the cool night air—he did so with a feeling that Mao was in his own way "a great man." China, he decided, had more than one potential leader among its population.

Mao gave Carlson the permission he wanted to travel through the Communist-held areas, but he did not want Carlson going alone. Carlson's previous interpreter Zhou Libo was not available, so Mao found Carlson a new companion—actually an entire crew of companions, for Carlson's new interpreter was part of a small cultural group of five young men who were about to make a tour through the rear base areas to document the life of the peasants and the army. As before, Carlson would move primarily by attaching himself to a series of military patrols, some Communist and others made up of provincial troops, each already traveling for its own reasons in a direction he wanted to go. But while the soldiers of those patrols would come and go in relative anonymity, his regular companions would be the

Carlson's traveling companions. Interpreter Ouyang Shanzun at far left.

cultural group. They were an eclectic bunch: Ouyang Shanzun, his interpreter, was a playwright, while the others included a novelist, a poet, a photographer, and a journalist. The novelist, Liu Baiyu, was the head of the group, while Ouyang was the only one who knew more than a few words of English, so he mediated between Carlson and the rest of the group as well as the other Chinese around them.

The "boys," as Carlson took to calling them, were in their teens and early twenties, the youngest being the same age as his estranged son. Along the way he taught them how to ride horseback, tended to their wounds when they got injured, told them stories, and serenaded them with his harmonica. They took to calling him their "foreign godfather." He hadn't wanted their company—he would have preferred to travel alone, or at least with only a single interpreter—but this was how Mao wanted it, and Carlson understood that their presence was a condition of his passage. At the same time, however, they were hardly high-level functionaries and they seemed completely lost as to how to act as his hosts.

There is no question the Communists saw a benefit to Carlson's presence. One of the Eighth Route Army generals explained to Ouyang Shanzun in June that he saw Carlson as an "overt" intelligence agent. Since Carlson was learning so much about the war conditions in different parts of China, he said, it would be useful to the Communists if Carlson could share that knowledge with people as he traveled. "Letting him run around like this will be beneficial to the United Front," the general predicted. At the same time, though, even as the Communists welcomed Carlson's presence in the north, the jury-rigged nature of his conveyances and the inexperience of his young handlers suggest that Mao did not consider Carlson's trip sufficiently important to merit the expenditure of more than a minimum of resources. The truck in which Carlson and the "boys" left Yan'an broke down within the day, and continued to break down until they abandoned it. They had difficulty obtaining even basic supplies like warm coats. His young companions kept falling off their horses. There was no Potemkin element to his trip, no imaginary reality cooked up for his benefit. Rather, for the most part, they muddled along on their own.

In the course of his second tour, Carlson abandoned any reservations he might have had about speaking to Chinese audiences. He wanted to share what he had seen in other parts of the country. Especially after visiting Hankow and witnessing the Battle of Taierzhuang, he was inspired to help encourage the people in the rear areas to support the United Front, which he saw as the key to their future—because the only way China could have any hope of finding victory against Japan was if the Communists and the KMT continued to work together. His role in that would be to help convince the people he met to trust the Chinese in other parties and regions than their own.

Threading his way through the northern provinces with his young handlers, he passed through areas under alternating forms of control—some under direct control of the Eighth Route Army, others governed by the KMT, and still others with a mixture of the two or other Chinese provincial authorities. When he was in the Communist-controlled areas, he assured the people he spoke with that they had the support and loyalty of Chiang Kai-shek in Hankow. In the areas where the KMT or their allied provincial administrators were dominant, he told his audiences that the Communists were fully committed to the United Front and supported the Generalissimo without question as the leader of the country. If the right words could help the cause of China's national unity, he thought, that was the least he could do to repay the leaders in both parties who had allowed him to travel in the hinterland and observe at will.

The truth, however, was that there were major tensions in the United Front, which Carlson could see most vividly in the places where the KMT was dominant. In late May he passed through Shenmu county in northern Shaanxi province, where anti-Red slogans were still painted on the walls of buildings ("Cut off the bandit areas/Don't let the Red Bandits spread!" "Suppress and extinguish the thoroughly evil Red Bandits!"). The county magistrate, who claimed not to belong to any party—though Ouyang Shanzun learned he was KMT—grilled Carlson skeptically about his meeting with Mao Zedong at Yan'an. Did Carlson really think Mao Zedong's ideals could be realized? Were they at all suitable for China's needs? Carlson asked the magistrate what he meant by "ideals." The Eighth Route Army was progressive and realistic, Carlson told him; they could get things done. They gave every sign of being sincere about their support for the United Front. Carlson said he couldn't see the future, but he told the magistrate what the Communists had told him: that they aimed to help build "a truly democratic collective government, a government made up of both the KMT and the CCP." The KMT man seemed unconvinced.

Given that his superior officer Harvey Overesch had warned him explicitly not to talk to Chinese audiences, Carlson tried to keep the speeches he made on this trip under his hat. He didn't refer to them in his formal report, or write anything in detail about them in his diary or in letters he later sent home—overall, he tried to leave no official trace of them, lest his superiors in the Navy Department get upset. But his interpreter, Ouyang Shanzun, kept a running account of them in his own diary, which he later published in Chinese, so Carlson's voice still found its place in a lasting form.

Some of these events were huge, with thousands of people—ten thousand on at least one occasion—standing in rows or sitting on the ground in front of whatever makeshift stage Carlson had been put on to speak. Most of the spectators were too far away to hear him, so after Ouyang Shanzun translated each part of the speech into Chinese, while Carlson was speaking in the English that most of the audience couldn't understand, the people in the front row would turn around and tell the people behind them what the interpreter had just said. Those in turn would tell the people behind them, and so his

Audience at a mass meeting. Photo by Carlson.

speech rippled out through the crowds, passed from person to person like a gigantic game of telephone.

He gave one of these speeches at the city of Kelan in northern Shanxi province, in a county at the confluence of three mountain valleys. It was June and the hillsides were green with new crops. The county was being administered cooperatively by Communists and KMT officials, so it posed something of a test case for the United Front. He arrived there on June 9, and the local authorities clearly had been preparing for him—the doorways of the houses were decorated with couplets welcoming him, and trained groups of children shouted English phrases of welcome when they saw him walking through the city.

On the afternoon of June 10, he addressed an audience of about 2,500 people outdoors in the pouring rain at a site outside the Kelan city wall. He spoke for an hour to give them encouragement, going on at length about what he saw as the decisive factors in the war of resistance: strengthening the military, expanding the guerrilla war, building the trust of the people, gaining support from foreign countries, and creating unity among the many groups and factions within China. He told them of his travels and what he had seen at Shanghai and Taierzhuang. Their fellow Chinese were prepared to suffer for the sake of their country, he told them—both in the hinterland and on the front lines. You are not alone, he assured them. He said that

Chiang Kai-shek and his wife were still at the central military head-quarters in Hankow even as the rest of the government had decamped for Chongqing, because Chiang wanted to lead the war personally.

He spoke to them as well about the outside world. He said that America, along with France and Britain and Russia, had always sup-ported China, even though their help might at times seem insuffi-cient. "However," he went on, "you all should understand that those countries all have their own internal problems to reckon with. My friends, you should think of it this way: if China's victory comes from her own strength, from her own struggle, then that victory will be all the greater, all the more significant, and all the more sweet!"

He ended by telling them that victory was within their grasp if they believed fully in their cause. "After the clouds part, the sun will come out," he promised them as the rain continued to pour down. "It is right there, behind the clouds, waiting for you." After the speech was over, he rode back to the city with Ouyang Shanzun, both of them soaked to the bone and shivering from the cold, but full of energy. As if on cue, just as their horses reached the gate to the city, the rain stopped, the clouds withdrew, and the sun shone down on them again.

On other occasions, Carlson compared China's war of resistance to the American Revolution. And whatever specific wording he may have used in English, Ouyang Shanzun translated Carlson's words into the terminology of the Chinese Communists. "My country, America, once had to fight a war for its independence," Carlson told an audience on May 25. "That war took seven years, and for the first two years it was just like this war in China—the chance of vic-tory seemed very small. But then we organized a number of guerrilla units, and the broad masses joined in the resistance, and in the end we achieved victory." He spoke as if he represented all of his country-men. "As an American, I can tell you that the people of the United States are all extremely sympathetic to China," he told them, "and they want to do everything they can to help you fulfill your mission of justice and world peace in this war of resistance."

Carlson knew that what he was doing was forbidden. Overesch the naval attaché would hit the roof if he knew about the speeches Carlson was giving to the organized peasant groups in North China, but he did not care. To his mind, the life-and-death struggle these people were waging against such dramatic odds was on a far higher moral plane than the pettifoggery of the Navy Department. He was especially moved by the young, selfless volunteers of the Eighth Route Army, who made him reflect on the nature of his own people. Could America's youth ever express such readiness to sacrifice themselves in order to remake their world? He wasn't so sure they could. He explored this question in his diary the day after his speech in the rain. "What slaves of personal comforts our modern civilization has made of us," he wrote. "When I see these young students full of energy and fire, consumed with the urge to sacrifice their lives, if need be, for their country, enduring hardships fearlessly and joyously, I am ashamed of many of my countrymen who allow personal convenience to influence their lives." It would "reenergize" young Americans, he went on, if they should be forced to do without their automobiles and their comfortable homes, if they could eat only the "coarsest" food, even just one day out of every seven. He wished that they could "become imbued with a new idealism which would fill them with the desire to live vigorous, simple useful lives."

But what would it take to get them to do that? He thought education might help, but more likely it would only come from their being "forced by dire necessity—as was the youth of China before this war started."

As Carlson and his youthful traveling companions made their way across North China, avoiding the cities and dodging the movements of Japanese forces in the region, Carlson took note of the efforts local officials were making to try to expand their support among the farming population. Most visibly, he saw Eighth Route Army soldiers helping farmers with manual labor, assisting them in plowing their fields and planting crops; come autumn, they said they would assist in the harvest. In the shadow of the Japanese occupation the Communists were cracking down heavily on corruption—shooting officials who took bribes over $500 and putting the lesser offenders in prison. Their efforts were effective enough to gain support even from Chinese who lived in areas under the direct control of the Japanese, who were in some cases sending tax payments to the resistance authorities and providing other assistance such as smuggling goods out of the cities. And always, whether outright or just under the surface, Carlson could sense the seething hatred the ordinary Chinese felt for the Japanese military. Some of them, perhaps apprehending Carlson's feelings of sympathy for their cause, mistook him for a foreign volunteer on his way to join the fight. "Kill a Japanese for me!" shouted one old man as Carlson rode past his town—"and bring him back tied to the tail of your horse!"

As he moved among districts under different kinds of Chinese authority, Carlson noted something that would matter a great deal in the years to come: namely, that the Communists were working much harder to win over the peasants in the areas under their control than were the KMT or other regional Chinese leaders. The support for the Communists felt palpable to him. "The people in the Communist controlled areas would undoubtably support the Communists in case of a schism," he wrote in his report after the trip, raising the prospect of a future resumption of the civil conflict. He realized that while the Communists seemed fully committed to the United Front, they were perfectly aware of the hatred many in the KMT still felt toward them. Further, they knew that right-wing factions of the KMT might try to make an alliance with the Japanese against them—so even as they organized for resistance, they were also laying the groundwork to fight alone, and for themselves, if the United Front should fall.

Carlson's second trip proved much more grueling than the first, and not just because it covered so much more ground. He suffered a recurring fever that he thought was malaria again, but it wouldn't respond to quinine. He contracted dysentery, and a case of trachoma bad enough for him to worry it would leave him blind. But he still pushed on, making notes and conducting interviews for his letters to FDR and his eventual reports. He continued to proselytize for the United Front to the officials and military commanders he met, and kept making his speeches about the sympathy Americans felt for China, until one unexpected episode near the end of his trip forced him to see things in a different light.

It was on the evening of July 17 in the city of Nangong in southern Hebei province, where Carlson had been delayed by heavy rains. In the late afternoon of his second day in the city, he met the future

Chinese leader Deng Xiaoping. At the time, Deng was a young veteran of the Long March working as Zhu De's assistant political director, and he was there on an inspection tour of his own. Carlson liked him quite a bit—Deng was "short, chunky, and physically tough," he wrote, "and his mind was as keen as mustard." Carlson and Deng talked about the usual things—the progress of the United Front, the status of the war in China, the international situation— but what unsettled Carlson was something Deng told him in passing, which he didn't at first believe: namely, that most of the war materials that Japan had imported in the past year had come from the United States. Carlson was shocked—this wasn't something he had heard before—but Deng insisted his information came from public sources. "Can this be true?" Carlson wrote in his diary that night.

It was. Carlson wouldn't be able to confirm it until he got back to Hankow, but in 1937, the first year of the Sino-Japanese War, resource-poor Japan had obtained three-quarters of its petroleum oil—including nearly all of its high-octane aviation fuel—from American exporters. American businessmen had sold Japan more than half of its imports of munitions and munition supplies, and a vast amount of metalworking machinery. More than a third of the steel used to build the tanks, warships, bombs, and artillery shells that Japan had unleashed on China had been produced using raw materials from the United States. And at the time Carlson met Deng Xiaoping, the trade was continuing to grow. As an American economist would argue in *Harper's Magazine* that summer, "The Japanese menace is made possible by American exports." Even as Carlson had been traveling through North China assuring his audiences that the American people supported them and sympathized with their plight, back home certain of his countrymen were making their fortunes by selling Japan the very means of China's destruction.

———

By the time Carlson got back to Hankow on August 7, the city's doom was written on the wall. There were still more than a million Chinese soldiers defending the city and the region surrounding it, but the Japanese army was making steady progress with only a quarter as many troops, supported by their superior artillery and airpower. So pronounced were Japan's advantages in training and equipment that outsiders estimated that, man for man, the Japanese military was at least three times as effective as the Chinese government's very best forces. When Carlson arrived, the Japanese were only about a hundred miles from Hankow and closing. Near-constant bombing raids had flattened large sections of the city, including Chiang Kai-shek's military headquarters.

The Chinese government had retreated from Hankow and moved farther up the Yangzi River to the city of Chongqing, another five hundred miles farther inland in Sichuan province, and most of the foreign population had followed them. Ambassador Nelson had moved the U.S. embassy to Chongqing, to follow the Chinese foreign office, and in the process of moving, Carlson's spare luggage— which he had left with the ambassador—got lost, so Carlson had nothing to change into. In what would be the last days of a free Hankow, Carlson was reduced to making his appearances about town in his summer traveling clothes: a pith helmet, khaki shorts, marching boots, and an old shirt from which he'd cut off the sleeves.

Carlson found a pervasive sense of listlessness in Hankow. In his first letter to Roosevelt once it was safe to send mail again, he lamented the contrast between the people in Hankow and those he had seen up north. "In the north, behind and within the Japanese lines all is optimism, enthusiasm," he said. "Here the Chinese drift along in an aura of defeatism, making no effort to extend themselves in the interest of the nation, attending tea parties, cocktail parties and cinemas, and looking very fat and prosperous."

He briefed Roosevelt about his visits with Mao Zedong and Chiang Kai-shek. Mao, he said, was "friendly and cordial" and Carlson relayed his message (verbatim) that the Chinese Communist Party did not intend to pursue class struggle or agrarian revolution until China had first gone through a period of development as a capitalist democracy. Mao said the Communists welcomed foreign investment in China, as long as it was on a basis of equality. At the same time, though, Carlson—who was perhaps the United Front's most enthusiastic Western supporter—remained doggedly favorable toward Chiang Kai-shek, telling FDR that "his spirit remains undaunted" (even as he confessed that Chiang seemed "aged" and was surrounded with "worthless rascals in his government"). Carlson said he had confidence in Chiang's integrity, and in his determination to continue resisting the Japanese. He told Roosevelt how crucial it was that the different parties in China should continue to work together. The Communists, from everything they had told him, seemed loyal to the central government, as well as to the leadership of Chiang Kai-shek, but he said they still felt the need to prepare for the possibility that they might be on their own after the fall of Hankow. He said he expected the Eighth Route Army would continue fighting the Japanese even if the KMT surrendered.

With Roosevelt, Carlson felt free to open up more fully and candidly than in his official report. He stressed the positive attitudes toward the United States he had encountered in the north. "Everywhere I found great enthusiasm for America and Americans," he wrote. "I discovered that the people don't expect America to come to their aid with troops and battleships, but they do want America's sympathetic understanding, and such moral and material assistance as she can give without jeopardizing her position of neutrality." He admitted to Roosevelt (and only to Roosevelt) that he had been telling the people he met in North China that the vast majority of people in America sympathized with them, and that America's "love of freedom and for all democratic peoples who are fighting for freedom from foreign domination is undiminished." He confessed that he now felt personally involved in trying to get the United States to pay attention to China's plight. "I try to be objective and impartial," he wrote, "but I must admit that my admiration for the courage and resourcefulness of these people, who are fighting against tremendous odds, is thoroughly aroused."

This, then, was his most candid appraisal of the course of the war, as he expressed it to the president. The Japanese were still unable to occupy North China properly. The local governments that the Chinese Communists were setting up behind Japanese lines had expanded their jurisdictions significantly since his visit to Wutaishan earlier in the year. These rural administrations were increasingly independent and self-sufficient, establishing banks and printing local currency and postage stamps. They were operating schools and training sites for partisans and self-defense corps in the rear areas. They were setting up small arsenals to produce ammunition, basic rifles, and 25-cent grenades. Furthermore, the guerrilla warfare the Eighth Route Army had been waging against Japanese lines of supply and communication had been successful enough to blunt Japan's expansion. While he admitted there was no way that guerrilla tactics could win the war on their own, he predicted they could delay Japan's progress and drag out the fighting long enough to ensure that the war cost the Japanese far more than they had bargained for. As Carlson saw it, Zhu De's guerrilla war could be the key to China's endurance; if it were expanded beyond just the Communist areas, it could buy the time Chiang Kai-shek needed for his armies to regroup and plan a major counteroffensive from Chongqing. China, he insisted, could survive.

But what of America's part? In a letter a few weeks later, Carlson told FDR directly that China needed foreign loans and war materials, and that it was "in the interest of the democratic powers to provide her with these sinews of war." Why was it in their interests? Because as long as the Japanese military remained tied down in China, it would help restrain them from setting their sights on other targets—such as America's Pacific territories. "I am not so sure that the statement that China is fighting our war for us is not right," he told the president. "Certain it is that the longer Japan is involved in China, the longer it will be before she is able to challenge us." In other words, Japan's war in China could be just a prelude to a war with the United States. "The independence of China is not merely a moral question," he concluded; "[it] is a condition which is essential to the future of the Pacific arena—which means the peace of America."

The small number of foreigners who remained in Hankow, most of them journalists, called themselves the "Last Ditchers." They were young and worldly and romantic, many with recent experience from the heartbreaking Spanish Civil War—in contrast to which even China's situation seemed more hopeful. They had no illusions that Hankow had more than a few weeks left, maybe a couple of months at the outside, but they intended to stay there until the Japanese tanks rolled in. They met once a week at a restaurant called Rosie's, and they happily welcomed Carlson into their club when he got back. Most of the group were men, since there hadn't been many foreign women in Hankow to start with, and those who were there by virtue of being someone's wife had long ago been shipped off to safety.

The women who remained were a sharply independent lot. Agnes Smedley was one of them, and through her introduction, Carlson befriended a bespectacled British writer named Freda Utley.

Utley formed an interesting counterpoint to Agnes Smedley. Like Agnes, she had never wanted to be the pretty girl. "Not only was I never beautiful," she wrote, "I scorned to be feminine. I wished I were a boy and always felt most flattered when told I have a man's mind." She was an accomplished writer like Agnes, but as well matched as the two women's minds may have been, their politics were irreconcilable. In contrast to Smedley's past flirtations with the Comintern, Utley had been a full-fledged Communist: first in Great Britain, where she joined the British Communist Party in 1927, then in the Soviet Union, where she lived for six years with a Russian husband she had met in England. But due to her much closer experience of the Soviet Union—where her beloved husband was one of the millions who disappeared in Stalin's purges—Utley was by 1938 far more cynical about the doctrine of communism than Smedley was, and held a much darker view of the Soviet Union in particular.

Even as she dismissed most of Agnes's politics as childish, Freda Utley adored Agnes as a friend and forgave her her faults because she was intelligent and funny and compelling in her own way. She reminded Freda of the early Bolsheviks, the idealistic men and women who had first attracted her to communism and the Soviet Union, the same ones whom Stalin was now butchering. "To me she seems a heroic and tragic figure," Utley later wrote, "doomed to destruction by her virtues, her courage, her compassion for human suffering, her integrity, and her romanticism." She enjoyed pressing Smedley on the hypocrisies of the Soviets, insisting that revolutionaries were only honest and self-sacrificing when they were still vying for power; once they succeeded, they turned into something altogether different. She told Agnes she was simply trying to toughen her up for the inevitable disappointment she would feel in the future. Agnes would have none of it. "Why do you try to make me lose my faith?" Agnes complained; "do you want me to marry a millionaire?"

Freda Utley also liked Carlson, whom she saw as honest and devout if a bit too wide-eyed for her tastes. ("Dear, innocent, kind, and courageous Evans Carlson," she called him.) She wrote in 1939 that his "deceptive air of simplicity, almost of *naïveté*, concealed an astute intelligence and a remarkable memory. He was a bit of a romantic, believing in the possibility of the good society and seeking all his life for the way to attain it." Smedley, Utley, and Carlson formed an awkward social triangle in Hankow, a trio of close friends with undertones of wishing to be something more. Agnes was in love with Carlson—Utley could see that as easily as anyone—though Carlson, it seemed to her, might be more attracted to Utley herself. "It was all rather mixed up," as she described it. It remained innocent enough, though apparently not everyone in their circle knew that Carlson was married; Freda Utley would later meet Etelle Carlson by chance, and upon hearing her last name asked if she was a relative of her friend Evans Carlson. "Only his wife!" replied Etelle.

Given her wrathful disenchantment with the Soviets, it is all the more remarkable that Utley (at least for the time being) saw the Chinese Communists in much the same light as Carlson did. "The Chinese Communist Party long ago abandoned the dream of establishing its own dictatorship," she wrote in 1939 after visiting Yan'an. "Now that its social basis is amongst the peasants of the most backward provinces in China, and amongst the middle-class youth and the liberal reformers, its aim has genuinely become social and political reform along capitalist and democratic lines." In contrast to the delusional misfits of the British and American communist parties, whom Utley saw as mere puppets of Stalin and the Comintern, the Chinese Communists were, she wrote, "sincere radicals who themselves believe what they proclaim to be their policy." They were authentic—true to themselves and their followers—and for that reason she judged that they would have "far greater influence in their country" than any of the poseurs in the Western communist parties could dream of.

By the end of August, Carlson's conversion was complete: his heart was firmly with the Chinese. "I have seen a new China in the making," he told his parents in his first letter to them in several months. "My sympathies [have] become very much involved because my natural tendency is to aid the under dog. In the present situation my sympathies are of course entirely with China, as are those of all fair minded and peace loving people." He told them about Zhu De's army and said he felt "devoted to the earnest men and women of this group"—devoted to the point that he no longer wanted to be just an outside observer, reporting on them to the U.S. government; now he wanted to find a way to help them directly. "You can probably understand my feeling, Dad," he told his father, "for it is the same feeling which has tied you to the ministry. . . . The point is that life is not worthwhile unless one is convinced he is making a definite contribution to human progress."

Echoing the thousands of Americans who had volunteered to fight on the side of the republicans against Franco in the Spanish Civil War, Carlson began to imagine himself joining the war in Asia on China's side, volunteering for the Eighth Route Army if they would have him. "My sympathies are so thoroughly involved that I have a strong urge to chuck everything and give them full time," he confided to Edgar Snow. To his parents, he wrote that he was "so thoroughly aroused to the righteousness of their cause and the fundamental honesty of their effort that I would cut my ties with our own civilization and throw in my lot with theirs, if I was not so conscious of material and moral obligations which have developed during my past life."

The American papers had been plugging Carlson's second trip from the moment he got back to Hankow. "China Runs 'Occupied' Area," read the *New York Times* headline two days after his return; "Capt. E. F. Carlson of U.S. Marines Makes 2,000-Mile Trip, Much of It Afoot." *Time* magazine wrote of "tall, bristly-haired, up-&-coming 42-year-old Captain Evans Fordyce Carlson of the U.S. Marine Corps," who had "traversed 2,000 miles with Chinese soldiers" and learned that "able-bodied men are being constantly trained for the guerrilla armies, whose morale is high." After his reprimand from Overesch back in April, Carlson knew he was not supposed to attract attention by giving interviews to the American and Chinese journalists in Hankow, but he did so anyway. "My view is that the truth about conditions in the rear areas should be made known," he told Snow. "It is favorable to China—and it is the truth." He wondered if the Marine Corps would pull him out of China on account of what he was saying about the Communists. "I can see some of the old fogies back in Washington lolling in their swivel chairs and saying 'Carlson is red as hell,'" he told Snow—though he no longer thought they knew what they meant when they used terms like that. Where the brass saw "Reds," Carlson saw the hopeful future of a free country.

Freda Utley was right—in the course of his journeys with the Eighth Route Army, Carlson had indeed turned into something of a "romantic, believing in the possibility of the good society and seeking . . . for the way to attain it." Others in the Last Ditchers group took to calling him "Evans Voice-in-the-Wilderness Carlson." But on that count, it was Agnes Smedley who captured him best at this moment in time. Later, looking back on the final days of Hankow before it fell to the Japanese, she imagined a play where her friends would be the main characters, each with their place in the drama. Of Carlson, she wrote: "Then there is Evans—where is he? Long and lanky and lovable, he shall be the man unconsciously reaching for the stars—but never touching them I fear. Yet that striving, alone, makes life worthwhile." Carlson was the dreamer, the idealist. And in her play, said Smedley, he would be the figure of tragedy.

It was only a matter of time before the hammer came down.

———

In the decade since Carlson had gotten his start in China as a novice intelligence officer, writing his early reports on the "notorious communist bandits," he had, by 1938, established himself as one of the leading China experts in the United States military. Aside from his still secret direct channel to the president, his official reports on the war in China were shared around the top ranks at the Navy Department, discussed at cabinet meetings in Washington, and circulated to America's allies. He had a range of experience in the country that no other American could touch. *The China Press* in Shanghai rightfully described him as being "generally credited with having seen more of the war in the Far East than any other foreigner." But his superiors had some concerns.

To be specific, Harvey Overesch, the square-jawed naval attaché, was now actively worried that Carlson had developed what he termed a "cause." In a letter to Admiral Harry Yarnell, the commander-in-chief of the United States Asiatic Fleet, Overesch warned of the "growing danger" that Carlson would compromise both the U.S. ambassador and Overesch himself, not just with all the publicity he was getting in the newspapers, but also by his "work and suggestions behind the scenes."

Overesch wasn't the only one who had misgivings. Some of his superiors in the Navy had expressed alarm when the news of Carlson's first trip appeared in the New York papers. The China desk officer at the Office of Naval Intelligence in Washington warned Overesch that both Carlson and James McHugh, the assistant attaché, were problematic—McHugh because he was so close to Chiang Kai-shek and his wife, and Carlson because of his enthusiasm for the Communists. He advised Overesch that "a gentle reminder now and again that they are working for Uncle Samuel, not China, the Soong Dynasty, or the 8th Route Army, will be beneficial to them as well as to the Department." He likewise noted his concern that a paragraph in one of Carlson's reports from Shanxi bore a striking resemblance to part of an article published by the radical Agnes Smedley. "We get all the propaganda we are looking for right here in the U.S.A.," he said, "without finding the selfsame thing in confidential dispatches."

That message from the China desk officer in Washington did not arrive in time for Overesch to act on it before Carlson left for his second trip, so by the time Carlson got back to Hankow in August, Overesch was already in a high state of agitation. And then, just as Carlson had done after his first trip, and in obvious violation of his promise to avoid publicity, he immediately started giving interviews to American and Chinese reporters. When the article about Carlson in *Time* magazine arrived in China in September, Overesch decided that he had to take action.

It was Carlson's sympathy for China that worried Overesch the most. Carlson had admitted that one of the reasons he gave his press interviews was because Chiang Kai-shek and the Communists both wanted the outside world to know about Japan's limited control in the north. "I think you will agree that Carlson had developed a 'cause,'" Overesch wrote to Harry Yarnell. "He quite frankly admits that both the Central Government and the Communist Party wish the facts made known to the public and he agrees that this is necessary. In other words, he took upon himself a new master and by virtue of his experiences and perception, had made himself capable of being an adviser to him." As Overesch saw it, Carlson might as well be working for the Chinese now.

Overesch had a great deal of respect for Carlson as an officer. In a separate letter around the same time, he wrote that Carlson "has endured hardships, disease, and trials that few white men can ever endure. He has done these things not only willingly but enthusiastically, bravely and almost heroically." All of his performance reports on Carlson gave him the highest marks of "outstanding," and he was, at that very moment, trying to get Carlson promoted to major without need of an examination, on the basis of his remarkable service during the war. Carlson was the most intrepid and fearless intelligence officer they had in China. But still, he needed to be reined in.

On September 18, Overesch sent Carlson a sharply worded radio message from Beijing informing him that his statements to the press had been "intolerable" and could not be repeated. Then he went a step further, and threatened that if any more publicity about Carlson's activities in China should appear in the newspapers—even if Carlson had not authenticated the reports himself—the Navy Department would hold him fully responsible.

Carlson exploded when he read the message. "I am tired of attempting to adjust my action to the arbitrary whims of a superior officer," he scribbled in his diary. As he saw it, the Navy Department was trying to force him to choose between his moral principles and his career: he could try to be helpful to China, or he could continue to perform his duties as a Marine, but it was clear that they would no longer allow him to do both. His old impetuousness kicked in, hard. Later that day, to the utter shock of Overesch—who, along with Yarnell, begged him to reconsider—Carlson submitted his resignation from the Marine Corps. He quit the service, abandoning his only source of income, and set himself free to follow his conscience.

PART III
AMERICAN INTERLUDE

CHAPTER 12

SYMPATHY

CARLSON SAID HIS GOODBYES in Hankow and wrote to Ambassador Johnson in Chongqing that he would miss working with him. "I feel very strongly on the subject of being able to say and write the truth," he told Johnson. "As you know, I am deeply sympathetic with the Chinese cause. As a public servant I realize that I am subject to certain restrictions which may be placed on my speech by my government. Hence, it follows that, being convinced that it is my duty to speak the truth, I have no alternative but to remove myself from association with the organization which controls me." He said he wasn't really sure what would come next, but he wanted to find some way to generate interest in China's struggle against Japan, and hopefully bring more aid to the country. Johnson was sorry to hear Carlson's news. "I have a profound belief in a man's ability to make his own decisions about life and work," he told Carlson, "otherwise I would be telling you that I think you are making a mistake."

The Last Ditchers threw Carlson a party before he left Hankow. Freda Utley was also planning to depart for the United States and the remaining members of the group staged an elaborate mock trial at Rosie's restaurant, where they charged Carlson and Utley with desertion and found them guilty. Some of the American reporters wrote articles about Carlson's dustup with Overesch, preferring to focus on Carlson's connection to the Chinese Communists. The correspondent for the *Chicago Daily News* blamed Carlson's departure on "Washington's disapproval of his public utterances on behalf of the Chinese Red Army"—which, he said, brought into "bold relief . . .

the American Navy's phobia against anything savoring of radical doctrine."

As a technical matter the Navy Department could not accept Carlson's resignation while he was still on foreign soil, so his superiors in China tried to get him to change his mind before he could leave for home. Admiral Yarnell, still based on his flagship at Shanghai, refused Carlson's initial message of resignation and said he would not transmit it to the Navy Department unless Carlson gave a fuller explanation of why he was leaving. Carlson complied. "Reason for resigning is desire to engage in literary career," he radioed back. "Am profoundly sympathetic with China's cause and feel that I can be of considerable moral support if I can write as a private citizen action taken after careful consideration and as the result of deep conviction."

Yarnell forwarded that one to Washington, but Carlson still had to get a transfer home, which brought him through Shanghai, where Yarnell and others tried to convince him in person to withdraw the resignation before it could take effect. "They seemed to think that the decision was made while I was depressed, and in gloomy circumstances—which was true," he told his parents. But he was a stubborn man, and he stuck with his decision. "The main point is that I have decided that I can no longer remain in the government service, where I am completely muzzled," he told Edgar Snow. "Now that I have very strong convictions I realize that my present situation is intolerable." With Emerson echoing in his head, Carlson recoiled from the "intolerable" feeling of being constrained by others—just as he had done when he ran away from home as a youth or fled from his marriage to Dorothy. This time, his yearning for freedom and self-reliance drove him to walk out on the most promising career he had ever had.

Agnes Smedley warned him that the "Powers-That-Be" would make a lot of trouble for him now that he had revealed his sympathies, but that was just Agnes being overdramatic. Truth be told, Carlson's view of the Chinese Communists wasn't really the issue. As far as the clash with Overesch went, it was the restriction on him talking to the press that caused the rift. Some of the other senior American military figures in China echoed Carlson's views on the CCP, even if they didn't share his sense of evangelism. Admiral Yarnell, for one, read Edgar Snow's *Red Star Over China* and in a letter to Snow he called it "a most timely book [that] will do much to clear the fog that has surrounded the 'Red Army' since 1932." He complimented Snow's "outstanding achievement" and told him *Red Star* should be "The Book of the Year." Colonel Joseph Stilwell, the military attaché in China (the Army's counterpart to Overesch), got to know Carlson at Hankow, and while he was cynical about just about everything under the sun—he had well earned his nickname "Vinegar Joe"—and though he disagreed that guerrilla warfare could make a difference against the Japanese in the long run, he echoed Carlson's assessment that the Chinese Communists were a different breed than the Soviets. "At present, judging by the acts of the Reds themselves, it is a mild form of socialism," Stilwell wrote in a 1938 intelligence report. "They insist on honesty in government, reduction of excessive rents, reduction of excessive interest rates, education for the masses, improvement of the standard of living, establishment of cooperatives, et cetera—an excellent program. If this is communism, China needs a lot of it."

As Carlson pushed on toward home, the question loomed of what he would do with himself as a civilian. He hadn't been out of the military since his days selling canned fruit. He had always dreamed of being a writer—and now he had stories to tell—but Edgar Snow warned him away from a literary career, telling him how hard it was to make a living that way. "I don't know how you are fixed financially," said Snow, "but I know from experience that real freedom is not unconnected with economic independence." He pointed out that all Carlson had to do was stay in the Marines for another year and a half and he would qualify for a pension, a guaranteed income he could live on while he wrote. But Carlson refused even that compromise. Snow said the Chinese Communists were wary of Carlson's decision to leave the service; he had discussed Carlson's case with Madame Sun Yat-sen, the primary Shanghai contact with Yan'an, and she said his decision to leave the Marines was "unnecessary and perhaps unwise." Snow warned Carlson that the Eighth Route Army might not trust him anymore—when he had come to them as an American intelligence officer, it was clear what he was. If he had no affiliation, they would probably treat him as a spy.

Helen Foster Snow, on the other hand, took an immediate proprietary interest in Carlson's writing career. She, like her husband, urged him not to resign from the Marines, though less for reasons of money than because she thought he would squander his credibility. To resign, she said, "would be a magnificent gesture, but might ruin your special effectiveness and prestige." In an effusive letter full of half-conceived ideas for Carlson's future—he should write his autobiography, in multiple volumes! He should write the definitive treatment of the war in China! He should write under the pen name "Col. F. Evans"!—Helen essentially told him what *she* wanted, which was for him to work as an agent of her own progressive political cause. After advising him to structure his multivolume life story as a gradual progression from conservative to revolutionary, she admitted, "I have had the idea of such a book in my mind for a long time, and hoped to find some progressive aviator or army or navy officer who could write it." Carlson fit the bill.

Etelle had been waiting for him patiently all along. From her room in the International House at Berkeley, ensconced in the Spanish-influenced dormitory on Pierpont Avenue, she had been working on a PhD in Far Eastern history with Woodbridge Bingham, a Berkeley professor she and Evans had known in Beijing. She socialized with the students and scholars from around the world who came to live at the International House, and was especially friendly with the students from China, with whom she convened a weekly Chinese language table.

As charming of a life as it was among the eucalyptus groves and year-round summer of Berkeley, however, all she really wanted was for her husband to come back to her. By 1938 they had been married fourteen years, and while they had been apart for much of that time, no period of absence had felt so long as this one. She kept in touch with her in-laws, sharing news from Carlson's occasional cables, and forwarding the articles on him she collected from newspapers and magazines. She wrote them with delight in June of 1938 that a pro-Japanese newspaper in Beijing had called him "that American upstart officer." She shared articles by Edgar Snow and reminisced about how she and Evans and the Snows would spend their weekends together in the Western Hills outside Beijing. And always, she tried to hide her loneliness behind a brave face. "I know you must be very proud as I am of what he is doing," she wrote in one letter to his parents, in which she explained that Evans was off on another adventure but would not tell her where he was going. "It is the sort of thing that only he could do."

She liked to follow his example, which was her way of being agreeable from a distance. She used his phrase of the "communists, so-called." She met with various Americans coming home from China and squeezed them for news about him. In Berkeley, she met Bishop Roots, who had just retired, as well as other of Carlson's more academic acquaintances—Owen Lattimore, a scholar of China destined for destruction in the McCarthy era; John King Fairbank, who would become Harvard's patron saint of Chinese studies. She was smart and knew a great deal—more than she would admit to herself—but she turned down requests from the Red Cross to give a series of talks on China in the Western states because she feared being controversial. There were Japanese students living at International House as well, and she did not want to poison the atmosphere where she lived, so she avoided writing or speaking about the war that so animated her husband. That was his subject, his own area, she would stay out of it. When his photograph appeared in *Time* magazine, she wrote to his parents again. "I am so proud of him," she said, "and you must be even more if possible."

Carlson's itinerary had him making landfall at San Francisco when he first arrived back in the United States, which meant a reunion with Etelle as soon as he disembarked from his ship. But the day that Etelle had been longing for was one he was dreading. "I shall see Etelle in San Francisco," he told his parents. "Don't bank on the result." He was at sea when he wrote the letter, en route from the Philippines to Hawaii and feeling the echoes of the past. He rode on the *Chaumont*, the same transport that had carried him to China on his first tour in 1927, and his arrival in Hawaii would mark twenty-five years since he had first gone there as a boy in the Army pretending he was a man. Later on in the letter, he touched on Etelle again. "I hope I can get out of San Francisco soon," he said. "Also hope that I don't have to deal with any nasty situations. I'm in no mood for temporizing."

When his ship docked at San Francisco, Etelle wasn't the only one waiting for him at the pier. He was also met by Major General Charles Lyman, the Marine Corps commander of the Department of the Pacific. Lyman had come to try to talk Carlson out of resigning— contrary to Agnes's prediction that they would give Carlson a hard time on account of his sympathies, the "Powers-That-Be" were actually doing everything they could to get him to stay in the Marines. While Lyman was waiting for the ship to arrive, he told Etelle that he wouldn't stand for Carlson *not* to be in the Corps. "The Marine Corps needs officers like him," he said. She, too, very much hoped Carlson would reconsider, for they would have nothing to live on otherwise. Fortunately for her, Lyman managed to sweet-talk Carlson, telling him that the conflict with Overesch had been a misunderstanding and he could write and say what he wanted while he was in the Marines. He offered Carlson a month's paid leave, followed by a position as intelligence officer with the Fleet Marine Force in San Diego. Carlson, who had no savings and no money other than what he could borrow from his life insurance policy, relented and said he would give it a try.

Along with Etelle and General Lyman, there was a third person who came down to greet Carlson, someone he hadn't expected to see: his son, Evans Junior. The little boy he had left with his mother when he was a toddler was now a tall, strapping young man of twenty-one, a student at San Francisco Junior College and physically a near-replica of his father. They had only seen each other a few times over the years, but the boy had watched Carlson's career from a distance and was thinking of following a similar path. He had joined a Marine officer's training course the previous summer, where he came out fifteenth in a class of fifty candidates, which was enough to impress his estranged father. The reason he had come to meet Carlson's ship was to tell him that he no longer needed to pay alimony to Dorothy. Young Evans knew his father was planning to resign from the Marines and would have no income, and he said he was willing to support his mother so that Carlson could be free from that financial burden.

Carlson was stunned by the man his son had become. "Evans junior has been the greatest surprise to me," he wrote later to his parents. "He has developed tremendously. . . . He is self-reliant, manly, strikes straight at the heart of things, and has an active and well-informed mind." It was the beginning of a new relationship between the two of them, and Carlson expressed an interest in being more of a father to him now that he was grown and independent. "I am gratified at his development," said Carlson, "and will see him through his last two years of college." While they were in San Francisco he helped young Evans find a place to live so he could transfer to Berkeley as a junior.

Etelle was delighted to be reunited with her husband. "How happy I am to have Evans back after this interminable—it seemed—separation," she wrote to Peg Snow. But the man who came home was not the same man who had left. His goals, his ambitions, his mindset, bore only a passing resemblance to the man who had married her. Peg encouraged Carlson to patch things up with Etelle and said he should try to make her more of a progressive. "Wish you could practice some evangelism on Etelle and convert her to the right line of thought," she wrote. "She is a person of good instincts and impulses and only needs to be convinced I think, and to lose interest in accumulating small properties in the bourgeois manner." She suggested Carlson give Etelle—a registered Republican—some new reading material, starting with George Bernard Shaw's socialist primer, *The Intelligent Woman's Guide to Socialism and Capitalism*. If Etelle ever did read it, one wonders how she might have reacted to Shaw's views on marriage, especially his assertion in that book that "At present a married woman is a female slave chained to a male one."

Everyone wanted Carlson to stay in the Marines—Etelle did, his friends and family did, and above all the leaders of the Marine Corps did—but Carlson only made it to March before he finalized his resignation. He just couldn't stand it anymore. "Since returning to San Diego I have tried to adapt myself to the Marine Corps way of life. But I am hemmed in at every turn," he told his parents, "and am wholly out of sympathy with the whole way of life. . . . The trouble is that my ideas and convictions refuse to be confined within the narrow limits of a Marine Officer's life. If I should continue I would lose my initiative and my idealism, and become a selfish and dogmatic old fool." He wrote to President Roosevelt to explain his decision. "As a civilian I can help to interpret to the American people the significance of events in the Far East," he said. "As an officer I cannot do so without embarrassing the government." He didn't know what would come next for him and Etelle, though the Institute of Pacific Relations, a think tank in New York, had offered him $500 to write a treatise on China's national army, so he thought they could live on that for a little while. "Henceforth Etelle and I will be leading the simple life," he told his parents.

It was tough going. They had almost no money and the Chinese army book was on a tight deadline, so all he could really do was write. He felt an impossible distance between himself and Etelle, though she tried her hardest to be supportive and loyal. "Life is indeed simpler since we have been out of the Corps," she wrote to Carlson's parents a couple months after his resignation, trying to make the best of their situation. "No calls to make, very little entertaining to do and no going out in the evening to dinner. . . . I am rather social minded, but, I thoroughly enjoy being at home, having time to read and write and having Evans at home." She claimed to be perfectly content that they had no money and no social life, and that their lives revolved entirely around Carlson's moods and his need to write. To the Snows, she was a little more direct. "I can't say I am very happy about it," she told them, "for like most women I enjoy a home and at least money enough to pay bills."

Other than an occasional outing to the movies, all of their time was spent at home. To keep busy, Etelle got involved with a Girl Scout troop at a nearby school and tried to find work as a Latin tutor to help support her husband. By May of 1939 she had found just one student. She was aware the situation could not last. "I know Evans will be getting the urge to be doing things," she told his parents, "he already has it, but he wants to do more. . . . I hate to contemplate another long separation but it can't be helped." She acknowledged that the two of them were just "marking time," and said she was grateful for all the housework she had to do because "it doesn't give me much time to wonder what next."

What came next was another separation. Carlson finished writing his thirty thousand words on the Chinese army and then moved to New York City without her. Deng Xiaoping's words about the enormous amount of raw materials and munitions the United States was selling to Japan had lodged firmly in his mind, and in New York he decided to focus on trying to get the American government to do something about that. So he rented a small apartment on the

Upper West Side and joined a campaign to build public support for an embargo on the sale of war materials to Japan.

———

Carlson was hardly the only American at the time who cared what was happening in China. Back on January 3, 1938, when Carlson was just a few days into his trip to Wutaishan with the Chinese Communists, Random House had released the first U.S. printing of Edgar Snow's *Red Star Over China*. It sold out completely by mid-afternoon. After a hasty series of reprintings, it made it onto the *New York Times* best-seller list by the end of the month. The book's sudden success was a surprise to all concerned, not least to Snow himself, who had told his agent that he didn't expect the American edition to find many readers. In Great Britain it did even better, selling 100,000 copies in its first few weeks alone.

There is a story behind its sales, though, which is an important one. It sold, by far, the most copies in Britain, where it was distributed by the Left Book Club, a publisher that appealed mainly to communists and other readers on the far left of the political spectrum. Snow found his audience, but it wasn't a mainstream one. In the United States, his situation was more complicated. Edgar Snow was no fan of either the Soviet Union or the Comintern, and several passages in the first edition of *Red Star* made that clear. "The Chinese Communists," he wrote at one point, "like Communists in every other country, have had to fall in line with, and usually subordinate themselves to, the broad strategic requirements of Soviet Russia, under the dictatorship of Stalin." Aside from calling Stalin's government a "dictatorship," he described the Comintern—which still purported to be an international organization—as being "virtually a Bureau of the Russian Communist Party." A few pages later, he called it "an instrument of the national policy of the Soviet Union." Snow's criticisms of Stalin and the Comintern did not sit well with the Communist Party of the USA, which immediately branded his book "Trotskyist poison" and published several scathing reviews in its allied publications as well as calling for a boycott, thus threatening Snow's ability to sell his book to the very audience that should have been the most receptive to it.

In response, Snow wrote a letter to Earl Browder, the head of the Communist Party of the USA, denying that he was a Trotskyite and challenging the CPUSA's decision to boycott *Red Star* and prevent the American communists from reading it. He said he was a sincere admirer of Browder's work but begged him to understand that *Red Star* was sympathetic not just to the Chinese revolutionaries but also to the worldwide revolutionary movement. The Chinese and British communists liked his book, he wrote, so why should the Americans alone oppose it? Didn't Browder think it strange that no foreign communists had ever gone to Shaanxi to write about the Chinese Red Army before—and yet when Snow, a non-communist, finally went in and wrote a sympathetic account, the Americans boycotted him! Attempting to muster a viable threat, Snow said he had collected a great deal of negative information about the Comintern that he had left out of the book, and might have used it "in a very harmful manner indeed" if he had known that the Communist Party of the USA would attack him.

Having stood up for himself, however, Snow then wilted. His letter turned conciliatory and he said, essentially, that he would do whatever the party wanted. "Some weeks ago," he told Browder, he "voluntarily" wrote to his publishers to ask that they "excise certain sentences from any new edition of my book—sentences which I thought might be offensive to the party." That is, he would censor the book, but he insisted that he had done so preemptively, of his own volition, and not because Browder and the party had boycotted him.

However, it is well worth noting that the letters he sent to his publisher with the "corrections" were dated in May 1938—two months *after* his letter to Browder, not "some weeks ago" as he had claimed. Snow's agent acknowledged the censorship as well, writing to him later that summer to say that Snow's changes hadn't made it into the most recent British edition but that was fine because "England didn't complain about your attitude toward Russia, and there isn't a great deal of harm in the book coming out there without the changes that were necessary for the United States." A sanitized version of *Red Star*, stripped of Snow's most negative comments about Stalin and the Comintern, came out soon afterward. With Browder's blessing it regained its place in America's leftist bookstores, and on the best-seller lists, and it is the basis of the edition that is sold to this day.

Shifting away from the ferocious internecine politics of the American left, there was a much wider, more mainstream American interest in China at the time that had little to do with questions of communism or Soviet influence. Even as Edgar Snow managed to get himself onto the *New York Times* nonfiction bestseller list for four weeks in 1938, a Chinese writer named Lin Yutang dominated the list for forty-six weeks that year, much of the time at number one, with the latest of his books: *The Importance of Living*, a gentle, whimsical rendering of early Chinese philosophy into a sort of self-help guide to the good life.

Lin, who had been born in 1895 in China's Fujian province, had a broad, international education and spent his life moving between China and America, writing prolifically for audiences in both countries. He was easily the most popular Chinese writer in the United States and published a long run of bestsellers, many of them interpretations of Chinese history and thought. He did not avoid political topics, but neither did he dwell exclusively on them, and above all he was playful and charming (and nonthreatening), so the accessibility of his writing made for an easy entrée to Chinese topics that American readers might otherwise have found alienating—his 1935 work, *My Country and My People*, for instance, was a primer on Chinese culture for the American reader that would resonate with particular power after the Japanese invasion.

Then there was the world of the returned missionaries and their children. A century of American Protestant missionary work in China had created a small class of white Americans who had grown up in China, some of whom occupied lofty positions in American culture. Pearl S. Buck, for one, was a massively prolific and successful interpreter of the country in which she had grown up. In the course of her career, she would publish more than forty novels and dozens of works of nonfiction about China. At the time when Carlson came home, the most famous of her books was *The Good Earth*, a sympathetic portrait of the unforgiving lives of Chinese peasants that sold more than four million copies and won the Pulitzer Prize in 1932. In 1937 it was made into a major Hollywood movie that would be watched by millions and win two Academy Awards. The following year marked a further high point in Pearl Buck's career when she was awarded the Nobel Prize in Literature for her "rich and truly epic descriptions of peasant life in China."

Buck's counterpart in journalism was Henry Luce, the founder and editor-in-chief of *Time*, *Life*, and *Fortune* magazines and the single most powerful American media figure in the pre-television age. Like Pearl Buck, he was the child of missionaries in China and he maintained a deep interest in the country of his birth that he carried to the pages of his flagship publications. As a conservative Republican and a devoted Christian, Luce was a vigorous supporter of Chiang Kai-shek, who had converted to Christianity in 1931 as a condition for marrying his wife, Soong Mei-ling. On January 3, 1938, the same day that *Red Star Over China* hit the bookstores, Luce's *Time* magazine featured Chiang Kai-shek and Soong Mei-ling on its cover as "Man and Wife of the Year." The issue included a long, adulatory summary of Chiang's life story, explaining that over the past year "the Chinese have been led—not without glory—by one supreme leader and his remarkable wife." It was the Generalissimo's sixth appearance on the cover of *Time*, the second for Soong Mei-ling, and more would come over the years as they enjoyed the unswerving support of Luce and his media empire.

All of which is to say that in 1938 China was hardly an unknown or distant topic for most Americans. Those who did not go out of their way to follow the war in the papers or read Snow's book on the Communists (or pick up one of that year's National Book Award winners, *400 Million Customers*, by an American adman based in Shanghai) might just as easily find themselves reading about the heroic Generalissimo in *Time* magazine, or thumbing through one of Lin Yutang's bestsellers, or at the very least flocking to the theaters with millions of others to see the tear-jerking blockbuster about Chinese peasants by the first American woman to win the Nobel Prize in literature. In 1938, in America, China mattered.

That did not, however, mean that aid was forthcoming. The dominant current of American public opinion vis-à-vis foreign affairs in the 1930s was isolationism. For a range of individual reasons—pacifism, the desire to focus on domestic issues during the Great Depression, the wish never to be drawn again into a distant conflict like the Great War—the majority of Americans strongly opposed any intervention in foreign wars. A Gallup poll in October of 1937, a few months into the war in Asia, found great sympathy for China: 59 percent of Americans supported the Chinese, while only 1 percent took the side of Japan (the remaining 40 percent were neutral). But their deeper isolationist sentiments became clear after the Japanese sank the *Panay* the following December. Against Carlson's expectation that the attack would provoke a war between America and Japan, it accomplished exactly the opposite: 70 percent of Americans surveyed after the *Panay* incident, far from calling for war, instead said that all American troops should be withdrawn from China in order to eliminate the risk of a conflict with Japan. In another survey a few months later, 68 percent of Americans opposed sending arms to China. Mainstream American support for China was, thus, of a sentimental yet passive kind—many felt sorry for China's suffering but they did not expect their government to do anything about it.

Against this mood of isolationism, Carlson set his shoulder. "I can't accustom myself to the indifference of people to the Far Eastern crisis," he wrote to Freda Utley in March of 1939. "We Anglo-Saxons are so terribly selfish and self-satisfied. When we are aroused we move, but it takes an army of Snow Whites and the Seven Dwarfs to wake us up." Fortunately he was not alone in his efforts. On October 1, 1937, for example, a group called the American League Against War and Fascism had convened a pro-China rally at Madison Square Garden that drew a crowd of ten thousand to denounce the Japanese invasion. Several Christian and Jewish religious leaders, including three Episcopalian bishops, shared the stage with the Chinese consul general, labor leaders, and the chairman of the ACLU to call for a boycott of Japanese goods and to raise money to send medical supplies to China. But as with Edgar Snow's readership, this group and others like it were based far to the left of the political spectrum. Both the American League Against War and Fascism and its cosponsor for the Madison Square Garden event, the American Friends of the Chinese People, were affiliated with the Communist Party of the USA and drew much of their support from its membership. Earl Browder allegedly referred to the American League as "a transmission belt of the Communist Party."

The far-left connections of these groups mattered because, in September of 1939, just before Carlson arrived in New York, Nazi Germany and the Soviet Union shocked the world by signing a mutual nonaggression pact. Hitler and Stalin pledged to avoid hostilities with each other (and secretly divided up Poland between themselves, among other things). Following that agreement, orders went out from the Comintern that the American Communists must immediately stop criticizing Hitler—their enemy henceforth would be the imperialists, not the fascists. The energy of the Communist-aligned anti-fascist groups in the United States was suddenly squelched, much to the dismay of those who had joined them in the mistaken belief that they were fighting for a cause rather than simply taking orders from Moscow. By the time Carlson arrived in New York, the American League Against War and Fascism and other groups like it had largely disappeared.

There were other options, though, which better appealed to his own views. A returned China missionary named Harry Price had recently formed a group called the American Committee for Non-Participation in Japanese Aggression. The name said it all: the sole purpose of the committee was to get Congress and the president to impose an embargo on the sale of war materials to Japan. The group was distinctive in its political stance, insofar as it was bipartisan and steered clear of involvement with antiwar groups connected to the Communists. To gain support from the isolationists, they argued that America—while avoiding direct involvement in the war in Asia—should at least decline to contribute its resources toward the furtherance of Japan's conquest.

The American Committee for Non-Participation in Japanese Aggression—or the "Price Committee" as it was also known (nobody particularly liked its full name)—was a perfect match for Carlson. It had an influential board including leaders of industry and education, former government officials, and social activists like Helen Keller. It was bipartisan but leaned Republican, and its honorary chairman was Henry Stimson, who had been President Hoover's secretary of state (and would be recalled into service as Roosevelt's secretary of war in 1940). One of its patrons in government was Stanley Hornbeck, the chief advisor on political relations at the State Department, who, according to a colleague, had two overriding passions: first, "a feeling of affection and sympathy for China," and second, "a pathological hatred of Japan and [all] things Japanese." The committee established dozens of local chapters and printed up thousands of copies of pamphlets with titles like "America's Share in Japan's War Guilt" and "Shall America Stop Arming Japan?" where they decried the phenomenon of "American-motored airplanes, fueled with American gasoline, dropping American metals to be blown into the bodies of Chinese men, women, and children who have traditionally regarded America as their best friend." They maintained a direct mailing list of 100,000 Protestant ministers, lobbied members of Congress, and established a speaker's bureau, which is where Carlson's main contribution came.

Carlson's goals matched seamlessly with those of the Price Committee and he brought to the group his own measure of influence in the government. President Roosevelt had discussed Carlson's reports from China at cabinet meetings, and after receiving Carlson's account of the battle at Taierzhuang, he had begun talking with his secretary of state and treasury secretary about how to help China financially. By the winter of 1938–1939, Roosevelt was approving China's first war loans as part of the new Lend-Lease program, inspired at least in part by Carlson's urging. Carlson also kept up a regular correspondence about China with other government figures including Stanley Hornbeck at the State Department. In one memo in FDR's personal files, Hornbeck said of Carlson that "He impresses me as being an American of the most wholesome type—rugged, courageous, conscientious, soft spoken, and committed to the 'good neighbor' policy both in private and public contacts."

Carlson became one of the Price Committee's most prominent public speakers. With the committee's support he traveled around the country giving talks about the war in China to civic and religious groups, including local chapters of organizations like the League of Women Voters and the Foreign Policy Association, as well as a host of smaller community forums. He spoke in church sanctuaries and high schools, in community halls and private homes on topics such as "Our Place in the Orient," "European Pacts and Chinese Prospects," and "Christianity and World Peace." He told his audiences he could give them stories of the Japanese invasion that would make their blood boil, but said it would be more productive to go into the policy aspects and explain why the embargo was necessary. China, he told them, had "the capacity to secure her own independence if the United States will cease helping Japan." He went on the radio to talk about his experiences in China, and wrote articles for a range of publications.

His style was unpolished, but his message was all the more compelling for that. "Carlson was not a fluent speaker, either in private or in public," wrote a journalist who heard him on several occasions. "He was hesitant and would grope for the right word. But his face could break into one of the most engaging smiles I ever saw, a smile that radiated good will, good temper, candor, and humbleness. But though he could not weave a magic spell of conversational narrative, he was one of the most convincing of men to listen to."

In his speeches for the Price Committee, Carlson made the case that the best way for America to avoid direct involvement in the war in Asia was to stop enabling Japan's invasion of China, for the longer it went on, the more emboldened Japan would become toward the United States. At the National Press Club in Washington on February 27, 1940, he argued that a Japanese victory in China would be only "a stepping stone to further aggression." An embargo, he insisted, was the only way to constrain them. "Sooner or later Japan would challenge us," he predicted, "and it might be very costly in wealth and lives to meet the challenge. But, today, we can make it physically impossible for Japan to go on, and do it with very little risk of war." If the United States would simply stop selling raw materials to Japan, he predicted, the war in Asia would grind to a halt in six months.

The main obstacle to an embargo was not the American business community (which did not, in fact, oppose the Price Committee's work) but rather the isolationist views of the voting public, which made the government wary of taking any actions at all. At the same time, there were also active propagandists for Japan at work, campaigning against the embargo. One of the most visible was an American named Carroll Lunt, a longtime Shanghai resident and publisher of the Chinese Who's Who, among other things, who had come home on a speaking tour of his own, calling for appeasement with Japan. Lunt, whom one offended publication called "a subservient flunky of Japanese interests," was a doughy man with a thin mustache that made him look something like a combination of Hitler and Walt Disney. Lunt was on tour in the United States for the purpose, as The China Weekly Review described it, of "advocating American cooperation with Japan in the exploitation of the riches of China." Among his favored talking points were that "aggression is a relative term" and "Japanese and Chinese are basically the same people."

Lunt gave his own audiences a wide variety of reasons why America should support Japan and continue trading with it without limitations. In San Francisco, he predicted Japan would see great financial returns from its efforts to "build up" China, and said that China would be better off, with "greater purchasing power and a high standard of living under Japanese control." If Americans wanted a piece of that prosperity, they needed to play along. In Honolulu, he declared that "when Chiang [Kai-shek] is beaten and the war is over, international trade in China will be better than ever under the benevolent rule of Japan." In New Jersey, he argued that "the best thing for China, in order to avoid further destruction, would be to accept the puppet government set up by Japan." On CBS radio, he blamed China for starting the war.

In January of 1940, Carlson and Lunt went head-to-head at a meeting of the Foreign Policy Association in Philadelphia. The main thrust of Lunt's argument was that what Japan was doing in China was no different from what the United States had done in Central America, so Americans had no right to judge or criticize. Carlson replied that Americans had repudiated those past interventions and the troops had been withdrawn. Americans, he said, had "attempted to profit from our mistakes in the past, and were endeavoring to progress." At another point in the back-and-forth, Lunt hammered on China's "culpability" in the conflict, insisting that China was to blame for provoking the war by boycotting Japanese trade. Carlson pointed out that the boycott came only after violence on the part of the Japanese military. Lunt then argued for the importance of protecting foreign interests in China, not just the interests of Japan, but those of Britain and America as well, to which Carlson asked: "How about the interests of the *Chinese* in China?"—and that brought the house down.

Between the talks, the travel, the radio interviews, and the articles he was writing, Carlson was busier than he had ever been in his life. At his apartment in New York, he worked late into the night, then fell into bed around one or two in the morning to sleep without dreaming. He was meeting the elites of the city—Roosevelts and Rockefellers and Carnegies. He lunched with the publisher and editorial staff of *The New York Times*, and dined with a core group of the Council on Foreign Relations, hosted by the newly retired Harry

Yarnell. Though the leaders of the Price Committee had not been able to get appointments with President Roosevelt, Carlson had his own access and Roosevelt welcomed him at the White House on several occasions to discuss China and the embargo. And the committee's lobbying paid off—according to Gallup, by February of 1940, 75 percent of Americans supported a ban on the sale of "arms, airplanes, gasoline and other war materials" to Japan. With public opinion shifting in the embargo's favor, Carlson's speaking venues became increasingly prominent; in the winter of 1940 he headlined at Boston's Symphony Hall and lectured at Harvard University, the locus of his childhood dreams of becoming a professor of literature. "Gosh, I don't know what happened," he wrote to his father, "but things seem to be breaking in my direction right now."

CHAPTER 13

UNHEARD WARNINGS

CARLSON'S ABIDING DREAM of becoming a writer came a step
closer to reality in February 1940 when a major New York publisher gave him a book contract. Dodd, Mead and Company
signed him up to write the story of his experiences with the Eighth
Route Army, but since it was urgent material, they gave him only
three months to finish the book. Up to that point he had only written
a few sample chapters—which Etelle, for one, thought were the best
things she had ever read. "It is a definite contribution to the world of
literature," she told his parents. "He has never written better. I have
read and reread it."

He didn't want Etelle's support, though, so when the time came
to pull back from his speaking engagements and leave New York to
focus on writing the book, instead of returning to his home with
Etelle in San Diego he went to live with his father in Plymouth,
Connecticut. His mother, Joetta, had died two months earlier, right
before Christmas. She had been wheelchair-bound for more than a
decade by that time, so her death had not been unexpected but Carlson's father was bereft as he adjusted to life without her. Carlson's
sister, Karen, had moved to Plymouth to take care of their father, and
Carlson felt the pull to come home and do his part as well, at least
for a while. His own grief for his mother's death was compounded by
the guilt he still carried for breaking her heart when he ran away as a
youth, and he decided to dedicate his book to her memory.

It would be the first time Carlson had lived under a roof with his
family since leaving home at age fourteen. He brought his suitcases
to his father's white clapboard parsonage on the Plymouth town

green, where he moved into an upstairs bedroom in the back, a quiet spot with a winter view of low mountains to the west. Downstairs, he worked in his father's study—the latest iteration of the one he remembered from his childhood, so full of books and radiant with the aura of his father's education. With a certain degree of pride that he now had a place there—and perhaps a life worthy of the books around him—he unpacked his notes and diaries from China and got to work.

Carlson became a familiar figure in the town of Plymouth over the following months. The neighbors remembered him as an amiable man with a sense of humor who loved to sit and talk. He enjoyed daily walks to the post office and sitting on the porch steps of the house chatting with his father and sister. Occasionally he gave the sermon at his father's church. The Reverend Thomas Carlson was planning to retire before long, and he thought his son might take over from him as minister—he suggested Evans start by serving as associate pastor, and study for the ministry at the Yale Divinity School thirty miles down the road in New Haven. Carlson was honored, but his heart was now set on a larger audience than the congregation of a small-town church could provide.

On Memorial Day of 1940, Carlson spoke at a ceremony on the Plymouth town green, a grassy plot in front of the church where Union soldiers had drilled in the Civil War. His topic was not China but democracy, and at the time he spoke the free countries of Europe were falling at a terrifying speed. Hitler's forces had smashed through Belgium, the Netherlands, and France, driving the retreating British and French armies to the edge of the sea at Dunkirk. France would surrender within weeks, and it seemed possible that all of Europe could be lost. Democracy, Carlson told the group assembled on the Plymouth green, "means the freedom to think, act, write and speak as we feel, as long as we do our neighbor no harm; it means that we claim the right to share equally with all men the rights, privileges and opportunities which our way of life may provide." It was not something to be taken for granted any longer. "Democracy is a state of mind," he told them, "a conviction which flows from within, and it can endure only so long as a majority of the people are determined that it shall be kept alive."

For all of his youthful dreams of literary fame, Carlson was no Martin Eden. He was a perfectly capable writer, but his greater gift was as a speaker. The book he wrote at Plymouth was informative and timely, and absolutely unique, though stylistically he tried a bit too hard to dramatize what was already an inherently dramatic story, so it contained much in the way of meaningful looks and twinkles in the eye. As he described the moment when Edgar Snow first told him about the Chinese Communists:

> "I believe," he assured me, "that the army leaders would welcome your inspection of their organization."
> "What sort of men are they?" I asked, inquisitively.
> A far-away look came into Ed's eyes. "They're different," he said slowly . . .

Some of the dialogue was formed in sentences that would never actually come out of a person's mouth. ("Take the Chinese habit of trying to 'save face,'" said Edgar Snow. "They endeavor to conquer it by inviting criticism and by severely criticizing themselves. Evasion and procrastination are their arch-enemies.") But considering Carlson's lack of formal education, it was an impressive feat to turn out a ninety-thousand-word book in just three months. And the literary quality wasn't the point, anyhow—the point was his message about China.

As for that, Carlson did nothing to disguise his admiration for the Eighth Route Army. He wrote that Mao Zedong's "kindly eyes regarded me thoughtfully from a face that suggested the dreamer." He described the Chinese Communist fighters as he had understood them—similar in spirit to Americans, engaged in a movement for freedom and equality that he thought his readers would naturally want to support. He described Zhu De as having "the kindliness of a Robert E. Lee, the humility of an Abraham Lincoln, and the tenacity of a U.S. Grant." He plotted out the route of his travels in American terms as well, superimposing an imaginary map of the United States over China to explain to his readers that, for instance, the return leg from his first journey to the Wutaishan area was equivalent to "striking west across the northern part of Lake Superior, with a view to moving south between Marquette and Duluth, Minnesota, and then returning to Green Bay, Wisconsin, where Zhu De's headquarters was located." He openly dismissed the possibility that the Chinese of the Eighth Route Army were communists in the sense that Americans understood the term. Certainly, he wrote in the introduction, they "seemed to possess characteristics quite different from the type of doctrine which we have come to associate with Russia."

But even as he praised the Chinese Communists, he did not intend for his book to be a partisan work like Snow's *Red Star Over China*. He wanted to help China as a whole, not just the party of Mao Zedong and Zhu De. So he wrote glowing passages about Chiang Kai-shek as well, and insisted that both political parties had crucial roles to play in the country's future. He described Chiang Kai-shek as the "central figure" of China's drama. "His experience, his devotion to the nation and his personal integrity have raised him above mere party interests," he wrote. He argued that Chiang's political party, the KMT, alone possessed "the ability to organize the resources of the nation on a vast scale," while the Communists had provided "the rich leavening of liberal thought and action, the insistence on recognition of the nobility and rights of the individual" that, when woven together with the organizational power of the KMT, could create in China "progress towards the goal of national independence, democracy, and a way of life which will bring economic sufficiency and happiness to all of its four hundred and fifty millions of citizens."

It was an incredibly optimistic book, reflecting the fact that it wasn't just a work of reportage or travel writing, it was political. Carlson wanted Americans to support China's war of resistance, and for that to happen, he had to convince them that if the United States stopped supplying Japan with raw materials then China would not only survive but triumph. Coming up with an appropriate title was difficult. Carlson wanted to call it "Backstage with China's Armies," or the more flowery "The Sons of Han Arise," though his publisher nixed both of those. In the end, to underscore Carlson's evenhanded support for the CCP and the KMT, the publisher went with an imitation of Edgar Snow's title and called Carlson's book *Twin Stars of China*, attempting to ride the coattails of Snow's success. If Edgar

Snow's "red star" was the Chinese Communist Party, Carlson's "twin stars" were the Communists and the KMT working together. The symbols of both parties were imprinted on the book's cover, and some editions had an image of Chiang Kai-shek and Mao Zedong superimposed over each other. In subject, in design, and in presentation, it was a work dedicated to the United Front.

The reviews were generally positive. *The Atlanta Constitution* called it "one of the most fascinating and fantastic books of travel ever written." A reviewer in *The Nation* said he wished the United States had more military officers "with the intelligence and breadth of interest with which Major Carlson is obviously endowed." *The New York Times*, in the book's most prominent notice, gave Carlson few points for literary style but commended his honest, unaffected writing. The reviewer echoed Carlson's American analogy, writing that the volunteers of the Eighth Route Army seemed to him "much like old-fashioned Americans, and their ways remind one a little of the soldiers of our own Civil War or Revolutionary War."

The fall of 1940, however, turned out to be a difficult time to publish a book about China. When Edgar Snow's book had done so well in 1938, China had just inherited from Spain the mantle of central front in the global struggle between freedom and fascism, and readers were hungry for books like his. By 1940, however, Europe was completely engulfed in war and the American public had little attention left over for Asia.

Joris Ivens and the History Today film crew ran up against this problem when the film they had shot in China, titled *The 400 Million*, failed to gain wide distribution upon its release in 1939. A documentary on Hitler's invasion of Czechoslovakia that came out the same week got all the prime theater showings and the lion's share of the reviews, and when the two films were reviewed together, the critics preferred the one on Europe. Ivens had pitched a bold framework for understanding the war in China—on one side, according to his opening montage, was "CHINA—which has enriched the world for 4000 years with its treasures of art and wisdom." On the other side was "JAPAN, determined to . . . seize the world for her empire." It was a powerful and vivid film, and might have caught the zeitgeist if it had come out in 1938, but by the time it was released in the United States all eyes were on Europe and, according to *Variety*, the few people who did go and see it in the theaters were mostly Chinese themselves, or hard-core sympathizers, so it is unlikely that it succeeded in changing anyone's mind.

Twin Stars faced headwinds for similar reasons, though its impact was also diminished by a more positive development: the campaign for an embargo had succeeded. In the summer of 1940, the Roosevelt administration began placing restrictions on the export of munitions and war supplies to Japan, with the result that by the time *Twin Stars* was published that fall, Carlson's primary talking point was moot. He also lost his public-speaking platform, because the Committee for Non-Participation in Japanese Aggression, which had sponsored his appearances, found itself in the enviable position of having succeeded in its objectives, and so it disbanded.

Carlson's speeches and writings and radio interviews up to that point had all boiled down to one fundamental promise: that if the United States stopped supplying Japan with the materials of war, then the people of China, welded together by the United Front, could fight back with unified vigor and eventually prevail against the Japanese Imperial Army. With the embargo in place, America was fulfilling its part of that bargain. But as Carlson was soon to find out, the other part of his argument was founded on a flawed premise, for in China, the United Front was already on the verge of collapse.

Carlson had been eager to go back to China as a private citizen after he quit the Marines, and once he was done writing *Twin Stars*, he used the money from the advance to buy his own ticket for the first time. The Snows were in the Philippines, and when he visited them on the way out they found a way to cover his expenses in China through an organization they had helped to found, Chinese Industrial Cooperatives (best known by the nickname Indusco). Founded in 1938, Indusco was dedicated to raising funds internationally to support small-scale industrial cooperatives in China as part of the war effort. The hope was that large numbers of bite-sized, mobile industrial enterprises in the Chinese countryside could make up for the loss of China's major industrial centers to Japan, by producing the basic consumer goods and military supplies that the free areas of China needed, while also being able to move safely out of reach of the Japanese when necessary. Carlson thought of the cooperatives as "guerrilla tactics applied to industry."

In the two years since Carlson had left, almost nothing had gone well for the Chinese government. Hankow fell in October of 1938, a month after his departure, and China's wartime capital and central military headquarters now resided in the final redoubt of Chongqing, far up the Yangzi in Sichuan province. Japanese planes bombed the city mercilessly, but it was protected by surrounding mountains and a climate that often gave it a heavy cloud cover. By September of 1940, Japan had conquered the most important seaports along China's southern coast, establishing a naval blockade that prevented the Chinese from importing supplies or war materials by sea. China's government in Chongqing was reduced to one lone route of supply, a treacherous, twisting mountain road from British-controlled Burma into China's Yunnan province. The Chinese government faced strangulation, even as the land war had ground down into a quagmire for the Japanese, who advanced deeper and deeper into China's interior in hopes of forcing a surrender.

The great guerrilla campaigns Carlson had imagined in 1938 had not materialized—if he had been able to retrace his steps in the north, which he could not, he might have seen that Mao was largely conserving his own forces by this time, preferring to focus on expanding his base of support while letting Chiang Kai-shek's armies bear the brunt of the fighting with Japan in central China. Meanwhile, there was now a second, smaller Communist army—the New Fourth Army—which had been grown from the remnants of the Communist forces that stayed behind on the Long March. It was made clear to Carlson when he first arrived in the country that worsening relations between the CCP and the KMT meant that he would not be allowed to travel freely between their areas of control as he had done in the past, so his journey this time focused

Carlson and Helen Foster (Peg) Snow in the Philippines, 1940.

mainly on rural areas still governed by KMT officials in the central and southern provinces of China—areas where the Japanese had a strong presence but limited control.

Since he no longer had any official status, Carlson received no particular welcome from either the Communists or the KMT on this trip. "I realize that I am in the curious position of being persona non grata all around," he wrote to Ambassador Johnson in Chongqing. "The reactionaries both here and in America think that I'm a Red, and the Reds think I'm a bourgeois spy. The truth is that I am simply a plain American who believes in real democracy, and who is particularly concerned with keeping Japan from becoming an imminent menace to the United States."

He traveled this time without bodyguards or interpreters, his lone companion being a New Zealander named Rewi Alley, one of the founders of Indusco, who had previously been a factory inspector at Shanghai and spoke excellent Chinese. They set off to try to visit as many of the nearly two thousand active cooperatives as they could reach, an experience that was exhausting and frustrating, but which gave Carlson his first broad view of the countryside south of the Communist areas. They walked, sometimes twenty or thirty miles a day, and packed themselves onto crowded buses and trains when they could. Due to wartime fuel shortages, many of the buses had been converted to burn charcoal, puffing their way slowly up the hills under power of steam boilers and making up time with gravity on the descents. Carlson no longer had his elaborate travel pass from Chiang Kai-shek, just a badge from the Chinese Industrial Cooperatives organization which hardly functioned as a passport. On one third-class train car, a young woman who spotted his Indusco badge accused him of being a spy, then spent the remainder of the trip loudly denouncing him to her fellow passengers.

He was reasonably impressed by the industrial cooperatives themselves—he and Rewi Alley visited hundreds of them, most of which made or processed a single product: shoes, umbrellas, soy sauce, hemp cloth, or any number of other goods for which they could find materials (the rubber for the soles of the shoes, for instance, came from worn-out truck tires). The co-ops sold their goods locally, as an alternative to the widely available Japanese products that were instrumental to Japan's goal of dominating the Chinese economy.

Carlson's interest had less to do with how well the cooperatives manufactured their products than with how they promoted a sense of social equality among their members—for the cooperatives were supposed to encourage Chinese peasants, officials, and refugees to work together as partners. They involved voting and shareholding and mutual responsibility, and were meant to act as laboratories from which a spirit of democracy could be grown. Such a grassroots sense of democracy could, Carlson believed, not just become a powerful weapon against the Japanese occupation but also help to ensure a more democratic future for China as a whole.

There were no great optimistic epiphanies as there had been on his tours with the Eighth Route Army. Instead, on this trip there were a lot of bureaucrats and local officials of varying levels of corruption. Some of the cooperative organizations seemed encouraging and effective while others were, as he described them in his diary, "lots of eye work, little real cooperation." As he traveled, he learned a great deal about the ongoing tensions between the KMT and the Communists. Faith in the United Front seemed to be on the decline. "Confidence of people destroyed," he wrote in his diary on October 16.

He was especially disturbed by the right-wing KMT officials he encountered—in a report to Roosevelt he described their tactics as "essentially fascist in character" and said they appeared to be pro-Japanese in their sentiments. He told FDR that the frictions between the KMT and CCP were far worse than anyone had reported previously. "Japan, of course, is taking full advantage of this state of affairs," he told the president, and her "present policy here seems to be aimed at breaking China's solidarity." In the worst cases, Japanese forces were singling out the Communist troops of the New Fourth Army for attack, while proto-fascist elements of the KMT harassed them from the rear. In their joint hatred of the Communists, the right-wing KMT and Japanese troops were operating practically as allies.

He found almost none of the hope he had seen two years earlier. "The situation here is disappointing," he wrote to Freda Utley from Guangxi province. "Gone is all the vim and enthusiasm of the early months of the war. In their place is conflict, profiteering and apathy." China's enthusiasm for resistance seemed to be fading, morale was sinking, the future was more uncertain than ever. To another corre-spondent, he wrote that "China is being destroyed by an ulcer from within." The overall mood of his tour was captured in a scene when he departed from a town in Fujian in October. The local cooperative staff made a big show of celebrating his departure, lighting off long strings of firecrackers as his diesel bus revved up to leave. But then the bus stalled. And the firecrackers petered out into silence. And he and his companion just sat there.

Amid the many disenchantments of the trip, something in Carlson's mind clicked at the beginning of December. He finally had his epiph-any, but it had nothing to do with the cooperatives. What struck him was a gut certainty that Japan was about to change directions in its war aims. It seemed to him that the military situation in China had deteriorated to the point where the Japanese could take advantage of the United Front's decline to relax their efforts on the Chinese main-land and devote their attentions elsewhere—specifically, he believed, to the conquest of resource-rich Southeast Asia as well as a challenge to America's supremacy in the Pacific region. War, he felt suddenly certain, was coming for America.

This realization came to him in the form of one of his hunches, as strong as any he had ever felt. It shook him badly enough that he abruptly canceled the rest of his tour of the cooperatives and took a succession of wheezing, broken-down buses to Chongqing for a final round of visits with the officials he had known from his past tours. On December 31, he met with Chiang Kai-shek at his offi-cial Chongqing residence. The Generalissimo looked to be in better health than he had been at Hankow, but he had a "sulky, bull dog expression" that Carlson didn't like. Chiang was aware of the role Carlson had played in lobbying for the embargo against Japan, and he expressed his appreciation for America's help. Carlson asked him how long he intended to keep up his resistance to the Japanese inva-sion, and Chiang assured him that China would resist until Japan withdrew or until President Roosevelt was ready to mediate.

Carlson pressed Chiang about the state of the United Front, ask-ing him about the rising unrest between the KMT and Communists. Chiang asked him where he had gotten his information, and Carlson said it was from people he met on his trip. The Generalissimo was dismissive. He said the Communists probably knew Carlson was coming and arranged for him to be misinformed. He said "no friction existed" between the two parties. Less than a week later, however, the tensions between KMT and New Fourth Army troops in Anhui province would erupt into open fighting that left thousands of Communist soldiers and civilians dead. Chiang's denials notwithstanding, the civil war in China was sparking back to life.

On January 3, Carlson flew from Chongqing down to Hong Kong. Planes could only fly at night now, in darkness, to avoid being shot down by Japanese forces who controlled the region just north of the British colony. In Hong Kong he bought an airplane ticket to Hawaii on Pan Am's transpacific clipper service to get himself back to the United States as quickly as possible. "I cut short my trip because of a hunch," he wrote to his father and sister from Hong Kong. "I feel that events in the international field are moving rapidly towards a point where it will be necessary for America to participate actively in the war." He did not want to be caught out of the country when that happened. He said he needed to share his intelligence with the authorities in Washington, but that was only part of his reason for coming home. "I must also be in a position to offer my services for active duty," he told them. It was one thing to quit the Marines impulsively on account of his moral feelings about the war in China, but at his core he was a patriot and if war came for America, then the only place in the world he wanted to be was back in the service.

Carlson was now positive that Japan was on the verge of a major new offensive that would involve an attack on U.S. interests. As he argued in an article for *Far Eastern Survey*, Japan had up until then built its empire in stages, willing to wait several years between major moves of expansion. The fall of France in 1940, however, opened an opportunity for Japan to seize France's colonial holdings in Indochina, giving it a base from which to launch a significant conquest in the neighboring region. He sensed that the halfhearted efforts of the Japanese army to consolidate its control over the Chinese countryside were because the Japanese militarists had never intended to conquer all of China—their original goal, he believed, was simply to capture the northern provinces as a prelude to a war for Siberia. But by the end of 1940, the Japanese had signed a neutrality agreement with the Soviets (who now recognized Manchukuo), and the Japanese army had been entangled for so long, and so expensively, in China that Carlson expected the militarists in Tokyo would be willing to accept "exceedingly liberal peace terms" there.

The possibility of a right-wing faction of the KMT breaking away from Chiang Kai-shek and making peace with Japan depended on how unified the country was in its will to resist. That, in turn, depended on the condition of the United Front. With the breakdown of cooperation between the KMT and the Communists already underway, the end to China's resistance might be closer than anyone thought. With Manchuria and China reasonably secure, Japan could launch the next stage of its ambition to dominate all of Asia.

Carlson also believed the timing was in Japan's favor for making a bold move in Southeast Asia because Britain's Royal Navy, which had long dominated the region from its bases at Singapore and Hong Kong, was now a shell of its former self as the British fought for their lives against Hitler back home. As Carlson saw it, the wars in Europe and Asia were far more deeply intertwined than most people realized. "It is true that China's fate depends in large measure on the outcome of the battle for Britain," Carlson wrote; "but it is equally true that the collapse of China would measurably improve the prospects of Herr Hitler in that battle. . . . China, the democracies of the West would soon discover, had been a formidable ally."

Carlson stopped over in the Philippines on his way home to share his concerns with the American military officials in Manila. He met with Douglas MacArthur, then the field marshal of the Philippine army, and urged him to prepare for a defense against a major Japanese attack on the islands. The two men went back a long ways; Carlson's first encounter with MacArthur had been at the end of World War I, when Carlson was investigating medal nominations in Europe and one of the cases that came across his desk was a nomination to give Douglas MacArthur the Medal of Honor. As Carlson noted at the time, MacArthur had nominated himself. (He didn't get the medal.) In 1941, the general was no less enamored of himself than he had been in 1918, and he saw no reason to worry about a Japanese attack on his watch. They had a cordial meeting but MacArthur paid no attention to Carlson's warning.

As the clipper planes progressed along their step-by-step course across the Pacific, they stopped to refuel at remote American-held islands like Wake and Midway that until then had mattered to few beyond the logistics officers at Pan Am Airways. From Hawaii, Carlson transferred to a ship, and the slowdown of his progress, combined with the frustration of being alone in his worries for the imminent future, left him with a sense of alienation as he watched the other American passengers cavorting about the upper decks. "The usual band playing the usual music," he wrote with bitterness in his diary. "And the usual people wearing faddish clothes acting in the usual lighthearted manner. Each only thinking of his own pleasure."

He reached California at the end of January and immediately began making his case for America to prepare for war. In a United Press interview the day after his arrival, he predicted a new crisis in the Far East within three months. His guess was that Japan—which was now a formal member of the Axis alliance—would take advantage of Hitler's assault on Britain to launch attacks into Thailand and the Dutch East Indies (today's Indonesia), while possibly also invading the Philippines "in order to protect her flank." The result would be war between the U.S. and Japan. "American-Japanese War in 90 Days Prophesied," announced the *Los Angeles Times*, which rehashed Carlson's message in football terms: "The United States and Japan will 'take to the gridiron in 90 days in an aerial and naval game, and the victor still will be all-American, but there'll be no time out between quarters.'" War with Japan was coming, Carlson repeated to anyone who would listen—but beyond a few newspaper reporters there was no way to know if anyone was paying attention.

After his resignation from the Marines, Carlson had kept in touch with the commandant of the Marine Corps, Major General Thomas Holcomb, who told Carlson back in the fall of 1939 that he would be welcome to an appointment in the reserves as long as his civilian activities were not "embarrassing" to the Navy Department. Carlson, of course, had bristled at the suggestion that there was anything embarrassing about his work. "My record since I left the Corps gives a pretty sound indication that I am endeavoring to serve humanity and my country in a wider field," he told Holcomb. They agreed then that Carlson should stay out of the service entirely for the time being, though Holcomb assured him that there would still be a place for him when he wanted it. "As they say in baseball," said

Holcomb, "don't sign up with any other team until you have talked to me!"

Carlson reconnected with Holcomb after he got back from China in 1941. "It looks to me as though we are pretty close to war, and when it comes I am prepared to do my part," he wrote to the commandant in March. Holcomb did not share Carlson's concerns about the prospect of hostilities with Japan, so he counseled Carlson to take his time. The ninety-day window for the start of the war that Carlson had predicted in Los Angeles came and went at the beginning of May 1941 without incident. Carlson traveled to Washington, D.C., to give a talk at the Army-Navy Club on the tenth of that month, and afterward Holcomb abandoned his reticence and formally offered Carlson a commission as a major in the Marine Corps Reserve. Carlson accepted, took his officer's exams the following week, and caught a train back out to California to report for duty.

One side effect of rejoining the Marine Corps was that it put him back in the orbit of Etelle. They were still married, after all, and now that he was an officer again it would be unseemly for them to live separately without a necessary reason. His orders posted him to the 2nd Marine Division at Camp Elliott just outside of San Diego, where, after talking the matter through, he and Etelle decided to move in together again and try to act the part of a Marine couple like they had been in Beijing. It did not go well at all. Carlson was intensely anxious—all of his alarm bells were going off, and even if the ninety days had passed, he felt no less certain that America and Japan were headed into a war that almost nobody in the United States, let alone its military command, believed could actually happen.

Etelle was immensely hopeful when they moved back in together. She put her best foot forward again, trying to be the wife that she thought he wanted her to be, hoping that the past year would be the last of their separations and maybe they could go back to the life they had shared in their little house surrounded by flower gardens at the air base in Pensacola. She planted zinnias and nasturtiums around the house in San Diego, which bloomed so quickly that she couldn't keep up with picking them. Evans was busy with his work for the Marines, which she thought made him happy (and that made her happy). She played her old, familiar part, hosting the wives of the other officers for lunch in the garden. She and Evans went camping once, and slept by the edge of a stream. "I haven't done that for a long time," she told his father, "and tried not to appear too inexperienced."

But Carlson did not want to go back to their old ways. In October of 1941 he moved them to La Jolla, just north of San Diego, to a larger rental house perched on a hillside on Castellana Road. Carlson was frustrated being back in the social culture of the Marine Corps, and he resented the financial pressure of taking care of Etelle. "I chafe at all the restraint," he told his father. "I had rather expected to be economically freer but Dorothy's stint plus the support of Etelle in the manner she has become accustomed to leave my bank account about zero at the end of the month." He had chosen the house in La Jolla because it was farther from the base and more secluded, but more to the point, because it had two bedrooms and two baths, which meant that he and Etelle could lead separate lives within it. They would live under one roof, but that was just for show. It cost more to have the extra space, he said, "But this enables us to fool the public, so I presume it is justifiable."

Carlson was assigned to a headquarters battalion, but he disliked the position because it meant spending all of his time with other officers when what he really wanted was to work with enlisted men. "I prefer to be with the troops somewhere near the front lines when the shooting starts," he told his father. He still insisted that it was just a matter of time. "For my part I'd like to get on with the Japanese war," he said. "It must come eventually." To another correspondent, he wrote that he felt morally cornered. "I understand the futility of war," he said, "but I also . . . realize that nothing I can do can prevent the use of war as an instrument to settle disputes. And if we fight I want my country to win. So here I am."

By the end of November there was still no war and he was fighting off another bout of depression—the old feeling of futility in his work, his wheels spinning without purchase. Nostalgic for the past, he drove up to Los Angeles to visit Agnes Smedley, who had just come back from China. They talked about the Eighth Route Army and Zhu De, and Hankow, and times gone by. It was intense, as it tended to be with her. ("Agnes is always a tonic, though I wouldn't want her for a diet," he told his father.) He asked the Marines for a new assignment, hoping to be transferred out of the headquarters staff so he could be closer to the ground troops, but it would be a while before he might hear anything about that. And he finally told Etelle that he wanted a divorce. Living in separate rooms in the same house wasn't working. They no longer had a relationship to speak of, though not for any lack of effort on her part. "I ignore her utterly," he told his father, "which must be humiliating, but is necessary." He said she wanted more than he could ever give her.

Carlson left Etelle for good on December 4. He packed up the car with his clothes and books and some of his furniture, and moved out of the house on Castellana Road they had shared for just two months. He moved into a rented bedroom in a private home less than a mile away. The room was so cramped he could barely fit his desk and books, but the house was quiet and had a view of the ocean and he thought he would be able to concentrate there. "I know that it is better for both of us to take this drastic action," he told his father. "I can accomplish nothing when I am with her." Etelle's composure, and her optimism, had held out already for so long and through so much with him, but she finally broke down on the morning he left, crying and begging him not to go. But he was a stubborn man when his mind was made up, and he did not look back.

Three days later, at a little before eight in the morning local time in the Central Pacific, the first wave of Japanese bombers dipped low out of the clouds on their run for the American naval base at Pearl Harbor.

PART IV
PACIFIC WAR

CHAPTER 14
NEW BEGINNINGS

I N THE WEEKS that followed Pearl Harbor, all momentum was on the side of Japan. Imperial Japanese naval and ground forces swept through the Pacific and Southeast Asia with dizzying speed, met in most cases by only slipshod resistance from local and Western imperial defenders. In the Pacific, the Japanese attacked U.S. forces on Guam and Wake Island on the same day as Pearl Harbor, taking Guam within two days and overwhelming the defenders of Wake by December 23. They invaded the Gilbert Islands, the Marianas, the Solomons, New Guinea, including the crucial port of Rabaul just off Australia, and established a foothold on the Aleutians en route to Alaska. In Southeast Asia they invaded and took control of Thailand, and the British colonies of Burma and Malaya, as well as the Dutch East Indies. In a shocking defeat to Britain's Royal Navy, the Japanese sank the battleship *Prince of Wales* and battle-cruiser *Repulse* on December 10 off the coast of Malaya, heralding the end of Britain's century of naval dominance in the region. Hong Kong—which the British had seized from China during the first Opium War almost exactly one hundred years earlier—fell to the Japanese on Christmas Day of 1941. Singapore, the "Gibraltar of the East" and Britain's most powerful naval and air base in Southeast Asia, followed two months later.

Simultaneously with their surprise raid on Pearl Harbor, the Japanese fulfilled Carlson's prediction with a massive invasion of the Philippines from Taiwan. Following bombing raids and intense and bloody urban warfare in the capital, MacArthur's underprepared American and Filipino forces abandoned Manila and fell back to the

Bataan Peninsula across the bay and, to its south, the tiny, heavily fortified island of Corregidor. MacArthur left the country on Roosevelt's orders in January of 1942 (promising, famously, to return), while the main body of American and Filipino forces continued to hold out. In April, the forces on Bataan surrendered to the Japanese, followed a month later by the remaining defenders of Corregidor. By the end of May, the Japanese had full control over the Philippines and had taken more than seventy thousand American and Filipino troops prisoner.

The U.S. forces in China fared no better. The 4th Marines—Carlson's old regiment of "China Marines"—had managed to hold their position in the International Settlement through the initial years of the Sino-Japanese War, even as the British left and the conquered Vichy French began cooperating with the Japanese. But by the late 1930s they numbered only about one thousand officers and men in two battalions, and it was obvious that a single, undersized regiment of Marines could do nothing to prevent the Japanese from taking control of the settlement if they so desired. In November of 1941, the 4th Marines were withdrawn to the Philippines for their safety, shipping out from Shanghai with astonishingly fortunate timing just a few days before Pearl Harbor. The storied American Legation Guards at Beijing were not so fortunate, however; they had planned to follow the 4th Marines but could not arrange transport until December 10, which meant they were left stranded in Beijing when the Japanese declared war on the U.S. On December 8, dramatically outnumbered, the entire Legation Guard surrendered without a fight. Meanwhile, the initial good fortune of the 4th Marines lasted only until they arrived in the Philippines, where their ranks were horribly ravaged in the defense of Corregidor. By the end of the battle for the Philippines, the remnants of their regiment, like the Legation Guard, surrendered en masse to the Japanese and would spend the rest of the war as prisoners.

For all that the isolationists had tried to ignore the situation in Asia while America's attention was focused on Europe, it was the Japanese who ultimately propelled America full-on into the European War. The United States declared war on Japan the day after Pearl Harbor, then on Germany and Italy three days later. The country was utterly unprepared. As recently as 1939 the United States had possessed only the nineteenth largest military in the world, behind Portugal and Romania. Due to its geographic position connecting the Atlantic to the Pacific, and the dramatic weakening of British overseas power, the United States became the only major belligerent in World War II to be invested so completely in both Europe and Asia. "I never wanted to have to fight this war on two fronts," FDR told Eleanor Roosevelt shortly after the attack. "We haven't got the Navy to fight in both the Atlantic and the Pacific . . . we will have to take a good many defeats before we can have a victory."

Inside the United States, where public sympathy for China had run high since the Japanese invasion in 1937, the Chinese were elevated almost overnight to an exalted status as America's main allies in Asia. By the same token the Japanese were reviled, and American citizens of Japanese descent attacked as potential agents of the Japanese Empire. For the sake of those Americans who couldn't tell the difference, and for whom all "Orientals" seemed basically the same, *Life* magazine ran a full-page spread two weeks after Pearl Harbor on "How to tell Japs from the Chinese." The article expressed concern that Americans showed "a distressing ignorance on the delicate question of how to tell a Chinese from a Jap," and so it proposed to teach the reader the "anthropomorphic conformations" that supposedly distinguished the two races. For illustration, it used a portrait of a friendly-looking KMT minister on one side and the scowling face of General Tojo, the Japanese premier, on the other. The Chinese official, the article suggested, had more civilized (read: European) features, with lighter-colored skin, a smooth complexion, delicate cheekbones, and a "finely bridged" nose. General Tojo, by comparison, was described as "aboriginal," with a "squat" and "bony" physique, "massive" cheekbones, a "flat, blob nose," an "earthy" complexion, and pronounced facial hair. The magazine said he was "representative of the Japanese people as a whole."

The *Life* article was hardly noble in its aims; it perpetuated nearly the same stereotypes it claimed to dispel (suggesting as it did that all Chinese looked basically the same, as did all Japanese) and it stoked the flames of hatred against Americans of Japanese descent—who, in a little over a month, would be rounded up by U.S. government orders and forced into detention camps in a race-based internment policy that would never be imposed on the many German and Italian Americans who likewise shared ancestry with an Axis power. *Life* apparently had no issue with public violence against Japanese Americans; it simply wanted to protect Chinese Americans from suffering the same fate. Nevertheless, the underlying message was one that Carlson had been preaching for years: that the Chinese were natural friends and allies of the United States.

In China's wartime capital of Chongqing, deep in the protective mountains of Sichuan province, the news of Pearl Harbor prompted celebrations with fireworks and dancing in the streets—for the attack meant that America would finally join the war against Japan; after four bloody years, China would no longer be fighting alone. To the minds of many in Chongqing, the entry of the United States was a promise of salvation. As one American diplomat stationed in China's wartime capital recalled, "The Chinese were beside themselves with excitement and pleasure, because to them this meant assurance of victory."

Another turn of the kaleidoscope and the pieces of Carlson's life fell back together again. America was now at war with Japan, taking up its own part in the conflict that had been consuming China since 1937—or, really, since the invasion of Manchuria in 1931. Carlson could finally join the fight as an ally of Zhu De, as he had wanted to do for so long. He was on the far side of the Pacific for now, though he hoped in time to be closer. On the broader scale, America and China would be allies against Japan, just as he and the Communist general had imagined on that cold December night in 1937, around the coal fire in Shanxi, when they thought the sinking of the *Panay* might bring the United States into the war. Now, four years later, they would get to see what could come of the alliance.

For the better part of a year, Carlson's superiors had dismissed his warnings about the threat from Japan, but he took little pleasure from his vindication. "There is not much comfort or satisfaction in being able to say 'I told you so,'" he wrote to Harry Yarnell. "When I think of lost opportunities at Hongkong, Luzon and Malaya it makes me ill." Nevertheless, he would carry a lasting grudge against the generals like MacArthur who had scoffed at him when he insisted they should prepare better for a Japanese attack.

To an acquaintance outside of the military—a radio journalist he had met in New York named Raymond Gram Swing—Carlson blamed America's failure to prepare for the war on the arrogance of the senior officer class and their smug, conformist social world. It was the same social world he had once embraced as an unmarried young lieutenant at Quantico but later came to resent. In January, seven weeks after Pearl Harbor, he told Swing that the initial losses in the Pacific were to be expected, but there was no excuse for the failure of America's military leaders to understand the basic causes of the Pearl Harbor disaster, or to conceive an effective solution.

The conditions that made Pearl Harbor possible, he told Swing, were rooted in the "system which has grown up in our military naval services of setting our officers apart as a privileged class." Here was his Emersonian self-reliance and his social resentment of the Marines all rolled into one. Carlson said the officers were like an "exclusive club," out of touch with reality. He knew from his own experience how younger officers were taught to conform, to fit in, and not to ask questions. They learned quickly that "rank is regarded as, ipso facto, clothing the incumbent with wisdom, knowledge and all ideas of merit." They learned that socializing with the senior officers was the key to advancement in the service. For a junior officer, he wrote, "as the years roll by almost unconsciously his objectives in life are narrowed to two: more rank, and more pay." As a professional culture it all but guaranteed that the senior officers' loyalty would be directed less toward their country than toward their particular branch of the service, and within that, to their social network of fellow officers.

The result, as he saw it, was a lack of any incentive to innovate or improve. The top ranks of the Navy and Marine Corps were filled with men who "fuss about rank and prestige instead of concentrating on their professional tasks," he wrote; "men who are intolerant of new ideas, and who judge their juniors by the same standards by which they were judged." They preferred blind obedience because it fed their egos. They were fearful of any experimentation that might threaten their appearance of infallibility or diminish their prestige. The country's military leadership was fundamentally undemocratic, he told Swing—and that was why no one had listened to him, and why America had been so badly blindsided on December 7.

But what could be done now? He had some ideas. In the weeks

246 · THE RAIDER

after Pearl Harbor, Carlson had been trying to imagine what would happen if the armed forces of the United States, fighting to preserve democracy, were themselves run in a more democratic fashion. The only way he could see that happening would be to take away the exclusive privileges of the officer class and change the standards by which they were selected and promoted. As in his earlier writing on leadership for the *Naval Institute Proceedings*, he wanted to break down the hierarchical barriers that set officers apart from the enlisted men. He wanted to promote officers who were true leaders, unafraid to innovate and take risks. To win the war, he told Swing, "an all out effort is not only indicated, but leadership must be dynamic, creative and inspired."

It was one thing to fantasize about changing the nature of American military command, another thing entirely to make such changes happen. But Carlson had the beginnings of a plan. He imagined starting small, with a single fighting unit that would be different from the traditional Marines. The men who served in this force would think differently, fight differently, carry themselves differently. They could be a microcosm from which to grow more meaningful change in the culture of the Marine Corps writ large, and eventually—once the war was over and the veterans returned home—to build a better and more democratic society for the country itself. At a more intimate level, what Carlson wanted to do was to take everything that he had admired about Zhu De's Eighth Route Army in China and transplant it onto American soil. Inspired by the Chinese Communists, he wanted to take a select group of United States Marines and turn them into a small, self-sufficient guerrilla force. The men would be volunteer fighters, stoic and strong, imbued with a sense of unity and purpose, driven by a shared vision for their nation's future. They would be highly mobile and tightly knit, and the officers and enlisted men would be as close as fathers and sons. That, he believed, was Zhu De's secret to fighting the Japanese. And he thought it could be America's as well.

———

Carlson's dream of building an American counterpart to the Eighth Route Army might have remained just the fantasy of a disaffected reserve officer if it hadn't been for a series of fortuitous accidents in early 1942. The first was that a few weeks after Pearl Harbor, James Roosevelt, the president's eldest son—by this time a captain in the Marine Corps Reserve—was transferred to Camp Elliott in San Diego, into the same intelligence section of the 2nd Marine Division where Carlson was based. The two men renewed their friendship from Carlson's stint at Warm Springs and started working together in a shared office that Roosevelt remembered as "a rather bleak room with a lot of maps and nothing else." As they worked together to prepare estimates of Japanese military strength in the Pacific, Carlson shared his thoughts about how the Marines could adapt the techniques of Chinese guerrilla warfare to their fight against the Japanese. James Roosevelt was the first person on record that Carlson shared these ideas with, and James, it turned out, was exactly the right person to talk to. He already looked up to Carlson, who was eleven years his senior, and Carlson was pleased to find that their minds seemed to be practically in lockstep. As Carlson later explained to the president, "I discovered to my great delight that [James] saw pretty much eye to eye with me on matters social, economic, political and military." Carlson gained an ally, and that ally was the son of the commander-in-chief.

The second fortunate coincidence was that, quite separately from Carlson's private ambition to build a more mobile and independent tactical unit, there were proposals already in circulation at the highest levels of the U.S. military to create some kind of an American commando force, inspired by the heroics of the British Commandos with their secret landings and lightning raids in Europe. Winston Churchill had urged Franklin Roosevelt to develop such a force, and right after Pearl Harbor a highly decorated World War I Army veteran named William Donovan—better known as "Wild Bill" Donovan—submitted a proposal to train and lead one himself. A spirited debate followed about what form the commando unit might take, where the best men for it could come from, and how it could be trained. It was a novel idea, though the Marine Corps was so strapped for manpower at the start of the war that one general suggested reaching outside of the service entirely and stocking the ranks of the commando force with professional football players.

Donovan's plan was never approved, for it ran aground on the shoals of interservice rivalry. The logical place for such a force was in the Marines, but Commandant Holcomb considered the prospect of Marines being commanded by an Army officer like Donovan to be an insult to his service. "I am terrified that I may be forced to take this man," Holcomb wrote to a colleague at the time. "I feel that it will be the worst slap in the face the Marine Corps ever was given." So in the end, Donovan failed to get his commando unit, though he suffered nothing professionally from the setback. He would soon become the founding director of the Office of Strategic Services, the progenitor to today's CIA, and would serve as America's spymaster for the duration of the war. Nevertheless, after Donovan's initiative petered out the idea of a commando force still had backers. And the third and final stroke of luck for Carlson was that James Roosevelt's prior assignment, just before he joined Carlson in San Diego, had been six months as an aide to Donovan. Which meant he arrived at Camp Elliott knowing exactly what sorts of ideas were circulating at the upper levels.

And so it was through James Roosevelt that Carlson's idea for a guerrilla force first went live. On January 13, 1942, James Roosevelt submitted a memo to Thomas Holcomb with the subject line: "Development within the Marine Corps of a unit for purposes similar to the British Commandos and the Chinese Guerrillas." In the memo, Roosevelt explained that the ideal function of a commando unit was to inflict, like a boxer, "surprise and swiftly moving blows" on the enemy, and by such means to "destroy confidence, disrupt well laid plans, create panic, fear and uncertainty." He briefly cited the success of the British Commandos in Europe before turning to the guerrillas of the Eighth Route Army in China—who, he wrote, had "proven an invaluable obstacle to any continued Japanese offensive." He said the Chinese guerrillas were uniquely effective against the Japanese, who had "not found it possible to withstand for any long period the pressure placed by these groups."

With Carlson whispering in his ear, Roosevelt recommended that a unit of Marines be trained on a similar model to the guerrillas in China, while being equipped with the best material resources America could offer. Transported by American submarines, these Marines could stage guerrilla raids on Japanese-held islands in the Pacific, then later maybe even land on the Philippines or the northern coast of Japan itself. Such a force, and such an approach, Roosevelt concluded, would be a natural course of action for the Marines—especially those with experience of jungle fighting in Nicaragua—and as a sweetener to Holcomb, he added that such a plan "fits the entire tradition of action and boldness held by the Marine Corps."

James Roosevelt may have written the proposal, but its words and its sentiments were entirely Carlson's. Carlson's voice was there, for instance, in Roosevelt's insistence that the guerrilla force must have an ideological foundation. "The appeal of adventure or the hope for glory are inadequate stimuli," he wrote. "These men must be indoctrinated with the conviction that their efforts and sacrifices are providing a vital contribution to the preservation of freedom in all its forms." Roosevelt said the force would depend on a much closer relationship between the officers and enlisted men than was customary. To this end, the officers would share the same material conditions as the fighters "without reservation." They would all learn to live off the land and to hike thirty to fifty miles a day. The Marines selected for the force would be physically strong, have above-average intelligence, and "possess at least a modicum of idealism." They would, in short, echo the volunteers Carlson had marched with in China's Eighth Route Army.

Holcomb's initial reaction was not enthusiastic. He questioned the need for an elite unit within the Marines—where, given their tougher recruitment standards compared to the Army, all of the men were arguably "elite" already. He also disliked the term "commando," which was too British for his tastes (its roots lay in colonial South Africa) and in any case, he saw it as "undesirable and superfluous." A United States Marine, he believed, was already a commando, ready for service at any time. But James Roosevelt had his father's ear. And Holcomb felt pressure from above to create *some* kind of commando force like the British had. So after James Roosevelt's proposal gained the support first of the president, then of the secretary of the navy and Admiral Chester Nimitz, the commander-in-chief of the United States Pacific Fleet, Holcomb had no choice but to act.

At the beginning of February 1942, Holcomb authorized the creation of two separate battalions of what would be, effectively, America's first modern special operations forces. He still disliked the name

"commandos," so after toying with suggestions like "destroyer battalions" and "shock battalions" he decided to call the new Marine
strike forces "raiders." The 1st Marine Raider battalion would be
formed on the East Coast at Quantico, and the 2nd in California at
Camp Elliott, where Carlson and James Roosevelt were stationed.
On the East Coast, Holcomb gave the command of the new unit
to Merritt Edson, an accomplished veteran of Nicaragua and China
who had overlapped with Carlson in Shanghai. On the West Coast,
the command went, almost inevitably, to Evans Carlson. With the
president's direct patronage, just two months after the attack on Pearl
Harbor Carlson found himself invested with near-complete autonomy to create and train the kind of guerrilla force he had imagined.
He appointed James Roosevelt to be his executive officer, or second
in command, and the two of them went to work on recruitment.

It was beyond anything he had dreamed. On February 5, 1942,
he reported to his father that he had just been given carte blanche to
train and indoctrinate a new fighting unit however he saw fit. "There
is nothing like it in existence in the country," he wrote. "Naturally I
am delighted. . . . Things seem to be moving in a direction I have so
long urged and had almost despaired of seeing materialize." The creation of the Raiders was a tightly held secret but Winston Churchill,
for one, was cheered to learn that they were preparing for service in
the Pacific. In a message to Roosevelt in early March of 1942, he said
that with regard to Asia, "When you told me about your intention to
form commando forces on a large scale on the California shore I felt
that you had the key. Once several good outfits are prepared, any one
can attack a Japanese-held base or island and beat the life out of the
garrison, all their islands will become hostages to fortune." A week
after Churchill's message, Roosevelt relayed his own excitement to
Carlson. "I am delighted . . . to know that all goes so well with you,"
he wrote. "The new outfit is most interesting and surely there will be
a chance to use it."

Carlson chose his men carefully, looking for tough, idealistic recruits
who could be taught to think of themselves not as brute warriors but
as defenders of Democracy with a capital "D." He wanted men who

could think and act on their own initiative on the battlefield without relying too heavily on their superiors. As he explained to Holcomb, "Men who learn to live by specific rules are inclined to wait for orders when they encounter perplexing problems in the field. They should be encouraged to think for themselves." To this end, the Marines of his Raider battalion would be trained for "initiative, resourcefulness, control of small groups in the jungles, stalking, instantaneous reaction in ambushes and aggressive action at all times." He wanted, as he later wrote, "to create and perfect a cohesive, smooth-functioning team which, by virtue of its harmony of action, unity of purpose and its invincible determination, would be able to outpoint the enemy on every count."

He called the guiding philosophy of his battalion "gung ho"— a term that he adapted from Chinese, where it wasn't a meaningful phrase on its own but simply the abbreviated name for the industrial cooperatives he had visited in 1940, using the first character of each word (like an acronym in English). In contemporary romanization it would be *gong he*, for the initial characters in *gongye hezuoshe*. The two characters carry the (very) rough meaning of "working together" and Carlson used the phrase to embody everything he admired about the spirit of the Chinese "so-called" Communists: working together in harmony, with an egalitarian, democratic sensibility, toward a shared mission. As he would later explain in a radio address, "Fundamentally, gung ho is an ideal. The ideal of complete cooperation and mutual trust and respect between men. Gung ho is tolerance, cooperation and equality. It is democracy at work."

Although the phrase would later take on the less-positive connotations of recklessness or overzealousness, its original meaning in English—as Carlson and his Marines used it—indicated an enthusiastic, selfless kind of cooperation that inspired acts of courage. "Any action was *gung ho* or it wasn't," Carlson told an interviewer later on in the war. "To help a man out of a tight spot, to jump in and do anything that needed doing without asking whose turn it was to do it—that was *gung ho*. Believe me, the farther we got into the jungle and hand-to-hand battle, the more we leaned on *gung ho*."

With James Roosevelt in his camp, Carlson got just about anything he asked for, which sparked no small amount of resentment from his fellow officers. He commandeered the best weapons, culled some of the best men from other units, and gathered scarce resources that alienated his rivals. Some derided the unorthodox trappings of his battalion as "Boy Scout equipment." Others envied his relationship with the commander-in-chief. As the joke went, referring to the president with his twenty-one-gun salute, the 2nd Raiders would never need artillery support because "Carlson's always got twenty-one guns in his hip pocket."

In particular, Carlson earned the lifelong resentment of his counterpart on the East Coast, Merritt Edson, a stocky, red-haired major known to his friends as "Red Mike." Edson, who had cut his teeth fighting the Sandinistas in Nicaragua like Carlson had, was building a much more conventional infantry force with his own Raider battalion (the 1st Raiders), and he had been experimenting with rubber-boat landings since before Pearl Harbor, so Thomas Holcomb saw his unit as the model Carlson should follow. In February of 1942, Holcomb made Edson send a company of his best Marines to California to lend some experience to Carlson's new outfit, but when they arrived, Carlson proceeded to reject most of them as not being up to his own standards. Edson would never forgive him the insult.

But Carlson wasn't trying to make friends. He had always had a difficult relationship with the Marine Corps, chafing at the conformity it demanded while embracing it as a springboard to explore the world and develop his own interests. He knew that many of the other officers considered him a Red on account of his exploits with the Communists in China, and few had really seemed to mourn him when he quit the Marines in 1938. Certainly Merritt Edson hadn't—after Carlson rejected most of his men, Edson wrote to the commanding general of the 2nd Marine Division that "Whatever Carlson's so-called standards may be, his refusal to accept three out of four of these men only confirmed my opinion that the Marine Corps had lost nothing by his resignation a few years ago and has gained nothing by his return to active duty as a reserve major."

Carlson's inspiration from the Chinese guerrillas would set him apart and become the basis of his mystique during the war, but it was also destined to haunt him. As late as 1979, long after the war was over and Carlson was forgotten by the public, James Roosevelt, by then an elderly man, still felt the need to defend Carlson against his critics in the Marine Corps, arguing at a Navy conference that Carlson should in no way be described as a "revolutionist" even though that was still "the general Marine Corps . . . characterization of him as a man." Even some of Carlson's admirers in the service would later come to assume that at some level he must have been a Red all along. "He was a very, very brave and capable man," recalled one retired general. "Just being a Communist doesn't mean that he wasn't a very brave man."

For many American troops in the Pacific War, their motivations were far from noble: revenge for Pearl Harbor, racial hatred of the Japanese, the excitement of being allowed to kill. And back home, in contrast to the common hindsight vision of a public united in common cause after Pearl Harbor, six months into the war a majority of Americans still said "they did not have a clear idea of what the war was about." Carlson, however, sought a higher purpose and clarity from the start, and he tried to indoctrinate the Raiders with a moral vision that reflected his own religiosity and idealism. Conventional soldiers were not asked to envision improvements to American society, but he asked his own men to do just that. It was awkward for some, the singing and the talk of social justice. But Carlson was adamant in his faith that if the Raiders knew what they were fighting for in a grand moral sense—that, as he taught them, this was a war between democracy and fascism, between freedom and tyranny—then they would be all the more effective on the battlefield.

Carlson also understood the importance of loyalty to one's fellow Marines, so he tried to instill that with his "gung ho" training, trying to re-create the sense of camaraderie he had found among the Chinese guerrillas. Following Zhu De, the tactics and ideology of his battalion were two sides of the same coin: the "guerrilla" methods of fighting were both derived from and depended on the spirit of flexibility and unified will within the group. From what he had seen in China, he believed that soldiers who could think for themselves in battle as well as work in close harmony with their tactical unit—those who could be creative and resourceful as circumstances required—would always have an advantage over the hidebound soldiers of totalitarian armies, who had difficulty operating outside of the rigid hierarchies that determined their lives.

Carlson did his work of "ethical indoctrination," as he called it, at the battalion's regular gung ho meetings. "Hope for glory will carry some men a long way in battle," he said at one meeting; "pride in the outfit and the desire not to let your buddies down is an even more potent force; but the force which impels men to carry on when the going is tough and victory appears to be remote is a deep spiritual conviction in the righteousness of the cause for which he fights." Each man in the Raiders, he insisted, needed not just to believe in the righteousness of America's cause but also to have an almost religious faith that victory would bring about an improved society where his loved ones and children would enjoy a brighter future than his own.

The training he put his men through at Jacques Farm in the hills northeast of San Diego was extraordinarily intense and grueling. One veteran called it "the most strenuous, back-breaking, soul-trying preparation any American fighting men had ever endured." The Raiders learned to suffer through exhaustion, discomfort, and deprivation. They honed their physical strength with fifty-mile overnight hikes and twelve to fourteen hours a day of intensive combat training. They learned to trust one another, especially the tightly knit three-man fire teams, who spent every minute of their training together and became like brothers. (One of the advantages of Carlson's fire team structure was that it simplified and strengthened communications on the battlefield. Instead of one squad officer having to give instructions to nine different Marines under his command, he only needed to maintain contact with the three fire team leaders, who took care of their own teams. It worked so well that it later became the standard for the Marine Corps as a whole.)

In a letter from Jacques Farm, Carlson told President Roosevelt that he now felt that his months of travel with the Chinese guerrillas had not been in vain. And as the weeks went by, he felt optimistic that his moral lessons were taking root. America's youth were not as weak as he had once feared. "My experience here has filled me with encouragement," he told Raymond Swing. "I have found that hundreds (and I dare say there are thousands) of young Americans have deep convictions about the equitable way of life, and are willing to make sacrifices to attain it." These were the men he had been looking for, the American companions to the young, idealistic Chinese of the Eighth Route Army. And he wanted them to lead the way not just for the war but for everything that would come after.

———

Carlson's battalion of nearly six hundred Marine Raiders embarked for Hawaii on the USS *Franklin Bell* from San Diego on May 8, 1942. He issued a general order to be read aloud to them at sea. "This battalion is now headed for the theatre of operations in the Pacific," he began. "We become the first of our land forces of our nation to carry the war to the enemy . . . we will set the pace and blaze the trail for those behind, inspiring them with confidence and showing them that we Americans have what it takes to win battles." The daunting nature of the task ahead became fully apparent when they entered Pearl Harbor and cruised slowly past the wreckage of the United States fleet. Even five months after the attack, damage from the Japanese raid was everywhere. In the face of the astounding succession of victories the Japanese had just achieved, and with the American fleet crippled, the war seemed all but unwinnable. Carlson, though, still thought his men could point the way forward.

It was an open question where Admiral Nimitz would send them first. Two companies of the Raiders were peeled off from the battalion to help defend Midway Island at the beginning of June. Though they were on hand for the epic battle that would give the United States its first victory against the Japanese navy, they had no role to play, as the fighting took place in the air, between swarms of fighters and bombers from carrier fleets that lay miles apart. By late June, the battalion was reunited but still waiting for an assignment that would align better with its training.

Carlson marveled at what lay ahead. "What a fantastic war this is," he wrote to his father from Hawaii, where he had just been promoted to lieutenant colonel. "When you think of the vast distances involved it almost leaves you breathless." In a certain sense, though, after his peripatetic life he felt as much at home in the Pacific as he did anywhere. "I have crossed and recrossed the Pacific, until I am as familiar with the mile posts as I am with the trail from your house to the post office," he told his father. The same was not true for the young enlisted men who had sailed with him from San Diego, most of whom had never been outside of the mainland United States. Nor was it true for the tens, later hundreds of thousands of other young American recruits who would, in time, be flung out into the infinite expanse of the Pacific—to Guadalcanal, to Tarawa, to Peleliu, to Iwo Jima—to live or die on islands most of them had never heard of before.

CHAPTER 15

MAKIN ISLAND

O N THE MORNING of August 16, 1942, the periscope of the USS *Nautilus* pierced the surface of the water two miles offshore from a sandy island deep in the Central Pacific. The island was Butaritari, part of the Makin Atoll, which lay at the northern end of the Gilbert Islands chain two thousand miles southwest of Hawaii. From inside the long, narrow hull of the submarine, Carlson took his turn peering through the scope at the flat strip of land that lay before them, a thin profile thickly fringed with palm trees. The *Nautilus* spent the rest of the day reconnoitering the island from periscope depth, only surfacing after the sun had gone down and there was no

Makin Island (Butaritari) through the periscope of the USS *Nautilus*.

danger of being seen. At a little after 9 p.m. it arrived at a designated rendezvous site where its sister vessel, the USS *Argonaut*, was waiting after its own eight-day journey from Pearl Harbor.

Between them, the two submarines carried 221 members of Carlson's battalion, which was less than half of the force but it was all they could fit into the vessels while still leaving space for the Navy crews that ran them. There were two companies present, A and B, though they were understrength and fifty-five of their members had to stay behind in Hawaii along with companies C and D. The *Nautilus* and *Argonaut* had not been designed to serve as transports, so to retrofit them for this mission the front torpedo rooms had been torn out, the torpedoes removed except for those already in the firing tubes, and in the hollowed-out space that remained a series of tight, makeshift bunks had been hammered together from two-by-fours. The Marines were crammed into these berths, three deep against each bulkhead, stacked five high with about a foot of clearance between them.

The *Nautilus* and *Argonaut* were the largest submarines in the U.S. Navy, but they could only travel at slow speeds underwater, so to make decent time they had to run on the surface for most of the trip. Unlike the cigar-shaped hulls of later submarines, they looked more like conventional ships—extremely long and narrow ones, to be sure, but with a flat upper deck that ran much of the length of the vessel so there was ample space topsides when they weren't submerged. Even so, since they had to be ready to dive immediately on any radar contact, Carlson's men were only allowed out on deck for twenty minutes a day to do calisthenics and breathe a bit of fresh air.

To help make the overcrowded conditions down below more bearable, the Navy had installed five-ton air-conditioning units on each of the subs but they did little to process the combined exhalations and body odor of the overloaded, unwashed men crammed inside. The air belowdecks was sweltering, over 90 degrees and humid. The Marines had to stay in their bunks most of the time to leave room for the submarine crews to do their work, and the men in the top bunks sweated through their clothes, soaking the thin mattresses, which dripped down on the men below them in turn. The captain allowed them to smoke, but at times there was so little oxygen it was difficult to get a match to light.

There were great hopes riding on them. President Roosevelt wanted Carlson's unit to pull off something spectacular in the Pacific. Four months earlier, in April of 1942, an Army Air Force colonel named James Doolittle had staged a daring and nearly suicidal air raid over Tokyo, in which sixteen American B-25 bombers without escorts were launched from an aircraft carrier near the main Japanese island of Honshu. Doolittle's pilots flew over Tokyo and other Japanese cities, unloaded their five-hundred-pound bombs, and then kept going until most of them ran out of fuel and crash-landed on the Chinese mainland. The air raid accomplished nothing strategically (in response, six Japanese army divisions mounted a vicious campaign to capture or destroy all of the airfields in eastern China within range of Tokyo) but it was an enormous boost for morale and earned Doolittle the Medal of Honor. Doolittle's raid had captivated the American public, but the prospect of a commando attack on the ground—face-to-face with the Japanese for the first time, rather than flying over and dropping bombs on them from the sky—would be something else entirely. And unlike the fanciful Doolittle raid, it was something that could be repeated if it worked.

Carlson had gotten little say in how his unit was first deployed; that decision ultimately rested with Admiral Nimitz and the senior Marine on his staff, Colonel Omar Pfeiffer. As they cast about for an

Raiders exercising on the deck of the USS *Nautilus*.

ideal target, the most tempting choice was Wake Island, which had been lost to the Japanese on December 23. But Navy intelligence thought there were now several thousand Japanese troops defending Wake, and they had taken over the American defensive infrastructure on the island, so it would be too much for two understrength companies of Marines to take on, no matter how well Carlson's men had been trained and equipped. Nimitz and Pfeiffer then toyed with the idea of landing Carlson's men on one of the Japanese home islands for a lightning demolition raid—either to destroy a Japanese steel mill on Hokkaido or blow up a couple of crucial railroad tunnels on the main island of Honshu.

The primary factor limiting their imaginations was the presence of James Roosevelt in the battalion. He had no combat experience, and it was hard to imagine a bigger windfall for Axis propaganda than for the Japanese to capture President Roosevelt's son right at the start of the war. Seeing James Roosevelt trotted out as a prisoner of war might be even worse for American morale than him getting killed. So Nimitz and Pfeiffer backed off from the main Japanese islands and decided to try instead for a smaller target in a more distant corner of Japan's Pacific expansion.

The Makin Atoll, at the northernmost end of the Gilberts chain, with its long, thin main island Butaritari (generally referred to just as Makin Island), fit the bill. The Gilberts marked the farthest point of Japanese penetration eastward into the Pacific, so getting there from Hawaii would not require travel through extensive areas of enemy control. The island was relatively isolated, about three hundred miles from the nearest Japanese air base in the Marshall Islands, so it would take time for reinforcements to get there. And the Gilberts had been a British colony until the Japanese invaded, so the mission's planners hoped that the thousand or so Gilbertese natives who lived on Makin would not feel any loyalty toward the Japanese and might even help the Raiders. The Americans had little information about the island other than a series of aerial photographs taken during a flyover in February. But as Makin Island was small—just eight miles long and about half a mile wide—the planners assumed there would be at most a few hundred Japanese soldiers in the garrison, which was a more promising matchup for two companies of Marine Raiders.

Strategically, Nimitz and Pfeiffer intended the raid to act as a diversion in support of Operation Watchtower, America's first major amphibious landing of the war. On August 7, more than ten thousand troops of the 1st Marine Division would be landed on Guadalcanal, in the Solomon Islands near Australia in the South Pacific. That was the real objective. Guadalcanal had a crucial airfield under construction by the Japanese that could be the key to projecting airpower over the sea lanes connecting the United States via Hawaii to Australia—meaning that if the Japanese held on to the island, they could cut off Australia entirely. If the Allies could capture it, however, they could not only keep open the route to Australia but also use the island's airfield to stage bombing missions against Japan's bases in the South Pacific. By sending Carlson's men more than a thousand miles northeast of the Solomons to stage a simultaneous attack on the Makin Atoll, Nimitz hoped to trick the Japanese into transferring resources to the Gilberts that might otherwise have gone to the Solomons, thus buying the Marines of the 1st Division an advantage in their fight for Guadalcanal and its coveted airfield.

That was the big picture. In a narrower sense, the immediate objectives of the Makin Raid as described in the operations order were simple: "destroying enemy troops and vital installations and [capturing] important documents and prisoners." The item about prisoners was pro forma; since there was barely room on the submarines for the Raiders themselves, there was no way to bring captives back with them and thus little point in taking prisoners in the first place. In essence, then, Carlson's mission was to annihilate the Japanese garrison on Butaritari. Even if the raid should fail to produce its desired effect on the Guadalcanal campaign, a successful, explosive show of force at Makin could, like the Doolittle Raid, serve as a boost to morale by proving that even when back on their heels, the Americans still had the capacity to strike at Japan without warning.

As for James Roosevelt, even the more modest target of Makin Island posed a serious danger to anyone involved in the raid, so Nimitz and Pfeiffer insisted that he stay behind. Carlson did not press the issue, for he felt personally responsible for James's safety—the president had written to him in March asking him to take good care of his son, who had a bad stomach and other vulnerabilities. Carlson had no desire to see young Roosevelt killed on his watch. Once the plans were complete, it fell to Omar Pfeiffer to inform James that he would have to stay behind in Hawaii with the remainder of the battalion during the raid. James, however, would have none of it. He first went over Pfeiffer's head to Admiral Nimitz, demanding that he be allowed to go with his men on the mission. When Nimitz balked, Roosevelt went to his father, who allegedly phoned his chief of naval operations, Admiral Ernest King, and told him: "Look, my son's an officer in that battalion; if he doesn't go, no one goes."

James Roosevelt wanted to prove his worth, no matter who his father was. He knew he was not a model of fitness—he had his bad stomach, his eyesight was poor, he had flat feet that required him to wear special shoes—but he thought those were not sufficient excuses for staying home. "I've thought so long on the angle of special interest and favoritism on this," he wrote to his mother, Eleanor, just before the Raiders were scheduled to leave Hawaii. "But after all any other officer would never have been given waivers on my defects (eyes 3-20th and stomach) and when this next job is done at least I'll feel I have stood the test of making it no matter what the odds." Under pressure from the president, Nimitz caved, and on August 8, James Roosevelt sailed for Makin with the group on the *Argonaut*.

To prepare for the raid, Carlson's battalion had spent much of July practicing beach landings on Oahu. Although the Marine Corps was well versed in the art of amphibious warfare, they had never attempted a landing from a submarine before, so Carlson's group had to invent as they went along. One of the biggest obstacles to their training was that the Navy needed the submarines for other service until Carlson's mission began, so the Raiders did not get a chance to train on the actual subs ahead of time. Instead, they had to use buoys to represent the *Nautilus* and *Argonaut*, anchoring them a little over a mile offshore and practicing how to pilot motorized rubber boats through the surf coming and going from the beach on Oahu. On land, they made mock-ups of the major buildings on Makin using target cloth to mark out their footprints so they could learn to orient themselves (even though most of them didn't know yet exactly which island they were going to).

At five o'clock in the morning of August 6, less than forty-eight hours before their scheduled departure and just as the American task force in the Solomons was about to begin its bombardment of Guadalcanal on the other side of the Date Line, the Raiders got their one and only chance to try landing from the actual submarines. The rehearsal went passably well. "B Company good, A Company fair," wrote Carlson in his diary. In a sign of how important their mission was to the military brass, Admiral Nimitz was there on the beach to observe them.

The men spent much of the long voyage out studying the aerial photographs of Makin from the earlier flyover, memorizing the placement of the buildings and roads. There weren't many of the latter, for the island was so narrow it had just one primary road running from end to end. The main body of the island was part of a larger triangular formation enclosing a protected lagoon in the center. Four wharves for loading cargo jutted out into the calm waters of the lagoon on the inside of the triangle, while a coral reef formed a protective barrier on the outer, ocean side of the island. Since the U.S. Navy assumed that the Japanese had installed shore batteries to protect the lagoon, the plan was for the Raiders to land instead on the ocean side, where they would be less expected.

Carlson was impressed with how well his men held up under the claustrophobic pressures of submarine transport. On the evening of August 12–13, as they crossed the International Date Line, he talked with some of them while they took air on the deck of the *Nautilus*. They were entering the seven-hundred-mile search radius of the nearest Japanese air base in the Marshalls so the submarines would have to spend their daylight hours underwater for the rest of the journey to avoid detection. The men were excited to be nearing their destination. "Happy-go-lucky life on board," Carlson wrote in his diary. "They're full of confidence and keen. No sign of nervousness or fear." In three days they would arrive at Makin.

This was the plan: at 3 a.m. on August 17, the submarines would surface about two miles from shore—far enough out that they expected to be invisible to Japanese radar on the island. The hatches would open and the Marines would climb up on deck with their equipment to start inflating a small fleet of rubber boats, all of which had to be filled using air hoses attached to pumps on the submarines. There were eight boats on the *Nautilus* and twelve on the *Argonaut*. Each boat could carry twelve men, and each man knew his exact station on the deck, his role in his own boat, every step rehearsed for a quick departure. It was too difficult to try to launch the boats directly into the water, which was several feet below deck level, so once each boat was inflated it would be moved to a designated spot on the deck. After all the boats were in place and the equipment was strapped in, the men would climb into their places and hold on tight as the *Nautilus* and *Argonaut* submerged, slipping into the water below them and leaving the fleet of rubber rafts to float on the surface.

Once the boats were launched, the men would fire up their outboards, sort themselves into companies, and motor in under cover of darkness. Companies A and B were to land at separate beaches about a half a mile apart and they intended to be in place, boats stowed and hidden, by 4 a.m., while it was still dark. The timing was planned with care so that the tide would hopefully be high enough to make it over the coral reef and the moon would have set hours before, giving them the darkest possible conditions. By the time the first rays of dawn began to illuminate the sky, the raid would be fully underway. The two Raider companies would each cross from their respective beaches over to the lagoon side and turn inward to converge on the heart of the island, which included the government house, the wharves, and the buildings where it was assumed the Japanese troops were quartered.

For equipment, they were bringing their full arsenal of weapons—Thompson submachine guns, Browning automatic rifles, and M1 Garand rifles for each fire team, along with grenades and some heavier weapons including several crew-served Browning machine guns with armor-piercing bullets and a couple of five-foot-long, .55-caliber Boys antitank rifles (which they called "elephant guns"). They would also bring medical equipment and stretchers, demolition explosives, and crates of extra ammunition. Each man had a uniform that was dyed black, and there was black paint available to camouflage their faces, though it turned out in practice that the black outfits were actually easier to see at night than their regular olive uniforms so most of the men left them behind.

True to Carlson's interest in novel equipment, the Raiders also carried a number of small, handheld SCR-536 radio-telephones, the earliest form of the walkie-talkie—this, at a time when the ordinary Marine units on Guadalcanal relied on sound-powered phones that

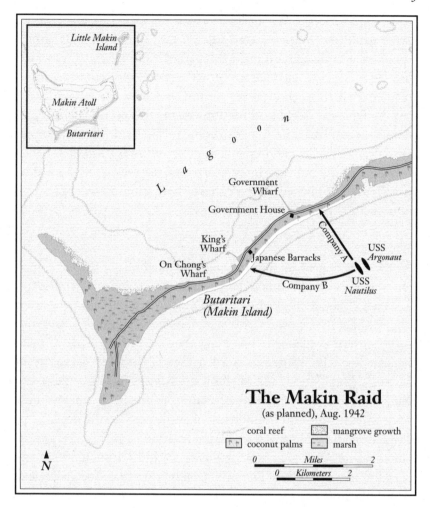

Little Makin
Island

Makin Atoll

Butaritari

L a g o o n

Government
Wharf

Government House

King's
Wharf

On Chong's
Wharf

Japanese Barracks

Company A

Company B

USS
Argonaut

USS
Nautilus

Butaritari
(Makin Island)

The Makin Raid
(as planned), Aug. 1942

coral reef   mangrove growth
coconut palms   marsh

0   Miles   2
0   Kilometers   2

N

required physical wiring to connect them back to their command posts, and when even the dashing British Commandos had to carry thirty-six-pound "portable" radio units. Weighing in at just five pounds each, the walkie-talkies would allow the Raiders to stay in contact wirelessly with one another and with the submarines once they were on land.

They didn't need much else. For food they would bring only a canteen of water and some military chocolate, because they wouldn't be staying long enough to need a meal; they intended to be back on board their submarines within a few hours, or by nightfall at the latest. The *Nautilus* and *Argonaut* were defenseless against air attack while they were on the surface, so if any Japanese planes should arrive while the Marines were still on the island, the submarines would have to dive and remain submerged until nightfall, in which case the Marines would take cover on the island and wait to return to them later that night. But that was it; if they took any longer than a day, the Japanese could land reinforcements from the Marshalls and there were no American forces to come to their aid. The Marines at Guadalcanal, twelve hundred miles to the southwest, had their hands completely full, and the closest American reserves were more than two thousand miles away at Pearl Harbor. They were entirely on their own.

On the morning of August 17 the men rolled out of their cramped bunks at 2 a.m. to fill themselves as best they could with coffee and breakfast. They rechecked their equipment and the ones who were religious said their prayers. At 3 a.m. the *Nautilus* and *Argonaut* rose to the surface as planned. The Navy crewmen made ready to open the hatches. The Marines, crowded together, waited nervously in the thick, humid air, ready to climb the ladders in single file, every man rehearsing in his mind exactly where he belonged, what he must carry, what he must do from the moment he reached the deck.

As soon as the hatches opened, it all started to go wrong. A squall had come up while they were submerged, and the submarines surfaced into a howling sea. The swells ran ten to fifteen feet from peak to trough, much worse than anyone had expected or planned for. Carlson conferred quickly with the Navy commodore in charge of the two submarines and decided to go ahead with the raid anyway— the window of timing was too narrow and too much was at stake to abandon the mission. The long, narrow bodies of the submarines pitched and rolled with the swells as the Marines climbed up through the hatches into the rain, nearly sweeping some of them overboard right off the bat. They could see almost nothing in the darkness of the storm, with mountains of water all around—at best, they could catch a brief glimpse of the distant island when they were at the top of a rise, before the ship rolled them down again into a black, swirling valley. Still, they followed their plan, working the air pumps to

Preparing to climb the ladder on the morning of the raid.

inflate each boat in turn as the decks groaned and the dark water rolled around them.

The ocean current was stronger than the planners had anticipated and it was pulling hard toward the island, so the submarines had to keep their propellers engaged and maneuver constantly to avoid getting dragged back onto the coral reef or into collision with one another. This meant the plan of having them slip peacefully into the water under the rubber boats was impossible. Instead, the submarines had to make way on the surface while the Marines tried to launch their boats into the roiling water and then board them by climbing or jumping down several feet from the deck, a dangerous endeavor in full battle dress with heavy equipment and no practice. Waves crashed over the submarine decks and water poured out through the limber holes, swamping the boats tied up below. Two of the boats were lost to the current along with their cargoes of medical equipment and ammunition, and spares had to be brought up from storage.

After the Raiders managed to get their boats inflated and launched and bailed out, the next step was to fire up the outboard motors—but when they started pulling the cords, in most cases nothing happened. The outboards were an Evinrude model that was popular with Amer-

ican sportsmen and though it was highly reliable under normal conditions, it had no means of keeping water out of the coils if the unit
should get drenched. The defect was well known, and it had worried
Carlson beforehand, but the Navy had been unable to get them anything better in the numbers they needed. In Hawaii they had tried
modifying the motors with protective canopies and metal shields, but
those measures failed in the high seas off Makin Island. Most of the
motors were now flooded with seawater and completely useless.

So they got out the paddles. Once everyone was in the water, the
boats assembled at the *Nautilus* and Carlson called for a change of
plans, shouting to be heard above the roar of the wind. The word
passed from boat to boat: they would paddle in under their own
power, all holding together rather than trying to divide by company.
Instead of A and B companies landing on separate beaches, they
would all land together. And off they went, paddling as hard as they
could, pulled forward by the unrelenting current.

The weather started to clear as they neared the island, but the
swells did not let up. The ocean floor had been deep where they
left the submarines, but it rose quickly as they approached the coral
reef and once they were within a couple of hundred yards of shore
the swells turned into large breakers that lifted the rafts up and spun
them out of control. Paddling hard, the boats slid one by one onto a
broad, smooth beach backed by a dense line of coconut palms. The
first men to reach ground fanned out to set a perimeter defense, just
as they had practiced on Oahu, though none of them knew if the
beach was mined. The others dragged their boats up past the tide
line into the palms and covered them in brush.

After the chaotic landing they had to sort themselves into platoons and companies on the beach, but in the darkness it was difficult
to figure out who belonged where and they couldn't shout to each
other without giving away their presence. It turned out three of the
manned boats had gone missing on the way in. Two of them had in
fact landed a little ways to the north and their crews would recon-
nect with the rest of the battalion soon enough, but the third, commanded by a lieutenant named Oscar Peatross, was half a mile to the
southwest, clear on the other side of the Japanese garrison (or at least
where they assumed the garrison would be).

It was not Peatross's fault. His boat had one of the only functioning motors, so he had used it to ferry some of the officers between the *Nautilus* and the *Argonaut*. But in the confusion of the departure they got delayed, and by the time his boat reached the rendezvous point the others had already left for the beach. Peatross and his men set out to follow them, using the orientation of the *Nautilus* to set their course for the unseen island. But the submarine had rotated as it fought the current, so they started out in the wrong direction— out to sea, with no compass to correct them. As the weather cleared, they realized there was no island ahead, so they turned back to the *Nautilus*. The captain pointed them the right way toward the island, but neglected to tell them about the change of plans, so they motored in toward their original planned destination, unaware that they were now separated from the rest of the battalion and heading for the wrong beach.

Everything took longer than planned, but by 5:13 a.m. the main body of Raiders was mostly sorted out and Carlson switched on his walkie-talkie to let the *Nautilus* know that they were safely on the beach. It was barely starting to get light, and the crashing of the surf had drowned out the sounds of their landing so they thought they had probably come in undetected. If that were the case, though, it didn't last long because about fifteen minutes later one of the enlisted men accidentally squeezed off a burst of .30-caliber rounds from his Browning Automatic Rifle, shattering the morning silence and alerting everyone within a couple of miles to their presence. Right after that, Carlson sent a second, brief communication to the *Nautilus*: "Everything lousy." That was nearly the last the submarines heard from him, for as soon as the Marines started moving inland from the beach, their fancy new wireless radios stopped working. Carlson thought maybe the signals couldn't penetrate the island's foliage. The raiding party soon found itself with no reliable means of communicating with the submarines, or with one another.

Carlson had to act quickly after the accidental discharge of the automatic rifle gave away their presence. There wasn't time to sort out the companies completely, so he scuttled the original plans in favor of continued improvisation and a reliance on all the "gung ho" indoctrination he had given his men to operate independently, on their own initiative. He sent a patrol from A Company across the island to pinpoint their location relative to the wharves, and fifteen minutes later they reported back that they had found the government house and it was empty. With the map of the island in his mind, Carlson then ordered A Company to move south toward the Japanese trading station, with B Company in reserve to protect their left flank.

The island was eerily quiet as the first squads moved through the brush alongside the main road in the early morning light, searching for signs of the Japanese and hoping to sneak up on their barracks undetected. They did not realize that the silence was because there were Japanese snipers all around them, well camouflaged, holding their fire until the Americans were as deep in amongst them as possible. Then, the growl of an engine. A truck appeared about three hundred yards up the road. Fifteen or twenty Japanese soldiers jumped out of the back, joined shortly by another dozen. They planted a flag and disappeared into the underbrush. The Raiders, preparing for their first engagement, fell back to slightly higher ground with a good field of fire and waited for the Japanese to advance toward them. They waited, and then the woods lit up with machine gun fire.

CHAPTER 16

SURVIVAL

For most of the young Marines it was their first experience of live fire, and it was nothing like they had envisioned. Nothing made sense, there was no order or clarity. They couldn't see where the bullets were coming from. "We had Japs in front of us, above us, alongside us to our left, and behind us also to our left," said one of them. "Two machine guns were sweeping the area above our heads; slugs were chunking into the bases of the palm trees." Nine of the Raiders were killed in the first thirty minutes.

They flattened themselves on the ground, below the raking of the machine guns, and tried to find a way to advance close enough to destroy them with grenades. But there were four of the guns, well placed and supported by infantry, so forward motion was nearly impossible. Staying still had its own risks because of the snipers in the trees, which nobody had anticipated. The machine guns were devastating enough, but the snipers were even more effective because they were spread out and so well camouflaged as to be invisible from the ground. When one of the Raiders managed to shoot one down from his perch, he turned out to have coconut shells sewn all over his uniform to help him blend in. As secretive as the Americans thought they were being in their approach, the Japanese were already on full alert as a blanket response to the American landing on Guadalcanal. The snipers had been strapped up in their trees for at least three days by the time the Raiders arrived.

The main body of Raiders got pinned down by the machine guns on the ground and the invisible snipers in the treetops. They hid behind trees and stumps, in taro pits and hollow spots. They couldn't move, at risk of attracting the snipers' attention or sparking a machine gun to open fire. One corporal was hit in the head and started raving deliriously, blood foaming out of his mouth. He got up and ran toward a Japanese machine gun emplacement, shooting frantically, until the gun opened fire and cut him down. A lieutenant named Le Francois was hit by five machine gun rounds, one an explosive bullet that blew out his shoulder. Another Marine was shot through the neck when he stood up to urinate against a tree. Still another was hit in the forehead and paralyzed. The battalion's Navy corpsmen quickly learned to remove their Red Cross armbands when they realized that the bright cloth just made them a better target for the snipers.

Carlson, however, was apparently charmed. Several of the men who were with him that day described him with varying tones of disbelief as walking calmly along the Raider lines, standing upright, unflinching as Japanese bullets pierced the air around him. As if taunting the snipers by making a better target of himself, he smoked his pipe freely. Whatever the magic that surrounded him, it was the same aura of untouchability he had carried since his time fighting Sandino's guerrillas in Nicaragua. His fatalism had stood him well through the war in China, and it was in full evidence on Makin.

Most of the young Marines viewed him with unreserved awe, but even the men on the island that day who in later years would turn against him most viciously still spoke with reverence about his composure in battle. ("His courage under fire was beyond question," wrote one of the Raider officers, in a 1956 memo otherwise savagely critical of his former commander. "He strolled around, smoking his pipe, with no apparent concern of danger.") Others were purely adulatory. "You ought to see him in battle," one of his men later told a Marine Corps correspondent. "He walks around, puffing that old pipe of his, and never gets excited. God, he's wonderful!" It was inspiring, though the magic did not necessarily accrue to those who served around him: a sergeant named Clyde Thomason—an exceptionally tall man who had needed special permission to join the Raiders because of his height—tried acting in much the same manner as Carlson, walking up and down his line, helping his platoon find targets even as they begged him to get down. The snipers shot him with ease.

Even as the progress of their mission ground down to a standstill, there were other threats to worry about. A little after 7 a.m. the Raiders spotted two Japanese ships motoring into the lagoon, one a gunboat and the other a transport. Carlson feared the transport might be carrying reinforcements for the Japanese garrison, so he sent James Roosevelt back to the ocean side to call for artillery support from the submarines, each of which had a pair of six-inch guns on its deck. In an improvised command post on the beach where they had landed, Roosevelt would be safely out of the area of fire (though at least one Marine thought his shiny, balding head made a perfect sniper's target). Even on the ocean side, though, the walkie-talkie signal was too weak and inconsistent for Roosevelt to communicate anything to the submarines beyond the basic fact that there were two Japanese vessels in the lagoon and to give a rough estimate of their positions relative to the government wharf.

After receiving Roosevelt's staticky message, the 371-foot leviathanic bulk of the *Nautilus* rose out of the depths, sloughing off the water that had concealed it, and the Navy sailors took up their battle stations at the deck guns. They had no line of sight on their targets, which were clear on the other side of the island, and without functioning communications they couldn't use the Marines on the lagoon side to guide their aim. So they started firing blindly, lobbing a succession of sixty-five shells over the island to explode in the water on the other side. To make up for the lack of a spotter, the gunners altered the range and deflection of each salvo to cover the lagoon as if walking their way through a chessboard—which, amazingly, worked. One of the shells (they had no idea which) hit the Japanese transport, which went up in flames and sank, and shortly after another hit the gunboat, which also sank with no visible survivors. It was impossible to tell how many people had been on board; some of the Gilbert Islanders the Raiders later encountered told them there were sixty Japanese marines on the transport, but it was unclear whether they were still on board when it sank or if they had already disembarked on the island.

The firefight continued sporadically through the morning until 11:30 a.m., when the drone of approaching aircraft broke the silence overhead. The Japanese commandant on Makin had gotten out a radio message of distress that morning—"We shall all die calmly"— which reached a Japanese air base in the Marshall Islands three hundred miles away. The Marshalls had been under Japanese control since long before the start of the war, and the base was well developed. Given the distance, it was about a two-hour flight for one of their reconnaissance aircraft to reach Makin, and these were the first responders. As the Marines hid from view and tried to remain motionless, two Japanese Type-95 reconnaissance seaplanes buzzed overhead and circled the island, trying to make out what was happening on the ground. In a day marked by an almost absurd intrusion of luck—both good and bad—after circling the island a few times the Japanese aircraft unwittingly dropped their bombs on an area occupied by Japanese troops instead of the Americans, then headed back to make their reports.

Two hours later another flight of Japanese aircraft arrived, this one larger than the first. There were twelve planes in total, including four of the agile Zero fighters, four reconnaissance bombers, two small Type 95 seaplanes, and a pair of large Kawanishi "flying boats" carrying what were likely to be reinforcements. The Zeros flew so low the Marines could see the faces of their pilots. Under cover of sustained bombing that shook the island for more than an hour, one of the flying boats landed in the lagoon accompanied by a Type 95 seaplane. The American submarines could not surface while Japanese fighters were in the air, so the Raiders took advantage of a lull in the bombing to set up the biggest weapons they had—three of the crew-served machine guns and one of the .55-caliber antitank rifles—and then they opened fire on the seaplanes. The smaller seaplane caught fire in the water and burned, while the Kawanishi flying boat circled "violently" several times and managed to lift off briefly before crashing in the lagoon. A cheer went through the Raider ranks.

The twelve men under Lieutenant Peatross who landed on the wrong beach found themselves that morning on the opposite side of the main Japanese force from the rest of the battalion. Their walkie-talkie didn't work either, even after one of them took it apart completely and reassembled it, so they had no way to communicate with the others. But they heard the accidental BAR discharge at 5:30 a.m., and were sufficiently experienced to identify the sound as one of their own guns (the Japanese used a slightly smaller-caliber round which made a slightly higher-pitched report). So they had a rough sense of where the others were. Exploring their end of the island, they came upon the main Japanese barracks, which was already emptied, but they surprised a straggler running out with his rifle. Three of them shot him dead at the same time. He was the first person they had encountered on the island and the first enemy they had seen in the war. He may also have been the first Japanese person they had seen in real life.

They then proceeded to join the attack from the enemy's rear. In the course of the day, they destroyed a radio installation, shot several Japanese messengers on bicycles who were bringing back reports from the skirmish line, destroyed one of the machine gun nests with a grenade, blew up a supply truck, and killed a man in a white shirt and sun helmet who—unbeknown to them—was the Japanese commandant. By the end of the day, three of Peatross's squad were dead and two had serious gunshot wounds but with their working outboard motor the survivors made it back to the *Nautilus* by the appointed hour of 7:30 p.m. Once safely on board, they learned that they were the only ones who had gotten back from the island.

The main body of Marines remained bogged down in a close-quarters battle for most of the afternoon, punctuated by yet another appearance of Japanese bombers. After that wave turned back toward the Marshalls around five o'clock, it was unlikely there would be any more that day. Given the distance from their base, any further sorties would not have time to get home before nightfall, so the soonest Carlson and his men could expect to see another Japanese aircraft would be the following morning, a couple of hours after sunrise. By that time they intended to be well on their way back to Hawaii.

They had failed to complete their mission. Although they had managed to destroy the machine guns and killed a substantial number of Japanese troops, they had no idea how many more remained on the island. They had shot down two seaplanes, and the submarines had sunk the two Japanese ships, but the Marines had gathered little if any intelligence, and since they had spent most of the day pinned down by the snipers they hadn't had any opportunity to sweep the island or hunt for radio equipment or fuel depots. But they couldn't stay any longer. Night was coming and the submarines were expecting them at 7:30 p.m., so Carlson had to call an end to the mission. After a quick gung ho conference with his officers and men, Carlson told them to withdraw to the beach where they had first landed. They pulled their boats out from under the foliage that had camouflaged them, lined them up on the beach, and strapped in the wounded men along with the equipment they were bringing back.

By 7:15 p.m. it was fully dark and the Raiders began launching their boats into the surf. The submarines surfaced as planned about a mile offshore. The *Nautilus* lit a green light as a beacon, the *Argonaut* a red one. Carlson stayed on the beach with a small covering force, ready to join them once all the boats were in the water.

What followed was the most demoralizing experience of his life.

———

They just couldn't get through the surf. The breakers had been difficult enough to manage on the way in, when the boats were buoyed by an onshore current and riding in the direction of the waves, but going against them to get off the island turned out to be almost impossible. High waves coming in rapid succession quickly swamped the boats, shorting out the motors again. They had to bail frantically. Several of the boats capsized, upending their contents into the water. An indeterminate number of Marines drowned, dragged to the bottom by the equipment attached to their webbing belts. Others stripped off their uniforms to swim, trying to push their rafts out past the breakers so they could climb back into them. When the motors failed they dumped them overboard to save weight and tried paddling. When they lost their oars, they paddled with rifle butts, with palm fronds, with their hands. They tried over and over, and most kept getting pushed back, swamped, capsized—six, seven, eight times. They lost their weapons. The wounded men, lashed into place, were in agony. An upended boat dumped the paralyzed man into the water, but someone managed to haul him back out before he could drown. For five exhausting, soul-crushing hours the Raiders tried to muscle their way through the oncoming surf, and nearly every time they did, the ocean would rise up like some giant monster and shove them violently back onto the beach.

By the end of the night only seven boats other than Peatross's made it past the breakers to the submarines—four to the *Nautilus* and three to the *Argonaut*. At least 120 men, more than half of the raiding force, remained on the beach. There was no effective means of communication between the submarines and the beach so they had no way to sort out who had gone missing. Peatross, who was already on board the *Nautilus*, described the "thousand-yard stare" of the survivors who arrived that night—silent, their eyes unfocused as if gazing at some distant horizon. And they were the lucky ones. After five hours fighting the waves, following a full day of battle, without a meal since breakfast at two the previous morning, the men on the beach were nearly catatonic. Most of their weapons had been lost in the sea during the repeated capsizing of the boats. Many of them had stripped off their uniforms to swim after being dumped overboard and now they wore only their underpants or were completely naked, wet and shivering in the nighttime breeze. They had no way to get off the island, and only a few had any means of defending themselves other than with their hands.

Carlson gave up for the night and set up a defensive perimeter in the coconut trees, assigning the few Marines who still had functioning rifles to act as sentries. At around 9 p.m., while some of the others were still trying to get through the surf, a private named Jess Hawkins spotted a Japanese patrol of eight men approaching the line and opened fire on them with his automatic rifle, killing three of them before the others shot him in the chest. Five members of the patrol escaped, so it was a fair assumption that the remaining Japanese forces on the island would soon know their location and could be expected to attack either overnight or in the morning. The rest of the men huddled together and tried to create shelter from the cold—one Raider simply dug himself a hole in the sand and covered himself with flat rocks to stay warm. They were miserable and terrified. There was nothing dashing or intrepid about that night, just

278 · THE RAIDER

a grueling, instinctual effort to survive until the next day. In whispered conversations they wondered how long it would take before they were captured or shot by the Japanese they knew were coming.

Carlson was desperate. Maybe if James Roosevelt had stayed behind in Hawaii like Nimitz had wanted him to, it wouldn't have been quite so bad. But the son of the president was now trapped with him on the hostile beach. Their outlook was wretched, and Carlson knew that if a well-armed Japanese force should challenge them when his men had no weapons, they would have no choice but to surrender. Carlson knew from China just how sadistically the Japanese treated their prisoners, but it was early enough in the war for him to imagine at some level that they might treat white Americans better than they did their fellow Asians.

He might have considered unarmed combat the better alternative if he had known what had happened to the remnants of his old regiment from China, the 4th Marines, after they surrendered in the Philippines. In what later came to be known as the Bataan Death March, the Japanese had driven tens of thousands of American and Filipino prisoners on a forced march of sixty miles through blazing tropical heat, savagely beating anyone who fell out of line. They shot men who stopped, or collapsed, or asked for water. They smashed prisoners' teeth to take their gold fillings. Some of the Japanese soldiers bayonetted their captives at whim, gutting them for sport or pleasure. All told, several thousand American and Filipino servicemen would suffer brutal deaths in the course of the march. But the outside world would not know of it until twelve survivors escaped from their prison camp in 1943 to tell what had happened, and in August of 1942 Carlson was still unaware of it.

What happened next is one of the most controversial incidents in the history of the World War II Marine Raiders. It is only partially verifiable from the conflicting accounts that survive, but a few things are clear. There is no question that Carlson considered surrender the only realistic option if his unarmed, exhausted Raiders should be attacked by a substantial Japanese force during the night. And at least some of the men stranded on Makin decided that their best option was to surrender preemptively: six separate Marines told a combat correspondent just after the mission that they had been part of a meeting that decided on surrendering to the Japanese, though the reporter withheld that information at the time because he knew the military censors would never allow it to be published.

And there was a note. A Japanese account of the war published in Tokyo the following year contained a facsimile of a scrawled message in cursive English that had been found on the island after the raid, addressed to the Japanese commandant. It read:

To the Commanding Officer, Japanese forces, Makin Island

Dear Sir.

I am a member of the American forces now on Makin.

> *We have suffered severe casualties and wish to make an end of the bloodshed and bombings.*

> *We wish to surrender according to the rules of military law and be treated as prisoners of war. We would also like to bury our dead and care for our wounded.*

> *There are approximately 60 of us left. We have all voted to surrender.*

> *I would like to see you as soon as possible to prevent future blood shed and bombing.*

Captain [name unreadable]

The signature on the note is obscured by a smudge of ink, but Captain Ralph Coyte, one of Carlson's two company commanders on Makin, later acknowledged writing it, and the shape and length of the ink smudge are consistent with his name.

From there, the evidence breaks down. It is unclear whether Carlson ordered Coyte to write the note (which Coyte claimed) or whether Coyte wrote it of his own initiative. It is also unclear how many of the Raiders on the beach Coyte actually represented; his note said only sixty, but there were twice that number still on the island. Most of the Marines later denied knowing anything about a decision to surrender. James Roosevelt said he knew of no such thing. Carlson said nothing publicly about it, and only told his superiors that he had considered it to be unavoidable if they were attacked. And lastly, it is unclear what happened to Coyte's surrender note after he wrote it. Coyte himself said that he gave the note to a Japanese soldier to deliver, but that shortly afterward another Raider, operating independently, shot that Japanese soldier dead. A more plausible explanation, from the Japanese source where the note was reproduced, was that he gave the note to one of the native islanders, who held on to it and turned it over to the Japanese forces who arrived to retake control of the island a few days later. Either way, the Japanese commandant to whom Coyte had addressed the note never received it, and would not have been able to act on it anyhow since he was dead.

So whether intentionally or not, the Marines stranded on Makin Island did not surrender that night—and as it turned out, there was no need for them even to have considered it. As Carlson would explain in his after-action report: "no matter how bad your own situation may appear to be, there is always the possibility that the situation of the enemy is much worse." After the sun came up the next morning and the Raiders began to probe again, they discovered that between their own weapons and the damage wrought by the Japanese planes' indiscriminate bombing—which apparently did more harm to the Japanese on the ground than to the Raiders—almost all of the enemy troops on the island were already dead. According to the islanders the Raiders encountered that morning, there was hardly anyone left to fight them.

They still had to get off the island, though. There were more than a hundred Marines left onshore and they knew the quiet would not last for long—the first Japanese planes would likely start arriving from the Marshalls by mid-morning. They had to get out to the submarines before then, because if an air raid came, the subs would have to dive yet again and stay under for the rest of the day. So at daylight on August 18 they tried again to battle the surf. This time, four of the boats made it through, loaded beyond their design capacity, with several men in the water holding on to their sides and swimming. Two of the boats continued on toward the *Nautilus* while the other two made way for the *Argonaut*. One of the boats for the *Argonaut* carried James Roosevelt, at Carlson's insistence, but Carlson himself stayed behind on the beach, intending to be the last man off the island.

Just as the rubber boats were nearing the submarines, a formation of aircraft appeared on the submarines' radar, approaching from several miles off. The *Nautilus* got everyone it could on board and dove immediately, but the *Argonaut* remained on the surface, waiting for the final boat from shore to reach it. The seventy Marines who remained on the beach watched from a distance as their comrades on the water paddled frantically to get to the submarine and climb on board just as the Japanese planes closed in. They weren't quite fast enough. At 9:17 a.m., the men on the beach watched in horror as the *Argonaut*—which had just taken James Roosevelt on board—launched into an emergency dive just as the first of the oncoming Japanese planes roared over the island. Moments after the *Argonaut* went under, the lead plane dropped two bombs squarely on the spot where its stern had just been. Two giant geysers blasted up from the water, followed by a pair of muffled explosions.

After the *Argonaut* dove under, there was still one rubber boat left out on the surface, with five men in it. They were part of the group that reached the *Nautilus* the night before, and they had volunteered to come back that morning to help the Raiders stranded on the island, bringing extra weapons and a line-throwing gun in hopes of pulling the remaining boats out through the surf. When the air raid came they were caught out in the open. One of the Japanese Zeros banked and came in low, strafing them with its machine guns, sinking the boat and leaving no trace of its crew. Watching helplessly from the beach as their rescuers were being killed, none of the men who remained knew how they could get off the island, or whether they even had a means of getting home if they did. And the clock was still ticking; Japanese ground reinforcements were almost certainly on their way by ship from the Marshalls.

Four squadrons of aircraft flew over Makin that day, bombing the island from end to end. But with no one left on the ground to direct the Japanese pilots' attacks, the Raiders managed to remain out of sight and unharmed. In the lulls between the air raids, the unarmed Raiders collected rifles and ammunition from dead Japanese soldiers as well as their own fallen comrades. Carlson ordered a thorough search of the island and his men found no organized resistance at all, just a handful of solitary Japanese who were now outnumbered. The Raiders shot the remaining Japanese dead—in spite of their fears of being captured the night before, and how they would have wanted to be treated had that happened.

Carlson and his men sifted through the main battlefield, collecting weapons and counting the corpses of eighty-three dead Japanese troops. They used TNT to blow up about a thousand barrels of aviation fuel, destroyed the main radio station, and ransacked the Japanese commandant's office to collect all the documents they could find. To the United States Navy's remarkably good fortune, the documents they brought back included not just intelligence on the Gilberts but also air defense maps of *all* Pacific islands under Japanese control, including information on the strength of their garrisons, their methods of alert, and their emergency operation plans.

The safer the Raiders became, the more absurd and feverish their explorations. They hunted in the barracks for trophies to bring home, loading up with abandoned flags and swords and helmets. One man found an officer's katana, which he insisted on calling a "Smirnoff sword" even after a friend tried to teach him the word "samurai." Searching for usable clothing, they raided a Japanese store on the island but found only silk underpants, in blue and pink, which they shared among themselves. Dressed in their colorful silk undies, marching around with swords and flags, they looked to one of the other Marines like "a child's picture-book version of a gang of pirates." They devoured cans of fish and corned beef from the Japanese store. More thrilling, they found beer. Carlson told them to ask the islanders what they wanted from the Japanese stores, give it to them, and then destroy everything else.

That evening around 6 p.m., Carlson tried again. Standing on the beach, looking out for lights in the water, he eventually spotted the green beacon of the *Nautilus* twinkling about a mile offshore, and then, to his unspeakable relief, a red one as well. The *Argonaut* had survived, only by a stroke of luck: the Japanese plane that bombed it was armed with antipersonnel ordnance meant for land targets rather than the depth charges that might have destroyed the submarine with ease. Since the bombs had been wired to explode on impact, they detonated as soon as they touched the surface of the water. Notwithstanding the visual spectacle of the explosions, the *Argonaut* had gotten far enough down to avoid harm, though there had been no way for it to communicate that fact to the anxious men on the island.

As much of a relief as it was to see that both submarines were still intact, Carlson did not want his men to risk the surf again. So the next challenge became how to communicate a new plan to the submarines when the walkie-talkies still didn't work. He managed to scare up a working flashlight, as well as an experienced signalman—the only one left, as the other four had all been killed the day before. With the signalman's help, Carlson flashed Morse-Code instructions to the *Nautilus* and *Argonaut* to meet them outside the mouth of the lagoon, on the opposite side of the island, where they wouldn't have to fight against the ocean surf. The captain of the *Nautilus* worried that the signal flashing from shore might be from Japanese forces luring them into an ambush, so he flashed back a challenge question, based on a conversation he and Carlson had had on board the submarine on the way out. Carlson passed.

Dragging their four remaining rubber boats across the island, the last vestiges of the Raider force lashed them together with a native outrigger canoe to create a makeshift raft that all seventy Marines crowded onto, among them several severely wounded men. They had two outboard motors, only one of which worked reliably, so for the most part the men had to paddle for the miles that lay between the beach and the area where the submarines were supposed to meet them. It was slow and painful going in the dark, but at least the water was relatively calm while they were still in the lagoon. Carlson navigated by the stars, but as they left the lagoon and entered into the rougher ocean waters beyond, they still had no visual sign of the submarines. If they couldn't find them, they would have to turn back or risk being lost at sea. The island faded into the darkness behind them as they paddled slowly on. An hour passed, then another hour, and then, out of the dark, they spotted the piercing green light of the *Nautilus*. One of the men began to cry. They reached the submarines a little after 11 p.m. and the men were brought on board—hollow, broken, and shivering. When Carlson came down the ladder on the *Nautilus*, Peatross thought he looked like he had aged ten years since the start of the raid. They were safe, though, and within the hour they were on their way back to Pearl Harbor.

It was a bleak journey home. As the submarines churned along on their separate courses back to Hawaii, Carlson had plenty of time to take stock of his losses. It was impossible to sort everyone out after the chaotic reembarkation onto the two subs, so they wouldn't be able to do a full head count until they were back at Pearl Harbor. The final tally would show that out of the 220 officers and enlisted men who had left with him for the mission, thirty failed to come home. Eighteen Marines were confirmed dead in the fighting; Carlson had paid the native chief of police on the island to bury them. The others were assumed to have drowned trying to get off the island, but there was no way to be sure. Several of the survivors had gunshot wounds, four of them stretcher cases, and the battalion's doctor was performing emergency surgeries on the dining table of the *Nautilus*'s wardroom.

The confidence and good spirits of the men heading into the raid had been shattered by their first experience of combat and the terror of being stranded on a hostile island with no means of escape. Most of their equipment was gone and would not be easy to replace—so scarce were American supplies at this stage in the war that the planners had expected the Raiders to bring back even their rubber boats, which they were supposed to slash with knives for rapid deflation and then patch up again once they were back in Hawaii. An armory's worth of powerful weapons was lying in the seawater off Makin, lost when the boats capsized in the surf. Many of the men had come back to the submarines nearly naked and now wore the black uniforms they had left behind or whatever ill-fitting clothing they could borrow from the Navy crewmen.

No one knew what to expect when they got home. They hadn't been beaten, one of the Marines recalled, but they weren't feeling very boastful either. On August 25, the *Nautilus*, sailing a day ahead of the *Argonaut*, reached Pearl Harbor after its two-thousand-mile journey from Makin and the scene that greeted the men as they turned out on deck—pale and blinking after a week without sunlight—was for some of them the most vivid memory they would carry for the entire war. All around them, on the decks of the gigantic Navy ships anchored in the harbor—on the destroyers, the cruisers, the battleships—were crowds of Navy sailors in their blue dress uniforms, cheering and shouting as the ships' bands played "From the Halls of Montezuma." As the *Nautilus* approached the crowded wharf, the men could make out an honor guard standing at attention and presenting arms, flanked by another brass band. All of the Raiders who had stayed behind were there, too, saluting them, along with a crowd of more high-ranking Navy and Marine Corps officers than they had ever seen in one place. The *Nautilus* glided up to its berth, the gangway came down, and Admiral Nimitz strode down onto the deck. He stood face-to-face with Carlson and held out his hand, grinning. Then the mob of reporters swarmed down on them all.

CHAPTER 17

FAME AND GLORY

THE RAIDERS WERE STARS. For a nation still in shock, looking for a way forward from its humiliations in the Pacific, the press happily relayed the news of their "two-day job of slaughter and destruction." They were "Raiders of Wrath," said one account, a "combination of sailor, soldier and something more—much more." It was an early taste of revenge for the country's losses. The *Honolulu Star-Bulletin* reported that "United States 'Kung Ho' marines—their memory of Wake still fresh—have completely leveled Makin island." Carlson and Roosevelt got much of the press's attention, though they gave all the credit to their men. Roosevelt said at a press conference that he didn't think there was a finer group of men in the world. When a reporter asked him whether he'd call them "rough riders" like Theodore Roosevelt's cavalry, James replied, "No, they're more like surf swimmers." They glossed happily over the slaughter at the end. "We wanted to take prisoners," said Carlson, "but we couldn't find any."

A Navy Department grateful for the war's first victorious ground mission—to say nothing of the sensation caused by the first submarine-based raid in American history—showered the veterans of the Makin Raid with honors, awarding twenty-three Navy Crosses as well as a posthumous Medal of Honor for Clyde Thomason, the tall sergeant who had been shot by snipers while helping his men find targets. He was the first enlisted Marine in World War II to earn the honor. Carlson received his second Navy Cross, a gold star to pin to the ribbon he got for fighting Sandino's guerrillas in Nicaragua. The secretary of the navy commended Carlson's "extraordinary heroism" and "high courage"—which, he said, "were in keeping with the finest traditions of the United States Naval Service."

The Marine Corps made hay of the raid. "In rigorous training these men become specialists in rubber-boat operations," read one of the press releases they sent out. "They learn every technique of gouging, strangling, knifing, bayoneting and otherwise putting an enemy out of action." They were, said the Marines, "a powerful force adept at close-range fighting and schooled in amphibious warfare." An article in *Liberty* magazine called them "Carlson's Immortal Raiders" and explained that they "were organized on a theory of group effort, of true co-operation on the part of every man in the outfit, officer and private alike. Their record shows the astounding results group effort can achieve."

For the final tally of Japanese dead, the Navy Department decided to go with the inflated (or at least highly wishful) figure of 350 enemy troops killed on Makin, a sum they reached by combining the very highest estimates of Japanese troop strength from the native islanders with a generous guess at how many Japanese might have been killed when the seaplane transport and the two ships were sunk in the lagoon. Carlson and Roosevelt played along, sharing that figure publicly even though it was much higher than the tally Carlson had used in his official reports, which was a little over eighty confirmed

Raiders and sailors on the USS *Nautilus* after returning from Makin.

dead. Japanese propagandists, for their part, reported that more than half of the Americans in the raiding party had been wiped out, with minimal Japanese casualties.

———

It was not an issue for either the Navy Department or the press that the Raiders had shot the last survivors of the Japanese garrison rather than taking them prisoner. Indeed, the press could hardly have been more delighted by the thoroughness of their killing. But there were moral implications to such actions, and the Raiders' celebrated slaughter of "Japs" on Makin was the beginning of a significant issue in the Pacific War. Simply put, while American troops were not supposed to kill surrendered, crippled, or disarmed Japanese combatants, many did, and they did so with the indulgence—even celebration—of their officers and the public back home. Admiral William Halsey famously erected a billboard on Tulagi, across from Guadalcanal, exhorting the arriving Marines to "Kill Japs, kill Japs, kill more Japs." Most Japanese soldiers preferred suicide to capture, leaving few who *could* be taken prisoner. Stories circulated among U.S. troops—some true, some not—describing incidents where Japanese soldiers pretended to surrender and then killed their captors, or pretended to be gravely injured, then pulled the pin on a grenade when a corpsman tried to help them. The belief thus became widespread among Marines in the Pacific that it was not just highly dangerous to take a Japanese prisoner, but also—because of that danger—not morally necessary. As the historian John Dower has argued, the remarkably low incidence of American units taking Japanese prisoners of war in the Pacific "was not official policy, and there were exceptions in certain places, but over wide reaches of the Asian battleground it was everyday practice."

Such a propensity to kill without mercy would be a hallmark of Carlson's battalion, a dark undercurrent to its stated idealism. The actual circumstances of how crippled or captured Japanese soldiers died at their hands are not clearly reflected in their recollections and memoirs—Carlson and his men may have committed war crimes; they also may just have hinted at such things to impress other Marines or play to the press. In either case, Carlson's humanitarian sympathy for the people of China did not by any means extend to the soldiers of Japan. Quite the opposite: the strength of his affection for the Chinese was precisely why his hatred for the Japanese was so unforgiving. Other Americans might want payback for Pearl Harbor, but Carlson also wanted to avenge what they had done to China.

Just as he had once been known as a bandit-hunter, Carlson would be celebrated as a killer of Japanese during the Pacific War, though he resisted the reputation. When one journalist asked him directly if he was a "Jap-hater," Carlson answered that No, he did not hate the Japanese people. He said the ordinary citizens of Japan were "just as sound fundamentally, and just as human" as any other nation. What he hated, he said, was the militarist clique that had started the war. Japan's war machine had to be destroyed before there could be an enduring peace, he said, and the only way to do that was through "the ruthless extinction of every Japanese who bears arms on the battlefield." In such a formulation, consideration for prisoners was irrelevant. One could be a humanitarian, Carlson believed, and still kill Japanese combatants without remorse—indeed, one could be a humanitarian *by* killing them. "No hate for the Japanese people is involved in this process," he told the reporter. "It is as impersonal as surgery."

The Makin Raid turned Carlson into one of the first American heroes of World War II. Reporters loved his China background, which they cited as evidence that he knew the "secret" for beating the Japanese. A front-page article in *The New York Times* on August 28 stressed how Carlson had beaten the Japanese by "using the guerrilla tactics he had learned as an observer with the Eighth Route Army." None of the disastrous elements of the raid were shared with the public; as the *Times* described it, the raid was done by 4 p.m. on the second day and the Marines spent the rest of their time "making friends with the cordial Polynesian natives." *Time* magazine echoed Carlson's prewar warnings about U.S. trade with Japan, noting that most of the Japanese supplies on the island were American: the barrels in the Japanese fuel depot on Makin bore the trademark of an American refiner. The trucks had been made in the United States. Even the canned beef in the Japanese store was American in origin. All of it, said *Time*, stood as "a record of pre-war U.S. policy."

As the press saw it, Carlson had been fighting this war for years already. The *New York Herald Tribune* credited him with being ahead of his time in his "crusading zeal for the anti-Japanese cause"—which, it said, was perhaps "untimely" when the United States was still neutral in Asia, but it was just what the Marines needed after Pearl Harbor. A United Press article explained that Carlson "learned how to fight the Japanese when he marched with the Chinese 8th Route Army the length and breadth of Shanxi Province in 1938." After quitting his commission in anger in 1939, he returned to the Marine Corps "when he saw that war between the United States and Japan was inevitable." Carlson, went the public narrative, was the Cassandra who had warned his country in vain of the war that was coming. And now, the incredible difficulty of establishing a foothold against Japan's forces in the Pacific—short on Marines, short on ships, short on armaments—was confirmation that America should have been listening to him all along.

Carlson's ideas about democracy in the armed forces also started making their way into the popular media after the raid. "Work Together Is New Cry of Carlson's Raiders," announced one Navy press release, which shared the words of the "battle-cry" of the Raiders, which was allegedly "shouted by the men as they go into action." It included such lyrics as:

> We are the raiders of the land and sea.
> We work together for democracy.
> Gung ho! Gung ho! Gung ho! Ho!
> . . .
> We are unbeatable—because we are right;
> Those Japs can't lick us—for we've got might.
> We're raiders—for democracy.
> We work together; that's why we're free.
> Gung ho! Gung ho! Gung ho! Ho!

Difficult as it may be to imagine a band of hard-bitten Marines chanting, "We're raiders for democracy" as they charged into battle (there is no evidence they actually sang it when fighting, just at their gung ho meetings), it perfectly encapsulated Carlson's vision for the Raiders—that they would not only fight their way to victory against Japan but would be the vanguard of a democratic awakening in the

Carlson and James Roosevelt with captured Japanese flag from Makin.

U.S. armed forces, and eventually lead the way for the country as a whole.

Behind the ecstatic press coverage and the public celebrations of the Raider victory, Carlson knew that the Makin Raid had been anything but an unqualified success—indeed, it had come incredibly close to ending in disaster. And while he did not talk about such things with reporters, neither did he try to hide them from his superiors in the military. In the initial draft of his formal report on the raid, Carlson wrote of his hopelessness on the night of August 17—the "spiritual low point of the expedition," he called it—when the men stranded on the beach were exhausted from their hours of fighting the surf, when they had no weapons and in many cases no clothing, and no apparent means of getting back to the submarines. He knew the following morning would bring renewed air raids, likely followed by the landing of Japanese reinforcements. He described his plan to try to get off the island via the lagoon the following day, but added, poignantly, "If we were attacked by a superior force in the meantime I believed that the wise course would be to surrender because we had no effective means of defending ourselves."

Admiral Nimitz hit the ceiling when he read Carlson's report. He called Omar Pfeiffer into his office, where he had Carlson's report on his desk, and shouted at him: "You take this report back and get ahold of that young man and tell him that no report from my command will have any word, or even idea, of surrender in it!" Pfeiffer called Carlson into his own office, where he told him to remove the line about how he had considered surrender. On principle, Carlson pushed back. "It's true, and it will stay in the report," he told Pfeiffer. Pfeiffer, by his own account, replied: "It comes out or you go out." Carlson had no desire to lose his command so early in the war, so he ruefully complied. The final version of the memo—the one that went up the ladder and stands as the official account of the raid—said nothing about how close Carlson thought they had come to surrendering half the raiding force, including President Roosevelt's son, to the Japanese.

Far worse, though, was what none of them knew at the time: that in the confusion of the repeated, failed attempts to get off the island, nine of the Raiders who had gone missing and were presumed to have drowned were, in fact, still alive, and they had been left behind on the island. It was never possible to pinpoint exactly what had happened to them—the Raiders had swept the island from end to end on their last day without seeing any sign of them. Some of the men speculated that they may have stayed behind deliberately. Or perhaps they survived the strafing of the rubber boat on the second day. Or when they were trying to get through the surf, their boat was pulled away by the current to an inaccessible part of the island. Japanese sources suggest that five of the stranded Marines had tried to make their own escape from Makin by stealing a 20-ton commercial vessel tied to one of the wharves on the lagoon side, but they ran aground at the western tip of the island. However it happened, when Japanese relief forces arrived on August 23 to take back control of the island, they found the nine stranded Americans and took them prisoner. (Remarkably, they would be the last Marines to be captured in a group for the rest of the war.)

Later in August, the captured Raiders were transferred to a Japanese base on Kwajalein, in the Marshall Islands group—where, on October 16, 1942, their captors beheaded all nine of them. The only way anyone would know of their fate was because the following year another American prisoner, a former Olympic track runner named Louis Zamperini, happened to be locked up in the same cell they had inhabited on Kwajalein, and he saw the words they had scratched into the wall: "Nine Marines marooned on Makin Island, August 18, 1942." In 1946, the Japanese commander on Kwajalein who ordered their executions would be tried for war crimes and hanged.

To the president, Carlson was more upbeat about the raid than he had been with Nimitz. In a letter to Roosevelt two days after his return to Hawaii, he said he had not anticipated how tough the fighting would be, but judged that in the end it had gone well. "This experience with the enemy has filled the men of this battalion with confidence," he wrote. "They know that in an even fight they can lick him hands down. And they have also learned that it is possible to outwit him." Carlson admitted that he had been apprehensive about taking James along on the raid, but since he had been so eager to go, Carlson had decided that the mission would provide a good opportunity for his "initial indoctrination in the mysteries of battle." James, he said, had acquitted himself well, staying "cool as the proverbial cucumber" in spite of all the fighting going on around him.

As far as the ideological indoctrination of the Raiders, Carlson attributed the victory at Makin to the "gung ho" spirit he and James had instilled in the men during their training. "It is a source of deep satisfaction to both of us to see our labors now receive general approbation," he told FDR. "Jim and I knew we had the right formula, but it was so unorthodox that the opposition for months was both virulent and persistent." The Raiders were starting to act like the Christian-democratic warriors Carlson wanted them to become. He told the president that most of the Marines who participated in the raid "got religion," and at their first group meeting after Makin, "the whole battalion sang the Doxology with a zest I have never seen or heard before."

It was a theme he echoed in other letters at the time: the religiosity of his Marines, as if they were his congregation and he were their pastor. "I told you my boys 'got' religion at Makin," he wrote to a friend in September. "It is of a more permanent nature than I had hoped for—and more extensive. Good bunch of lads. They make you proud to be a human being." The day after his return from

Makin, Carlson held a memorial service in Hawaii for the members of the battalion who had died on Makin. Playing the role of his father the minister, he gave a eulogy on sacrifice. He listed the names of the dead, describing them as he remembered them—one with a "boyish grin," another with a "lumbering stride and eager, half embarrassed manner." "They loved each other, these comrades of ours," he said. "They were vital, eager, thoughtful, realistic. They had convictions even to the point of sacrificing their lives." They had died for their ideals, he said, and for the survivors, the work was just beginning. "It behooves those of us who remain to rededicate ourselves to the task that lies ahead," he concluded. "The convictions of these comrades are our convictions. . . . With the memory of their sacrifices in mind, let us rededicate ourselves to the task of bringing into reality the ideals for which they died."

A few weeks after Carlson gave his eulogy service in Hawaii, back in New England the Reverend Thomas Carlson gave his final sermon at the Plymouth congregational church where he had been minister for sixteen years, by far the longest tenure of his fifty-year career. As if having his son in mind, the theme of Thomas Carlson's farewell sermon was, likewise, sacrifice. "Jesus knew that fulfillment in the great thing we call life includes a sacrifice as a normal element," he told his congregation. "If there is to be any solution of social . . . and international relations, it can come only through sacrificial principles." His son was now sufficiently famous that when *The Hartford Courant* reported on Thomas Carlson's retirement, it described him in its headline not as a long-serving local minister but simply as "Carlson's Father."

The Raiders enjoyed a couple of months of recuperation and training after Makin, first for two weeks on Hawaii and then in a camp—which they naturally christened "Camp Gung Ho"—on the island of Espiritu Santo in the New Hebrides about six hundred miles southeast of Guadalcanal. There had been some changes in the meantime. Prompted by the success of the Makin operation—and the parallel heroics of the 1st Raider Battalion under Merritt Edson, who fought in support of the 1st Marine Division on Tulagi and Guadalcanal—two new Raider battalions, the 3rd and the 4th, were created in

American Samoa and at Camp Pendleton in California, respectively. James Roosevelt was put in charge of the 4th, which bode well for the future of the concept though it would separate Roosevelt and Carlson for the rest of the war. Carlson also worked to increase the strength of his battalion, making up for the losses at Makin through new recruitments and additions of veterans from other units, as well as adding two more companies, E and F, to bring the total strength of the battalion to 46 officers and 1,062 enlisted men. They got replacements for the weapons that were lost at Makin and were issued the "Gung Ho Knife"—a huge, Bowie-style survival knife with a 9.5-inch blade that Navy pilots had previously packed as emergency gear with their parachutes.

Among Carlson's new officers was one Marine who had wanted to be part of the battalion since it was formed, and who wanted to serve under him more eagerly than anyone else: his son. In the years since Carlson had reconnected with him on the dock at San Francisco, Evans Junior had finished his education and in the summer of 1942 he was commissioned as a lieutenant in the Marine Corps. Immediately afterward, he tried to get into his father's Raider battalion, which by then was already in Hawaii.

Ironically, considering how Carlson thought of the young enlisted men who served under him like his own sons, it turned out that the last person he wanted in his battalion was his actual son. Carlson turned him down. By way of explanation, Carlson wrote to his father in Plymouth that he did not think it would be good either for himself or Evans Junior if he let his son into the Raiders. He didn't want the taint of nepotism—if the boy did something heroic, he wouldn't be able to nominate him for a medal since it was his own son—and he also didn't want to put himself in the situation of having to give Evans Junior orders that might get him killed. So he refused to accept him into the Raiders and told him that he would be better off under a different commander. Still, the young man persisted. He applied a second time to join the Raiders, and Carlson turned him down again. Finally, some of the Raider officers who knew young Evans personally managed to persuade Carlson to let him in. Father and son—nearly mirror images of each other—were reunited.

Carlson felt himself growing again through the experience of leading the Raiders, becoming more of a father figure to his young charges, experiencing a deeper sense of responsibility than he had ever felt before. In war, he told his sister in a letter from Espiritu Santo, the fighting was in some ways the easy part. It was the waiting and uncertainty, the homesickness, that drove his men to the edge. "Youth, especially, is impatient," he told her. "Youth is filled with dash, the spirit of adventure, the desire to get it over with, whatever 'it' may be. And it is difficult, so difficult, for youth to learn the virtue of patience." But he was learning how to keep his men in line. "When all others are distressed and distraught I must be calmly even of temper and optimistic of outlook," he told her. "In my younger years I would have been unable to do it. I, too, would have sought escape, as I have so many times in my career."

Looking back on his life, he could see the broader themes—how he had always run away from his frustrations, whether it was leaving home at an early age, or abandoning Dorothy and then Etelle, or his impulsive resignation from the Marines in 1938. Whenever he felt stuck, or restricted in his motions, he fled. But now he was in a role where he felt he could remain fixed in place, both physically and mentally—he had a job with responsibilities he could not run from. "Fortunately a degree of wisdom and fortitude come with maturity," he told Karen. "How slow I have been to mature."

For all the fame and hype about the "guerrilla" Raiders, the truth is that there had been little about the Makin Raid that matched with what Carlson had learned in China, nor with the training he gave his men. There were no long hikes, no living off the land, no feinting maneuvers or carefully sprung surprise attacks, no melting into the forest. The fighting had been a relative free-for-all with little overall cohesion. It had not by any means been an ideal mission for the battalion he had created. But with Makin behind him, and his reputation not just salvaged but enhanced by a nation eager for good news from the war, Carlson was able to look ahead for a new mission that would match more closely with the philosophy and training of his Raiders, one that would play more to their strengths. He would get that opportunity soon enough, on Guadalcanal.

CHAPTER 18

INTO THE JUNGLE

O PERATION WATCHTOWER, the American assault on Guadal-canal that began on the morning of August 7, had started off auspiciously enough, with an uncontested landing of the 1st Marine Division and their quick establishment of control over the airstrip, adjacent to the coast, which they named Henderson Field after a Marine pilot killed at Midway. But in the darkness after midnight on August 9, the Japanese navy struck back. In the space of less than an hour, a Japanese task force sank four Allied heavy cruisers, permanently crippled an American destroyer, and killed more than 1,300 American and Australian sailors in one of the worst defeats the United States Navy had ever suffered. The remainder of the Allied fleet had to retreat for its own safety, leaving the Marines stranded on the island with no naval support. The Japanese controlled the nighttime seas, and the Marines on Guadalcanal found themselves with almost no artillery, and vulnerable to naval bombardment—especially at night when their aircraft from Henderson Field couldn't defend them. To make matters worse, the Japanese attack had come when they were still transferring supplies from their ships to the beach, so the sixteen thousand Allied troops on the ground were left with only about half of the food rations, ammunition, and other supplies they had expected to need for the operation. General A. A. Vande-grift, the commander of the division, estimated their food supplies would last them only ten days.

On land, the Allies controlled only about ten square miles of Guadalcanal—roughly half a percent of its total area. They held a tight perimeter around Henderson Field, while Japanese troops roamed with impunity elsewhere in the densely jungled, mountainous island. Over the months to come, Japanese land forces would make repeated, ferocious attempts to recapture the airstrip—in September, the 1st Raider Battalion under Merritt Edson held off an hours-long attack overnight on a ridge just above the airfield. Six weeks later, in October, a force under the command of Lewis "Chesty" Puller held its position against a two-night onslaught, after which the remaining Japanese disappeared back into the jungle. Vandegrift had his perimeter, a tiny cutout on the north end of the two-thousand-square-mile island, but there was no information on what the Japanese were preparing in the areas beyond, and the American forces were sufficiently scant that sending large patrols into the jungle risked weakening their hold on the airfield. The situation was barely tenable, but at least those higher up on the chain of command agreed on the importance of the island; on October 24 President Roosevelt ordered the Joint Chiefs of Staff to reinforce Guadalcanal immediately. That was where Carlson came in.

Carlson made two trips to Guadalcanal from the Raider camp on Espiritu Santo, and he returned from the second one in late October with a plan in place. He would take two companies of his Raiders—a third of the battalion's total strength—and land with them at Aola Bay, forty miles to the east of Henderson Field and the Marine perimeter. There, they would provide security for the Navy Seabees as they landed materials and heavy equipment to begin the construction of a second airfield. It was to be a short mission, just a day or two until Army forces arrived to relieve them, but at least it was better than whiling away the days at camp.

The night before the landing, Carlson wrote a letter to his father and sister back in Plymouth. "Another one of these zero hours," he began. "Always there is the same suspense—the wondering about the shape events will take when the landing occurs. From the standpoint of pure adventure there is nothing to equal it. But the issues at stake place this far above sensational adventure. It is another blow in the succession that must accumulate before the final victory can be won." He assured them of his continued sense of fatalism, which had served him well so far. "I am really more at peace with myself now than I have ever been," he said. "Not that I am satisfied with my work—or that I feel that my work is done. Far from it. But—my conscience is clear. I have been honest in my effort. And I have tried to follow the inner light. My faith in Divine guidance is supreme."

The mission would turn out to be far more than just a couple of days' worth of security for the Seabees. General Vandegrift—who had been Carlson's battalion commander when he first went to China in 1927—was extremely hard-pressed in his campaign to establish control of Guadalcanal. As the American and Japanese navies fought a series of desperate, pitched battles that lit up the night sky with explosions, the vagaries of their struggle determined what supplies could reach the Americans, and what reinforcements the Japanese were able to land. Henderson Field was barely in hand, and there were Japanese artillery positions in the jungle—collectively dubbed "Pistol Pete" by the Americans—that regularly shelled the airfield, but the Americans could not figure out their locations because they were so well hidden. While the Navy fought for mastery of the coastal waters, Vandegrift needed a ground force that could take the fight to the Japanese in the jungle, and that was the opportunity Carlson's Raiders afforded him.

For this mission, Vandegrift decided to let Carlson off his leash. Lieutenant Colonel Merrill Twining, an operations officer for the 1st Marine Division, would be Carlson's point of contact at Vandegrift's headquarters, monitoring the course of his mission. As Twining recalled: "I was told only that there would be a raid, that Carlson would report by radio, and that under no circumstances was I to give him anything whatever in the way of orders or instructions." Carlson called in three more companies of his Raiders, leaving one in reserve on Espiritu Santo, to lead a patrol in force through the forty miles of dense, unmapped jungle between Aola and the Marine perimeter at Henderson Field. By the time the mission was done, they would cover nearly four times that distance. The goal was to root out Japanese forces encamped in the jungle, to harass newly landed reinforcements, to find the trails the Japanese were using to move men and supplies, and if possible, to find the "Pistol Pete" installations and destroy them. Under the umbrella of that mission, Carlson had full autonomy to lead his Raiders as he saw fit.

This time, the Raiders landed on the shore at Aola in the shallow-draft, motorized landing craft known as Higgins boats, no more rubber rafts for them. Beacons burned on shore as they approached,

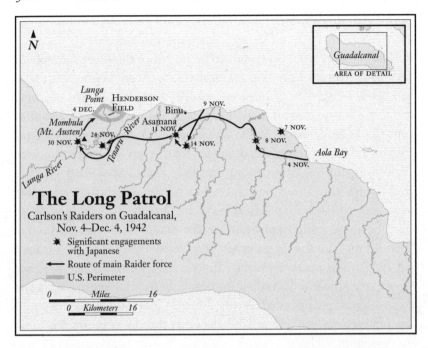

N

Guadalcanal
AREA OF DETAIL

Lunga
Point   HENDERSON
4 DEC.   FIELD   Binu.   9 NOV.
Mombula   Asamana
(Mt. Austen)   11 NOV.   7 NOV.
30 NOV.   24 NOV.   8 NOV.
                                        Aola Bay
Lunga River   4 NOV.

The Long Patrol
Carlson's Raiders on Guadalcanal,
Nov. 4–Dec. 4, 1942

✴ Significant engagements
   with Japanese
← Route of main Raider force
   U.S. Perimeter

0   Miles   16

0   Kilometers   16

twelve-foot-high bonfires to show them the way to the landing site. A small group of men waited for them on the dark gray volcanic sand of the beach. Their leader was Martin Clemens, a coastwatcher for the British Colonial Service who had become a major asset to the Allied campaign due to his familiarity with the geography of Guadalcanal and his ability to recruit islanders for intelligence work against the Japanese. As the Raiders arrived, Clemens was ready with a group of 150 Solomon Islanders to provide support for them— fifty as scouts and a hundred as porters to help the Marines carry the food and ammunition they would need.

Carlson had no map other than a mimeographed outline of the island with a few rivers sketched in, so his men would have to rely entirely on their native guides to find their way through the jungle. In the metaphors of his own mind, the islanders on Guadalcanal were to his Marines what the peasants had been to the Eighth Route Army in China: the ordinary people so often invisible in military accounts who, if they were treated with kindness and respect, could provide guidance and logistical support—and who, with their detailed knowledge of the local area, could be a decisive source of advantage over an enemy who alienated them with cruelty.

A case in point was Jacob Vouza, the leader of Carlson's scouts. Vouza, a Solomon Islander, was a native police sergeant who had been captured by the Japanese just after the initial American landing in August 1942. They tortured him for information about the disposition of American forces, bayoneted him, and left him for dead. As Vouza told it in a letter to a New Zealand friend after the war, "Well I was caughted by the Japs and one of the Japanese Naval Officer questioned me but I was refuse to answer & I was bayoneted by a long sword twice on my chest, through my throught, a cutted the side of my tongue." Vouza survived the attack and dragged himself on the ground through several miles of jungle to reach the American lines, where he warned them of the coming Japanese attack. Vouza was treated for his wounds at the American field hospital—including replacement of the three-quarters of a gallon of blood he had lost—and after he recovered he became a fierce ally through the campaign on Guadalcanal, helping to organize and rally the islanders to support the Allied efforts against the Japanese. As Vouza himself put it, "After I wad discharged from the hospital, I wad do my fighting with the Japs & paid back all what they have done with me." Vouza was far from being the only islander to suffer from Japanese violence, and the scouts carried their own long knives which—when opportunities arose—they intended to use for their own acts of revenge.

It was essential to Carlson's vision that the islanders be treated as equals, and in the course of the mission his Marines would form close bonds with their guides and porters that lasted long after the war. "I am proud to say, we dearly loved Vouza and all of his brave men," recalled one of the Marines years later. In the 1970s, the surviving veterans of Carlson's Raiders collected thirty-seven tons of school supplies to send to Guadalcanal and funded a scholarship in Jacob Vouza's name to support boys and girls from the Solomons to receive a secondary education in the capital.

In a segregated United States military, there were no Black soldiers in Carlson's column, but the force that entered the jungle was otherwise as integrated as it could be, and Carlson liked it that way. Among his Marines were several Mexican Americans and others of Hispanic and Latino descent, along with Filipino Americans, Armenians, Jews, and pretty much anyone who was not kept out by segregation rules. One of the Mexican Americans in Carlson's battalion

Raider column on Guadalcanal, guided by Solomon Islanders.

recalled, "Being Marines was kind of a melting pot, and we all got together, it was like being in a mini–United States. You've got Jews, you've got Italians, you've got Indians, and they all learned to live together." Along with the Marines there were also the 150 Solomon Islanders in the column as support personnel and scouts, while two Navajos came along as code-talkers for radio communications with the Marine headquarters at Henderson Field.

Of only three Koreans in the U.S. military at the time, two were attached to Carlson's battalion as Japanese interpreters. The younger of the two, forty-year-old Yong Hak Park, had been a minister at the Korean Methodist Church in Oakland, California, but he put his religious calling on hold to serve in the war. "I must tell my people that those of us residing outside Korea must sacrifice everything to win freedom for our beloved country," he explained to a reporter. Both men had learned Japanese while growing up in annexed Korea before they fled separately to the United States, and though they weren't commissioned in the military (because Asian immigrants still weren't allowed to become U.S. citizens) they held honorary officer's rank as second lieutenants. They were popular with the Raiders, who gave them the affectionate if cringeworthy nicknames "Gung" and "Ho." A photo of the two men appeared in the papers afterward with Carlson, his arms around their shoulders. Their main duty was to

Interpreter Yong Hak Park (left) having breakfast as the porters pack up for the day's march.

interrogate captured Japanese soldiers, though they later said that they didn't get much work to do because the Raiders took so few prisoners—and when they did, the captives "didn't last that long."

The jungle was loud, filled with screeches and howls and human-sounding noises at night. Land crabs and lizards skittered and rustled on leaves. Marines described birds that barked like a dog and others that sounded like someone banging two blocks of wood together. The woods were filled with dangers that had nothing to do with the war: barbed vines, disease-carrying insects, crocodiles. The jungle reached high overhead and was so dense with vegetation that when you were in it you could only see a few feet in either direction unless you were looking straight down a trail, and then only until the trail turned out of sight. Open spaces that offered a wider field of view were rare, but they included rivers, occasional coconut plantations that had been carved out of the jungle (now abandoned because of the war), and fields of sharp kunai grass, which grew to several feet high. Hiding places were everywhere, and even without the skills of the Japanese at camouflage an enemy could be unseeable at a distance of only a few yards. A machine gun could be hidden in the interwoven roots of a banyan tree. An ambush could be set just around the corner of a tight turn in a trail. A man could move on his stomach through the fields of high kunai grass while barely making a ripple on the surface—even more invisibly if there was a breeze in the air. In short, there was no such thing as a feeling of safety, anywhere.

Between the five companies of Marines and the native support personnel Carlson had about a thousand mouths to feed. Canned C-rations would have been impossibly heavy and cumbersome, and since the number of porters was limited, every sack of food they brought along represented a crate of ammunition that had to be left behind. So he followed the example of the Chinese guerrillas with their grain-filled socks slung over their shoulders on the march. Each man in Carlson's battalion was issued extra socks filled with four days' nonperishable rations: mainly rice, along with allotments of salt pork, raisins, and coffee or tea. The men cooked for themselves as they had been trained at Jacques Farm, using their helmets as pots to boil water and cook rice. Whatever tin cans they happened to possess became prized objects, as having one meant you could boil water for coffee at the same time you were making rice. Every four days Carlson would arrange by radio for a Higgins boat to deliver another shipment of rations at an agreed-upon landing site along the coast. A patrol with a group of native porters would meet the boat and carry the supplies back to camp, where they were doled out into the men's socks. Within days, the men started complaining about the

Twilight patrol on Guadalcanal.

monotony of the rice, though the islanders were reportedly unbothered since it was one of their staple foods already.

When the Raiders were on the move they traveled as a column, single file on the narrow trails, each man walking a few feet behind the man in front of him. A single company of nearly 150 men would stretch out for a quarter of a mile. When they had to move at night they stayed closer together, each man with a hand resting on the pack of the man in front of him. Carlson's strategy was to set a succession of base camps, where he would establish a temporary headquarters for the battalion and send company-sized patrols to fan out in different directions to try to find signs of Japanese activity. If a patrol made contact with the enemy, it would radio back to Carlson at the base and he would in turn radio one of the other companies to close in on their position from a different direction, to hit the Japanese force from the flank or the rear. Once the area was clear, they would move on to the next camp.

Carlson applied what he had learned from Zhu De about disguising one's numbers, using a small, platoon-sized advance force with automatic weapons to pin down the enemy and make them think they had found the main body of American troops, while the bulk of the company crept wide through the jungle to come around and attack from the side. They would win most of their skirmishes this way—remarkably, since the Japanese simply did not seem to catch

Carlson washing his feet in a river on Guadalcanal.

on to Carlson's ruse, even after he had used it multiple times. It confirmed his impressions from China, that Japanese troops—for all of their bravery and willingness to die—were not trained for creativity on the battlefield and had difficulty adapting on the fly.

The Raiders were not always successful, though. One of their deadliest encounters was on November 11, a week into the mission, when they lost ten men. C Company was patrolling a trail that led from their base camp to the village of Asamana, in an area where the native scouts had reported Japanese sightings. The trail emerged from the jungle into an abandoned coconut plantation, overgrown with rotten coconuts and palm fronds littering the ground near a few deserted, crumbling shacks. They saw empty Japanese ration containers on the ground and other signs of recent activity. Ahead was an open field of kunai grass about three feet high, and beyond the grassy clearing was the jungle again. The heat was oppressive, and the Marines in the patrol were miles from camp with hardly any water. A point squad moved ahead, inching along the trail into the open field, which was surrounded on three sides by the jungle. There was no sign of the enemy so the main column moved forward in single file behind them, sending flankers out to the sides.

Once they were fully exposed in the field and the point squad had just reached the jungle at the other side, they heard the first rifle shots. The Raiders formed up into a skirmish line and ran, as hard as they could, toward the jungle, firing back, but the shooting from the jungle exploded into a cacophony of machine guns and rifles, mortar shells and hand grenades. The first few men were killed instantly and the others dove to the ground and rolled into the grass as bullets hissed all around them.

They had stumbled onto a Japanese force that numbered in the hundreds, far larger than they had been expecting, so all they could do was to try to get back to the coconut grove and radio for support. The men took turns moving and giving one another covering fire. Every third man would get up, sprint in a zigzag pattern for a few steps, and then dive back into the grass. They started running out of ammunition. More wounded fell. A private named Lowell Bulger crawled on his stomach through the long grass, hoping there were no snipers in the trees who could see him. He came across an injured Raider who was nearly delirious from loss of blood. He waited for a lull in the shooting when he might be able to carry the wounded man back, but when the lull didn't come he gave up and grabbed another Marine to help him drag the injured man along the ground toward the coconut grove, crouching low as machine gun bullets cut the grass above their heads. "No death could be worse than the agonizing exhaustion and pain of trying to drag a man as you are creepin and crawlin," he recalled. Mortar shells whistled down and exploded as they hauled the man to safety, but fortunately for them, the one that fell closest was a dud that hit the ground with a thump and failed to detonate.

The rest of the patrol behind them set up mortars to provide covering fire, while the radioman made contact with Carlson back at the base three miles away. Carlson told them to try to hold their position and directed the others to come to their aid from the rear of the Japanese force. Two other companies, D and E, had encounters of their own, though—apparently the force pinning down Company C was a rear guard protecting a larger movement of Japanese troops to the west. The fighting in different quarters lasted through the day and into the late afternoon. Carlson hiked up to Company C's location from the base camp, arriving around 4:30 p.m. Given the apparent size of the Japanese force there, he decided to call in an air strike. He collected everyone's white T-shirts, then sent Bulger and another unwounded Raider back out into the field to lay them out in an arrow formation, pointing the planes toward the concentration of Japanese in the jungle. Ten minutes later, a squadron of two dive-bombers and four fighter planes from Henderson Field roared overhead and bombed the Japanese position, then the fighters came back for repeated strafing runs.

Under cover of the air attack, the Raiders tried to bring in their wounded but they couldn't find all of the injured men before night fell. A private named James Clusker remained out in the field, shot in the back and unable to move, drifting in and out of consciousness. He spent the night lying in the tall grass hoping to avoid discovery. There was another wounded Raider nearby, a private named Owen Barber (known to his friends as "Little Chick") who lay within earshot but neither of them could move so they couldn't help each other. During the night, a Japanese patrol discovered Barber. Private Clusker lay still in his hiding spot, listening helplessly as Barber screamed. Eventually it became quiet, and the patrol moved on. In the light of the morning, Clusker was rescued by a party of Raiders looking for the wounded. They found the mutilated body of Little Chick nearby where the enemy patrol had left it. The Japanese had cut off his genitals and stuffed them into his mouth before they killed him.

Even as Carlson's men were retrieving their dead and wounded from that battle, back home Raymond Gram Swing was making the Raiders the centerpiece of his Armistice Day broadcast. Carlson's acquaintance from New York was by this point one of the most prominent radio news commentators of the war era, with listeners at more than one hundred stations around the country. In memory of the end of World War I, he decided to tell his audience what he knew about the Raiders and their potential to help lead America to victory in the current conflict. "The Marines are tough," said Swing, "but there is a special branch of the Marines which is especially tough. These men are called Carlson's Raiders." He recounted how Carlson had trudged thousands of miles behind Japanese lines in North China as a Marine intelligence officer, how he gave speeches on behalf of the Chinese before Pearl Harbor. Now, he said, Carlson was helping lead the way in the fight against Japan. "Carlson's Raiders have learned to combine guerrilla fighting as perfected by the Chinese, with the Indian fighting of our own history, and to conduct it on the two dimensions of amphibious warfare," he said. "They are a peculiarly American brand of commandos, and I repeat that they are tougher than marines, if there can be such a thing."

In Carlson's style of leadership, Swing saw hope for America's future. Not just to win the war, but to build a peace that would be more enduring than the Armistice of 1918. Such a peace required not just the courage to defeat the enemy, said Swing, but also the humility to recognize our inadequacies in the past. He talked about Carlson's gung ho meetings—how Carlson taught his Marines about democracy and the reasons why they fought, how he empowered his men to act as individuals, gave them dignity, encouraged them to think of their own stake in defending America's freedoms. Carlson was not just teaching his Raiders how to fight, said Swing, he was also teaching them wisdom. "So it *can* be done," he concluded. "War can be fought by sharpening the intelligence, by increasing, rather than diminishing the democratic fellowship with human beings." There were many groups in America and abroad working to bring a better world into being, he said, but "there is none more inspiring than these tough raiders under Evans Carlson. . . . They are a steady invitation to all civilian Americans to think as hard and live as hard for true democracy as they are doing it in Guadalcanal."

———

Be that as it may, up close there was little that was abstract or high-minded about what Carlson's men were doing on Guadalcanal. It was raw and it was brutal. Wearing cotton fatigues through daily drenching rains, sleeping in the mud in their wet, dissolving clothes, the men were literally rotting. Jungle sores festered and oozed on their bodies, covering their backs and arms and genitals. Their feet swelled so severely that some of the men cut their boots off and wore wraps of dirty cloth instead. Swarms of mosquitoes covered every sliver of exposed skin. Since the Japanese now controlled most of the world's quinine supply for preventing malaria, American troops in the South Pacific had to rely on Atabrine, a synthetic, foul-tasting medication that turned the skin and eyes a sickly lemon color and was rumored among the men to cause sterility. Many chose to skip it, with dire results; more than a hundred of the Raiders had to be evacuated for malaria even as others stayed on to fight in spite of it, their aim trembling as they shivered with fever. One Marine had chills so severe he rolled himself on the ashes of a campfire to try to warm himself up. They suffered from constant diarrhea in spite of the iodine they used to treat their drinking water. They were hungry all the time and could hardly think about anything else. They had almost no sanitary products and brushed their teeth with dirt, using their fingers. They were filthy, and smelled horrible.

The Japanese, though, were no better off. The first enemy soldiers Carlson's men killed seemed strong and healthy, but as the weeks ground on and the Raiders became weakened and malnourished, the men they shot appeared sicker and sicker as well. As the American and Japanese naval forces fought for control of the maritime channels to Guadalcanal, their respective ground forces were left to suffer from chronic shortages of food and ammunition. On one afternoon, up a river gorge, a platoon of Raiders came upon ten Japanese at a campfire on a spit that jutted into the river. The Marines killed all of them, then inspected the bodies. They were "a pitiful sight," recalled one, "emaciated beyond words, pale and sickly-looking." Some of them were crippled—one had a crutch, another a makeshift splint on his leg. They still had their rifles, but almost no ammunition. Not one of them had a full magazine.

It seemed the enemy was never far off. The evidence of their passage ahead of the Raiders was visible in paths they had cut with machetes, in abandoned campsites, in ration containers with Japanese script strewn on the ground of empty villages. Sometimes, the only signs of them were the bodies of their dead. In mid-November, Oscar Peatross—he of the errant boat at Makin, now a captain and commander of Company B—was so exhausted when he returned to the Raider base camp in an abandoned native village that he lay his blanket on the ground in an empty thatched hut and went to sleep without digging a foxhole first. But the camp came under fire in the middle of the night, so he got up and started wearily digging with his helmet in a patch of soft ground at the edge of the hut. A few inches down, he uncovered a forehead, and then a face. Japanese. He moved to a different part of the hut and started digging again. His helmet struck something hard and he uncovered part of another man. He tried again and found another, then another. But it was too dangerous to move from where he was, so he finally lay back down on the dirt floor and went back to sleep, with the remains of the enemy dead rotting beneath him.

Death became ordinary and matter-of-fact. Carlson made few notations in his diary while he was in the jungle, but the occasional fragments speak well enough for the routine. On one day late in the mission he scribbled: "0950. Killed Jap on trail coming in our direction. Nothing of importance found on body." Less than an hour later: "1025 Killed 2nd Jap on trail coming in our direction. Neither Jap was armed but showed signs of starving to death or dysentery. Nothing found." They killed without mercy, even as the deteriorating condition of the enemy would haunt some of them later on. Sometimes, when searching the body of a dead Japanese soldier, a Marine would find a photograph of the man's wife, perhaps with a baby. And then, for a fleeting moment, the enemy became human. But only for a moment, and they returned to the task they were given. Because even for what may have been the most high-minded and idealistic battalion under American command, war, at its essence, was butchery.

On some days, their mission in the jungle seemed like it would never end and all they could think about was the food they weren't getting enough of. There were instances of theft among the men, and Carlson worried about a breakdown of group trust if it continued. Although he encouraged a spirit of equality between officers and enlisted men, he was still responsible for discipline. One day a young man who had been a hunter back at home led an expedition to hunt for wild game, and came back to the camp with fresh meat for their dinner. When he got there, though, his tin can for boiling coffee had gone missing. Carlson called a group meeting and explained what had happened. He said he wouldn't tolerate theft, and if any Raider was caught stealing from another, the others should shoot him. "Or if you can't shoot a buddy," he told them, "bring him to me and I'll shoot him."

On other days, things went quickly, and the long hours of dread and uncertainty gave way to sudden, explosive slaughter. On November 30, an understrength squad of six Raiders patrolling in a heavy rain happened onto a bivouac site where a large body of what they estimated to be a hundred Japanese soldiers were huddled under shelters from the downpour. Their weapons were stacked against trees to the side, out of reach. The six Marines charged the camp with their BARs and Tommy guns on automatic, gunning down every man they could see. A few got away, and they hunted them down in the woods like animals. When they were done there were more than seventy dead Japanese strewn about the campsite or lying in the nearby jungle. The squad of Raiders suffered no casualties at all, not a single wound.

The mission only got harder the longer it went on. After a couple of weeks, Carlson had shifted their route inland, to make a full circuit around the Marine perimeter at Henderson Field, a few miles beyond the line of control. As they moved deeper into the jungle in search of scattered enemy forces it became impossible to continue receiving supplies by boat along the coast—it was just too far for the porters to carry them—so Carlson arranged by radio for an air drop. On the first run, an American cargo plane from Henderson Field dropped crates of food with attached parachutes, which floated down to land in impossible-to-reach places. So the flight crew returned to try again, this time skipping the parachutes and just shoving fifty-pound sacks of rice and five-gallon cans of hardtack and raisins out the side of the plane at low altitude. Some of the sacks fell into the river and could not be retrieved. Some were lost to the jungle no matter how hard the Raiders hunted for them. And as always, they were never alone. While searching for one of the cans of food, a private named Glenn Mitchell was shot dead by a Japanese sniper.

Their food rations declining, and their strength eroded by disease and infections, Carlson's men still pushed on. Just beyond the Marine perimeter stood a sharp, forbidding peak called Mombula, or Mount Austen, which had a clear view over the Allied base area. It was the most likely site for the "Pistol Pete" artillery that had been hammering the airfield. The Raiders climbed the mountain in the pouring rain, on a route so steep they had to tie ropes to themselves to pull their equipment and one another up the side. They eventually found what they were looking for, following a Japanese telephone wire near the top which led them into a ravine where they found an artillery position with a 75mm mountain gun and a 37mm antitank gun. Nearby they found another site. They dismantled the guns, scattering the pieces down the side of a cliff, and destroyed the ammunition.

On December 2, Vandegrift ordered the Raiders home. Their work was done: they had effectively cleared the immediate region outside the Marine perimeter of Japanese forces; they had destroyed the artillery that threatened the U.S. airfield; and they had intercepted and mapped the trails by which the Japanese had been moving men and information. Henderson Field was now secure and the broader battle for Guadalcanal was running well enough in the Allies' favor that the remaining Japanese troops on the island were cut off from supplies; by February the Japanese would abandon the island altogether. Carlson called a gung ho meeting on the morning of December 3 to share the news with his men that their month-long mission was complete. He led the Raiders in singing the Marines' Hymn, followed by "Onward Christian Soldiers." The indigenous scouts, who had learned the second song from missionaries, joined in the singing. Carlson told the men how much their service had meant. "You men here are the creme de la creme," he told them. "You have proved yourselves among the best fighting men in this war."

On the afternoon of December 4, 1942, after thirty days in the jungle, Carlson finally led his men back out through the Marine perimeter at Henderson Field. They walked in a single-file column just as they had moved through the jungle. The men were painfully thin and jaundiced, skin covered in sores. Some had no boots. Most had grown rough beards like castaways and their uniforms were filthy and tattered. It took a moment for the sentry on duty to recognize them. Then: "Holy CAT!" he shouted, "Here come Carlson's boys!" They carried a few wounded men in stretchers, and these were loaded into waiting ambulances that the 1st Marine Division had prepared for them. It was still eight miles to their bivouac site but Carlson declined the offer of motor transport for the rest of his men. We walked in, said Carlson, and we'll walk out.

CHAPTER 19

HOME FRONTS

L IVING IN A HOTEL in New York and revising her new book for publication, Agnes Smedley made the rounds of cocktail parties in the fall of 1942 with Freda Utley, her friend from China. After twenty years abroad, Smedley had finally returned to the United States in the summer of 1941, driven out of China by depression and her fear of the Japanese. She had also run out of money and had to borrow funds for her passage home from Carlson, who saw her briefly in Hong Kong that January when he was on his way home from visiting the cooperatives. She was afraid of being detained by the Japanese if she stayed in China any longer, but it wasn't easy to come home to an America where people seemed like foreigners to her. Yet she had nowhere else to go. "I had become a part of the vast struggle of China," she wrote in her book, "yet I remained American in many ways. I had, in truth, become one of those creatures who have no home anywhere."

She often felt like an outsider when she mingled with the intellectual urbanites of New York, as if they inhabited different worlds. Over sherry and highballs one evening at Freda Utley's apartment in Greenwich Village, she was enraged by several fashionable women who refused to believe that the Japanese had ever committed any atrocities in China. Nothing Agnes could say would change their minds. A man trying to be provocative accused her and Freda of being condescending to the Chinese because, as he suggested, the only possible reason someone would claim to "like China" was to feed their own ego. Later, she found herself cornered by an older man who had once been a high-ranking figure in the Communist

Party of the USA but resigned after the purges in the Soviet Union. He was bitter and disillusioned now, and assumed that she was, too. He kept trying to get her to reminisce about the days when they were younger and had revolutionary dreams. "Agnes," he told her, "you and I will never live through such glorious days as in the past, will we?" But she still had faith—not in the Soviets anymore, but in the Chinese, in Zhu De and his Eighth Route Army, though none of the cocktail-party set wanted to hear it. The Chinese bored them. Freda Utley, who had been disillusioned with the Soviet Union since Agnes first met her in Hankow, kept talking over Agnes to the old ex-Communist, insisting, "Oh, she feels just the same as we do, but will not admit it." Agnes was sick of it all.

If the anti-Communists made for poor company, the Communists themselves—the American variety, at least—were even worse. Agnes met a group of them at a different New York party and was revolted by their smug self-satisfaction. "With withering scorn they condemned everyone else to perdition—as 'half-baked liberals, corny illiterates, Fascists,'" she wrote to a friend. "They say everybody is running to them now to get knowledge and wisdom and they are dispensing it to the worthy. I decided that I am not worthy to associate with the American Communists; and I shall not seek their company nor tolerate it in the future." The only Communists she liked were the Chinese kind.

The war drove a wedge between the Americans whose lives involved China. You had to take sides, either Chiang Kai-shek or the Communists. Nobody pretended there was a United Front anymore. The publishing magnate Henry Luce was still Chiang's most influential supporter in the United States, and Agnes met him for the first time in November of 1942, around the time Carlson was leading his men into the jungle at Guadalcanal. They met at a New York party hosted by her publisher, Blanche Knopf, and she spent an hour talking with him on the couch. Mostly, they argued about China. Knopf told Agnes afterward that the only reason Henry Luce had come to the party was because he'd been wanting to meet her. "He's amazingly attractive," Agnes reported to a friend; "which is rather distressing when you consider that I so thoroughly disagree with all his ideas." But at least Henry Luce was entertaining; Freda Utley merely depressed her. "Never in my life have I seen a woman in whose heart and mind every hope on earth has been slain, as has hers," she wrote to the same friend a couple of weeks later. "She used to be a leading British Communist; now a black-minded cynic. She believes in nothing at all, absolutely nothing."

Agnes still dreamed of Carlson. She kept a scrapbook of newspaper clippings about him, which she hoped to give to him someday. She held on to his memory not just because she was quietly in love with him but also because he was the only person who truly saw eye to eye with her about Zhu De and the Eighth Route Army. She wrote about him in the book she was working on, a memoir titled *Battle Hymn of China*. In it, she told the story of how she met Carlson at the basketball game, how they shared their days at Zhu De's headquarters in December of 1937. "He was of Norwegian descent, the son of a Connecticut pastor, and had a profound strain of religious ethics running through his character," she wrote. "His principles were rooted in early American Jeffersonian democracy; that must have been why he felt at home in the political and ethical atmosphere of the Eighth Route Army." She wrote about the Christmas Eve they spent together in Shanxi—how he played his harmonica and they sang "Battle Hymn of the Republic" together. Ever since then, she said, she had always thought of him when she heard the words from the song: "As He died to make men holy, let us die to make men free."

Carlson was far away now, and there was no hope of seeing him in person. But there was one uncanny moment, on a cold and snowy Manhattan afternoon in February of 1943, when Agnes ventured out to a theater to see a film and suddenly there he was—up on the screen, a dozen feet tall, in a newsreel about Guadalcanal. She studied him closely on the flickering screen through a series of clips—standing with a group of Solomon Islanders, saluting a passing jeep, grinning his trademark grin, sitting and talking with his son, who now had a mustache. She could see how much the war was grinding him down. "Evans stood, ragged, bare-headed, as haggard as a rail," she wrote afterward. "He seems to have turned almost gray. . . . Evans has aged ten or fifteen years since he went into the field."

They stayed in contact by mail, but Agnes habitually destroyed her correspondence and Carlson did not take much care with his own, so only a few accidental letters survive. In one of them, a few

Carlson and his son on Guadalcanal.

months after Guadalcanal, he vented about his resentment of the military command to one of the few people he thought would understand him. "I am continually in hot water, even in the midst of a peculiarly vicious war, because I am excruciatingly frank and honest in my criticism and action," he told her. "The only reason I hold my job in the service is because Destiny has graced me with the ability to accomplish results in military affairs."

He told Agnes that he felt frustrated most of the time. He could practically see the future when it came to the war, he said, but that made no difference because none of his superiors would listen to him or follow his lead. For all of his accomplishments, he was still an outsider. "I am as impotent now as I was in the pre-war period," he complained. He said he was "constantly being sabotaged" by senior officers who did not understand that "men are inspired to fight with all that is in them only by leadership based on merit, a profound knowledge of the reasons why they fight, and the conviction that the things for which they fight are worth fighting for."

Carlson had always envisioned his Raiders as the starting point for a broader cultural change in the U.S. military, but that was not happening. He told Agnes he thought the United States would win in the end because of its economic strength, regardless of how the war was conducted. But unless the military adopted his "gung ho" philosophy and started training more of the troops on the model of his Raiders, and unless the American people fully embraced the personal sacrifices needed to defeat Japan, then the cost of the war in blood and treasure would be far out of proportion to what it could be if Americans just understood that there was "no smooth road to freedom."

The alliance between China and the United States would never be one of equals. Even without their history of one-sided treaties and Opium Wars and Anglo dominance in Shanghai, the governments of the United States and Great Britain simply did not consider China a full partner in World War II. An influential member of the Senate Foreign Relations Committee described the Big Four alliance of the U.S., Britain, China, and Russia as being a "three-power alliance (with China added as a pleasant gesture)." Britain's primary concern was Hitler, not the Japanese, so Churchill mainly wanted China to protect Britain's colonies in Asia if it could—beyond that, he called it "an absolute farce" that China should be treated as one of the great powers. General George Marshall, the U.S. Army's chief of staff, likewise viewed the fight in Europe as the primary one, so to his mind China's role was simply to keep as many Japanese troops as possible occupied so they couldn't be used in the Pacific or against Russia.

Roosevelt and Marshall never expected the Chinese to prevail against Japan—a U.S. Joint Intelligence Committee report in June of 1942 stated that China's army "has so many inherent weaknesses that it will not be able to stage a major offensive." Nevertheless, two-thirds of Japan's military manpower was committed to the occupation of China and Manchuria, and a collapse of Chiang Kai-shek's government or a revolt from hard-line KMT factions could lead to peace terms with Japan, which would free much of that vast Japanese army for redeployment.

America's military support for China was thus oriented mainly toward keeping China alive and at least partially independent, while also using it as an air base in hopes of bombing Japan. As the Japanese cut off almost all routes of supply to the wartime capital of Chongqing—including the 715-mile overland road from Burma that the Chinese had constructed earlier in the war as a last-ditch supply line—the United States was reduced to flying military supplies from India into China on a spectacularly dangerous air route over the Himalayas as the only means of keeping Chiang Kai-shek in the fight. Later, the United States would send fifteen thousand troops—mostly segregated Black engineering battalions, who were typically assigned the most difficult manual labor—to join Indian, Chinese, and Burmese workers in the backbreaking effort of carving a new road from Ledo, India, through the jungles and mountains of northern Burma to reestablish an overland supply route into southwest China. American forces in China proper, however, would be minimal until the very end of the war.

The ranking American officer in China was Joseph Stilwell, President Roosevelt's military liaison to Chiang Kai-shek. He was the sharp-tongued Army general who had been military attaché when Carlson was in China, and now he served as the overall commander of American ground forces in the China-Burma-India theater (though that was not saying much, for there were hardly any U.S. troops in China; even the Caribbean had a higher priority for supplies from Washington than the CBI theater did). Without American forces of his own to command, much of the tension between Stilwell and Chiang revolved around Stilwell's efforts to take command of Chinese armies himself. Chiang found Stilwell arrogant and imperious, while Stilwell, for his part, saw Chiang as corrupt, self-interested, and unable to lead China's troops effectively against Japan. In his diary, Stilwell described the Chinese government as "a structure based on fear and favor, in the hands of an ignorant, arbitrary, stubborn man."

For all of the rancor between Stilwell and Chiang Kai-shek, at least the United States maintained direct relations with the KMT government in Chongqing. They sent no one to liaise with the Communist forces in northern China until nearly the end of the war. After the breakdown of the anti-Japanese United Front in 1941, Chiang had established an economic and military blockade of the north to cut the Communists off from communication with the outside world, and he refused to allow any American weapons or other aid to go to their base areas. The United States still might have insisted that its aid be shared among all significant military factions in China that were fighting Japan, but under pressure from Chiang's government it did not.

As a result, U.S. military aid to China in World War II went exclusively to Chiang Kai-shek, who used some of it to fight the Japanese, and the rest to blockade the Communists and strengthen his own position domestically against other factions of the KMT. For fear of losing Chiang's cooperation against Japan, Roosevelt's emissaries (Stilwell excepted) generally tried to appease him. They went out of their way to avoid communicating with the Communists—for example, when Roosevelt's administrative assistant Lauchlin Currie visited Chongqing in the late summer of 1942, he pointedly refused to meet with Zhou Enlai, the Communists' representative in Chongqing, calling it "impolitic." The Communists invited the United States to send one or more representatives to visit the areas of North China that were under their control, but Currie ignored that as well.

By the beginning of 1943 some American diplomats could see that a resumption of the civil war in China was inevitable. "The 'United Front' is now definitely a thing of the past," reported U.S. embassy staff member John Service on January 23, "and it is impossible to find any optimism regarding the possibility of its resurrection as long as the present tendencies continue and the present leadership of the Kuomintang [KMT], both civil and military, remains in power. Far from improving, the situation is deteriorating." He noted how much of the KMT army's best resources had been diverted from the fight against the Japanese in order to blockade the Communists. Furthermore, as it had done in the time of the White Terror in the late 1920s, the KMT government showed a growing obsession with suppressing anything it deemed communist or subversive, to the point that it was abandoning even the pretense of trying to build a democratic form of government after the war. The question, said Service, wasn't whether civil war in China could be avoided, but whether it could at least be delayed until after Japan was defeated. Because if it couldn't, he predicted it would have "disastrous" consequences for America's campaigns in the Pacific.

Nevertheless, all suggestions that the United States try to ensure that some of the Lend-Lease supplies it shipped to China be shared with Zhu De and Mao Zedong were met with stiff resistance from Chiang's supporters in the United States, especially those with connections to the missionary community. Henry Luce was the organizer of United China Relief, the largest nongovernmental organization to collect public donations for China during the war, and he insisted that all of its funds go to Chiang's government in Chongqing. Chiang was indeed a Methodist, but even if his personal beliefs were sincere, there was little that was outwardly "Christian" about his governance. Nevertheless, the alternative, as his American supporters saw it, was godless communists.

These supporters argued that any aid to Mao and Zhu De to help them fight the Japanese would only undermine Chiang Kai-shek. As Stanley Hornbeck, the State Department's advisor on political relations, put it in January of 1943, giving military aid to the Chinese Communists "would launch us on a course of playing both sides in a foreign country, which we never have followed, which I trust we will never follow, and which, if followed, would be both vicious and stupid." The United Front alliance between the KMT and the CCP may still have existed on paper, but to American officials like Hornbeck it was clear that the two parties in China were enemies, and if the United States was to be involved in China at all, it had to choose between them.

Chiang Kai-shek's prestige in the eyes of the American public was greatly enhanced when his wife, Soong Mei-ling—a graduate of Wellesley College and a fluent English speaker—visited the United States for medical treatment in the late fall of 1942 and used the opportunity to go on a six-week speaking tour on behalf of her husband. On February 18, 1943, she became the first person of Chinese descent, and only the second woman of any race, to speak before a joint session of Congress. She spoke with passion about the need for America to support China's heroic resistance against Japan, and "China," in her formulation, meant Chiang Kai-shek and his Nationalist Party.

Soong Mei-ling's speech brought the wartime Congress to its feet in wild applause. "Goddam it," said one congressman afterward, "I never saw anything like it. Madame Chiang had me on the verge of bursting into tears." Thanks to crowds in the tens of thousands who turned out for her speaking engagements, amplified by fawning radio and print coverage of her tour (which landed her once again on the cover of *Time* magazine), China's resistance to Japan gained a visible face in America—a cultured, eloquent, feminine, Christian-Chinese face—and support for Soong Mei-ling meant support for her husband. The Chinese Communists, by contrast, would never have a representative in the United States with anything even remotely approaching her stature, and so they would never benefit from the same public admiration as their KMT rivals. That difference would matter.

From their capital at Yan'an, isolated from the Allies by Chiang's blockade, the leaders of the Chinese Communist Party continued to proclaim their support for a democratic, coalition government even as the chances of actually creating one seemed increasingly remote. At the opening of the Central Party School at Yan'an in August of 1943, Mao spoke of building a "new democratic society." Unlike the transition to democracy in Europe, he said, which was led by elites, China's "new democracy" would involve the peasants and be led by multiple parties, though it would still be capitalist. Private property should eventually be abolished, but that could wait until the Communists had sufficient control over the country. Until then, there would be not one but two revolutions: the democratic revolution of the present, and the socialist revolution of the future. To put it another way, Mao's party would fight for power in China not on a platform of communism or socialism, but rather on a broad promise of democracy.

Zhu De supported him fully. In a July 1943 article in the Yan'an *Liberation Daily* newspaper, the general argued that one of the reasons the Communists had managed not just to survive but to expand their power during the war, in spite of Chiang Kai-shek's refusal to share weapons and other supplies with them, was because they had used democracy—and specifically *not* socialism—to unify the people in the base areas. "We have practiced complete democracy," he wrote, "so that all anti-Japanese people can enjoy the freedoms of speech, the press, assembly and association and of arming themselves, and we have protected their human and political rights as well as their right to own land and other lawful property." The organization of the general population had succeeded by incorporating other parties, not by excluding them. "Obviously," he explained, "our base areas in the enemy's rear would have disintegrated long ago if we had acted otherwise and practiced a one-party dictatorship."

Mao and Zhu De both recognized in 1943 that the party's most potent appeal was as the bringer of democratic government to China. That was what the educated Chinese liberals wanted, and in a basic form it was what the ordinary people wanted as well—a voice in their own government, at least at the local level, and an end to corruption and oppression—this, in contrast to the increasingly dictatorial conduct of Chiang Kai-shek and the KMT. Few in 1943 advocated directly for communism in China, though in Mao's long-range vision it always lay just behind the public promises of democracy, a latter stage of revolution waiting patiently for its day to come.

As the wartime Chinese Communists devoted themselves to building mass support by trying to give people what they most desired, they formed a vivid contrast to the practices of Chiang Kai-shek's military, which brought little but terror to the Chinese peasants in the areas under KMT control. An American intelligence report from the summer of 1945 captured the horror of the KMT press gangs that kidnapped peasants and forced them to fight the Japanese. "Conscription comes to the Chinese peasant like famine or flood, only more regularly—every year twice—and claims more victims," it said. "You are working in the field looking after your rice . . . [there come] a number of uniformed men who tie your hands behind your back and take you with them. . . . Hoe and plough rust in the field, the wife runs to the magistrate to cry and beg for her husband, the children starve." The report described KMT officials who would seize ten men for every conscript they needed to provide, then force the other nine to purchase their freedom. It described private dealers in conscripts who were barely a degree removed from slave traders, purchasing men from "starved families who need rice more urgently than sons" and selling them for military service. Of well over a million Chinese men who were drafted by the KMT armies in 1943, it is estimated that nearly half died or disappeared before they could join their assigned units to fight the Japanese.

With no news coming in or out from behind the KMT blockade, the Communists and their activities in North China were once again a cipher to the outside world. Edgar Snow worked as a global correspondent for *The Saturday Evening Post* during the war and came back to China in 1943 to collect material for a new book (which he dedicated to Carlson) but he found it impossible to cross the lines to visit Yan'an as he had done in 1936. He reported on breathtaking inflation and low morale in the areas under KMT control—prices had risen 20,000 percent since the start of the war and hoarding was rampant. But with respect to the Communists he was as blind as anyone—until he encountered a group of foreigners who had escaped Beijing just after Pearl Harbor and made their way back to safety by way of the guerrilla base areas. The group included various American and European bankers, businessmen, and professors who had been working in Beijing. One of them, an Oxford scholar named Michael Lindsay, was so taken with the Communists that he stayed behind in the rear areas and would work for them as a radio operator for the rest of the war.

Snow learned from these foreigners that the Communists' organization of the peasant population for military resistance that had so captured Carlson's imagination had not just continued in the shadow of the Japanese occupation but grown dramatically. As Snow put it, "Guerrilla China has become the scene of the broadest effort at mass mobilization and mass education in Chinese history." The basic schematics of organization were the same as when Carlson had been there: the Eighth Route Army and the New Fourth Army were still the regular military of the Communists. Below them were guerrilla units in each county, and below them were the local militias—farmers with some training who operated in their home areas, armed mainly with homemade weapons. At the broadest level, there were the village self-defense forces Carlson had visited, who spied on the Japanese and provided logistical help for the regular army. It was the same basic scheme of organization that Carlson had witnessed, and according to Michael Lindsay, there were now nearly 620,000 militia members just in the base area where he lived.

But the Communists still faced tremendous material difficulties. They did not have enough weapons to arm all of their soldiers (and though not all Communist fighters were volunteers, the coercion they used was nothing compared to the KMT press gangs). Ammunition shortages were chronic. Even as the Chinese Communists received none of the American aid that was going to Chiang Kai-shek, they also got nothing from the Soviet Union because Stalin had abruptly ended his military aid to China in June of 1941, after Hitler's surprise attack on Russia, because he had to focus all of his resources on the war with Germany. As when Carlson was with them, the Chinese Communists still relied mainly on what they could capture from the Japanese, along with such ammunition as they could produce in primitive arsenals in the mountains.

Indeed, so acute were the Communists' shortages of military supplies, Lindsay reported, that the Eighth Route Army could only engage in battles it was certain it could win with minimal use of resources. "If the Chinese had better supplies of ammunition," he wrote, "the whole situation in North China would be changed." In any case, whether the reason was a lack of supplies and equipment— or something more strategic—the Chinese Communists simply did not engage in any further large-scale campaigns against the Japanese after 1940. Notwithstanding the outward impression that they were, as a U.S. diplomat at Chongqing described them in 1944, the most "cohesive, disciplined and aggressively anti-Japanese regime in China," the focus of the Communists after Pearl Harbor was less on confronting the Japanese than on growing their own numbers while letting the KMT bear the brunt of the fighting. One Soviet advisor at Yan'an reported to his superiors that the Communist armies in North China had essentially "folded up military operations since 1941."

Instead, they played to their advantages—small guerrilla attacks against isolated enemy columns, harassment, focusing their energies on making it as costly as possible for the Japanese to establish control in the countryside. This allowed the Communists to devote themselves to the consolidation and expansion of their influence among the rural populations in the base areas, thereby preserving and increasing their strength rather than risking it in the kind of positional warfare that was killing unfathomable numbers of Nationalist soldiers in central China.

Such restraint was perfectly in keeping with the Eighth Route Army's doctrine. As Zhu De had written in 1938 in a treatise on guerrilla warfare, "Even though the anti-Japanese guerrillas have poor weapons, they need not fear the enemy. . . . They should engage in night assaults, ambushes, surprise attacks, and cutting off the enemy communications. They should never risk their lives against the

326 · THE RAIDER

enemy's weapons." Avoiding positional warfare also served the Communists' longer-term purposes; Mao wrote with some frequency on his theory of "protracted war," advising that the Communists must bide their time patiently and build their strength in preparation for a major counterattack in the future—a counterattack that, when it finally came in 1947, would be unleashed not on the Japanese, who were already gone, but on Chiang Kai-shek.

This dramatic expansion of the Chinese Communist Party's influence in North China came at the expense of what Carlson had always seen as its most alluring feature: the free-spirited egalitarianism of its members. As the party grew and expanded, Mao consolidated his own political power within its leadership and began to assert an increasing level of control over its ideology. Taking particular aim at his rivals like Wang Ming and anyone who criticized the CCP's policies or leadership, he launched a "Rectification Campaign" in 1942 to eradicate ideological dissent. Overlapping with a counter-espionage campaign to root out KMT spies at Yan'an, by its end the following year the campaign would effectively rebrand any disagreement with the party's policies as an act of treason.

Party members singled out for attack in the Rectification Campaign were subjected to "struggle sessions"—mass events spanning multiple days where shouting crowds denounced the victims, then forced them to censure themselves by writing extensive self-confessions of their ideological sins. Those who complied were welcomed back into the fold; those who resisted were beaten and abused, some executed or hounded to commit suicide, others forced to do hard labor to "rectify" their thinking. Starting in Yan'an, the campaign spread outward through the areas controlled by the Communists, affecting not just high-level functionaries but party members of all levels, including even elementary school teachers. Those who were not themselves targets had to take part in the denunciation of others and engage in intense small-group study of documents reflecting Mao's political thought. Almost no actual traitors were discovered in the course of the campaign, but many party members confessed imaginary offenses simply to avoid greater punishment. It set a precedent for the mass movements and "thought reform" that would distinguish Mao's rule in the future.

Evans Carlson was quite confident in his judgment that the Chinese Communists were not really communists, and that they were fundamentally democratic. But his impressions, forged in the course of his travels in 1938, had always been based on outward appearances, which by this point were starting to diverge from reality. For on the one hand, the Chinese Communist Party—with its public espousal of democracy—was indeed succeeding in winning mass support from China's peasantry in ways the KMT could never dream of replicating. But at the same time, internally, and far from the view of the likes of Carlson, it was also beginning to exhibit the hallmarks of the much more centralized, authoritarian—and yes, Stalinist—organization that it would become.

CHAPTER 20

BACKLASH

THE PRESS HAD a hard time trying to pin Carlson down after Guadalcanal—he just didn't fit any conventional model of a military hero. "Lt. Col. Evans Fordyce Carlson writes books, kills Japs, plays the harmonica and speaks Chinese," read one profile. "He can deliver polished lectures on Asiatic problems, swim an ice-flecked river naked and exist on a half-sock of rice a day. He wears five rows of campaign ribbons and decorations. . . . He is a fighter, a philosopher, a man of action and an intellectual." It was one of many adulatory profiles of Carlson that appeared in American magazines and newspapers after the Raiders got back from Guadalcanal. This particular one quoted one of his men, who declared, "I have been to hell and back, and I will go to hell and back again, if I can follow one man—Col. Carlson."

Carlson by this point was a leathery, crowlike, sun-beaten creature. He had become so thin his uniform hung loose and baggy on his narrow frame. Even his rough skin seemed a size too large; deep, vertical furrows appeared in each cheek and across his brow when he smiled his broad, friendly grin. His hair was gray and close-cropped. Other than in his imposing height, gone was any resemblance to the blond, ruddy-cheeked young officer who had made the hearts of the colonels' daughters swoon in Quantico twenty years earlier. He looked at least a decade older than his forty-seven years. But still, he crackled with energy.

The wartime press adored the Raiders. *Newsweek* called them "America's first trained guerrillas, whose boast was that they 'know how to do anything,' and who could prove it." A paper in Hawaii predicted that they were destined to become as famous as Rogers' Rangers from the French and Indian War. A paper in New York related with delight that they "swung through jungled islands of the Solomons like bands of Tarzans," and they "tommy-gunned, bayonetted, knifed, hacked, gouged and strangled with a fury that bowled the 'little men' over like nine pins." A Navy sailor who had seen their handiwork declared: "Those Raiders didn't seem to give a damn whether they lived or died, as long as they died shooting Japs!"

Carlson on Guadalcanal.

Amid the torrent of blood-and-guts accounts of the Raiders, Carlson's idealistic side—his passion for democracy, his love of Emerson, his hope for a more equitable future in America—often got lost, though not always. "Colonel Carlson is a true warrior of democracy," wrote an admirer to *The Minneapolis Star* in January of 1943. "In teaching his tough marine raiders, Col. Carlson has made use of democratic philosophy and the humanities as well as the bayonet. Political theory, literature, and—yes—symphony music, have accompanied the Chinese guerrilla and American Indian tactics in the fashioning of a Carlson raider."

Through Carlson and his Raiders, "gung ho" became a permanent feature of the English language, though it took some getting used to. When one of the Raiders wrote a letter home with the postmark Gung Ho, for his camp, it mystified his parents. "We thought it must be an island in the Pacific and were disappointed when we could not find it," his mother told her local paper. Eventually she figured it out. "How wonderful to learn it means 'work together,'" she said, "which is what we all have to do to help our boys win the war."

Inspired by Carlson, the phrase appeared in advertisements for service companies, banks, railroads, and farmers' organizations as a celebration of the importance of working together for the nation's war effort. As they saw it, cooperation in local-level organizations was the way to bring American society together and enable the troops to cooperate in winning the war. "Start practicing 'GUNG HO' at home by supporting and strengthening your farm cooperatives," read one advertisement. "Americans may not understand Chinese," read another, "but they DO understand the meaning of 'Gung Ho!'"

The phrase also started taking on its more enduring connotation of reckless enthusiasm. Just before Christmas in 1942, the nationally syndicated Sergeant Stony Craig comic strip featured a pair of Marines charging into a Japanese camp with their weapons ablaze, bellowing: "Come on, you Raiders! Yippie!!! Gung Ho! GUNG HO!" And by one highly dubious report, even some of the Japanese troops in the Pacific had begun shouting "Gung ho!" instead of "Banzai!" when they charged—to which, according to a Navy Department press release, the U.S. Marines shouted back: "We'll Gung Ho you, you blankety-blanks!"

In early January 1943, Carlson gave a eulogy for the Raiders who had died on Guadalcanal. The service was a quiet event with his men sitting on the ground among the palms of their camp on Espiritu Santo, but his audience grew as the Navy sent out the full text of his speech as a press release, which was excerpted in newspapers from coast to coast. Then the Office of War Information picked it up and engaged Fredric March, one of the leading actors of the time, to perform a dramatic reading of it to be broadcast to the American forces overseas. So his words were literally heard around the world.

"What of the future for those of us who remain?" Carlson asked toward the end of his speech. "Our course is clear. It is for us at this moment, with the memory of the sacrifices of our brothers still fresh, to dedicate again our hearts, our minds and our bodies to the great task that lies ahead. The future of America—yes, the future condition of all peoples, rests in our hands." That much might have been said by others, but the passage that followed, on the transformation of American society, was distinctly Carlson. "We must go further," he continued, "and dedicate ourselves also to the monumental task of assuring that the peace which follows this holocaust will be a just and equitable and conclusive peace. And beyond that lies the mission of making certain that the social order which we bequeath to our sons and daughters is truly based on the four freedoms for which these men died."

His words on sacrifice carried a particular resonance for the public back home—who, if they did not have a family member in uniform, were likely to be more preoccupied with the day-to-day inconveniences of ration coupons and product shortages than they were with the hardships of the Marines fighting in the Pacific. "These men are realists, as all must be under such circumstances," said *The New York Times* when it published Carlson's speech. "We might give them a thought some day soon when we have bread but not enough butter, a motor car but not quite enough gasoline. They can teach us something if we are wise and humble enough to learn." A man from North Carolina who read the eulogy was moved to write in response: "Are not these young men—the cream of the nation—in their death the seed corn of something greater than the nation itself, do they not set forth the greatness of spirit upon which our very civilization grows to deeper grace?"

By almost any measure the Guadalcanal mission had been a success. In contrast to the stumbling near-failure of the Makin Raid, there was no need to inflate its outcome for the press. The Raiders killed 488 Japanese while losing only 16 of their own in combat—an astonishing kill ratio of more than thirty to one. Over a month of near-daily engagements with the enemy on Guadalcanal, the guerrilla tactics they had used gave them the advantage of surprise in all but two of the encounters. Merrill Twining, the operations officer who supervised Carlson's mission from Vandegrift's headquarters, called it a "superbly commanded operation" and regretted only that the transcripts of Carlson's daily radio reports had all been burned when Vandegrift thought his headquarters might be overrun by the Japanese.

General Vandegrift gave the battalion a blanket citation, making them only the second unit in World War II to receive such an honor, after the defenders of Wake Island a year earlier. As he wrote in the citation:

For a period of thirty days this battalion, moving through difficult terrain, pursued, harried and, by repeated attacks, destroyed an enemy force of equal or greater size and drove the remnants from the area of operations. During this period the battalion, as a whole or by detachments, attacked the enemy whenever and wherever he could be found in a repeated series of carefully planned and well executed surprise attacks. . . . For the consummate skill displayed in the conduct of operations, for the training, stamina and fortitude displayed by all members of the battalion and for its commendably aggressive spirit and high morale, the Commanding General cites to the Division the Commanding Officer, Officers and Men of the Raider Battalion.

Carlson earned his third Navy Cross for the Guadalcanal mission, adding to the ones he had earned for Makin and Nicaragua. In Marine Corps lore, the Raiders' thirty days in the jungle would be remembered with reverence as "The Long Patrol."

The stunning ratio of dead Japanese to dead Americans in the Raiders' Guadalcanal mission did not, however, account for the casualties of disease, and more than a fifth of Carlson's men wound up being evacuated for malaria, jaundice, malnutrition, infections, and dysentery. So they hardly came through unscathed—and Carlson,

Carlson receiving Navy Cross from Chester Nimitz. A. A. Vandegrift is at far left.

who had both malaria and jaundice, was no exception. But what Carlson's men did *not* appear to suffer from was psychiatric trauma. Across the United States military in World War II, 40 percent of casualties involved traumatic stress—"shell shock" or "combat fatigue" as it was often called. And those casualties were mainly concentrated among the minority of servicemembers who served as combat troops, more than a quarter of whom had to be admitted for psychiatric treatment each year. But during the month-long guerrilla patrol of Carlson's battalion—in spite of the constant stress of danger, the invisibility of the enemy in the jungle, the near-daily firefights, and the malnutrition and abysmal sanitary conditions—only one of Carlson's men had to leave because of a mental health crisis. The morale and confidence of his battalion were among the highest in the war.

A year after Carlson's patrol on Guadalcanal, *Fortune* magazine ran an article on the psychiatric toll of warfare that highlighted the rare success of the 2nd Marine Raider Battalion. It observed that at the time of writing, in December of 1943, half of the VA beds in the United States were still occupied by the psychiatric casualties of World War I, but the pressures of the current war were shaping up to be even worse. Men "are sustained largely by their will to fight," it said. "But this will is far less solidly felt in 1943 than it was in 1917.... Today Americans fight, unclear in their purpose, apprehensive of the future, with a dogged determination to get it over with and get home." At that point in World War II—two years beyond Pearl Harbor but not yet into the grinding bloodbaths of Saipan, Iwo Jima, and Okinawa, to say nothing of Normandy or the Battle of the Bulge in Europe—already about one-third of the American casualties being sent home from overseas were for reasons of mental trauma, while in some areas of combat the ratio was running as high as 50 percent.

The magazine gave credit for the Raiders' remarkable success on this count to Carlson's unique training methods: the gung ho meetings that empowered individuals and built cohesion within the group, his insistence that the men understand why they were doing what they did. The Raiders had suffered virtually no psychiatric casualties, it explained, because Carlson "prepared the men for what they might expect; because he considered their opinions and feelings; because they were convinced he would never sacrifice a man need-lessly; because he provided an outlet for terror and tension; because his men understood what they were fighting for; because the Raiders trusted him implicitly." Carlson may have been a renegade, a maverick, a radical in the eyes of his peers, but it was clear that his methods worked.

A Yale psychologist named John Dollard would come to a similar conclusion when he investigated Carlson's work in 1944 as part of a consulting project for the War Department on morale in the armed forces. Like the authors of the *Fortune* article, Dollard came away convinced that Carlson's unique leadership style had been the secret to the mental resilience of his men. When they had to sleep in the mud on Guadalcanal, Dollard reported, Carlson "went through the ranks and said to one and another, 'I told you it was going to be like this.' Without exception they answered something reassuring. Most said, 'We asked for it.'" He analyzed Carlson's moral training, how he taught the men "You must know what's right and then go ahead. Don't let others kid or shame you out of it." Dollard believed that Carlson's philosophy of "gung ho" resembled old-fashioned Christian charity—and though many gave lip service to that concept, he said, "Witch-faced, gaunt Carlson really has it." Similarly, Dollard was impressed by Carlson's sense of religious fatalism—the root of his fearlessness in battle—as well as the influence of Christianity in Carlson's moral indoctrination of his men. In a series of interviews, Carlson took him back to the beginning, talking about the roots of his philosophy of self-reliance from Emerson and the influence of his father the Congregationalist minister. Dollard's conclusion in his report to the War Department was that Evans Carlson was "a sort of military saint or old fashioned Christian soldier."

All the same, by 1943 Carlson was growing weary of the fighting. "All I do is kill, kill, kill," he wrote to Helen Foster Snow after Guadalcanal. He was so intent on his work with the Raiders that he had little time to think about the larger themes that had always preoccupied him. China, his great passion, was on the back burner for the time being. His sole focus was on his men. True to his father's calling, he pushed them to be better Christians. "Back on Guadalcanal, most of you were praying and promising to lead good Christian lives, like

Carlson and some of the Raiders after their Guadalcanal mission.

you should," he told them at a gung ho meeting on Espiritu Santo. "That was fine, and I'm for it. But a lot of good it does to pray only when you're scared. Think the Lord appreciates that? Hell, no, he doesn't. Why not try praying a little bit now, when there's no Jap with a bayonet in your belly, and no sniper taking pot shots at you from the trees. I think the Lord would like it. I really think he would."

Carlson hoped his training methods might catch on more widely in the U.S. military now that he had shown their worth on Guadalcanal. "I wish you could see our Raiders now," he wrote to James Roosevelt. "You would be proud of your handiwork and mine. Gung Ho is here to stay—proved in the crucible of protracted jungle fighting." He said Vandegrift was "unstinting in his praise and vows he will have his whole division trained this way."

This wasn't just optimism for Roosevelt's sake—a 1943 War Office training pamphlet, *Fighting on Guadalcanal*, which collected the advice of a number of officers and enlisted men who had served on the island, found several of them advocating for Carlson's methods without citing him by name. Vandegrift, in the introduction, called for more guerrilla-type training, saying that America's troops must "go back to the tactics of French and Indian days. . . . I refer to the tactics and leadership of the days of ROGERS' RANGERS." An Army infantry captain said if he could train his men again, "I would have some maneuvers on which the men were deprived of food, water and comforts in order to find out which NCO's and men can't take it." Several officers said the enlisted men needed to be taught to act on their own initiative, without waiting for an NCO to tell them what to do. Even Merritt Edson, who had been promoted from his own Raider battalion to a regimental command, said that if he had to retrain his unit, "I would stress small group training and the training of the individual even more than we did." He also recommended increasing the number of automatic weapons in each squad.

General Vandegrift's information officer Herbert Merillat was more explicit in his praise for Carlson's methods. Calling the Raiders "a great bunch of soldiers," he later wrote that "They had demonstrated that well-trained, jungle-wise troops, living on light rations (raisins, bacon, tea, and rice), disposing of heavy firepower, could operate independently and with deadly effectiveness away from an established supply base." Merrill Twining, the operations officer who had been Carlson's point of radio contact, likewise said he was "convinced that marines in general could learn much from the practices and tactics of Carlson's Raiders." (Much later, as a retired general, Twining would cite Carlson's use of native scouts and supply drops to enable his battalion's mobility as the inspiration for the U.S. military's use of helicopters in Korea.)

Carlson was proud of his men and wanted to believe that the rest of the Marine Corps could learn to endure what the Raiders had in their jungle mission. But he wasn't sure they could. After a short vacation in New Zealand he wrote to his father: "It was good to see old friends, but I was also appalled by the general note of apathy— the disinclination to get up on the firing line. Can't understand it except that it must be a sure index of the deterioration of American character and stamina. . . . Under these conditions it is difficult to continue to convince my men that they should carry the torch." He compared the United States to the declining Roman Empire. "We're going down to perdition unless people can be aroused to the need for the sacrifice of comfort, convenience, and life," he told his father.

Carlson's fixation on discomfort had made the Guadalcanal operation harder than it needed to be—he could have ordered more rations, and a greater variety than rice, bacon, and raisins. They didn't have to starve the way they did. With the hundred native porters the Raiders had working for them, and the well-orchestrated landings of supplies, Carlson might have given them mosquito nets and better sanitation equipment. Their thirty days in the jungle were the toughest assignment any American unit had yet undertaken in the war, Carlson was sure of that. But that was also the point of it. Anything that made his men more comfortable, he believed, would weaken them. His insight was flirting with obsession.

But his men still loved him, especially once they were safely out of the jungle. A Marine Corps correspondent named Jim Lucas tracked down the Raiders at their Gung Ho Camp in early 1943. He had searched out Carlson mainly to find out if he was real. "I knew that he was a strange character, almost out of fiction," he wrote, "and because Colonel Carlson was almost a legend, because the stories about him were told in every port and printed in every newspaper, I didn't quite believe in him." Lucas arrived on Espiritu Santo in a candid, carefree moment in early 1943 when the Raiders were out of danger and newly decorated, loafing around and enjoying one another's company. They could joke about their experiences now. One of the men wrote a song about all the rice they'd had to eat in the jungle:

> I'm a rice eating raider
> Back from Guadalcanal
> While we were there
> We gave those Japs hell
> The Japs were half starved
> It was plain to see
> But none of them were
> Half as hungry as me
>
> Now we'd hike all the day
> And then rest for a spell
> And leave all those Japs
> On the trail where they fell
> Then hunt up a bivouac
> And cook up some chow
> I used to like rice
> But I don't like it now

Carlson had been trying to get the men to talk about social issues when Lucas arrived—a couple of days earlier he'd led them in a discussion of the kind of social order they wanted to see in America after the war. They agreed it should be based on a "fair-deal principle." Another time, the men had argued about whether soldiers stationed overseas should have the right to vote by mail and Carlson impressed upon them the importance of being politically engaged when they got home so that, as he put it, they could "gain those things for which we are now fighting." The discussions were freewheeling and spontaneous, and the men didn't always follow Carlson's lead. At one meeting, they argued over a proposal to limit American household incomes during the war to $25,000 per year (over a million in annual income today)—Carlson was in favor of it, but most of the men were not, which surprised him because so many of them came from low-income families. They said it was because they didn't want to see anyone held back.

The ethos of the battalion was clear from the moment Lucas first entered their camp, with its welcome sign bearing the Raiders' new logo—a fierce-looking skull with glaring eyes and a downturned mouth, with a Gung Ho Knife behind it crossed with a lightning bolt. The men had also painted the insignia on their gear and field jackets. (In another, less intimidating craft project, they had recently painted coconuts different colors and hung them on a tree for Christmas.)

Over the course of several days, Lucas lounged with the Raiders at their camp, sailed with them on a submarine, sat in on their gung ho meetings, and listened to the men sing their Raider songs. By this time, they had an entire booklet of them, written mostly by the men with their commander's encouragement. (Carlson also encouraged them to write poetry, which was fitting with his lifelong literary interests. As he explained to a different reporter: "When you get a platoon sergeant going into the jungle with a sock of rice and a jungle knife and a tommy gun and coming out with a poem, you've got something!") Along with the singing and training and other activities they also held nondenominational church services every Sunday, as per a battalion memo, "to bring to [the] men of the battalion concrete examples of the practical benefits of religious experience." Carlson did much of the preaching.

Lucas talked with the Raiders about their gung ho meetings,

Carlson (left) at the entrance to Camp Gung Ho on Espiritu Santo.

how the enlisted men were welcome to raise complaints and suggestions, how they could even question their officers' past orders and
the officers would be called on to explain their decisions. It was Carlson's egalitarian democracy in action and to Lucas their camaraderie
seemed unparalleled. "The men literally worship 'the old man,'" he
reported. But Lucas saw the ruthless side of Carlson as well, a part of
him that only the men who had served with him on Guadalcanal had
seen up close. "We never take a prisoner," Carlson told him. "That's
not our job. I tell my men to kill every Jap they meet—lame, halt and
well. We've no accommodations to care for prisoners." He said he
had learned this from experience. "They're too treacherous, for one
thing. They killed most of our medical corpsmen who tried to help
them, so we take no chances."

All this was more than the public was meant to know at the time.
Someone deleted the paragraph in Lucas's report about Carlson
instructing his men to kill every Japanese they encountered; certainly, the amoral violence of it was jarring in an article otherwise
concerned with singing songs, praying, and debating politics. However, the upper-level staff of the Marine Corps public relations office
were apparently less concerned by the killing of crippled Japanese
soldiers than they were by the kind of egalitarian relationship Carlson
encouraged between the officers and enlisted men in his battalion—
which risked making Marines in other units want the same thing. A

captain in the Marine Corps Division of Public Relations flagged Lucas's article for review by the colonel in charge, with a note that "since it is about Raiders and deals with informality between officers and enlisted personnel, thought you'd like to look it over." On those grounds, the colonel killed the piece entirely. "Better keep this on ice," he replied.

Lucas had caught Carlson at the most hopeful moment since the initial formation of his Raider battalion in the wake of Pearl Harbor. The men were relaxed and proud, recovering from the unquestionable success of their Guadalcanal operation. Unlike the Makin Raid, Carlson had actually been able to lead his men like a band of guerrillas, through the jungle, fighting the Japanese from their rear like the Chinese Communists would have done. "The last operation on Guadalcanal was tough," Carlson wrote to Helen Foster Snow. "I used Eighth Route Army tactics almost exclusively. The old master's philosophy is the guiding force in my organization." The "old master," of course, was Zhu De.

Carlson was getting closer to his vision of an American counterpart to the army of the Chinese Communists (or "so-called communists," as he still thought of them) and it felt like great things were in store. Looking ahead, his greatest hope was to take the Raiders with him back to China, where they would join forces with Zhu De and the Eighth Route Army to drive the Japanese invaders back out to sea. The men were thrilled with the idea and they told Lucas they wouldn't consider their mission a success until "the old man takes us back."

"Colonel," asked one of the enlisted men at a gung ho meeting, "what's chances of going to China?"

"Very good, lad, very good," Carlson told him, grinning, "but I'm not saying when."

When never came.

On March 22, Carlson was removed from command. It came in the form of an unwanted promotion that put him out of reach of the enlisted men who had been his pet project. He was "kicked upstairs," as he resentfully put it. Up to that point, his Raider battalion had been operating under Navy command with great autonomy, and

Admiral Nimitz and General Vandegrift had been happy to let Carlson do his work as he wished, so long as it got results. But after Guadalcanal, the Marine Corps set up a headquarters in the South Pacific and with that reorganization Carlson's unit came back under Marine Corps control, where his battalion was combined with the three other raider battalions (including Edson's former unit) into a Marine Raider Regiment. It was to the headquarters of this regimental command that Carlson was "promoted"—though he was only made the executive officer there, a staff post where he would have no control over how the Raiders were trained or commanded in the future.

Carlson's superiors were too diplomatic to humiliate him publicly—he was a hero in the eyes of the American public, after all—but their resentment of his methods had reached the breaking point. They were sick of his "gung ho" philosophy and his personal fame and they wanted to make sure that he wouldn't have any more contact with the enlisted Marines who (as Jim Lucas put it) literally worshipped him. The officer who took over Carlson's command of the 2nd Raider Battalion was his polar opposite, a Naval Academy graduate and football star named Alan Shapley who had little overseas experience and was perfectly comfortable with the officer culture as it existed. Carlson saw Shapley as "an orthodox line man . . . with orders to wipe out the 'Gung Ho' spirit." And that was accurate enough, for Shapley immediately set about turning the Raiders back into a conventional infantry force. In one of his first addresses to the men, Shapley told them that from now on they were going to be Marines instead of Boy Scouts.

Many in the upper ranks of the Marine Corps applauded the demise of Carlson's Raiders. Aside from the general resentment toward all Raider battalions for being elites with better equipment and their pick of personnel, Carlson's unit was an object of particular hostility. His personal fame, his idealistic politics, his refusal to fit in, his blurring of the boundaries between officers and enlisted men—all of these had made him enemies in the Corps. "There could be no discipline and no morale in such an organization," said Omar Pfeiffer, who insisted after the war that Carlson's Raiders were "imbued with purely and simply communist doctrine and procedure." He said he wanted to throw up whenever he heard the words "gung ho." Others viewed Carlson's antagonism to the traditions of the Marine Corps as being in itself a form of disloyalty. Charles Lamb, an unhappy lieutenant in the 2nd Raiders who came to despise Carlson, later said he "could not understand or digest Carlson's double talk and ridicule of the Marine Corps and its methods." Not everyone in the Corps celebrated the clipping of Carlson's wings, though. Merrill Twining, the operations officer who had followed Carlson's mission on Guadalcanal more closely than anyone, wrote that Carlson's removal from command "gives a momentary glimpse of the dark side of the upper levels of the Marine Corps showing its inflexibility of thought and a compulsive suspicion of all things new and untried."

Carlson knew what was said about him behind his back. "I am considered a radical, of course," he wrote to his father. He said a friend who had been party to the creation of the Raider regiment told him he was the natural choice for its commander "but that the high command was afraid of me—afraid that I would change the technique of the Corps." Carlson tried to find a way forward, though. On a personal level he liked the man who was picked in his stead as regimental commander, a colonel named Harry Liversedge who previously led the 3rd Raider Battalion, and Carlson thought maybe he could find some way to continue influencing the Raiders from his new position. "You know me," he told his father. "It is the cause that counts, not the individual. . . . I am far from being through fighting."

As for the 2nd Raiders themselves, Jim Lucas the Marine Corps correspondent happened to be there at their camp on Espiritu Santo when Carlson's men got the news that their beloved colonel would no longer be leading them. They were heartbroken. "I stumbled with them up the beach, tears in their eyes, and heard them curse the fate that had robbed them of their old man," Lucas wrote. "I sat in their tents and heard them cry like babies."

CHAPTER 21

THE MAW

C ARLSON WAS CONSUMED with bitterness after losing his command. "I am often beside myself with a feeling of impotence and frustration," he wrote to Peg Snow. "I am such small potatoes, and so thoroughly feared and hated in certain quarters, that I am really impotent." There was no interest in continuing Carlson's project at the regimental level. Liversedge, the commander, joked about Carlson's methods to his superiors, reporting in one memo that the organization of the Raider Regiment was going well "considering that we had nothing to start with except 'Gung Ho' and a campsite." In any case, Carlson did not last long in the regimental headquarters; his malaria had come back in force, and eleven days after being removed from command of the 2nd Raiders he was hospitalized and then evacuated home for medical treatment. Just two weeks after the Raider Regiment's creation, Liversedge was already putting out feelers for a new executive officer to replace him.

Even without their "gung ho" leader, the Marine Raiders would continue to fight with inordinate courage and success through most of the following year. But the needs of the Pacific War were changing. As America's wartime industrial output built toward its peak, the Navy increasingly relied on vast fleets of overwhelming size to deliver landing forces of a division or more—a strategy that obviated the need for small, independent special-operations-type forces, even as the general envy of the Raiders' elite status continued to antagonize the rest of the Corps. "Handpicked outfits, such as these troops, are detrimental to morale of other troops," read one internal memo in December of 1943 that advocated their termination. "The

Marine Corps has always had 'esprit de corps,' but separating a certain group and telling them that they are better than the rest is not conducive to that 'do or die' spirit which has been the essence of the Corps." By early January of 1944, the Raider designation would be abandoned completely and the most visible remnants of Carlson's wartime experiment faded away.

It would take seventy years, but the Raider title would, in the end, find a new life in an entirely different era. In the summer of 2014, the Marine Corps officially renamed its twenty-first-century special operations forces after their World War II forebears: the Marine Raiders would ride again. This was not a decision made without controversy, though the Raiders had always been controversial within the Corps and there was no reason this should have been less true in 2014 than it was in 1944. But if the tactics and training of today's Marine Forces Special Operations Command (MARSOC) bear only a passing resemblance to the Raiders of World War II, their linkage is above all an honorary one, less about specific methods than about inspiration and esprit de corps. It highlights the point of pride that the World War II Raiders were, in the view of MARSOC, "the United States' first special operations units." And it gives today's Marine special forces a firm historical tradition—establishing, in the words of the commandant in 2014, "the official continuation of our Corps' special operations heritage from the Raiders of World War II to our modern day Marines."

Carlson came home angry and tired. At the naval hospital in San Diego where he arrived in May of 1943, they gave him a diagnosis of "extreme emotional fatigue" and told him not to have any visitors. By early June, his malaria was in remission so he felt well enough to travel east to visit his father and sister in Connecticut. It was a restorative trip, the best sleep he had enjoyed in months. He stayed a week in Plymouth and attended church with his father, then traveled down to New York and Washington, where he had lunch with President Roosevelt. In New York City, his anger was on full display when he spoke to a group of bankers and industrialists and reminded them of the speeches he had given before the war. "I don't know precisely why I am here," he told them, "because I stopped talking December seventh largely out of a feeling of frustration occasioned by the fact that I had talked to many of you gentlemen in 1939 and 1940. Then I told you of what I was convinced—that the Japanese intended to war on us. And I pleaded with you to stop the stupid practice of arming Japan. You did nothing."

He had a return of the old feeling of futility in his work, that nothing he had done mattered—though occasionally, something would cut through the gloom and show him otherwise. After his visit with Roosevelt, Carlson got an invitation from the undersecretary of the navy, James Forrestal, to fly with him out to Oregon to speak at a newspaper publishers' convention. At the banquet in Eugene, which was attended by the state governor and Supreme Court justices as well as the leaders of Oregon's journalism industry, Forrestal introduced Carlson as being, along with Admirals Chester Nimitz and Ernest King, "typical of the men who are winning the war for us." Carlson stood up and walked over to the podium to speak, and the room came to its feet. The governor, the justices, the newspaper publishers, the military entourage—the whole of the crowded banquet hall—stood and applauded and shouted for him in an ovation that went on for a full three minutes. By the time it died down, Carlson's eyes were wet with tears.

He could no longer influence his Raiders, but Carlson's temporary return home did give him a chance to connect with the American public more widely. Universal Pictures had optioned the story of the Makin Raid and since Carlson was home from the war, the Navy Department gave him permission to serve as a technical advisor on set (in the Navy's eyes, it was good publicity and it took care of the question of what to do with him for the time being). So after the banquet in Oregon, he went down to Hollywood to work on a movie. It was a big-budget film for the time, spearheaded by an influential producer named Walter Wanger, who was president of the Academy of Motion Picture Arts and Sciences. Manly-man heartthrob Randolph Scott was cast in the lead, and the young Robert Mitchum found a role in it as well, as a fictional Raider named "Pig Iron" Matthews. Some of the actual Raiders who were based at Camp Pendleton were cast in supporting roles, and Wanger initially tried to get Carlson to play himself in the film but that was more than the Navy would tolerate. For the movie's title, the studio went with the obvious choice and called it *Gung Ho!*

The Navy Department welcomed the publicity the movie would bring, but it had certain limits. One was that the studio was forbidden to represent Carlson or James Roosevelt personally in the film, so the writers dropped Roosevelt entirely from the script and turned Carlson into a fictional colonel named Thorwald. Still, it was obvious to everyone who saw the film who Randolph Scott's Colonel Thorwald actually was; the movie's subtitle was "The Story of Carlson's Makin Island Raiders," and in case that wasn't clear enough, *Life* magazine explained that "Col. Thorwald is a movie copy of fabulous Lieut. Col. Evans Carlson."

It was not the kind of wartime movie to withstand the test of time. Viewed in hindsight, it was awful—full of caricatures of buck-toothed Japanese strafing the island and pious, sentimental speeches on patriotism and sacrifice. The enemy troops (none, for obvious reasons, played by Japanese actors) spoke some kind of gibberish that barely sounded like Japanese. The many scenes of shooting, throttling, and blowing up Japanese soldiers were filmed with particular relish. A 1980s history of the American wartime film industry would sum it up as "one of the most rabid 'hate the Jap' films made in Hollywood."

But in its own moment it made quite a splash. It was *Life* magazine's pick for movie of the week on February 7, 1944. They called it "the most literal war movie yet produced," and said it presented "the most factual and intelligent sequence on a segment of Central Pacific fighting yet seen." (Which was quite a stretch, given that much of the film was fictionalized.) A columnist in *The Hartford Courant* challenged his readers: "See 'Gung Ho' and if you don't buy bonds then, you never will!" *The New York Times* called it a "lurid action film" and said Universal Pictures hardly had to dress the events up for Hollywood, because the actual raid "was almost as boldly theatrical as this new film." The *Times* reviewer also said—somewhat preciously for a time when humans were killing one another by the millions in Europe and Asia—that the movie was so violent it should only be viewed by people with "strong stomachs and a taste for the submachine gun."

The movie followed Carlson and his Raiders from the initial creation and training of the battalion in California, through their jour-

Gung Ho! in Chicago.

ney to the wreckage of Pearl Harbor, and finally to the promised payoff: the submarine-based raid on Makin Island. In the Hollywood version of events, everything that went wrong on the actual raid went right: the weather barely concerned them, no boats got lost, the walkie-talkies worked perfectly. In the extended dramatic climax of the movie, the Raiders shoot, strangle, and bludgeon their way through the Japanese garrison in an unabashed, giddy bloodbath. In one drawn-out (and entirely imaginary) scene, a resourceful Raider commandeers a steamroller and uses it to crush a Japanese radio installation with several men inside. In another fanciful sequence, Carlson's men trick the Japanese pilots into bombing their own troops by secretly painting an American flag on the roof of the Japanese barracks. By the end, the Raiders kill everyone in sight, blow up a few buildings, night falls, and they paddle back out to the submarines through placid water, just as neat as you please.

Carlson's hand in shaping the script revealed itself in places where the action film shifted unexpectedly into didactic explorations of his "gung ho" philosophy. This was deliberate on Carlson's part. As he explained in a letter to Raymond Swing while he was working on the film, he saw *Gung Ho!* as a means of introducing his philosophy to ordinary people. He was actively rewriting parts of the script with Walter Wanger's indulgence, and hoped that through the film he could reach a wider audience than the Marines he was no longer allowed to command. "The major emphasis at present must be on winning the war as quickly as possible," he told Swing. "But equally important is the conditioning of our young men for the post-war period."

Carlson's influence was most obvious at the very end of the movie. On board the *Nautilus* as it powers home from the successful raid, Carlson's avatar Colonel Thorwald is talking with a group of Raiders gathered around him when he turns and looks straight into the camera, addressing the viewer directly. With a level gaze, he repeats almost verbatim the central passage of Carlson's eulogy for the Raiders who died on Guadalcanal, transposing it to the earlier Makin Raid. "Our course is clear," he says. "It is for us at this moment, with the memory of the sacrifices of our brothers still fresh, to dedicate again our hearts, our minds, and our bodies, to the great task that lies ahead. We must go further, and dedicate ourselves also to the monumental task of assuring that the peace which follows this holocaust will be a just, equitable and conclusive peace." A chorus of Marines singing a Raider ballad swells in the background as Thorwald/Carlson builds to his dramatic conclusion. "And beyond that," he intones, "lies the mission of making certain that the social order which we bequeath to our sons and daughters is truly based on freedom, for which these men died." The camera pans back, the Raiders shout "Gung ho!" in unison, and Colonel Thorwald takes a thoughtful sip of his coffee. The film fades to black as the chorus of singing Marines rises to full volume and carries over into the closing credits.

———

Life magazine did a profile of Carlson while the movie was in production. It led off with a half-page spread of photographs of him folded uncomfortably into a director's chair in different positions—still photos of a man in constant motion. He wears his service uniform with a sharp crease in his pants and a chest bulging with decorations. He radiates a restless energy, his enthusiasm for his cause overwhelming any capacity to sit still. "His voice rises and falls to accent facts," said the article; "his hands and body are mobile and he uses them unconsciously for emphasis. . . . Talking about his Raiders or China he is intense, leans forward frequently, runs his hands through his closely cropped gray hair. He looks awkward and finds it hard to confine his

6-ft. body within the confines of a chair in a set position. Yet he has about him a certain rugged gracefulness."

The profile in *Life*, then the most widely circulated magazine in the United States, represented Carlson to the American public in the way he liked to think of himself: as an outsider, a maverick, a humanitarian whose hopes for the peace were at least as strong as his hopes for the war. "Some of the older, more orthodox Marine officers considered him a fanatic," said the

Carlson in *Life* magazine.

magazine, "and, though the Raiders' record has justified his training techniques, they still have misgivings about his ideology. But to Carlson it is just as important that his men know why they are bayoneting a Jap as that they know the best way to do it."

In spite of Henry Luce's strong partisanship for Chiang Kai-shek over the Communists in China, *Life* made no effort to paper over the controversial side of Carlson's leadership style—it ran an old photo of Carlson with Zhu De, explaining that he had gotten his ideas for the political organization of the Raiders from the Eighth Route Army. In the interview, Carlson told *Life* that Zhu De's army was "the best-organized, best-led fighting force in the world for its size and purpose." He gave the Chinese Communists full credit for his training philosophy. "I was trying to build up the same sort of working spirit I had seen in China, where all the soldiers dedicated themselves to one idea and worked together to put that idea over," he said. "I told the boys about it again and again."

By that point, after four months back in the United States, Carlson was done recovering from his bout of malaria, the filming of the movie was complete, and he was on the verge of being sent back into the war. *Life* predicted that "The Marine Corps as a whole is not likely to follow Carlson's pattern of ideological training, nor to adopt *Gung Ho* as its motto." And they were correct—at least in the first part, that the Marines wanted nothing to do with his ideology. "Gung ho," however, would live on as an unofficial motto of the Marine Corps, albeit with a different meaning than Carlson intended.

———

Two months later, Carlson was back in the Central Pacific, in the thick of the heaviest fighting the Marine Corps had ever seen. He was on the Tarawa Atoll, in the Gilbert Islands just a hundred miles south of Makin. In the year that had passed since Carlson's raid on Makin, the Japanese had built up their defensive fortifications in the Gilberts and increased the strength of their garrisons by orders of magnitude beyond what his Raiders encountered in August of 1942. Where there had been dozens of defenders before, now there were thousands. Carlson had volunteered to come back as an observer with the 2nd Marine Division as it tried to stage an invasion of Tarawa's main island, Betio—a tiny patch of sand just one square mile in size with an airstrip and nearly three thousand of the Japanese military's best troops dug into it. His goal was to observe the battle firsthand, take note of what worked and what didn't, and then relay that information to the planning officers in his own division (the 4th). It was the first time any amphibious force had tried to land on a heavily fortified atoll, and if successful it would be the first step in a new U.S. campaign to drive across the Central Pacific, leapfrogging from one strategic island to the next, in an effort to reach Japan.

In contrast to the two paltry submarines that supported the Raiders in the summer of 1942, the assault on Tarawa opened on November 20, 1943, with a naval artillery barrage of unprecedented scale. It was one of the most concrete images one can get of the enormous material and industrial advantages the United States enjoyed over resource-strapped Japan. Over the course of three hours, the vast U.S. assault fleet poured two thousand tons of artillery shells onto the tiny island. Planes launched from the fleet's seventeen aircraft carriers blanketed the island with bombs and strafed the visible Japanese installations with millions of rounds of ammunition.

The hope was that such overwhelming artillery and airpower would obliterate the Japanese defenses and smooth the way for an easy amphibious landing by the twelve thousand Marines of the 2nd Division. But the Japanese were far better prepared than the American planners had anticipated. They were protected by fortified bunkers and pillboxes built of heavy, half-buried coconut logs and reinforced concrete with four feet of sand on top, marvels of engineering that allowed the men inside to withstand the conflagration of artillery and bombing mostly unscathed. When the naval shelling quieted down and the first wave of amphibian tractors approached the coral reef with the assault force, the defenders opened up on them with a storm of machine gun and artillery fire of their own from above the beach.

More Americans would die in the grinding, four-day fight for tiny Betio Island than in any amphibious battle since the founding of the Marine Corps: fully one quarter of the landing force would be killed or wounded, most of them on the first day. The plans went awry almost from the start. The Navy had expected the tide to be high enough for the landing craft to clear the reef, but it wasn't, and they couldn't. So while the amphibian tractors that carried the first wave could crawl over the coral and continue on their way toward shore (only, in many cases, to be destroyed by close-range artillery fire once they got to the beach), the Higgins boats that came after them ran hard aground on the reef more than five hundred yards out. Thousands of Marines had to abandon their motorized transports and wade, unprotected, through shoulder-deep water toward shore, in clear view of Japanese machine-gunners who mowed them down like insects.

There was no room for being a mere observer. Half an hour after the first assault wave hit the beach, Carlson was headed for shore in the same landing craft as the commander of the 2nd Marine Regiment, Colonel David Shoup—a short, stocky officer with no previous combat experience who had been thrust into command of the landing force after his superior suffered a breakdown on the way to Tarawa. Their Higgins boat ran aground on the reef like the others had done, so they exchanged it for a nearby amphibian tractor that was carrying wounded back to the ships. After they transferred the wounded men to another vessel, the amphtrac started with Carlson and Shoup toward shore but quickly came under a heavy crossfire of machine guns and antitank guns, so the driver steered away from the beach and into the shelter of a stone and wood pier that jutted five hundred yards out into the water. Halfway in, the damaged amphtrac's engine stalled and they had to get out and wade the rest of the way, through water choked with dead fish from the bombs, crouching in the lee of the pier to try to avoid the enfilading enemy fire. One shell hit so close that it nearly killed Colonel Shoup, who was briefly knocked senseless by the concussion and suffered shrapnel wounds in both legs. Carlson helped him get up out of the water and they continued crawling toward shore. Carlson himself, as always, remained untouched.

Shoup set up his command post in the shallow water underneath the pier at first, then moved it to the beach, up against a protective seawall that contained an active enemy bunker on the opposite side. The regiment's hold on the beach was tenuous, encompassing an area of only seventy-five by three hundred yards, with withering enemy fire coming from multiple directions. Communication between the Marines on the beach and the naval fleet broke down due to the soaking of radio equipment in seawater so Carlson volunteered to act as Shoup's courier, carrying messages back and forth from the command post onshore to the flagship beyond the reef, through heavy shelling and small-arms fire. He also relayed the crucial message from Shoup—a future Marine Corps commandant who would earn the Medal of Honor for his conduct on Tarawa—that no matter how bad it got "we intend to stick here and fight it out."

Carlson told his father that he didn't know how he survived the battle. "Thought that I would go ashore with the regimental commander as an observer, take a few notes and that would be that," he wrote. "But—I never worked so hard in my life for the first three days. . . . I have been in many battles, and I've had a lot of lead and steel thrown in my direction. But I don't believe that more lead was ever flowing around me at one time than during the first two days of Tarawa. How I got through unscathed is a miracle." Through the horrific storm of machine gun and mortar fire, he made repeated trips from the beach over the coral shelf, ferrying wounded men and information back to the ships, and helping conduct reinforcements and supplies forward to the beach. He commandeered an amphibian tractor to rescue men who were trapped under the pier, unable to advance. In the middle of the explosive cacophony one mortar round burst just over his head, only an arm's length away, but somehow the shrapnel failed to connect with his body. Another time, a Japanese sniper's bullet punched

Tarawa.

through his trousers, between his legs, but only grazed his inner thigh and left nothing more than a minor burn.

One of the thousands of American servicemen on the beach at Tarawa was the young actor Eddie Albert (who would later star as Eva Gabor's farmer husband in *Green Acres*, among many other roles). Albert was a Navy coxswain for a landing craft who came ashore on Betio to help the Marines, and he recalled that on the second or third night of the battle, he took shelter in a hollow crater on the beach. As soon as he lay down, another man fell on top of him. The two of them spent the night together in the hole with explosions lighting up the darkness above and a cannon just behind them firing toward the Japanese installations above the beach. Amid all the noise and chaos the other man, to Albert's bewilderment, calmly removed his pants, folded them neatly, and laid them down before going to sleep. Albert asked him why he did that, and the man said he might as well try to stay sharp. Early the next morning, while it was still dark, the man got up and put on his pants, pointed out to Albert where the Japanese snipers were, said, "Here I go!" and took off. Albert spotted him again later that day on the beach. "I saw him," said Albert, "it was getting a little light—he was smoking a little pipe. I mean that fellow was cool. He was helping the wounded and going everywhere where he could be of service. I was huddling there with a Marine and

I said, 'Who's that guy, do you know who that is?' He said, 'Yah, that's Colonel Carlson from Carlson's Raiders.'"

It was exceptionally rare for an officer of Carlson's age to be where he was. He was a World War I veteran, after all, and he did not need to be there, on the beach at Tarawa, on the front line of one of the bloodiest battles of the Pacific War. Most of the enlisted Marines were teenagers, early twenties at most, and the young noncommissioned officers in the assault waves weren't much older. Even the overall commander of the American landing force, David Shoup, was almost a decade younger than Carlson. In another part of the war, during the battle for Peleliu, a gray-haired officer named Paul Douglas who was a few years older than Carlson appeared out of nowhere to help some Marines unload supplies from an amphibian tractor near the front. One of them, E. B. Sledge, later wrote about Douglas in one of the best known first-person accounts of the Pacific War, *With the Old Breed*. "What astonished us was that he looked to be more than 50 years old," wrote Sledge. "When he took off his helmet to mop his brow, we saw his gray hair." After Douglas left, one of the privates asked what that "crazy old gray-headed guy" was doing so close to the fighting.

The middle-aged Douglas, who had been an economics professor before the war, went on to an eighteen-year career as a liberal senator for Illinois, greatly helped in his political career by his military service. But the mere fact that his appearance at a relatively quiet spot near the front on Peleliu should have occasioned such amazement from Sledge and his fellow enlisted men gives a sense of what it meant that at the comparatively advanced age of forty-seven, with his own head of gray hair, Carlson readily volunteered to throw himself into the midst of the excruciating firefight on Tarawa. His courage was not lost on his fellow Marines at the time—even on those who scorned his politics, as witnessed by the widely repeated quip, attributed to David Shoup at the Tarawa landing, that "Carlson may be Red but he's not yellow."

By the end of the seventy-six-hour battle, the Tarawa beach was covered in dead American Marines—facedown, twisted into grotesque shapes, torn into pieces. Half-naked corpses bobbed in the tide, washing gently against the shore. Inland from the beach, through the stench of rotting flesh and swarms of flies, almost all of the Japanese defenders were dead, many by their own hands or burned to cinders when the Marines blasted out their pillboxes with flamethrowers. The island was unrecognizable—burned, bombed, and defoliated. The Seabees had landed with their heavy construction equipment and were excavating and bulldozing the final pillboxes, cutting trenches for mass graves, and reestablishing the heavily damaged airstrip. Within twenty-four hours of the battle's end the first American planes were landing, the war's planners turning already toward the next step in their gruesome march across the Central Pacific to Japan. The sheer scale of the killing, though, would cause a reckoning back home. A war correspondent for the Combined American Press judged that "No victory in American military history was ever attained at a higher price." Merritt Edson came onshore after the battle and said it was the toughest fight the Marines had ever seen: "Nothing in any previous war or this one can compare with it," he said. Carlson agreed. "It was really a blood-and-guts battle," he told another reporter, "just blood and guts."

As was his wont, Carlson judged the battle less by the plans of the officers in command than by the spirit of individual Marines forced to act on their own when those plans fell apart. In a Marine Corps radio broadcast after the battle that went out to an audience of millions, Carlson cited instances of individual heroism he had seen on Tarawa. "I saw a man with half his face blown off, still conscious and on his feet, endeavoring to make his way up to the front with his weapon," he said. "I saw a young lieutenant shot through the shoulder who refused evacuation for three days and for those three days was at the head of a group which sneaked up and dynamited enemy strong points. I saw a doctor working over wounded, utterly oblivious of the machine gun and sniper fire which was bent on killing him and his patient." He was especially moved by the courage of the young enlisted men. "I found boys with serious chest and abdominal wounds imploring doctors to permit them to return to the beach and join in the struggle," he said. "This is the spirit that has made the Marine Corps what it is and which, in the years to come, will assure it a secure place in history."

Carlson believed those words, but privately he also saw the battle as further proof that the Marines needed more of the kind of training he had given his Raiders, especially in teaching the enlisted men to act on their own initiative on the battlefield. Unrecorded in the public accounts of Tarawa were how many terrified young men had been paralyzed and refused to fight (Colonel Shoup dragged one such Marine out from his hiding place in a pile of rubble by beating him on his feet, then told him his mother would be ashamed of him). "Tarawa provided abundant evidence of the need for teaching our men *why* they fight and endure and sacrifice," Carlson wrote to Raymond Swing, "and for developing a system of discipline based on *knowledge* and *reason* rather than on blind obedience." He echoed the same themes in his after-action report for the Marine Corps, where he advised that "intensive training and psychological indoctrination of small combat groups cannot be overemphasized. Men must . . . be imbued with confidence in their ability to prevail against the enemy, even when officers and NCO's are absent."

When Carlson helped plan his own division's assault two months later on the Kwajalein Atoll, in the heart of the Marshall Islands seven hundred miles farther on toward Japan (and the location of the prison where, still unknown to him, nine of his Raiders had been beheaded the year before), he felt that some lessons had been learned. There was more "gung ho" on the battlefield, more individual initiative, less waiting for orders than on Tarawa, and the battle went better as a result. With the Kwajalein Atoll in hand, the island-hopping campaign in the Central Pacific gathered momentum. The next major targets would be the islands of Saipan, Tinian, and Guam in the Marianas, which—if the Allies could capture them—would be close enough to the Japanese home islands to put Tokyo within reach of the new, long-range B-29 Superfortress bombers that were just beginning to roll out from assembly plants in Wichita, Kansas, and Renton, Washington.

———

While all this was going on, Carlson somehow found the time to get married again. After he had walked out on Etelle just before Pearl Harbor, the national emergency had scuttled any chance of their filing divorce paperwork right away. There was just too much else to do. So when Carlson first went into the Pacific, they were still legally married, and Etelle still considered herself his wife, sending news about her husband's exploits at Makin to her college sorority's alumni magazine. It took more than a year, but he eventually pressured her to put in for the divorce, which was granted in January of 1943. Etelle would keep his name, and would never remarry. Things did not turn out so badly for her, though. She wound up returning to the International House at Berkeley and making a career there. For nearly twenty years she would be a mainstay of the University of California international community, welcoming students from abroad (not "foreigners," she said, for she knew from her time in China how bad it felt to be called by that word). As social director for the International House, she hosted wedding receptions for students at her home, took them on tours of California, placed them in homestays, and helped to make the "I-House" a home for all comers, working her way into the hearts of its residents until her retirement in 1961.

For Carlson, the divorce meant that when he was on the set of the *Gung Ho!* movie in the summer of 1943 he was free to court the woman who would become his third wife: Peggy Tatum. Peggy (he finally found a Peg of his own) was the daughter of an Army colonel, a beauty who, in contrast to Etelle, was so far left on the political spectrum that she made Carlson look like a reactionary. She was nearly twenty years younger than him and had an eight-year-old son, Tony, from a previous marriage whom she raised on such classics of Soviet children's literature as *New Russia's Primer: The Story of the Five-Year Plan*. ("Practically every page carries the mark of genius," crowed the translator's introduction. "Gigantic tasks of social reconstruction are brought into intimate relation with the interests of boys and girls.")

Evans and Peggy had met during the brief window between when he left Etelle and when he shipped off for Hawaii with the Raiders. Though he was taken with her right off the bat, she had been more standoffish; after all, he was just an ordinary Marine officer (and a married one, to boot). But once he became a national figure, and after his divorce from Etelle finally came through, she warmed up to him and agreed to get married.

The divorce required a one-year waiting period, but once it passed, Carlson got a brief leave—right after the Kwajalein campaign—to come home and marry Peggy. They signed their papers in La Jolla, California, on February 29, 1944. His family was not enthused. It had been hard enough for Carlson to get his parents to accept Etelle when he first married her as his second wife in 1924, but they had eventually done so, and came to adore her. Carlson's son had gotten to know Etelle in California and loved her like a second mother. There was no such acceptance for Carlson's third wife; his family all suspected Peggy of being an opportunist. It did not help that Carlson gushed about her in the exact same sappy, love-as-literature, perfect-harmony language he had used to describe his relationship with Etelle twenty years earlier. ("In the middle of the night, last night, she got up to write a poem," he wrote to his father and sister. "We are in perfect harmony on all major matters.") The rest of Carlson's family remained devoted to Etelle and would never really accept Peggy as one of their own.

The president, at least, sent his heartiest congratulations when he saw the wedding announcement in the papers, as did Roosevelt's secretary (a new one, Grace Tully, for Missy LeHand had suffered a stroke). "I read much about the wonderful job you are doing in this war," she told Carlson, "and I must say that I am very proud to know you." Evans and Peggy spent their brief honeymoon in Hollywood, where Walter Wanger gave them tickets to the Academy Awards. They got to see *Casablanca* win best picture. Then it was back to the war.

———

Carlson spent the spring of 1944 helping to plan the assault on Saipan, part of a massive collective effort for the Marianas campaign to orchestrate the supplies and movements of a fleet totaling some six hundred ships carrying more than 300,000 sailors, airmen, soldiers, and Marines. In spite of the relative anonymity of any individual in such an enterprise, Carlson's personal contribution stood out enough that he was awarded the Legion of Merit for it, with a citation that called him a "brilliant tactician and indomitable fighter" who was "schooled by grim experience in the art of countering Japanese strategy." (Carlson, pleased by the "tactician" part, told Edgar Snow it was the first time the Navy Department had admitted in writing that he could do anything besides baring his chest to a machine gun.)

Looking ahead to yet another bloody island campaign, he reflected on everything he had seen. "I am weary with war," he wrote to Raymond Swing. He said that with every new operation, he felt more depressed by the thought of the thousands of earnest young men who "stream doggedly into the maw, some to remain, others to return mutilated in body, all to bear the scars on their souls forevermore of this destructive episode of their lives." He had written nearly the same thing in his China diary in 1938, watching the trains full of young KMT soldiers departing for the Xuzhou front, singing their patriotic songs as the cars carrying the wounded and disfigured returned from the opposite direction. "I felt this during the battles in China," he now told Swing; "and I have felt it more poignantly in this war about our own men."

Carlson still held close to China in his mind, even as his immediate job was to help defeat Japan in the Pacific. But for him, China's war and America's war had always been two sides of the same coin. "I've been fighting the Japs since 1937, which is a hell of a long time ago," he wrote to Agnes Smedley. "Think of what the Chinese people have been through in that time." It made him furious how little regard Zhu De and the Eighth Route Army were getting from the Allied powers. But as long as he was in the service he could say nothing publicly about China, and due to military censorship he also had to be careful what he wrote in private letters. But she knew exactly what he thought.

The president also knew, and sympathized. Earlier that spring, Roosevelt had responded positively to a letter where Carlson suggested that he would like to be sent to North China as a liaison officer with the Eighth Route Army. "The time may be ripe for ground work to be done in North China by someone with my experience," wrote Carlson (knowing that there was literally no one else with his experience), "looking to the time when we can link up East and West through our Pacific operations." He hoped it might be time for the U.S. military to start coordinating with the Chinese Communists in their mutual fight against Japan. Roosevelt had met recently with Chiang Kai-shek in Cairo, Egypt, where he pressured Chiang to stop fighting the CCP and form a unity government with them instead. He replied to Carlson that he felt they were going through a "transition period" with regard to North China but he hoped something could be worked out. "I have done my best to keep some of the Chinese leaders from taking more positive action against the Eighth

Route Army," he said, "but it seems to go hard with the Generalissimo. I am sure, however, that the time will come when we will all
want you back there."

On June 22, 1944, the eighth day of the American assault on Saipan,
Carlson's luck finally ran out. He was embedded as an observer
with the landing forces of the 4th Marine Division as they fought
hard across the southeastern portion of the island against heavily
entrenched Japanese resistance. On that particular day they were
advancing northward into the foothills of Saipan's tallest peak, a
1,500-foot mountain honeycombed with caves and camouflaged
machine gun nests. Carlson was at the front with an assault battalion,
relaying observations by radio to the division commander. The force
entered a ravine that lay perpendicular to its line of advance and
ended in a sheer cliff about 250 yards to the left. As the advance platoons crept down into the ravine, Carlson watched from just behind
the crest of the hill along with the young battalion commander and
his radioman.

A Japanese machine-gunner was perched, just out of view, in the
cliff to their left. He opened fire on their observation post, hitting
the radio operator, a twenty-one-year-old private from Brooklyn
named Vito Cassaro, who fell with a bullet in his left thigh that broke
the femur. Cassaro writhed on the ground, struggling to crawl out
of the way, but he couldn't move because of the bulky radio apparatus strapped to his back. The battalion commander waved in an
artillery half-track to fire on the machine gun emplacement while
Carlson—driven by the same instinct that had sent him up the side
of the blood-dripping water tower in Shanghai back in 1937—dove
in to help the radioman without missing a beat.

Carlson lifted Cassaro partway up from the ground and started
dragging him back, crouched low, but he only made it a few yards
before the machine gun opened up again. One round hit him in
the thigh with a sledgehammer blow. In the same instant another
smashed into his right forearm, shattering the bones. After the better
part of thirty years in the Army and Marines, through multiple wars
without even a scratch, Carlson finally went down, bleeding heavily
from his arm and leg. Once the machine gun was destroyed, a Navy

corpsman and a stretcher-bearer rushed over to help the two men. They knelt down and got to work on Carlson's wounds first, because he was the senior officer and that was his privilege, but he told them to stop and take care of Private Cassaro instead. "Vic was wounded first," he told them. "Take him back first."

The medics patched up Vito Cassaro and evacuated him, then they came back for Carlson, cutting open his uniform, injecting him with morphine, tying a tourniquet on his arm, and wrapping his wounds in gauze. They lifted him onto a stretcher and carried him to a waiting jeep ambulance that brought him half a mile down the reverse slope to the battalion aid station, which was set up inside an old stable. Mortar shells started exploding around them as they reached the makeshift hospital but the medics got him inside, where Carlson lay on his stretcher, bleeding and drugged as the mortars rained down, thinking peacefully that if the Japanese hadn't been able to kill him on the hilltop, they probably weren't going to get him now.

PART V
HOMECOMING

CHAPTER 22

INTO THE POSTWAR

T HAT WAS THE END of the war for Carlson. His arm was shattered and a series of operations and bone grafts would only make things worse. His leg would heal up enough for him to walk short distances, with difficulty, but he developed gangrene in his right arm and would never regain the full use of it again. That was his last trip to the Pacific. There would be no more battles, no more landings, no more presence on the front lines of the war. For all intents and purposes, it was over.

Carlson's star only rose with the enlisted men after he risked his life to help a wounded private. "Youth's Life Saved by Col. Carlson" read the headline in the *Marine Corps Chevron*, the service's in-house newspaper out of San Diego. A flock of reporters interviewed Vito Cassaro in his bed at the naval hospital in Oakland, California, where he gave Carlson full credit for saving his life. "I know if he hadn't carried me away from that spot I would certainly have been hit again and probably killed," he said. He told them how Carlson had ordered the medics to take him first, even though Carlson was hurt even worse. "They don't come any better than the colonel," said Cassaro. "He has won the respect and admiration of all who have served with him." A United Press war correspondent on Saipan went even further, reporting in a wire piece that went out across the country that after this incident, Carlson "could be called the most beloved officer by the enlisted men of the Marine Corps."

Eleanor Roosevelt came to see him in the naval hospital in San Diego in a surprise visit that brought whooping cheers from the

throngs of wounded Marines and sailors who had just started returning from Saipan. Her son James came with her. She reported afterward in her syndicated newspaper column that Carlson "looks thin
and shows the strain of his wounds and the experience which he went
through." Under cover of heavy secrecy, revealed only after the fact,
President Roosevelt made his own visit to the hospital two days later
and had Carlson's bed wheeled out to the side of his car so he could
pay his respects in private.

Carlson was deluged with mail from well-wishers as he recuper-
ated in the hospital, and when they weren't sure how to contact him
directly, they wrote to the Marine Corps instead. One self-described
"12-year old future Marine" wrote a heavily underlined letter to the
commandant in Washington: "I have read the experiances of <u>Lt. Col.
Evans F. Carlson</u> on <u>Tarawa, Guadalcanal, + Saipan</u>. And I think he
deserves <u>more</u> credit. I think he is <u>illigible</u> for promotion to <u>Brig.
Gen</u>, or at least <u>Col</u>. I think also that he should be awarded the <u>Cong.
Med. Hon</u>. for his leadership on <u>Tarawa, Guadalcanal</u> etc. or the
<u>Legion of Merit</u>."

Of all the letters Carlson received in the hospital, the most unexpected and gratifying was from Zhu De. It was their first contact since
Carlson had watched the general's column disappear into the moun-

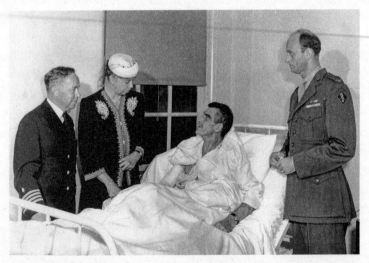

Eleanor Roosevelt visiting Carlson in the San Diego Naval Hospital.
Also pictured: Secretary of the Navy Frank Knox (far left) and
James Roosevelt (far right).

tains in 1938. "It is a long time since we have communicated and in the meantime the United States has gone to war against our enemy," wrote Zhu De. He said he knew of Carlson's efforts to emulate the Eighth Route Army in the Pacific. "You yourself have distinguished yourself repeatedly in action as the head of a force trained in partisan tactics and the spirit of the democratic people's war," he wrote. In a promising development, the first official American observers since Carlson's time had just arrived at the Communist capital of Yan'an—a small group of diplomatic and military officers known colloquially as the "Dixie Mission." The members of the mission were there to sound out the possibility of working with the Communists against Japan, and their arrival at Yan'an gave Zhu De his first opportunity to write to Carlson since before the Pacific War.

Zhu De indicated that he also knew about Carlson's efforts on behalf of China before Pearl Harbor, when he campaigned for the embargo and tried to raise public sympathy for the country. "One of the causes of our confidence," said the general, "was the knowledge that friends like you, true representations of American democracy, were speaking, writing and working to make the truth of our struggle and the opportunities for cooperation evident to all honest people who desire the defeat of Fascism." He told Carlson that they were thinking of him in China. "Many of your friends are now gathered in Yan'an," said Zhu. "We were proud of your successes and distressed to hear of your wound, from which we hope you have now fully recovered. We were happy to hear of your marriage which we hope will bring you joy. We have long wanted to send you a word of greeting and comradeship in the anti-Fascist struggle and now the opportunity has come."

The Dixie Mission embodied all of the hopes Carlson had held during the war for an alliance between the United States and the Chinese Communists. It originated with an American diplomat named John Paton Davies, who, based on Carlson's reports from the late 1930s, believed that reaching out to Mao Zedong would be in America's interest. At the time Davies began making his proposals in 1943, Carlson was still the only official U.S. observer who had ever been to Yan'an, and Davies thought this should be rectified. He argued that in the Communists' capital the U.S. would surely find a wealth of intelligence on the Japanese army, as well as a well-organized and highly disciplined anti-Japanese fighting force and "the single greatest challenge in China to the Chiang Kai-shek government." Given that the Chinese Communists had repeatedly extended invitations to American officials that had always been rebuffed, Davies thought the United States should act, and quickly, before the course of the war shifted.

Roosevelt managed to push through the Dixie Mission against Chiang Kai-shek's initial resistance, and the American observers started arriving in Yan'an in July of 1944. They were impressed by what they found. Six days after reaching the Communist capital, John Service, another U.S. diplomat involved with the mission, reported: "All of our party have had the same feeling—that we have come into a different country and are meeting a different people." His observations echoed the letters Carlson had sent to Roosevelt six years earlier: the absence of formality at Yan'an, the frankness of speech of the Communists, the openness of their personalities, the simplicity of their clothing and food, the pervasive sense of democracy and equality among them. And above all, their enthusiastic spirits in comparison to Chongqing. "Morale is very high," reported Service. "The war seems close and real. There is no defeatism, but rather confidence. There is no war-weariness." He summed up the group's experience by quoting a foreign journalist who had arrived just before him: "We have come to the mountains of North Shaanxi, to find the most modern place in China."

Mao Zedong told the visiting Americans exactly what they wanted to hear. Speaking to a group of Chinese and foreign reporters just before the Dixie Mission's arrival, Mao said that one of China's greatest deficiencies was its lack of democracy. "Only democracy can achieve victory in the War of Resistance, enable us to build a good country, and guarantee continued unity in China after the war," he said. "Only with the addition of democracy can China move forward."

This wasn't just a line Mao invented for the Americans, though, for it was central to his internal speeches as well. At the Chinese Communist Party's 7th Congress the following April, Mao said in his opening speech that after Japan's defeat, two Chinese futures were possible: "Either a China that is independent, free, democratic, united, prosperous, and strong or a China that is semicolonial, semifeudal, divided, poor, and weak." The goal of the party, he said, must be to unify the people of China to defeat Japan and "to build a new democratic state in the future." In his political report to the Party Congress, Mao argued that with Japan's eventual defeat a near-certainty, a coalition government should be established in China. There should be "a national assembly on a broad democratic basis," he said, and "a formally constituted democratic government, which . . . will lead the liberated people of the whole nation in building an independent, free, democratic, united, rich and powerful new nation."

Mao still believed in socialism, but for the time being, he said, it was "impossible for the Chinese people to institute a socialist state system, and therefore they should not even try to do so." Instead, he urged the preservation of capitalist incentives and individual freedoms "to guarantee that the people can freely develop their individuality within the framework of society." He pledged that the current era would be one of building a strong capitalist democracy—specifically *not* a dictatorship of the proletariat, and not a one-party state. The government would protect what he called "the people's most important freedoms": freedom of speech, of the press, of assembly and association, of religious belief, and of thought.

By the time Mao made that report on democracy and coalition government to the 7th Party Congress, he was speaking from a position of greater strength than he, or his party, had ever wielded before in China. Back in 1921 when he attended the first meeting of the Chinese Communist Party, there had been only twelve people present. Their numbers had grown in the following years, only to be decimated during the 1927 White Terror, then the encirclement campaigns, and then the loss of roughly 90 percent of their army in the Long March. But by the time Mao gave his speech to the Party Congress in 1945, their efforts at expansion and growth during the war had paid off stunningly well. Zhu De commanded more than 900,000 Communist soldiers in the Eighth Route and New Fourth armies, supported by two million militia troops. The party had more than a million members and controlled base areas encompassing a population of some 95 million people, greater than all of Japan. They were upstarts no more.

The Dixie Mission reawakened Carlson's hope that the United States could cooperate with the Chinese Communists, but the time remaining to the American overture was limited. In what should have been the mission's most hopeful moment, on January 9, 1945, the acting chief of the American group forwarded to the U.S. ambassador in Chongqing the startling news that Mao Zedong had expressed his willingness to travel to Washington, D.C., for an "exploratory conference" with President Roosevelt. It would have been Mao's first visit to a foreign country—he had never even been to Russia to meet Stalin. But the invitation never reached Roosevelt; the U.S. ambassador at the time, Patrick Hurley, buried the message in his files and never sent it on to the White House.

A backlash against the Dixie Mission from Chiang and his supporters was already underway, and it would ensure that nothing came from the mission other than a brief window of possibility—and the grounds for the destruction in the McCarthy era of the careers of John Paton Davies, John Service, and others in the mission who had spoken positively of the Chinese Communists. In the end, the only concrete result of the mission was a series of tentative agreements for cooperation between U.S. Army and OSS forces with the Communists—among them, for American paratroopers to help arm and command Chinese guerrilla forces and to supply 100,000 one-shot pistols to the militias—which the United States quickly abandoned as soon as Chiang Kai-shek objected to them. All this simply fueled a deeper sense of betrayal on the part of the Communists.

Meanwhile, even as the Dixie Mission was digging into its work at Yan'an and Carlson was recovering from his wounds in the summer of 1944, relations between Joseph Stilwell and Chiang Kai-shek were breaking down irretrievably. The central disagreement was on how China's troops should be commanded and how American aid should be used. Stilwell's singular focus was on recovering northern Burma in order to reestablish an overland supply route into Yunnan province. Chiang viewed that campaign as far less important than the fight against the Japanese in central China. Stilwell countered that Chiang's forces would be sufficient for both if he weren't wasting half a million of his troops blockading the Communists. The Generalissimo found Stilwell high-handed and typical of the Western imperialists, while Stilwell saw Chiang as passive and overly dependent on American support. Now Stilwell demanded that he be given total control over China's armies and urged the United States to consider backing a different leader in China. Roosevelt, supported by George Marshall, agreed with the first part, and sent a telegram to Chiang in September informing him that he must put Joseph Stilwell "in unrestricted command of all your forces." In his diary, Chiang described that message from Roosevelt as the greatest humiliation of his entire life.

This struggle between Stilwell and Chiang took place against the backdrop of a major Japanese campaign into central and south China—the Ichigo Offensive—that aimed to destroy a series of air bases that the American 14th Air Force was preparing for the launch of B-29 bombers toward Japan. It was the largest Japanese offensive in China since 1941, and by the end of the summer of 1944 it appeared more likely than ever that Japan would finally achieve victory in China. The autumn found Franklin Roosevelt in a heated campaign for his fourth term as president, and in that campaign China became a political liability. Pro-KMT Republicans attacked Roosevelt for not giving Chiang Kai-shek enough support. Roosevelt realized that he did not want his fortunes tied too closely to Chiang—if China should fall to Japan before November, and if Stilwell were in command of China's armies when that happened, Roosevelt would be blamed.

So FDR backed off from his demand that Chiang put Stilwell in charge of China's armies, and when the Generalissimo replied with an ultimatum of his own that Stilwell must be recalled from China, threatening to step down as China's leader if he remained, Roosevelt saw an escape. He complied, and ordered Stilwell home in October 1944. Stilwell came back full of piss and vinegar toward Chiang Kai-shek and the Nationalists, but in recalling him from Chongqing, Roosevelt successfully defused Republican attacks on his China policy and distanced himself from the Generalissimo in time to win the election.

Carlson's heart had been with China's Communists since his first tour with them in 1938, but he still maintained that a multiparty United Front had to be the basis for a future democratic government there. In his writings and speeches he had generally tried to be equally supportive of Chiang Kai-shek (the other "star" of his *Twin*

Stars of China). But by the time Stilwell was recalled home, Carlson was ready to throw in the towel. "The fact is that there is nothing democratic about the Kuomintang Party or the government which it administers," he wrote to Agnes Smedley. "The only organized group in China which labors to improve the welfare of the people is the Chinese Communist Party." (Even then, though, he could not imagine a China ruled by the Communists alone—in a postscript, he clarified: "What China needs right now is immediate restoration of freedom of speech and of the press and the establishment of a coalition government with Communist and Progressive Kuomintang leaders as well as representation from the Right Wing Kuomintang and the other minority parties.")

Carlson and Stilwell had known each other since Hankow in 1938, when the straitlaced Stilwell enjoyed mocking Carlson's odd sartorial tastes in his diary. ("Carlson has made shorts by cutting off long khakis," he noted in one entry. "He wears high shoes with them and his stockings hang loose—Terrible." After the banquet for Carlson's farewell, Stilwell wrote with astonishment, "Carlson had on a white suit!") Stilwell liked Carlson on the whole, and privately nicknamed him "Captain Courageous." When Carlson was in the hospital, Stilwell sent his sympathy, telling him, "I know it is useless to advise you to take it easy and let the war take care of itself for a while, for the simple reason that you aren't built that way." He was responding to a letter in which Carlson had shared the same concerns about the antidemocratic nature of the KMT that he had sent to Agnes. "What you say about Chiang is, I am afraid, very much to the point," Stilwell replied. He said he appreciated Carlson's moral support "because you know the conditions we have been up against in China."

Back in 1927 when Chiang first turned on the Communists, unleashing his violent purge of left-wing KMT members and labor organizers, Carlson had celebrated the wisdom and foresight of Chiang's move and wrote for years afterward that the White Terror was a necessary step toward distancing China from the Soviets and improving relations with the United States and Great Britain. From his hospital bed in 1944, he finally reversed that judgment. "As I see the picture," he wrote to Agnes, "China is now reaping the whirlwind as a result of Chiang Kai-shek's betrayal of the Chinese people in

1927, when he purged the liberal elements from the Kuomintang in order to gain favor with the Shanghai bankers and the foreign powers." Since 1928, he continued, "I know of not one measure which has been promulgated by the KMT which is designed to prepare the people for assuming the role of citizens of a democracy."

Carlson forwarded a copy of his letter from Zhu De to Franklin Roosevelt, hoping the president would read it in the same light that he did: as further confirmation that the Chinese Communists were sincere in their desire to cooperate with the United States. "I am delighted to see those letters," Roosevelt wrote back on November 15, a week after his reelection. "Things in Chongqing look a little better, and I am hoping and praying for a real working out of the situation with the so-called Communists." His use of "so-called Communists" was music to Carlson's ears, for it was exactly what Carlson had been trying to convince the president of since his mission to China in 1937: that the Chinese of the Eighth Route Army were "communist" in name only. If Roosevelt shared Carlson's openness toward them, and if, as his note implied, he might use America's influence to help push for a détente between them and the KMT—rather than just blindly supporting Chiang Kai-shek—then perhaps the eventual victory against Japan could be followed in China not by a civil war but by the birth of a democracy. But Roosevelt said nothing further on that. It was a brief note and he was an incredibly busy man. "Take care of that arm," he told Carlson. "I hope to see you some day soon." He died a few months later.

The death of President Roosevelt was for Carlson the darkest moment in the entire war. "You know how dearly I loved your father and how devoted I was to him and to his ideals," he wrote to James Roosevelt the day after. "Your father's friendship is the greatest inspiration of my life." As he had told Missy LeHand in one of his secret missives in the late 1930s, "I am devoted to him not only as our President, but also (and primarily) because of the things he stands for as a man." Carlson's relationship with Franklin Roosevelt had been the greatest honor of his life, and now he felt like he was on a ship without a rudder. "I know of no one else whose leadership I could follow with the supreme confidence with which I followed FDR," he wrote to another friend. "I was so certain of his integrity—of his concern for the welfare of all the people."

Along with his grief for Roosevelt the man, when the president died, Carlson's dreams for the future of America and China began to die as well. All of Carlson's hopes for China to avoid a civil war had depended on Roosevelt's willingness to mediate if necessary and push Chiang toward a power-sharing arrangement. Roosevelt had indicated a certain amount of sympathy toward the "so-called Communists" in China, and seemed to accept Carlson's description of them as fundamentally democratic and open to cooperation, even as he balanced those views against the complex exigencies of the war and the demands of Chiang Kai-shek's powerful supporters in the United States. But at least Carlson knew that his voice was being heard. After Roosevelt's death, Carlson no longer had any kind of access to the White House; he would be just another outsider again. "I fear for things in China now," he wrote to Edgar Snow.

When he first came home in 1944, Carlson (like many other military observers) had expected that the war in the Pacific would last at least two more years—and that was if the European War should end quickly so that all of America's resources could be brought to bear against Japan. He feared that American troops had not yet encountered what he considered "the cream of the Japanese army" in China. Even if the Japanese home islands were conquered, he believed the Kwantung Army could still hold out independently in Manchuria.

But major, unexpected transitions lay ahead. First was the death of President Roosevelt and the ascension of the untested, inexperienced junior senator from Missouri Harry Truman into the seat of power in Washington. Then came the ghastly fire-bombings of Tokyo and dozens of other Japanese cities that spring and summer: vast, relentless, low-flying waves of B-29 Superfortresses launched from the Marianas unloaded millions of pounds of napalm incendiaries onto Japan's dense, wood-structured neighborhoods, igniting firestorms that consumed entire city districts and burned hundreds of thousands of civilians to ash. Then, when Japan would not surrender, came the stunning detonation of the first atomic bomb over Hiroshima on August 6, a single weapon that killed as many as eighty thousand people in an instant. Even after the horrific demonstration of America's nuclear capacity at Hiroshima—compounding the destruction of the fire-bombing campaigns that had preceded it—it took the Soviet Red Army's invasion of Manchuria on August 9 (by prior agreement between Stalin and Roosevelt), followed shortly by the detonation of a second nuclear bomb at Nagasaki, to force an end to the war. On August 15, 1945, Emperor Hirohito made a radio broadcast to his nation announcing Japan's surrender.

The accelerated ending of the war just four months after Roosevelt's death opened a scramble for power in China that many had anticipated but no one had fully prepared for. Russian, Chinese Communist, and KMT troops rushed from different directions into North China to try to be the first to take control from the defeated Japanese. There were more than a million Japanese troops in China proper, and nearly a million more in Manchuria, as well as the better part of two million Japanese civilians who had to be somehow repatriated home. Whichever army's troops arrived first to accept surrender from the Japanese could potentially secure their weapons and supplies and take control of their regions of influence. The areas of Japan's conquest in China—above all Manchuria, with its fourteen years of industrial development as a Japanese puppet state—now became gigantic vacuums of power, enormous prizes for whoever could seize them first.

And so came the return of the United States Marines to China—this time without Carlson. Fifty thousand Marines from the III Amphibious Corps, which had been training for the ground invasion of Tokyo that never took place, were landed instead on mainland China in September of 1945 to help manage the surrender of the Japanese combatants and civilians there. They were given an equally crucial secondary mission, however, which was one of intervention: to ensure that it would be Chiang Kai-shek's armies, rather than the Communists, who established control in the occupied areas.

Other than the limited, ineffectual overture of the Dixie Mission, the United States had never really been neutral in China during the war; America's overwhelming focus on the Pacific over the Chinese mainland led the Roosevelt administration to tolerate Chiang's monopolization of U.S. funding and military aid at the expense of the Communists. Now, in the aftermath of Japan's defeat, even the pretense of neutrality was abandoned. There was a new administration in Washington, and Truman had none of the ties to China that Roosevelt had, nor the understanding of its history. He thought little of Chiang Kai-shek, but nevertheless took an active hand in trying to strengthen the Generalissimo's position in China as a hedge against Stalin, who had aggressively resumed the expansion of his Soviet empire in the final months of the war.

Consequently, on the day after Japan's surrender in August 1945, Douglas MacArthur's General Order No. 1 instructed Japanese army forces in mainland China to surrender only to Chiang Kai-shek, cutting out the Communists entirely. The Communists protested, but to no avail. As the U.S. Marines landed in China, they accepted the surrender of Japanese forces on Chiang Kai-shek's behalf and held their positions until KMT troops could arrive to take over from them. By October of 1945, American military planes had begun airlifting several hundred thousand of Chiang's Nationalist troops from central and southwest China to the centers of Japanese occupation in the northeast—a baldly partisan effort to forestall the overland advance of Zhu De's Communist troops into the region.

In cities where there were not enough KMT or American troops to maintain control, Chiang Kai-shek's military authorized Japanese army forces to remain in place—*with* all of their weapons—to maintain security against the Communists. And not only were the Japanese allowed to hold defensive positions; they were also authorized and encouraged to undertake offensive operations against areas already under Communist control, which they did, fighting now as allies of Chiang Kai-shek. A staggering seven thousand Japanese troops would die fighting the Communists *after* Japan's formal surrender, operating on behalf of the KMT to prevent them from gaining ground. As the Americans and Japanese actively took the side of the Nationalists, even Stalin withheld support for Mao, preferring instead to ink a new treaty with Chiang, based on a secret agreement with Roosevelt from the Yalta Conference in February, that would give the Soviet Union many of Russia's old tsarist rights in Manchuria that had been lost to Japan in the Russo-Japanese War of 1904–1905. Far from welcoming their fellow Communists into Manchuria in 1945, Russia's Red Army instead operated on behalf of Chiang Kai-shek to keep them out of its cities.

Most of the Marines who landed in China at the end of World

War II had little idea what an explosive situation they were entering. Fresh from the horrors of Okinawa, the young men of the
1st Marine Division who entered Beijing in 1945 looked forward to
comfortable peacetime service in a friendly country. As their trucks
rolled into the old capital past cheering crowds of Chinese people,
one Marine stood, fist raised high, shouting "Gung ho! Gung ho!"
over and over until he went red in the face—much to the delight of
the Chinese spectators, who thought he was shouting "Ding hao!"
("Very good!").

Hastily composed training materials encouraged the men to think
positively about the shared history of China and America. "The U.S.
Marine Corps has never made a hostile landing in China," said an
intelligence pamphlet for the Marines heading to North China in
1945, which conveniently left out the Boxer Rebellion. "Our numer-
ous trips and stays ashore, whether long or short, have been to preserve order and to protect the lives and property of Americans." It
explained that the Chinese had always been America's allies, and the
Marines should look forward to a pleasant stay in the country—hardly
an occupation or invasion, more like an invitation from friends. The
history of the United States and China, it said, was one of "high spots
only" and the two countries had been "on most friendly terms for
many years."

The pamphlet echoed Carlson's earlier efforts to cut through
American stereotypes about China when he was with the Legation
Guard in Beijing. "We Americans know very little about China and
the Chinese," it said. "We studied the geography of Asia when we
were in grade school and have a foggy idea of the extent of the country." It explained that the Chinese were "essentially democratic" and
encouraged the men to think positively about the Chinese people
themselves, that Americans could learn from them and they were
"not just another kind of 'gook.'" It also encouraged the men to
respect Chinese culture. "The Chinese are civilized," it said. "Don't
get the idea they aren't because they do so many things just the opposite from our way. Maybe they are nearer right than we are; at least
their way has a much longer history back of it." There was nothing
in the pamphlet to alert the troops to the fact that they were stepping
into what many diplomats expected would be the beginning of an
all-out civil war.

The end of World War II found Agnes Smedley living in upstate New York at the Yaddo writers' colony in Saratoga Springs, which had taken her in in 1943 after she ran out of money in New York City. All told, she would spend the better part of five years enjoying the peace and beauty of its four hundred acres of landscaped grounds, working on her writing, living rent-free in the upstairs of an old farmhouse, and socializing with fellow residents like Langston Hughes and Carson McCullers. She ventured out occasionally for speaking tours to promote *Battle Hymn of China*, but always returned with relief to her refuge at Yaddo. In the fall of 1944, she had tried to arrange a fellowship for Carlson to come live there as well—the director of Yaddo said she would be happy to sponsor a convalescing Marine who needed a quiet place to write—but he declined, saying there was too much he couldn't say in print while he was still in uniform. (He may also have sensed an ulterior motive; his response went on at conspicuous length about his new wife, Peggy, whom he emphasized was a great admirer of Agnes. He said he hoped they could be friends.)

At Yaddo, Agnes finally started writing the biography of Zhu De for which she had been collecting materials since before she and Carlson met. It was slow going, though, and it was no longer possible to interview him in person. She was frustrated. "I'm working on my new book," she wrote to a friend, "and, as usual, wish I'd never been born." It wasn't until the summer of 1946 that Zhu De would send her more materials by courier to work with. When he did, he enclosed a letter thanking Agnes and other "American friends of China" for making possible the hope for a democratic government in China after the Japanese defeat. "American democratic activities have considerably strengthened the friendship between the Chinese and the American people," Zhu De told her. He asked her to keep her faith in China and said he would likewise continue to believe in the American people. He said he doubted that his life was worth writing about, for he was just "a very small part of the life of the Chinese peasants and soldiers." But he obliged her request for sources and enclosed a draft biography of himself in Chinese written by Liu Baiyu, one of the five "boys" Carlson had traveled with in 1938, along with his own writings from the period of the war. He asked her to give his best wishes to Carlson and Stilwell. "The Chinese people all remember his righteous efforts," he said.

With the war ending, and with Carlson slated for retirement from the Marines on the basis of his injuries, it was practically a foregone conclusion that he would run for office. He had a public profile in America matched by few in the Marine Corps. Along with General Vandegrift, Lewis "Chesty" Puller, and the late Smedley Butler (who died in 1940), Carlson was a household name. *Time* magazine described his chest in 1945 as being "one of the world's most bemedaled." The *Marine Corps Chevron* called him "one of the most experienced of all Marine officers." The *Chicago Sunday Tribune* ran a full-page color portrait of him in February of 1945 on the front page of its graphic section, wearing his service uniform, set against an American flag background. The accompanying story called him "just about one of the toughest United States marines" and one of the "most decorated leathernecks in history." It catalogued his wounds from Saipan, adding: "The colonel does not need to fight any more. He has earned enough campaign ribbons and medals to last any self-respecting American family three generations."

The California Democratic Party had an opening on their ticket for the 1946 U.S. Senate election, and they sounded Carlson out on his willingness to run. James Roosevelt, who was based in Los Angeles, started convening focus groups to test the idea. The donors Roosevelt talked to loved the idea—Carlson was a war hero, a humanitarian, and a political liberal. To a public accustomed to war, he commanded an authority few outside of the

Front page of *Chicago Sunday Tribune* graphic section, February 18, 1945.

military could match. Hollywood adored him, as did multitudes of young war veterans coming home from the Pacific.

By the spring of 1945, rumors of a "draft Carlson" movement were feeding out into the press. The *San Francisco News* relayed the talk of his potential Senate run with excitement. "Some glamor that would give California politics," it said—"not to mention the up-pepping that could follow if 'Gung ho!' ever became the slogan of 'the most exclusive gentlemen's club in the world'!" There were plenty of other men in uniform who intended to run for office, it noted, but with Carlson it was the real deal: with him, "it would be a case of an authentic hero getting into politics."

In October of 1945, six weeks after Japan's formal surrender, Carlson acknowledged publicly for the first time that he intended to run for Senate. Speaking from a hospital bed where he had just undergone an operation on his right hand, he told a reporter that he hoped to enter politics as soon as his retirement from the Marines was finalized, which he expected would take place in January. The fighting was done and now—as he had repeated so many times in his eulogies and speeches during the war—it was time to look to the future. "I felt it was important to win the war with Japan to assure conditions that would be favorable for pressing for the realization of democratic ideals," he told the reporter. "I now feel the importance of putting my efforts into the elimination of discrimination, and the establishment of equality of opportunity. In other words, working for the reality of the things we told the men we were fighting for."

A Hollywood screenwriter named Michael Blankfort had been trying to write a biography of Carlson since 1943, though Carlson, who was fiercely protective of his personal life, was initially hostile to his overtures; he told Blankfort bluntly in 1944 to stop trying to interview his wife and father without his permission. Carlson's brother, Tom, also rejected Blankfort's entreaties, telling him in a salty letter that he didn't trust people who wrote biographies "ever since Agnes Smedley wrote that Evans had really done remarkably well in life considering his poor family background." After Carlson came back from the war, however, his wife, Peggy, helped win him over to the view that it might be good for his political career to have such a book published.

Blankfort wanted to call it *The Big Yankee*, to describe Carlson as he imagined the Chinese saw him. He was up against a lot in working on Carlson's story, though—an executive at Harcourt, Brace & Co. rejected Blankfort's book proposal, telling him that Carlson was a perfectly good writer and the book would "carry a far greater urgency" if he wrote it himself. But eventually *The Big Yankee* found a home at Little, Brown & Co., and Carlson gave Blankfort access to some of his correspondence as well as permission to talk to his family and friends. Helen Foster Snow, for one, liked the idea of the book being a launching pad for Carlson's political career. "Michael—let's start building him up for President in 1948," she wrote to Blankfort. "I'm deadly serious." She said the biography could be the first step in that plan. "But keep this confidential," she insisted, "so Evans won't be embarrassed by it."

To Carlson himself, Peg Snow (who had always loved giving him firm and opinionated advice) sent a warning not to say too much about his life to Blankfort, so as to ensure that the biography was written "as a campaign document only." Its sole purpose, she said, should be to make Carlson "respected by the general public." He could write the full details of his life in his own book later, or others could tell the story of his life "after you are long dead etc." But for now, he should try to remain a "dark horse." Carlson was unique in his appeal to both liberals and conservatives, she said, and he was possibly the only person who could build a bridge between the twelve million returning war veterans and the members of the labor unions whose jobs they would soon be trying to take back. She said he should especially avoid taking a stand on any controversial issues like Black civil rights that might cause the Southern Democrats to oppose him.

Carlson didn't want advice, though. He insisted that he would not be anyone's puppet, and when he started making political speeches he refused to work with ghostwriters. If he was going to serve in public office, he said, he would do it as himself. "I may use the wrong words and the wrong technique, but they are my words and my technique," he wrote to Blankfort. "I have said that I will accept a Senatorship provided it is the will of the people that I serve. However, in presenting my views to the people I shall use my own words, and in representing the people I shall use my own methods. . . . Either they take me as I am, or not at all." A month later he added, "I want above all that the people be convinced they can place their confidence in me without fear of being sold down the river."

The Nation came on board with Carlson's candidacy in December of 1945. The left-wing magazine liked his progressive consciousness, his ideas for democratizing the armed forces, and his deep-seated moral convictions. It also noted approvingly that a senator who could speak both Chinese and Spanish would be "a rather exceptional figure on the hill." But the clincher was what Carlson's men said about him. The magazine asked one of his Raiders, a staff sergeant, for his thoughts on his former commander. "I find that words are of no use to me," said the Marine. "When the Colonel is mentioned you don't think, you feel things inside of you that you were not aware of, that become a part of your life while you are with him." The magazine concluded that any man who could inspire such feelings in those he commanded had more than proven his potential for democratic leadership.

The press was starstruck. One journalist who interviewed him in San Francisco remembered: "as we walked down Market Street, I could see people stopping and staring at this magnificent tall handsome marine general with all those medals. . . . I was so pleased to be with him." On December 4, 1945, Carlson took the stage at

Carlson, arm in sling, speaking at a rally after the war.

Madison Square Garden to speak out against Truman's China policy as part of a program on the significance of the atomic bomb for world affairs. When Carlson came up to the podium, limping and withered, his right arm hanging useless in a sling, 22,000 people rose to their feet in a standing ovation, chanting in unison: "Gung! Ho! Gung! Ho! Gung! Ho!"

Carlson ignored Peg Snow's advice to steer clear of controversy. At a CIO union conference in Los Angeles, he championed a resolution to withdraw all American forces from China immediately, insisting that the United States must maintain neutrality between the KMT and the Communists. "I can't say much about the Chinese situation while in uniform but I could tell you plenty if I wasn't," Carlson told his audience. "It is not compatible with our democracy to intervene in other people's affairs." Elsewhere, he spoke out passionately in favor of veterans' rights, and against racial discrimination. In a foreword for a book on the moral imperative to end segregation in the military, he wrote: "We must mend the fences of our democratic society, and one of the gaps most in need of attention is the prejudice practiced in many communities against the Negro citizen." He could not have cared less what the Southern Democrats thought.

By Christmas of 1945, Carlson's Senate candidacy was all but a lock. James Roosevelt's circle of Hollywood donors closed ranks around him. Robert Kenny, the California attorney general and head of the state Democratic Party apparatus, wrote to Michael Blankfort on December 26 that "the prospects are now excellent for the Colonel to get the Democratic nomination at the June 4th election." Elsewhere, Kenny shared his opinion that Carlson was the only man in California politics who was "literally able to move his hearers to tears." He was the perfect Democratic candidate—fully acceptable to the left, while the right, as Kenny saw it, "was unprepared to oppose the political mystique of an undeniable hero of the war just fought and won." Kenny told Blankfort that if *The Big Yankee* could be timed to come out in print right after Carlson received the party's nomination that summer, it would be a boon heading into the November general election.

Everything was going according to plan, until Carlson had his first heart attack.

CHAPTER 23

SHIFTING GROUNDS

C ARLSON HAD SUFFERED from chest pains for weeks, but he thought they were just lingering tenderness from a bout of pneumonia so he kept at his work. The momentum of his Senate candidacy was still building. On January 13, *The Washington Post* called him "Lincolnesque" and raved about him as a political newcomer. "The war in the Pacific, which left him physically crippled, was a personal triumph for Colonel Carlson," it said. "Although he can no longer serve his country as a Marine, Carlson hopes to serve in another role—Senator from California." The paper described him as an "Ace Marine Raider" who "led and inspired one of the greatest fighting forces of the Nation."

But his heart could not take the strain. The heart attack came on January 29, 1946, and it landed him back in the San Diego Naval Hospital for six weeks. He survived, but his political career was over before it could begin. In early February, still in the hospital, he withdrew his name from consideration for the Senate nomination. It went instead to a far less compelling candidate—Will Rogers, Jr., son of the humorist Will Rogers—who went on to lose by nearly ten points to the Republican incumbent.

Carlson was bedridden for the better part of four months after he left the hospital, and with his campaign for Senate derailed, he found himself with plenty of time to brood over the news from China. He felt a growing anger at what he saw as the injustice of Truman's interference there, but he was still not retired from the Marines so he had to be careful what he said to reporters. To friends he could be candid, though. "Actually we are using the disarming and repatriation of Japanese troops as a device for supporting the government of Chiang Kai-shek," he wrote to Agnes Smedley. "I am convinced that the present administration in Washington has no more desire for a people's government in China than does Chiang Kai-shek or any of his mealy mouthed and parasitical ministers."

Carlson was finally freed to speak his mind publicly on July 1, 1946, when his retirement came through. As a farewell honor, in recognition of his Navy Crosses, the Marines retired him at the rank of brigadier general—henceforth he would be known as "General Carlson." For the first time since Pearl Harbor he could weigh in on issues of foreign policy without fear of censure, and as he regained his strength he devoted what energy he had to the situation in China, where he denounced Truman's policy of intervention as "a vigorously conducted campaign for economic domination of Eastern Asia by American industrial interests." The United States should support democracy abroad, he argued, but by propping up Chiang Kai-shek and his corrupt Nationalist Party they were doing exactly the opposite.

Up until the end of World War II, it had been an easy case to make that the Chinese Communists owed little to the Soviet Union. Although Mao had always bent toward Stalin ideologically, the Soviet leader gave him almost nothing in return. Not only did most Soviet aid go to Chiang Kai-shek during the war instead of to Mao and Zhu De, the treaty Stalin signed with Chiang's government immediately after the Japanese surrender left the Communists out entirely. Stalin pledged to give "moral, material and military" support exclusively to the KMT, and in return the Soviet Union would regain the tsar's colonial rights to railway lines and warm-water ports in Manchuria, as well as control over Mongolia. Edgar Snow, for one, was appalled at the crassness of Stalin's move: "This is the last and final proof that Moscow's policies are determined solely and only by national considerations," he wrote in his diary at the time. The Chinese Communists pretended publicly to support the treaty, repeating their calls for a coalition government in China, but privately they were furious at what was merely the latest insult from their ostensible ideological allies next door.

At Chiang Kai-shek's request, Stalin left his forces in Manchuria for three months after the Japanese surrender to prevent the Chinese Communists from gaining ground there. But when those three months had passed and the Red Army showed no signs of abandoning its hold on the region, President Truman sent George Marshall to China in an attempt to broker a peace agreement between the Communists and the KMT and hopefully help them establish a coalition government, while also pressuring the Soviets to leave Manchuria. In Truman's words, it was "in the most vital interest of the United States and all the United Nations that the people of China overlook no opportunity to adjust their internal differences promptly by methods of peaceful negotiation."

Marshall met with some initial success upon his arrival in January of 1946. He managed to get the two parties to agree to a cease-fire and set up meetings to discuss the outlines of a new constitution in which they would share power, though it took a threat from Truman to withhold American aid and military supplies from the KMT to make Chiang cooperate. The Soviets, meanwhile, bowed to U.S. pressure and began withdrawing their troops from Manchuria (after looting the region's industrial base, breaking down entire factories and shipping them back to Russia by train). But as Stalin relinquished his grip on Manchuria he also, finally, started supplying arms to the Chinese Communists as a hedge for the future.

Marshall would remain in China for a year, a rather unhappy one from his point of view, but even this attempt at American neutrality in China, with Marshall playing the role of peacemaker, was notably one-sided. Soon after his arrival, Marshall assured Chiang he would confide only in him, not the other side. Marshall had little contact with the Communists, who were required to send their negotiators to Chongqing and later Nanjing, conducting their meetings in Chiang's house, as it were. Marshall and his wife spent much of their time at Chiang's luxurious mountain residences, socializing with the Generalissimo's family and playing endless rounds of Chinese checkers. He visited Yan'an just once, for less than twenty-four hours. And though Marshall insisted that both sides must halt their troop movements in China proper, he did not make the same demand for Manchuria, where Chiang's forces alone were allowed to move in and take over from the Soviet Red Army. By the summer of 1946, Mao concluded that Marshall's mission was nothing more than "a smoke screen for strengthening Chiang Kai-shek." It was obvious to both sides that the United States did not want to see the Communists hold any significant power in China. Truman was far from enthused about Chiang Kai-shek, but the Generalissimo was still America's man—for better or for worse—and the pressure from the United States for him to enter a coalition government with the CCP was intended at least partly to protect him from a civil war he might not win.

Under these circumstances, Carlson saw no hope for the Marshall Mission. In July of 1946, he predicted that Truman's attempt at mediation in China would do nothing to prevent another war, and might only make matters worse. He believed that mediation between the two parties was meaningless as long as the United States kept supplying arms to Chiang that he could use against the Communists. "No one could succeed under these conditions," said Carlson. He was certain that as long as Chiang felt assured of continued support from Truman, he would never agree to a compromise with the Communists, and down that road lay a resumption of violence. If a full-scale civil war should erupt in China with the United States taking the side of Chiang Kai-shek even indirectly, Carlson warned in a speech on July 24, it would be "the powder keg for the precipitation of a third World War."

Joseph Stilwell avoided talking to the press after he came home from China, so it was Carlson who emerged as the most outspoken and authoritative voice of condemnation for Truman's policy of supporting Chiang—a policy he called "patently imperialistic in concept and practice." He channeled the ghost of Smedley Butler when he told a group of returned veterans in August 1946 that the only reason the Marines were in China was for the sake of U.S. business interests. "They are there today," he said, "because Wall-Street interests want to see a certain government maintained in China so they can get many returns from their commitments." Carlson said the war was over and there was no reason the Marines shouldn't come home; the Chinese were perfectly capable of settling their own affairs. Two months later, he headlined a three-day rally in California calling for the United States to remove its troops from China and stop providing military aid to the KMT. Representatives of Chiang's government in San Francisco labeled the rally "another Communist front outfit hoping to arouse public opinion."

The situation in China spiraled. In a last-ditch attempt to restrain

Chiang from attacking the Communists, Truman temporarily halted the shipment of new U.S. weapons to the KMT in the summer of 1946. But that embargo had no effect. Carlson's prediction that the Marshall Mission was doomed proved correct, and by January of 1947 the failure of American mediation was clear enough that Truman ordered Marshall home from China. Within months, U.S. supplies for the KMT would resume in even grander fashion—between 1947 and 1949, the Truman administration would sell Chiang Kai-shek more than a billion dollars of American arms to use against the Communists and supply him with $2 billion in loans and credits, more aid than the United States gave to any of the nations in Western Europe.

By the time Marshall returned home from China, the negotiations for a new political structure had broken down intractably. Fighting had resumed between the KMT and CCP—now with the novel, complicating factor of Soviet military aid to the Communists to offset America's supply of weapons and funding to Chiang Kai-shek. The United States proved no more capable of imposing a democracy on China than it had done in Nicaragua. In the end, George Marshall left China even more unstable than he had found it.

Now that Carlson was retired, he needed to find a place to settle down. He and Peggy could not afford to buy anything in Southern California, where they had been renting a tiny one-bedroom house in Escondido since his return from the Pacific, but they no longer needed to be near a Marine base, so in the summer of 1946 they set out across the country to look for a new place to live. Carlson thought fondly about Montana, which he remembered from his canned-fruit days, or else somewhere in the Northeast where their friends and his family lived. He preferred a place with a warmer climate for the sake of his heart, but refused to consider living in the segregated, Jim Crow South, which he found morally abhorrent.

Their long trip across the country to find a home was, by Peggy's description, "grueling." Carlson was still too weak to climb stairs, so they could only stay in hotels that had elevators, but he tolerated the driving well enough. Setting out in August they started across the country by way of New Mexico, Oklahoma, and Tennessee. In Athens, Tennessee, Carlson spoke to a mass meeting of war veterans who had converged from across the state to take part in the overthrow of a corrupt local political boss who had been falsifying elections. Praising the veterans, Carlson called the incident "the most hopeful yet experienced in this country." He had always believed in the power of young veterans to effect positive social and political change after the war, and he saw the events in Tennessee as a first step on that path. He urged the men in Athens to organize other veterans from surrounding communities and build "a spearhead for good government" that could attack corruption on a wider scale. "I'm for the boys," he told a reporter, "and feel that such an organization with integrity and good government as a goal will be of great value to our country."

From Tennessee, he and Peggy continued on to the Northeast, back to his roots. In upstate New York, they tracked down the parsonage where he had been born, though he left unrecorded how he felt upon seeing for the first time the home where his itinerant life had begun. They continued on to the Yaddo writers' colony in Saratoga Springs, where they spent a couple of days with Agnes Smedley, strolling the lush grounds and listening to her stories.

Carlson also reconnected for the first time in years with Edgar Snow, who had been out of the country for much of the war pursuing his reporting. As was the case for most Marine officers who had spent as long in active service as Carlson had, his military career had left him with almost no money to buy a home. Snow's *Red Star* sales, on the other hand, had bought him not just six acres and a colonial farmhouse in the coastal enclave of Madison, Connecticut, but also an apartment in Manhattan's Upper East Side, which the Carlsons borrowed as a base for exploring the city.

New York was ground zero for progressive politics and as a liberal war hero Carlson was beset by a swarm of organizations that wanted him to speak at their functions and help them raise funds. He agreed to serve with the Black singer and activist Paul Robeson as cochairman of the National Committee to Win the Peace, a far-left group (descended from the Communist-affiliated American League Against War and Fascism) that he supported because, among other causes, it called for the withdrawal of American forces from China. He and Robeson gave a joint press conference in New York where they charged that Truman's actions were strengthening fascism in

China. Carlson compared Chiang Kai-shek's government to that of Hitler or Mussolini, and said it was only in power because the United States was supporting it. If the Chinese could vote, he said, "the first thing they would do would be to kick Chiang and his Kuomintang group out of office." He told *The New York Times* that in China "the only democratic force—the only organization aiming to benefit the broad mass of people there—is that being fostered by the Chinese Communists."

In spite of the presence of his friends and family, Carlson ultimately decided against making a home in the Northeast. The winters would be cold, and it had in common with Southern California that it was too expensive. But Carlson also worried about the stress on his heart if he should live too close to Washington and New York City, with all of the demands people there wanted to make on his time and energy. Agnes Smedley and Edgar Snow told him he should seek solitude and quiet, and he agreed with them. "I'm going to hole up and read and write," he told his father. "No speaking." So he and Peggy trekked back across the northern reaches of the United States in search of somewhere more peaceful.

They found what they were looking for in Oregon, as they were driving across the Wapinitia Pass on their way to Portland in October. It was a small town called Brightwood on the lower slopes of Mount Hood. There was a little polished-log cottage for sale there with a large stone fireplace and an acre of land on the east bank of a rushing stream full of trout. It was cozy, but it had a large porch and a garden with ferns and tall rhododendrons, and as far as Carlson was concerned, it was perfect. It was far from the demands of the East Coast, surrounded by towering forests of cedar and fir, with a temperate climate below the snow line. There was no telephone, but the post office was only a quarter mile away. It seemed like a place where he could recover in peace.

They only needed $5,500 to buy the cottage, but they did not have that much in their savings and when Carlson tried to get a loan from the banks in Portland, they all turned him down. After all he had done for his country, their refusal to give him a mortgage made his blood boil. Those bankers, he wrote to Agnes Smedley, were "perfectly willing that young fellows shall go out and get killed to protect their right to make money, but not willing to finance homes for them if they come back." If a retired officer like himself couldn't get a loan, he told Agnes, "you can imagine what the average G.I. is up against." It is unclear why he did not resort to a federal loan through the G.I. Bill, but pride may have played a part. In the end he wound up borrowing the money from Edgar Snow, who had plenty to spare.

When they moved into the Brightwood cottage, Carlson looked forward to hunting in the surrounding forests and fishing in the stream that flowed behind their yard. He planned to spend much of his time reading, and thought that maybe he would write another book about China. He decorated the living room with photos and memorabilia he had collected over the years—artifacts of the richer and more meaningful life he had dreamed of finding in his younger years. Among them were his military decorations, a "gung ho" sign, and a portrait of Zhu De. With another loan from Edgar Snow, he purchased a full set of the *Encyclopaedia Britannica*. He and Peggy adopted a luxurious, long-haired black cat they named "Raider," who kept the mice at bay, and a neighbor gave them a dog, which Peggy's son, Tony (the one raised on Soviet children's literature), named "Comrade." The locals were glad to have a war hero in the neighborhood.

Carlson made it less than a month in his new home before he suffered another heart attack, followed in the hospital by a minor stroke. When he got back to the Brightwood cottage at the end of December he could barely walk, let alone hunt or fish. He turned fifty-one on February 26, 1947, but his health was so fragile he might as well have been four decades older. Along with the heart attacks, the stroke, the bone grafts, and the pneumonia, he also suffered from recurrences of malaria. His right arm was in a sling and he could only walk very short distances, slowly, before he reached the point of exhaustion. His teeth were falling out. His eyesight was failing. After multiple operations his right hand still barely worked. Even a slight amount of exertion or emotional stress could give him chest pains, leaving him bedridden for days. He complained in the hospital that when he got out, the only thing he would be able to do safely would be to play with a model train set. Peggy, taking him literally, bought him one for his birthday.

And yet the demands kept coming. Back in 1938 when Carlson resigned from the Marine Corps, Edgar Snow had warned him not to get his name associated with any political groups in the United States. He said that Carlson occupied a fragile position as a respected military officer who also believed in liberal causes, and Snow did not want to see him typecast as a zealot or bound by obligations to any group or organization. "Your greatest value as a writer is to present facts, I think," Snow told him, "not to polemicize. . . . You can't afford to isolate yourself, by tying up with anyone."

It was sound advice, and Carlson had followed it back then. The only group he had connected himself with was the Price Committee, which was a genuinely bipartisan group with the single purpose of passing an embargo against Japan, so he supported every aspect of its work. After the war, however, he was so famous that there were a great number of groups that wanted to use his name, and after the heart attack made his direct participation in politics impossible, he started agreeing to invitations from them—to serve in honorary capacities on their boards, to supply quotations for their publications, to be a figurehead for their organizations. As he explained to Raymond Swing in a letter from Brightwood, "While fuming in the hospital last spring with the heart ailment I had joined a lot of committees as an effort to make some contribution to straight thinking and decent action about domestic and foreign problems." If he couldn't make the changes himself, he would let others do it in his name.

And so down he went, into the rabbit hole of progressive activism. A more pragmatic man might have taken more care to steer clear of association with communists, but Carlson had never been much for pragmatism. Once he signaled his willingness to lend his stature as a war hero to the groups he agreed with, he was hounded by a wide range of organizations with highly similar-sounding names, all wanting his stamp of approval and his name on their stationery—the National Citizens Political Action Committee, the National Committee to Win the Peace, American Youth for Democracy, the Progressive Citizens of America, the Committee for a Democratic Far Eastern Policy, and the list went on.

As long as he supported their outward platforms, he was inclined to help them. But since his primary cause was American neutrality in China—and since the Soviet Union was now supporting the Chinese Communists against American-backed Chiang Kai-shek—this meant that he found himself in alignment with several groups connected behind the scenes to the American Communists, who saw in him a champion. Carlson and the Communists came to the issue from very different directions; Carlson wanted the U.S. out of China on principle, for the sake of neutrality and self-determination, while they wanted U.S. troops out of China so the Soviets could shape the outcome there. On the surface, though, it became nearly impossible to distinguish between them.

It was a stark departure from just a year earlier, when he told Blankfort that he would only ever speak for himself. Now, in his weakened state, there were so many groups using his name he could barely keep them straight. He had no manager or public relations agent (other than his wife and caretaker, Peggy, who was even further left than he was), so as long as the organizations stood for the same things he did—as long as they supported racial equality, opposed U.S. military intervention in China, and viewed the war veterans as a force of democratic change—he was willing to lend them his name and likeness, regardless of who else might fall under their umbrella. Though he did draw the line when one of the groups asked if it could make a rubber stamp of his signature. His reaction to that involved what Peggy described delicately as "some rather strong words." Incapacitated as he was, he still refused to let anyone use him as a puppet.

Of all the groups he joined, Carlson gave the most of his fading energies to the Committee for a Democratic Far Eastern Policy, an organization that lobbied Congress to stop military aid to Chiang Kai-shek, advocated for the removal of U.S. troops from China, held remembrances for Joseph Stilwell (who died in October 1946), and published an English translation of Chiang's book *China's Destiny*, which they hoped would demonstrate to the reading public that he was a dictator and no friend of America. The group was based in New York but had branches around the country, including in Los Angeles, where one of its sponsors was Ronald Reagan. In August of 1946 Carlson agreed to be its honorary chairman.

Given the rising fears of Soviet infiltration in the United States, the CDFEP's executive director, Maud Russell, held the view that the committee should make clear that it was not a communist front, but at the same time it should not succumb to red-baiting by refusing to work with individual communists who happened to support its work. As Russell explained to a donor who was worried about communist influence in their organization, the committee focused on issues, and it would work with anyone who felt the same way about those issues, regardless of their background. "If some one points out there is a communist around," she said, "so what?" (Maud Russell was almost certainly a secret Communist Party member herself.)

As chairman, even if only in an honorary capacity—and communicating only by letter, since he lived thousands of miles away and had no phone—Carlson tried to steer a fair course for the organization. "We should not regard ourselves as a propaganda organization, though the opposition will always so label us," he wrote to Maud Russell. He said the committee should focus on promoting a foreign policy "consonant with the democratic ideals and principles which we, the American people, profess, and which are a solid part of our American faith." Anticipating the attacks that would surely be coming their way from Republicans, he said they must be careful always to act in such a way "as to leave no room for doubt that by advancing democratic practises and institutions abroad we are serving the paramount interests of the American people."

It was a treacherous time to be a critic of American foreign policy. Carlson urged the committee to respond vigorously to those who charged that removing U.S. troops from China would simply allow the Soviets to sweep in to take their place. His view was that no outside power—be it the United States or the Soviet Union—was capable of altering the course of events in China in any significant way. The country was simply too big, the fault lines too vast, and the historical struggle between the Nationalists and the Communists too deeply rooted, to depend on the near-term interventions of foreigners. The Chinese would determine their own fate—he was certain of that—and the United States must ensure that when they did, it did not make itself an enemy by trying to stand in the way.

The public was largely on Carlson's side. A University of Chicago survey in October 1946 found just 18 percent of respondents wanting the United States to help the KMT in China, while 69 percent said the U.S. should remain neutral. But Carlson no longer had the strength to go on speaking tours like he had done before Pearl Harbor. In press releases from the committee—dictated to Peggy, then mailed to Maud Russell in New York—he brought all of his life's experience to bear on this one, final cause. Chiang Kai-shek's troops would never be able to defeat the Chinese Communists, he insisted, because the KMT armies did not have the same kind of support from the ordinary people. They were not conditioned "physically, professionally, spiritually or morally" for the kind of grueling campaign that would be necessary for them to achieve victory. In the final count, Carlson declared, Truman's intervention on behalf of Chiang Kai-shek was nothing less than a "betrayal of the Chinese people by the American Government." He predicted that it would go down as one of the greatest mistakes ever made in American diplomacy.

J. Edgar Hoover's FBI had been keeping a file for quite some time on what it called "the Communist tendencies of Lieutenant Colonel Evans Fordyce Carlson." One of the memos in the file relates to a 1943 profile of Carlson in the magazine *Current Biography* that discussed how Carlson "abolished officer's privileges" and how "the raiders wore the same clothes, carried the same equipment and lived alike." It reported, furthermore, that "Colonel Carlson has adopted the Eighth Route's method of group meetings where problems were threshed out and the men heard talks on Democracy, freedom of speech, press and religion." The following paragraph in the memo, which presumably contained an informant's commentary on the significance of the magazine profile, was, like much of the file, blacked out in its entirety before it was released in response to a Freedom of Information Act request—though its redacted contents were insidious enough to merit a comment in Hoover's own handwriting at the bottom of the page: "A surprising connection and of course a dangerous one because it would be least suspected."

Carlson was unaware that J. Edgar Hoover had taken an interest in him, but even if he had known of the FBI file, he surely would not have acted any differently because he refused to play along with the Red Scare. He was adamant that the freedoms he had fought for in the Pacific gave him the right to think, to read, to say whatever he wanted. That was the America to which he had given himself. It would not help his Cold War reputation that he was such a darling of the progressive left, or that the actual Communists in the United States admired him as much as anyone did. But he did nothing to hide those connections, and would have considered any advice to distance himself from them as an act of cowardice. Among the many publications he and Peggy followed from their home in Brightwood was the *Daily People's World*—a small-circulation communist paper published in San Francisco—and he enjoyed it sufficiently well that when he renewed his subscription in 1946 he sent a note to the editors, thanking them for their "courageous and factual reporting" and the "high quality of journalism" they were providing to the people of the West Coast. The paper proudly ran a facsimile of his message, looping signature and all, under the headline "A Letter from Col. Carlson." A copy, of course, ended up in his FBI file.

Henry Luce turned on him as soon as he started speaking out against Chiang Kai-shek. In a September 1946 article titled "Win the Peace for Whom?" *Time* magazine all but accused Carlson of being a Soviet agent. "Everyone knew that retired Brigadier General Evans F. Carlson was a Marine, and a good one," it said. "Not so many U.S. citizens knew that General Carlson had also long been an apostle of Communistic causes and Communist-fringe groups." The article focused on his service with Paul Robeson as cochairman of the National Committee to Win the Peace, and said he "made his ideology perfectly clear" when he said in one of his speeches that "the only democratic force [in China] is that being fostered by the Communists." The committee had a "strong Russian accent," said the magazine, and "seemed hell-bent on highballing down the Communist Party Line."

Carlson saw that piece in *Time* magazine and it made his stomach turn. He called it a "putrid article" and told his father that it was to be expected "because I am probably the most potent opponent of the ambitions of Henry Luce in China there is in America today." He wrote back to Luce's magazine to defend himself. "I am not a member of the Communist Party, nor am I an apostle for Communist causes," he said in a letter *Time* published three weeks later. "I am a free American citizen who has spent over 30 years in the armed services fighting in defense of the right of American citizens to enjoy life, liberty, the pursuit of happiness and the four freedoms." He added that he was retired as a result of wounds received in action, and by joining the National Committee to Win the Peace he was simply "exercising the right, common to all citizens, of expressing my opinions and working for those objectives which I am convinced are beneficial to my countrymen and humanity."

Time got the final word. Below his letter, the editor simply commented: "*TIME* did not say that distinguished Marine Carlson was a member of the Communist Party, [but] did make the indisputable point that his political views often take him into Communist-front organizations."

———

When *The Big Yankee* finally came out in February of 1947, it was banned for sale on Marine bases. *The New York Times* said it was "very useful and important, if not precisely objective." It got a gushing review from the Communist *Daily Worker*, which called Carlson "a real democratic hero of our time." At the other end of the political spectrum, a caustic review from the right called it "easily the most pretentiously literary work that has come out of the war." The latter critic, who praised Carlson's war record while scoffing at his politics, found the biography far too ideological. "A fighting man should have a fighting biography," he said, "not a tract." J. Edgar Hoover learned about the book from one of his agents, who described its publisher, Little, Brown & Co., as a hotbed of radicalism. He said Carlson was "well-regarded by the Communist and left-wing assortment of personnel which are presently operating the publishing company."

There is no question that the book was a sepia-toned exercise in hagiography. It was aimed squarely at a progressive readership, and its tone was adoring and uncritical. Even Blankfort's editor found it cloying. Michael Blankfort was in deep thrall to his subject (who would be reading it) and he took liberties with his writing to create dramatic effect—inventing dialogue and scenery, changing the wording of his sources to make them read better. The resulting book was baldly didactic, determined to show a Hollywood-smooth evolution in Carlson's character from starched conservative to a flawless, democratic leader of men. But all that was perhaps understandable, given that the book's main purpose had been to launch Carlson's Senate campaign.

But by the time *The Big Yankee* was published, not only was there no longer any Senate campaign for it to launch, Carlson could not even read anymore. He had suffered another stroke in February of 1947 that left him temporarily paralyzed. When his copy of *The Big Yankee* arrived at the Brightwood post office a few weeks later, Peggy had to read short passages from it aloud to him during the brief periods when he was awake. She tried to guess at his reactions by studying his facial expressions, since he could not speak coherently. Even then, the mere effort of concentrating on her voice quickly exhausted him. At age fifty-one, the "Big Yankee" was falling to pieces in his mountain retreat.

Two days before Carlson died of his final heart attack, he was visited in his Brightwood cottage by Henry Wallace. Wallace had been Roosevelt's vice president for his third term, until FDR dropped him for Truman in his fourth campaign, on account of Wallace's politics being so far to the left of the American mainstream (his followers were known to other Democrats as "the lunatic fringe"). Wallace was now the editor of *The New Republic*, and their meeting would be the last interview Carlson gave. At the time, Wallace was on the verge of launching an ill-fated, third-party presidential run for the 1948 election that would see him capture less than 3 percent of the vote for his far-left Progressive Party, which most people understood as being simply a front for the communists. (Even *The New Republic*'s publisher, Michael Straight, who accompanied Wallace on his visit to Carlson and would later confess to having once been a KGB spy, considered Wallace a communist front man and on that basis endorsed Truman over him for the 1948 election.)

During the visit, an account of which Michael Straight wrote up for *The New Republic*, the bedridden Carlson told Wallace what he expected was coming next in China. "The Yan'an and Shanxi forces of the Communists are going to unite with the forces in Manchuria and Chiang can't stop them," he said. "One day these forces will advance down into China on the same road the Manchus took. There will be years of fighting and famine and exhaustion if this war continues, and at the end the Communists will win." Less than a year later, the forces of the Chinese Communists would indeed consolidate their control over Manchuria and drive southward into the Chinese heartland, through the same corridor that the Manchus of the

Qing dynasty had used to conquer China from the Ming in 1644. By 1949, the vast Communist armies that had grown up from the seeds Zhu De had planted in North China in the 1930s would achieve victory across the full span of the Chinese mainland. Chiang Kai-shek, his government, and the remains of his Nationalist armies would flee under American protection into retreat on Taiwan, never to reclaim their mantle to rule China again. Carlson's final hunch was one of his most accurate.

CHAPTER 24

FORGETTING

AFTER CARLSON DIED, the government refused to cover the cost of transporting his body across the country to be buried at Arlington National Cemetery. His widow, Peggy, did not have enough money to ship it herself, for she and Evans had always been badly strapped for cash. Even if she'd had the money to send his coffin, she would not have had enough to buy her own ticket to accompany it and attend the funeral. Not knowing what else to do, she turned to James Roosevelt for help. Outraged on her behalf, he took up a collection from some of Carlson's wealthier admirers, including *Gung Ho!* producer Walter Wanger, to cover the costs of her journey. They came up with a total of $812.95, which was sufficient to get her to Washington with the coffin. It is not clear who donated the ninety-five cents.

The funeral on June 4, 1947, was impeccable from the standpoint of etiquette. Carlson was buried in Arlington National Cemetery on a sunny, late-spring morning. A black caisson rolled slowly through the cemetery carrying his flag-draped coffin, followed by a black horse with an empty saddle and a pair of gleaming-black boots turned backwards in its stirrups. At the grave, a detachment of the Marine Corps Band played "Nearer, My God, to Thee." An honor guard fired a salute as his coffin was lowered into the ground. General Vandegrift, now commandant of the Marine Corps, presented Carlson's grieving widow with the flag that had draped his coffin.

The ceremony followed every protocol, but in its heart it was empty. It was sparsely attended, because almost no one had been notified about it ahead of time. Hardly any of the generals who had served with Carlson over his long career chose to come. The four platoons of Marines who accompanied the procession were not his Raiders, they were simply men who happened to be near at hand. Only a few of Carlson's friends managed to learn in advance that the funeral was being held. Raymond Swing, the radio news anchor, was one of them, and he was appalled by how far it fell short of the kind of honor he thought Carlson deserved. The funeral "left nothing to be desired in piety and correctness," Swing wrote to *The Washington Post* the next day. "But one had no sense that a grateful Nation was lovingly saying farewell to one of its rarest heroes."

Swing had no informants within the Marine Corps, but he strongly suspected that the same in-house resentments that had brought about Carlson's removal from command at the peak of his success with the Raiders were now responsible for the obscurity of his funeral. "I venture to estimate that a generation from now Evans Carlson will be one of the best known and best loved Americans of the war," Swing told the *Post*, "not only for his intrepid skill and courage but because he redeemed so much that was lacking in democratic faith among his contemporaries." But there was no indication of any of that in the way Carlson's funeral service had been handled. Swing questioned whether the Marine Corps, the Navy Department, or even the U.S. government really knew "how to value the great men who have served them."

Swing's instinct was not far from the mark. Some would respond to his complaint by citing the litany of formal honors that had been part of the ceremony, but that was not the point. Formalities were not the same as heartfelt sentiment. Commandant Vandegrift had been reduced to twisting arms to coerce enough senior officers from the Washington area to come to Carlson's burial to make it look proper. Among those who resisted his entreaties was Merritt Edson, founder of the 1st Raider Battalion, who still carried a grudge against Carlson from the time when their rival units were created. When Vandegrift asked him to chair the funeral service, Edson refused, saying, "I have never been nor am I now an ardent admirer of General Carlson's. Although I respected his bravery as an individual, I have never agreed with the doctrines and policies which he espoused." According to William Worton, one of the few generals who attended the service, Vandegrift went through all the formalities of giving Carlson a textbook funeral at Arlington—"gave him the works," as Worton put it—and then, when it was over, he said with relief, "Thank God, he's gone."

The closed nature of the funeral made it difficult for those who loved him best to grieve. A group of Raider families in Chicago had pooled their money to buy a large floral wreath in the shape of the Raiders' blaze to lay on his grave, but they could not find out where to send it. The public relations department at the Marine Corps told them they couldn't share any information about the funeral and the families should contact the commandant's office instead. The person they spoke to at the commandant's office said they didn't know anything about a funeral. By the time they finally learned the date of Carlson's service it was only one day away, so there was no way to send the flowers to Washington on time. Fortunately Peggy Carlson changed trains in Chicago on her way across the country with Carlson's coffin, so they were able to give her the wreath at the train station, but they could not afford to come along with her.

Agnes Smedley led a more personal memorial service for him, organized by the Committee for a Democratic Far Eastern Policy on January 25, 1948. Speaking in front of a large, blown-up photograph of Carlson in uniform, she read aloud some of the passages he had marked in his worn copy of Emerson's *Essays*, the moral and spiritual guide he had carried with him for most of his life. Peggy had loaned her his copy. One passage in particular resonated with the changes he had undergone in his life, how his beliefs and principles had transformed in the course of his experiences in Nicaragua, China, and the Pacific. It was from Emerson's essay on self-reliance, and Carlson had underlined almost the entire passage:

> The other terror that scares us from self-trust is our consistency; a reverence for our past act or word. . . . Speak what you think now in hard words and to-morrow speak what to-morrow thinks in hard words again, though it contradict everything you said today.—"Ah, so you shall be sure to be misunderstood?" Is it so bad, then, to be misunderstood? . . . To be great is to be misunderstood.

Agnes talked about Carlson's love for his men, and their love for him. She recounted a conversation she'd had with a Raider who told her that Carlson died of a broken heart. "His heart began to break when he was removed from command of our Battalion," he said. "And ours did too." Agnes tried to sum up why she herself had loved Evans so deeply. She settled on his integrity, his honesty, and his deep religious convictions, which gave him, in her words, "a humility of soul such as I have never known in any other person except General Zhu De of China." Americans were used to thinking of gentle, humble men as being "soft and sloppy," she said, but Carlson was the opposite. "Carlson loved good people," she said, "he loved youth, he was gentle and humble, but he was capable of hard and fierce action in defense of good people and good policies. He was slow to speech and slow to anger, but when once convinced of the righteousness of his course of action, he was capable of any sacrifice."

Many at the time saw him as a martyr. The *Baltimore Sun*, in a piece titled "Death of a Rebel" two days after his death, commented that Carlson was in many ways "the black sheep of the United States Marine Corps." Referring to his removal from command in 1943, the *Sun* said "it was generally recognized in military circles that Evans Carlson was too unorthodox to suit his superior officers, and his ideas were receiving far too much publicity." After the war he had continued to be a thorn in the side of the military establishment with his activism among veterans. "General Carlson had learned a lesson in the remote regions of China that he never forgot," the paper concluded. "He devoted the last years of his life to spreading that gospel . . . he was a popular hero, and this is perhaps what most irked those who opposed his views."

The Washington Post denounced the "shabby treatment accorded General Carlson," calling the government's refusal to pay for his body to be transported to Washington a deliberate insult to one of America's great heroes. "The only consolation," it said, "lies in the sure knowledge that the imprint of General Carlson's valor and democratic faith is not something that can be eradicated." *The New York Times*, which had covered him since his first tour with the Eighth Route Army in 1938, devoted an editorial titled "Semper Fidelis" to him the day after he died. It quoted at length from his eulogy for the Raiders who died on Guadalcanal—the eulogy where he said that the reason for fighting the war was to ensure that the social order his men handed down to their children would be founded on the freedoms for which their brothers had died. "This was his creed and he never wavered from it," said the *Times.* "He was quite a man, this Carlson, faithful to himself and to that which he believed."

His friends knew what was likely coming. A few months after his death, Raymond Swing wrote to James Roosevelt, remarking on how many different committees and causes had tried to exploit Carlson's fame for their own purposes at the end of his life. "I hope Evans can be saved from being made a Communist *after* his death," he said. But the Red Scare had only just gotten started. One by one, the U.S. Attorney General's office listed the committees to which Carlson had lent his name in the final months of his life as communist, subversive organizations: the National Committee to Win the Peace was targeted a few months after his death in 1947. The Committee for a Democratic Far Eastern Policy was so listed in 1949. One of the founders of the latter organization admitted to being a Communist and testified before the Senate Internal Security Subcommittee that the group had been created at the direct instigation of the Communist Party of the USA. It is unclear whether Carlson was aware of the connection—Maud Russell denied it under oath and it shows up in none of his correspondence with the group—but then, even if he was aware of it, he probably wouldn't have cared as long as the committee championed a China policy that he agreed with.

Look magazine captured the rising hysteria of the time when it ran an article just before Carlson's death on "How to Spot an American Communist." It was not mere liberalism or progressive politics the magazine's readers should be worried about, it said, but actual Soviet agents in their midst. "The real Communist is not a liberal or a progressive," it said. "He believes in Russia first and a Soviet America. He accepts the doctrines of dictatorship as practiced in Russia. And he is prepared to use a dictator's tactics of lies and violence to realise his ambitions." None of that described Carlson, but the measures that the article recommended for detecting someone's secret Communist identity very much did. One of the warning signs, it said, was "Continually receiving favourable publicity in such Communist publications as the *Daily Worker* and the *New Masses*"—which Carlson regularly did. Likewise, it said, one should take note if a person appeared "as sponsor or co-worker of such known Communist-front groups as the Committee to Win the Peace." Carlson, of course, had been that group's cochairman.

Carlson's close engagement with the Chinese Communists had been the making of him, and it would be the destruction of him as well. In the spring of 1950, Louis Budenz, an ex-Communist and former editor of the *Daily Worker,* denounced Carlson along with dozens of others to the Senate subcommittee investigating Communist infiltration of the U.S. government. He gave no evidence other than his own (often faulty and inconsistent) memory, when he said Carlson "was a Communist before he was a general." Asked to repeat himself, Budenz said, "I know he was a general. Therefore he was part of the governmental machinery." A Democratic senator from Connecticut pressed him, "On Carlson, you know he was a Communist?" and Budenz confessed that he had only been introduced once to Carlson, during Carlson's hiatus from the Marine Corps when he was speaking on behalf of China. "Was he introduced to you as a Communist?" the senator asked. "Yes, sir," said Budenz. "And he accepted the introduction?" "Yes, sir."

In later testimony, Budenz added new details, placing the introduction in "the middle forties," and claiming that Carlson "has been a Communist for a long time according to the official reports made in the Politbureau and to me." (Budenz never produced those reports.) He also claimed in sworn testimony that "General Carlson was very widely discussed just before I left the party as the man who would lead the movement for a Red China in the United States."

When Budenz's testimony faltered, he attacked Carlson's biographer instead. "As a matter of fact, his life, gentlemen, is written up by a Communist under order of the Communist Party, by Michael Blankfort," said Budenz. Budenz cited passages from *Twin Stars of China* about Carlson's admiration for Zhu De and Mao as evidence that Carlson had clearly been producing "Communist propaganda" in order to subvert Chiang Kai-shek and hand China over to the Soviets. Blankfort was later called to testify and successfully defended himself against Budenz's accusations. But Carlson, being dead, could no longer speak for himself.

The tide was turning, and by the autumn of 1950, Carlson no longer had defenders when critics referred to him casually in print as "a notorious Pro-Communist." By 1951, Senator Joseph McCarthy would be singling him out by name; in *America's Retreat from Victory*, McCarthy's diatribe against George Marshall and what McCarthy saw as a massive conspiracy to undermine Chiang Kai-shek and hand China over to the Communists, he lumped Carlson together with Joseph Stilwell—who he believed was central to that conspiracy—writing, "I would remind the reader that Stilwell and Carlson are the Communist heroes of our war in the Far East, that both were and are honored in the *Daily Worker* and throughout the Communist movement in this country." McCarthy had read Freda Utley's memoir of life in Hankow, and from it he knew of Carlson's friendship with Agnes Smedley, whom he described as an "effective agent of Russian imperialism" who "dominated" the American expatriate community. McCarthy concluded that Smedley was the link that connected both Carlson and Stilwell to the Soviets. Evans Carlson, he pronounced in the end, had been nothing more than Agnes Smedley's "disciple."

In case it needs to be said, Carlson was not a communist, and no evidence has ever come to light that would suggest he tried in any way to undermine the government or political system of his home country. He was a patriot to his roots, who gave his life in service to a vision of freedom, democracy, and equality he had grown up on in New England. His admiration for what he called the "so-called" Chinese Communists was based on a willful interpretation on his part, that they were unwitting Christian democrats who, in their attention to the poorest classes of people of China, were doing the work of Jesus Christ without knowing it. It was an idealization, understanding them at least partly in his own terms—though the same can be said of many who claim to find deep commonalities across vastly different cultures. The point, though, is that Carlson admired the Chinese of the Eighth Route Army not because they were communists, but because deep down he felt certain that they weren't.

Carlson had been sufficiently controversial during his own lifetime, but in the years that followed his death, as the Cold War surged toward its peak, the insinuations about his "Communist tendencies" were enough to destroy his legacy and erase the memory of nearly everything he had done. By the Navy Department's own reckoning, he died as one of the most decorated officers in the Marine Corps. He had earned three Navy Crosses, two Purple Hearts, the Legion of Merit, three Presidential Unit Citations (for Guadalcanal, Tarawa, and Saipan), two medals from the president of Nicaragua, and nearly a dozen campaign decorations for operations in China, Nicaragua, and the two world wars. Today, however, there is nothing to commemorate him other than his tombstone. In contrast to the other Marine heroes of World War II—including some of the Raiders who served under him—there has never been a naval vessel of any kind named for Evans Carlson. There is no camp, no training site, no barracks, no veterans' care center, no road, no parade ground, no outbuilding, not even a recreation hall named in his honor.

The public would soon forget about him, though they might have done so anyway as their interest in the war faded. But as times continued to change, his memory would be revived now and then by military historians and others with similarly specialized interests. In 1987, forty years after his death, a profile of Carlson in the *Marine Corps Gazette* reintroduced his unorthodox methods to a new generation of

officers. Crediting him with "techniques and concepts of leadership that were many years ahead of their time," the article prompted a flood of responses from active and retired Marines, several of whom viewed him through the lens of the Vietnam War. One respondent asked whether Carlson wasn't the key to understanding what had gone wrong in that conflict. "What motivated the average North Vietnamese soldier to keep up his struggle against the Americans with our vastly superior logistics, artillery firepower, and air power?" he asked. "What

A haunted-looking Carlson after receiving the Legion of Merit.

was the North Vietnamese 'ethical indoctrination'?" Another Marine commented that "Ironically, it was the Gung Ho principle the Vietnamese used all too well against our forces," which he thought was "the price we paid, perhaps, for jettisoning too much of Col. Carlson's legacy." In the judgment of that veteran, the long-forgotten Evans Carlson was "the ultimate human being. . . . He was, to paraphrase Churchill, An American Worthy."

Carlson died before he could see the worst of the Red Scare, but his friends would suffer its full effects. By the late 1940s both Agnes Smedley and Edgar Snow were finding it difficult to get any of their writing published, or to secure invitations for speaking engagements. Helen Foster Snow, who was divorced from Edgar in 1949, found that she had to stop writing about China altogether if she wanted to publish anything at all. A front-page article in *The New York Times* in 1953 described Edgar Snow as one of a "mixed crew of communists and liberals" who had misled Americans about the Chinese Communists. *The Saturday Evening Post*, which had been his most regular employer, severed its relationship with him. In 1959, he left the country and moved with his second wife to Switzerland.

Agnes Smedley's past finally caught up to her in the winter of 1948, when the story came to light of her past relationship with Richard Sorge—"Sorgie," her lover from her early years in China, the devilishly handsome Soviet agent she would cling to as he drove his motorcycle at wild speeds through the streets of Shanghai. After he left China, never to see Agnes again, Sorge posed as a Nazi and successfully infiltrated the German embassy in Tokyo, where he became its press officer and a close confidant of Hitler's ambassador to Japan. He worked in collaboration with a journalist named Hotsumi Ozaki who served as an unofficial advisor to the Japanese cabinet. Agnes had introduced them to each other in Shanghai (Ozaki was the translator of her memoir *Daughter of Earth* into Japanese). With Ozaki's help, Sorge had funneled information from the highest levels of the Japanese government and the German diplomatic mission to Stalin, including advance notice that Hitler planned to throw more than 170 divisions into a surprise attack on the Soviet Union's western border on June 20, 1941 (Sorge's date for Operation Barbarossa was off by only two days).

Even more critically, Sorge was able to inform Stalin that the Japanese had no plans to launch a simultaneous attack on Russia from the east, via Manchuria, which reputedly freed Stalin to transfer his best Siberian forces to Russia's western front and throw the full weight of the Red Army against Hitler, thus changing the course of World War II. Sorge's intelligence coup was unrivaled in the annals of spycraft—though in truth, Stalin was likely too paranoid to have put that much stock in the word of one lone spy, no matter how good his information. Nevertheless, in the words of the espionage novelist John le Carré, Richard Sorge was "The spy to end spies." He was caught by the Japanese police in 1941 and hanged in 1944. Just before his execution, he wrote a confession in which he named Agnes Smedley as his most valuable collaborator in Shanghai.

The FBI had long had its eyes on Agnes. In 1944, J. Edgar Hoover described her internally as "one of the principal propagandists for the Soviets writing in the English language." But although the secretary at Yaddo had been secretly feeding them information about Smedley's visitors and activities for years, nothing public had emerged from the FBI's ongoing surveillance. Then, in January of 1948, the *Chicago Tribune* published the first report on her connection to Sorge. A month later, the Yaddo colony asked Smedley to pack up her belongings and move out so they would not be tainted by association with her. The real bombshell landed a year later, in February of 1949, when the U.S. Army made public a 32,000-word intelligence report from Tokyo on the Sorge spy ring that identified Agnes Smedley as one of the core members of what it declared to be the "most successful and complete spying operation in Japan's history." Douglas MacArthur warned that its members might be continuing their work in other countries. Smedley found herself on the front page of the national newspapers, publicly accused by MacArthur's intelligence division of being a spy and an agent of the Soviets. The accusation was far-fetched and somewhat paradoxical, given that Sorge had been spying only on the Japanese and Germans—America's enemies—on behalf of the Soviets, who were America's allies at the time, but in the postwar zeitgeist that distinction was meaningless.

Hounded by the press, evicted from her home at Yaddo, and facing the likelihood of formal charges before the House Un-American Activities Committee, Smedley fled the country, moving to England in 1949 in hopes of finding peace there. But the U.S. State Department would only grant her a one-year passport, to ensure that she would have to come home again. Before it could expire, however, she died in England from botched surgery for an ulcer. Ironically, one of her actual spy friends from Shanghai days, Ursula Kuczynski—now "Agent Sonja"—whom Agnes had recruited for Sorge back in 1930, was living right near her in England in 1949, posing as a British housewife. Although she knew Agnes was there, she avoided reaching out because Agnes's devotion to Stalin had for so long been suspect and Kuczynski was at that point running one of the largest networks of Soviet spies in Europe.

One of the most cherished memories of Agnes's life had always been the Christmas Eve she and Carlson spent together in Shanxi in 1937, sharing coffee and peanuts and singing hymns together by candlelight. In *Battle Hymn of China* she wrote that her friendship with Carlson was "the firmest of my life, welded in the fires of war." After she died, one of her close friends from Yaddo, the writer Katherine Anne Porter, wrote to a mutual acquaintance that she hoped that after all of the suffering and disappointment Agnes had endured in her life, she might have an afterlife in a place where she could be reunited with Evans Carlson again. "They were two brave soldiers if I ever saw any," said Porter. "She loved him so dearly I always hoped he loved her as well."

Beginning in the summer of 1950, less than two months after Agnes Smedley's death, the consequences of Truman's failed intervention in China played out to their darkest conclusion when a war on the Korean Peninsula drew the United States and the People's Republic of China into full-scale battlefield combat against each other for the first (and as yet only) time in their history. Had there at least been rudimentary diplomatic relations between the two countries at the time—which likely would have been the case if the United States had not alienated itself so thoroughly from the Chinese Communists by actively siding with their enemy both during and after the civil war—there might have been a chance for a détente. As it was, in the absence of any viable line of communication, both sides fatefully misjudged the intentions of the other and launched themselves into a war of far greater scale, and far more negligible accomplishment, than either expected. In the three years it took for them to fight each other to a standstill, tens of thousands of Americans and more than a hundred thousand Chinese would die at each other's hands in the Korean War, leaving a legacy of enmity and mistrust between the two countries that has never fully dissipated.

Back in 1937 on that wistful Christmas Eve in Shanxi, Evans and Agnes had not been alone for the entire evening. At one point, Zhu De had been walking past Carlson's quarters when he heard the sound of their music from outside. Curious, he came in to listen for a while as Agnes sang her spirituals and Carlson played his harmonica. When they came to a resting place, Zhu De stood up and sang for them a slow, plaintive ballad he remembered from his childhood in Sichuan. It was a moment of transcendence, when the affection of the three seemed to herald a future of promise for their two nations. "Here," said Zhu De when his song was done, "we have the brotherhood of man." Thirteen years later, the gentle, self-effacing general with the liquid-brown eyes would be the supreme commander of the People's Liberation Army as China's volunteers marched to war in Korea.

Carlson and Smedley were both fortunate, in a sense, to die with their ideals about the Chinese Communists intact. They did not have to test their faith against the horrors of Mao at his peak, during the mass campaigns of the 1950s and '60s when tens of millions of people in China would starve to death or have their lives destroyed to suit his ideological whims. Agnes Smedley had already gone through that in the 1930s with Stalin's purges and the shattering of her hopes for the Soviet Union; she did not expect that the same would come in China, no matter how many times Freda Utley told her it was just a matter of time.

Edgar Snow, however, did live on through the 1950s, and the 1960s, and to his lasting disgrace it would turn out that his career as a journalist was so heavily yoked to his unique access to the Chinese

Communist leaders that he would hold fast to his original judgments no matter what transformations took place. And those transformations came quickly after the Korean War. The war enabled Mao to centralize his power over a Chinese population that was now fully united behind him against what it saw as the existential threat of the United States. (Indeed, such a consolidation of domestic power may have been the primary reason he went to war in Korea in the first place.) This dramatic expansion of Mao's political control gave him an opening to press forward toward the vision of socialism that had always lain just behind his public promises of democracy during World War II.

In 1953, against the misgivings of more moderate party leaders like Liu Shaoqi and Zhou Enlai, Mao cast aside the "new democracy" that had helped the Communists win the civil war, and launched China headlong into what he had always said would be the eventual, later stage of the revolution: the total transformation of China into a socialist state, en route to communism. In a Politburo speech in June of 1953 attacking his comrades who continued to support private enterprise and market reforms, Mao said: "There are some who, after the victory of the democratic revolution, are still marking time. They do not realize that the nature of the revolution has changed, and instead of socialist reforms they continue to dabble at their precious 'new democracy.'" Hardly anyone, including the other leaders of the party, had expected that the next stage would come so soon.

In 1960, living in self-imposed exile from the United States with his writing career on the rocks, Edgar Snow was invited to come back to China for the first time since the founding of the People's Republic, to revisit his interviews with Mao and the other leaders from *Red Star* days. He wound up spending five months in China during the worst depths of the Great Leap famine, a time when Chinese peasants were starving by the millions in the countryside as a result of Mao's horrifically, willfully failed drive for total agricultural collectivization. But during Snow's carefully curated tour of the country he was allowed to see none of that. Now that the Communists controlled the whole of China, including near-total power over the movement of people and information, they had the capacity to project their own reality to a visitor like Snow in a way they could only have dreamed of in the 1930s, when they were just a small party of revolutionaries in a vast country controlled mainly by their enemies.

In Snow's naïve continued faith in Mao's regime, and in spite of what he had known of the Soviet Union, he took everything his handlers showed him at face value. Abandoning even basic journalistic responsibility, he treated the fact that he did not personally witness starvation as sufficient proof that there *was* none. "I saw no starving people in China," he wrote in the mammoth, eight-hundred-page book that resulted from the trip. "I do not believe there is famine in China at this writing. . . . Isolated instances of starvation due to neglect or failure of the rationing system were possible. Considerable malnutrition undoubtedly existed. Mass starvation? No." The famine was, he reported, simply a creation of anti-Chinese propagandists. He cited information he had gotten from his (approved) interviews that in fact the food situation in China was far better now than it had been in the past. "What is new," he wrote, "is that millions of people are not starving, as they did throughout chronic famine in the twenties, thirties and forties."

Even then, Snow was not content simply to deny the existence of mass starvation in China; he also went out of his way to ridicule foreign reports of the famine, some based on the accounts of refugees who had escaped to Hong Kong, that testified to the suffering. One such report had concluded that the average Chinese person was probably getting only six hundred calories a day, prompting Snow to joke that if such a "childish exaggeration" were true, then all the Chinese would simply vanish from the face of the earth by April of 1962. The Chinese did not, of course, vanish, but by that date as many as 36 million of them would be dead from the famine Snow so mockingly dismissed.

But Edgar Snow had always been pliable, going back to his readiness to edit *Red Star Over China* to please Earl Browder and the Communist Party of the USA in order to improve his book sales. In that sense it is perhaps consistent that Snow would further compromise himself by clinging so strongly to the message about the Chinese Communists that made him famous, even as it turned him into a propagandist for a monstrous regime. One hopes that Agnes Smedley or Evans Carlson, had they lived, would not have followed him that far—Smedley, given her abandonment of the Russians for similar reasons in the 1930s, and Carlson, because his faith in the Chinese Communists had always been based on a certain amount of illusion—an illusion that was consistent with the hopes and outward appearances of the 1930s, but that would become utterly irreconcilable with the reality of Mao's China in the future.

Freda Utley, at least, forgave Carlson his sympathies. By the early 1950s, his onetime friend from Hankow had established herself as one of the leading anticommunist writers in the United States, running in the same social circles as William F. Buckley and Ayn Rand. It was her account of Hankow that McCarthy used in attacking Carlson. In 1951 she published *The China Story*, a ruthless denunciation of the Americans who had admired the Chinese Communists in the 1930s and '40s, many of them her former friends. But she drew a clear distinction in that book between Evans Carlson and Edgar Snow. Carlson, she said, had always been naïve and idealistic, but his humanitarian sentiments were genuine. He had been taken in by the Chinese Communists, she believed, because he sincerely cared about the Chinese people. In that, he was a true liberal, and as much as she detested liberals, she allowed that excuses could be made for such people. She would brook no excuses, however, for the likes of Edgar Snow—who, she wrote, had been guided all along not by any internal moral compass, but only by the desire to advance his own career.

———

Peggy Tatum Carlson was ruined financially by the cost of a gastrectomy operation in 1958. She lost the little house in Brightwood, Oregon, that she and Evans had stretched their finances to purchase after the war, and by the time the medical liens were satisfied she didn't even have enough money to get her furniture out of hock. She also lost control over the storage space where she had kept her late husband's property after his death. In 1964, his diaries and a number of his personal effects turned up in the possession of an antique dealer in Seattle. The collection included Carlson's journals from China, his passports and award citations, and some correspondence as well as his Navy Cross and Legion of Merit medals. The dealer had gotten them in trade for some Civil War memorabilia, and once he recognized their value, he intended to sell them at auction for a tidy profit. However, a Navy lieutenant who heard about the planned sale notified Carlson's son, Evans Junior, who by that time was a decorated Korean War veteran stationed in California. Young Evans (no longer so young) came up to Seattle and convinced the dealer to sell him his father's effects at cost so they could be returned to the family.

After she lost her home and her possessions, Peggy Carlson worked for a time as a clerk at the naval air station at Oak Harbor, Washington, making less than minimum wage. She remarried, and eventually found better work managing a gift shop at the Timberline Lodge, the grand, sprawling WPA hotel on Oregon's Mount Hood where Stanley Kubrick would later film *The Shining*. She retired from the gift shop in 1974 after thirteen years of service. In 1976, nearly thirty years after her Marine husband's death and four years after Nixon's visit with Mao finally reopened the door between China and the United States, she made a trip to China with a tour group to retrace the path of Carlson's 1938 journey with the Eighth Route Army. In Beijing she visited the graves of Edgar Snow and Agnes Smedley, both of whom had asked to be buried in China, the land upon which—for better or for worse—they had built their lives. Edgar Snow had designated that half of his ashes be buried there; Smedley, fittingly, wanted China for her entirety.

Considering the disappointment Carlson had felt at the end of his life, one might wonder whether, if given the choice, he would have wanted the same. But that leads us back to the most essential difference between him and his two closest friends from China days. Because for Agnes Smedley and Edgar Snow, who, like Carlson, had discovered new and better versions of themselves in China in the 1930s, China had become an escape, a means of letting go of the land of their birth and leaving their old lives behind. China made Edgar Snow into a star, and he would never feel fully at home in America again. Agnes Smedley, who had never felt at home in America to begin with, found in China a place and a people she could love without cynicism. But for Carlson it was different. His experience of China made him more worldly, yes, but ultimately it wedded him ever more fiercely to the ideals of his home, at least as he understood them. He subsumed his experience of China into his own sense of patriotism, and that made him the man he was destined to be.

The fundamental inspiration that Carlson brought home from

China (and he was never fully aware just how much of it had come from within himself) was that a more just and equal society, a fuller participation in democracy for all of America's people, and a willingness to sacrifice personal comfort for the sake of the greater whole—all of this could be born from the crucible of the battlefield. As he taught his beloved Raiders under the palm trees of Espiritu Santo, they were fighting not just for victory but for a better future. They were fighting for a world that would better match their own ideals. They were sacrificing their own lives to create a better destiny for their daughters and sons.

And so, while Agnes Smedley was getting into arguments at cocktail parties in New York and Edgar Snow was traveling the world to file his travel reports, Carlson was exactly where he wanted to be: putting his body on the line in the Pacific, slogging through mud and mosquitoes, dodging mortar rounds and raking machine gun fire, because he thought it would lead to a better future for his country. As disillusioned as he would be by the end, there is no more appropriate resting place for his broken remains than under the rolling hills of Arlington Cemetery, surrounded on all sides by the multitudes of others, under identical white headstones, who gave their lives to that same elusive cause.

God will not have his work made manifest by cowards.
—Ralph Waldo Emerson, "Self-Reliance"

ACKNOWLEDGMENTS

In researching Evans Carlson's life, my greatest debt of gratitude is to his granddaughter, Karen Carlson Loving. During a 2019 visit to her South Carolina home, watched over by her English mastiffs and their puppies, Karen generously shared her grandfather's family letters and other privately held papers with me. I hope that I have merited her trust. The family sources in her possession complemented the many publicly available archival materials on Carlson's career to make possible a three-dimensional portrait of a man who was both a remarkable public figure and also quite guarded about his personal life. I could not have written this book the same way without her help, and for that I am immensely grateful. I only wish I could have brought home one of the puppies.

I am grateful as well to the National Endowment for the Humanities for funding the research for this book with a grant from their Public Scholars program. This is the second of my books to benefit from NEH support, and their largesse is all the more meaningful at a time when so many sources of funding for research in the humanities have been scaled back or eliminated altogether.

It is impossible to overstate the importance of draft readers, and for this book I benefitted from the generosity of several fellow historians who took on the laborious task of reading part or all of the raw manuscript. But before I gave it to any of the specialists, I did what every serious author should do: I gave a copy to my high school English teacher. Thank you, Robert Bonneau, for being my first reader on this project and for all you taught me about writing and reading back when I was a teenager who still thought he wanted to be a mathematician.

Although my primary background as a historian is modern China, the World War II era was new for me, so I am grateful to Stephen MacKinnon, Rana Mitter, and John Delury for their readings of the manuscript, their questions and corrections, and their help in navigating the complex field of recent scholarship on China's experience of WWII. Thank you also to Joel Wolfe and Michael Gorra for reading chapters, to Barak Kushner and Jeremy Yellen for generous help with Japanese sources, and to Lei Duan for vetting my Chinese translations.

On the Marine Corps side, I was fortunate to have two sharp-eyed veterans of the USMC History Division go through my draft manuscript to check the military details. I am profoundly grateful to Frank Kalesnik and Reed Bonadonna for their questions, corrections, and (especially) challenges. The book is far stronger for their help, though it goes without saying that any errors of fact or interpretation that remain are my responsibility alone.

As all historians know, it is easy enough to find an interesting topic; the hard part is finding good sources. The spark that really set this project in motion was the discovery that a partial collection of Carlson's personal papers had been microfilmed in the 1970s by an arrangement between Carlson's son and the Cal State Fullerton Library—which held on to them quietly for decades without making them publicly available until recently. Thank you to Patricia Prestinary and Guillermina Vega for sending the microfilm reels to Massachusetts for me to read when I was just beginning to explore whether a book on Carlson could be done. Seeing those sources, which included Carlson's China diaries with their tiny, almost inscrutable handwriting, made the book seem realistic for the first time.

At the United States Marine Corps History Division in Quantico, VA, thank you to Alisa Whitley, Annette Amerman, and Dominic Ameral for their help in navigating the holdings of the Archives Branch. Thank you also to Michael Westermeier in the Reference Branch for his assistance and for talking with me about the memory of Carlson in the Marines today. At the National Museum of the Marine Corps, Kater Miller kindly gave up an otherwise productive afternoon to take me on base for a personal tour of the Marine Raider Museum he curates.

At the National Archives in College Park, Maryland, I benefitted from the patient assistance of Todd Crumley, as well as Heather Sulier, William Green, Alexis Hill, and Kevin Quinn. At the main National Archives site in Washington, D.C., thank you to Katherine Vollen for making an exception to the reservation policy and creating room for me at the last minute during one of my research trips. Harrison Behl and Eric Graf of the Library of Congress Recorded Sound Research Center helped me find a 1940 NBC radio interview with Carlson that allowed me to hear his voice for the first time. Thank you to Gillian Lusins at NBC Universal for permission to digitize that recording.

For assistance with in-person research, thank you to Jane Parr at the Howard Gotlieb Archival Research Center at Boston University; Sarah L. Malcolm at the FDR Library in Hyde Park, NY; Shannon Walker, Matthew Messbarger, Robert Spindler, and Ralph Gabbard at Arizona State University; Tara Craig at the Columbia University Rare Book and Manuscript Library; and the ever-helpful Sharon Domier at UMass–Amherst. For answering email queries, thank you to Carol Ferland and Denise Clapsaddle at the First Congregational Church of Plymouth, CT, and Judy Giguere, the Plymouth Town Historian.

Much of the research and writing for this book took place during the pandemic, which threw up unprecedented challenges to the old ways of doing things. I am grateful to those who bent the rules or enacted new policies that make it possible for people like me to keep moving forward, if slowly. The Sterling Memorial Library at Yale University mailed me books from its collection. Archivists and special-collections librarians arranged scans of entire folders of material. Among those who went out of their way to help me were Cindy Brightenburg at Brigham Young University; Sarah Patton at the Hoover Institution; Meg Langford at the Oregon Health and Science University; Cynthia Franco at Southern Methodist University; Valoise Armstrong at the Dwight D. Eisenhower Presidential Library and Museum; Lauren Leeman at the State Historical Society of Missouri; and Cheri Kinnick at the University of Washington. Thank you to Sian Snow for permission to use the Edgar Snow Papers at the University of Missouri–Kansas City, and to Stuart Hinds, the university archivist, for having scans made for me of the Carlson-Snow correspondence.

For help with illustrations, I am grateful to Tony Dudek, Jessica Harrison-Hall, Yang Chia-ling, and Henry Howard-Sneyd. Thank you also to Greg Wilsbacher at the University of South Carolina for alerting me to the amazing collection of historical Marine Corps footage USC has digitized, including rare color footage of Carlson and his Raiders.

For helpful conversations and advice about the Pacific War, Carlson's Raiders, US–China relations, and the craft of biography, thank you to Ronald Spector, Barak Kushner, Nicholas Reynolds, T. J. Stiles, Rana Mitter, Julia Lovell, Jon Hoffman, Niu Ke, Janice Nimura, Andy Mertha, Tobie Meyer-Fong, Qi Haotian, Jeff Wasserstrom, Yu Tiejun, and innumerable others. When I was in Arizona for research in the Agnes Smedley papers, Stephen MacKinnon and Anne Feldhaus gave me a lovely evening of dinner and conversation at their Tempe home and sent me home with an armload of lemons from the garden. Over coffee in Brattleboro, Vermont, Evan Taylor shared a spreadsheet with locations of the documents he had found in his own research on Carlson; I am grateful for his collegiality and look forward to the culmination of his project. John Grady has been a constant source of encouragement and his generous introductions helped open more doors than I can count. For other crucial introductions, thank you to Nicholas Reynolds and Kate Kaup.

For general writing and moral support, I thank my fellow members of the Biographers International military history writing group as well as the other millworkers at the Writers' Mill in Florence, MA. Thank you also to Geri, Lisa, and Molly at Bread Euphoria in Haydenville, MA, for coffee, bagels, and a meditative place to write.

I was fortunate with this book to have been able to work with two spectacular editors at Knopf. Todd Portnowitz kindly took on the project after my longtime editor Andrew Miller moved to a new position, and the transition could not have been smoother. The editing I've gotten at Knopf has always been stellar, and this time it was doubly so, as the handing of the baton from Andrew to Todd meant I got the benefit of full readings from both of them. Along with Todd and Andrew, Tiara Sharma gave the manuscript a brilliant close reading, with line edits that were some of the most insightful I've had.

Writing and editing aside, a book like this cannot be published without an enormous amount of additional work behind the scenes. My enduring thanks to everyone else at Knopf who has worked on this book: Jordan Pavlin the Knopf publisher, Chip Kidd the jacket designer, production manager Lisa Montebello, text designer Marisa Nakasone, publicists Kelly Shi and Anne Noone, Todd's assistants Ben Shields and Margot Lee, and attorney Dan Novack—and those are just the people whose contributions I am aware of at this time. It was always a dream of mine to publish with Knopf, and as my third book with them comes to completion they continue to surpass even my highest hopes. Finally, thank you to my agent, Brettne Bloom, the lion in my corner, for her enduring support and encouragement over more than fifteen years of working together.

I would probably be a crumpled mess on the floor if it weren't for the support of my family. They bring the joy, the distraction, the inspiration, and the grounding in the real world that keep my life in balance and save me from getting swallowed up by the solitude of writing. I dedicate this book to them. The companionship of my wife, Francie Lin, means the world to me; I simply couldn't have done this without her. Our children, Lucy and Eliot, were the model of patience as I ran endless title/subtitle ideas past them, told them stories about Agnes Smedley punching Mao's wife, and gave mini lectures about WWII history at dinnertime. This may not be the kind of book they would check out from the library, at least not at this point in their lives, but they never made me think it was anything less than captivating.

NOTE ON ROMANIZATION

In rendering Chinese words into English in this book, I have primarily used the Hanyu Pinyin system of romanization that is standard in mainland China and the United States today. So: Beijing rather than Peking, Mao Zedong rather than Mao Tse-tung, etc.

Exceptions were made for a handful of names and terms that are still best known in English by their mid-twentieth-century romanizations. These include: Chiang Kai-shek (rather than Jiang Jieshi); Sun Yat-sen (rather than Sun Zhongshan); the KMT or Kuomintang (rather than GMD/Guomindang); Soong Mei-ling (Song Meiling); Canton (Guangzhou); and Hankow (Hankou).

In any instance where, for the sake of consistency, I have changed the romanization of a Chinese word in a direct quotation, the change is explained in the source note.

SOURCE NOTES

ABBREVIATIONS IN NOTES

ASASU Agnes Smedley Collection, MSS-122, Arizona State University Archives, Tempe, AZ.

CSUF Papers of Evans Fordyce Carlson, Brig. Gen., USMC, Special Collections, California State University, Fullerton, CA. 3 microfilm reels.

ECFP Evans Carlson Family Papers, in private possession of family.

ESUM Edgar Parks Snow Papers, Dr. Kenneth J. LaBudde Department of Special Collections, University of Missouri-Kansas City, Kansas City, MO.

FDRL Franklin D. Roosevelt Library, Hyde Park, NY.

HFSBYU Helen Foster Snow Papers, MSS 2219, L. Tom Perry Special Collections, Brigham Young University, Provo, UT.

HIA Hoover Institution Library and Archives, Stanford, CA.

LOC Library of Congress, Washington, DC.

MBBU Michael Blankfort Collection, SPE-24, Howard Gotlieb Archival Research Center, Boston University Libraries, Boston, MA.

MRNYPL Maud Russell Papers, MssColl 2649, Manuscripts and Archives Division, New York Public Library.

NARA I National Archives, Washington, DC.

NARA II National Archives, College Park, MD.

SMASU Smedley-MacKinnon Collection, MSS-123, Arizona State University Archives, Tempe, AZ.

SMPA Shanghai Municipal Police Archives.

USMCA Archives Branch, Marine Corps History Division, Quantico, VA.

USMCR Reference Branch, Marine Corps History Division, Quantico, VA.

INTRODUCTION

xi most beloved: "'Gung Ho' Carlson Wounded Rescuing Marine Companion," United Press, July 7, 1944.

xi "the black sheep": "Death of a Rebel," *Baltimore Sun*, May 29, 1947.

xii conformity and obedience: Aaron B. O'Connell, *Underdogs: The Making of the Modern Marine Corps* (Cambridge, MA: Harvard University Press, 2012), p. 28: "More so than in the other services, membership in the Marine Corps required an ideological commitment, the abandonment of previous civilian identities, and the adoption of a new set of stories and priorities. One officer put it well a decade after World War II: 'The Marine Corps must seek to possess the souls of its personnel as earnestly as it strives to condition their bodies.'"

xiii "forgotten" theater: Rana Mitter, *Forgotten Ally: China's World War II, 1937–1945* (Boston: Houghton Mifflin Harcourt, 2013). For a broad-based survey that does a fine job of incorporating recent scholarship on China's centrality to the Asia-Pacific theater of World War II, see Richard B. Frank, *Tower of Skulls: A History of the Asia-Pacific War, July 1937–May 1942* (New York: W. W. Norton, 2020).

PROLOGUE: THE GREAT ADVENTURE

3 One of the men in line: The prologue is a composite drawn from various histories of the 2nd Raiders, including accounts in the *Raider Patch* newsletter over the years and oral histories, including: Ben Carson (National Museum of the Pacific War, 2001); Frank Duesler (Wisconsin Veterans Museum Research Center, 2002); Kenneth Merrill (National Museum of the Pacific War, 2016); Dean Voight (Wisconsin Veterans Museum Research Center, 1995); and Charles W. Lindberg (University of North Texas Oral History Collection, No. 1224, 1998).

3 "I want men": Charles W. Lindberg oral history, February 19, 1998. University of North Texas Oral History Collection, No. 1224, p. 6.

4 One of the men said: Michael Blankfort, *The Big Yankee: The Life of Carlson of the Raiders* (Boston: Little, Brown, 1947), p. 10.

4 we won't be asking for mercy: Blankfort, *The Big Yankee*, p. 12.

4 Six hundred recruits: Evans Carlson to FDR, March 2, 1942, PPF 4951, FDR Papers, *FDRL*.

5 "The morale of that outfit": Charles W. Lindberg oral history, p. 7.

5 "It is a crack outfit": Jack Miller to his mother, March 1, 1942, Jack Miller Papers, Southern Methodist University.

5 One of them had just come back: Samuel B. Griffith oral history transcript (interviewed by Benis Frank in 1976), History and Museums Division, Headquarters, U.S. Marine Corps, Washington, DC, pp. 51, 52 (copy held at Columbia University Special Collections).

6 Within each fire team: John F. Wukovits, *American Commando: Evans Carlson, His WWII Marine Raiders, and America's First Special Forces Mission* (New York: NAL Caliber, 2009), p. 60.

6 effectively outgunned: George W. Smith, *Carlson's Raid* (New York: Berkley Books, 2001), p. 53.

6   "And at the end": Smith, *Carlson's Raid*, p. 56.
6   "You kind of felt good there": Charles W. Lindberg oral history, p. 7.
6   "He would do anything": Smith, *Carlson's Raid*, p. 56.
6   "A corker": Wukovits, *American Commando*, p. 50.
6   "This Major Carlson": Jack Miller to his mother, March 17, 1942, Jack Miller Papers, Southern Methodist University.
7   "Singing helps a man": Jim Lucas article typescript, in Carlson Personal File, PC56/Coll. 3146, *USMCA*.
8   "a striking force": Wukovits, *American Commando*, p. 66.
8   "Dear Mr. President": EFC to FDR, April 29, 1942, PPF 4951, FDR Papers, *FDRL*.

CHAPTER 1: THE TELEGRAM

11   Like Carlson, most of the 1,200 Marines: Evans Carlson, "Shoulder to Shoulder with the Coldstream Guards," *Leatherneck*, October 1927, pp. 8, 50.
12   waving and blown kisses: The crowd on the pier is described in "Devil Dogs Bring Back War Memory," *The Bulletin* (Pomona, CA), February 4, 1927.
12   "Hope to get out": EFC to father, May 4, 1922, *ECFP*.
12   As a child, he ran away: "The Autobiography of Evans Carlson," unpublished typescript, as told to Helen Foster Snow, Carlson Personal File, Published Materials, *USMCR*.
12   Carlson's Norwegian grandfather: Thomas A. Carlson to Michael Blankfort, May 24, 1945, Box 85, Folder 3, *MBBU*.
13   "adventurous": Lewis H. Mattoon article (no title) from *Waterbury Republican*, December 1942, typescript in Box 8, Folder 4, *MBBU*.
13   His father's salary: "The Man Whose Picture Is on Our Cover" (Thomas A. Carlson family history), *Congregational Connecticut*, Vol. 7, No. 9 (November 1942), p. 42. One of Carlson's brothers would die of the flu epidemic in 1918, so for most of his life he had just one brother and one sister.
13   She claimed to trace: Carlson, "Autobiography."
13   as Evans later came to see it: EFC to Etta Mae Wallace, October 10, 1939, *ECFP*. "She had been reared in comparative luxury, and when she had succumbed to Dad's charm and married him she felt that she had made a supreme sacrifice. She never allowed him to forget it, and in a thousand subtle ways she commanded his attention and his devotion to the point where he had little time for his parish work."
13   He was the very picture: "Lieut. Col. Evans Carlson, Son of Humble Plymouth Minister, Philippine Service Veteran at 19, a National Hero at 46," *Waterbury Republican*, September 6, 1942.
14   One of the earliest memories: Carlson, "Autobiography."
14   An essay survives: Carlson school essay, quoted in Michael Blankfort, *The Big Yankee: The Life of Carlson of the Raiders* (Boston: Little, Brown, 1947), p. 87.
15   "To believe your own thought": Ralph Waldo Emerson, "Self-Reliance," in *Emerson: Essays and Lectures* (New York: Library of America, 1983), pp. 259–82; quotations on pp. 259, 261, 282.
15   "We were, of course, never happy": Thomas A. Carlson to Michael Blankfort, April 30, 1945, Box 85, Folder 3, *MBBU*.

15 "almost failed to appear": "Lieut. Col. Evans F. Carlson," *Enterprise and Vermonter* (Vergennes, VT), September 3, 1942.

16 "Say dad": EFC to his father, October 13, 1912, Box 8, Folder 10, *MBBU*.

16 "Go to the field artillery": Carlson, "Autobiography."

16 Evans's parents were shocked: Lewis H. Mattoon article (no title) from *Waterbury Republican*, December 1942, *MBBU*.

17 "Manila 1913": Notes from physical examination, December 14, 1922, Carlson military personnel file, RG 127, Series: Official Military Personnel Files, National Archives, St. Louis, MO.

17 "scums": Carlson, "Autobiography."

17 "one of the best soldiers": P. D. Glassford letter of recommendation for Evans Carlson, October 25, 1915, *CSUF*, microfilm reel 2.

18 "time hangs heavy": Carlson letter to an unnamed friend back home, published under headline "Soldier Life in Hawaii" in *Middlebury Register*, October 1, 1915.

19 "an adventure or nothing": Carlson, "Autobiography."

19 "ever increasing regret": EFC to Karen Carlson, January 23, 1919, *ECFP*.

19 Carlson left the Army: Carlson, "Autobiography."

20 "Our home is the happiest": EFC to parents, February 22 and March 31, 1920, *ECFP*.

20 "mental inferiors": EFC to parents, from Oakland, CA, February 22, 1920, *ECFP*.

20 "My one ambition": EFC to parents, from Missoula, MT, April 18, 1920, *ECFP*.

21 When he reported: EFC to parents, May 4, 1922, *ECFP*.

22 "imperial America's": Dennis E. Showalter, "Evolution of the U.S. Marine Corps as a Military Elite," *Marine Corps Gazette*, November 1979, pp. 44–58; quotation on p. 49.

22 he wouldn't have to pay: EFC to father, May 7, 1922, *ECFP*.

22 "Well I'm back": EFC to father, May 7, 1922, *ECFP*.

23 It was a legendarily comfortable: Allan R. Millett, *Semper Fidelis: The History of the United States Marine Corps* (New York: Free Press, 1991), p. 216.

23 "He was like a god": Carlson, "Autobiography."

24 His winter dress uniform: EFC to parents, January 20, 1923, *ECFP*.

24 "I am right in my element": EFC to parents, February 3, 1923, *ECFP*.

24 "When my week's work is over": EFC to mother, March 4, 1923, *ECFP*.

24 "chain lightning": EFC to parents, March 18, 1923, *ECFP*.

24 "I have a suspicion": EFC to parents, November 9, 1923, *ECFP*.

24 "She typifies": EFC to parents, December 2, 1923, *ECFP*.

25 "the quintessence": Helen Foster Snow, "Remembering the Autobiography of Evans F. Carlson," unpublished manuscript, 1979, Box 175, Folder 15, *HFSBYU*.

25 "Etelle loves me": EFC to parents, February 18, 1924, *ECFP*.

25 "a turning point": EFC to parents, February 25, 1924, *ECFP*.

25 "She was meant for me": EFC to father, March 15, 1924, *ECFP*.

25 "You probably think me": EFC to parents, February 27, 1924, *ECFP*.

25 neither of Carlson's parents: Blankfort, *The Big Yankee*, p. 131.

26 His mother: EFC to father, May 15, 1924, *ECFP*; Blankfort, *The Big Yankee*, p. 130.

26 "My hunches": EFC to parents, March 15, 1924, *ECFP.*

26 Recently, for instance: EFC to parents, November 29, 1923, *ECFP.*

CHAPTER 2: SHANGHAI

29 "If an American": *Commercial Traveler's Guide to the Far East,* U.S. Department of Commerce, 1932, p. 94.

30 "regard Chinese lives": Jay Taylor, *The Generalissimo: Chiang Kai-shek and the Struggle for Modern China* (Cambridge, MA: Belknap Press of Harvard University Press, 2009), p. 49; Hans van de Ven, *China at War: Triumph and Tragedy in the Emergence of the New China* (Cambridge, MA: Harvard University Press, 2018), p. 24.

30 Coolidge was uncomfortable: "Coolidge Considers an Inquiry on China," *New York Times,* February 2, 1927.

31 Abraham Lincoln's minister to China: Stephen R. Platt, *Autumn in the Heavenly Kingdom: China, the West, and the Epic Story of the Taiping Civil War* (New York: Alfred A. Knopf, 2012), pp. 319–20.

32 Chinese were not allowed: James L. Huskey, "The Cosmopolitan Connection: Americans and Chinese in Shanghai During the Interwar Years," *Diplomatic History,* Vol. 11, No. 3 (Summer 1987): 227–42; see p. 236.

33 many of them saw it instead: Huskey, "The Cosmopolitan Connection," pp. 227–28.

33 "taming": Evans Carlson, "Shoulder to Shoulder with the Coldstream Guards," *Leatherneck,* October 1927, p. 8.

33 A foreign missionary: Harry A. Franck, *Roving Through Southern China* (New York: Century Company, 1925), p. 16; Stella Dong, *Shanghai: The Rise and Fall of a Decadent City, 1842–1949* (New York: Perennial, 2001), p. 1.

34 "Oh, we all": Lt. Col. Arthur J. Burks, "China Side 1927," *Marine Corps Gazette,* April 1949, p. 48.

34 "very fine impression": "Canteens for the Soldiers," *North-China Herald,* February 26, 1927.

34 "impress the Chinese": Carlson, "Shoulder to Shoulder with the Coldstream Guards," p. 8.

34 "The flash": EFC to parents, April 9, 1927, *ECFP.*

35 "choked with thousands": "US Marines Are Cheered in Parade on Nanking Road," *North-China Herald,* February 26, 1927.

36 "blood is thicker": "We Must Act with British if Fighting Comes," editorial, *New York Evening Post,* January 31, 1927.

36 "poor and ignorant": "Blames the Soviet for Events in China," *New York Times,* March 26, 1927.

36 "first of the Western nations": "Forces at Work in China," editorial, *New York Times,* March 24, 1927.

37 As they hoofed: Carlson, "Shoulder to Shoulder with the Coldstream Guards," p. 8.

37 Visually, the scene: EFC to parents, March 3, 1927, *ECFP.*

37 "depredations of Chinese mobs": Carlson, "Shoulder to Shoulder with the Coldstream Guards," p. 8.

37 "the front lines held": "Protection of American Interests," *Marine Corps Gazette,* September 1927, pp. 175–83; quotation on p. 181.

37 A few weeks earlier: Donald A. Jordan, *The Northern Expedition: China's National Revolution of 1926–1928* (Honolulu: University of Hawaii Press, 1976), p. 130.

37 "You Americans": Charles Allen Peckham, "The Northern Expedition, the Nanking Incident, and the Protection of American Nationals" (PhD diss., Ohio State University, 1973), pp. 55–73.

38 "Well, we're here": EFC to father, April 9, 1927, *ECFP.*

38 "It is a great show": EFC to parents, March 24, 1927, *ECFP.*

39 "remarkably quiet": EFC to father, April 18, 1927, *ECFP.*

40 Acting at the instigation: Anthony Saich, "A Dutchman's Fantasy: Henricus Sneevliet's United Front for the Chinese Communist Party," in Timothy Cheek et al., eds., *The Chinese Communist Party: A Century in Ten Lives* (Cambridge, UK: Cambridge University Press, 2021), p. 15.

41 "like a squeezed-out lemon": As quoted in Jordan, *The Northern Expedition*, p. 142.

42 On September 7 he was promoted: Evans Carlson certificates of promotion, *CSUF,* microfilm reel 2.

42 "It is largely": EFC to parents, March 3, 1927, *ECFP.*

43 "crowds of curious": EFC and Etelle to parents, March 21, 1928, *ECFP*; also EFC to parents, November 16, 1927, *ECFP.*

43 "teach these slant eyed": EFC to father, April 18, 1927, *ECFP.*

44 "I feel detached": EFC to mother, January 22, 1929, *ECFP.*

44 "The Nationalists have accomplished": EFC to parents, March 21, 1928, *ECFP.*

46 "intensification": Evans F. Carlson, "Intelligence Memorandum 14: Proposed Communist Uprising," October 13, 1928, Carlson Personal File, Intelligence Memorandums, PC56/Coll. 3146, *USMCA.*

47 "hardy ruffians": Evans F. Carlson, "Intelligence Summary Week Ending 24 March, 1929," Office of the Intelligence Officer, Fourth Regiment, U.S. Marine Corps, Carlson Personal File, Intelligence Memorandums, PC56/Coll. 3146, *USMCA.*

47 "both well trained": Evans F. Carlson, "Communist Activities: Report #1," February 15, 1929, Carlson Personal File, Intelligence Memorandums, PC56/Coll. 3146, *USMCA.*

47 "considerable murder": Evans F. Carlson, "Communist Activities: Report #9," June 30, 1929, Carlson Personal File, Intelligence Memorandums, PC56/Coll. 3146, *USMCA.*

47 They said that might be possible: EFC to parents, December 31, 1929, *ECFP.*

48 "systematic and laborious": "Lt. Carlson to Leave for Home," *Walla Walla*, September 7, 1929.

48 "Few officers": "Lieut. Carlson, Intelligence Officer, Completes Service Here," *China Weekly Review*, September 14, 1929.

48 It was nearly Christmas: Michael Blankfort, *The Big Yankee: The Life of Carlson of the Raiders* (Boston: Little, Brown, 1947), p. 157; EFC to parents, December 31, 1929, and October 3, 1930, *ECFP.* In the latter, he wrote: "Christmas has never meant anything to me till last year. Somehow or other that celebration we had last year got under my hide. I would give a good deal to go through it again."

CHAPTER 3: BANDITS

49 "bandit country": EFC to parents, May 30, 1930, *ECFP.*

49 "Only a fool": EFC to parents, June 19, 1930, *ECFP.*

50 Compared to opulent Shanghai: EFC to parents, October 3, 1930, *ECFP.*

50 Dorothy learned: Congressman Albert E. Carter to Brig. Gen. Ben H. Fuller, September 6, 1930, Carlson military personnel file, Series: Official Military Personnel Files, RG 127, National Archives, St. Louis, MO.

50 The Navy Department found: The correspondence relating to this incident is in his military personnel file at the National Archives in St. Louis, MO (cited above), and the "Correspondence and Memos" folder of Carlson's Personal File, *USMCA.*

50 after the Wall Street crash: Alan L. McPherson, *The Invaded: How Latin Americans and Their Allies Fought and Ended U.S. Occupations* (New York: Oxford University Press, 2014), p. 231.

50 still under American control: Richard Leroy Millett, "The History of the Guardia Nacional de Nicaragua, 1925–1965" (PhD diss., University of New Mexico, 1966), pp. 171–72.

51 Sandino's followers: McPherson, *The Invaded*, p. 229.

51 demonstrators carried: Michel Gobat, *Confronting the American Dream: Nicaragua Under U.S. Imperial Rule* (Durham, NC: Duke University Press, 2005), p. 236.

51 "kill all Americans": McPherson, *The Invaded*, p. 230.

52 The first time Carlson was nearly shot: Evans F. Carlson, "The Autobiography of Evans Carlson," unpublished typescript, as told to Helen Foster Snow, Carlson Personal File, Published Materials, *USMCR.*

53 "I try not to imply": EFC to family, August 16, 1932, *ECFP.*

53 "I feel that": EFC to Thomas Carlson (brother), June 19, 1930, *ECFP.*

53 "What a sweet hike": EFC to parents, May 30, 1930, *ECFP.*

53 "It is a great life": EFC to parents, October 3, 1930, *ECFP.*

54 Instead of turning back: The official report on the engagement is in Carlson's personnel file from the Guardia Nacional, Inventory Entry Number 193, RG 127, *NARA I.*

54 Carlson's men were vastly: Commendation, by order of Gen. D. C. McDougal, Jefe Director of Guardia Nacional (general order no. 50–1930), July 18, 1930, *ECFP.* The original document listed two dead and seven wounded; this was corrected in Carlson's hand based on later information to five dead and eight wounded.

55 "extraordinary heroism": Citation for award of Navy Cross, October 1, 1930, *CSUF,* microfilm reel 2.

55 second-highest: While the Navy Cross was the second-highest combat decoration for which a Marine could qualify at this time, it was actually the third-highest decoration overall, ranked below the Navy Distinguished Service Medal, which was not a combat medal and was reserved largely for senior Navy flag officers or Marine generals who performed distinguished service in positions of great responsibility. In 1942, the rankings of the two decorations would be reversed, making the Navy Cross the second highest overall after the Medal of Honor. The equivalent decoration in the Army was (and is) the Distinguished Service Cross.

55 "hardly the kind of place": "Spoils of Battle with Nicaraguan Bandits Housed in Quiet Plymouth Parsonage," clipping in *ECFP*. No date, no info on publication.

55 "Gosh": EFC to parents, November 19, 1931, *ECFP*.

56 "The change in climate": EFC to family, December 27, 1930, *ECFP*.

56 happiest day of his life: EFC to mother, March 1, 1931, *ECFP*.

57 March 31, 1931: This section based on John Creigh Hendrickson, "El Terremoto," *Leatherneck*, April 1987, pp. 22–31.

57 Three-quarters of its sixty thousand residents: Hendrickson, "El Terremoto"; EFC to family, April 8, 1931, *ECFP*.

58 "I am not flattered": EFC to parents, November 19, 1931, *ECFP*.

59 He even went so far: EFC to parents, February 14, 1932, *ECFP*.

59 "subversive literature": Millett, "The History of the Guardia Nacional," p. 264, quoting Carlson report to Jefe Director, February 22, 1932. To his parents, he called it "communistic literature": EFC to parents, February 28, 1932, *ECFP*.

59 Carlson confided to his parents: EFC to parents, February 28, 1932, *ECFP*.

59 "lost all mental stimulus": EFC to family, August 16, 1932, *ECFP*.

59 "I accept God": EFC to family, August 16, 1932, ECFP.

60 "without regard for his personal interest": Citation for Nicaraguan Presidential Medal of Merit, *CSUF*, microfilm reel 2.

60 most people would later assume: See, for example, Carlson's Marine Corps biography in his Personal File ("Biographies" folder) at *USMCR*, which states incorrectly: "During World War I he saw action in France, and was awarded the Purple Heart for wounds received in action."

61 As chief of police: Carlson, "Autobiography."

61 "A curious silence": Evans F. Carlson, "The Guardia Nacional de Nicaragua," *Marine Corps Gazette*, August 1937, pp. 7–20; see p. 20.

61 Major General Smedley Butler: Jonathan M. Katz, *Gangsters of Capitalism: Smedley Butler, the Marines, and the Making and Breaking of America's Empire* (New York: St. Martin's Press, 2022).

61 "It's because we've got": Herb Richardson, "Giants of the Corps," *Leatherneck*, March 1977, p. 40.

61 "a hell of a good officer": Smedley Butler to Evans Carlson, January 3, 1927, *CSUF*, microfilm reel 2.

62 "lifelong favorites": Merrill Twining, *No Bended Knee: The Battle for Guadalcanal* (Novato, CA: Presidio Press, 1996), p. 177.

62 By one reckoning: "Gen. Butler to Head Marines in China," *New York Times*, February 27, 1927.

62 "I spent 33 years": Smedley Darlington Butler, "America's Armed Forces," Part 2, *Common Sense*, November 1935, pp. 8–12; quotation on p. 8.

62 he had reported in an intelligence memo: Millett, "The History of the Guardia Nacional," p. 303.

63 Carlson had worked: EFC to parents, November 23, 1932, *ECFP*.

CHAPTER 4: THE OLD CAPITAL

64 "I plan now to make": EFC to parents, 1933, rest of date unclear (February 7?), *ECFP*.

65   most profitable corporation in Asia: Louise Young, *Japan's Total Empire: Manchuria and the Culture of Wartime Imperialism* (Berkeley: University of California Press, 1998), pp. 31–34.

66   The tipping point: Rana Mitter, *Forgotten Ally: China's World War II, 1937–1945* (Boston: Houghton Mifflin Harcourt, 2013), p. 61.

67   "First unity, then resistance": Hans J. van de Ven, *China at War: Triumph and Tragedy in the Emergence of the New China* (Cambridge, MA: Harvard University Press, 2018), p. 32.

68   Japan withdrew from the League: Saburō Ienaga, *The Pacific War: World War II and the Japanese, 1931–1945* (New York: Pantheon, 1978), p. 66.

68   In a bloody month-long episode: Mitter, *Forgotten Ally*, p. 64.

69   "I feel more in the center": EFC to parents, March 16, 1933, *ECFP*.

69   "many friends": *Shanghai Times*, April 20, 1933.

69   "blocks and blocks": Etelle to Carlsons, April 14, 1933, *ECFP*.

70   The centerpiece of Chiang's anti-Communist strategy: Donald S. Sutton, "German Advice and Residual Warlordism in the Nanking Decade: Influences on Nationalist Military Training and Strategy," *China Quarterly*, No. 91 (September 1982): 386–410; see p. 398.

72   "Dynasties and revolutions": EFC to parents, September 10, 1933, *ECFP*.

72   "the China you read about": Oscar F. Peatross, *Bless 'Em All: The Marine Raiders of World War II* (Tampa: Raider Publishing, 1995), p. 6.

72   same college sorority: Etelle to Carlsons, May 13, 1934, *ECFP*.

73   "I have many personal ideas": EFC to parents, July 19, 1933, *ECFP*.

73   "Not much money": EFC to parents, February 6, 1934, *ECFP*.

73   the Shanghai Municipal Police: Notes from a Nelson Johnson memorandum, Carlson Personal File, Charges of Radical Activity Against Edgar Snow, PC56/Coll. 3146, *USMCA*.

74   "a lovely Southern girl": Edgar Snow to his mother, quoted in S. Bernard Thomas, *Season of High Adventure: Edgar Snow in China* (Berkeley: University of California Press, 1996), p. 57.

75   "Evans wouldn't like it": Helen Foster Snow, manuscript intro to "Carlson of (The 'Gung Ho') Carlson's Raiders: His Own Sketch," unpublished, n.d., Box 175, Folder 15, *HFSBYU*.

75   "We are in accord": EFC to parents, March 15, 1924, *ECFP*.

75   borrow his typewriter: Etelle to Karen Carlson, November 25, 1934, *ECFP*.

75   "Keep criticizing and pushing Ed": Thomas, *Season of High Adventure*, p. 101.

75    $750 advance: Thomas, *Season of High Adventure*, p. 110.

76   "a moment of optimism": Edgar Snow to Nelson Johnson, February 6, 1937, Nelson T. Johnson Papers, Box 31, *LOC*.

76   "The human heart": EFC to family, August 16, 1932, *ECFP*.

77   "Life can be made": "Editorial Grist," *Legation Guard News*, March 1, 1935, p. 1.

77   he started a museum: "Ming Coins Found," *South China Morning Post*, July 28, 1934; "Early Chinese Relics Found Near Legation," *China Press*, July 24, 1934 (via Reuters).

78   "the curator": EFC to parents, October 7, 1934, *ECFP*.

78   Chinese history contest: *Legation Guard News*, February 1, 1935, *ECFP*.

78   As evidence of at least modest success: Carlson, "Autobiography"; Peatross, *Bless 'Em All*, p. 6.

78   a "new life" in Beijing: "Marine-Chinese Friendship in Peiping Grows," *China Press*, December 17, 1934 (reprinted from *China Weekly Review*).

78   "We're supposed to be here": "Marine-Chinese Friendship in Peiping Grows," *China Press*.

79   box and play baseball: *Legation Guard News*, July 1, 1935, p. 7.

79   "Evans and I had our first Chinese dinner": Etelle to Carlsons, April 14, 1933, *ECFP*.

80   Etelle was seated: Etelle to Carlsons, May 13, 1934, *ECFP*.

80   "The Chinese were overcome": EFC to parents, May 13, 1934, *ECFP*.

80   "quintessential American Christian officer": Helen Foster Snow, "Evans Carlson, Who Put the Term 'Gung Ho' into English Dictionaries," unpublished manuscript, p. 3, Box 175, Folder 15, *HFSBYU*.

80   "it indicates": EFC to parents, August 3, 1935, *ECFP*.

CHAPTER 5: WARM SPRINGS

82   "the most magnificent": EFC to parents, August 30, 1935, *ECFP*.

83   "Looks like Roosevelt": EFC to parents, October 20, 1932, *ECFP*.

83   he credited Roosevelt's statesmanship: EFC to parents, December 2, 1934, *ECFP*.

83   "Camp Roosevelt": On the Marines at Warm Springs, see Chico, "Camp Roosevelt Vignettes," *Leatherneck*, Vol. 19, No. 1 (January 1936), pp. 7, 50–51.

84   There were surprise visits: Ibid.

84   Roosevelt had spent a substantial portion: Jean Edward Smith, *FDR* (New York: Random House, 2007), pp. 215–17. According to Smith, the purchase of Warm Springs cost about two-thirds of FDR's fortune.

85   "He's a great man": EFC to parents, November 24, 1935, *ECFP*.

85   "Not bad": EFC to parents, February 6, 1936, *ECFP*.

85   "I was shocked": Michael Blankfort, *The Big Yankee: The Life of Carlson of the Raiders* (Boston: Little, Brown, 1947), p. 170.

85   he had even singled Carlson out: EFC to parents, January 24, 1936, *ECFP*.

86   "prove, by virtue": EFC to parents, November 8, 1936, *ECFP*.

86   "I would go to hell for him": EFC to parents, November 8, 1936, *ECFP*.

86   "It is almost too good": Carlson to Nelson Johnson, February 21, 1937, Nelson T. Johnson Papers, Box 31, *LOC*.

86   proper place in the sun: EFC to Nelson Johnson, April 11, 1937, Nelson T. Johnson Papers, Box 31, *LOC*.

86   "Tell mother": EFC to father, July 8, 1937, *ECFP*.

86   "My separation from Etelle": EFC to father, July 31, 1937, *ECFP*.

87   She enrolled in a graduate program: Etelle Carlson to Helen Foster Snow, January 2, 1939, Box 130, Folder 14, *HFSBYU*.

87   Not long afterward: EFC to Karen Carlson, August 2, 1937, *ECFP*.

88   Roosevelt told the story: EFC to Nelson Johnson, April 11, 1937, Nelson T. Johnson Papers, Box 31, *LOC*. FDR's descendant Frederic D. Grant, Jr., who has done substantial research on the old China trade and his own family's connections to it, believes FDR made this story up and it did not actu-

ally take place, at least not as FDR told it during the dinner with Carlson. Author's conversation with F. D. Grant, April 2024.

88   That evening was one of the most memorable: EFC to parents, March 18, 1937, *ECFP*; EFC to Marguerite LeHand, June 17, 1937, PPF 4951, FDR Papers, *FDRL*.

89   "Future developments are unpredictable": "3,000,000 Men Await Tokyo Call to Arms," *Washington Post*, July 15, 1937.

CHAPTER 6: INTO THE CATACLYSM

93   The bombers droned high: The description of Carlson's arrival is based on Evans F. Carlson, *Twin Stars of China: A Behind-the-Scenes Story of China's Valiant Struggle for Existence* (New York: Dodd, Mead, 1940), p. 1.

94   "Let them come": Jay Taylor, *The Generalissimo: Chiang Kai-shek and the Struggle for Modern China* (Cambridge, MA: Belknap Press of Harvard University Press, 2009), p. 127 (exclamation point added as source describes him "shouting").

94   shooting dozens of his guards: Alexander V. Pantsov, *Victorious in Defeat: The Life and Times of Chiang Kai-shek, China, 1887–1975*, trans. Steven I. Levine (New Haven: Yale University Press, 2023), p. 245.

94   "I am the Generalissimo": Taylor, *The Generalissimo*, p. 127; Xu Youwei and Philip Billingsley, "Behind the Scenes of the Xi'an Incident: The Case of the Lixingshe," *China Quarterly*, No. 154 (June 1998), pp. 283–307.

95   "like mad": Pantsov, *Victorious in Defeat*, p. 247, quoting Zhang Guotao.

95   And that need for protection: John W. Garver, "Mao, the Comintern, and the Second United Front," *China Quarterly*, No. 129 (March 1992), pp. 171–79; see p. 174.

95   Stalin feared: Hans J. van de Ven, *China at War: Triumph and Tragedy in the Emergence of the New China* (Cambridge, MA: Harvard University Press, 2018), pp. 61–62, on Xi'an Incident.

95   Stalin's fears were well founded: Taylor, *The Generalissimo*, pp. 130–31.

96   Chiang hoped: van de Ven, *China at War*, p. 63.

96   The Communists, for their part: Michael Sheng, "Mao, Stalin, and the Formation of the Anti-Japanese United Front: 1935–1937," *China Quarterly*, No. 129 (March 1992), pp. 149–70.

97   "This is not": EFC to parents, September 11, 1937, *ECFP*. Details on his arrival from Carlson, *Twin Stars of China*, p. 4; and EFC to LeHand, August 20, 1937, PPF 4951, FDR Papers, *FDRL*.

98   "Language Student Officer": Semi-Annual Report from the Naval Attaché to the Director of Naval Intelligence, Peiping, China, July 16, 1938, A9-2 (716), Naval Attaché Reports, RG 38, *NARA I*.

98   "assistant to the Assistant": EFC to parents, September 11, 1937, *ECFP*.

98   "There was a tremendous, sickening lurch": Hallett Abend, *My Life in China, 1926–1941* (New York: Harcourt, Brace, 1943), quoted in van de Ven, *China at War*, p. 83.

99   "Nowhere else is a great": Edgar Snow, *The Battle for Asia* (New York: Random House, 1941), p. 45.

99   "Never to my dying day": EFC to LeHand, November 13, 1937, PPF 4951, FDR Papers, *FDRL*.

438 · *Source Notes*

100 "the greatest show": EFC to parents, September 11, 1937, *ECFP.*

100 As he saw it, Japan's ultimate goal: EFC to LeHand, August 27, 1937, PPF 4951, FDR Papers, *FDRL.*

101 Snow had witnessed: Bernard S. Thomas, *Season of High Adventure: Edgar Snow in China* (Berkeley: University of California Press, 1996), pp. 166–67.

101 "sense of fatalism": Snow, *The Battle for Asia*, p. 50.

101 "When my time comes": EFC to father and Karen, December 5, 1943, *ECFP.*

103 "prompt action":"Japanese Kill British Writer Watching Fight," *New York Herald Tribune*, November 12, 1937. The article has no byline but was almost certainly written by Edgar Snow.

103 "If I had not done so": EFC to LeHand, November 13, 1937, PPF 4951, FDR Papers, *FDRL.*

103 red poppy: Snow, *The Battle for Asia*, pp. 53–54.

103 "the heaviest concentration": Snow, The *Battle for Asia*, p. 50.

104 "One phase of this war": Admiral William Leahy to President Roosevelt, quoting letter from Admiral Yarnell, January 6, 1938, President's Secretary's File, Diplomatic Correspondence, China, 1938, FDR Papers, *FDRL.*

104 As an example, he forwarded: Memorandum included as attachment to Leahy to FDR, above.

104 "The Japanese have found": EFC to parents, September 11, 1937, *ECFP.*

105 Long after he finished spending: Helen Foster Snow to Evans and Etelle Carlson, March 21, 1936, Box 130, Folder 14, *HFSBYU.*

105 "the significance of Red China": R. L. Duffus, "A Remarkable Survey of the Red in the Map of China," *New York Times*, January 9, 1938, quoted in Thomas, *Season of High Adventure*, p. 173.

106 "a world scoop": Snow to Nelson Johnson, February 6, 1937, Nelson T. Johnson Papers, Box 31, Part 2, *LOC.*

106 From the outset he envisioned: Thomas, *Season of High Adventure*, p. 133.

106 Zhu De was away: Thomas, *Season of High Adventure*, p. 162.

106 "a quiet, modest, soft-spoken": Edgar Snow, *Red Star Over China* (New York: Random House, 1938; first printing), p. 354.

106 "an extremely competent": China (Military) Situation Report, March 30–April 12, 1935, Report No. 9098 from U.S. Army Military Attaché, China, p. 2.

106 "a very clever and able": China (Military) Situation Report, December 6–19, 1934, Report No. 9004 from U.S. Army Military Attaché, China, p. 2.

106 "It would be naïve": Snow, *Red Star Over China*, pp. 354–55. This was one of the passages deleted from later editions of the book, as part of the changes Snow made to please the Communist Party of the USA; see Chapter 12.

107 it was at least partially engineered for him: Anne-Marie Brady, *Making the Foreign Serve China: Managing Foreigners in the People's Republic* (Lanham, MD: Rowman & Littlefield, 2003), pp. 43–44.

107 "The Generalissimo displays": EFC to LeHand, November 29, 1937, PPF 4951, FDR Papers, *FDRL.*

109 Carlson caught a steamer: Carlson, *Twin Stars of China*, pp. 37–38.

109 "Gran": William M. Leary, "Portrait of an Intelligence Officer: James McHugh in China, 1937–1942," *Naval History*, 1988, pp. 249–63; see p. 252.

110 "Never touch the stuff!": W. H. Auden and Christopher Isherwood, *Journey to a War* (London: Faber & Faber, 1973), p. 46.

110 "this man Carlson": James McHugh notes on meeting with Donald, 1937, Carlson Personal File, Carlson with Red Army, PC56/Coll. 3146, *USMCA;* McHugh unpublished manuscript, "The Carlson Incident," in Carlson Personal File, The Carlson Incident, PC56/Coll. 3146, *USMCA.*

111 "queer duck": James McHugh notes in Carlson Personal File, Carlson with Red Chinese Army, PC56/Coll. 3146, *USMCA;* McHugh, "The Carlson Incident."

111 McHugh's mood at the time: James McHugh to Nelson Johnson, February 4, 1938, Nelson T. Johnson Papers, Box 35, *LOC.* (The doctors in Hong Kong were able to identify the stomach bug that had been causing him such flatulence.)

111 most valuable intelligence asset: Leary, "Portrait of an Intelligence Officer," p. 250.

111 explaining to Donald: McHugh notes in Carlson Personal File, Carlson with Red Chinese Army, PC56/Coll. 3146, *USMCA.*

111 It took a few days: Evans Carlson diary, November 27, 1937, *CSUF,* microfilm reel 1.

112 never found a publisher: Leary, "Portrait of an Intelligence Officer," p. 262. The manuscript of his memoir is in the James McHugh Papers at Cornell University.

112 "he almost burst": McHugh, second draft of "The Carlson Incident," in Carlson Personal File, PC56/Coll. 3146, *USMCA.*

112 The general had vowed publicly: EFC to LeHand, November 29, 1937, PPF 4951, FDR Papers, *FDRL.*

112 he planned to make the Japanese pay dearly: Carlson diary, November 27, 1937, *CSUF,* microfilm reel 1.

CHAPTER 7: THE REDS

113 "smart looking crowd": Carlson diary, December 4, 1937. All Carlson diary entries referred to in this chapter are from his December 1937–February 1938 diary in *CSUF,* microfilm reel 1.

114 The students spent their mornings: Evans F. Carlson, *Twin Stars of China: A Behind-the-Scenes Story of China's Valiant Struggle for Existence* (New York: Dodd, Mead, 1940), p. 56.

114 Part of Chiang Kai-shek's rationale: Peter Harmsen, *Shanghai 1937: Stalingrad on the Yangtze* (Havertown, PA: Casemate, 2015), p. 31.

114 Carlson saw convoys: Evans F. Carlson, "Notes on the Politico-Military Situation Made by Captain E. F. Carlson, USMC, from Observations Made While En Route from Shanghai to Sianfu, 19 November to 7 December, 1937," Naval Attaché Reports, 1886–1939, Box 527, Register No. 18240, RG 38, *NARA I.*

114 prompting the Communists to complain: Otto Braun, *A Comintern Agent in China, 1932–1939* (Stanford: Stanford University Press, 1982), p. 209.

115 "None speaks English": Carlson diary, December 10, 1937.

115 "All of these people": Carlson diary, December 13, 1937.

115 As for what Carlson: Stuart Browne, "A Professor Quits the Communist Party," *Reader's Digest*, Vol. 31, No. 185 (September 1937), pp. 10–14; Carlson lists the September 1937 issue of *Reader's Digest* as being the one he brought along for this trip in *Twin Stars of China*, p. 176.

116 The run turned into a race: Carlson, *Twin Stars of China*, p. 64.

116 "a stocky short man": Carlson diary, December 15, 1937 (changing "Chu Teh" to "Zhu De," "comdr" to "commander," and "8th Route Army" to "Eighth Route Army").

117 five of whom they drowned: Zhu De, "Memories of My Mother," in *Selected Works of Zhu De* (Beijing: Foreign Languages Press, 1986), p. 116; Agnes Smedley, *The Great Road: The Life and Times of Chu Teh* (New York: Monthly Review Press, 1956), p. 12.

118 He would never return: Zhu De, "Memories of My Mother," p. 119.

118 Zhu's first taste: Guo Junning, *Zhu De yu Fan Shisheng* [Zhu De and Fan Shisheng] (Beijing: Huawen chubanshe, 2001), pp. 105–6.

119 By the 1920s: Matthew William Russell, "From Imperial Soldier to Communist General: The Early Career of Zhu De and His Influence on the Formation of the Chinese Red Army" (PhD diss., George Washington University, 2009), pp. 264, 267.

119 "good relations": Nym Wales (Helen Foster Snow), *Inside Red China* (New York: Doubleday, Doran, 1939), p. 116.

119 In 1922: Nym Wales, *Inside Red China*, p. 117.

120 "volunteer farmers": Nym Wales, *Inside Red China*, p. 121; I. Pozhilov, "Zhu De: The Early Days of a Commander," *Far Eastern Affairs*, 1987, No. 1 (1987), pp. 91–99; see p. 95.

120 Twice, he was arrested: Pozhilov, "Zhu De: The Early Days," p. 99.

120 "Zhu-Mao": Lucien Bianco, *Origins of the Chinese Revolution, 1915–1949* (Stanford: Stanford University Press, 1971), p. 64, n. 10.

121 "that rare kind of personality": Nym Wales, *Inside Red China*, p. 112.

122 "the true leader practices": Evans F. Carlson, "Military Leadership," *United States Naval Institute Proceedings*, Vol. 63, No. 11, Whole No. 417 (November 1937), p. 1587.

122 "to rid China": Carlson diary, December 15, 1937.

123 "I felt that I had found": Carlson diary, December 15, 1937.

123 When Carlson encountered: T'ien-wei Wu, "The Chinese Communist Movement," in James C. Hsiung and Steven I. Levine, eds., *China's Bitter Victory: The War with Japan, 1937–1945* (Armonk, NY: M. E. Sharpe, 1992), p. 80.

124 "Communism will be put into practice": Mao Zedong, "Urgent Tasks of the Chinese Revolution Following the Establishment of Guomindang-Communist Cooperation," September 29, 1937, trans. in Stuart Schram, ed., *Mao's Road to Power: Revolutionary Writings, 1912–1949* (Armonk, NY: M. E. Sharpe, 1992), Vol. 6 ("The New Stage; August 1937–1938"), p. 73.

124 "united democratic government": Mao Zedong, interview with British Journalist James Bertram, October 25, 1937, published in *Liberation Daily* (*Jiefang ribao*), November 13, 1937, trans. in Schram, ed., *Mao's Road to Power*, Vol. 6, pp. 122, 125.

124 Behind the scenes, however: Frederick C. Teiwes and Warren Sun, "From a Leninist to a Charismatic Party: The CCP's Changing Leadership, 1937–

1945," in Tony Saich and Hans van de Ven, eds., *New Perspectives on the Chinese Communist Revolution* (Armonk, NY: M. E. Sharpe, 1995).

125 "Up early today": Carlson diary, December 16, 1937.

125 "gruff in manner": Evans Carlson, *The Chinese Army: Its Organization and Military Efficiency* (New York: Institute of Pacific Relations, 1940), p. 40; Carlson's book *Twin Stars of China* (p. 74) cites both Peng and Lin being present at this meeting, while his diary lists only Lin Biao.

125 "I gave it to them": Carlson diary, December 16, 1937.

125 "I have never seen Chinese so interested": Carlson diary, December 16, 1937.

126 After making the rounds: Carlson diary, December 17, 1937; EFC to LeHand, December 23, 1937, PPF 4951, FDR Papers, *FDRL*.

127 "ingenuity and imagination": Carlson diary, December 18, 1937.

127 "political training": EFC to LeHand, December 24, 1937, PPF 4951, FDR Papers, *FDRL*.

128 "thrilling": Carlson diary, December 20, 1937.

128 battle at Pingxing Pass: T'ien-wei Wu, "The Chinese Communist Movement," pp. 83–84.

129 He asked Zhu De for permission: Carlson, *Twin Stars of China*, pp. 84–85, 115; from Carlson's diary it is clear he got permission by December 18.

129 "So we sat around the charcoal fire": Carlson diary, December 23, 1937.

130 "clear bond of friendship": Carlson diary, December 23, 1937.

CHAPTER 8: AGNES

131 Agnes had been born: Ruth Price, *The Lives of Agnes Smedley* (New York: Oxford University Press, 2005), pp. 22–30.

132 "ugly and poor": Price, *The Lives of Agnes Smedley*, p. 30.

132 Later, as a student: Price, *The Lives of Agnes Smedley*, pp. 34–37.

132 "I began to see": Agnes Smedley, *Daughter of Earth* (New York: Coward-McCann, 1929), pp. 180–81.

133 Smedley arrived: Ben Macintyre, *Agent Sonya: Moscow's Most Daring Wartime Spy* (New York: Crown, 2020), p. 35.

133 "Out here I've had": Agnes Smedley to Florence Becker Lennon, July 19, 1930, quoted in Price, *The Lives of Agnes Smedley*, p. 191.

133 "take sex like a man": Janice MacKinnon and Stephen MacKinnon, *Agnes Smedley: The Life and Times of an American Radical* (Berkeley: University of California Press, 1988), p. 141.

133 "an idiot": Price, *The Lives of Agnes Smedley*, p. 250.

133 "a very high standing": Price, *The Lives of Agnes Smedley*, p. 188.

134 "a well known radical": Document 7333, Box 59, Reel 28, *SMPA*.

134 "notorious American anarchist": Extract from French Police Intelligence Report, May 31, 1932, Document 3703, Box 29, Reel 11, *SMPA*.

134 "an American who represents": Document 7675 (translated from pro-KMT Chinese press reports), Box 62, Reel 31, *SMPA*.

134 "grand and glorious": Price, *The Lives of Agnes Smedley*, p. 200.

134 "I'm married, child": MacKinnon and MacKinnon, *Agnes Smedley*, p. 147.

134 "the most formidable": Promotional copy for Owen Matthews, *An Impeccable Spy: Richard Sorge, Stalin's Master Agent* (London: Bloomsbury, 2019).

134   "mutual acquaintance": Price, *The Lives of Agnes Smedley*, p. 198.

134   too headstrong and impetuous: John Sexton, *Red Friends: Internationalists in China's Struggle for Liberation* (New York: Verso Press, 2023), p. 66.

135   "I could not understand": Macintyre, *Agent Sonya*, p. 37.

135   Once Agnes was certain: For the story of Ursula Kuczynski, see Macintyre, *Agent Sonya*. On Kuczynski's relationship with Smedley, see especially pp. 31–50, and on Smedley's jealousy, p. 59.

136   "The fighters love him": Edgar A. Porter, *The People's Doctor: George Hatem and China's Revolution* (Honolulu: University of Hawaii Press, 1997), p. 103.

136   "kissed him resoundingly": Agnes Smedley, *Battle Hymn of China* (New York: Alfred A. Knopf, 1943), p. 164.

136   "ran his hand": Porter, *The People's Doctor*, p. 103; Smedley, *Battle Hymn of China*, p. 164.

137   "reliable sources": "American Woman Aids Chinese Rising," *New York Times*, January 8, 1937.

137   "Mao's American ally": Price, *The Lives of Agnes Smedley*, p. 303; "First Pictures of China's Roving Communists," *Life*, Vol. 1, No. 4 (January 25, 1937), p. 9.

137   "a young schoolteacher": Upton Sinclair, "America's Amazing Woman Rebel in China," *Liberty*, March 13, 1937.

137   "These statements": "A Disclaimer from Agnes Smedley," *China Weekly Review*, April 10, 1937.

138   "She is grand": Carlson diary, December 15, 1937, *CSUF*, microfilm reel 1.

138   "When I heard": Smedley, *Battle Hymn of China*, p. 197.

138   "While the 8th Route": Agnes Smedley to Michael Blankfort, May 28, 1946, Box 85, Folder 3, *MBBU*.

139   "Carlson was a very long": Smedley, *Battle Hymn of China*, p. 197.

139   "Agnes Smedley and I": Carlson diary, December 19, 1937, *CSUF*, microfilm reel 1.

139   "accepted without question": Agnes Smedley, *China Fights Back: An American Woman with the Eighth Route Army* (New York: Vanguard Press, 1938), pp. 246–47.

139   "He, like so many": Smedley, *China Fights Back*, p. 247.

140   As late as 1979: Helen Foster Snow to Evans C. Carlson, August 22, 1979, Box 130, Folder 14, *HFSBYU*.

140   "hymn-singing": Agnes Smedley, *The Great Road: The Life and Times of Chu Teh* (New York: Monthly Review Press, 1956), p. 368.

141   Agnes wanted to go: Smedley, *China Fights Back*, p. 250.

141   "I'll shoot": Carlson diary, December 18, 1937, *CSUF*, microfilm reel 1.

141   Back in the spring of 1937: MacKinnon and MacKinnon, *Agnes Smedley*, p. 186.

142   "The rule was": See p. 6 of her 1979 epilogue to the autobiography of Evans Carlson, *HFSBYU*, Box 175, Folder 15. She plugged this line repeatedly—see, for example, p. 4 of Snow's 1987 introduction to Margaret Stanley's "Foreigners in Areas of China Under Communist Jurisdiction Before 1949," where she writes that Agnes went to Yan'an in 1937 from Xi'an "where she had been repudiated by the American Communist Party with wide publicity, and with serious harm to her psychiatric condition."

142 She set up a phonograph: MacKinnon and MacKinnon, *Agnes Smedley*, p. 187.

142 "I have a reputation": Price, *The Lives of Agnes Smedley*, p. 3.

143 "Imperialist bitch!": MacKinnon and MacKinnon, *Agnes Smedley*, pp. 190–91; Adalbert Tomasz Grunfeld, "Friends of the Revolution: American Supporters of China's Communists, 1926–1939" (PhD diss., New York University, 1985), p. 137.

143 "I cannot tell you how interested": Marguerite LeHand to EFC, October 21, 1937, PPF 4951, FDR Papers, *FDRL*.

143 "and we are all interested": Marguerite LeHand to EFC, November 27, 1937, PPF 4951, FDR Papers, *FDRL*.

143 "We are all thinking about you": Marguerite LeHand to EFC, December 23, 1937 (envelope marked return to sender), PPF 4951, FDR Papers, *FDRL*.

144 In the letter, he said he had just learned: LeHand to EFC, October 21, 1937, and November 27, 1937; EFC to LeHand, December 24, 1937, PPF 4951, FDR Papers, *FDRL*.

144 "a style of military tactics": EFC to LeHand, December 24, 1937, PPF 4951, FDR Papers, *FDRL*.

144 "quite unorthodox": EFC to LeHand, December 24, 1937.

145 "The knowledge which our American people possess": EFC to LeHand, December 24, 1937.

146 "I must *see* how these ideas": EFC to LeHand, December 24, 1937 (changing "practise" to "practice").

146 On Christmas Eve: Carlson diary, December 24, 1937; Evans F. Carlson, *Twin Stars of China: A Behind-the-Scenes Story of China's Valiant Struggle for Existence* (New York: Dodd, Mead, 1940), p. 85; Smedley, *Battle Hymn of China*, p. 199; Michael Blankfort, *The Big Yankee: The Life of Carlson of the Raiders* (Boston: Little, Brown, 1947), pp. 210–12; MacKinnon and MacKinnon, *Agnes Smedley*, pp. 200–201.

147 "This is Christmas Eve": Carlson diary, December 24, 1937, *CSUF*, microfilm reel 1.

147 "This is probably the most interesting": EFC to Nelson Johnson, December 18, 1937, Nelson T. Johnson Papers, Box 33, *LOC*.

148 As if to amplify: Smedley, *Battle Hymn of China*, p. 206.

CHAPTER 9: INTO THE NORTH

149 Up early: Carlson diary, December 26, 1937. All Carlson diary entries referred to in this chapter are from his December 1937–February 1938 diary in *CSUF*, microfilm reel 1.

149 Between the soldiers of the patrol: Agnes Smedley, *China Fights Back: An American Woman with the Eighth Route Army* (New York: Vanguard Press, 1938), p. 249.

149 As they were getting ready to depart: Evans F. Carlson, *Twin Stars of China: A Behind-the-Scenes Story of China's Valiant Struggle for Existence* (New York: Dodd, Mead, 1940), pp. 87–88; Carlson diary, December 26, 1937.

150 Desolate, treeless: Zhou Libo, *Zhandi riji* [War zone diary] (Shanghai: Shanghai zazhi gongsi, 1938), p. 5.

150 Some offered the soldiers walnuts: Zhou, *Zhandi riji*, p. 6.

150 "shifty-eyed fellows": Carlson diary, December 28 and 29, 1937.

151 "very well behaved": Ernest M. Wampler, *China Suffers: Or, My Six Years of Work During the Incident* (Elgin, IL: Brethren Publishing House, 1945), p. 32.

152 "a very pleasant man": Wampler, *China Suffers*, p. 33.

152 "honest, earnest": Carlson diary, January 1, 1938.

152 "Jesus was a social activist": Zhou, *Zhandi riji*, p. 18.

152 put on a grand show: Carlson diary, January 2, 1938; Zhou, *Zhandi riji*, p. 17; Carlson, *Twin Stars of China*, p. 95.

153 "keqi": Carlson diary January 2–3, 1937. As he romanized it: "k'e ch'i" or "ke ch'i."

153 "bowing and scraping": Carlson, *Twin Stars of China*, p. 96.

153 One of the boys: Zhou Libo, *Jin Cha Ji bianqu yinxiang ji* [Impressions of the Jin-Cha-Ji border region] (Washington, DC: Center for Chinese Research Materials, 1971), p. 19.

155 Carlson wanted to encourage: Zhou, *Zhandi riji*, pp. 29–31.

155 "people came pouring": Carlson diary, January 4, 1938.

156 "Welcome, American patriots": Zhou, *Zhandi riji*, p. 23.

156 Such assumptions of American involvement: Zhou, *Zhandi riji*, p. 24.

156 "They would usually still murmur": EFC to LeHand, March 4, 1938, PPF 4951, FDR Papers, *FDRL*.

157 "very sympathetic": Carlson diary, January 5, 1938.

157 "First you need": Zhou, *Zhandi riji*, p. 3.

157 "I am not bound to win": Zhou, *Zhandi riji*, pp. 117–18.

157 "He shared some of his war experience": Zhou, *Zhandi riji*, pp. 115–16.

158 "simple and pure faith": Zhou, *Zhandi riji*, p. 116.

158 the self-defense forces: EFC to LeHand, March 4, 1938, PPF 4951, FDR Papers, *FDRL*.

159 In one village, a group of old men: Carlson, *Twin Stars of China*, pp. 105–6.

160 "What vandals!": Carlson diary, January 21, 1938.

160 the local girls' primary school: Zhou, *Zhandi riji*, p. 49.

160 In another village farther north: Zhou, *Zhandi riji*, p. 50; Carlson diary, January 13, 1938.

160 Japanese soldiers had killed: Zhou, *Jin Cha Ji bianqu*, p. 21.

160 a middle-aged farmer came out to the road: Zhou, *Zhandi riji*, p. 68.

161 The ranking officer: As per Carlson's official report, "A Report on Military Activities in the Northwest of China, with Special Regard to the Organization and Tactics of the Chinese Eighth Route Army (Ex-Communist)," March 23, 1938, Carlson Personal File, PC56/Coll. 3146, *USMCA*.

161 Carlson said he would prefer to come along: Carlson diary, January 15, 1938.

161 Carlson could hear the firing: Zhou, *Zhandi riji*, p. 55; Carlson diary, January 15, 1938.

163 "He is right, of course": Carlson diary, January 16, 1938.

163 The dogs started barking: This final section of the chapter is based on Carlson's diary for January 22, 1938; Carlson, *Twin Stars of China*, pp. 106–109; and EFC to LeHand, March 4, 1938.

CHAPTER 10: THE OTHER SIDE

166 "Those are good mountains": Zhou Libo, *Zhandi riji* [War zone diary] (Shanghai: Shanghai zazhi gongsi, 1938), p. 45.

167 "I was very much affected": Carlson diary, January 26, 1938. All Carlson diary entries referred to in this chapter are from his December 1937–February 1938 and February–October 1938 diaries in *CSUF*, microfilm reel 1.

167 On February 6: Carlson diary, February 6, 1938.

168 The provincial soldiers looked terrified: Evans F. Carlson, *Twin Stars of China: A Behind-the-Scenes Story of China's Valiant Struggle for Existence* (New York: Dodd, Mead, 1940), p. 120.

168 Carlson's truck periodically: Carlson diary, February 18, 1938; Zhou, *Zhandi riji*, p. 111.

169 "the poorest of the lot": Carlson diary, February 20, 1938.

169 "I have met few men": Carlson diary, February 20, 1938 (hyphen added to "self-effacing").

169 Carlson walked with Zhu: Carlson diary, February 20, 1938; Carlson, *Twin Stars of China*, p. 121.

169 It was a period, wrote Agnes Smedley: Agnes Smedley, *Battle Hymn of China* (New York: Alfred A. Knopf, 1943), p. 205.

170 "All kinds of people": W. H. Auden and Christopher Isherwood, *Journey to a War* (London: Faber & Faber, 1973), p. 40 (changing "Chou En-lai" to "Zhou Enlai").

170 "Comrade Bishop": Ilona Ralf Sues, *Shark's Fins and Millet* (Boston: Little, Brown, 1944), pp. 174, 192.

170 "My parents": Sues, *Shark's Fins and Millet*, p. 194.

171 "he either puffed": Sues, *Shark's Fins and Millet*, pp. 300–301.

171 From the 45,000 soldiers: Chiu Sin-ming, "A History of the Chinese Communist Army" (PhD diss., University of Southern California, 1958), p. 75.

171 "The Chinese Communist group": EFC letter to LeHand, March 4, 1938, PPF 4951, FDR Papers, *FDRL*.

172 "most mobile": Edgar Snow, "The Sun Also Sets," *Saturday Evening Post*, June 4, 1938.

172 A Chinese journalist: "Ka'erxun shi Huabei lüxing tan," [Mr. Carlson speaks about his travels in North China], *Xinwen bao*, March 2, 1938.

172 "has sworn to fight": "Chu Teh and U.S. Marine," *Daily Worker*, April 26, 1938.

172 "where during the past": "American Tours Shansi War Zone," *New York Times*, March 1, 1938.

173 "I am 42 years old today": Carlson diary, February 26, 1938.

175 "one hundred times more difficulties": Thomas Waugh, *The Conscience of Cinema: The Works of Joris Ivens, 1926–1989* (Amsterdam: Amsterdam University Press, 2016), p. 222.

175 The film crew arrived: Waugh, The *Conscience of Cinema*, p. 219.

175 "the first defeat": "The Ambassador in China (Johnson) to the Secretary of State," April 19, 1938, in *Foreign Relations of the United States: Diplomatic Papers, 1938*, Vol. III, *The Far East* (Washington, DC: U.S. Government Printing Office, 1954), pp. 153–54.

176 The battle for Taierzhuang: Rana Mitter, *Forgotten Ally: China's World War II, 1937–1945* (Boston: Houghton Mifflin Harcourt, 2013), p. 152, quoting Chinese journalist Sheng Cheng.

176 Carlson hadn't seen: Carlson diary, April 7, 1938; EFC to LeHand, April 15, 1938, PPF 4951, FDR Papers, *FDRL*. Carlson's formal report on the fighting, "Observations on the Sino-Japanese Armies During the Battle of Taierchwang (Shantung)," April 22, 1938, is in Naval Attaché Reports, 1886–1939, Box 527, Register No. 18240, RG 38, *NARA I*.

176 "The Japanese infantry": Carlson, *Twin Stars of China*, p. 143.

177 Carlson passed by the spot: Carlson diary, April 8, 1938.

177 "I tell the Generalissimo": Carlson, *Twin Stars of China*, p. 151.

178 Hitler had recently recognized: Fu Pao-Jen, "The German Military Mission in Nanking, 1928–1938: A Bridge Connecting China and Germany" (PhD diss., Syracuse University, 1989), pp. 192–93.

178 In the final count: Ambassador Johnson telegrams to Secretary of State, June 18 and 23, 1938, in *FRUS*, 1938, Vol. III, documents 188 and 192. On the history of the German mission, see Fu Pao-Jen, "The German Military Mission in Nanking."

178 Other intelligence officers: Freda Utley, *The China Story* (Chicago: H. Regnery, 1951), p. 107, describes him being ridiculed by John Davies and Pinkie Dorn.

178 One admiral joked: Letter from James McHugh to unnamed general, October 6, 1938, from McHugh Papers (originals at Cornell University), copy in Carlson Personal File, Carlson with Red Army, PC56/Coll. 3146, *USMCA*.

179 "Spend less time": Ouyang Shanzun, "San yue riji" [A three months' diary], in Zhongguo guoji youren yanjiuhui, ed. *Zhongguo zhi you Ka Erxun* [China's friend, Evans Carlson] (Shenyang: Liaoning renmin chubanshe, 1996), p. 145.

179 "These people are prepared to resist": EFC to FDR, March 31, 1938, PPF 4951, FDR Papers, *FDRL*.

179 "We didn't have much": Michael Blankfort, *The Big Yankee: The Life of Carlson of the Raiders* (Boston: Little, Brown, 1947), p. 230.

180 Overesch assured Carlson: Carlson diary, April 14, 1938.

180 On the whole, their conversation was friendly: H. E. Overesch to H. E. Yarnell, September 22, 1938, Harry E. Yarnell Papers, Box 3, *LOC*. Overesch described all of his interactions with Carlson as being "extremely friendly."

CHAPTER 11: CROSSROADS

181 "It gets under my skin": Carlson diary, April 26, 1938. All Carlson diary entries referred to in this chapter are from his February–October 1938 diary in *CSUF*, microfilm reel 1.

181 he also had a more personal goal in mind: Ouyang Shanzun, "San yue riji" [A three months' diary], in Zhongguo guoji youren yanjiuhui, ed. *Zhongguo zhi you Ka Erxun* [China's friend, Evans Carlson] (Shenyang: Liaoning renmin chubanshe, 1996), p. 124. His more formal mission is given at the outset of his report, "Chinese Resistance to Japanese Invasion of North China," 1938, U.K. National Archives, FO 676/397. My gratitude to Evan Taylor,

who tracked down a copy of this report in the U.K. National Archives after he discovered it to be missing from its folder in the U.S. National Archives.

182 "In Yan'an": Freda Utley, *Last Chance in China* (New York: Bobbs-Merrill, 1947), p. 140.

183 "I do not want to pry": Rewi Alley, *At 90: Memoirs of My China Years* (Beijing: New World Press, 1986), p. 133.

183 He appeared younger: Carlson diary, May 5, 1938.

185 "they realize he is a genius": Carlson, "Chinese Resistance to Japanese Invasion of North China," U.K. National Archives, FO 676/397.

185 "dreamer": EFC to LeHand, August 15, 1938, PPF 4951, FDR Papers, *FDRL*.

186 "foreign godfather": Ouyang, "San yue riji," p. 135.

187 "Letting him run around like this": Ouyang, "San yue riji," p. 178.

188 "Cut off the bandit areas": Ouyang, "San yue riji," p. 137.

188 But his interpreter: Ouyang, "San yue riji," p. 137.

189 He arrived there on June 9: Ouyang, "San yue riji," p. 168.

189 On the afternoon of June 10: Ouyang, "San yue riji," p. 172.

190 "you all should understand": Ouyang, "San yue riji," p. 172.

190 "My country, America": Ouyang, "San yue riji," pp. 140–41.

191 "What slaves of personal comforts": Carlson diary, June 11, 1938.

191 As Carlson and his youthful traveling companions: Evans F. Carlson, "A Report on Military Activities in the Northwest of China, with Special Regard to the Organization and Tactics of the Chinese Eighth Route Army (Ex-Communist)," March 23, 1938, Carlson Personal File, PC56/Coll. 3146, *USMCA*.

192 "Kill a Japanese for me!": EFC to LeHand, August 15, 1938, PPF 4951, FDR Papers, *FDRL*.

192 "The people in the Communist controlled areas": Carlson, "A Report on Military Activities in the Northwest of China."

193 "short, chunky": Evans F. Carlson, *Twin Stars of China: A Behind-the-Scenes Story of China's Valiant Struggle for Existence* (New York: Dodd, Mead, 1940), p. 252; Carlson diary, July 17, 1938.

193 "Can this be true?": Carlson diary, July 17, 1938.

193 "The Japanese menace": Donald J. Friedman, *The Road from Isolation* (Cambridge, MA: Harvard University Asia Center, 1968), p. 1; Eliot Janeway, "Japan's Partner: Japanese Dependence upon the United States," *Harper's Magazine*, Vol. 177 (June 1938), pp. 1–8; see p. 8.

193 So pronounced were Japan's advantages: Stephen MacKinnon, *Wuhan, 1938: War, Refugees, and the Making of Modern China* (Berkeley: University of California Press, 2008), p. 25.

194 When Carlson arrived: Carlson, *Twin Stars of China*, p. 269; MacKinnon, *Wuhan, 1938*, p. 122.

194 Carlson was reduced to making his appearances: Freda Utley, *China at War* (London: Faber & Faber, 1939), p. 210.

194 "In the north": EFC to LeHand, August 15, 1938, PPF 4951, FDR Papers, *FDRL*.

194 "his spirit remains undaunted": EFC to LeHand, August 15, 1938, PPF 4951, FDR Papers, *FDRL*.

195 "Everywhere I found": EFC to LeHand, August 15, 1938, PPF 4951, FDR Papers, *FDRL*.

196 "in the interest": EFC to LeHand, September 23, 1938, PPF 4951, FDR Papers, *FDRL*.

196 "The independence of China": EFC to LeHand, November 15, 1938, PPF 4951, FDR Papers, *FDRL*.

196 The small number of foreigners: Stephen MacKinnon, "Romantic Hankow, 1938," in Stephen MacKinnon and Oris Friesen, *China Reporting: An Oral History of American Journalism in the 1930s and 1940s* (Berkeley: University of California Press, 1987), p. 38.

197 "Not only was I never beautiful": Freda Utley, *Odyssey of a Liberal: Memoirs* (Washington, DC: Washington National Press, 1970), p. 9.

197 "Why do you try": Utley, *Odyssey of a Liberal*, p. 204.

197 "Dear, innocent": Utley, *Odyssey of a Liberal*, p. 203.

197 "deceptive air": Utley, *China at War*, p. 211.

198 "It was all rather mixed up": Utley, *Odyssey of a Liberal*, p. 202.

198 "Only his wife!": Utley, *Odyssey of a Liberal*, p. 203.

198 "The Chinese Communist Party long ago abandoned": Utley, *China at War*, p. 254.

198 "I have seen a new China": EFC to parents, August 27, 1938, *ECFP*.

199 "My sympathies are so thoroughly involved" EFC to Edgar Snow, August 31, 1938, Folder 13, *ESUM*.

199 "so thoroughly aroused": EFC to parents, August 27, 1938, *ECFP*.

199 "Capt. E. F. Carlson of U.S Marines": "Finds China Runs 'Occupied' Area," *New York Times*, August 9, 1938.

199 "tall, bristly-haired": "Behind the Lines," *Time*, Vol. 32, No. 8 (August 22, 1938).

199 "My view is that the truth": EFC to Edgar Snow, August 16, 1938, Folder 13, *ESUM*.

199 "I can see some of the old fogies": EFC to Edgar Snow, August 31, 1938, Folder 13, *ESUM*.

200 "romantic, believing": Utley, *China at War*, p. 211

200 "Evans Voice-in-the-Wilderness": MacKinnon, "Romantic Hankow, 1938," p. 46.

200 "Then there is Evans": Agnes Smedley, quoted in MacKinnon, "Romantic Hankow, 1938," p. 42.

200 "generally credited": "Pres. Coolidge Arrives with Many Notables," *China Press*, October 24, 1938.

200 "growing danger": H. E. Overesch to H. E. Yarnell, September 22, 1938, Harry E. Yarnell Papers, Box 3, *LOC*. Unless otherwise indicated, all quotations from here to the end of the chapter are from this document, which contains substantial quotations from other letters written by, or received by, Overesch, relating to Carlson.

202 trying to get Carlson promoted: Carlson military personnel file, Series: Official Military Personnel Files, RG 127, National Archives, St. Louis, MO.

202 "intolerable": EFC to Nelson Johnson, September 20, 1938, Nelson T. Johnson Papers, Box 34, *LOC*.

202 "I am tired": Carlson diary, September 18, 1938; Carlson's resignation is relayed in a Navy Department communication of September 21, 1938,

from the Naval Attaché's office to the Secretary of the Navy, Carlson Personal File, Office of Naval Intelligence Memos (copies), PC56/Coll. 3146, *USMCA.*

CHAPTER 12: SYMPATHY

205   "I feel very strongly on the subject": EFC to Nelson Johnson, September 20, 1938, Nelson T. Johnson Papers, Box 34, *LOC.*

205   "I have a profound belief": Johnson to EFC, September 23, 1938, Nelson T. Johnson Papers, Box 34, *LOC.*

205   The Last Ditchers threw: Stephen MacKinnon and Oris Friesen, *China Reporting: An Oral History of American Journalism in the 1930s and 1940s* (Berkeley: University of California Press, 1987), pp. 46–47.

205   "Washington's disapproval": "Captain to Quit; 'Red' Talk Cited," *Evening Star* (Washington, DC), via *Chicago Daily News*, September 24, 1938.

206   "Reason for resigning": Coded radio from Commander of Yangtze Patrol to Commander-in-Chief, Asia Fleet, September 21, 1938, National Archives, digitized copy accessed via University of Southern California digital collections, Pedro Loureiro Collection, item identifier: lou-asiatic-111-002.

206   "They seemed to think": EFC to Carlsons, December 12, 1938, *ECFP.*

206   "The main point is": EFC to Edgar Snow, September 19, 1938, Folder 13, *ESUM.*

206   "Powers-That-Be": Carlson relating conversation with Agnes Smedley in letter to Edgar Snow, September 19, 1938, Folder 13, *ESUM.*

207   "a most timely book": Yarnell to Edgar Snow, February 24, 1938, Folder 12, *ESUM.*

207   "At present": "Notes on Guerrilla Activities," report from Military Attaché, China (David D. Barrett, Assistant Military Attaché, forwarding report by Joseph Stilwell), Report No. 9695, November 9, 1938, *ECFP.*

207   "I don't know how you are fixed": Edgar Snow to EFC, December 8, 1938, from Baguio, Philippines, Box 175, Folder 15, *HFSBYU.*

208   "would be a magnificent gesture": Helen Foster Snow to EFC, December 4, 1938, Box 175, Folder 15, *HFSBYU.*

208   From her room in the International House: Etelle Carlson to Helen Foster Snow, January 2, 1939, Box 130, Folder 14, *HFSBYU.*

208   "that American upstart officer": Etelle to Carlsons, June 5, 1938, *ECFP.*

209   "I know you must be very proud": Etelle to Carlsons, June 5, 1938, *ECFP.*

209   "I am so proud of him": Etelle to Carlsons, August 22, 1938, *ECFP.*

209   "I shall see Etelle in San Francisco": EFC to Carlsons, December 12, 1938, *ECFP.*

210   "The Marine Corps needs": Etelle Carlson to Helen Foster Snow, January 2, 1939, Box 130, Folder 14, *HFSBYU.*

210   "Evans junior has been": EFC to parents, December 31, 1938, *ECFP.*

211   While they were in San Francisco: EFC to parents, January 22, 1939, *ECFP.*

211   "How happy I am": Etelle Carlson to Helen Foster Snow, January 2, 1939, Box 130, Folder 14, *HFSBYU.*

211   "Wish you could practice some evangelism": Helen Foster Snow to EFC, January 30, 1939, Box 130, Folder 14, *HFSBYU.*

450 · *Source Notes*

211 "At present a married woman": George Bernard Shaw, *The Intelligent Woman's Guide to Socialism and Communism* (New Brunswick, NJ: Transaction Publishers, 2005), p. 407.

211 "Since returning to San Diego": EFC to parents, March 24, 1939, *ECFP.*

211 "As a civilian I can help": EFC to Le Hand, March 17, 1939, PPF 4951, FDR Papers, *FDRL.*

212 He felt an impossible distance: EFC to father, March 24, 1939, *ECFP.*

212 "Life is indeed simpler": Etelle to Carlsons, May 5, 1939, *ECFP.*

212 "I can't say I am very happy": Etelle to Snows, May 1, 1939, Box 130, Folder 14, *HFSBYU.*

213 The book's sudden success: "Book Notes," *New York Times,* January 4, 1938; "Book Notes," *New York Times,* January 26, 1938.

213 In Great Britain it did even better: Bernard S. Thomas, *Season of High Adventure: Edgar Snow in China* (Berkeley: University of California Press, 1996), p. 170.

213 "The Chinese Communists": Edgar Snow, *Red Star Over China* (New York: Random House, 1938; first printing), p. 374.

213 "virtually a Bureau": Snow, *Red Star Over China* (1938; first printing), pp. 374, 376.

213 "Trotskyist poison": Harvey Klehr, *The Soviet World of American Communism* (New Haven: Yale University Press, 1998), pp. 336–37.

214 "in a very harmful manner indeed": Edgar Snow to Earl Browder, March 20, 1938, quoted in Thomas, *Season of High Adventure*, p. 180.

214 "Some weeks ago": Edgar Snow to Earl Browder, March 20, 1938, quoted in Thomas, *Season of High Adventure*, p. 180.

214 two months *after* his letter to Browder: Letter from Agent (Henriette Herz) to Edgar Snow, June 14, 1938 (referring to his letters with corrections of May 15 and May 21, 1938), Folder 12, *ESUM.*

214 "England didn't complain": Henriette Herz to Edgar Snow, July 28, 1938, Folder 12, *ESUM.*

215 "rich and truly epic": Pearl S. Buck Nobel Prize citation, 1938.

216 "the Chinese have been led": "Man and Wife of the Year," *Time,* January 3, 1938.

217 Against Carlson's expectation: Andrew Johnstone, *Against Immediate Evil: American Internationalists and the Four Freedoms on the Eve of World War II* (Ithaca, NY: Cornell University Press, 2014), p. 18.

217 "I can't accustom myself": EFC to Freda Utley, March 7, 1939, Carlson Correspondence File, Freda Utley Papers, *HIA.*

217 On October 1, 1937: "Japan Denounced at Rally of 10,000," *New York Times,* October 2, 1937.

217 "a transmission belt": United States Congress House Committee on Un-American Activities, *Hearings 1953/54,* Vol. III, p. 3622, n. 5.

218 "a feeling of affection": Sidney L. Pash, *The Currents of War: A New History of American-Japanese Relations, 1899–1941* (Lexington: University Press of Kentucky, 2014), p. 85, citing Eugene Dooman oral history, Butler Library, Columbia University Rare Books and Manuscripts, New York, NY.

218 "American-motored airplanes": American Committee for Non-Participation in Japanese Aggression, *Shall America Stop Arming Japan?* (New York, 1940), p. 25.

219 They maintained: Donald J. Friedman, *The Road from Isolation* (Cambridge, MA: Harvard University Asia Center, 1968), pp. 22–24.

219 By the winter of 1938–1939: Sun Youli, "Chinese Military Resistance and Changing American Perceptions, 1937–1938," in Robert David Johnson, ed., *On Cultural Ground: Essays in International History* (Chicago: Imprint Publications, 1994), p. 89; Stephen MacKinnon, *Wuhan, 1938: War, Refugees, and the Making of Modern China* (Berkeley: University of California Press, 2008), pp. 99, 103.

219 "He impresses me as being": Hornbeck to [appears to be Welles], December 7, 1939, Evans Carlson Folder, Stanley Hornbeck Papers, *HIA*.

219 He spoke in church sanctuaries: "Services Tomorrow," *Pittsburgh Press*, January 13, 1940; "Ex-Marine Officer to Talk at Forum," *Pittsburgh Press*, January 14, 1940.

219 make their blood boil: "Ex-Marine Officer Talks on Japan War," *Pittsburgh Post-Gazette*, January 16, 1940.

219 "the capacity to secure": "Ban on War Goods to Japan Is Urged," *Baltimore Sun*, February 7, 1940.

220 "Carlson was not a fluent speaker": Raymond Gram Swing, "The Man Who Will Become a Legend," *Saturday Review of Literature*, Vol. 30 (October 1947), pp. 26–27.

220 "a stepping stone": "Ex-Observer Asks Embargo on Japan," *Washington Post*, February 28, 1940.

220 did not, in fact, oppose: Friedman, The *Road from Isolation*, p. 63.

220 "a subservient flunky": "Carroll Lunt Registers as a Japanese Propagandist," *China Weekly Review*, July 20, 1940.

220 "advocating American cooperation": "Lunt Says Japanese 'Built-up' China Will Bring Handsome Returns!," *China Weekly Review*, September 30, 1939.

220 "aggression is a relative term": "Editor Backs Japan Policy," *Los Angeles Times*, July 16, 1940.

221 "When Chiang [Kai-shek] is beaten": "Former Honolulan Now World Affairs Lecturer," *Honolulu Advertiser*, July 26, 1940.

221 "the best thing for China": "Mt. Holly Fortnightly Hears Talk on China," *Courier-Post* (Camden, NJ), April 12, 1940.

221 On CBS radio: Memo in Agnes Smedley FBI file, *SMASU*.

221 Carlson and Lunt went head-to-head: "Optional Embargo of Japan is Urged," *New York Times*, January 13, 1940.

221 "attempted to profit": EFC to Le Hand, January 13, 1940, PPF 4951, FDR Papers, *FDRL*.

222 "arms, airplanes, gasoline": American Committee for Non-Participation in Japanese Aggression, *Shall America Stop Arming Japan?*, p. 35.

222 "Gosh, I don't know": EFC to father and Karen, January 21, 1940, *ECFP*.

CHAPTER 13: UNHEARD WARNINGS

223 "It is a definite contribution": Etelle to Carlsons, May 5, 1939, *ECFP*.

224 The neighbors remembered him: "Outspoken War Hero Stirred Controversy with Critical Views," *Hartford Courant*, March 20, 1977.

224 The Reverend Thomas Carlson was planning: EFC to Etta Mae Wallace, November 21, 1939, *ECFP*.

224   "means the freedom to think": Michael Blankfort, *The Big Yankee: The Life of Carlson of the Raiders* (Boston: Little, Brown, 1947), p. 278.

225   "'I believe,' he assured me": Evans F. Carlson, *Twin Stars of China: A Behind-the-Scenes Story of China's Valiant Struggle for Existence* (New York: Dodd, Mead, 1940), p. 35.

225   "Take the Chinese habit": Carlson, *Twin Stars of China*, p. 35.

225   "kindly eyes": Carlson, *Twin Stars of China*, p. 167.

225   "the kindliness of a Robert E. Lee": Carlson, *Twin Stars of China*, p. 66.

226   "striking west across": Carlson, *Twin Stars of China*, p. 116 (changing "Chu Teh" to "Zhu De").

226   "seemed to possess": Carlson, *Twin Stars of China*, p. viii.

226   "central figure": Carlson, *Twin Stars of China*, p. 318.

226   "the ability to organize": Carlson, *Twin Stars of China*, pp. 318–19.

226   Carlson wanted to call it: EFC to Etta Mae Wallace, April 30, 1940, *ECFP.*

227   "one of the most fascinating": "Light on China War," *Atlanta Constitution*, October 7, 1940.

227   "with the intelligence": "Report from the Front," *The Nation*, October 5, 1940.

227   "much like old-fashioned Americans": "An American Marine Reports on China," *New York Times*, September 22, 1940.

227   the critics preferred: Thomas Waugh, *The Conscience of Cinema: The Works of Joris Ivens, 1926–1989* (Amsterdam: Amsterdam University Press, 2016), p. 253.

227   "CHINA—which has enriched": Joris Ivens (director), *The 400 Million*, History Today, 1939.

227   according to *Variety*: Waugh, *The Conscience of Cinema*, p. 253.

228   and so it disbanded: Akio Tsuchida, "China's 'Public Diplomacy' Toward the United States Before Pearl Harbor," *The Journal of American-East Asian Relations*, Vol. 17, No. 1 (2010), pp. 35–55; p. 54 (ACNPJA shuts down) and p. 52 (export restrictions).

229   "guerrilla tactics applied to industry": EFC to LeHand, June 13, 1939, PPF 4951, FDR Papers, *FDRL.*

230   "I realize that I am": EFC to Nelson Johnson, September 8, 1940, Carlson Personal File, Correspondence and Memos, PC56/Coll. 3146, *USMCA.*

230   On one third-class train car: Carlson diary, October 14, 1940. All Carlson diary entries referred to in this chapter are from his August 1940–January 1941 diary in *CSUF*, microfilm reel 1.

231   "lots of eye work": Carlson diary, October 10, 1940.

231   "Confidence of people": Carlson diary, October 16, 1940.

231   "essentially fascist": EFC to LeHand, November 29, 1940, PPF 4951, FDR Papers, *FDRL.*

231   "The situation here is disappointing": EFC to Freda Utley, November 28, 1940, Carlson correspondence file, Freda Utley papers, *HIA.*

232   "China is being destroyed": EFC to Etta Mae Wallace, March 1, 1941, *ECFP.*

232   The local cooperative staff: Carlson diary, October 11, 1940.

232   "sulky, bull dog": Carlson diary, December 31, 1940.

233   "no friction existed": Carlson diary, December 31, 1940.

233   "I cut short my trip": EFC to family, January 6, 1941, *ECFP.*

234 "exceedingly liberal": Evans F. Carlson, "Strategy of the Sino-Japanese War," *Far Eastern Survey*, Vol. 10, No. 9 (May 19, 1941), pp. 99–105.

234 The two men went back: Evans F. Carlson, "The Autobiography of Evans Carlson," unpublished typescript, as told to Helen Foster Snow, Carlson Personal File, Published Materials, *USMCR*.

235 "The usual band": Carlson diary, January 24, 1941.

235 "in order to protect": "Crisis in Far East to Come Within 90 Days According to Major Evans Carlson," *North China Daily News*, January 31, 1941 (from United Press wire report dated January 30).

235 "The United States and Japan": "American-Japanese War in 90 Days Prophesied," *Los Angeles Times*, January 30, 1941.

235 "embarrassing": Thomas Holcomb to EFC, November 15, 1939, Carlson Personal File, Correspondence and Memos, PC56/Coll. 3146, *USMCA*.

235 "My record since I left the Corps": EFC to Holcomb, November 19, 1939, from Plymouth, CT, Carlson Personal File, Correspondence and Memos, PC56/Coll. 3146, *USMCA*.

235 "As they say in baseball": Holcomb to EFC, November 27, 1939, Carlson Personal File, Correspondence and Memos, PC56/Coll. 3146, *USMCA*.

236 "It looks to me as though": EFC to Holcomb, March 3, 1941, Carlson Personal File, Correspondence and Memos, PC56/Coll. 3146, *USMCA*.

237 "I haven't done that": Etelle to Thomas Carlson, August 24, 1941, *ECFP*.

237 "I chafe at all the restraint": EFC to father and Karen, October 6, 1941, *ECFP* (changing "E" to "Etelle").

237 "I prefer to be with the troops": EFC to father and Karen, November 19, 1941, *ECFP*.

237 "I understand the futility": EFC to Etta Mae Wallace, November 16, 1941, *ECFP*.

237 "Agnes is always a tonic": EFC to father, December 1, 1941, *ECFP*.

238 "I know that it is better": EFC to father and Karen, December 4, 1941, *ECFP*.

CHAPTER 14: NEW BEGINNINGS

242 The U.S. forces in China: George B. Clark, *Treading Softly: U.S. Marines in China, 1819–1949* (Westport, CT: Praeger, 2001), pp. 122–25; James S. Santelli, *A Brief History of the 4th Marines*, Marine Corps Historical Reference Pamphlet (Washington, DC: Headquarters, U.S. Marine Corps, 1970), p. 21.

242 As recently as 1939: Hans J. van de Ven, *War and Nationalism in China: 1925–1945* (London: Routledge Curzon, 2003), p. 24.

243 "I never wanted to have to fight": Eleanor Roosevelt oral history, quoted in James Scott, *Target Tokyo: Jimmy Doolittle and the Raid That Avenged Pearl Harbor* (New York: W. W. Norton, 2015), p. 25.

243 "a distressing ignorance": "How to Tell Japs from the Chinese," *Life*, December 22, 1941, p. 81.

244 "The Chinese were beside themselves": John S. Service oral history, Truman Library, https://www.trumanlibrary.gov/library/oral-histories/service2 #186.

244 "There is not much comfort": EFC to Yarnell, July 18, 1942, Harry E. Yarnell Papers, Box 1, Folder 4, *LOC*.

245 To an acquaintance: EFC to Raymond Gram Swing, January 26, 1942, Raymond Swing Papers, Box 40, Folder 6, *LOC;* David H. Culbert, "Radio's Raymond Gram Swing: 'He Isn't the Kind of Man You Would Call Ray," *The Historian,* Vol. 35, No. 4 (August 1973), pp. 587–606; see p. 587.

247 "a rather bleak room": James Roosevelt, "Evans Carlson: A Personal Memoir," in *New Aspects of Naval History: Selected Papers Presented at the Fourth Naval History Symposium, United States Naval Academy, 25–26 October 1979,* ed. Craig L. Symonds et al. (Annapolis, MD: Naval Institute Press, 1981), p. 387.

247 "I discovered to my great delight": EFC to FDR, March 2, 1942, PPF 4951, FDR Papers, *FDRL.*

247 professional football players: Maj. Gen. Charles Price to Commandant Holcomb, January 16, 1942, reprinted in Robert E. Mattingly, "Herringbone Cloak—GI Dagger: Marines of the OSS," Occasional Paper, History and Museums Division, Headquarters, U.S. Marine Corps, Washington, DC, 1989, p. 250.

248 "I am terrified": Holcomb to Samuel Week, January 19, 1942, in Mattingly, "Herringbone Cloak," p. 254.

248 James Roosevelt's prior assignment: Robert E. Mattingly, "The Worst Slap in the Face," *Marine Corps Gazette,* March 1983, pp. 58–66; see p. 61.

248 "surprise and swiftly moving blows": James Roosevelt, "Development within the Marine Corps of a unit for purposes similar to the British Commandos and the Chinese Guerrillas," January 13, 1942, "Midway" folder, Box 75, James Roosevelt Papers, *FDRL.*

249 "undesirable and superfluous": Joseph Alexander, *Edson's Raiders: The 1st Marine Raider Battalion in World War II* (Annapolis, MD: Naval Institute Press, 2001), p. 27; David J. Ulbrich, *Preparing for Victory: Thomas Holcomb and the Making of the Modern Marine Corps, 1936–1943* (Annapolis, MD: Naval Institute Press, 2011), pp. 124–25.

249 And Holcomb felt pressure: Thomas Holcomb to Holland Smith, February 11, 1942, AO-283-njp (03A4242), in Mattingly, "Herringbone Cloak," pp. 269–72. Regarding the commando plan and the apparent end of Donovan's candidacy to lead it, Holcomb wrote, "I fear . . . that the idea is too strongly imbedded to remain dormant very long unless we move promptly to broaden our amphibious training in such a way as to head off any outside interference."

249 Holcomb had no choice: Ulbrich, *Preparing for Victory,* p. 125.

250 toying with suggestions: Jon T. Hoffman, *Once a Legend: "Red Mike" Edson of the Marine Raiders* (Novato, CA: Presidio Press, 1994), p. 153; H. H. Smith to Thomas Holcomb, February 9, 1942 (2385 02/106 061), in Mattingly, "Herringbone Cloak."

250 "There is nothing like it": EFC to father, February 5, 1942, quoted in Michael Blankfort, *The Big Yankee: The Life of Carlson of the Raiders* (Boston: Little, Brown, 1947), p. 8.

250 "When you told me about your intention": Churchill to FDR, March 4, 1942, in Francis L. Loewenheim, Harold D. Langley, and Manfred Jonas, eds., *Roosevelt and Churchill: Their Secret Wartime Correspondence* (New York: Saturday Review Press, 1975), p. 185.

250 "The new outfit is most interesting": FDR to EFC, March 12, 1942, PPF 4951, FDR Papers, *FDRL*.

251 "Men who learn": Carlson to Holcomb, January 27, 1943, "2nd Raider Bn (Carlson)—WWII" file, *USMCR*.

251 "to create and perfect": Evans Carlson, "Address of the Commanding Officer . . . ," February 1943, Carlson Personal File, PC56/Coll. 3146, *USMCA*.

251 "Fundamentally, gung ho is an ideal": Carlson national radio address on First Line, quoted in raw transcript for History Channel program on Raiders, *ECFP* (changing "Gung-Ho" to "gung ho").

251 "To help a man": "Carlson's Immortal Raiders," *Liberty*, November 20, 1943.

252 "Boy Scout equipment": Lt. Gen. Alan Shapley oral history (interviewed by Maj. Thomas E. Donnelly), History and Museums Division, Headquarters, U.S. Marine Corps, Washington, DC, 1976 (copy held at Columbia University Special Collections), p. 74.

252 "Carlson's always got": Merrill Twining, *No Bended Knee: The Battle for Guadalcanal* (Novato, CA: Presidio Press, 1996), p. 178.

252 "Whatever Carlson's so-called standards": Merritt Edson to Maj. Gen. Charles Price, February 20, 1942, Merritt Austin Edson Papers, Box 4, *LOC*.

253 "revolutionist": James Roosevelt, "Evans Carlson: A Personal Memoir," p. 386.

253 "He was a very": Maj. Gen. William Arthur Worton oral history (interviewed by Benis Frank in 1967, 1969), History and Museums Division, Headquarters, U.S. Marine Corps, Washington, DC, p. 154 (copy held at Columbia University Special Collections).

253 "they did not have a clear idea": Elizabeth D. Samet, *Looking for the Good War: American Amnesia and the Violent Pursuit of Happiness* (New York: Farrar, Straus & Giroux, 2021), p. 55.

254 "Hope for glory": Evans Carlson, "Address of the Commanding Officer . . . ," February 1943, Carlson Personal File, PC56/Coll. 3146, *USMCA*.

254 "the most strenuous, back-breaking": W. S. Le Francois, "We Mopped Up Makin Island," Part I, *Saturday Evening Post*, December 4, 1943, p. 20.

254 They honed their physical strength: George W. Smith, *Carlson's Raid: The Daring Marine Assault on Makin* (New York: Berkley Books, 2003), p. 61.

254 In a letter from Jacques Farm: EFC to FDR, March 2, 1942, PPF 4951, FDR Papers, *FDRL*.

254 "My experience here": EFC to Raymond Gram Swing, n.d. (February or March 1942), Raymond Swing Papers, Box 40, Folder 6, *LOC*.

255 "This battalion is now headed": Carlson, Battalion General Order, Number 5-42, quoted in Blankfort, *The Big Yankee*, p. 35.

255 "What a fantastic war this is": EFC to father and Karen, June 25, 1942, *ECFP*.

CHAPTER 15: MAKIN ISLAND

257 On the morning of August 16: Unless otherwise cited, the basic details on the raid in this chapter and the next come from Oscar F. Peatross, *Bless*

'Em All: The Marine Raiders of World War II (Tampa: Raider Publishing, 1995); and John F. Wukovits, *American Commando: Evans Carlson, His WWII Marine Raiders, and America's First Special Forces Mission* (New York: NAL Caliber, 2009). Of the many overview accounts out there, these two are the most reliable.

259   the prospect of a commando attack: Peatross, *Bless 'Em All*, p. 89.

259   As they cast about: George W. Smith, *Carlson's Raid: The Daring Marine Assault on Makin* (New York: Berkley Books, 2003), p. 77.

260   Nimitz and Pfeiffer then toyed: Maj. Gen. Omar Pfeiffer oral history (interviewed by L. E. Tatem), History and Museums Division, Headquarters, U.S. Marine Corps, Washington, DC, 1974 (copy held at Columbia University Special Collections), p. 195.

261   "destroying enemy troops": Operation Order Number 1-42 (Makin), August 7, 1942, Carlson Personal File, PC56/Coll. 3146, *USMCA*.

261   the president had written to him: FDR to EFC, March 12, 1942, PPF 4951, FDR Papers, *FDRL*.

262   "Look, my son's an officer": Smith, *Carlson's Raid*, p. 89.

262   "I've thought so long": Eleanor Roosevelt, *This I Remember* (New York: Harper & Brothers, 1949), pp. 289–90.

262   Under pressure from the president: Omar Pfeiffer oral history, p. 196.

263   "B Company good": Carlson WWII diary, August 6, 1942, *CSUF*, microfilm reel 1.

263   "Happy-go-lucky": Carlson WWII diary, August 12, 1942, *CSUF*, microfilm reel 1.

264   The timing was planned: Makin Island Raid Collection, Operation Plans, Coll/4384, *USMCA*.

268   The first men to reach ground: Kenneth H. Merrill oral history, January 18, 2016, Nimitz Education and Research Center, National Museum of the Pacific War, Fredericksburg, TX, p. 11.

268   It was not Peatross's fault: Peatross, *Bless 'Em All*, pp. 54–55.

269   Carlson switched on his walkie-talkie: Carlson Personal File, Extract From *Nautilus* War Diary (Raid on Makin Island), PC56/Coll. 3146, *USMCA*.

270   They did not realize: James Faulkner interview in *The Raider Patch*, March 1977, p. 6.

270   Fifteen or twenty Japanese soldiers: Smith, *Carlson's Raid*, p. 121.

CHAPTER 16: SURVIVAL

271   "We had Japs": John F. Wukovits, *American Commando: Evans Carlson, His WWII Marine Raiders, and America's First Special Forces Mission* (New York: NAL Caliber, 2009), p. 111; Oscar F. Peatross, *Bless 'Em All: The Marine Raiders of World War II* (Tampa: Raider Publishing, 1995), p. 72.

271   Nine of the Raiders were killed: Wukovits, *American Commando*, p. 111.

271   The snipers had been: Wukovits, *American Commando*, p. 109.

272   The battalion's Navy corpsmen: George W. Smith, *Carlson's Raid: The Daring Marine Assault on Makin* (New York: Berkley Books, 2003), pp. 124–29.

272   "His courage under fire": Lt. Col. Charles Lamb, "Comments on the Raid on Makin Island Manuscript," p. 9, Carlson Personal File, PC56/Coll. 3146, *USMCA*.

272 "You ought to see him in battle": Typescript of article by Jim Lucas, Carlson Personal File, PC56/Coll. 3146, *USMCA*.

273 at least one Marine thought: W. S. Le Francois, "We Mopped Up Makin Island," Part 1, *Saturday Evening Post*, December 4, 1943, p. 41; Smith, *Carlson's Raid*, p. 134.

273 It was impossible to tell: Carlson Personal File, Extract from *Nautilus* War Diary (Raid on Makin Island), PC56/Coll. 3146, *USMCA*; Peatross, *Bless 'Em All*, p. 76.

274 "We shall all die calmly": Matome Ugaki, *Fading Victory: The Diary of Admiral Matome Ugaki, 1941–1945* (Pittsburgh: University of Pittsburgh Press, 1991), p. 184.

274 The Zeros flew so low: Melvin Spotts account of Makin Raid, *The Raider Patch*, July 1980, pp. 13–16; see p. 14.

274 "violently": Evans Carlson, "Operations on MAKIN, August 17–18, 1942," Carlson Personal File, Report of the Commanding Officer, PC56/Coll. 3146, *USMCA*.

275 He was the first person: Peatross, *Bless 'Em All*, p. 56.

275 In the course of the day: "Only 2 Japanese Out of 350 Escaped American Marines in Makin Blitz," *Honolulu Star-Bulletin*, August 28, 1942.

277 "thousand-yard stare": Peatross, *Bless 'Em All*, p. 61.

277 dug himself a hole: Spotts account in *The Raider Patch*, July 1980, p. 15.

278 In whispered conversations: Wukovits, *American Commando*, pp. 137–38, quoting Kenneth Seaton account from *The Raider Patch*, March 1982.

278 There is no question: Carlson draft report on Makin Raid, August 21, 1942, Carlson Personal File, Reports of Raider Expedition against Makin, PC56/Coll. 3146, *USMCA*.

278 six separate Marines told: Samuel E. Stavinsky, *Marine Combat Correspondent: World War II in the Pacific* (New York: Ballantine, 1999), p. 37.

279 "To the Commanding Officer": Handwritten note published in facsimile in Hotta Yoshiaki et al., *Dai Tōa senshi* [History of the Great East Asia War] (Tokyo: Kōbundō Shoten, 1942–1943), Vol. 2, p. 470. NB: not all editions of this work contain the note. A copy of the edition that does have it is held at the Library of Congress, Asian Reading Room, call number D755.4 .H67.

279 later acknowledged writing it: For Coyte's telling of the story, as related to his fellow Raider Oscar Peatross, see Peatross, *Bless 'Em All*, pp. 80–81.

279 Coyte himself said: Peatross, *Bless 'Em All*, p. 81.

280 A more plausible explanation: Hotta Yoshiaki et al., *Dai Tōa senshi*, Vol. 2, p. 470.

280 "no matter how bad": Carlson, "Operations on MAKIN, August 17–18, 1942," Carlson Personal File, PC56/Coll. 3146, *USMCA*.

281 the men on the beach watched in horror: Wukovits, *American Commando*, p. 62.

281 Two giant geysers: W. S. LeFrancois, "We Mopped Up Makin Island," Part 2, *Saturday Evening Post*, December 11, 1943, p. 41.

282 eighty-three dead Japanese troops: Carlson, "Operations on MAKIN, August 17–18, 1942," Carlson Personal File, PC56/Coll. 3146, *USMCA*.

282 the documents they brought back: Greg Bradsher, "Seventy Years Ago: The Makin Island Raid, August 1942," *The Text Message*, National Archives blog, November 14, 2012.

282 "Smirnoff sword": Le Francois, "We Mopped Up," Part 2, p. 43.

282 "a child's picture-book": Le Francois, "We Mopped Up," Part 2, p. 43.

282 Carlson told them to ask: Spotts account in *The Raider Patch*, July 1980, p. 16.

283 He managed to scare up: Smith, *Carlson's Raid*, p. 170.

283 When Carlson came down: Peatross, *Bless 'Em All*, p. 84.

284 paid the native chief of police: Wukovits, *American Commando*, pp. 148–49.

284 slash with knives: Makin Island Raid Collection, Operation Plans, COLL/4384, *USMCA*.

284 No one knew: Most details in this final paragraph are from Buck Stidham, "Comments on Returning from the Makin Raid," *The Raider Patch*, January 1993, pp. 12–13; also, archival film footage of the return of the *Nautilus*, RG 428, NAID: 75303, Local ID: 428-NPC-28, *NARA II*; and Wukovits, *American Commando*, pp. 152–53.

284 most vivid memory: Stephen Stigler account in Patrick K. O'Donnell, *Into the Rising Sun: In Their Own Words, World War II's Pacific Veterans Reveal the Heart of Combat* (New York: Free Press, 2002), p. 35.

CHAPTER 17: FAME AND GLORY

286 "two-day job of slaughter": "Defense Force of 350 Japs Wiped Out in Makin Raid," *Evening Star* (Washington, DC), via AP, August 28, 1942.

286 "Raiders of Wrath": "Marines' 'Raiders of Wrath' Are Combination of Sailor, Soldier and Something More—Much More," *Dunkirk Evening Observer* (NY), November 10, 1942.

286 "United States 'Kung Ho' marines": "Only 2 Japanese Out of 350 Escaped American Marines in Makin Blitz," *Honolulu Star-Bulletin*, August 28, 1942.

286 Roosevelt said at a press conference: "Defense Force of 350 Japs Wiped Out in Makin Raid," *Evening Star* (Washington, DC), via AP.

286 "No, they're more like surf swimmers": "Eyewitness Account of US Raid on Makin," *St. Louis Post-Dispatch*, August 28, 1942.

286 "We wanted to take prisoners": "Forty Hours on Makin," *Time*, September 7, 1942.

286 first enlisted Marine: As a technical matter, while Thomason's actions to earn the Medal of Honor were the first of any enlisted Marine in World War II, the medal itself was not presented to his mother until five months after the raid, in January of 1943, by which time another Marine (John Basilone) had received it as well. So to be precise, Thomason was the first enlisted Marine in WWII to earn the Medal of Honor but the second to be awarded it.

286 "extraordinary heroism": Citation for Navy Cross Star for Lt. Col. Evans F. Carlson, October 1942, Carlson Personal File, Award Citations, *USMCR*.

287 "In rigorous training": "Marine Corps 'Raider' Battalions Employed in Solomons Offensive," *New York Times*, August 26, 1942.

287 "were organized on a theory": "Carlson's Immortal Raiders," *Liberty*, November 20, 1943.

288 Japanese propagandists: "Half of Marines Killed in Makin Raid, Japs Claim," *Evening Star* (Washington, DC), via AP, September 7, 1942. Japanese records suggest that even the figure of 83 Japanese killed may have

been an overstatement. According to the official Japanese account of the war, published in the 1970s, the number of Japanese in the Makin garrison at the start of the raid was only 73 men, some of whom, unknown to the Americans, survived by hiding or escaping to a nearby island. That number does not, however, account for any Japanese personnel on the two seaplanes and two ships that the Raiders destroyed. Bōeichō Bōei Kenshūjo, *Chūbū Taiheiyō hōmen Kaigun sakusen* [Naval operations in the Central Pacific] (Tokyo: Asagumo Shinbunsha, 1970–1973), Vol. 2, p. 108. Thank you to Jeremy Yellen for pointing me to this source and helping me interpret it.

288 "Kill Japs, kill Japs": Joseph Wheelan, *Midnight in the Pacific: Guadalcanal: The World War II Battle That Turned the Tide of War* (Boston: Da Capo, 2017), p. 173.

288 The belief thus became widespread: Craig M. Cameron, *American Samurai: Myth, Imagination, and the Conduct of Battle in the First Marine Division, 1941–1952* (New York: Cambridge University Press, 1994), pp. 112–13.

288 "was not official policy": John W. Dower, *War Without Mercy: Race and Power in the Pacific War* (New York: Pantheon, 1986), p. 68.

288 The actual circumstances: Oscar Peatross, an officer in the 2nd Raiders who later compiled the most comprehensive and balanced history of their missions, based on his own recollections and interviews with his fellow veterans, refers to the death of a Japanese prisoner in Carlson's custody on Guadalcanal, though even he was unable to determine whether the man had been shot while trying to escape, or simply "as a means to rid ourselves of an encumbrance to movement." Oscar F. Peatross, *Bless 'Em All: The Marine Raiders of World War II* (Tampa: Raider Publishing, 1995), pp. 143, 152.

289 "just as sound fundamentally": EFC to Raymond Gram Swing, December 15, 1942, Raymond Swing Papers, Box 40, Folder 6, *LOC*.

289 "using the guerrilla tactics": "Marines Wiped Out Japanese on Makin Isle in Hot Fighting," *New York Times*, August 28, 1942.

289 "a record of pre-war U.S. policy": "Forty Hours on Makin," *Time*, September 7, 1942.

290 "crusading zeal": "Carlson of the Raiders," *New York Herald Tribune*, August 29, 1942.

290 "learned how to fight": "Carlson, Who Led Makin Attack, Veteran Fighter," United Press article, *Boston Globe*, August 22, 1942.

290 "We are the raiders": "Work Together Is New Cry of Carlson's Raiders Who Have Doctrine for Invaders," *Austin American*, September 8, 1942.

291 "If we were attacked": Carlson draft report on Makin Raid, August 21, 1942, Carlson Personal File, Reports of Raider Expedition Against Makin, PC56/ Coll. 3146, *USMCA*.

292 "You take this report back": Maj. Gen. Omar Pfeiffer oral history (interviewed by L. E. Tatem), History and Museums Division, Headquarters, U.S. Marine Corps, Washington, DC, 1974 (copy held at Columbia University Special Collections), p. 198. Carlson confirmed this story in an interview with John Dollard in 1944, where he said he was told to remove the line about surrender "because it reflected on the Service." Digest of Dollard Report in Box 8, Folder 4, *MBBU*.

292 Far worse, though: A fine effort to piece together the fates of these nine men

is Tripp Wiles, *Forgotten Raiders of '42: The Fate of the Marines Left Behind on Makin* (Washington, DC: Potomac Books, 2007).

292 five of the stranded Marines had tried: *Chūbū Taiheiyō hōmen Kaigun sakusen*, Vol. 2, pp. 122, 124.

292 last Marines to be captured in a group: Benis M. Frank and Henry I. Shaw, *Victory and Occupation*, Vol. 5 of *History of U.S. Marine Corps Operations in World War II* (Washington, DC: Historical Branch, G-3 Division, Headquarters, U.S. Marine Corps, 1968), p. 744.

293 "Nine Marines marooned": Laura Hillenbrand, *Unbroken: A World War II Story of Survival, Resilience, and Redemption* (New York: Random House, 2010), p. 175.

293 "This experience with the enemy": EFC to FDR, August 27, 1942, "Makin Island" folder, Box 75, James Roosevelt Papers, *FDRL*.

293 "I told you my boys": EFC to Etta Mae Wallace, September 15, 1942, *ECFP*.

294 "boyish grin": Peatross, *Bless 'Em All*, p. 122.

294 "Jesus knew that": "Carlson's Father Gives Final Sermon," *Hartford Courant*, September 14, 1942.

295 total strength of the battalion: Charles L. Updegraph, *U.S. Marine Corps Special Units of World War II* (Washington, DC: History and Museums Division, Headquarters, U.S. Marine Corps, 1972), p. 22.

295 "Gung Ho Knife": "The Carlson Raider Gung Ho Knife," *The Raider Patch*, November 1980, pp. 12–13. A more recent, extremely thorough attempt to pin down the details of how and when these knives were issued can be found in J. Doug Bailey, "The Carlson Raider Gung Ho Knife: A Forty Year Study," *The Raider Patch*, No. 157 (4th Quarter 2022), pp. 8–15.

295 By way of explanation: As related by his father in "Two Carlson Heroes Make Pastor Proud," *Hartford Courant*, April 13, 1943.

296 "Youth, especially, is impatient": EFC to sister Karen, March 7, 1943, *ECFP*.

CHAPTER 18: INTO THE JUNGLE

297 To make matters worse: Ian W. Toll, *The Conquering Tide: War in the Pacific Islands, 1942–1944* (New York: W. W. Norton, 2015), p. 61.

298 The situation was barely tenable: Oscar F. Peatross, *Bless 'Em All: The Marine Raiders of World War II* (Tampa: Raider Publishing, 1995), p. 131.

298 "Another one of these zero hours": EFC to father and Karen, November 4, 1942, *ECFP*.

299 "I was told only that": Merrill Twining, *No Bended Knee: The Battle for Guadalcanal* (Novato, CA: Presidio Press, 1996), p. 179.

299 This time, the Raiders: Martin Clemens, *Alone on Guadalcanal: A Coastwatcher's Story* (Annapolis, MD: Naval Institute Press, 1998), p. 277.

301 "Well I was caughted": John Lee Zimmerman, *The Guadalcanal Campaign* (Washington, DC: Historical Division, Headquarters, U.S. Marine Corps, 1949), pp. 67–68.

301 "I am proud to say": "Vouza Heroics," *The Raider Patch*, May 1977.

302 "Being Marines was": William Lansford interview in Ken Burns documentary series, *The War* (PBS, 2007).

302 "I must tell my people": "Korean Marines Tell Experiences on Guadalcanal," *Korean National Herald—Pacific Weekly*, June 2, 1943.

303 "didn't last that long": "Korean Interpreters Tell Jap Optimism," *Daily News* (Los Angeles), May 5, 1943.

303 The jungle was loud: *Fighting on Guadalcanal* (Washington, DC: U.S. Government Printing Office, 1943), p. 13.

305 Carlson's strategy: Evans Carlson, "Report of the operations of this battalion on Guadalcanal between 4 November and 4 December, 1942," p. 3, Carlson Personal File, Second Raider Battalion Reports, PC56/Coll. 3146, *USMCA*.

305 Carlson applied: John Apergis recollections of 2nd Marine Raider Battalion (in form of letter to Archie B. Rackerby, June 10, 1991), John Apergis Papers, *USMCA*.

306 Once they were fully exposed: Lowell Bulger, "The Second Marine Raider Battalion on Guadalcanal," Part 2, *The Raider Patch*, May–July 1981.

307 "No death could be worse": Bulger, "The Second Marine Raider Battalion," Part 2.

307 A private named James Clusker: "The Bullsheet," *The Raider Patch*, March 1977, p. 16.

308 more than one hundred stations: Robert Reinehr and Jon D. Swartz, *The A to Z of Old–Time Radio* (Plymouth, UK: Scarecrow Press, 2008), p. 250. On Swing, see also David H. Culbert, "Radio's Raymond Gram Swing: 'He Isn't the Kind of Man You Would Call Ray,'" *The Historian*, Vol. 35, No. 4 (August 1973), pp. 587–606.

308 "The Marines are tough": Raymond Gram Swing radio broadcast for November 11, 1942, Raymond Swing Papers, Box 20, Folder 4, *LOC*.

309 cause sterility: Bulger, "The Second Marine Raider Battalion on Guadalcanal," Part 1, *The Raider Patch*, March 1981.

309 One Marine had chills: John F. Wukovits, *American Commando: Evans Carlson, His WWII Marine Raiders, and America's First Special Forces Mission* (New York: NAL Caliber, 2009), p. 231.

310 "a pitiful sight": Peatross, *Bless 'Em All*, p. 164.

310 Some of them were crippled: Peatross, *Bless 'Em All*, p. 164.

310 A few inches down, he uncovered: Peatross, *Bless 'Em All*, p. 150.

310 "0950": Carlson World War II notebook with fragmentary comments on Guadalcanal operations, *CSUF*, microfilm reel 2.

310 Sometimes, when searching: Peatross says this of himself. Peatross, *Bless 'Em All*, p. 165.

311 "Or if you can't shoot a buddy": Digest of Dollard Report, Box 8, Folder 4, *MBBU*; Bulger, "The Second Marine Raider Battalion," Part 2.

311 On November 30: Peatross, *Bless 'Em All*, p. 161; Bulger, "The Second Marine Raider Battalion," *The Raider Patch*, Part 4, November 1981.

312 While searching: Bulger, "The Second Marine Raider Battalion," Part 4, pp. 12–13.

312 They eventually found: Peatross, *Bless 'Em All*, p. 160; Carlson, "Report of the operations of this battalion," pp. 9–10.

313 "You men here": Bulger, "The Second Marine Raider Battalion," *The Raider Patch*, Part 4, p. 13.

313 "Holy CAT!": "No. 1 guerrilla," *American Magazine*, Vol. 135 (June 1943), p. 112; "Carlson's Boys," *Newsweek*, December 28, 1942. "Cat" is almost certainly not the actual word the sentry used.

313 It was still eight miles: Carlson, "Report of the operations of this battalion," p. 12.

313 We walked in: Wukovits, *American Commando*, p. 249 (based on interview with Sgt. Rhel Cook).

CHAPTER 19: HOME FRONTS

314 She had also run out of money: Ruth Price, *The Lives of Agnes Smedley* (New York: Oxford University Press, 2005), p. 346.

314 "I had become a part": Agnes Smedley, *Battle Hymn of China* (New York: Alfred A. Knopf, 1943), pp. 526–27.

315 "Oh, she feels": Agnes Smedley to Aino Taylor, December 4, [1942?], Box 1, Folder 12, *SMASU*.

315 "With withering scorn": Agnes Smedley to Aino Taylor, December 24, 1942, quoted in Janice MacKinnon and Stephen MacKinnon, *Agnes Smedley: The Life and Times of an American Radical* (Berkeley: University of California Press, 1988), p. 251.

315 "He's amazingly attractive": Agnes Smedley to Aino Taylor, November 20, [1942?], Box 1, Folder 12, *SMASU*.

315 "Never in my life": Agnes Smedley to Aino and Elviira Taylor, December 2, 1942, Box 1, Folder 12, *SMASU*.

316 She kept a scrapbook: Agnes Smedley to Aino and Elviira Taylor, November 20, [1942?].

316 Ever since then: Smedley, *Battle Hymn of China*, p. 199.

316 "Evans stood": Agnes Smedley to Aino and Elviira Taylor, February 7, 1943, Box 1, Folder 12a, *SMASU*.

317 "I am continually in hot water": EFC to Agnes Smedley, March 26, 1943, Vol. 25, *ASASU*.

318 "three-power alliance": Daniel Kurtz-Phelan, *The China Mission: George C. Marshall's Unfinished War, 1945–1947* (New York: W. W. Norton, 2018), p. 19.

318 "an absolute farce": Hans J. van de Ven, *War and Nationalism in China: 1925–1945* (London: Routledge Curzon, 2003), p. 42.

318 "has so many inherent weaknesses": van de Ven, *War and Nationalism in China*, p. 34.

319 even the Caribbean: Joseph Stilwell, *The Stilwell Papers*, ed. Theodore H. White (New York: Da Capo, 1991), p. 119.

319 "a structure based": Stilwell diary, June 19, 1942, *The Stilwell Papers*, pp. 115–16.

320 "impolitic": Michael Schaller, *The U.S. Crusade in China, 1938–1945* (New York: Columbia University Press, 1979), p. 112; John Paton Davies, "Memorandum by the Second Secretary of Embassy in China (Davies) to Mr. Lauchlin Currie, Administrative Assistant to President Roosevelt," August 6, 1942, *Foreign Relations of the United States: Diplomatic Papers, 1942, China* (Washington, DC: U.S. Government Printing Office, 1956), pp. 226–28.

320 "The 'United Front' is now": John Service, "Memorandum by the Third Secretary of Embassy in China (Service), Temporarily in the United States," January 23, 1943, *Foreign Relations of the United States: Diplomatic Papers,*

1943, China (Washington, DC: U.S. Government Printing Office, 1957), pp. 193–99.

321 "would launch us": Stanley Hornbeck, "Memorandum by the Adviser on Political Relations (Hornbeck)," January 30, 1943, *Foreign Relations of the United States: Diplomatic Papers, 1943, China,* p. 201.

321 "Goddam it": Hannah Pakula, *The Last Empress: Madame Chiang Kai-Shek and the Birth of Modern China* (New York: Simon & Schuster, 2009), p. 421 (changing "Mme." to "Madame").

322 "new democratic society": Mao Zedong, "Talk at the Opening Ceremony for the Second Class of the Central Party School," trans. in Stuart Schram, ed., *Mao's Road to Power: Revolutionary Writings, 1912–1949,* Vol. 8 (Armonk, NY: M. E. Sharpe, 1992), pp. 409–15; see p. 412.

322 a broad promise of democracy: Alexander Pantsov and Steven Levine, *Mao: The Real Story* (New York: Simon & Schuster, 2012), p. 353.

322 "We have practiced": Zhu De, "We Have the Means to Fight On Till Victory," July 5, 1943, in *Selected Works of Zhu De* (Beijing: Foreign Languages Press, 1986), pp. 91–101; quotation on p. 100 (changing "practised" to "practiced"); originally published in *Jiefang ribao* [Liberation Daily], Yan'an, July 5, 1943.

323 "Conscription comes": Charles F. Romanus and Riley Sunderland, *Time Runs Out in CBI* (Washington, DC: Center of Military History, U.S. Army, 1999), p. 369.

323 "starved families": Memo 678-7, Wedemeyer for Generalissimo, 5 August 45, Item 25, Bk 8, Wedemeyer Corresp. with Chinese, quoted in Charles F. Romanus and Riley Sunderland, *Time Runs Out in CBI* (Washington, DC: Center of Military History, U.S. Army, 1999), pp. 369–71.

323 Of well over a million: Jonathan Spence, *The Search for Modern China* (New York: W. W. Norton, 2013), p. 427.

324 prices had risen 20,000 percent: Edgar Snow, *People on Our Side* (New York: Random House, 1944), p. 279.

324 One of them, an Oxford scholar: Michael Lindsay, "The North China Front: A Study of Chinese Guerrillas in Action," Part 1, *Amerasia,* Vol. 8, No. 7 (March 31, 1944), pp. 99–110; Part 2, *Amerasia,* Vol. 8, No. 8 (April 14, 1944), pp. 117–25.

324 "Guerrilla China": Snow, *People on Our Side,* p. 288.

324 nearly 620,000: Lindsay, "The North China Front," Part 1.

324 Stalin had abruptly ended: Maochun Yu, *The Dragon's War: Allied Operations and the Fate of China, 1937–1947* (Annapolis, MD: Naval Institute Press, 2006), pp. 14, 23.

325 the Chinese Communists still relied: Lindsay, "The North China Front," Part 1, p. 104.

325 simply did not engage: Klaus Mühlhahn, *Making China Modern: From the Great Qing to Xi Jinping* (Cambridge, MA: Harvard University Press, 2019), p. 319.

325 "cohesive, disciplined": John Paton Davies, "Memorandum by the Second Secretary of Embassy in China (Davies)," January 15, 1944, *Foreign Relations of the United States, Diplomatic Papers, 1944,* Vol. VI, *China* (Washington, DC: U.S. Government Printing Office, 1967), pp. 307–8.

325 "folded up military operations": Rana Mitter, *Forgotten Ally: China's World War II, 1937–1945* (Boston: Houghton Mifflin Harcourt, 2013), p. 331; P. P. Vladimirov, *The Vladimirov Diaries: Yenan, China, 1942–1945* (Garden City, NY: Doubleday, 1975), p. 252.

325 "Even though the anti-Japanese guerrillas": Zhu De, "On Anti-Japanese Guerrilla War," *Selected Works of Zhu De* (Beijing: Foreign Languages Press, 1986), p. 61.

326 "Rectification Campaign": Peter Seybolt, "Terror and Conformity: Counterespionage Campaigns, Rectification, and Mass Movements, 1942–1943," *Modern China*, Vol. 12, No. 1 (January 1986), pp. 39–73; see pp. 39, 59.

326 Those who complied: Seybolt, "Terror and Conformity," p. 60.

326 Starting in Yan'an: Seybolt, "Terror and Conformity," p. 51.

326 Almost no actual traitors: Mühlhahn, *Making China Modern*, p. 323; Anthony Saich and David Apter, *Revolutionary Discourse in Mao's Republic* (Cambridge, MA: Harvard University Press, 1994), pp. 163–92.

327 But at the same time: on Stalinist methods in the Rectification Campaign, see Saich and Apter, *Revolutionary Discourse in Mao's Republic*.

CHAPTER 20: BACKLASH

328 "Lt. Col. Evans Fordyce Carlson writes books": Wesley Price, "Raider Carlson," *Picture News*, January 2, 1944.

328 "America's first trained guerrillas": "Carlson's Boys," *Newsweek*, December 28, 1942.

328 A paper in Hawaii: Editor's note to "Marine Raiders Outfight Japs in Pacific Jungle Warfare," *Honolulu Advertiser*, December 26, 1942.

329 "swung through jungled islands": "Marines' 'Raiders of Wrath' Are Combination of Sailor, Soldier and Something More—Much More," *Dunkirk Evening Observer* (NY), November 10, 1942.

329 "Colonel Carlson is a true warrior": "What It Takes to Make a Soldier," *Minneapolis Star*, January 9, 1943.

329 "We thought it must be": "Learns Meaning of 'Gung Ho,'" *Courier-Post* (Camden, NJ), March 30, 1943.

330 "Start practicing 'GUNG HO'": Advertisement for the Washington Cooperative Egg and Poultry Association, *Daily Chronicle* (Centralia, WA), October 23, 1942.

330 "Americans may not understand Chinese": Advertisement for the Pennsylvania-Reading Seashore Lines, *Daily Journal* (Vineland, NJ), October 9, 1942.

330 "Come on, you Raiders!": Sergeant Stony Craig comic, December 23, 1942.

330 "We'll Gung Ho you": Raiders press releases, Carlson's Raider Guadalcanal General Information, *USMCR*.

330 "What of the future": Carlson eulogy, Carlson Personal File, Speeches, *USMCR*.

331 "These men are realists": "A Soldier Speaks," *New York Times*, January 10, 1943.

331 "Are not these young men": "Chaplain's Remark Evokes Observations on Sacrifice," *New York Times*, January 24, 1943.

331 The Raiders killed: Casualty figures and statement on use of surprise are from Evans Carlson, "Report of the operations of this battalion on Guadalcanal between 4 November and 4 December, 1942," p. 13, Carlson Personal File, Second Raider Battalion Reports, PC56/Coll. 3146, *USMCA*.

331 "superbly commanded": Merrill Twining, *No Bended Knee: The Battle for Guadalcanal* (Novato, CA: Presidio Press, 1996), p. 182.

331 had all been burned: Twining, *No Bended Knee*, p. 192.

332 "For a period of thirty days": "Carlson's Raiders Cited," Navy press release of December, 26, 1942, Carlson's Raiders folder, Box 18, RG 428, *NARA II*.

333 Across the United States military: Duane Schultz, "Combat Fatigue: How Stress in Battle Was Felt (and Treated) in WWII," *Warfare History Network*, https://warfarehistorynetwork.com/combat-fatigue-how-stress-in-battle-was-felt-and-treated-in-wwii (accessed September 27, 2023); Larry Decuers, "WWII Post Traumatic Stress," National World War II Museum, New Orleans, LA, June, 2020, https://www.nationalww2museum.org/war/articles/wwii-post-traumatic-stress (accessed September 27, 2023).

333 more than a quarter of whom: Norman Q. Brill et al., "Age and Resistance to Military Stress," *United States Armed Forces Medical Journal*, Vol. 4, No. 1 (January 1953), pp. 1247–66; see p. 1256. Their figure for combat troops was 285 breakdowns per 1,000 men per year.

333 "are sustained largely": "The Psychiatric Toll of Warfare," *Fortune*, Vol. 28, No. 6 (December 1943), pp. 141, 274–82.

334 "went through the ranks": Dollard Report, Box 8, Folder 4, *MBBU*.

334 "All I do is kill, kill, kill": EFC to Helen Foster Snow, January 13, 1943, Box 175, Folder 15, *HFSBYU*.

334 "Back on Guadalcanal, most of you": Jim Lucas article typescript, Carlson Personal File, PC56/Coll. 3146, *USMCA*.

335 "unstinting in his praise: EFC to James Roosevelt, December 15, 1942, Box 76, James Roosevelt Papers, *FDRL*.

335 "go back to the tactics": *Fighting on Guadalcanal*, p. v (correcting "Roger's" to "Rogers'").

335 "I would have some maneuvers": *Fighting on Guadalcanal*, p. 54.

336 "I would stress": *Fighting on Guadalcanal*, p. 14.

336 "a great bunch of soldiers": Herbert C. Merillat, *Guadalcanal Remembered* (New York: Avon, 1982), pp. 238, 241.

336 "convinced that marines in general": Merillat, *Guadalcanal Remembered*, p. 241, describing Merrill Twining.

336 Twining would cite Carlson's use: Twining, *No Bended Knee*, pp. 184, 243–44.

336 "It was good to see old friends": EFC to father and Karen, February 20, 1943, *ECFP*.

337 "I knew that he was a strange character": Lt. Jim Lucas, *Combat Correspondent* (New York: Reynal & Hitchcock, 1944), p. 99.

337 "I'm a rice eating raider": "Rice-eating Raider," by T. M. Buckman (to the tune of "Strawberry Roan"), *CSUF*, microfilm reel 2.

338 "gain those things for which": EFC to Helen Foster Snow, January 13, 1943, Box 175, Folder 15, *HFSBYU*.

338 At one meeting, they argued: James Roosevelt oral history interview, August 7, 1942, "California Democrats in the Earl Warren Era," Regional

Oral History Office, University of California, Berkeley. Conversion of the $25,000 income to today's dollars is from measuringworth.com, using the figure for relative income.

338 The ethos of the battalion: *The Raider Patch*, March 1980, p. 5.

338 In another, less intimidating: John Apergis recollections of 2nd Marine Raider Battalion (in form of letter to Archie B. Rackerby, June 10, 1991), John Apergis Papers, *USMCA*.

338 "When you get a platoon sergeant": "You Can Write Poetry—and Enjoy It!," Christian Science Publication Society, condensed from the *Christian Science Monitor*, August 18, 1945.

338 "to bring to [the] men": Battalion Special Order Number 6-43, January 5, 1943, *CSUF*, microfilm reel 2.

339 "The men literally worship": Jim Lucas article typescript, Carlson Personal File, PC56/Coll. 3146, *USMCA*.

339 "We never take a prisoner": This was a slight exaggeration; the Raiders did take one prisoner during the Guadalcanal operation, who was transported back to the 1st Marine Division for further interrogation. Carlson, "Report of the operations of this battalion," p. 14.

340 "since it is about Raiders": Note attached to Lucas article typescript, Carlson Personal File, PC56/Coll. 3146, *USMCA*.

340 "The last operation on Guadalcanal": EFC to Helen Foster Snow, January 13, 1943, Box 175, Folder 15, *HFSBYU* [changing "era (Eighth Route Army)" to "Eighth Route Army"].

340 "Colonel," asked one of the enlisted men: Jim Lucas article typescript, Carlson Personal File, PC56/Coll. 3146, *USMCA*.

340 "kicked upstairs": EFC to Helen Foster Snow, March 26, 1943, Box 175, Folder 15, *HFSBYU*.

341 "an orthodox line man": EFC to Raymond Swing, July 21, 1943, Raymond Swing Papers, Box 40, Folder 6, *LOC*.

341 Shapley immediately set about: Lt. Gen. Alan Shapley oral history (interviewed by Maj. Thomas E. Donnelly), History and Museums Division, Headquarters, U.S. Marine Corps, Washington, DC, 1976 (copy held at Columbia University Special Collections), p. 77. Shapley recalled: "I just changed things completely, and made it into a regular battalion."

341 In one of his first addresses: Carlson response to Dollard, Box 8, Folder 4, *MBBU*; William Lansford interview, raw transcript for History Channel program on Raiders, *ECFP*.

341 "There could be no discipline": Maj. Gen. Omar Pfeiffer oral history (interviewed by L. E. Tatem), History and Museums Division, Headquarters, U.S. Marine Corps, Washington, DC, 1974 (copy held at Columbia University Special Collections), pp. 198–99.

342 "could not understand or digest": Lt. Col. Charles Lamb, "Comments on the Raid on Makin Island Manuscript," Carlson Personal File, PC56/Coll. 3146, *USMCA*.

342 "gives a momentary glimpse": Twining, *No Bended Knee*, p. 184.

342 "I am considered a radical": EFC to father and Karen, March 23, 1943, *ECFP*.

342 "I stumbled with them": Lt. Jim Lucas, *Combat Correspondent*, p. 105.

CHAPTER 21: THE MAW

343 "I am often beside myself": EFC to Helen Foster Snow, March 26, 1943, Box 175, Folder 15, *HFSBYU*.

343 "considering that we had nothing": Liversedge memo for C-3, I MAC, April 6, 1943, Raiders File, Official Archival Materials, *USMCR* (changing "camp sight" to "campsite").

343 "Handpicked outfits, such as these": Raiders File, Official Archival Materials, *USMCR*.

344 not a decision made without controversy: Frank Kalesnik makes the point that the Raiders in 1944 had been reorganized as the 4th Marine Regiment (coincidentally, Carlson's original regiment from when he first went to China in 1927) and the 4th Marines still very much existed in 2014. Furthermore, he holds that the tactical roots of today's special forces owe far more to the OSS guerrilla forces in World War II than to the Marine Raiders under Carlson and Edson. From email conversation with Frank Kalesnik, former Chief Historian of the Marine Corps, June 19, 2024.

344 "the United States' first": Gunnery Sgt. Josh Higgins, Marine Corps Forces Special Operations Command, "The Past Aligned with the Future: MARSOC Becomes Marine Raiders," August 6, 2014, https://www.marsoc.marines.mil/. For an overview history of the other early special operations forces in World War II, see Mark Moyar, *Oppose Any Foe: The Rise of America's Special Operations Forces* (New York: Basic Books, 2017), pp. 1–95.

344 "the official continuation": "Marine Corps to Adopt Iconic Raiders Name for Its Special Operations Troops," *Washington Post*, August 6, 2014.

344 "extreme emotional fatigue": EFC to father, May 23, 1943, *ECFP*.

344 It was a restorative trip: "Col. Carlson Is Home for Brief Rest," *Hartford Courant*, June 9, 1943.

344 lunch with President Roosevelt: "The Day in Washington," *New York Times*, June 17, 1943. Also see FDR daily log, http://www.fdrlibrary.marist.edu/daybyday/daylog/june-16th-1943.

344 "I don't know precisely why I am here": Michael Blankfort, *The Big Yankee: The Life of Carlson of the Raiders* (Boston: Little, Brown, 1947), p. 322.

345 "typical of the men": EFC to father, June 20, 1943, *ECFP*.

346 One was that the studio was forbidden: Matthew Bernstein and Robert Wise, *Walter Wanger: Hollywood Independent* (St. Paul: University of Minnesota Press, 2000), pp. 191–92.

346 "Col. Thorwald is a movie copy": "Movie of the Week: Gung Ho!," *Life*, February 7, 1944, p. 77.

346 "one of the most rabid": Clayton R. Koppes and Gregory D. Black, *Hollywood Goes to War: How Politics, Profits and Propaganda Shaped World War II Movies* (New York: Free Press, 1987), p. 264.

346 "the most literal war movie": "Movie of the Week: Gung Ho!," *Life*, p. 77.

346 "See 'Gung Ho'": "Informing You," *Hartford Courant*, February 9, 1944.

346 "lurid action film": "'Gung Ho!' a Lurid Action Film About the Makin Island Raid, with Randolph Scott, Opens at the Criterion Theatre," *New York Times*, January 26, 1944.

348 "The major emphasis at present": EFC to Raymond Gram Swing, July 21, 1943, Raymond Swing Papers, Box 40, Folder 6, *LOC*.

348 "Our course is clear": *"Gung Ho!": The Story of Carlson's Makin Island Raiders*, Universal Pictures, 1943.

348 "His voice rises and falls": "Carlson of the Raiders," *Life*, September 20, 1943.

350 It was the first time any amphibious force: See A. A. Vandegrift introduction to Capt. James R. Stockman, *The Battle for Tarawa* (Washington, DC: Historical Section, Division of Public Information, Headquarters, U.S. Marine Corps, 1947), p. ii.

350 In contrast to the two paltry submarines: Evans Carlson, Halls of Montezuma radio interview, Carlson Personal File, Published Materials, *USMCR*.

351 Thousands of Marines had to abandon: Joseph Alexander, *Utmost Savagery: The Three Days of Tarawa* (Annapolis, MD: Naval Institute Press, 1995), p. 73.

351 a short, stocky officer: Ian W. Toll, *The Conquering Tide: War in the Pacific Islands, 1942–1944* (New York: W. W. Norton, 2015), p. 350.

351 Their Higgins boat ran aground: Stockman, *The Battle for Tarawa*, p. 17.

352 One shell hit so close: Alexander, *Utmost Savagery*, p. 136.

352 "we intend to stick here": David M. Shoup letter to Raymond Gram Swing, November 7, 1947, Raymond Swing Papers, Box 40, Folder 8, *LOC*.

352 "Thought that I would go ashore": EFC to father and Karen, December 5, 1943, *ECFP*.

352 He commandeered: Stockton, *The Battle for Tarawa*, p. 25.

353 "I saw him": Eddie Albert oral history interview, May 1993, National Museum of the Pacific War, Fredericksburg, TX.

354 "What astonished us": E. B. Sledge, *With the Old Breed: At Peleliu and Okinawa* (New York: Ballantine, 1981), p. 89.

354 "Carlson may be Red": This quotation appears in print in many, many places, but I have not been able to find an original source for it. Even if it is apocryphal, which seems likely, the degree to which it has been repeated is itself a testament to the respect for Carlson's bravery even by those who ridiculed his political views.

355 "No victory in American military history": Richard W. Johnston report for Combined American Press. See, for example, "Our Blood Bath at Tarawa," *Indianapolis News*, November 27, 1943.

355 "Nothing in any previous war": Johnston, "Our Blood Bath at Tarawa."

355 "It was really a blood-and-guts battle": "Col. Roosevelt and Carlson Tell of Following Bombs onto Makin," *Boston Globe*, November 27, 1943.

355 In a Marine Corps radio broadcast: Lauren Bowers, "'The Song They Lived By,' The 'Marines' Hymn' During World War II," *Marine Corps History*, Vol. 8, No. 2 (Winter 2022–2023), pp. 23–42; see p. 41. According to a 1942 press release, the Halls of Montezuma radio broadcast was carried on about 140 stations with a combined audience of seven million people.

355 "I saw a man with half his face": "Carlson Relates Heroic Deeds in Tarawa Conquest," *Hartford Courant*, December 10, 1943; Halls of Montezuma interview, Carlson Personal File, Published Materials, *USMCR*.

356 Unrecorded in the public accounts: John F. Wukovits, *One Square Mile of Hell: The Battle for Tarawa* (New York: NAL Caliber, 2006), p. 165. In an

interview with John Dollard in 1944, Carlson said "all combat officers at Tarawa knew of the 'sit-down'" but he doubted it was in any of the official reports. Digest of Dollard interview with Carlson, Box 8, Folder 4, *MBBU*.

356 "Tarawa provided abundant evidence": EFC to Raymond Gram Swing, January 2, 1944 (erroneously dated 1943), Raymond Swing Papers, Box 40, Folder 6, *LOC*.

356 "intensive training and psychological indoctrination": Headquarters V Amphibious Corps, Report by Special Observers on Galvanic, Report by Lt. Col. E. F. Carlson, *USMCR*, Carlson Personal File, Correspondence and Memos, PC56/Coll. 3146, *USMCA*.

356 sending news about her husband's exploits: See, for example, *The Arrow of Pi Beta Phi*, Vol. 59, No. 2 (December 1942), p. 164.

357 not "foreigners": Etelle Carlson to Helen Foster Snow, September 14, 1942, Box 130, Folder 14, *HFSBYU*.

357 As social director: "Rotarians Honor Mrs. Carlson," *Record Searchlight* (Redding, CA), August 19, 1961; "Etelle Carlson," *Berkeley Gazette*, October 22, 1974.

357 For Carlson, the divorce meant: EFC to father, March 23, 1943, *ECFP*.

357 "Practically every page": George S. Counts and Nicua P. Lodge, trans., *New Russia's Primer: The Story of the Five-Year Plan* (by M. Ilin) (Boston: Houghton Mifflin, 1931), pp. v, vii–viii. On young Tony reading the primer (and, according to Peggy, taking notes on it), see EFC to the Snows, March 7, 1944, Box 130, Folder 14, *HFSBYU*.

357 They signed their papers: Evans Carlson–Peggy Tatum Whyte marriage certificate, *CSUF*, microfilm reel 2.

358 Carlson's son had gotten to know: Helen Foster Snow, "Remembering the Autobiography of Evans F. Carlson," unpublished manuscript, 1979, Box 175, Folder 15, *HFSBYU*.

358 "In the middle of the night": EFC to father and Karen, February 16, 1944, *ECFP*.

358 The president, at least: FDR to EFC, March 2, 1944, in Elliott Roosevelt, ed., *F.D.R.: His Personal Letters, 1928–1945* (New York: Duell, Sloan & Pearce, 1950), p. 1497.

358 "I read much about": Grace Tully to EFC, March 7, 1944, PPF 4951, FDR Papers, *FDRL*.

358 massive collective effort: Toll, *The Conquering Tide*, p. 457.

358 "brilliant tactician": Carlson Legion of Merit citation, *CSUF*, microfilm reel 2. NB: there were two different forms of his Legion of Merit citation; the quotation is from the later one.

358 pleased by the "tactician" part: EFC to Edgar Snow, July 27, 1946, Folder 13, *ESUM*.

358 "I am weary with war": EFC to Raymond Gram Swing, May 11, 1944, Raymond Swing Papers, Box 40, Folder 6, *LOC*.

359 "I've been fighting the Japs": EFC to Agnes Smedley, May 11, 1944, Vol. 25, *ASASU*.

359 "The time may be ripe": EFC to President Roosevelt, February 23, 1944, President's Secretary's File, FDR Diplomatic Correspondence, China, January–June 1944, FDR Papers, *FDRL*.

359 Roosevelt had met: Alexander V. Pantsov, *Victorious in Defeat: The Life and*

Times of Chiang Kai-shek, China, 1887–1975, trans. Steven I. Levine (New Haven: Yale University Press, 2023), p. 364.

359 "transition period": FDR to EFC, March 2, 1944, in Elliott Roosevelt, ed., *F.D.R.: His Personal Letters, 1928–1945*, p. 1498.

360 One round hit: The nature of Carlson's wounds is described in his medical history, in his military personnel folder at the National Archives in St. Louis, MO. An examining doctor later thought both wounds may have been caused by one bullet that went through the thigh and into his arm.

361 "Vic was wounded first": "'Gung Ho' Carlson Wounded Rescuing Marine Companion," *Honolulu Daily Advertiser*, July 7, 1944.

361 The medics patched: Carlson's account is from a Halls of Montezuma radio broadcast, December 8, 1944. Transcript in Carlson Personal File, Speeches, *USMCR*.

CHAPTER 22: INTO THE POSTWAR

365 "I know if he hadn't carried me": "Saipan Marine Lauds Col. Carlson, Rescuer," *New York Times*, September 18, 1944; "Carlson Rescues Wounded Hero," *Oakland Tribune*, September 18, 1944.

365 "They don't come any better": "Youth's Life Saved by Col. Carlson," *Marine Corps Chevron*, September 23, 1944.

365 "could be called the most beloved": "'Gung Ho' Carlson Wounded Rescuing Marine Companion," UP article in, for example, *Press Democrat* (Santa Rosa, CA), July 7, 1944, *Honolulu Advertiser*, and *The Pittsburgh Press*, same date.

366 "looks thin": Eleanor Roosevelt, "My Day" column for July 27, 1944. See also "Roosevelt Visits San Diego to See Colonel Carlson," AP article in *Sacramento Bee*, July 29, 1944.

366 Under cover of heavy secrecy: "Roosevelt Visits San Diego to See Colonel Carlson," *Sacramento Bee*; "Lt. Col. Carlson Visited by FDR," *Marine Corps Chevron*, August 5, 1944; FDR to Eleanor Roosevelt, July 21, 1944, in Elliott Roosevelt, ed., *F.D.R.: His Personal Letters, 1928–1945* (New York: Duell, Sloan & Pearce, 1950), p. 1525. Roosevelt was on his way to Hawaii to meet with his Pacific commanders.

366 "12-year old future Marine": David E. Shulz to Marine Corps Headquarters, rec'd August 24, 1944, Carlson military personnel file, RG 127, Series: Official Military Personnel Files, National Archives, St. Louis, MO.

367 "One of the causes of our confidence": Letter from Zhu De, Zhou Enlai, Ye Jianying, and Nie Rongzhen to Evans Carlson, August 14, 1944. Copy in President's Secretary's File, Diplomatic Correspondence, China, July–December 1944, FDR Papers, *FDRL* (changing "Yenan" to "Yan'an").

368 "the single greatest challenge": John Paton Davies, "Memorandum by the Second Secretary of Embassy in China (Davies)," January 15, 1944, *Foreign Relations of the United States: Diplomatic Papers, 1944*, Vol. 6, *China* (Washington, DC: U.S. Government Printing Office, 1967), pp. 307–8.

368 "All of our party have had": John Service, "Report by the Second Secretary of Embassy in China (Service)," July 28, 1944, *Foreign Relations of the United States: Diplomatic Papers, 1944*, Vol. 6, *China*, pp. 517–520; Rana Mitter, *For-*

gotten Ally: China's World War II, 1937–1945 (Boston: Houghton Mifflin Harcourt, 2013), p. 328.

368 "We have come to the mountains": Service, "Report by the Second Secretary," July 28, 1944 (changing "Shensi" to "Shaanxi").

368 "Only democracy can achieve": Mao Zedong, "Talk While Meeting with the Delegation of Chinese and Foreign Reporters Visiting the Northwest," June 12, 1944, trans. in Stuart Schram, ed., *Mao's Road to Power: Revolutionary Writings, 1912–1949*, Vol. 8 (Armonk, NY: M. E. Sharpe, 1992), p. 570.

368 "Either a China that is independent": Mao Zedong, "Comrade Mao Zedong's Opening Speech at the Seventh National Congress," April 23, 1945, *Mao's Road to Power*, Vol. 8, p. 757.

369 "a national assembly": Mao Zedong, "On Coalition Government," April 24, 1945, *Mao's Road to Power*, Vol. 8, p. 759.

369 "impossible for the Chinese people": Mao Zedong, "On Coalition Government," p. 784.

369 "the people's most important freedoms": Mao Zedong, "On Coalition Government," p. 796.

370 In what should have been: Barbara Tuchman, "If Mao Had Come to Washington," *Foreign Affairs*, Vol. 51, No. 1 (October 1972), pp. 44–64; see pp. 44–45.

371 "in unrestricted command": Hans J. van de Ven, *China at War: Triumph and Tragedy in the Emergence of the New China* (Cambridge, MA: Harvard University Press, 2018), p. 192.

371 In his diary: Alexander V. Pantsov, *Victorious in Defeat: The Life and Times of Chiang Kai-shek, China, 1887–1975*, trans. Steven I. Levine (New Haven: Yale University Press, 2023), p. 380.

371 Roosevelt realized: Hans J. van de Ven, *War and Nationalism in China: 1925–1945* (London: Routledge Curzon, 2003), p. 21.

372 "The fact is that there is nothing": EFC to Agnes Smedley, November 13, 1944, Vol. 25, *ASASU.*

372 "Carlson has made shorts": Stilwell diary entries for April 17 and August 28, 1938, Diaries of General Joseph W. Stilwell, *HIA.*

372 "Captain Courageous": Barbara Tuchman, *Stilwell and the American Experience of China* (New York: Grove Press, 1971), p. 184.

372 "I know it is useless": Joseph Stilwell to EFC, November 14, 1944, *CSUF*, microfilm reel 2.

372 "As I see the picture": EFC to Agnes Smedley, November 14, 1944, Vol. 25, *ASASU.*

373 "I am delighted to see": FDR to Evans Carlson, November 15, 1944, President's Secretary's File, Diplomatic Correspondence, China, July–December 1944, FDR Papers, *FDRL* (changing "Chungking" to "Chongqing").

373 "You know how dearly": EFC to James Roosevelt, April 12, 1945, Box 76, "Evans Carlson 1943–1951" folder, James Roosevelt Papers, *FDRL.*

373 "I am devoted to him not only": EFC to Marguerite LeHand, January 1, 1939, PPF 4951, FDR Papers, *FDRL.*

373 "I know of no one else": EFC to Michael Blankfort, April 13, 1945, Box 85, Folder 3, *MBBU.*

374 "I fear for things": EFC to Edgar Snow, April 13, 1945, Folder 13, *ESUM*.

374 two more years: "Carlson Sees 2 More Years of Pacific War," *New York Herald Tribune*, March 12, 1944.

374 "the cream of the Japanese army": "Pacific War Seen Lasting into 1946," *New York Times*, March 12, 1944.

376 Truman had none of the ties to China: In 1911, Truman wrote to his future wife, "I think one man is just as good as another so long as he's honest and decent and not a n——r or a Chinaman. . . . I am strongly of the opinion that negroes ought to be in Africa, yellow men in Asia, and white men in Europe and America." Harry S. Truman to Bess Wallace, June 22, 1911, Truman Papers, Truman Library, cited in Pantsov, *Victorious in Defeat*, p. 611, n. 68.

376 In cities where there were not enough: Douglas MacArthur General Order No. 1; Jonathan Spence, *The Search for Modern China* (New York: W. W. Norton, 2013), p. 434; Suzanne Pepper, *Civil War in China: The Political Struggle, 1945–1949* (Berkeley: University of California Press, 1978), p. 10.

376 A staggering seven thousand Japanese troops: van de Ven, *China at War*, p. 211.

376 Far from welcoming: van de Ven, *China at War*, p. 212; Alexander Pantsov and Steven Levine, *Mao: The Real Story* (New York: Simon & Schuster, 2012), p. 347.

377 As their trucks rolled: E. B. Sledge, *China Marine: An Infantryman's Life After World War II* (New York: Oxford University Press, 2002), p. 21.

377 "The U.S. Marine Corps has never": *A Marine's Guide to North China* (September 1945), Box 22, Folder 17, A. T. Steele Papers, MSS-349, University Archives, Arizona State University, Tempe, AZ.

378 The end of World War II found: Janice MacKinnon and Stephen MacKinnon, *Agnes Smedley: The Life and Times of an American Radical* (Berkeley: University of California Press, 1988), pp. 266–67.

378 In the fall of 1944, she had tried: EFC to Agnes Smedley, November 5, 1944, Vol. 25, *ASASU*; Telegram from Elizabeth Ames at Yaddo to EFC, March 13, 1944, *ECFP*.

378 "I'm working on my new book": MacKinnon and MacKinnon, *Agnes Smedley*, p. 276.

378 "American democratic activities": Zhu De letter to Agnes Smedley, July 1, 1946, in *Selected Works of Zhu De* (Beijing: Foreign Languages Press, 1986), p. 194.

379 "one of the world's most bemedaled": "Men of Merit," *Time*, Vol. 45, No. 7 (February 12, 1945).

379 "one of the most experienced": "Tarawa Just 'Sideshow' Compared with Saipan," *Marine Corps Chevron*, July 15, 1944.

379 "just about one of the toughest": "Carlson of the Marines," *Chicago Sunday Tribune*, February 18, 1945.

379 The donors Roosevelt talked to: Material on Roosevelt's groundwork for Carlson's Senate campaign can be found in Box 76, "Evans Carlson 1943–1951" folder, James Roosevelt Papers, *FDRL*.

380 "Some glamor": "Col. Carlson for Senate?," *Ventura County Star-Free Press* (reprinting from *San Francisco News*), April 3, 1945.

380 "I felt it was important": "Carlson Plans Civilian Life; May Be Politics," *Times-Advocate* (Escondido, CA), October 19, 1945.

380 he told Blankfort bluntly: EFC to Michael Blankfort, May 26, 1944, Box 85, Folder 3, *MBBU*.

380 "ever since Agnes Smedley": Thomas Carlson to Michael Blankfort, April 26, 1944, Box 85, Folder 3, *MBBU*.

381 "carry a far greater urgency": Harcourt, Brace & Co. to Michael Blankfort, November 11, 1943, Box 85, Folder 3, *MBBU*.

381 "Michael—let's start building": Helen Foster Snow to Michael Blankfort, November 1, 1945, Box 85, Folder 3, *MBBU*.

381 "as a campaign document": Helen Foster Snow to EFC, February 25, 1945, Box 130, Folder 14, *HFSBYU*.

381 "I may use the wrong words": EFC to Blankfort, July 20, 1945, Box 85, Folder 3, *MBBU*.

382 "I want above all": EFC to Blankfort, August 28, 1945, Box 85, Folder 3, *MBBU*.

382 "a rather exceptional figure": Carey McWilliams, "The Education of Evans Carlson," *The Nation*, December 1, 1945, pp. 577–79.

382 "as we walked down Market Street": Sidney Roger oral interview, "A Liberal Journalist on the Air and on the Waterfront: Labor and Political Issues, 1932–1990," Archive of California, https://oac.cdlib.org/view?docId =kt10000013q.

382 When Carlson came up to the podium: Capt. Shepard Traube to Michael Blankfort, December 5, 1945, Box 85, Folder 3, *MBBU*. See also "The Autobiography of Evans Carlson," unpublished typescript, as told to Helen Foster Snow, Carlson Personal File, Published Materials, *USMCR*.

383 "I can't say much about": "Marine Colonel Congratulates CIO on Aid to Vets," *Herald* (Provo, UT), via UP, December 9, 1945.

383 "We must mend the fences": Carlson foreword to Seymour J. Schoenfeld, *The Negro in the Armed Forces: His Value and Status, Past, Present and Potential* (Washington, DC: Associated Publishers, 1945), p. viii.

383 "the prospects are now excellent": Robert W. Kenny to Michael Blankfort, December 26, 1945, Box 85, Folder 3, *MBBU*.

383 "literally able": Robert W. Kenny, "My First Forty Years in California Politics: 1922–1962," n.d., oral history transcript at Bancroft Library, University of California, Berkeley, p. 240.

383 "was unprepared to oppose": Kenny, "My First Forty Years in California Politics," p. 264.

CHAPTER 23: SHIFTING GROUNDS

384 "Lincolnesque": "Ace Marine Raider Eyes Senate Beachhead," *Washington Post*, January 13, 1946.

384 "Actually we are using": EFC to Agnes Smedley, January 21, 1946, Box 85, Folder 3, *MBBU*.

385 "a vigorously conducted campaign": Committee for a Democratic Far Eastern Policy press release, May 31, 1947, Box 130, Folder 14, *HFSBYU*.

385 "This is the last": Bernard S. Thomas, *Season of High Adventure: Edgar Snow in China* (Berkeley: University of California Press, 1996), p. 271.

386 "in the most vital interest": Henry I. Shaw, Jr., *The United States Marines in North China, 1945–1949* (Washington, DC: Historical Branch, G-3 Division Headquarters, U.S. Marine Corps, 1968), p. 11.

386 The Soviets, meanwhile, bowed: Daniel Kurtz-Phelan, *The China Mission: George C. Marshall's Unfinished War, 1945–1947* (New York: W. W. Norton, 2018), p. 231.

386 But as Stalin: Hans J. van de Ven, *China at War: Triumph and Tragedy in the Emergence of the New China* (Cambridge, MA: Harvard University Press, 2018), p. 232; Alexander Pantsov and Steven Levine, *Mao: The Real Story* (New York: Simon & Schuster, 2012), pp. 347–48.

386 socializing with the Generalissimo's family: Kurtz-Phelan, *The China Mission*, pp. 47, 227–29, 233, 236, 255.

386 "a smoke screen": Kurtz-Phelan, *The China Mission*, p. 286; Tang Tsou, *America's Failure in China, 1941–50* (Chicago: University of Chicago Press, 1963), p. 433.

387 "No one could succeed": "Chinese Policy Hit by Carlson," *Muncie Evening Press*, October 25, 1946.

387 "the powder keg": "Gen. Carlson Warns of U.S. Policy in China," *Times-Herald* (Washington, DC), July 25, 1946.

387 "patently imperialistic": EFC to Raymond Gram Swing, December 5, 1946, Carlson Personal File, Correspondence and Memos, PC56/Coll. 3146, *USMCA*.

387 "They are there today": "Vets Declare War on Boss Crump," *Washington Daily News*, August 20, 1946.

387 "another Communist front": "'Get Out of China' Group Opens 3-Day Parley Here," San Francisco news clipping, publication data unclear, Carlson Personal File, Published Materials, *USMCR*.

388 between 1947 and 1949: Alexander V. Pantsov, *Victorious in Defeat: The Life and Times of Chiang Kai-shek, China, 1887–1975*, trans. Steven I. Levine (New Haven: Yale University Press, 2023), pp. 409, 421.

388 He preferred a place: EFC to Raymond Gram Swing, December 5, 1946, Carlson Personal File, Correspondence and Memos, PC56/Coll. 3146, *USMCA*.

388 "grueling": Peggy Carlson to James Roosevelt, December 12, 1946, Box 153, James Roosevelt Papers, *FDRL*.

388 In Athens, Tennessee: On the Athens, Tennessee, actions, see Robert Francis Saxe, "Settling Down: Domesticating World War II Veterans' Challenge to the Postwar Consensus" (PhD diss., University of Illinois at Urbana-Champaign, 2002), p. 72.

389 "the most hopeful yet experienced": "Gen. Carlson Praises Action of Athens Vets," *Knoxville Journal*, August 23, 1946.

389 "a spearhead for good government": EFC to father and Karen, August 23, 1946, *ECFP.*

389 "I'm for the boys": "Vets' Political Conquests Blessed by Marine Hero," *Columbus Enquirer* (Columbus, GA, via AP), August 20, 1946.

389 As was the case for most Marine officers: Col. K. W. Benner to Bruce E. West, June 30, 1947. "Further, from personal experience, I can assure you that the status of being with 'few funds' is a usual and chronic one with most officers who spend as many years in active service as did Briga-

dier General Carlson." Carlson military personnel file, National Archives, St. Louis, MO.

389 an apartment in Manhattan's Upper East Side: EFC to father and Karen, August 31, 1946, *ECFP.*

390 "the first thing they would do": "U.S. Supports Chiang's Fascism, Carlson Charges," *The Gazette and Daily* (York, PA, via Federated Press), September 7, 1946.

390 "the only democratic force": "Wants American Troops in China Brought Home," *New York Times,* September 6, 1946.

390 "I'm going to hole up": EFC to father and Karen, August 31, 1946, *ECFP.*

390 They found: "Famed Marine Raider Finds Peace in Oregon," *Sunday Oregonian,* November 17, 1946; Peggy Carlson to Helen Foster Snow, October 4, 1946, Box 130, Folder 14, *HFSBYU.*

390 "perfectly willing that young fellows": Agnes Smedley, "In Memoriam—Evans Carlson," *Social Questions Bulletin,* May 1948.

391 In the end he wound up borrowing: Helen Foster Snow, "Carlson of (the 'Gung Ho') Carlson's Raiders: His Own Sketch," p. 12, Carlson Personal File, Published Materials, *USMCR.*

391 With another loan: Peggy Tatum Carlson to Edgar Snow, June 10, 1947, Folder 13, *ESUM.*

391 The locals were glad: "Famed Marine Raider Finds Peace in Oregon," *Sunday Oregonian.*

391 Carlson made it less than a month: Carlson medical file in the Charles M. Grossman Papers, Oregon Health and Science University, Historical Collections & Archives, Portland, OR.

391 teeth were falling out: EFC to father and Karen, May 4, 1944, *ECFP.*

391 He complained in the hospital: Peggy Carlson to Edgar Snow, December 9, 1946, Box 130, Folder 14, *HFSBYU.*

392 "Your greatest value as a writer": Edgar Snow to EFC, December 4, 1938, Box 175, Folder 15, *HFSBYU.*

392 "While fuming in the hospital": EFC to Raymond Gram Swing, December 5, 1946, Carlson Personal File, Correspondence and Memos, PC56/ Coll. 3146, *USMCA.*

392 Once he signaled: Kenneth E. Shewmaker, "The American Liberal Dream: Evans F. Carlson and the Chinese Communists, 1937–1947," *Pacific Historical Review,* Vol. 38, No. 2 (May 1969), pp. 207–16; see p. 208.

393 rubber stamp: Maud Russell to EFC, November 21, 1946, Box 5, Evans Carlson Correspondence, *MRNYPL.*

393 "some rather strong words": Peggy Carlson to Maud Russell, December 6, 1946, Box 5, Evans Carlson Correspondence, *MRNYPL.*

393 Of all the groups: Harold Fletcher to EFC, February 7, 1946, Box 5, Evans Carlson Correspondence, *MRNYPL.*

394 "If some one points out": Maud Russell to EFC, October 2, 1946, Box 5, Evans Carlson Correspondence, *MRNYPL.*

394 Maud Russell was almost certainly: Karen Garner, *Precious Fire: Maud Russell and the Chinese Revolution* (Amherst: University of Massachusetts Press, 2003), pp. 187, 267, n. 5.

394 "We should not regard ourselves": EFC to Maud Russell, July 27, 1946, Box 5, Evans Carlson Correspondence, *MRNYPL.*

394 Carlson urged the committee: EFC to Maud Russell, May 8, 1947, Box 5, Evans Carlson Correspondence, *MRNYPL*.

394 A University of Chicago survey: Kurtz-Phelan, *The China Mission*, p. 287, citing National Opinion Research Center Foreign Affairs Survey, University of Chicago, October 1946.

395 "physically, professionally": Committee for a Democratic Far Eastern Policy press release, May 31, 1947, Box 130, Folder 14, *HFSBYU*.

395 "the Communist tendencies": Carlson FBI file. A copy of the file as released in response to a FOIA request in 1993 is in the Charles M. Grossman Papers, Oregon Health and Science University, Portland, OR.

396 "courageous and factual": "A Letter from Col. Carlson," *Daily People's World*, July 9, 1946, United States newspaper collection, Box 859, *HIA*.

396 "Everyone knew": "Win the Peace for Whom?," *Time*, September 16, 1946.

396 "putrid article": EFC to father and Karen, September 13, 1946, *ECFP*.

396 "I am not a member of the Communist Party": Evans Carlson, "What Is a Front?," *Time*, October 7, 1946.

397 banned for sale: Michael Blankfort to John Maxwell Hamilton, April 7, 1974, Box 85, Folder 4, *MBBU*.

397 "very useful and important": "General Carlson's Story: Or the Philosophy of 'Gung Ho,'" *New York Times*, March 9, 1947.

397 "a real democratic hero": "Carlson of the Raiders, Democratic Hero of Our Time," *Daily Worker*, May 2, 1947.

397 "easily the most pretentiously": "Carlson as a Preacher," *World War* (?), March 1947, clipping in Carlson folder, Alfred Kohlberg Papers, *HIA*.

397 "well-regarded by the Communist": J. Edgar Hoover to Senator Claude Pepper, April 24, 1947, Carlson FBI file, Grossman Papers, OHSU.

397 Even Blankfort's editor: Angus Cameron to Michael Blankfort, March 4, 1946, Box 85, Folder 4, *MBBU*. Cameron (the editor) found it "breathless" and complained that Blankfort's "hero-worship attitude . . . detracts from the readability of the script."

398 When his copy: Peggy Carlson to Michael Blankfort, March 24, 1947, Box 85, Folder 4, *MBBU*.

398 "lunatic fringe": A. J. Baime, *The Accidental President: Harry S. Truman and the Four Months That Changed the World* (Boston: Houghton Mifflin Harcourt, 2017), p. 93.

398 Even *The New Republic*'s publisher: "Michael Straight Dies," *Washington Post*, January 6, 2004.

398 "The Yan'an and Shanxi forces": Michael Straight, "The Faith of a Raider," *The New Republic*, June 9, 1947 (changing Yenan and Shansi to Yan'an and Shanxi). According to Peggy, Carlson found Wallace embarrassing as a politician "though he felt he should support his efforts against the Truman doctrine." The purpose of their conversation was to give Wallace something to say about China at a speech he was giving that night. Peggy Tatum Carlson to Edgar Snow, June 10, 1947, Folder 13, *ESUM*.

CHAPTER 24: FORGETTING

400 he took up a collection: Relevant correspondence is in Box 76, "Evans Carlson, 1943–1951" folder, James Roosevelt Papers, *FDRL*.

400   A black caisson: "They Did Right by Gen. Carlson: They Buried Him Without the Officers," *Washington Daily News*, June 5, 1947; "Full Military Honors Are Paid Carlson at Arlington Rites," clipping from *The Washington Post*, June 5, 1947, Carlson Personal File, Newspaper Articles, PC56/Coll. 3146, *USMCA*.

400   At the grave: Thomas A. Carlson describes the burial in a letter to Michael Blankfort, June 12, 1947, Box 85, Folder 4, *MBBU*.

401   "left nothing to be desired": Raymond Swing, Letter to the Editor, *Washington Post*, June 5, 1947.

401   Some would respond: See, for example, Maj. R. D. Heinl, "Wronged with Weasel Words," Letter to the Editor, *Saturday Review of Literature*, Vol. 20 (December 1947), p. 21, where he writes, "If the Arlington funeral of a Marine general officer, attended by a provisional regiment of Marines and sailors, the United States Marine Band, and the firing of minute-guns, can be considered 'stealthy,' I wish I could ascertain Mr. Swing's definition of ostentation."

401   "I have never been nor am I now": Jon T. Hoffman, *Once a Legend: "Red Mike" Edson of the Marine Raiders* (Novato, CA: Presidio Press, 1994), p. 400.

402   "gave him the works": Maj. Gen. William Arthur Worton oral history (interviewed by Benis Frank in 1967, 1969), History and Museums Division, Headquarters, U.S. Marine Corps, Washington, DC, p. 154 (copy held at Columbia University Special Collections). Attendance of officers at the funeral is detailed in a memo from the Commandant's Office, June 9, 1947, in Carlson's official military personnel file at the National Archives, St. Louis, MO.

402   A group of Raider families: Peggy Carlson to Michael Blankfort, June 13, 1947; and Thomas Hermanek (of Carlson's Marine Raiders Family Club) to Michael Blankfort, June 19, 1947, Box 85, Folder 4, *MBBU*.

402   "The other terror": Ralph Waldo Emerson, "Self-Reliance." Underlining is described in Smedley, "In Memoriam—Evans Carlson," *Social Questions Bulletin*, May 1948.

403   "a humility of soul": Smedley, "In Memoriam" (changing "Chu Teh" to "Zhu De").

403   "the black sheep": "Death of a Rebel," *Baltimore Sun*, May 29, 1947.

403   "shabby treatment": "Honor Slighted," *Washington Post*, June 5, 1947. Clipping in Box 153, James Roosevelt Papers, *FDRL*.

404   "This was his creed": "Semper Fidelis," *New York Times*, May 28, 1947.

404   "I hope Evans can be saved": Raymond Gram Swing to James Roosevelt, November 7, 1947, Box 76, James Roosevelt Papers, *FDRL*.

404   One of the founders: The founder in question was Max Yergan. See *U.S. Communist Party Assistance to Foreign Communist Governments (Testimony of Maud Russell): Hearing Before the Committee on Un-American Activities, House of Representatives* (Committee on Un-American Activities, March 6, 1963), p. 22.

404   "The real Communist": "How to Spot a Communist," *Look*, March 4, 1947.

405   "was a Communist before he was a general": Budenz testimony on the afternoon of April 25, 1950, *State Department Employee Loyalty Investigation: Hearings Before a Subcommittee of the Committee on Foreign Relations, United*

States Senate . . . Part 1 (Washington, DC: Committee on Foreign Relations, 1950), pp. 586–87.

405 "General Carlson was very widely discussed": Budenz testimony on afternoon of August 22, 1951, *Institute of Pacific Relations: Hearings Before the Subcommittee to Investigate the Administration of the Internal Security Act and Other Internal Security Laws of the Committee on the Judiciary, United States Senate, Eighty-First Congress, First Session, on The Institute of Pacific Relations* (Washington, DC: U.S. Government Printing Office, 1951), Part 1, p. 581.

405 "As a matter of fact": *Hearings Before a Subcommittee of the Committee on Foreign Relations, United States Senate, Eighty-First Congress, Second Session, pursuant to S. Res. 231* (Washington, DC: U.S. Government Printing Office, 1950), Part 1, pp. 586–87 (changing "Blankford" to "Blankfort").

406 "a notorious Pro-Communist": Westbrook Pegler, "Surely He Has Nothing to Fear," *Atlanta Constitution*, October 9, 1950.

406 "I would remind the reader": Joseph R. McCarthy, *America's Retreat from Victory: The Story of George Catlett Marshall* (New York: Devin-Adair, 1951), pp. 68, 118.

407 one of the most decorated: The Marine Corps press release with Carlson's obituary listed all of his honors and called him "One of the Marine Corps' most decorated officers." Carlson Personal File, Press Releases, *USMCR*.

407 He had earned: Carlson Personal File, Award Citations, *USMCR*.

407 "techniques and concepts": Robert J. Dalton, "The Legacy of Evans Carlson," *Marine Corps Gazette*, August 1987, pp. 29–30.

407 "What motivated the average North Vietnamese": "Carlson & Leadership," *Marine Corps Gazette*, December, 1987, p. 28.

408 "mixed crew of communists": "John Paton Davies' Motives Mystery in 'Tawny Pipit' Case," *New York Times*, December 9, 1953; "The Davies Case" (letter to the editor from Edgar Snow), *New York Times*, December 12, 1953.

408 severed its relationship: Adalbert Tomasz Grunfeld, "Friends of the Revolution: American Supporters of China's Communists, 1926–1939" (PhD diss., New York University, 1985), p. 310.

409 "The spy to end spies": John le Carré, "The Spy to End Spies: On Richard Sorge," *Encounter*, November 1966, pp. 88–89.

409 most valuable collaborator: Ruth Price, *The Lives of Agnes Smedley* (New York: Oxford University Press, 2005), p. 375.

409 "one of the principal": Janice MacKinnon and Stephen MacKinnon, *Agnes Smedley: The Life and Times of an American Radical* (Berkeley: University of California Press, 1988), p. 285.

409 the Yaddo colony asked Smedley: Price, *The Lives of Agnes Smedley*, pp. 385–86.

409 "most successful and complete": "Tokyo War Secrets Stolen by Soviet Spy Ring in 1941," *New York Times*, February 11, 1949.

410 one of her actual spy friends: Price, *The Lives of Agnes Smedley*, p. 414. For Kuczynski's activities in Britain at this time, see Ben Macintyre, *Agent Sonya: Moscow's Most Daring Wartime Spy* (New York: Crown, 2020).

410 "the firmest of my life": Agnes Smedley, *Battle Hymn of China* (New York: Alfred A. Knopf, 1943), p. 198.

410 "They were two brave soldiers": Price, *The Lives of Agnes Smedley*, p. 415.

411 a chance for a détente: Thomas J. Christenson, "A 'Lost Chance' for

What? Rethinking the Origins of U.S.-PRC Confrontation," *The Journal of American-East Asian Relations*, Vol. 4, No. 3 (Fall 1995), pp. 249–78.

411   fatefully misjudged: see Qing Simei, *From Allies to Enemies: Visions of Modernity, Identity, and U.S.–China Diplomacy, 1945–1960* (Cambridge, MA: Harvard University Press, 2007), pp. 143–68.

411   "the brotherhood of man": Evans F. Carlson, *Twin Stars of China: A Behind-the-Scenes Story of China's Valiant Struggle for Existence* (New York: Dodd, Mead, 1940), p. 86.

411   to his lasting disgrace: The following section is indebted to Jonathan Mirsky, "Message from Mao," review of *Edgar Snow: A Biography*, by John Maxwell Hamilton, *New York Review of Books*, February 16, 1989.

412   may have been the primary reason: Chen Jian, *China's Road to the Korean War: The Making of the Sino-American Confrontation* (New York: Columbia University Press, 1994).

412   "There are some who": Arlen Meliksetov, " 'New Democracy' and China's Search for Socio-Economic Development Routes (1949–1953)," *Far Eastern Affairs*, No. 1 (1996), pp. 75–92; quotation on p. 83; Marc Blecher, "New Democracy," in Christian Sorace, Ivan Franceschini, and Nicholas Loubere, eds., *Afterlives of Chinese Communism* (New York: Verso, 2019), pp. 155–59.

413   "I saw no starving people in China": Edgar Snow, *The Other Side of the River: Red China Today* (New York: Random House, 1962), pp. 619–20; Bernard S. Thomas, *Season of High Adventure: Edgar Snow in China* (Berkeley: University of California Press, 1996), p. 307.

413   "millions of people are not starving": Snow, *The Other Side of the River*, p. 620.

413   "childish exaggeration": Snow, *The Other Side of the River*, pp. 614, 618.

413   as many as 36 million: Yang Jisheng, *Tombstone: The Great Chinese Famine, 1958–1962*, trans. Stacy Mosher and Guo Jian (New York: Farrar, Straus & Giroux, 2012).

414   had established herself: Daniel James Klotz, "Freda Utley: From Communist to Anti-Communist" (PhD diss., Yale University, 1987), pp. 4, 242–43.

414   to advance his own career: Freda Utley, *The China Story* (Chicago: H. Regnery, 1951), p. 157.

414   was ruined financially: Peggy Carlson to Michael Blankfort, November 16, 1961, Box 85, Folder 4, *MBBU*.

414   In 1964, his diaries: "Gen. Carlson's Effects Found," *Hartford Courant*, January 9, 1964.

415   After she lost her home: Peggy (Carlson) Ellwood to Michael Blankfort, September 29, 1976, Box 85, Folder 4, *MBBU*.

BIBLIOGRAPHY

Abend, Hallett. *My Life in China, 1926–1941.* New York: Harcourt, Brace, 1943.

Alexander, Joseph. *Edson's Raiders: The 1st Marine Raider Battalion in World War II.* Annapolis, MD: Naval Institute Press, 2001.

———. *Utmost Savagery: The Three Days of Tarawa.* Annapolis, MD: Naval Institute Press, 1995.

Alley, Rewi. *At 90: Memoirs of My China Years.* Beijing: New World Press, 1986.

American Committee for Non-Participation in Japanese Aggression. *America's Share in Japan's War Guilt.* New York: Academy Press, 1938.

———. *Shall America Stop Arming Japan?* New York, 1940.

Arnold, Julean. *China: A Commercial and Industrial Handbook.* U.S. Department of Commerce, Trade Promotion Series No. 38. Washington, DC: U.S. Government Printing Office, 1926.

Auden, W. H., and Christopher Isherwood. *Journey to a War.* London: Faber & Faber, 1973.

Averill, Stephen C. *Revolution in the Highlands: China's Jinggangshan Base Area.* Lanham, MD: Rowman & Littlefield, 2006.

Bailey, J. Doug. "The Carlson Raider Gung Ho Knife: A Forty Year Study." *The Raider Patch,* No. 157 (4th Quarter 2022): 8–15.

Baime, A. J. *The Accidental President: Harry S. Truman and the Four Months That Changed the World.* Boston: Houghton Mifflin Harcourt, 2017.

Barrett, David D. *Dixie Mission: The United States Army Observer Group in Yenan, 1944.* Berkeley: Center for Chinese Studies, University of California, Berkeley, 1970.

Belden, Jack. *China Shakes the World.* Beijing: Foreign Languages Press, 2003.

———. *Still Time to Die.* New York: Harper & Brothers, 1944.

Bentley, Eric, ed. *Thirty Years of Treason: Excerpts from Hearings Before the House Committee on Un-American Activities, 1938–1968.* New York: Viking, 1971.

Bernstein, Matthew, and Robert Wise. *Walter Wanger: Hollywood Independent.* St. Paul: University of Minnesota Press, 2000.

Bianco, Lucien. *Origins of the Chinese Revolution, 1915–1949.* Stanford: Stanford University Press, 1971.

Blankfort, Michael. *The Big Yankee: The Life of Carlson of the Raiders.* Boston: Little, Brown, 1947.

Blecher, Marc. "New Democracy." In Christian Sorace et al., eds., *Afterlives of Chinese Communism*. New York: Verso, 2019.

Bōeichō Bōei Kenshūjo. *Chūbū Taiheiyō hōmen Kaigun sakusen* [Naval operations in the Central Pacific]. 2 Vols. Tokyo: Asagumo Shinbunsha, 1970–1973.

Borg, Dorothy. *The United States and the Far Eastern Crisis of 1933–1938: From the Manchurian Incident Through the Initial Stage of the Undeclared Sino-Japanese War*. Cambridge, MA: Harvard University Press, 1964.

Bowers, Lauren. "'The Song They Lived By,' The 'Marines' Hymn' During World War II." *Marine Corps History*, Vol. 8, No. 2 (Winter 2022–2023): 23–42.

Brady, Anne-Marie. *Making the Foreign Serve China: Managing Foreigners in the People's Republic*. Lanham, MD: Rowman & Littlefield, 2003.

———. "Who Friend, Who Enemy? Rewi Alley and the Friends of China." *China Quarterly*, No. 161 (September 1997): 614–32.

Braun, Otto. *A Comintern Agent in China, 1932–1939*. Stanford: Stanford University Press, 1982.

Brill, Norman Q. et al. "Age and Resistance to Military Stress." *United States Armed Forces Medical Journal*, Vol. 4, No. 1 (January 1953): 1247–66.

Browne, Stuart. "A Professor Quits the Communist Party." *Reader's Digest*, Vol. 31, No. 185 (September 1937): 10–14.

Bulger, Lowell. "The Second Marine Raider Battalion on Guadalcanal." *The Raider Patch*, four parts: March 1981; May–July 1981; September 1981; November 1981.

Burks, Lt. Col. Arthur J. "China Side 1927." *Marine Corps Gazette* (April 1949): 46–52.

Butler, Smedley Darlington. "America's Armed Forces." Part 2. *Common Sense*, November 1935, pp. 8–12.

———. *War Is a Racket*. New York: Round Table Press, 1935.

Cameron, Craig M. *American Samurai: Myth, Imagination, and the Conduct of Battle in the First Marine Division, 1941–1952*. New York: Cambridge University Press, 1994.

Carlson, Evans F. "America Faces Crisis in the Orient." *Amerasia*, Vol. 3 (February 1940): 555–60.

———. "The Autobiography of Evans Carlson," unpublished typescript, as told to Helen Foster Snow. Carlson Personal File, Published Materials, Reference Branch, Marine Corps History Division, Quantico, VA.

———. "The Autobiography of Evans Carlson of 'Carlson's Raiders,'" unpublished typescript, 1940, in Helen Foster Snow papers, MSS 2219, Box 175, Folder 15, L. Tom Perry Special Collections, Brigham Young University, Provo, UT.

———. *The Chinese Army: Its Organization and Military Efficiency*. New York: Institute of Pacific Relations, 1940.

———. "The Chinese Mongol Front in Suiyuan." *Pacific Affairs*, Vol. 12, No. 3 (September 1939): 278–84.

———. "The Guardia Nacional de Nicaragua." *Marine Corps Gazette* (August 1937): 7–20.

———. "Legal Bases for the Use of Foreign Armed Forces in China." *Proceedings of the United States Naval Institute*, Vol. 62, No. 405 (November 1936): 1544–56.

———. "Marines as an Aid to Diplomacy in China." *Marine Corps Gazette* (February 1936): 27–30, 47–53.

———. "Military Leadership." *United States Naval Institute Proceedings*, Vol. 63, No. 11, Whole No. 417 (November 1937): 1587.

———. "Shoulder to Shoulder with the Coldstream Guards." *Leatherneck* (October 1927): 8, 50.

———. "Strategy of the Sino-Japanese War." *Far Eastern Survey*, Vol. 10, No. 9 (May 19, 1941): 99–105.

———. *Twin Stars of China: A Behind-the-Scenes Story of China's Valiant Struggle for Existence*. New York: Dodd, Mead, 1940.

Carter, Carolle J. *Mission to Yenan: American Liaison with the Chinese Communists, 1944–1947*. Lexington: University Press of Kentucky, 1997.

Castro, Sara Bush. "Improvising Tradecraft: The Evolving U.S. Intelligence Regime and the Chinese Communist Party in the 1940s." PhD diss., University of North Carolina Chapel Hill, 2016.

Chen Jian. *China's Road to the Korean War: The Making of the Sino-American Confrontation*. New York: Columbia University Press, 1994.

———. "The Myth of America's 'Lost Chance' in China: A Chinese Perspective in Light of New Evidence." *Diplomatic History*, Vol. 21, No. 1 (Winter 1997): 77–86.

———. "The Ward Case and the Emergence of Sino-American Confrontation, 1948–1950." *The Australian Journal of Chinese Affairs*, No. 30 (July 1993): 149–70.

Chern, Kenneth S. "Politics of American China Policy, 1945: Roots of the Cold War in Asia." *Political Science Quarterly*, Vol. 91, No. 4 (Winter 1976–1977): 631–47.

Chiang Kai-shek. *China's Destiny*, trans. Wang Chung-hui. New York: Macmillan, 1947.

Chico. "Camp Roosevelt Vignettes." *Leatherneck*, Vol. 19, No. 1 (January 1936): 7, 50–51.

Chinese Ministry of Information. *China Handbook, 1937–1943: A Comprehensive Survey of Major Developments in China in Six Years of War*. New York: Macmillan, 1943.

Chiu Sin-ming. "A History of the Chinese Communist Army." PhD diss., University of Southern California, 1958.

Christenson, Thomas J. "A 'Lost Chance' for What? Rethinking the Origins of U.S.-PRC Confrontation." *The Journal of American-East Asian Relations*, Vol. 4, No. 3 (Fall 1995): 249–78.

———. *Useful Adversaries: Grand Strategy, Domestic Mobilization, and Sino-American Conflict, 1947–1958*. Princeton: Princeton University Press, 1996.

Clark, George B. *Treading Softly: U.S. Marines in China, 1819–1949*. Westport, CT: Praeger, 2001.

Clegg, Jenny. "Mass- and Elite-Based Strategies for Cooperative Development in Wartime Nationalist China: Western Views on the 'Gung Ho' Industrial Cooperative Experience." *European Journal of East Asian Studies*, Vol. 11, No. 2 (2012): 305–27.

Clemens, Martin. *Alone on Guadalcanal: A Coastwatcher's Story*. Annapolis, MD: Naval Institute Press, 1998.

Cliver, Robert. *Red Silk: Class, Gender, and Revolution in China's Yangzi Delta Silk Industry*. Cambridge, MA: Harvard University Asia Center, 2020.

Coble, Parks. *Facing Japan: Chinese Politics and Japanese Imperialism, 1931–1937*. Cambridge, MA: Council on East Asian Studies, 1991.

———. "The Legacy of China's Wartime Reporting, 1937–1945: Can the Past Serve the Present?" *Modern China*, Vol. 36, No. 4 (July 2010): 435–60.

Cohen, Warren I. "Was There a Lost Chance in China?" *Diplomatic History*, Vol. 21, No. 1 (Winter 1997): 71–75.

Condit, Kenneth W., and Edwin T. Turnbladh. *Hold High the Torch: A History of the 4th Marines*. Washington, DC: Historical Branch, G-3 Division, Headquarters, U.S. Marine Corps, 1960.

Cook, Haruko Tàyà, and Theodore F. Cook. *Japan at War: An Oral History*. New York: The New Press, 1992.

Culbert, David H. "Radio's Raymond Gram Swing: 'He Isn't the Kind of Man You Would Call Ray.'" *The Historian*, Vol. 35, No. 4 (August 1973): 587–606.

Dalton, Robert J. "The Legacy of Evans Carlson," *Marine Corps Gazette* (August 1987).

Deane, Hugh, ed. *Evans F. Carlson on China at War, 1937–1941*. Beijing: Foreign Languages Press, 1993.

Delury, John T. *Agents of Subversion: The Fate of John T. Downey and the CIA's Covert War in China*. Ithaca, NY: Cornell University Press, 2022.

Dimitrov, Georgi. *The Diary of Georgi Dimitrov, 1933–1949*, ed. Ivo Banac. New Haven: Yale University Press, 2003.

Doenecke, Justus D. "Rehearsal for Cold War: United States Anti-Interventionists and the Soviet Union, 1939–1941." *International Journal of Politics, Culture, and Society*, Vol. 7, No. 3 (Spring 1994): 375–92.

Dong, Stella. *Shanghai: The Rise and Fall of a Decadent City, 1842–1949*. New York: Perennial, 2001.

Dower, John W. *War Without Mercy: Race and Power in the Pacific War*. New York: Pantheon, 1986.

Dreyer, Edward. *China at War, 1901–1949*. London: Longman, 1995.

Du Chunmei. "Occupational Hazard: American Servicemen's Sensory Encounters with China, 1945–1949." *Diplomatic History*, Vol. 47, No. 1 (January 2023): 55–84.

Eldridge, David. *American Culture in the 1930's*. Edinburgh: Edinburgh University Press, 2008.

Emerson, Ralph Waldo. *Emerson: Essays and Lectures*. New York: Library of America, 1983.

Epstein, Israel. *My China Eye: Memoirs of a Jew and a Journalist*. San Francisco: Long River Press, 2005.

Esherick, Joseph. *Accidental Holy Land: The Communist Revolution in Northwest China*. Oakland: University of California Press, 2022.

Esherick, Joseph, and Matthew T. Combs, eds. *1943: China at the Crossroads*. Ithaca, NY: Cornell University East Asia Program, 2015.

Ferenz, Adam. "Joseph McCarthy and the Loss of China: A Study in Fear and Panic." PhD diss., University of Michigan-Flint, 2014.

Fighting on Guadalcanal. Washington, DC: U.S. Government Printing Office, 1943.

Firsov, Fridrikh Igorevich. *Secret Cables of the Comintern, 1933–1943.* New Haven: Yale University Press, 2014.

Foreign Relations of the United States: Diplomatic Papers, 1938, Vol. III: *The Far East.* Washington, DC: U.S. Government Printing Office, 1954.

Foreign Relations of the United States: Diplomatic Papers, 1942, China. Washington, DC: U.S. Government Printing Office, 1956.

Foreign Relations of the United States: Diplomatic Papers, 1943, China. Washington, DC: U.S. Government Printing Office, 1957.

Foreign Relations of the United States, Diplomatic Papers, 1944, Vol. VI: *China.* Washington, DC: U.S. Government Printing Office, 1967.

Forman, Harrison. *Report from Red China.* New York: Henry Holt, 1945.

Franck, Harry A. *Roving Through Southern China.* New York: Century Company, 1925.

Frank, Benis M., and Henry I. Shaw. *Victory and Occupation,* Vol. 5, *History of U.S. Marine Corps Operations in World War II.* Washington, DC: Historical Branch, G-3 Division, Headquarters, U.S. Marine Corps, 1968.

Frank, Richard B. *Tower of Skulls: A History of the Asia-Pacific War, July 1937–May 1942.* New York: W. W. Norton, 2020.

Fredman, Zach. *The Tormented Alliance: American Servicemen and the Occupation of China, 1941–1949.* Chapel Hill: University of North Carolina Press, 2022.

Friedman, Donald J. *The Road from Isolation.* Cambridge, MA: Harvard University Asia Center, 1968.

Fu Pao-Jen. "The German Military Mission in Nanking, 1928–1938: A Bridge Connecting China and Germany." PhD diss., Syracuse University, 1989.

Gao Hua. *How the Red Sun Rose: The Origins and Development of the Yan'an Rectification Movement, 1930–1945.* Hong Kong: Chinese University of Hong Kong Press, 2018.

Garner, Karen. "The 'Chinese Connection' to American Radicalism." *The Journal of American-East Asian Relations,* Vol. 3, No. 2 (Summer 1994): 127–53.

———. *Precious Fire: Maud Russell and the Chinese Revolution.* Amherst: University of Massachusetts Press, 2003.

Garver, John W. "Little Chance." *Diplomatic History,* Vol. 21, No. 1 (Winter 1997): 87–94.

———. "Mao, the Comintern, and the Second United Front." *China Quarterly,* No. 129 (March 1992): 171–79.

———. "The Origins of the Second United Front: The Comintern and the Chinese Communist Party." *China Quarterly,* No. 113 (March 1988): 29–59.

———. "The Soviet Union and the Xi'an Incident." *The Australian Journal of Chinese Affairs,* No. 26 (July 1991): 145–75.

Gobat, Michel. *Confronting the American Dream: Nicaragua Under U.S. Imperial Rule.* Durham, NC: Duke University Press, 2005.

Gomrick, Maj. Kathleen M. "Gung Ho, Raider! The Philosophy and Methods of Brig Gen Evans F. Carlson, Marine Corps Raider." Research report, Air Command and Staff College, Maxwell Air Force Base, AL, 1999.

Grunfeld, Adalbert Tomasz. "Friends of the Revolution: American Supporters of China's Communists, 1926–1939." PhD diss., New York University, 1985.

Guo Junning. *Zhu De yu Fan Shisheng* [Zhu De and Fan Shisheng]. Beijing: Huawen chubanshe, 2001.

Hahn, Emily. *China to Me: A Partial Autobiography.* Garden City, NY: Doubleday, Doran, 1945.

Hanson, Haldore. *"Humane Endeavor": The Story of the China War.* New York: Farrar & Rinehart, 1939.

Harmsen, Peter. *Shanghai 1937: Stalingrad on the Yangtze.* Havertown, PA: Casemate, 2015.

———. *War in the Far East*, Vol. 1, *Storm Clouds over the Pacific, 1931–1941.* Philadelphia: Casemate, 2018.

Hartford, Kathleen J. "Step by Step: Reform, Resistance, and Revolution in Chin-Ch'a-Chi Border Region, 1937–1945." PhD diss., Stanford University, 1980.

Hendrickson, John Creigh. "El Terremoto." *Leatherneck* (April 1987).

Hillenbrand, Laura. *Unbroken: A World War II Story of Survival, Resilience, and Redemption.* New York: Random House, 2010.

Hochschild, Adam. *Spain in Our Hearts: Americans in the Spanish Civil War, 1936–1939.* Boston: Houghton Mifflin Harcourt, 2016.

Hoefer, Peter D. "A David Against Goliath: The American Veterans Committee's Challenge to the American Legion in the 1950s." PhD diss., University of Maryland, College Park, 2010.

Hoffman, Jon T. *From Makin to Bougainville: Marine Raiders in the Pacific War.* Washington, DC: Marine Corps Historical Center, 1993.

———. *Once a Legend: "Red Mike" Edson of the Marine Raiders.* Novato, CA: Presidio Press, 1994.

Hotta Yoshiaki et al. *Dai Tōa senshi* [History of the Great East Asia War]. 2 Vols. Tokyo: Kōbundō shoten, 1942–1943.

Hough, Lt. Col. Frank O., Maj. Verle E. Ludwig, and Henry I. Shaw. *History of U.S. Marine Corps Operations in World War II.* 5 Vols. Washington, DC: Historical Branch, G-3 Division, Headquarters, U.S. Marine Corps, 1958.

Houseknecht, Stephen Mark. "The Elite of the Elites: The U.S. Marine Raider Battalions, 1942–1944: A Case Study in Elite Military Organizations." MA thesis, Missouri State University, 2015.

Hsiung, James C., and Steven I. Levine, eds. *China's Bitter Victory: The War with Japan, 1937–1945.* Armonk, NY: M. E. Sharpe, 1992.

Hsu, Hua. "Pacific Crossings: China, the United States, and the Transpacific Imagination." PhD diss., Harvard University, 2008.

Hu Guoqiang, ed. *Zhu De shi xuan zhu* [The annotated poetry of Zhu De]. Chongqing: Xinan shifan daxue chubanshe, 1986.

Hu Zhefeng. *Zhu De bing fa* [Zhu De's art of war]. Zhengzhou: Zhongyuan nongmin chubanshe, 1996.

Hudak, Joshua J. "Through Crimson Tides: Tarawa's Effect on Military Tactics and Public Perception of War." MA thesis, Clemson University, 2014.

Huskey, James L. "The Cosmopolitan Connection: Americans and Chinese in Shanghai During the Interwar Years." *Diplomatic History*, Vol. 11, No. 3 (Summer 1987): 227–42.

Ienaga, Saburō. *The Pacific War: World War II and the Japanese, 1931–1945.* New York: Pantheon, 1978.

Ilin, M. *New Russia's Primer: The Story of the Five-Year Plan*, trans. George S. Counts and Nicua P. Lodge. Boston: Houghton Mifflin, 1931.

Janeway, Eliot. "Japan's Partner: Japanese Dependence upon the United States." *Harper's Magazine*, Vol. 177 (June 1938): 1–8.

Jesperson, Christopher T. *American Images of China, 1931–1949*. Stanford: Stanford University Press, 1996.

Johnstone, Andrew. *Against Immediate Evil: American Internationalists and the Four Freedoms on the Eve of World War II*. Ithaca, NY: Cornell University Press, 2014.

Jones, James. *The Thin Red Line*. New York: Scribner, 1962.

Jordan, Donald A. *The Northern Expedition: China's National Revolution of 1926–1928*. Honolulu: University of Hawaii Press, 1976.

Karl, Rebecca E. *Mao Zedong and China in the Twentieth-Century World: A Concise History*. Durham, NC: Duke University Press, 2010.

Katz, Jonathan M. *Gangsters of Capitalism: Smedley Butler, the Marines, and the Making and Breaking of America's Empire*. New York: St. Martin's Press, 2022.

Keating, Pauline. "The Yan'an Way of Co-Operativization." *China Quarterly*, No. 140 (December 1994): 1025–51.

Keeley, Joseph C. *The China Lobby Man: The Story of Alfred Kohlberg*. New Rochelle, NY: Arlington House, 1969.

Kennedy, Andrew Bingham. "Can the Weak Defeat the Strong? Mao's Evolving Approach to Asymmetric Warfare in Yan'an." *China Quarterly*, No. 196 (December 2008): 884–99.

Kim, Donggil. "China's Intervention in the Korean War Revisited." *Diplomatic History*, Vol. 40, No. 5 (November 2016): 1002–26.

Klehr, Harvey. *The Soviet World of American Communism*. New Haven: Yale University Press, 1998.

Klotz, Daniel James. "Freda Utley: From Communist to Anti-Communist." PhD diss., Yale University, 1987.

Koppes, Clayton R., and Gregory D. Black. *Hollywood Goes to War: How Politics, Profits and Propaganda Shaped World War II Movies*. New York: Free Press, 1987.

Kotkin, Stephen. *Stalin: Waiting for Hitler, 1929–1941*. New York: Penguin, 2017.

Kublin, Michael Baru. "The Role of China in American Military Strategy from Pearl Harbor to the Fall of 1944." PhD diss., New York University, 1981.

Kurtz-Phelan, Daniel. *The China Mission: George C. Marshall's Unfinished War, 1945–1947*. New York: W. W. Norton, 2018.

Kushner, Barak. *The Thought War: Japanese Imperial Propaganda*. Honolulu: University of Hawaii Press, 2006.

Lary, Diana. *China's Civil War: A Social History, 1945–1949*. Cambridge, UK: Cambridge University Press, 2015.

Leary, William M. "Portrait of an Intelligence Officer: James McHugh in China, 1937–1942." *Naval History* (1988): 249–63.

le Carré, John. "The Spy to End Spies: On Richard Sorge." *Encounter* (November 1966): 88–89.

Le Francois, Lt. W. S. "We Mopped Up Makin Island." *Saturday Evening Post*. Part 1: December 4, 1943; Part 2: December 11, 1943.

Li Fangchun. "Mass Democracy, Class Struggle, and Remolding the Party and Government During the Land Reform Movement in North China." *Modern China*, Vol. 38, No. 4 (July 2012): 411–45.

Li Xiaobing. *A History of the Modern Chinese Army*. Lexington: University Press of Kentucky, 2007.

Li Yuzhen. "Chiang Kai-Shek and Joseph Stalin During World War II." In Hans van de Ven, Diana Lary, and Stephen MacKinnon, eds., *Negotiating China's Destiny in World War II*. Stanford: Stanford University Press, 2015.

Lindsay, Michael. "The North China Front: A Study of Chinese Guerrillas in Action." Part 1, *Amerasia*, Vol. 8, No. 7 (March 31, 1944): 99–110; Part 2, *Amerasia*, Vol. 8, No. 8 (April 14, 1944): 117–25.

Loewenheim, Francis L., Harold D. Langley, and Manfred Jonas, eds. *Roosevelt and Churchill: Their Secret Wartime Correspondence*. New York: Saturday Review Press, 1975.

Long, Kelly Ann. *Helen Foster Snow: An American Woman in Revolutionary China*. Boulder: University Press of Colorado, 2006.

Loureiro, Pedro Anthony. "Intelligence Success: The Evolution of Navy and Marine Intelligence Operations in China, 1931–1941." PhD diss., University of Southern California, 1995.

Lovell, Julia. *Maoism: A Global History*. New York: Alfred A. Knopf, 2019.

Lucas, Lt. Jim. *Combat Correspondent*. New York: Reynal & Hitchcock, 1944.

Lunt, Carroll. *China, Star of Asia's Drama*. Los Angeles: Walton & Wright, 1941.

Ma Xiaohua. "The Sino-American Alliance During World War II and the Lifting of the Chinese Exclusion Acts." *American Studies International*, Vol. 38, No. 2 (June 2000): 39–61.

Macintyre, Ben. *Agent Sonya: Moscow's Most Daring Wartime Spy*. New York: Crown, 2020.

———. *Rogue Heroes: The History of the SAS, Britain's Secret Special Forces Unit That Sabotaged the Nazis and Changed the Nature of War*. New York: Crown, 2016.

MacKinnon, Janice, and Stephen MacKinnon. *Agnes Smedley: The Life and Times of an American Radical*. Berkeley: University of California Press, 1988.

MacKinnon, Stephen. "The Tragedy of Wuhan, 1938." *Modern Asian Studies*, Vol. 30, No. 4 (October 1996): 931–43.

———. *Wuhan, 1938: War, Refugees, and the Making of Modern China*. Berkeley: University of California Press, 2008.

MacKinnon, Stephen, and Oris Friesen. *China Reporting: An Oral History of American Journalism in the 1930s and 1940s*. Berkeley: University of California Press, 1987.

Makos, Adam. *Voices of the Pacific: Untold Stories from the Marine Heroes of World War II*. New York: Dutton Caliber, 2021.

Manser, Richard L. "Roosevelt and China: From Cairo to Yalta." PhD diss., Temple University, 1987.

Mao Zedong. *On Guerrilla Warfare*, trans. Samuel B. Griffith II. Washington, DC: U.S. Marine Corps, 1989.

"A Marine's Guide to North China" (September 1945). Pamphlet in the A. T. Steele Papers, MSS—349, Box 22, Folder 17. Arizona State University Archives, Tempe, AZ.

Markey, Gregory Thomas. "The United States in China, 1941–1944: The Perspective from the State Department." 2 Vols. PhD diss., Georgetown University, 1985.

Mason, John T., ed. *The Pacific War Remembered: An Oral History Collection*. Annapolis, MD: Naval Institute Press, 1986.

Matthews, Owen. *An Impeccable Spy: Richard Sorge, Stalin's Master Agent*. London: Bloomsbury, 2019.

Mattingly, Maj. Robert E. "Herringbone Cloak—GI Dagger: Marines of the OSS." Occasional Paper, History and Museums Division, Headquarters, U.S. Marine Corps, Washington, DC, 1989.

———. "The Worst Slap in the Face." *Marine Corps Gazette* (March 1983): 58–66.

McCarthy, Joseph R. *America's Retreat from Victory: The Story of George Catlett Marshall.* New York: Devin-Adair, 1951.

McHugh, James. "The Carlson Incident," unpublished typescript from James McHugh Papers, Cornell University. Copy in Carlson Personal File, PC56/Coll. 3146, *USMCA.*

McPherson, Alan L. *The Invaded: How Latin Americans and Their Allies Fought and Ended U.S. Occupations.* New York: Oxford University Press, 2014.

McWilliams, Carey. "The Education of Evans Carlson." *The Nation* (December 1, 1945).

Meliksetov, Arlen. "'New Democracy' and China's Search for Socio-Economic Development Routes (1949–1953)." *Far Eastern Affairs* (1996) 1:75–92.

Merillat, Herbert C. *Guadalcanal Remembered.* New York: Avon, 1982.

Millar, Thomas J. "Americans and the Issue of China: The Passion and Dispassion of American Opinions About China, 1930 to 1944." PhD diss., University of California, Los Angeles, 1998.

Miller, John. *Guadalcanal: The First Offensive.* Part of series, United States Army in World War II. Washington, DC: Center of Military History, United States Army, 1995.

Millett, Allan R. *Semper Fidelis: The History of the United States Marine Corps.* New York: Free Press, 1991.

Millett, Richard Leroy. "The History of the Guardia Nacional de Nicaragua, 1925–1965." PhD diss., University of New Mexico, 1966.

Mirsky, Jonathan. "Message from Mao." (Review of *Edgar Snow: A Biography* by John Maxwell Hamilton.) *New York Review of Books* (February 16, 1989).

Mitter, Rana. *China's Good War: How World War II Is Shaping a New Nationalism.* Cambridge, MA: Harvard University Press, 2020.

———. *Forgotten Ally: China's World War II, 1937–1945.* Boston: Houghton Mifflin Harcourt, 2013.

Moe, Albert F. "Gung Ho." *American Speech*, Vol. 42, No. 1 (February 1967): 19–30.

Moore, Aaron William. *Writing War: Soldiers Record the Japanese Empire.* Cambridge, MA: Harvard University Press, 2013.

Moyar, Mark. *Oppose Any Foe: The Rise of America's Special Operations Forces.* New York: Basic Books, 2017.

Mühlhahn, Klaus. *Making China Modern: From the Great Qing to Xi Jinping.* Cambridge, MA: Harvard University Press, 2019.

Nichter, Matthew F. "Rethinking the Origins of the Civil Rights Movement: Radicals, Repression, and the Black Freedom Struggle." PhD diss., University of Wisconsin–Madison, 2014.

O'Connell, Aaron B. *Underdogs: The Making of the Modern Marine Corps.* Cambridge, MA: Harvard University Press, 2012.

O'Donnell, Patrick K. *Into the Rising Sun: In Their Own Words, World War II's Pacific Veterans Reveal the Heart of Combat.* New York: Free Press, 2002.

Opper, Marc. *People's Wars in China, Malaya, and Vietnam.* Ann Arbor: University of Michigan Press, 2019.

Ouyang Shanzun. "San yue riji" [A three months' diary]. In Zhongguo guoji youren yanjiuhui, ed. *Zhongguo zhi you Ka Erxun* [China's friend, Evans Carlson]. Shenyang: Liaoning renmin chubanshe, 1996.

Pakula, Hannah. *The Last Empress: Madame Chiang Kai-Shek and the Birth of Modern China.* New York: Simon & Schuster, 2009.

Pantsov, Alexander V. *The Bolsheviks and the Chinese Revolution, 1919–1927.* Honolulu: University of Hawaii Press, 2000.

Pantsov, Alexander V. *Victorious in Defeat: The Life and Times of Chiang Kai-shek, China, 1887–1975.* Translated by Steven I. Levine. New Haven: Yale University Press, 2023.

Pantsov, Alexander V., and Steven I. Levine. *Mao: The Real Story.* New York: Simon & Schuster, 2012.

Pash, Sidney L. *The Currents of War: A New History of American-Japanese Relations, 1899–1941.* Lexington: University Press of Kentucky, 2014.

Peatross, Oscar F. *Bless 'Em All: The Marine Raiders of World War II.* Tampa: Raider Publishing, 1995.

———. "The Raid on Makin Island." *Leatherneck* (August 1992): 32–41; (September 1992): 30–39.

Peattie, Mark, Edward Drea, and Hans van de Ven, eds. *The Battle for China: Essays on the Military History of the Sino-Japanese War of 1937–1945.* Stanford: Stanford University Press, 2011.

Peckham, Charles Allen. "The Northern Expedition, the Nanking Incident, and the Protection of American Nationals." PhD diss., Ohio State University, 1973.

Pepper, Suzanne. *Civil War in China: The Political Struggle, 1945–1949.* Berkeley: University of California Press, 1978.

Phillips, Cabell. *The 1940's: Decade of Triumph and Trouble.* New York: Macmillan, 1975.

Platt, Stephen R. *Autumn in the Heavenly Kingdom: China, the West, and the Epic Story of the Taiping Civil War.* New York: Alfred A. Knopf, 2012.

Porter, Edgar A. *The People's Doctor: George Hatem and China's Revolution.* Honolulu: University of Hawaii Press, 1997.

Powers, Richard G. *Not Without Honor: The History of American Anticommunism.* New York: Free Press, 1995.

Pozhilov, I. "Zhu De: The Early Days of a Commander." *Far Eastern Affairs,* No. 1 (1987): 91–99.

Prange, Gordon William. *Target Tokyo: The Story of the Sorge Spy Ring.* New York: McGraw-Hill, 1984.

Price, Ruth. *The Lives of Agnes Smedley.* New York: Oxford University Press, 2005.

Price, Wesley. "Raider Carlson," *Picture News* (January 2, 1944).

"The Psychiatric Toll of Warfare." *Fortune,* Vol. 28, No. 6 (December 1943): 141, 274–82.

Qian Suoqiao. "Representing China: Lin Yutang vs. American 'China Hands' in the 1940s." *The Journal of American-East Asian Relations,* Vol. 17, No. 2 (2010): 99–117.

Qing Simei. *From Allies to Enemies: Visions of Modernity, Identity, and U.S.–China Diplomacy, 1945–1960.* Cambridge, MA: Harvard University Press, 2007.

Reynolds, Douglas Robertson. "The Chinese Industrial Cooperative Movement and the Political Polarization of Wartime China, 1938–1945." PhD diss., Columbia University, 1975.

Richardson, Herb. "Giants of the Corps." *Leatherneck* (March 1977): 38–41.

Rielly, Maj. Robert J. "Confronting the Tiger: Small Unit Cohesion in Battle." *Military Review* (November–December 2000): 61–65.

Romanus, Charles F., and Riley Sunderland. *Stilwell's Command Problems*. Part of series United States Army in World War II: China–Burma–India Theater. Washington, DC: Center of Military History, United States Army, 1987.

———. *Stilwell's Mission to China*. Part of series United States Army in World War II: China–Burma–India Theater. Washington, DC: Center of Military History, United States Army, 1987.

———. *Time Runs Out in CBI*. Part of series United States Army in World War II: China–Burma–India Theater. Washington, DC: Center of Military History, United States Army, 1999.

Roosevelt, Eleanor. *This I Remember*. New York: Harper & Brothers, 1949.

Roosevelt, Franklin. *F.D.R.: His Personal Letters, 1928–1945*, ed. Elliott Roosevelt. 2 Vols. New York: Duell, Sloan & Pearce, 1950.

Roosevelt, James. "Development Within the Marine Corps of a Unit for Purposes Similar to the British Commandos and the Chinese Guerrillas." January 13, 1942. In "Midway" folder, Box 75, James Roosevelt Papers, Franklin D. Roosevelt Library, Hyde Park, NY.

———. "Evans Carlson: A Personal Memoir." In Craig L. Symonds et al., eds., *New Aspects of Naval History: Selected Papers Presented at the Fourth Naval History Symposium, United States Naval Academy, 25–26 October 1979*. Annapolis, MD: Naval Institute Press, 1981.

———. *My Parents: A Differing View*. Chicago: Playboy Press, 1976.

Rose, Lisle A. *The Cold War Comes to Main Street*. Lawrence: University Press of Kansas, 1999.

Russell, Matthew William. "From Imperial Soldier to Communist General: The Early Career of Zhu De and His Influence on the Formation of the Chinese Red Army." PhD diss., George Washington University, 2009.

Saich, Anthony. "The Chinese Communist Party and the Anti-Japanese War Base Areas." *China Quarterly*, No. 140 (December 1994): 1000–1006.

———. "A Dutchman's Fantasy: Henricus Sneevliet's United Front for the Chinese Communist Party," in Timothy Cheek et al., eds., *The Chinese Communist Party: A Century in Ten Lives*. Cambridge: Cambridge University Press, 2021.

Saich, Anthony, and David Apter. *Revolutionary Discourse in Mao's Republic*. Cambridge, MA: Harvard University Press, 1994.

Samet, Elizabeth D. *Looking for the Good War: American Amnesia and the Violent Pursuit of Happiness*. New York: Farrar, Straus & Giroux, 2021.

Santelli, James S. *A Brief History of the 4th Marines*. Marine Corps Historical Reference Pamphlet. Washington, DC: Headquarters, U.S. Marine Corps, 1970.

Sasaki, Yutaka. "The Struggle for Scholarly Objectivity: Unofficial Diplomacy and the Institute of Pacific Relations from the Sino-Japanese War to the McCarthy Era." PhD diss., Rutgers University, 2005.

Saxe, Robert Francis. "Settling Down: Domesticating World War II Veterans' Challenge to the Postwar Consensus." PhD diss., University of Illinois, Urbana-Champaign, 2002.

Schaller, Michael. *The U.S. Crusade in China, 1938–1945*. New York: Columbia University Press, 1979.

Schmidt, Hans. *Maverick Marine: General Smedley D. Butler and the Contradictions of American Military History*. Lexington: University Press of Kentucky, 1987.

Schoenfeld, Seymour J. *The Negro in the Armed Forces: His Value and Status, Past, Present and Potential.* Washington, DC: The Associated Publishers, 1945. (Foreword by Evans Carlson.)

Schom, Alan. *The Eagle and the Rising Sun: The Japanese-American War, 1941–1943: Pearl Harbor Through Guadalcanal.* New York: W. W. Norton, 2004.

Schram, Stuart, ed. *Mao's Road to Power: Revolutionary Writings, 1912–1949.* 10 Vols. Armonk, NY: M. E. Sharpe, 1992.

Schram, Stuart. *The Thought of Mao Tse-Tung.* New York: Cambridge University Press, 1989.

Schreindl, David Robert. "Sowing the Seeds of War: The New York Times' Coverage of Japanese-American Tensions, A Prelude to Conflict in the Pacific, 1920–1941." MA thesis, Brigham Young University, 2004.

Schultz, Duane. *Evans Carlson, Marine Raider: The Man Who Commanded America's First Special Forces.* Yardley, PA: Westholme Publishing, 2014.

Scott, James. *Target Tokyo: Jimmy Doolittle and the Raid That Avenged Pearl Harbor.* New York: W. W. Norton, 2015.

Selden, Mark. "Yan'an Communism Reconsidered." *Modern China*, Vol. 21, No. 1 (January 1995): 8–44.

———. *The Yenan Way in Revolutionary China.* Cambridge, MA: Harvard University Press, 1971.

Sexton, John. *Red Friends: Internationalists in China's Struggle for Liberation.* New York: Verso Press, 2023.

Seybolt, Peter. "Terror and Conformity: Counterespionage Campaigns, Rectification, and Mass Movements, 1942–1943." *Modern China*, Vol. 12, No. 1 (January 1986): 39–73.

Shaw, Chonghai Petey. *The Role of the United States in Chinese Civil Conflicts, 1944–1949.* Salt Lake City: C. Schlacks Jr., 1991.

Shaw, George Bernard. *The Intelligent Woman's Guide to Socialism and Communism.* New Brunswick, NJ: Transaction Publishers, 2005.

Shaw, Henry I. *The United States Marines in North China, 1945–1949.* Washington, DC: Historical Branch, G-3 Division Headquarters, United States Marine Corps, 1968.

Sheng, Michael M. "America's Lost Chance in China? A Reappraisal of Chinese Communist Policy Toward the United States Before 1945." *The Australian Journal of Chinese Affairs*, No. 29 (January 1993): 135–57.

———. "Mao, Stalin, and the Formation of the Anti-Japanese United Front: 1935–1937." *China Quarterly*, No. 129 (March 1992): 149–70.

———. "The United States, the Chinese Communist Party, and the Soviet Union, 1948–1950: A Reappraisal." *Pacific Historical Review*, Vol. 63, No. 4 (November 1994): 521–36.

Sherrod, Robert. *Tarawa: The Incredible Story of One of World War II's Bloodiest Battles.* New York: Skyhorse Publishing, 2013.

Shewmaker, Kenneth E. *Americans and Chinese Communists, 1927–1945: A Persuading Encounter.* Ithaca, NY: Cornell University Press, 1971.

———. "The American Liberal Dream: Evans F. Carlson and the Chinese Communists, 1937–1947." *Pacific Historical Review*, Vol. 38, No. 2 (May 1969): 207–16.

Showalter, Dennis E. "Evolution of the U.S. Marine Corps as a Military Elite." *Marine Corps Gazette* (November 1979): 44–58.

Shu Zhang and Zhao Yue, eds. *Taiyang zhengzai shengqi: Ka Erxun qinli de Zhong-guo kangzhan* [The sun is rising: Evans Carlson's experience of China's War of Resistance]. Beijing: Beijing chubanshe, 2016.

Sinclair, Upton. "America's Amazing Woman Rebel in China." *Liberty* (March 13, 1937).

Sledge, E. B. *China Marine: An Infantryman's Life After World War II*. New York: Oxford University Press, 2002.

———. *With the Old Breed: At Peleliu and Okinawa*. New York: Ballantine, 1981.

Smedley, Agnes. *Battle Hymn of China*. New York: Alfred A. Knopf, 1943.

———. *China Fights Back: An American Woman with the Eighth Route Army*. New York: Vanguard Press, 1938.

———. *Chinese Destinies: Sketches of Present-Day China*. New York: Vanguard Press, 1933.

———. *Daughter of Earth*. New York: Coward-McCann, 1929.

———. *The Great Road: The Life and Times of Chu Teh*. New York: Monthly Review Press, 1956.

———. "In Memoriam—Evans Carlson." *Social Questions Bulletin* (May 1948).

Smith, George W. *Carlson's Raid: The Daring Marine Assault on Makin*. New York: Berkley Books, 2003.

Smith, Gen. Holland M., and Percy Finch. *Coral and Brass*. New York: Scribner, 1949.

Smith, Jean Edward. *FDR*. New York: Random House, 2007.

Smith, Richard H. *OSS: The Secret History of America's First Central Intelligence Agency*. Berkeley: University of California Press, 1981.

Snow, Edgar. *The Battle for Asia*. New York: Random House, 1941.

———. *The Other Side of the River: Red China Today*. New York: Random House, 1962.

———. *People on Our Side*. New York: Random House, 1944.

———. *Red Star Over China*. New York: Random House, 1938; first printing.

———. "The Sun Also Sets." *Saturday Evening Post* (June 4, 1938).

Snow, Helen Foster. "Carlson of (the 'Gung Ho') Carlson's Raiders: His Own Sketch." Carlson Personal File, Published Materials, Reference Branch, Marine Corps History Division, Quantico, VA.

———. "Evans Carlson, Who Put the Term 'Gung Ho' into English Diction-aries," unpublished manuscript. Helen Foster Snow papers, MSS 2219, Box 175, Folder 15, L. Tom Perry Special Collections, Brigham Young University, Provo, UT.

———. (as Nym Wales). *Inside Red China*. New York: Doubleday, Doran, 1939.

———. (as Nym Wales). *My China Years: A Memoir*. New York: Morrow, 1984.

———. "Remembering the Autobiography of Evans F. Carlson," unpublished manuscript, 1979. Helen Foster Snow papers, MSS 2219, Box 175, Folder 15, L. Tom Perry Special Collections, Brigham Young University, Provo, UT.

Sorace, Christian, et al., eds. *Afterlives of Chinese Communism: Political Concepts from Mao to Xi*. New York: Verso, 2019.

Spector, Ronald H. *A Continent Erupts: Decolonization, Civil War, and Massacre in Postwar Asia, 1945–1955*. New York: W. W. Norton, 2022.

———. *Eagle Against the Sun: The American War with Japan*. New York: Vintage, 1985.

Spence, Jonathan. *The Search for Modern China*. New York: W. W. Norton, 2013.

Stanley, Margaret. "Foreigners in Areas of China Under Communist Jurisdiction Before 1949: Biographical Notes and a Comprehensive Bibliography of the *Yenan Hui.*" Reference Series, No. 3, Center for East Asian Studies, University of Kansas, 1987.

Stavinsky, Samuel E. *Marine Combat Correspondent: World War II in the Pacific.* New York: Ballantine, 1999.

Stidham, Buck. "Comments on Returning from the Makin Raid." *The Raider Patch*, January 1993.

Stilwell, Joseph. *The Stilwell Papers.* Edited by Theodore H. White. New York: Da Capo, 1991.

Stockman, Capt. James R., USMC. *The Battle for Tarawa.* Washington, DC: Historical Section, Division of Public Information, Headquarters, U.S. Marine Corps, 1947.

Straight, Michael. "The Faith of a Raider." *The New Republic* (June 9, 1947).

Sues, Ilona Ralf. *Shark's Fins and Millet.* Boston: Little, Brown, 1944.

Sun Shuyun. *The Long March: The True History of Communist China's Founding Myth.* New York: Anchor, 2008.

Sun Youli. "Chinese Military Resistance and Changing American Perceptions, 1937–1938." In Robert David Johnson, ed., *On Cultural Ground: Essays in International History.* Chicago: Imprint Publications, 1994.

Sutton, Donald S. "German Advice and Residual Warlordism in the Nanking Decade: Influences on Nationalist Military Training and Strategy." *China Quarterly*, No. 91 (September 1982): 386–410.

Swing, Raymond Gram. "The Man Who Will Become a Legend." *Saturday Review of Literature*, Vol. 30 (October 1947): 26–27.

Tao Wenzhao, Yang Kuisong, and Wang Jianlang. *Kang Ri zhanzheng shiqi Zhongguo dui wai guanxi* [China's foreign relations during the War of Resistance against Japan]. Beijing: Zhonggong dangshi chubanshe, 1995.

Taylor, Jay. *The Generalissimo: Chiang Kai-shek and the Struggle for Modern China.* Cambridge, MA: Belknap Press of Harvard University Press, 2009.

Teiwes, Frederick C., and Warren Sun. "From a Leninist to a Charismatic Party: The CCP's Changing Leadership, 1937–1945." In Tony Saich and Hans van de Ven, eds., *New Perspectives on the Chinese Communist Revolution.* Armonk, NY: M. E. Sharpe, 1995.

Terkel, Studs. *The Good War: An Oral History of World War Two.* New York: Pantheon, 1984.

Thomas, Bernard S. *Season of High Adventure: Edgar Snow in China.* Berkeley: University of California Press, 1996.

Toland, John. *The Rising Sun: The Decline and Fall of the Japanese Empire, 1936–1945.* New York: Random House, 1970.

Toll, Ian W. *The Conquering Tide: War in the Pacific Islands, 1942–1944.* New York: W. W. Norton, 2015.

Tozer, Warren W. "The Foreign Correspondents' Visit to Yenan in 1944: A Reassessment." *Pacific Historical Review*, Vol. 41, No. 2 (May 1972): 207–24.

Tregaskis, Richard. *Guadalcanal Diary.* New York: Random House, 1943.

Tsou Tang. *America's Failure in China, 1941–50.* Chicago: University of Chicago Press, 1963.

Tsuchida, Akio. "China's 'Public Diplomacy' Toward the United States Before

Pearl Harbor." *The Journal of American-East Asian Relations*, Vol. 17, No. 1 (2010): 35–55.

Tuchman, Barbara. "If Mao Had Come to Washington: An Essay in Alternatives." *Foreign Affairs*, Vol. 51, No. 1 (October 1972): 44–64.

———. *Stilwell and the American Experience in China*. New York: Grove Press, 1971.

Tucker, Robert C. *Stalin in Power: The Revolution from Above, 1928–1941*. New York: W. W. Norton, 1990.

Twining, Merrill. *No Bended Knee: The Battle for Guadalcanal*. Novato, CA: Presidio Press, 1996.

Ugaki, Matome. *Fading Victory: The Diary of Admiral Matome Ugaki, 1941–1945*. Pittsburgh: University of Pittsburgh Press, 1991.

Ulbrich, David J. *Preparing for Victory: Thomas Holcomb and the Making of the Modern Marine Corps, 1936–1943*. Annapolis, MD: Naval Institute Press, 2011.

United States Department of Commerce. *Commercial Travelers' Guide to the Far East*. Washington, DC: U.S. Government Printing Office, 1932.

United States Department of State. *The China White Paper, August 1949*. 2 Vols. Stanford: Stanford University Press, 1967.

Updegraph, Charles L. *U.S. Marine Corps Special Units of World War II*. Washington, DC: History and Museums Division, Headquarters, U.S. Marine Corps, 1972.

Utley, Freda. *China at War*. London: Faber & Faber, 1939.

———. *The China Story*. Chicago: H. Regnery, 1951.

———. *The Dream We Lost: Soviet Russia Then and Now*. New York: John Day, 1940.

———. *Last Chance in China*. New York: Bobbs-Merrill, 1947.

———. *Odyssey of a Liberal: Memoirs*. Washington, DC: Washington National Press, 1970.

van de Ven, Hans J. *China at War: Triumph and Tragedy in the Emergence of the New China*. Cambridge, MA: Harvard University Press, 2018.

———. *War and Nationalism in China: 1925–1945*. London: Routledge Curzon, 2003.

Van Edgerton, F. "The Carlson Intelligence Mission to China." *Michigan Academician*, Vol. 9, No. 4 (April 1977): 419–32.

Vladimirov, P. P. *The Vladimirov Diaries: Yenan, China, 1942–1945*. Garden City, NY: Doubleday, 1975.

Vogel, Ezra. *Deng Xiaoping and the Transformation of China*. Cambridge, MA: Harvard University Press, 2011.

Wakeman, Frederic. *Policing Shanghai, 1927–1937*. Berkeley: University of California Press, 1995.

Wampler, Ernest M. *China Suffers: Or, My Six Years of Work During the Incident*. Elgin, IL: Brethren Publishing House, 1945.

Wang Jingbin. "No Lost Chance in China: The False Realism of American Foreign Service Officers, 1943–1945." *The Journal of American-East Asian Relations*, Vol. 17, No. 2 (2010): 118–45.

Waugh, Thomas. *The Conscience of Cinema: The Works of Joris Ivens, 1926–1989*. Amsterdam: Amsterdam University Press, 2016.

Wei, William. "'Political Power Grows out of the Barrel of a Gun': Mao and the Red Army." In David A. Graff and Robin Higham, eds., *A Military History of China*. Lexington: University Press of Kentucky, 2012.

Westad, Odd Arne. *Decisive Encounters: The Chinese Civil War, 1946–1950*. Stanford: Stanford University Press, 2003.

———. "Losses, Chances, and Myths: The United States and the Creation of the Sino-Soviet Alliance, 1945–1950." *Diplomatic History*, Vol. 21, No. 1 (Winter 1997): 105–15.

Weyl, Walter. *Tired Radicals and Other Papers*. New York: B. W. Huebesch, 1921.

Wheelan, Joseph. *Midnight in the Pacific: Guadalcanal: The World War II Battle That Turned the Tide of War*. Boston: Da Capo, 2017.

Whymant, Robert. *Stalin's Spy: Richard Sorge and the Tokyo Espionage Ring*. New York: St. Martin's Press, 1998.

Whyte, William H. *A Time of War: Remembering Guadalcanal, A Battle Without Maps*. New York: Fordham University Press, 2000.

Wiles, Tripp. *Forgotten Raiders of '42: The Fate of the Marines Left Behind on Makin*. Washington, DC: Potomac Books, 2007.

Wu, T'ien-wei. "The Chinese Communist Movement." In James Chieh Hsiung and Steven I. Levine, eds., *China's Bitter Victory: The War with Japan, 1937–1945*. Armonk, NY: M. E. Sharpe, 1992.

Wukovits, John F. *American Commando: Evans Carlson, His WWII Marine Raiders, and America's First Special Forces Mission*. New York: NAL Caliber, 2009.

———. *One Square Mile of Hell: The Battle for Tarawa*. New York: NAL Caliber, 2006.

Xu Youwei and Philip Billingsley. "Behind the Scenes of the Xi'an Incident: The Case of the Lixingshe." *China Quarterly*, No. 154 (June 1998): 283–307.

Yang, Benjamin. "The Making of a Pragmatic Communist: The Early Life of Deng Xiaoping, 1904–49." *China Quarterly*, No. 135 (September 1993): 444–56.

Yang, Jisheng. *Tombstone: The Great Chinese Famine, 1958–1962*. Translated by Stacy Mosher and Guo Jian. New York: Farrar, Straus & Giroux, 2012.

Yang, Kuisong. "The Evolution of the Relationship Between the Chinese Communist Party and the Comintern During the Sino-Japanese War." In Hans van de Ven, Diana Lary, and Stephen MacKinnon, eds., *Negotiating China's Destiny in World War II*. Stanford: Stanford University Press, 2015.

Young, Louise. *Japan's Total Empire: Manchuria and the Culture of Wartime Imperialism*. Berkeley: University of California Press, 1998.

Yu, Maochun. *The Dragon's War: Allied Operations and the Fate of China, 1937–1947*. Annapolis, MD: Naval Institute Press, 2006.

———. *OSS in China: Prelude to Cold War*. New Haven: Yale University Press, 1996.

Zeng Dehou. *Kouqin yu bishou: Ka Erxun zhuan* [Harmonica and dagger: a biography of Evans Carlson]. Beijing: Zhongguo qingnian chubanshe, 1991.

Zhao Yifan. "Agnes Smedley: An American Intellectual Pilgrim in China." PhD diss., Harvard University, 1989.

Zhongguo guoji youren yanjiuhui, ed. *Zhongguo zhi you Ka Erxun* [China's friend, Evans Carlson]. Liaoning renmin chubanshe, 1996.

Zhou Libo. *Jin Cha Ji bianqu yinxiang ji* [Impressions of the Jin-Cha-Ji border region]. Washington, DC: Center for Chinese Research Materials, 1971.

———. *Zhandi riji* [War zone diary]. Shanghai: Shanghai zazhi gongsi, 1938.

Zhu De. *Selected Works of Zhu De*. Beijing: Foreign Languages Press, 1986.

———. *Zhu De shi xuan ji* [The selected poems of Zhu De]. Beijing: Renmin wenxue chubanshe, 1977.

————. *Zhu De xuan ji* [Selected works of Zhu De]. Beijing: Renmin chubanshe, 1983.

————. *Zhu De zi shu* [The autobiography of Zhu De]. Beijing: Guoji wenhua chuban gongsi, 2009.

Zhu Min. *Wode fuqin Zhu De* [My father, Zhu De]. Beijing: Renmin chubanshe, 2009.

Zimmerman, John Lee. *The Guadalcanal Campaign*. Washington, DC: History Division, Headquarters, U.S. Marine Corps, 1949.

Zimmerman, Phyllis A. "Military Missionary: The Riddle Wrapped in a Mystery Inside an Enigma That Was Evans F. Carlson." In Craig L. Symonds, et al., eds., *New Interpretations in Naval History: Selected Papers from the Fourteenth Naval History Symposium*. Annapolis, MD: Naval Institute Press, 2001.

INDEX

Page numbers in *italics* refer to illustrations.

ILLUSTRATION CREDITS

522 · *Illustration Credits*

186 Evans F. Carlson, *Twin Stars of China: A Behind-the-Scenes Story of China's Valiant Struggle for Existence*. New York: Dodd, Mead, 1940

189 Courtesy National Archives, RG 38, Entry 98, Naval Attaché Reports, 1880–1904, Box 527, Folder C-10-h, Register No. 18240, photograph by Evans Carlson

229 Helen Foster Snow Papers (MS 2219), L. Tom Perry Special Collections, Harold B. Lee Library, Brigham Young University, Provo, Utah

257 Courtesy National Archives, photo no. 80-G-11720

259 Courtesy National Archives, photo no. 80-G-34493

267 Courtesy National Archives, photo no. 80-G-11722

287 Courtesy National Archives, photo no. 80-G-11729

291 Courtesy National Archives, photo no. 127-GW-1240

302 Official USMC Photograph, Thayer Soule Collection (COLL/2266), Archives Branch, Marine Corps History Division

303 Courtesy Naval History and Heritage Command, photo no. NH-49168

304 Official USMC Photograph, Thayer Soule Collection (COLL/2266), Archives Branch, Marine Corps History Division

305 Courtesy National Archives, RG 127-N, photo no. A701546

317 Official USMC Photograph, Thayer Soule Collection (COLL/2266), Archives Branch, Marine Corps History Division

329 Official USMC Photograph, Thayer Soule Collection (COLL/2266), Archives Branch, Marine Corps History Division

332 Courtesy Naval History and Heritage Command, photo no. NH-62278

335 Official USMC Photograph, Thayer Soule Collection (COLL/2266), Archives Branch, Marine Corps History Division

339 Courtesy National Archives, official U.S. Navy photo no. 67598

347 Shutterstock, Inc.

349 Shutterstock, Inc.

353 Marine Corps Photo No. 2-17, Frederick R. Findtner Collection (COLL/3890), Marine Corps Archives and Special Collections

366 Courtesy National Archives, photo no. 7330169

379 Chicago Tribune/TCA

382 Courtesy Karen Carlson Loving

407 Courtesy National Archives, RG-208-PU-31

A NOTE ABOUT THE AUTHOR

Stephen R. Platt is an award-winning historian of China and the West whose books include *Imperial Twilight* (Knopf, 2018) and *Autumn in the Heavenly Kingdom* (Knopf, 2012), the latter of which won the Cundill History Prize. He is a professor at the University of Massachusetts, Amherst and holds a PhD from Yale. He lives with his family in Northampton, Massachusetts.

A NOTE ON THE TYPE

This book was set in Janson, a typeface named for the Dutchman Anton Janson but actually the work of Nicholas Kis (1650–1702). The type is an excellent example of the influential and sturdy Dutch types that prevailed in England up to the time William Caslon (1692–1766) developed his own incomparable designs from them.

Typeset by North Market Street Graphics,
Lancaster, Pennsylvania

Designed by Marisa Nakasone